Snakes of the
United States and Canada

DEDICATION

This book is dedicated to our families and our teachers. Specifically it is dedicated to our brothers and sisters, Scott and Marilee Somerville, Ricky and Odelia Rossi, Rosalind Rossi, and Eva Rossi, Tim and Victoria Dillman, Michael Rossi, Roy Williams, Edwin and Beelyn Williams, LuAnn and the late Ronald Williams. The senior author would also like to dedicate this book to his professors, Dr. Margaret M. Stewart, Dr. Robert Jaeger, Dr. Dale Jackson, and Dr. Roy McDiarmid. They led by example, inspired with their enthusiasm, and gave of their tremendous knowledge.

It is also dedicated to Ernest Hernandez and Brenda Carlson, whose loving and caring ways enriched our lives and the lives of all who knew them.

Snakes of the
United States and Canada
Natural History and Care in Captivity

John V. Rossi, DVM, MA
and
Roxanne Rossi

KRIEGER PUBLISHING COMPANY
Malabar, Florida
2003

All photos are by David G Campbell unless marked otherwise.

Original Edition, 2003

Printed and Published by
KRIEGER PUBLISHING COMPANY
KRIEGER DRIVE
MALABAR, FLORIDA 32950

FROM A DECLARATION OF PRINCIPLES JOINTLY ADOPTED BY A COMMITTEE OF THE AMERICAN BAR ASSOCIATION AND A COMMITTEE OF PUBLISHERS:

This publication is designed to provide accurate and authoritative information in regard to the subject matter covered. It is sold with the understanding that the publisher is not engaged in rendering legal, accounting, or other professional service. If legal advice or other expert assistance is required, the services of a competent professional should be sought.

Library of Congress Cataloging-in-Publication Data

Rossi, John, 1955–
    Snakes of the United States and Canada : natural history and care in captivity / John V.
Rossi, Roxanne Rossi.
        p. cm.
    Includes bibliographical references (p.   ) and index.
    ISBN 1-57524-031-9 (hc : alk. paper)
        1. Captive snakes.   2. Snakes—United States.   3. Snakes—Canada.   I. Rossi, Roxanne.   II.
Title.

SF515.5.S64 R68 2003
639.3'96'097—dc21
                                                                99-086782

10   9   8   7   6   5   4   3   2

CONTENTS

LIST OF TABLES

ACKNOWLEDGMENTS

The authors would like to thank all of the amateur and professional herpetologists who shared their experiences caring for North America's snakes. These include Fred Antonio, Robert Applegate, Randy Babb, James Badman, Joleen Barry, Bernard Bechtel, Pat Burchfield, Rob Crabtree, Doug Duerre, Kevin Enge, Greg Ewald, Doug Finnegan, Neil Ford, James C. Goodwin, Robert Hansen, Richard Hoyer, Dana Knepper, Howard Lawler, Chris and Nicole Lechowitz, Greg LePera, Rick Lewis, Bill and Cathy Love, Sean McKeown, Tony Mills, Paul Moler, Vic Morgan, Larry Nienaber, August Rentfro, Cecil Schwalbe, Richard Stengle, George Van Horne, Jerry Salmon, Norman Scott, Winchester Seyle, and Mike Welker.

Bill Snead of Phoenix, Arizona, led us on repeated expeditions into the Chiricahua, Huachuca, and Pinaleno (Graham) Mountains of Arizona. Jerrold Feldner and his son Marty helped us collect snakes in southern California and donated a number of valuable specimens for this work. Doug Finnigan guided us into the Sierra Nevadas and collected numerous animals on our behalf. Dennis Sheridan waded with us down numerous cold water streams in central coastal California in search of two-striped garter snakes. Randy Babb, biologist with the Arizona Game and Fish Commission, shared with us some of his numerous experiences with both captive and wild Arizona snakes, and helped us acquire several important specimens.

David Campbell, wildlife photographer and biologist, brought so many of our native snakes to life among the pages of this book. His efforts included numerous photo sessions with our captives, assistance in the field, and independent trips and collection of desperately needed snakes. He also researched several species independently and shared his results with us.

The other photographers and biologists, particularly Ray Ashton, Robert Hansen, Pat Burchfield, Sean McKeown, Steve Barten, Scott Cushnir, Cecil Schwalbe, John Murphy, Patrick Briggs, Jim Rorabaugh, R. D. Bartlett, Harold Voris, and R. Wayne Van Devender all contributed beautiful photographs, which are so important in a book of this nature.

Many other individuals assisted us in the field or sent us specimens they had collected. These included Greg Watts, John and Etta Staeck, Sean and Wendy McKeown, Mike Terrell, Greg Ewald, Vic Morgan, John Brandt, Lynn Campbell, Chris and Nicole Lechowitz, Art Nohlberg, Charles Metcalf, Manny Rubio, Scott Solar, Al and Ruth Wolf, Eric Thiss, Bill and Billy Griswold, Pat Day, Stuart James, Jimmy Waters, Louis Porras, Richard Marriott, Don Lorenzo, Tim Hofnagle, Kevin Enge, Eugene Trescott, Joe Butler, Mike Miller, Wayne Howell, Jim Hartman, Paul Moler, John C. Rossi, Robert Rossi, Dennis Sargent, Chris Woodcock, Richard Wells, Michael Wells, and Steve Barten. Eugene Trescott helped us acquire extremely difficult-to-find snakes. His skill and good fortune in the field have been translated into a wealth of information with captive snakes. He also made a number of valuable suggestions which we have utilized in evaluating foods for these snakes.

Aside from providing information, a number of individuals actually assisted us in caring for some of the snakes in our collection. First and foremost among these was Richard Wells. Other individuals who helped us maintain animals in captivity included Dean and Elizabeth Medeiros, Charles and Susan Metcalf, John Brandt, Skip Ferguson, Scott Cushnir, Don Muttillo, and Patrick Bevan.

Sean McKeown, Howard Lawler, Dana Knepper, Randy Babb, Norman Scott, Cecil Schwalbe, Doug Finnigan, Ed Ely, Phil Brown,

Jim Kane, Pat Burchfield, Larry Nienaber, Robert Hansen, Joleen Berry, Doug Duerre, William Mara, and Mike Welker shared with us their knowledge of natural history and experience caring for some of North America's unusual snakes. This information was invaluable in helping us to understand these animals and forming a better foundation for their care.

We are again indebted to Wanda Loutsenheizer for her skilled portraits of some of North America's least known snakes in action.

Eric Thiss of Serpent's Tale Books lent us a large number of rare, and in some cases, expensive books for an extended period. These books proved tremendously useful in researching information about some of the least known snakes.

A number of individuals donated money or food items to help with this research. These included Brown's Bait and Tackle, Thrifty Bait and Tackle of Jacksonville, Rick Lewis, and Mike Duffy. The Central Florida Herpetological Society awarded us a sizeable grant which helped bring this book to completion.

The late Jim Hartman donated a large number of cages, books, and equipment, which helped us immensely in our work with these snakes.

In attempting to better understand the captive requirements of many of these snakes, we drew heavily on the published natural history works of prominent herpetologists. Most notable among these publications are the publications of Barry Armstrong, Roger Barbour, Alvin Braswell, Edmund Brodie, Philip Brown, Jonathan Campbell, Sheldon Campbell, Joseph Collins, Roger Conant, William Degenhardt, James Dixon, Harold Dundee, Carl Ernst, Henry Fitch, Neil Ford, Jack Fowlie, Howard Gloyd, James Harding, Malcom Hunter, Terry Johnson, Laurence Klauber, Michael Klemmens, William Lamar, Charles Lowe, Sherman Minton, Joseph Mitchell, John Moriarty, Robert Mount, James Murphy, Charles Painter, William Palmer, William Preston, Andrew Price, Douglas Rossman, Manny Rubio, Richard Seigel, Charles Shaw, Robert Stebbins, Robert Storm, Alan Tennant, Robert Webb, and John Werler.

We would like to thank our parents, Dr. and Mrs. Roscoe Rossi and Mr. and Mrs. Ronald H. Williams, for the encouragement needed to bring this book to completion, as well as our grandmothers, Mrs. John Grieco and Mrs. John Rossi.

We are indebted to the former Hogtown Herpetological Supply in Gainesville, Florida, who kindly allowed us to photograph numerous snakes in their care, and shared with us clutch sizes, incubation times, and other information. Tom Crutchfield also donated a number of unusual snakes for this study.

The Texas Parks and Wildlife Dept. granted us a permit to conduct research and guided us toward other sources of information.

We are indebted to the many fine people at Krieger Publishing Company, who encouraged us and assisted us in bringing this book to completion, and put up with our sometimes illegible additions to the text.

We are also grateful to Sean and Wendy McKeown for making many major suggestions and reviewing some of the text. Sean, who passed away recently, was a true pioneer in herpetoculture. He will be missed.

Furthermore, from our travels and our research we gained a deep appreciation for the colossal work of Albert and Anna Wright some 47 years earlier. We are thoroughly indebted to them and remain in awe of their *Handbook of Snakes*, which has served and will continue to serve as the foundation of American ophiology.

Lastly, we would like to recognize the effort put forth by each other and the encouragement we derived from each other during this long, and at times, difficult task, for there is no way either one of us could have done this alone.

FOREWORD

Most of you who use this book or read this foreword probably own snakes or are contemplating snake ownership. As such, you would find a visit to the home of John and Roxanne Rossi to be awe-inspiring. Several of my herpetology classes have been dazzled by their collection. The house is a single-story white rectangle with two bedrooms and no more than 1000 square feet of floor space. Located in a rural area of Jacksonville, Florida, it is nestled among several huge pecan trees, and the yard is surrounded by cow pasture. It is within this serene setting that most of the information in this book was gathered and assimilated into a powerful tool that will benefit herpetoculturists, field biologists, and others who would keep and study snakes.

Every time I visit John and Roxanne there are more and different animals. The count as of this writing is about 200 snakes representing 100 different species. One first enters the living room to find shelves arranged four-high along all walls, and on them the many terraria that house the snakes. Cages are kept meticulously clean, which is a continuous and herculean feat with so many to care for.

From the living room with over 50 cages, one can then enter the actual "snake room." Again all walls are covered with shelves and terraria, and there is a double row of shelves down the center of the room. In most homes this would be the master bedroom, but John and Roxanne sleep in the smaller room, and there are some snakes in there as well.

The kitchen used to have snakes on only one wall; the stacks of shoe box cages were for neonates. Most recently, however, more adult cages have taken up another wall. Egg clutches are incubated in several of the lower cabinets and in the linen closet. The only room in the house without snakes is the bathroom, and I have never asked why.

John and Roxanne Rossi know more about caring for North American snakes than any other two people I know. They have actually kept most North American species. They have successfully bred about half of all the North American species including first-time captive breeding of smooth earth snakes, rough earth snakes, night snakes, Sonoran whipsnakes, Mexican vine snakes, pine woods snakes, southern hognose snakes, and mangrove salt marsh snakes. Presently, they are raising several rare and protected snakes and hope to breed them this spring.

On many evenings and days off, when the Rossis are not writing books they are out collecting snake food. Mice can be purchased, of course, but the Rossis also need a supply of small lizards for neonate scarlet kingsnakes, frogs and toads for pine woods snakes, some water snakes and hognoses, sirens for rainbow and mud snakes, earthworms and slugs for worm snakes and redbellies, spiders and insects for green snakes, and even centipedes for crowned snakes. Now they also keep several western species that prefer scorpions! Between forays these items are stored in a special freezer. Most of us snake keepers have strange things in our freezers from time to time, but I will never forget the first time Roxanne handed me a sandwich bag from the freezer filled with dead wolf spiders with legs all inwardly curled!

During their years of field work and snake husbandry the Rossis have discovered many previously unknown life history facts about their subjects. It behooves all scientists to seek novel information and make their findings available to the scientific community. John and Roxanne have published their work in herpetocultural series such as *The Vivarium* and *Reptiles Magazine*, and John wrote the monthly column entitled "Ask the Vet" for the League of Florida Herpetological Societies. Some of their more technical work is found in highly respected professional journals such as *American Midland Naturalist*, *Herpetologica*, and *Herpetological Review*. This volume on the care of captive North American snakes represents an integration of knowledge gleaned from years of field work and caring for captive snakes. As such, it represents an educational link between herpetoculturists and field biologists, two groups that will gain by sharing each other's knowledge. This synergism is perhaps the only hope for the future of an entire group of fascinating animals that we all love and respect.

Joseph A. Butler, PhD
Professor of Biology
University of North Florida

INTRODUCTION

This is one of the first books in over 40 years to discuss the natural history of almost all North American snakes in one volume. It is an outgrowth of earlier volumes, which sought primarily to educate herpetoculturists on the maintenance and breeding of North American snakes. However, a knowledge of natural history is often critical to the successful maintenance of a species, and in some cases, captive reproduction. Therefore, the natural history of each species was researched and incorporated. The details include geographic range, preferred habitat, known prey, known and potential predators, thermal preferences, mating seasons, incubation and gestation periods, clutch sizes, some aspects of behavior, and more. Certainly, there was no current summary of the natural history of all North American snakes. Information was widely dispersed or very scarce. In some cases, amateurs were sitting on unpublished gold mines of herpetological information, and professional herpetologists were publishing excellent information in places unlikely to be seen by many. Hence, the focus of this book has shifted from being purely herpetocultural education to being education in general. Our goal was to bring together in one convenient form as much basic natural history information on each species as possible within the constraints of space. Given those constraints, we did not include detailed meristic characters, micromorphological details, or detailed subspecies descriptions. We also did not add tables of raw data. In spite of this, there is a great deal of original research presented among the pages of this book. We have made many natural history observations in our years of observing these snakes in the field. We have also presented a fair number of the original field observations of other amateur and professional herpetologists. We have also discussed and compared a great deal of information from regional publications (i.e., books dealing with the reptiles of a state, province, or geographic region). Thanks to the encouragement of Neil Ford, we have begun collecting data in a slightly different manner, and this may be reflected in future editions. However, he also impressed upon us that while there was great value to captive behavior and reproductive information, it needed to be distinguished from such observations in wild specimens. Hence, every section starts with observations of wild snakes, and then discusses captivity and the observations made there.

Indeed, we have recognized the concerns of many professional herpetologists that "captive snakes are not the same as wild snakes." We are aware that a great deal of research measuring the intricate complexities of snake ecology and behavior exists, and that captivity may truly create domestic snakes after several generations because of major selective forces. We are also aware that early studies examining the survivorship of released individuals indicate that survivorship has been fairly low. Hence, the conservation benefits of captive breeding efforts may be somewhat limited. Certainly, as we come to better understand the complexities of the environment and dietary selection, we may be better prepared to breed snakes for release, similar to stocking fish, or "head-starting" turtles. But this effort would require species survival teams to pair up expert field biologists with expert herpetoculturists and veterinarians. Perhaps as captive environments, including outdoor enclosures, become more complex, the survivorship of released individuals will improve, and our understanding of captive requirements will eventually become a force for conservation. See the discussion on Brazos water snakes. With this in mind, we have presented our observations on the herpetoculture of North American snakes separate from and clearly differentiated from observations of wild snakes, even though they are presented in the same chapters.

A great deal has been learned about the herpetoculture of North American snakes since Volumes I and II (Rossi 1992; Rossi and Rossi, 1995b) were published. We and others made observations that would change our approaches to a number of problems faced by captive snakes in general and certain species in particular. We have made every attempt possible to include some of these changes in the general care section and, where applicable, in the individual species sections of this book. Once again, we firmly believe there are a number of means to an end in this young science; hence there is usually more than just one "right" cage design or feeding program. Similarly, there is probably no single "correct" breeding program for any one species, even though many of the approaches used have worked relatively well. We have therefore tried to discuss environments and diets that have worked for us and those we interviewed.

In the course of preparing this book, we tried to maintain every species of snake native to the United States and Canada and to breed as many as possible. At the time of this writing, there were only a handful of species (three or four including the genus *Tantilla*) that we were unsuccessful in obtaining, either because they are exceedingly rare or are protected. Our efforts required that we obtain permits from a large number of states, including Florida, Texas, New Mexico, Arizona, and California, and the paperwork alone was formidable, not to mention the actual traveling and collecting of our study animals. Our study collection exceeded 250 snakes representing more than 90 species at one time, even though this varied over the years. As might be expected, this was a massive undertaking for us. Maintenance of many of these species was reasonably difficult, as many required more than just a basic cage; furthermore, many required unusual food items, including centipedes, slugs, ant eggs, termites, or crayfish, that were time-consuming to feed and, at times, difficult to procure. Medical problems, parasitological examinations, and breeding efforts demanded even more time; therefore,

many questions remain unanswered regarding the captive maintenance of North American snakes. We have made good progress with some, but have barely scratched the surface of what we need to know with others, hence, some chapters remain virtually unchanged while others show dramatic changes and revisions when compared to our previous works, Volumes I and II.

As mentioned above, in addition to actually maintaining and breeding a large number of species ourselves, we have interviewed many professional and amateur herpetologists about their experiences and/or opinions on the captive maintenance of a number of species. We have reviewed as much of the literature available to us as possible regarding the species discussed herein, and referred readers to it where applicable. In addition, we had the opportunity to visit a number of reptile wholesalers, and actually see the conditions to which many of these animals are exposed prior to their ultimate destination. The senior author's experience in treating reptiles over the last several years, especially many of those species of snakes discussed, is also well represented. In this way, we hoped we would avoid some of the commonly replicated errors that occur in reference works.

Herpetoculturists need to extend their interests to those reptiles and amphibians that are not large and showy; this includes the vast majority of reptiles and most of the snakes "in our own backyard." It is only in this way that we can truly claim that herpetoculture has the potential to aid in the conservation of reptiles and amphibians. Certainly, the breeding of tricolored kingsnakes has not suffered from a shortage of volunteers; however, we know little more about the captive reproduction of leafnose snakes than we did 50 years ago. A number of other snakes fall into this category as well. In fact, the vast majority of North American snakes are virtually unknown to many avid herpetoculturists. To many of these people, there are only kingsnakes and rat snakes, boas and pythons. Everything else is a "junk" snake. The truth of the matter is there is no such thing as a "junk" snake, and by limiting our studies to just four or five genera out of 50, we have literally put blinders on. Because of this, we have a one- or two-dimensional picture of the proper environment for captive snakes, when in fact, most snakes have multidimensional environments. We need to realize that not every species of snake will survive under the conditions we have so vigorously preached for captive kingsnakes and rat snakes over the last 20 years. For many of these snakes, environmental factors not even considered in the captive maintenance of those commonly maintained species are critical for their survival. Factors such as light intensity, branch diameter, humidity, barometric pressure fluctuations, substrate pH, and moisture gradients are definitely important parameters of the physical environment for many of our snakes and need to be considered when creating a captive environment.

Yet, herpetoculturists are in many ways driven by the laws of economics. Many people cannot afford to maintain large collections of snakes, nor do they have the time. For many, captive breeding must pay the bills, therefore, they must maintain and breed desirable snakes. For others it is only a hobby they will pursue even though it may not be economically rewarding. Both groups can contribute a great deal to our knowledge about the captive requirements of snakes. Those with large operations have the skill and resources necessary to work with and succeed with many species. Those who do not maintain large collections may have the patience and time necessary to succeed with many others. There is still so much to learn that even those maintaining only one or two animals may contribute tremendously by careful observation of the animals in their care.

Unfortunately, the realities of human population growth have placed many of these animals in jeopardy. More and more reptiles and amphibians are being placed on state and federal lists as endangered, threatened, or species of special concern. These animals then receive some degree of protection in that they may not be collected indiscriminately or, in some cases, at all. Indeed, the intent of these laws and of various state agencies is to preserve as many of these animals in the wild as possible. The collection of any specimen from the wild may

affect the local population and imparts a serious responsibility to the collector. Therefore, limited collection of some of these animals (and their captive breeding) is necessary, in our opinion. Responsible collecting of some species is a positive and prudent undertaking that should not be completely stifled by state and federal governments. Certainly, it is becoming apparent that the only animals that will survive the next century will be those that are considered valuable enough to be bred in captivity or fortunate enough to be living on protected lands (a very small percentage of the original land inhabited by these animals). Even those species that are considered common and have large geographic ranges may be at some risk. Indeed, it is hard to imagine how a species as widespread as the night snake, *Hypsiglena torquata*, could become extinct in the wild; yet, it is not habitat destruction alone that must be considered when we think about extinction. Even in the middle of the pristine desert hundreds of miles from the nearest large city, the evidence of our presence can be seen. Pollution, in the form of smog, reaches far out into the desert and may exert its deadly influence in ways unknown to us, long before we know exactly what is happening or can take measures to stop it. We are already aware that hundreds of species of amphibians and fishes have experienced drastic reductions in numbers over the last several years. It is inconceivable that reptiles (including snakes), birds, and mammals will not be affected; after all, one does not need to look too far for evidence that even extremely common animals may become extinct (e.g., the passenger pigeon in North America).

Thus, state and provincial fish and game commissions should not consider all herpetoculturists as pests who need to be kept at bay, but as a valuable resource for information that may possibly aid in the preservation of many species of herps. To purists, the preservation of a species is meaningless if they are not in their proper habitat. Animals removed from the wild, and those bred in captivity, are often not considered ''real animals'' in conservation efforts by purists. The fact is that the products of captive breeding help provide valuable information and may themselves become an extremely valuable resource, especially if they have been bred true (to animals from the same geographic area). Certainly, in a world where habitat is being destroyed at phenomenal rates, they are better than the alternative, which is no animals at all. In addition, how many "pure" habitats are left? We already know that a large number of exotic grasses and trees are invading numerous habitats across North America, and by doing so are changing those environments. Wouldn't it be a very pleasant surprise if someone had a large captive population of California red-legged frogs right now, and could reintroduce them into suitable habitats if they could be found?

Nevertheless, we must demand that herpetoculturists live within the law. We have been disgusted by habitats that have been thoroughly shredded in efforts to find valuable snakes. In certain areas, collectors—not just with crowbars, but backhoes—have destroyed crevice habitats that were needed by snakes to survive in that area. In the south, where rocks are scarce, some have entirely stripped fallen trees of their bark in efforts to find snakes. Logs and rocks are often left overturned and far too many animals are collected. This must not continue. We encourage herpers to adopt a sportsmanlike, conservation-minded attitude toward these animals; enjoy the thrill of finding that rare snake, and then release it; collect a single individual or pair if you must, when it is legal, but that is all; respect the law with regard to those species that have very small populations, such as the montane rattlesnakes.

Laws protecting these animals should be based upon fact or at least common sense. There are numerous examples of animals, especially reptiles, but also mammals, that are easily bred in captivity but extremely rare in the wild. Thus, they are protected from collection and are not allowed to be maintained or bred in captivity, even though their habitat may be destroyed by land developers, and they may be killed by cars as they attempt to cross roads. At the time of their extinction in the wild, so few are in captivity and so little is known about their captive maintenance or medical problems that they are much more likely to be totally exterminated than if captive breeding were

allowed back when their numbers (and therefore gene pool) would have allowed the establishment of a stable population. An extremely good example of the failure of the system is that of the Florida panther. It was basically "managed" into near extinction by an overprotective bureaucracy that prevented captive breeding until it was too late. The same can be said for the California condor, although it now appears to be making a slow recovery. Will this be said about the indigo snake, giant garter snake, or ridgenose rattlesnake in the years to come? Will we learn from past mistakes and allow a sustainable yield for research and serious captive breeding efforts of those animals that can be captive-bred?

It is important to note that there are many more people opposed to herpetoculture than just those in government agencies. These people are constantly proposing legislation banning the captive maintenance of reptiles and amphibians, usually by evoking fear in the general population. The three major proposed threats are as follows: (1) the animals in question are dangerous; (2) the animals in question carry dangerous diseases; and (3) the animals in question are being totally eliminated by the pet trade. Some of these things are simply not true. Horses and dogs injure thousands of people every year. Pythons may injure at most a few hundred. Fast food restaurants give hundreds more people *Salmonella* food poisoning than reptiles do. And lastly, if the pet trade is the problem, then prevent the *sale* of reptiles. Legislation against all collection and captive maintenance is not a logical approach to the problem. Educate, don't legislate.

The previous discussion should in no way be construed as an argument in support of poaching rare and endangered animals. However, it is an argument for their legal harvesting (at levels that wild populations can support) and captive propagation. This is analogous to what hunters are allowed to do, except that those reptiles harvested are not being killed, only collected and bred in captivity.

One of the goals of this book is to continue to introduce some of North America's less commonly known snakes, and to discuss their natural history and captive maintenance. It is hoped that this work will be a convenient reference source on almost all of our native snakes. We also hope that it will be useful for both amateurs and professionals, working together to better understand and preserve these animals in whatever ways are necessary, as well as to help veterinarians who are called upon to treat these animals.

Please note that the range maps are merely approximations of the ranges of these snake. For more accurate or detailed range information, we advise the use of local field guides. Particularly useful among these are regional books which include county localities.

We have made every attempt possible to advise the feeding of captive-bred and -reared animals to captive snakes. If this is not possible, we have advised the feeding of non-native introduced or more commonly occurring natural food items, particularly those that do well around human habitation.

The recent explosion of publications and the proliferation of information on the internet has made it difficult to keep up with all that is going on in the field of herpetology. Certain books published in the last year of the production of this book were extremely significant contributions to this field, and the authors postponed the completion of this book in order to incorporate some of this new information. Perhaps the most significant of these recent books, in terms of understanding the ecology of North American snakes, is Henry Fitch's 50-year summary of observations on Kansas snakes, *A Kansas Snake Community: Composition and Changes over 50 Years*. The authors strongly recommend this book. Another highly significant work is Manny Rubio's 1998 book, *Rattlesnake, Portrait of a Predator*, which has a tremendous amount of useful information about rattlesnakes.

Lastly, we primarily utilized the common and scientific names found in *Standard Common and Current Scientific Names For North American Amphibians and Reptiles* by Joseph T. Collins, Fourth Edition (1997). However, at the time of this writing, there was still some debate over some of the newer names, and some confusion over the specific or subspecific status of a number of snakes. Some of the newer names are listed in parentheses next to the older names, or else the proposed changes have been discussed in the text. By doing so, we hope to avoid losing continuity with the literature published previously and perhaps to form a bridge to that which will follow. We feel that this approach is especially important for amateur herpetologists, who may not have access to all of the most recent literature. As mentioned above, there is still some debate over many of the newer names, and we have therefore chosen to include both the old and new names in some species accounts until the matter is settled by systematic herpetologists.

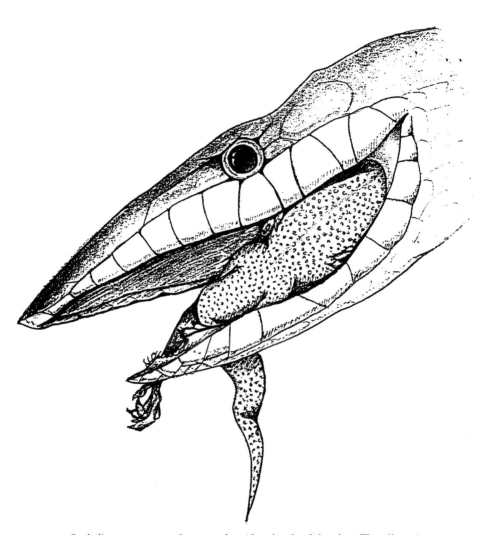

Oxybelis aenus consuming a gecko. (drawing by Johnathan Thomlinson)

NATURAL HISTORY NOTES ON SNAKES
AN OVERVIEW

Snakes are legless reptiles believed to have evolved from monitorlike lizards sometime in the Cretaceous Period, about 120 million years ago. During this time, the dinosaurs still ruled the surface of the earth, but there were many small burrowing mamals. Snakes may have evolved to take advantage of this fossorial food source; indeed, the loss of limbs and the fusion of the upper and lower eyelids would benefit a burrowing animal. Most other adaptations seen in snakes are probably directly or indirectly related to the legless condition. Without paws or claws to hold their prey or tear it apart, recurved teeth and distensible jaws developed. The skull and jaws became highly kinetic, or capable of movement; snakes became able to "walk" their jaws over prey items that were very large. As larger and more dangerous prey were taken, some snakes evolved the ability to constrict the prey, or developed potent saliva called venom and the means to deliver it—elongated teeth which were grooved or hollow. These are called fangs and the type of venom and fangs vary with the type of prey consumed. Snakes which consume primarily ectothermic prey are generally more likely to have neurotoxic venom, while those consuming mammalian prey are more likely to have primarily hemotoxic venom. Actually, there is a great deal of overlap, with many snakes possessing venom with both components. The Mojave rattlesnake and canebrake rattlesnake are two examples of snakes with such venoms. Other snakes developed constriction as a method of subduing prey. Venom, fangs, and means of constriction appear to have been developed independently in several groups of snakes. The great herpetologist Sherman Minton frequently asked the question: Are there really any nonvenomous snakes? Basically, he believed that all snakes were in the process of developing venom, even those that are still harmless to humans.

Indeed, many of our North American snakes appear to produce locally severe bites if we let them hang on and chew when they bite us.

If we classify the kinds of venom delivery systems among snakes, they generally fall into three groups referred to as opisthoglyphs, proteroglyphs, and solenoglyphs. Opisthoglyphous snakes are those with grooved enlarged rear teeth. Examples among North American snakes are numerous and include many snakes that are harmless to humans. Examples include ringneck snakes, crowned snakes, night snakes, cateyed snakes, Mexican vine snakes, lyre snakes, and black-striped snakes. Proteroglyphous snakes have fixed, hollow fangs in the front·of the mouth, and examples of snakes that possess this tooth arrangements are the coral snakes. The advanced weaponry among snakes belongs to the solenoglyphous snakes. These snakes possess hollow fangs that fold up when not in use. This allows a greater fang length, which is important if they must penetrate fur or feathers before they reach their target. The North American solenoglyphs include the rattlesnakes, copperheads, and cottonmouths.

The other obvious characteristic of snakes that differentiates them from the lizards is the absence of an observable external or middle ear. There is a bone called the columella which connects the jawbone to the inner ear. Whether or not snakes can hear has been a question for centuries. Most herpetologists believe that snakes do not hear airborne sounds as most other animals do, but that they can feel vibrations. Sound travels through solids or liquids faster than it does through air, and snakes are usually in contact with one or the other. Do they have an acute sense of vibration reception? Can the loosely attached bones of the skull and overlying elastic skin function as the bones of the middle ear and overlying tympanic membrane in other animals do?

While the acuity of snake hearing may be questionable, there is little doubt as to the presence of an effective sense of smell. That leads us to a discussion of another obvious external characteristic of snakes, the constantly flicking forked tongue. Previous researchers have shown that the tongue picks up particles in the environment and brings them into the mouth. Certain areas of on the floor of the mouth are then pushed upward to contact the openings of Jacobson's organ (a specialized structure lined with sensory epithelium), whereupon the snake effectively smells or tastes the particles. Snakes are excellent trackers; they can identify the scent trails of both prey and mates extremely well. Rattlesnakes have been reported to locate rodent trails by scent and then wait in ambush for the prey to come by again. Numerous studies by Dr. David Chiszar and others have shown just how accurate this sense is. From their work it is apparent that rattlesnakes can distinguish which rodent they have bitten, and can use the scent of their venom to help trail their prey. We have demonstrated that water snakes will spend more time in fish-scented locations than nonscented locations, and that they are capable of following a trail made by dragging a fish along the substrate. In fact, a number of researchers have shown that newborn snakes will tongue flick more quickly when the odor of their preferred prey is presented on a cotton swab than when a nonprey-scented swab is presented. Some of these innate preferences differ from population to population within a species, or even among individuals in the same clutch or litter, e.g., one population of prairie ringneck may prefer earthworms, while another may prefer smaller snakes; certain neonate corn snakes in the same clutch may prefer pinky mice, while others prefer lizards. Another interesting fact about olfaction in snakes is that their preferences appear to change with age. A 1-year-old snake may tongue flick more frequently when presented with rodent scent than lizard scent, just the opposite of when it was a hatchling.

Another sense identified in snakes is that of heat sensing or thermoreception. Vipers and boids have developed this sense independently, and both groups demonstrate heat pits. In the North American vipers, including rattlesnakes, copperhead, and cottonmouth, there is a single pit on each side of the face between the eye and nostril; thus, they are called pit vipers. These pits can accurately sense minute temperature differences and provide the snake with an infrared picture of its prey in total darkness, allowing the snake to accurately strike prey in low light conditions.

As mentioned above, the eyes of snakes have a clear shield over them, which was formed by the fusion of the eyelids. This epidermal shield is called the spectacle or brille, and is thought to represent an adaptation to a fossorial, or burrowing life style. Those snakes which remained fossorial have very reduced eyes, while those that are diurnal surface hunters have the largest eyes among snakes. Those snakes which are largely nocturnal tend to have elliptical pupils, but there are many exceptions such as hooknose snakes, leafnose snakes, and scarlet snakes. A number of aquatic snakes are largely nocturnal, yet they have round pupils. One snake, the glossy crayfish snake, appears to have extremely thick spectacles (eye shields), which may be an adaptation to prevent injuries from its hard-shelled prey or to help it see better under water.

Most snakes lack remnants of a pelvis, which is understandable since most snakes lack legs. Only the boas among North American snakes may have spurs where legs used to be, and remnants of a pelvic girdle. All snakes lack a sternum, or breast bone, which is also understandable since the ribs need increased mobility; furthermore, all snakes lack bladders and most lack a functional left lung. These latter two observations are believed to be associated with the economy of limited space in the elongated body plan of snakes. This elongated shape and flexibility of the skeleton has allowed snakes to move in a number of ways. There are four kinds of locomotion described including the "caterpillar crawl" or rectilinear motion, serpentine motion, sidewinding, and concertina locomotion. The caterpillar crawl is often used by heavy-bodied snakes as they crawl in a straight line. Different groups of scutes (enlarged belly scales) are lifted and moved forward, then placed down against the substrate and pulled backwards. Serpentine motion is used by most snakes at one time or another, and this involves a lateral motion that pushes against objects in the enviroment. Swimming is a form of serpentine motion. Sidewinding involves throwing a loop of the body forward and rapidly placing this loop down and pulling the tail and head forward. This rapid motion allows relatively rapid motion on smooth or loose surfaces, and has benefits in reducing body contact on extremely hot surfaces. It is used by some desert vipers, one of which bears the name sidewinder, as well as many snakes when they are placed on a very smooth surface and forced to move rapidly. Concertina motion is usually used by a medium- to heavy-bodied snake to climb a tree or other rough-surfaced object. It involves using several loops of the posterior body to push forward the front of the body, whereupon the front of the body grasps the surface with several loops and pulls the posterior part forward. The whole process is then repeated.

There are approximately 2700 species of snakes worldwide. These snakes are placed into 15 families, 5 of which are represented in the United States and Canada. These include the blind snakes, Leptotyphlopidae; the two boas, Boidae; the rattlesnakes, copperheads, and cottonmouths, Viperidae; coral snakes and the yellow-belly sea snake, Elapidae; and the vast majority of North American snakes, Colubridae. The colubrids include brown snakes, ground snakes, water snakes, garter snakes, kingsnakes, rat snakes, hognose snakes, leafnose snakes, patchnose snakes, longnose snakes, worm snakes, ringneck snakes, whipsnakes, racers, and a variety of other snakes. One introduced species has become established in the United States, the Brahminy blind snake, which is an all-female species that reproduces parthenogenetically. They are commonly transported in potted plants. These snakes are representative of the family Typhlopidae, another group of blind snakes.

Snakes basically exist because they are predators that can get where other predators can't. In addition, they are ectothermic, meaning that they derive the majority of their body heat from external sources, and generally have a lower metabolic rate than competing mammalian predators. This means they can go much longer between meals than mammals and birds. Combined with the fact that they are adapted to swallow relatively large meals by virtue of their jaw structure, survival and reproduction can be accomplished with very few meals. Indeed, studies of snake metabolism and observations of the feeding of wild snakes suggest that a snake only needs to consume between 2 and 4 times its weight on an annual basis for maintenance purposes. For a snake weighing half a kilogram (1 pound) this amounts to about 20–40 mice weighing 50 grams each or 3–6 rats weighing 330 grams each, or 1–2 rabbits weighing 1000 grams. Certainly a mammalian predator would starve on such a paltry diet. Hence, snakes have exploited a niche unused by mammals in a very efficient manner. Imagine surviving on 1–2 meals a year!

Yet snakes are also in the middle of most food chains (or webs), and they therefore form an important food source for larger predators. North American predators known to prey upon snakes include moles, shrews, weasels, otters, raccoons, skunks, foxes, coyotes, wolves, badgers, bobcats, lynx, cougars, jaguars, coatimundis, bears, wild hogs, eagles, hawks, falcons, crows, ravens, jays, shrikes, snapping turtles, alligators, large frogs, and other snakes. This makes snakes particularly susceptible to elimination from certain habitats, i.e., the habitat must be suitable for prey and it must also provide sufficient hiding areas for snakes. In addition, the habitat must not be severely polluted, since their prey may either be eliminated or else may bioconcentrate toxins, resulting in even higher levels in the snakes. This is one of the theories proposed for the disappearance of the smooth green snake, a terrestrial insectivore, from many areas. Successional changes to more mature plant cover are detrimental to certain species of snakes but may be beneficial to others (Fitch, 1999).

If one examines the distribution of snakes in the area covered by this book, it appears that there are five areas that harbor large numbers of endemic species of snakes. These areas include Florida, southern Texas, western Texas, Arizona, and California. Peninsular Florida has a

The Mojave Desert, perhaps the driest and most barren of America's true deserts, is nonetheless rich in reptile life, particularly snakes such as the Mojave rattlesnake, Mojave sidewinder, Mojave patchnose, Mojave glossy snake, Mojave shovelnose, speckled rattlesnake, spotted leafnose, rosy boa, coachwhip, longnose snake, and common kingsnake, among others. Shown here is the richest part of the Mojave Desert, dominated by Joshua trees. (photo by John Rossi)

The Chihuahuan Desert does not appear to be a hospitable place, but is home to many species of snakes, including ground snakes, hooknose snakes, glossy snakes, longnose snakes, bullsnakes, whipsnakes, kingsnakes (both common kingsnakes, the gray-banded kingsnake), and the Trans-Pecos rat snake, among others. (photo by John Rossi)

The Sonoran Desert, which extends into Arizona, is the richest desert in the United States, and has many species of snakes as well. These include: the banded sand snake, leafnose snakes (two species), shovelnose snakes (two species), the desert hooknose, Arizona coral snake, tiger rattlesnake, green rat snake, and Sonoran whipsnake, among others. (photo by John Rossi)

Grasslands are a major habitat type for North American snakes. Massasaugas, prairie rattlesnakes, prairie kingsnakes, prairie ringnecks, Kirtland's snakes (in moist areas), bullsnakes, plains garter snakes, and lined snakes are found primarily in this habitat type. This particular picture was taken at the Tall Grass Prairie Preserve in Oklahoma. (photo by John Rossi)

relatively warm climate, and at least in geological terms has been isolated from the mainland, and this would help to explain the present snakes species diversity. Southern Texas, near the Rio Grande, is referred to as the "Valley," and numerous Tamalupian species range into this area from the south. West Texas is part of the Chihuahuan Desert, and there are many endemic species of reptiles there. The Sonoran Desert, richest of all deserts in terms of plant and animal life, is found in southern and central Arizona. Arizona also possesses numerous mountain "islands" in the desert which harbor a number of endemic species. Lastly, Califor-

This is the Central Valley of California. Dominated by bunchgrass, this habitat appears to be somwehat inhospitable to many kinds of snakes, whose ranges encircle this unique grassland. However, generalists such as the kingsnake, racer, glossy snake, longnose snake, night snake, and some garter snakes are found here. The giant garter snake, formerly found along heavily vegetated waterways throughout this valley, is now found in only a small portion of the Central Valley. (photo by John Rossi)

Wet prairie vegetation near a pond in Ohio. This kind of habitat is dwindling rapidly, and with it some of the snake species commonly associated with this habitat, e.g., Kirtland's snake and Butler's garter snake. (photo by John Rossi)

Open, prickly-pear-dominated savanna in south Texas. Half desert, half grassland, this savanna is rich in snake species, although there are few species endemic to this area. The Texas indigo snake and whipsnakes seem to thrive in this sandy, open habitat. (photo by John Rossi)

Desert mountain ranges are islands of diversity, with many endemic species. Pictured here are forested hillsides in the Huachuca Mountains of southern Arizona. Rock rattlesnakes, blacktail rattlesnakes, and ridgenose rattlesnakes are found here, as well as a number of other snakes. (photo by John Rossi)

nia, with its tremendous habitat diversity, from coastal rain forests to the harsh Mojave Desert, is home to a great variety of snakes.

Indeed, the distribution of North American snakes demonstrates a pattern common for reptiles, with the largest number of species found closer to the equator, and a gradual reduction in that species diversity as one travels northward. Within that framework, species diversity is also affected by geological features, such as mountain ranges, lakes, and rivers, and climatic factors, such as annual rainfall, all of which combine to form a number of micro-habitats. Like latitude, the elevation has a huge

Forested rocky hillsides in the Sierra Nevada mountains of California are home to a variety of western North American snakes, including rubber boas, sharptail snakes, California mountain kingsnakes, and Sierra garter snakes. (photo by John Rossi)

Sand hill turkey oak habitat is seen commonly in the southeast. It is commonly occupied by scarlet kingsnakes, coachwhips, racers, southern and eastern hognose snakes, Florida pine snakes, and, in central Florida, the short-tailed snake. (photo by John Rossi)

Rich broadleaf deciduous forests dominate much of the eastern and central part of North America. Many small woodland species such as worm snakes, brown snakes, redbelly snakes, and smooth green snakes are found in suitable areas in these forests. (photo by John Rossi)

Pine flatwoods are widespread throughout the southeastern United States. Corn snakes, kingsnakes, earth snakes, southern ringneck snakes, and pine woods snakes may be common here. (photo by John Rossi)

effect on the temperature and humidity of an area. The geological and biological history of the area are also critical factors in determining the number of species present. The biogeography of many North American amphibians and reptiles is discussed in a number of herpetology reference books and will not be discussed here. In any case, habitats of importance for North American snakes include the four major deserts, Mojave, Sonoran, Chihuahua, and Great Basin, the midwestern moist prairies and grasslands, the major mountain ranges that travel north and south, the riverine communities, the pine dominated flatlands and swamps of the southeastern United States, the coniferous forests of the western and northern parts of the continent, and the deciduous forests of the eastern and central areas of North America.

A large number of North American snake species can probably be placed into artificial groups based upon habitat and prey similarities. These might include the following: (1) moist soil-dwelling invertebrate predators like worm snakes, earth snakes, lined snakes, ringneck snakes, and smooth green snakes; (2) dry sandy soil-dwelling invertebrate predators such as shovelnose snakes, banded sand snakes, hooknose snakes, and ground snakes; (3) woodland vertebrate predators such as pine woods snakes, certain milk snakes, common rat snakes, eastern and southern hognose snakes, eastern coral snakes, and timber rattlesnakes; (4) plains vertebrate predators such as great plains rat snakes, prairie kingsnakes, prairie rattlesnakes, massasaugas, and fox snakes; and (5) desert vertebrate predators such as night snakes, lyre snakes, desert kingsnakes, mojave rattlesnakes, speckled rattlesnakes, rock rattlesnakes, sidewinders, whipsnakes, and the two desert rat snakes. These groups are not inclusive and there are a number of species that are habitat and dietary generalists. The bullsnake, racer, and western rattlesnake are such species. These species are found in a variety of habitats. Others are so specialized that they don't fall into these broad groups either. Some species survive only on mountaintops, others in certain valleys; some are highly arboreal, such as the rough green snake and Mexican vine snake; and some specialize on a single food item like centipedes or spiders. There are also large groups of aquatic snakes, some of which are

Snakes, like other predators, may be classified as either generalists or specialists. The cat-eyed snake shown here is eating a fish, but this species has been reported to consume a wide variety of prey items including amphibians and their eggs, small snakes, and mammals. Hence, it might be considered to be a dietary generalist, even though it is specialized with regard to its habitat preference. (photo by John Rossi)

specialized upon particular food items such as crayfish or aquatic salamanders, while others seem to be generalized feeders, consuming anything in the right size range. Garter snakes, a very diverse transcontinental group, possess species which occupy all of the niches discussed above. Some species seem very plastic and occupy different niches in different areas. The racer and ringneck are examples of such species. Other species, such as the scarlet snake in the east and the leafnose snakes in the west, appear to be specialized upon reptile eggs and occur wherever the eggs are common. Basically, every habitat type in the warmer parts of North America is occupied by snakes and most animals from ant eggs and termites up to medium-sized mammals and birds are potential prey for some species of snake.

No two species of snake appear to occupy the exact same niche in the same area, i.e., if they live in the same habitat, they don't usually eat the same food (or at least not at the same time of day). This is called the principle of competitive exclusion by ecologists. However, habitats change and animals evolve, so sometimes snakes compete with each other for food or space. Competition between snakes may be intraspecific (between members of the same species) or interspecific (between members of two different species). If similar food items are consumed, snakes may actually fight over a food item, and the smaller one either lets go or may be eaten by the larger snake. Competition may also occur over territories or mates. The ritualized "dances" we have mentioned elsewhere are an example of intraspecific competition over a territory or a mate. In some instances, snakes may compete for a limited number of hiding areas or shelters. When habitat changes occur, either natural or manmade, those species specialized for a certain habitat, or severely restricted in range, are placed in danger of extinction. This is accelerated by the invasion of generalist species into the new habitat whereby competition occurs. An example is occurring in the Brazos River of central Texas. When dams were placed in the fast-flowing rocky river, they slowed down the water flow and allowed silt to be deposited along the river's edge. Vegetation started grow-

Rivers and lakes provide critical habitat for many species of snakes along their shores and in nearby moist areas. Most water snakes and garter snakes, all crayfish snakes, black swamp snakes, and fox snakes are some of the snakes found along the water's edge. This is the Brazos River in central Texas, home of the endangered Brazos water snake. The river has been changed by damming, thereby threatening the endemic species even more. (photo by John Rossi)

ing right down to the edge of the slower moving river, and many rocks were buried. Large heavy-bodied water snakes increased in number and the Brazos water snake, adapted to fast-flowing waters with lots of rocks for cover, began to dwindle in number. See that section for a detailed discussion.

Snakes are known for their innate preferences for certain food and, as mentioned above, this may vary within a species from one geographic location to another, i.e., some garter snakes prefer worms, others slugs at birth. Snakes also demonstrate ontogenetic food shifts, with young snakes of a species preferring one food, while maturing snakes prefer another. Some species also seem to demonstrate dietary preferences that differ to some extent between the sexes. Female snakes are often less selective than males; it has been hypothesized that this may be related to their higher energy demands for reproduction. Some snakes appear to demonstrate seasonal food preferences, even though this may be based upon changing food availability from season to season. Another factor entering into this picture is the selection of different microhabitats by different age and size groups of snakes. The young may prefer moister environments, resulting in an entirely different variety of available prey. Similarly, young snakes are often active on the surface both earlier and later than adults of the same species. This may indicate either a greater tolerance for lower temperatures or the ability to heat up faster their than larger relatives. Certainly, food items ingested by smaller species are not only smaller but also more easily digested than larger food items. Indeed, there are few species of large snakes in northern areas; many in the south.

Reproduction in North American snakes generally falls into several patterns. The majority mate in the spring or fall, ovulation occurs in the spring, and young are born mid- to late summer. The gestation period of most live-bearing snakes varies from 90 to 150 days while the gestation period for egg laying species (the time from mating to laying eggs) usually varies from 30 to 45 days. Incubation periods of these eggs have ranged from an unusually short 4 days to 120 days, with the eggs of most species averaging around 60 days. Some of the larger species in the north may take as many as 5–7 years to reach sexual maturity, while smaller species in the south may reach sexual maturity in 1 year. Timber rattlesnakes in New York may take as many as 7 years to reach maturity, and may breed only every 2 or 3 years. Earth snakes and brown snakes in Florida may reach maturity in 1 year and breed annually. Perhaps the most unusual reproduction pattern of any North American snake is that of the lined snake.

Rocky streams provide suitable microhabitats for many species, particularly the queen snake and Graham's crayfish snake, as well as the rainbow snake and mud snake. (photo by John Rossi)

Breeding occurs immediately after the female gives birth, almost invariably in mid-August. Sperm is stored and ovulation occurs the following spring, so that neonates are born again the following August. Many mountain rattlesnakes also mate in the fall, and give birth the following fall after a delayed ovulation. Lowland rattlesnakes often mate in the spring and give birth the same fall. At least one species follows a very tropical pattern, mating in the winer. Indigo snakes mate in December and January, resulting in eggs being deposited in April or May. The mating season of a number of North American snakes is unknown. The short-tailed snake of central Florida is still a mystery, with most of its natural history largely unknown. Most female snakes generally invest about one-third of their body weight into annual reproduction, i.e., a litter or clutch will weigh about 33% of the female's weight prior to delivery. Natricine snakes such as water snakes and garter snakes, lined snakes, brown snakes, earth snakes, redbelly snakes, and Kirtland's snake, as well as vipers and boas, bear live young, and some placental exchange is thought to occur. The rest of the North American snakes are egg bearers, and these include

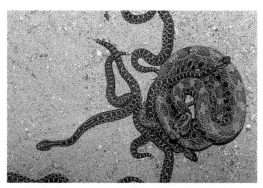

All North American vipers are live bearers. Shown here is a Massasauga with her clutch. It should be noted that the babies of many species of rattlesnake have now been observed to remain with the mother for a prolonged period of time after they are born. They may also remain with their siblings long after the mother is gone. The reasons for this are not yet known, but hypothetically it confers increased survival value. (photo by Steve Barten)

not only all of the popular pet snakes such as kingsnakes and rat snakes, but many other less well-known snakes. Herpetologists have argued for years over why some snakes lay eggs and others bear live young. See the discussion below.

Regarding clutch size, it is generally accepted that the larger the female snake is, the larger the clutch. Neonate size may also be larger with larger females, but this is not always the case. Maternal care is poorly known in snakes and not presently believed to be significant. It is known that young vipers will often spend up to several weeks in the vicinity of the mother. Young colubrids usually do not. Perhaps there is some selective value for the young vipers if the presence of the mother deters potential predators. However, young colubrid siblings often demonstrate a mutual affinity for each other. They may remain with each other and sometimes travel together for weeks. The benefit of this behavior is unknown, but many other small vertebrates are known to remain in groups for the protection that such groups confer.

Other complex behaviors have been observed in snakes. Many people are familiar with the "mating dances" of snakes in the spring. These usually involve two males each trying to test the strength of the other by attempting to knock each other down. The winner maintains the territory and presumably the mating rights to females entering that territory. Interestingly, this behavior has been observed in females as well. Generally speaking, those species displaying intermale aggression have larger males than females.

Mating pairs of snakes have been known to remain together for many weeks, although true monogamy lasting longer than one season is not believed to occur in North American snakes. In fact, both sexes may mate with multiple partners each season. The mating season for most species appears to be the spring, but another peak of mating activity occurs in the fall. Some species such as cottonmouths may mate all year except in the dead of winter, while others such as the lined snake mate right after a litter is born. If mating occurs in the fall, delayed ovulation usually occurs the following spring utilizing the sperm stored over the winter. Herpetologists also believe that long-term sperm storage (LTSS) may occur and that sperm may be stored for several years. However, the recent findings that some colubrid and viperid snakes may reproduce parthenogenetically have made some of the reports of LTSS (e.g., 7 years in a cat-eyed snake) questionable. Typically, if parthenogenesis occurs in vipers or colubrids, very small litters consisting of all males are produced. We have observed this in eastern garter snakes that were raised in captivity and had never been with a male, and in a narrowhead garter snake, where normal spring mating was unsuccessful and one or two males would be born at unusual times of the year. This "opportunistic" parthenogenesis in normally sexually reproducing species is different from the obligate parthenogenesis which occurs in the Brahminy blind snake. In this species, like in some lizards, only females are produced.

Once mating has occurred, eggs or live young may be produced. Snakes that produce live young are called ovoviviparous (although some are nearly totally placental, which would be termed viviparous), while those that produce eggs are called oviparous. Oviparous or egg laying species include kingsnakes, rat snakes, hognose snakes, worm snakes, ground snakes, leafnose snakes, hooknose snakes, lyre snakes, night snakes, glossy snakes, shovelnose snakes, longnose snakes, and others. Examples of live-bearing snakes include garter snakes, ribbon snakes, water snakes, crayfish snakes, swamp snakes, earth snakes, brown snakes, redbelly snakes, the yellowbelly sea snake, and all of the North American vipers. The evolutionary forces that have produced this division of reproductive strategies are not entirely understood. One can certainly see the benefit of live birth to snakes that live in cold climates. There the mother may behaviorally regulate her body temperature to "incubate" the eggs in a safer and more consistent fashion. Additional nutrition may also be provided to the young as it becomes available. However, we believe that the driving force for most live-bearing among colubrid snakes is their invasion of aquatic environments. Indeed, only the aquatic or semi-aquatic colubrids in North America bear live

young. One can argue that the earth snake, brown snake, or redbelly snake are not aquatic, but they are certainly close relatives of those that are. Furthermore, they are often found in moist environments that may flood, thus making egg laying more risky. In addition, there is a greater likelihood for predation around aquatic environments, especially by invertebrates. Indeed, the only truly aquatic North American snakes that lay eggs are mud snakes and rainbow snakes, and note that they guard them. The two hypothetical explanations for this behavior include protection from predation and assistance with nest humidity. One of the possible explanations for this is that these snakes are xenodontine snakes, which as a group are largely terrestrial egg layers, and that they just evolved a different way of reproducing when they invaded an aquatic environment.

The behavior of snakes is dependent upon many things, for they are much more complex animals than we previously imagined (Gillingham, 1987). One of the most important physical factors of their environment that helps determine behavior is the temperature. As ectotherms—animals which derive the majority of body heat from outside the body—they depend upon achieving a certain body temperature to accomplish different tasks. They are not totally at the mercy of the environment, how

The need to regulate body temperature is critical to many snakes, such as this gravid Brazos water snake. Many snakes will attempt to maintain a very narrow range of body temperature for various functions, such as digestion, immune system function, or reproduction. (photo by John Rossi)

ever; they can choose where they go and how long they stay there; they can choose to remain exposed on the surface or just under a sun-warmed rock; if it gets too hot during the day, they can move around and hunt at night. Herpetologists refer to this as behavioral thermoregulation. If they are visually oriented diurnal predators, they can choose to hunt in the morning and late afternoon rather than at midday. It is probably not a coincidence that many large snakes living in northern latitudes are dark-colored, while those from southern areas of North America are light-colored. Dark objects absorb heat faster, light-colored objects may reflect more light and heat. Even when the exterior of a snake is light-colored, the lining of the uterus and tissue over the uterus in a live-bearing snake is often darkly pigmented, suggesting that a "radiation-absorbing incubator" is present.

The ultimate temperature control is the ability to survive the extremes. Most snakes brumate (hibernate) during extremely cold weather. Those from northern areas or high altitudes usually migrate to "safe places" such as deep fissures in rock outcroppings. In the case of rattlesnakes, it is often near the area where they were born. These communal dens often house hundreds of snakes representing many different species. The dens may have been used for hundreds of years and, unfortunately, once they are found, they are susceptible to easy destruction or disturbance by man. Snakes from warmer climates often brumate on the run. They seek shelters wherever they may be available and may stay there for only a short period of time. Other species or individuals may or may not be there. As soon as a warming trend arrives, they may move on to another site. Those in the north do not eat during this time, while those in the south might. The greatest danger to a hibernating snake is dehydration, with predation by rodents or other predators being another major risk. Freezing to death is probably rare, since most hibernaculums provide enough insulation from the cold and most North American snakes can tolerate near freezing temperatures. Eastern diamondback rattlesnakes often get caught on the surface when freezing weather occurs in South Carolina.

They have been observed with frost on them, but they seem to recover. One of our friends once placed a small injured diamondback in the freezer for several days to finish the task started by the automobile that hit the snake. He pulled the apparently frozen and stiff snake out of the freezer 2 days later and let it thaw on his kitchen table. When he went to pick it up several hours later, it rattled and struck at him. Fortunately, it missed, but you can imagine his surprise. Indeed, North American snakes appear well adapted to handle the cold. Intense heat is also a threat, and many snakes will become inactive for weeks during these hot times also. This process of summer inactivity has been referred to as estivation.

In summary, snakes are fascinating animals. North American snakes are perhaps the most well-known snakes in the world, yet many are still poorly understood. The natural history of these animals, the basic information about their lives, is summarized at the beginning of each species discussion. These discussions include habitat, predators and prey, some notes on thermal ecology, and reproductive data. Some notes on behavior are included as well. If a species is threatened or endangered, we have often included a discussion of some of the present threats to this species. We have relied on many references to create these summaries, however, a large number of our own field observations and a good deal of original breeding data are presented here for the first time. In addition to including much of our own research, we have included some original research done by amateur herpetologists around North America. For some species, the discussion is very detailed. For other species, not much is known or we have chosen to shorten the summary in order to save space. The Society for the Study of Amphibians and Reptiles (SSAR) publishes a series of species summaries which are excellent sources of information. The professional journals such as the *Journal of Herpetology*, *Copeia*, and *Herpetologica* are wealths of information as well. *Herpetological Review* is usually heavily laden with original field observations of North American snakes, and the *Bulletin of the Chicago Herpetological Society* typically has a variety of very good original research and summaries of some of the recent professional work. The reader is referred to these sources for more details on the species in question. It is beyond the scope of this book to provide detailed systematic and ecological discussions on each species of snake. Detailed discussions of snake ecology are presented in Seigel et al., 1987, Seigel and Collins, 1993, and Fitch, 1999. Readers may also gain a great deal of insight about the evolution of North American snakes by reading *Fossil Snakes of North America* by J. Allen Holman (Holman, 2000).

CONSERVATION

At the time of this writing, most species of North American snakes appear stable. However, there are a number of species that are already threatened and many, many more that are on the verge of achieving some form of threatened status. Some species are threatened in some states but common in others. Many populations are in rapid decline in some areas but appear to be thriving in other areas. What are the major forces shaping the future of North American snakes and what can be done to protect them?

The major threats to our snake populations appear to be habitat destruction, habitat fragmentation, automobiles, pollution, fear and ignorance, and overcollection. The relative importance of these factors varies from species to species and even from place to place for the same species. For example, montane rattlesnakes and kingsnakes are heavily collected in spite of legal protection, even though their mountain habitats are relatively stable. On the other hand, many lowland species face major

Huge areas of North America remain agricultural. Several species of snakes seem to thrive in these areas, when enough cover is left for them to hide and thin corridors of undisturbed habitat remain. This photo was taken in southern Texas. (photo by John Rossi)

habitat destruction, habitat fragmentation by road construction, pollution, and persecution by fearful and ignorant people. Some species actually appear to be spreading and may thrive around human habitation, but these species are certainly in the minority.

Attempting to conserve our native snakes will be a challenge. Snakes do not engender the positive public support more commonly reserved for the "warm, fuzzy creatures." Without public support and education, even government projects will not guarantee the continued survival of many species; therefore, public education is considered by these authors to be the most important tool for conservation of snakes. We need to make people aware of the beauty and diversity of these fascinating animals, an awareness that should stimulate an interest in preserving snakes and reduce the needless killing. Indeed, there is no other group of wild animals so persecuted as snakes.

Other conservation measures need to concentrate on preserving habitats, especially those that are environmentally sensitive and those that contain large numbers of snakes. Perhaps the most sensitive habitats are wetlands, mountains, and prairies. All too commonly, swamps or marshes are drained or filled in for development. Mitigation should consist of setting aside some of the original high quality wetlands, not the creation of artificial and low diversity wetlands. Mountains also provide a great deal of refuge for our wildlife, and this habitat is important. Another habitat under siege is the prairie. Large preserves usually work well for both large and small species. The authors had the opportunity to visit the Tall Grass Prairie Preserve in Oklahoma, and marvel at its wildlife. We are now indeed aware that many species of snakes have much larger home ranges than we thought, sometimes as much as several hundred acres.

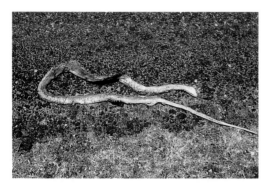

A dead Ruthven's whipsnake in south Texas. Roads are one of the greatest threats to snakes. Not only are many snakes killed by motor vehicles, many populations of snakes are isolated on smaller and smaller "islands" formed by the increasing number of roads. This has a destabilizing effect on these populations and allows progressive localized extinctions to occur. (photo by John Rossi)

Every effort should be made to conserve as much land as possible, but perhaps another important issue is that of habitat fragmentation. Contiguous preserves—or at least preserves that have natural corridors between them—will help tremendously to conserve species diversity and population stability. Roads are the worst habitat-fragmenting agents. Those passing through environmentally sensitive areas should have drift fences and underground tunnels to allow the wildlife to cross unharmed.

This is being done extensively in Europe now, and if they are built in at the time of the original construction they are not that much more costly. Remember, the size of these tunnels need not be large.

Pollution and pesticides may have seriously affected our native snakes, even though this is not known with certainty. Terrestrial insect-eating snakes, such as smooth green snakes, would be particularly susceptible because of their increased exposure; however, all reptiles must be considered as very sensitive to pollutants, especially organophosphate insecticides. Experienced snake collectors in the Midwest have shared an ominous observation. They say if the land has ever been sprayed or "turned over," you won't find smooth green snakes there. Hence, the use of pesticides, particularly long-lived organophosphates and fertilizers, should be restricted in some areas.

Overcollection has been a problem in recent years. The time has come for bag limits and possession limits to be put into effect in most states and provinces. While this is not popular with many herpetoculturists, it is a prudent and timely course of action, the intent of which is to preserve these animals for a sustainable yield so collectors in the future may enjoy the sport of hunting and collecting snakes, much as those today are doing. Success will involve the adoption of a sportsmanlike attitude on the part of collectors, and a game management attitude in the wildlife agencies

The Mexican garter snake is believed to be going extinct in the United States because of the introduction of another predator to the west—the bullfrog! (photo by Cecil Schwalbe)

Texas Indigos hatching. Captive breeding may become a valuable tool in future conservation efforts. (photo by David G. Campbell)

that control those areas. Aside from bag limits, management techniques may also include open and closed seasons, alternate open years, size limits, and the maintenance of some areas that are closed to hunting. Restocking may even be an option at some point in the future, and the cost of reptile/snake hunting permits may need to be raised to help with these management efforts. There are some species which need a great deal of protection, and others which, at this time, do not. However, most species could withstand some limited harvest, particularly if only the young were legal and the adults had to be "thrown back." Snake hunters should indeed adopt a "bird watching" or sport fishing mentality: study about it, find its habitat, enjoy the sport of finding it, photograph it, and release it. We have observed over the years that we get the same satisfaction from finding that rare snake and photographing it as we used to when we collected it.

Perhaps the most deplorable snake-related activities in North America are the rattlesnake roundups. Like passenger pigeon and buffalo shoots, these have no place in the 21st century and they should be outlawed. Any cultural events surrounding this time of the year could continue without the collection and inhumane treatment of these animals. This has been done successfully in some areas of Florida, where rattlesnake festivals are held, not roundups.

Conserving snakes will be a challenge. We know that snakes are wonderful and fascinating creatures. We know they are important in most food webs and help provide stability to many ecosystems. We know they are complex and highly evolved animals with complicated behaviors. We know that they are shy and nonaggressive toward people and do not need to be feared. Lastly, we know they are very sensitive to human activities. What we don't yet know is how to preserve them, and whether we can educate the public about these valuable animals before it is too late.

NORTH AMERICAN SNAKE GENERA

At the time of this writing there are at least 51 genera of Serpentes (snakes) that are native to North America (north of Mexico). The genus name is listed first, followed by the common name and number of species.

Agkistrodon—copperhead and cottonmouth (2 species)
Arizona—glossy snake (1 species)
Bogertophis—desert rat snakes (2 species)
Carphophis—worm snake (2 species)
Cemophora—scarlet snake (1 species)
Charina—rubber boa (1 species)
Chilomeniscus—sand snake (1 species)
Chionactis—shovelnose snakes (3 species)
Clonophis—Kirtland's snake (1 species)
Coluber—racers (1 species)
Coniophanes—black-striped snakes (1 species)
Contia—sharptail snake (1 species)
Crotalus—rattlesnakes (13 species)
Diadophis—ringneck snake (1 species)
Drymarchon—indigo snake (2 species)
Drymobius—speckled racers (1 species)
Elaphe—rat snakes and fox snakes (5+ species)
Farancia—mud snake and rainbow snake (2 species)
Ficimia—Mexican hooknose snakes (1 species)
Gyalopion—plateau hooknose snakes (2 species)
Heterodon—hognose snakes (3 species)
Hypsiglena—night snakes (1 species)
Lampropeltis—kingsnakes and milk snake (6 species)
Leptodeira—cat-eyed snakes (1 species)
Leptotyphlops—blind snakes (2 species)
Lichanura—rosy boa (1 species)

Masticophis—whipsnakes, striped racer, and coachwhip (4 species)
Micruroides—western coral snake (1 species)
Micrurus—eastern coral snake (1 species)
Nerodia—water and salt marsh snakes (10 species)
Opheodrys (*Liochlorophis*)—green snakes (2 species)
Oxybelis—vine snakes (1 species)
Pelamis—sea snake (1 species)
Phyllorhynchus—leafnose snakes (2 species)
Pituophis—bullsnake, pine snake, and gopher snake (2 species)
Regina—crayfish snakes (4 species)
Rhadinaea—pine woods snakes (1 species)
Rhinocheilus—longnose snake (1 species)
Salvadora—patchnose snakes (3 species)
Seminatrix—swamp snake (1 species)
Senticolis—mountain rat snake (1 species)
Sistrurus—pigmy rattlesnakes and massasauga (2 species)
Sonora—ground snakes (1 species)
Stilosoma—short-tailed snake (1 species)
Storeria—brown and redbelly snakes (2 species)
Tantilla—blackhead, flathead, and crowned snakes (11 species)
Thamnophis—garter and ribbon snakes (16 species)
Trimorphodon—lyre snakes (1 species)
Tropidoclonion—lined snake (1 species)
Virginia—earth snakes (2 species)

At the time of this writing, there is one introduced genus.
Ramphotyphlops—Brahminy blind snake (1 species)

PART I

KEEPING SNAKES
GENERAL CARE

Housing

This section has been placed first because, ideally, the enclosure should be set up before the snake arrives. Of course, you will need to have some idea of what kind of snake you are getting and how big it is before arranging the enclosure for it, so do read the section on choosing a snake if you have not already made your decision.

The first part of the housing discussion will center on the basics such as size, shape, and materials useful in the construction of snake enclosures. The second part of the housing section will discuss different arrangements of substrate (enclosure floor materials) and cage accessories. These arrangements are referred to as "setups," and each setup is discussed in some detail. Be sure to see the individual species sections for specifics and more details on particular species.

The Basics

In general, all cages should have smooth waterproof sides and bottoms. This facilitates cleaning, disinfection, and mite or other ectoparasite elimination. Glass, fiberglass, plastic, and rustproof metal are all ideal. Wood should be used only if treated in such a way as to make it smooth and waterproof. You can sand it finely and use water sealant or lacquer for this purpose, but make sure it is thoroughly dry and does not smell of chemicals at all before you place the snake in it. Untreated wood is abrasive, drying, and porous, therefore, it is nearly impossible to disinfect and it often has cracks that are almost impossible to rid of mites.

Glass aquariums with grooved, sliding, tight-fitting (or locking) tops will work very well for most snakes. Pegboard can be substituted for screen as long as you cut it to fit tightly and secure it properly; however, remember that pegboard may restrict ventilation significantly and can hold moisture, and therefore support bacteria and mold. It also restricts the flow of light into the enclosure. The newer metal-rimmed screens with metal clips work well. The older plastic tops and clips that tighten with turn screws will also work but are a bit

more tricky. If you aren't very careful to push these down all the way before you tighten the screws, small snakes will escape. These types of lids should be avoided for kingsnakes, rat snakes, young whipsnakes, lyre snakes, and night snakes as all of these are extremely adept at escaping (all snakes are good at escaping, but in our experience with U.S. snakes, these are the most likely to do so). Modified aquariums with groove-fitting sliding tops are far superior to clip-on or screw-on lids when it comes to preventing escapes, especially in the climbing muscular species mentioned above. Set pins are strongly recommended. Of course, venomous species must be maintained in locked terraria.

Fiberglass cages are now available with sliding glass fronts that work well. Wooden snake cages, also available commercially, can be used provided they are treated as outlined above.

The size and shape of the enclosure are just as important as the material used to construct it. In general, the length of the cage should at least be equal to the length of the snake and be a minimum of one-half as wide as it is long. Enclosures slightly smaller than this can work for the more sedentary species, including many of the kingsnakes, rat snakes, boas, and hognose snakes. Larger enclosures will be fine for most, but may be essential for the more active species such as coachwhip, whipsnakes, and racers. Remember that the larger the enclosure, the more difficult it will be for snakes that are fed live prey to find their food, especially those in more natural arrangements. However, most snakes are fed using feeding tongs.

One must also take into account if feeding and breeding will be accomplished in smaller enclosures. Some of the larger species may require a large area in which to mate easily (e.g., coachwhip, bullsnake, and pine snake).

Use Table 1 to determine enclosure size for the average-sized adult of the respective species. Juveniles of the larger species can, of course, be started in smaller enclosures and moved up as they grow.

Once the style, shape, and size of the enclosure is determined, it is ready to be set up in an appropriate manner. The setup will vary considerably based on the snake's natural environ-

Table 1. Suitable Enclosure Sizes (Gallon Aquarium) for Snakes of the United States and Canada

Species	10 gal	20 gal	30L gal	40L gal	DC
Black-striped snake	×				
Blackhead/Crowned/Flathead snake	×				
Blind snake	×				
Brown snake	×				
Eastern ribbon snake	×				
Ground snake	×				
Hooknose snake (all)	×				
Kirtland's snake	×				
Lined snake	×				
Night snake	×				
Pine woods snake	×				
Redbelly snake	×				
Rough earth snake	×				
Sand snake	×				
Scarlet snake	×				
Scarlet kingsnake	×				
Sharptail snake	×				
Shorthead snake	×				
Shovelnose snake	×				
Smooth earth snake	×				
Smooth green snake	×				
Southern hognose snake	×				
Swamp snake	×				
Worm snake	×				
Cat-eyed snake	×	×			
Coral snake	×	×			
Crayfish/Queen snake	×	×			
Eastern hognose snake	×	×			
Garter snake (all)	×	×			
Glossy snake	×	×			
Gray-banded kingsnake	×	×			
Leafnose snake (all)	×	×			
Longnose snake	×	×			
Lyre snake	×	×			
Massasauga rattlesnake	×	×			
Mountain kingsnake	×	×			
Ridgenose rattlesnake	×	×			
Rock rattlesnake	×	×			
Rosy boa	×	×			
Short-tailed snake	×	×			
Sidewinder	×	×			
Tiger rattlesnake	×	×			
Trans-Pecos rat snake	×	×			
Twin-spotted rattlesnake	×	×			
Western ribbon snake	×	×			
Water snake (all)	×	×	×		
Rough green snake		× (H)			
Common kingsnake		×	×		
Copperhead		×	×		

Table 1. Suitable Enclosure Sizes (Gallon Aquarium) for Snakes of the United States and Canada (continued)

Species	10 gal	20 gal	30L gal	40L gal	DC
Giant garter snake		×	×		
Patchnose snake (all)		×	×		
Prairie kingsnake		×	×		
Racer		×	×		
Rat snake (all)		×	×		
Speckled racer		×	×		
Western rattlesnake		×	×		
Speckled rattlesnake		×	×	×	
Whipsnake		×	×	×	
Blacktail rattlesnake			×	×	
Mojave rattlesnake			×	×	
Mud snake			×	×	
Rainbow snake			×	×	
Red diamond rattlesnake			×	×	
Bull-/Gopher snake			×	×	×
Green rat snake			×	×	×
Western diamondback rattlesnake			×	×	×
Coachwhip				×	×
Cottonmouth				×	×
Eastern diamondback rattlesnake				×	×
Indigo snake				×	×
Pine snake				×	×
Timber rattlesnake				×	×
Mexican vine snake					×

DC = display cases or homemade cage (see individual for size). L = long (as opposed to high aquariums. H = high (as opposed to long aquariums).

ment and its adaptability. Those terrestrial snakes that are adaptable will often thrive in artificial arrangements, while very secretive, burrowing (fossorial), or aquatic snakes will require more complex arrangements that often approximate their natural environment and that provide suitable microhabitats.

Basic Enclosure Setup

The basic setup is perhaps the most commonly used arrangement for captive snakes today. It is highly artificial, although it can be very attractive, and is the easiest to clean of all of the enclosure interiors. It consists of one kind of substrate, usually an artificial one such as indoor-outdoor carpet, artificial turf, or newspaper, a hide box, and a water bowl. A variety of other substrates—including aspen shavings,

pine shavings, orchid bark, smooth gravel top-soil, and clay beads—have been successfully used for these enclosures.

Other enclosure accessories that appear to benefit the captive snake and also improve the attractiveness of the enclosure for humans include branches, rocks, and plastic or cloth plants. These plants often look very realistic and are less likely to be flattened by a wandering snake than real plants are. In addition, these artificial plants are disinfectable and rarely if ever carry parasites or bacteria that may be harmful to snakes. In very dry environments, live plants hold humidity and may be ideal for very small snakes, but watch for soil mites that opportunistically feed on snakes.

Many species of the larger terrestrial snakes, such as kingsnakes, rat snakes, garter snakes, bullsnakes, gopher snakes, and pine snakes,

Basic setup. Simple and clean arrangements will work well for many North American snakes. Indoor-outdoor carpet or newspaper will serve as a suitable substrate. Also important are a place to hide, a ventral heat source, a water source, and good ventilation (a screen top works well). (photo by David G. Campbell)

Wet/dry setup. Placing a dry burrowing medium on one side (wood chips) and moist burrowing medium on the other (soil) gives the snake a choice. This setup works well for many of our small fossorial snakes. (photo by David G. Campbell)

Simple fossorial snake setup. A layer of a burrowing medium, such as cypress mulch alone, is often suitable for many secretive snakes. Other cage accessories such as plastic plants, rocks, and water bowl can result in a very functional and attractive cage. (photo by David G. Campbell)

misting with water every day. Recently, we determined that an impermeable barrier such as a sheet of plastic or glass or even a flat rock placed over the soil will reduce the need for misting the soil to as little as once per week, depending on air humidity and species being managed.

It is imperative that these kinds of enclosures have good ventilation. Otherwise, the humidity in the cage will rapidly reach unhealthy levels.

The purpose of this arrangement is to provide a horizontal moisture gradient in the cage that will allow a snake to select the preferred microenvironment. Once again, plastic plants, rocks, and branches can be excellent enclosure

Wet/dry setup with plastic box over soil. The plastic holds the moisture in the soil and reduces the need for misting it as frequently. (photo by David G. Campbell)

and almost all of the rattlesnakes and others will do very well in this type of cage.

Wet/Dry Enclosure Setup

These enclosures usually contain at least two kinds of substrate, but even if only one substrate is used they all have both a moist and dry area. Generally, cypress mulch or pine mulch works well as the dry substrate, while soil works well as the moist substrate for most species. Uncovered soil may require a good accessories for snakes. This setup is particularly suitable for small, secretive, or fossorial snakes of moist woodlands and fields, e.g., lined snakes, Butler's garter snake, earth snakes, brown snakes, ringneck snakes, redbelly snakes, and sharptail snakes.

For small desert species of snakes, dry sand may be a suitable substrate, but one area of the enclosure may contain sand moistened by overflow from a water bowl. Intermittent overflows may mimic their natural substrate even more, and many desert snakes seem used to this.

Three-Layer Enclosure Setup

The three-layer enclosure consists of a layer of gravel over which a thick layer of sand and a thin layer of mulch is placed. Water is added to the gravel and is drawn by capillary action into the lower layer of the sand. If an intense heat source, such as an incandescent bulb, is placed over the surface of this arrangement, a vertical temperature and moisture gradient is created. This arrangement allows the snake to stay dry and warm at the surface or move deeper for more moisture and cooler temperatures. This setup was initially developed for members of the genus *Tantilla* (e.g., crowned snakes) and appears to work well for them although several

other cage arrangements have worked for them as well. See the discussion on *Tantilla* in the nonvenomous species care section for more details.

The standard cage accessories (e.g., rocks, plastic plants, and branches) may be used in this setup also. Pieces of bark placed on the surface of the sand or mulch will also provide surface refuges.

Desert Enclosure Setup

Sand is the major ingredient for success in the desert setup. Five to 10 centimeters (2 to 4 inches) of warm dry sand appears to be all that is required for certain small desert snakes. Stable rocks and plastic cacti can be added to create extremely attractive as well as functional terraria. Snakes, such as the shovelnose snakes and the banded sand snake, will do well in these simple enclosures as long as they are very well ventilated. The same can be said for most sidewinders. Ground snakes and hooknose snakes will also do well if managed in this manner, although they will often do equally well in a basic setup. In fact, many of the larger desert snakes commonly housed in a basic setup will also do very nicely in a well-ventilated desert setup.

Three-layer cage setup. Placing gravel on the bottom, sand in the middle, and wood chips or other objects on the surface results in a vertical moisture gradient that may be useful with many small snakes. This cage was developed for members of the genus *Tantilla* (blackhead snakes) but may have many other applications as well. (photo by David G. Campbell)

Desert setup. Dry, loose sand is the main ingredient for success with our shovelnose and banded sand snakes. It also works well for sidewinders. Good ventilation and heat from above are critical for long-term success, however. (photo by David G. Campbell)

A small moist area of sand in a desert enclosure is not necessarily a bad idea, as long as the enclosure ventilation is adequate. In fact, many desert snakes seem to benefit tremendously from occasional access to moist retreats. These retreats can vary from something as simple as a moist patch near an overflowing water bowl to something as permanent as a submerged humidity box with moist sphagnum moss in it. Indeed, this will allow a desert snake to seek out high moisture areas at times when it may be beneficial, such as during ecdysis (shedding), or times when it may be necessary, such as during oviposition (egg laying). Remember, however, that the majority of the enclosure needs to remain dry and during the day the surface layers need to be warm.

Swamp Tea Setup

Many species of swamp-dwelling snakes will rapidly develop a bacterial dermatitis (blister disease) if they are placed in enclosures containing plain tap water. If not placed in an aquatic medium, however, they will often refuse to eat. Therefore, the use of an acidic medium such as tea is suggested as a means to provide an acidic medium that would mimic the acidity of the swamps from which most of these snakes come and thereby prevent blister disease. This setup is discussed in detail in the

Swamp tea setup. Dilute tea may be used to create an acidic medium for swamp-dwelling snakes such as the Graham's crayfish snake. Plastic plants, heated water, and light from above also appear important when maintaining these snakes. (photo by David G. Campbell)

section on the striped crayfish snake, *Regina alleni*.

Natural Setups and Outdoor Enclosures

The use of real plants and soil to re-create a snake's natural environment is actually the ultimate goal of many herpetoculturists. What better setup could there be than the real thing? Indeed, the more natural arrangements are more pleasing to the eye of the keeper and presumably less stressful to the captive; however, the more complex and natural the enclosure is, the harder it will be to maintain and keep clean, and the greater the likelihood for an outbreak of an infectious disease. The average person may not have the time or resources necessary to maintain a room-sized natural exhibit featuring a breeding colony of one species of snake, 10 species of plants, and natural prey species of a sufficient density to feed the snakes. This may be possible with smaller species of snakes but would be very difficult with larger species, although, one could maintain a substantial breeding colony of many snake species relatively easily by using a number of basic enclosure setups as described above. In addition, the likelihood of the spread of an infectious disease would be minimized using separate enclosures. Consider, for instance, the problem with parasites in a small natural enclosure. Those parasites with a direct life cycle would increase in number to a point where their host (the snake) may be exposed to a concentration of parasites thousands of times higher than that found in nature. This would be unlikely in the frequently cleaned basic cage setup where the substrate was replaced or disinfected regularly.

Even though natural enclosures are theoretically and intellectually the best kinds of enclosures, in reality they are generally more difficult to maintain. In fact, the largest zoos are now starting to use large amounts of realistic-appearing fiberglass to form the bottoms and sides of their reptile enclosures—essentially producing very fancy basic cage setups that are easy to clean and disinfect.

If one chooses to utilize a natural vivarium, there are several things which must be taken

Natural setup. Although beautiful and apparently satisfying to both some snakes and owners, these cages are often very difficult to maintain and clean. They are easiest to provide for very small snakes, and this is one of the benefits of maintaining small snakes. (photo by David G. Campbell)

Outdoor enclosures are the ultimate captive environment for snakes, and may be necessary for some of the most difficult species, such as crayfish snakes and leafnose snakes. This outdoor enclosure at the Haap Reptile Zoo in Klagenfurt, Austria, housed six species of snakes. (photo by John Rossi)

into consideration. First, ventilation is critical because natural substrates retain moisture. Second, toxic plants must not be used. Plants that are safe for use with snakes are pothos, Chinese evergreen, *Aglaonema*, arrowhead, *Syngonium*, weeping fig, *Ficus benjamina*, and wax-leaved peperomia, *Peperomia obtusifolia* (de Vosjoli, 1995). These plants can either be added in pots or planted directly in a natural potting soil and bark mixture as long as there is a layer of pea gravel for adequate drainage. Ferns, *Nephrolepis*, have also been used for small snakes.

Outdoor enclosures have recently become very popular for reptiles and amphibians. Those who have used them state that snakes housed in these enclosures feed better and may be more likely to breed than those in indoor enclosures. Fred Antonio, an experienced reptile curator, believes that the snakes he housed in outdoor enclosures maintained much better body tone than those housed indoors. In our experience with Brazos water snakes, those maintained outside grew faster and had greater flight distances than those maintained indoors. Perhaps this is a function of living outdoors, or possibly it is just a function of enclosure size. No one knows yet.

The problem with snakes in terms of outdoor enclosures is their tremendous ability to escape. Those who have worked with outdoor snake

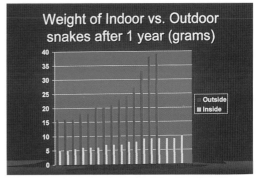

Graph showing the weights of snakes housed outdoors versus weights of their siblings housed indoors after 1 year. The causes of this difference are hypothesized to include a greater ability to thermoregulate outdoors (even though inside animals had access to a ventral heat source) and greater food availability (even though those outside had to hunt). The long-term benefits of an outdoor enclosure are still under investigation (Rossi and Rossi, in press).

enclosures suggest that wire mesh should completely enclose any outdoor facility, including under the bottom. This usually requires that the mesh be buried at least 0.6–1.5 meters (2–5 feet) deep in order to prevent escapes, allow the drainage of water, and maintain the natural appearance of the ground in the enclosure. The wire mesh (hardware cloth) also aids in the

The authors' outdoor enclosure is 9.75 meters (32 feet) long by 7.3 meters (24 feet) wide. It has an artificial waterfall, stream, and pond, as well as a rock face with four hibernaculums built in. The pen appears to have provided 20 Brazos water snakes (born in captivity) with an environment conducive to growth, since those in the pen grew to three times the weight of their siblings housed inside during the same time. We believe the outdoor enclosure is the most powerful tool in herpetoculture, and holds the answer for many difficult snake species. (photo by John Rossi)

exclusion of predatory mammals and birds such as rats, cats, raccoons, opossums, crows, and jays. Insects, especially ants, must also be controlled carefully in reptile enclosures, as ants and other insects may destroy nests and even kill adults. We have had success with many snakes by using half-inch 4 × 8 foot plywood sheets buried 20.3 cm (8 inches) deep and packed with small gravel and soil. The gravel makes it difficult for them to burrow underneath the wood.

Other problems must be solved when planning for an outdoor snake enclosure. Over much of North America, even in the extreme southern parts of the United States, temperatures may drop into the freezing range for some length of time. Therefore, the outdoor enclosure must have a suitable hibernaculum (brumaculum). For snakes, this may be constructed by excavating a hole 1.5–3 meters (5–10 feet) deep and about equally as wide, and filling it with debris such as stones and logs. The height of this brumaculum may also exceed 1.5 meters (5 feet) above ground level, and this is advisable in colder climates. If a suitable material such as mulch or leaf litter is added to this

structure, the brumaculum may also serve as an egg deposition site in the spring.

Another difficulty experienced with these enclosures is the control of parasites. Large numbers of snakes confined to a small area with natural soil may shed parasites, to such an extent that those with direct life cycles can easily reinfect the snakes in that enclosure. This problem may be controlled by replacing the contaminated topsoil every year or two and by frequent fecal exams of the snakes and repeated dewormings, if necessary.

Insects, gastropods, fish, amphibians, other reptiles, birds, and mammals may all serve as intermediate hosts for parasites with indirect life cycles, something that is not a problem in an indoor cage. Furthermore, mosquitoes, some true bugs, and ticks may transmit blood parasites. These are typically a rarity in indoor collections.

Snakekeepers should be aware that turtles and tortoises often carry protozoans that may have little effect on them, but may be devastating to snakes, therefore, turtles and tortoises should be excluded from a professional snake enclosure. In addition, understand that snakes from one area may carry parasites or be harboring bacteria that are normal for them but are not normal for snakes from other areas. These snakes may not be able to mount an effective immune response and could be very seriously affected, thus, snakes from different geographic regions should not be housed together.

Certain species of snakes should not be housed together even if they are from the same area. Many species of snakes are opportunistic feeders and will unpleasantly surprise their keepers by swallowing a similar-sized captive of the same or different species. Two of the worst offenders in this regard are cottonmouths and any kind of kingsnake. Either may greedily devour another snake.

Outdoor enclosures can nevertheless be remarkably successful for maintaining snakes and may be extremely rewarding for the keeper. Certainly, outdoor enclosures have been used in the south for years with a great deal of success, and snakes which seem to do especially well in these enclosures are the natricines (water and garter snakes) and the pit vipers (rattlesnakes, cottonmouth, and copperhead). In fact, successful captive breeding of both natricines and xenodontines (e.g., the eastern hognose snake) has been reported in snakes housed in outdoor enclosures. It is possible that outdoor enclosures may be a practical approach to the captive breeding of snakes that require environments difficult to re-create indoors, e.g., crayfish snakes, *Regina*, or snakes that have unusual food requirements, e.g., mud snakes, *Farancia*.

In our experience, outdoor enclosures have been very satisfying. A large enclosure may house a number of species, and their behavior in an outdoor enclosure is believed to be more similar to that of wild snakes than those housed in indoor cages. The 1998 International Herpetological Symposium featured a number of papers emphasizing the differences between wild snakes and captive snakes, and a large outdoor enclosure may be a happy compromise. In addition to leaner body mass, those snakes maintained in an outdoor enclosure may be better hunters, better hiders, and better at surviving if they were to be released, than those raised in small indoor cages. Hence, outdoor enclosures may be one of our best tools for producing snakes for the purpose of restocking or head starting certain species of snakes. These pens also provide tremendous photographic and research opportunities and may be one of the only ways to easily maintain difficult species. An outdoor enclosure should include a source of water, hiding areas such as rocks, and perhaps most importantly, a wood pile. Food should be stocked regularly, unless the food occurs naturally in the pen and reproduces sufficiently in order to maintain sufficient levels. We carefully monitored for evidence of pests and used rat poison in our hibernaculums during the winter in order to protect the inactive snakes. Apart from all the extra work and the concerns over predation, there is no feeling like seeing a captive-born and -raised snake experience hunting for the first time, and "learn" how to do it better, or the thrill of seeing a territorial display, or even the satisfaction of seeing several snakes basking on a protected ledge. Outdoor enclosures may well represent the next generation of snake herpetoculture.

Choosing a Snake

Species

The choice of the right species of snake for you is critical to your success in keeping it. If you don't have much time to spend on your snakes or much experience maintaining snakes, you should stick with the larger, terrestrial, rodent-eating species. Small, fossorial, aquatic, or nonmammal-eating snakes tend to have higher maintenance requirements as they tend to eat more frequently and defecate more frequently. The only exception may be the desert insectivores (e.g., shovelnoses), which are incredibly easy to maintain. In addition, the captive environments of these small snakes may be more difficult to provide and keep clean. See the discussion on different cage setups in the housing section.

Many of these small nonmammal-eating species are also more likely to be parasitized than strict mammalvores, especially if they have not been captive-bred (see the discussion below on captive versus wild-caught).

Furthermore, their food is often more difficult to procure, although this is not as much of a problem as it was in the past when most of the food consumed by these kinds of snakes needed to be collected in the great outdoors. This was not only time-consuming but risky because of the threat of parasitism or chemical toxins (see the discussion under food quality). Now, however, a wide variety of captive-raised insects, worms, and fish is available. This makes the task of maintaining what may have been previously considered difficult species much less labor-intensive, although perhaps not quite as easy as the large terrestrial rodent feeders.

Having made the distinction between terrestrial mammal-eating snakes and the others in terms of their maintenance difficulty, or lack thereof, it is important to be aware that the majority of North American snakes will eat domestic rodents. For example, most garter snakes and water snakes, hognose snakes, patchnose snakes, glossy snakes, longnose snakes, night snakes, lyre snakes, most whipsnakes, most rattlesnakes, copperheads, cottonmouths, and others either readily accept domestic mice or rats as food or can be easily trained to do so. Admittedly, some snakes may require a little more training than others, but in general most of these snakes will switch quickly to rodents and become excellent feeders.

Since they will consume domestic rodents, they can generally be fed with the same frequency as the commonly kept kingsnakes, rat snakes, and boas and, therefore, defecate with equal frequency and produce stools that are of the same consistency (and relatively mild odor) as those of kingsnakes and rat snakes fed a similar diet. In addition, most of these snakes can be successfully housed in a basic cage arrangement. Many more species than were previously thought are similar in their captive maintenance requirements to those that are commonly maintained at present, i.e., kingsnakes, rat snakes, and boas. Yet, the majority of herpetoculturists have been unable or unwilling to maintain many of these animals because of somewhat misleading and often outdated notions about the maintenance and feeding requirements of these snakes. The common beliefs that all garter snakes eat only fish, frogs, and worms, and rarely mice, are more messy and smelly than other snakes, and require a good deal of water in their enclosure are simply not accurate.

In summary, the authors strongly encourage zoo keepers, professional herpetologists, and experienced herpetoculturists to maintain and breed many more species than they have, including many of the species mentioned above. These snakes need to be studied. Those who are not very experienced in keeping snakes are encouraged to start off with the old standards, those snakes that are known to be good-feeding, relatively gentle-natured, and handleable animals. These include kingsnakes and rat snakes.

Throughout the individual species sections, the species information boxes contain a heading called the Maintenance Difficulty Index (MDI), which is followed by a number. This number is a subjective comparative rating, based on our experience, of how difficult various species are to maintain in captivity. The lower the number, the easier the snake is to maintain. The highest number is 5, and these

snakes may be extremely difficult to maintain in captivity, even for expert herpetoculturists. Those without much experience in snakekeeping may wish to check the MDI prior to purchasing or collecting a new pet and choose a snake with a low number. On the other hand, advanced herpetoculturists may wish to seek out those species that are more difficult to maintain (higher MDI) in order to research their captive requirements further. Of course, it is somewhat dangerous to generalize about the difficulty of maintaining members of an entire species on the basis of the captive observations of a handful of individuals. There is a tremendous amount of variability within a species depending upon their age at capture, sex, and geographic origin, and whether or not they were captive-born.

Captive versus Wild-Caught/Hatchling versus Adult

There is often a major difference between captive-bred snakes and wild-caught snakes, even if they are of the same species. Captive-bred snakes are less likely to be parasitized and much more likely to feed well than wild-caught snakes. They also tend to have a slightly calmer disposition, even though no baby snakes are especially calm. On the other hand, a personally collected wild-caught snake is less likely to have been exposed to a wide variety of pathogens (harmful bacteria) than a wild-caught snake from some pet shops or poorly managed dealerships. Therefore, purchase captive-bred snakes from a clean reputable breeder or capture the animals yourself. The top investments are probably well-started (which is breeder terminology for feeding on their own) snakes that are still fairly young, perhaps 3–12 months old. These large juveniles and subadults still have their entire adult lives ahead of them, including their best breeding years, and are young enough that they are adaptable, yet more reasonably priced than adults. This compares favorably with purchasing hatchlings, which may be cheaper but may not eat readily, or adults, which are more expensive and may have questionable histories, including either behavioral or breeding difficulties. Of course, the key word here is *may*, and many hatchlings and adults will do just fine in captivity.

Single Snakes versus Pairs

Once you have chosen a species to keep, select the individual male and female. We advise the maintenance of a pair (in separate cages most of the year) because we encourage captive breeding.[1] Captive breeding is often an enjoyable and educational experience for both the snake and the keeper.

With regard to buying a breeding pair, ascertain the geographic origin of the parent stock, which may be important in management decisions later on. It is also wise to ask if the pair is related. It would be best to purchase an unrelated pair in order to avoid the potentially dangerous problems of inbreeding. If siblings are purchased, one can be traded later in order to avoid this problem. See the section on breeding.

Male versus Female

It has been our experience with most North American snakes (including colubrids, viperids, and elapids) that females are usually more likely to be consistent feeders than males. Perhaps the energy demands on females in the wild mean they can't be as selective in choosing meals as males are. This may carry over to some extent in captivity. Hence, if faced with the prospect of choosing only one specimen of a species for an exhibit, a female would probably represent less of a challenge than a male.

When purchasing hatchlings from breeders, however, do not be surprised if they refuse to sell a single female. The reason for this is they usually prefer to sell pairs (one male and one female) or trios (one of one sex and two of the other) to another serious breeder, rather than sell females alone. And since the sex ratio of most snakes at birth is statistically 50:50, they will rarely sell females alone. One solution for those who are not anticipating breeding the pair is to purchase the pair but sell one to someone

else who is not interested in breeding right away.

Geographic Origin

In general, those snakes that originate from more northern latitudes or higher altitudes (colder climates) tend to show a strong seasonal pattern in captivity. In many cases, even those young hatched in captivity may go off feed in preparation for brumation (winter cooldown) about the same time every year whether they are exposed to cooler temperatures or not. This is considered by us to be a self-protective mechanism; it prevents food from being trapped in a gut that is suddenly turned off by a sharp drop in ambient temperature in the fall. Nevertheless, it is a source of major concern and confusion for many inexperienced snakekeepers who do not understand why their snake suddenly stops eating in August or September even under ideal conditions. This is a factor even within a species when one compares lowland and mountain individuals, so one is strongly encouraged to research the species in question thoroughly prior to purchase.

Disposition

Snakes that are overly aggressive are not necessarily bad investments (unless they have severely injured their mouths) since many will calm down with time and become good captives. However, they may represent more of a challenge if their nervous disposition prevents them from eating and they constantly travel the perimeter of the cage looking to escape. Some of these snakes will never adapt to captivity. On the other hand, aggressive hatchlings are often aggressive feeders while shy hatchlings are often not.

Aggressive snakes would definitely not be a good choice for a beginner or someone wishing to handle the snake frequently.

Health

Last, but certainly not least, the health of your chosen snake(s) needs to be determined. In order to help determine whether or not a snake

---

[1]Many snakes breed better if two males are available for managed, limited male-to-male contact. This is especially true for boids and viperids.

is healthy, it will be necessary for you to perform a prepurchase exam.

Prepurchase Exam

If you are purchasing snakes rather than capturing, examine them carefully to make sure they are healthy. In most cases it will be advisable to choose the healthiest individuals available rather than sickly individuals you may feel sorry for. Some have gone so far as to discourage the purchase of even a healthy-appearing snake if it is housed with a sickly one. In addition, the attractiveness of an animal should not be placed ahead of health when choosing a snake unless you are an experienced breeder willing to take a risk for the sake of those particularly attractive characteristics you have selected.

Observe the snakes you are considering from a distance at first. Choose the snakes that are in good flesh with clear eyes and smooth skin, and that are alert and actively tongue flicking. Check the skin closely for wrinkles or abnormalities in scalation as this may indicate a serious underlying problem. Look for obvious scars, parasites, or excessive folds of skin. Scars and ticks usually indicate a snake is wild-caught, while mites represent a serious (and contagious) health risk to that snake and others. Visible folds of skin running longitudinally usually indicate dehydration or long-term anorexia.

Watch the snake move. Is it coordinated? Is its tongue flicking rapidly and regularly or slowly and irregularly? Is the head held at a normal angle (parallel to the ground for most snakes)? Is the snake breathing rapidly and with some difficulty or slowly and easily? Generally, it is normal for a snake to be tongue flicking rapidly, breathing with no difficulty, and holding its head evenly. However, excited snakes of different species may protrude their tongues abnormally (as part of a threat display), demonstrate hyperpnea (rapid breathing), or even feign death as part of their normal behavioral repertoire.

After the initial observation, ask to see the snake eat or take a look at the feeding record.

This may not always be possible and some breeders or pet shop owners will not be able or willing to oblige your request, but if they do, you will learn a great deal about the snake you are considering purchasing. A snake that eats readily is telling you that his mouth and digestive system are in good shape (as is his attitude toward captivity), and is also unlikely to have any serious systemic diseases. If the snake eats, fine; if it doesn't, that doesn't necessarily mean it is sick. Other reasons for not eating include:

1. It has not yet adjusted to captivity.
2. It is too cold.
3. It is handled or disturbed too frequently.
4. It is getting ready to shed, brumate, or mate.
5. It is gravid.
6. It has just eaten (pet store owners always tell you this but be wary).
7. It is not interested in the same food item (or you didn't offer the snake what it wanted).

Next, ask if you can hold the snake. Do this carefully if the snake has just eaten. Check for lumps or bumps, raw spots, abnormal coloration or roughness of the skin, clarity of the eyes, normal closure of the mouth, and especially for lesions on the belly or any respiratory signs (head-raising, blowing bubbles, wheezing, or open-mouth breathing). If the seller will allow, gently open the mouth with a flattened blunt

Opening the mouth of a snake for tube-feeding. Note the clean pink interior of this kingsnake. The mouth is easily and gently opened with a smooth blunt object. (photo by David G. Campbell)

probe and look inside. Generally, the mouth should be clean and pink, although it can be naturally pale in some snakes (e.g., cottonmouths). Work your way from front to back, feeling for firm masses in the abdomen and take note of the snake's muscle tone. Most snakes should have a reasonably good grip. Drape the snake over one finger. If the snake is thin or has poor muscle tone, it will often appear flat over that finger. Finally, examine the cloaca by gently lifting the anal scale. It should appear clean and pink. Swelling, redness, or crustiness in this area may indicate cloacitis, an inflammation of the cloaca, which is a potentially serious problem.

If possible, ask if your purchase may be contingent on the snake passing an exam by your reptile veterinarian. You should also request this contingency if you need to have a certain sex and you or the seller are not very experienced at sexing. Your reptile veterinarian or an experienced breeder can usually probe the snake to determine this. The veterinarian will also examine the snake and do a fecal exam to check for parasites.

Capturing a Snake

Capturing a snake and removing it from nature have become a serious matter. Many populations of snakes may be more fragile than we would like to think. Therefore, when you remove these animals, you are taking upon yourself the responsibility of potentially damaging a population and the responsibility of caring for that animal to the best of your ability. You should take no more animals than you need or than you can take care of properly, however tempting it may be. Where bag limits apply, you should not exceed them and where they don't, exercise some good judgment. Remember that rocks, logs, bark, and other objects (including trash if it is usable habitat) should be replaced in their original positions. This is an important and useful microhabitat that is necessary not only for the continued existence of many of those species you are seeking but for many other species as well.

Admittedly, collecting snakes is more than just a means to an end. It has become a sport for many. Indeed, it is called "snake hunting" by many and is very similar to other types of hunting or fishing in that it requires some skill and often a great deal of knowledge about the quarry. Yet, it is superior to hunting with a gun because you are not killing that which you seek. A notable exception is rattlesnake hunting for rattlesnake rodeos in which large numbers are killed.

If you are capturing a snake, make every effort to reduce trauma and stressing during and immediately following the capture process. Grasp the snake (with your hand or lift with a snake hook) quickly and gently and place the snake by itself in a clean dry pillowcase which has previously been inspected for small holes. Remember that tongs can damage skin and spines. Carry the bag rather than hang it from your belt, so as not to traumatize the snake even further. Venomous snakes should, of course, be placed in a clearly labeled and locked box after being placed in the pillowcase. Do not disturb the snake while traveling in the car and remember the importance of a styrofoam container (discussed in the transportation section). When you arrive home, place the snake, still in the pillowcase, in its prepared cage. Then after several hours open the pillowcase. The snake will eventually find its way out of the bag and will be in a much more peaceful state of mind. Remove the pillowcase later. This reduction in capture stress may be very important in the way a snake adjusts to captivity, especially some of the pitvipers (Morgan, pers. comm., 1990). Captured snakes, although usually fairly healthy, should also be placed in quarantine, then checked for internal and external parasites and examined by your veterinarian. Quarantine should last at least 3 months, but preferably 6 months.

Transportation/Shipping

Transportation should be accomplished in a clean pillowcase. After the snake has been placed in the pillowcase, twist the top of the pillowcase and tie it upon itself, making sure not to include the snake in the knot. Then place

Transporting a snake. Bagged snakes are best placed inside styrofoam (or other) coolers for transportation, even for short trips. Plastic containers with ice in them may also be placed in the cooler on hot days, and a digital indoor-outdoor thermometer may be used to monitor the temperature frequently. (photo by David G. Campbell)

the snake, inside of the pillowcase, into a styrofoam box into which several holes have been punched (you don't need many). We usually use a pencil or a pen and punch about three or four holes in each side of the container, a few inches below the top since heat rises. The styrofoam box will protect the snake to some extent from direct sun and from temperature extremes in both summer and winter. A chill of even a short duration can lead to a respiratory infection while a few minutes in a hot car, especially with the windows up, can quickly kill a snake. WARNING: Very few coolers will protect snakes if they are in direct sunlight, and the sun will often shine in through a car window at such an angle that the driver is unaware of how hot it is becoming in the cooler. It is very important to keep coolers out of the sun, and it usually is a very good idea to place some ice in a watertight container somewhere in the cooler. Jerry Feldner, an experienced desert herpetologist, insists that you will never kill a reptile that is properly covered in a cooler that contains ice. He also feels that the plastic coolers are much safer than styrofoam coolers and refers to the styrofoam coolers as "warmer coolers." The "koolatron," an insulated cooling device that plugs into a car lighter, is the

high-tech answer for transporting snakes in harsh environments.

Small battery-operated, digital indoor/outdoor thermometers with probes can be purchased relatively inexpensively and used to monitor the temperature in the coolers while you are driving. This has saved many a snake for us.

Small snakes will also benefit from the addition of slightly moistened shredded newspaper or paper towels. The paper serves as a cushion and helps prevent desiccation.

Regardless of the type of cooler, packing material, or thermometer used, it is prudent to avoid leaving reptiles inside a parked car in direct or partial sunlight. Park in the shade whenever possible, take the coolers into a building when you will be there for an extended period of time (such as for a meal in a restaurant). If you are near home or a base camp, it may be wise to leave your previously captured snakes there rather than bring them with you in the cooler. Be warned, however, that a tent can also be a dangerous place to leave snakes, especially if they are in direct sunlight.

For shipping purposes, the styrofoam box should be placed inside a cardboard box that is clearly marked "Live Reptiles: Avoid Extreme Heat or Cold." Also, the snake must be properly identified. By law, venomous reptiles will need to be shipped in a double wooden crate that has metal corners and metal strapping.

The best way to ship snakes is via air freight. It is fast, relatively safe for the snakes, and legal (although only some airlines will ship venomous reptiles). And, although it is relatively expensive compared to several other forms of shipping, air freight is much less expensive if the animals arrive alive. It is illegal to send any snake via the U.S. Postal Service at this time.

Upon arrival, the snake should be removed from the crate as soon as possible, examined quickly for mites, signs of dehydration, or heat stress, and placed in a cage for acclimation and quarantine. *THE SNAKE SHOULD BE QUARANTINED FOR 3–6 MONTHS IN A SEPARATE ROOM FROM OTHER SNAKES (AND PREFERABLY ROOMS NOT EXCHANGING AIR WITH EACH OTHER)!* The cage should be disinfected regularly (see the section on cleaning and disinfection) and you should always wash your hands before and after handling this or any snake or its cage, especially before you eat and before you handle any other snakes in your care.

Cleaning and Disinfection

Regardless of species, cleanliness is one of the most important factors of successful snake maintenance.

Cleaning the enclosure implies the removal of organic matter such as fecal material, uric acid and breakdown products, undigested food, etc., from the cage. Usually some kind of soap or detergent is necessary for this process (we have successfully used dishwashing detergent for years), since these products are bipolar and aid in the emulsification of fatty substances and the suspension of dirt. It is important to note that these soaps or detergents should be removed by rinsing thoroughly because many disinfectants will also be inactivated by them. Thus, a thorough cleaning and rinsing is absolutely the most important first step in controlling bacteria, because almost every disinfectant available will be inactivated by large amounts of organic matter or large amounts of soap. Therefore, for all intents and purposes, no disinfection is possible without first thoroughly cleaning.

Other agents that are useful for cleaning purposes are various salts such as sodium bicarbonate (baking soda) or sodium chloride (table salt). Susan Barnard, head reptile keeper at the Atlanta Zoo, says that table salt is a good cleanser and that it removes mineral deposits, fish oils, and algae.

Disinfection, which is the destruction of bacteria, is the second step in the cage-cleaning process and may be carried out by either physical or chemical means. Examples of physical disinfection are steam cleaning or boiling, while chemical means include the use of harsh substances known as disinfectants. The more common approach in herpetoculture has been to use disinfectants. These disinfectants include alcohol, ammonia, centrimide, chlorine compounds (bleach and Nolvasan®), glutaraldehyde, iodophors (Betadine®), phenols (Lysol®),

quaternary ammonium chloride compounds (Roccal®), and various organic compounds.

Most of these widely used disinfectants have a broad spectrum of activity but will not kill bacterial spores, fungi, or viruses; one should therefore not develop a false sense of security when using these products. They are not a substitute for a good disease control program, the most important part of which include housing animals singly, controlling the entry of new animals into a collection, and keeping the cages clean. Nevertheless, disinfectants are an important and integral part of any disease control program. They will be discussed here in some detail. See Barnard's rules below.

It is widely accepted at this time that the cheapest and one of the most effective disinfectants for reptile cages is a 3–10% solution (roughly 1–3 ounces per quart of water) of sodium hypochlorite (household bleach). Betadine® (or povidone-iodine) solution is a good disinfectant. Chris Mattison (1987) also recommends centrimide (diluted as indicated) or ordinary washing soda (sodium carbonate). Chlorhexidine (Nolvasan®) is not effective against many reptile pathogens (harmful bacteria) and both phenols and coal tar derivatives may be toxic to reptiles, so avoid these disinfectants.

Regardless of disinfectant used, disease will be more likely to occur and spread if common sense practices are not followed. Keeper Barnard has several simple rules that help prevent the spread of infection:

1. Remove all uneaten food, fecal material, and shed skins as soon as possible.
2. Avoid transferring items from one cage to another (this includes uneaten food).
3. Always wash hands after handling each animal.

Maintain a bucket with dilute bleach near your snake cages and make a habit of rinsing your hands with this solution, after washing, when going from cage to cage. Change it frequently, preferably daily. We have successfully used this approach for more than 8 years and have not had any major outbreaks during that time. Indeed, a program including frequent washing of the hands between cages may be the difference between a major outbreak in your collection or just one sick snake. Once the necessity of cleanliness is understood, attention should be turned to providing the correct physical environment. This includes the correct temperature, humidity, lighting, substrate (flooring material), and sufficient room. Remember that the substrate used, complexity of the cage, and the material used to construct the cage will affect how well the cage can be cleaned. Wooden cages are more likely to retain moisture, fungi, and bacteria and provide more hiding places for mites than glass or metal cages. In fact, untreated wood is basically undisinfectable. This is discussed in more detail under the section on substrate.

The frequency of cleaning will depend upon the type of snake, what it is eating, how frequently it is eating, the temperature at which it is kept, and the age of the snake. The substrate and the humidity in the cage will also dictate the frequency of cleaning. In general, spot cleaning or wiping out the cage should immediately follow defecation, while a thorough cleansing and disinfection may only be needed every 1–3 months. For instance, water snakes eating fish frequently and being kept at high temperatures will defecate almost daily, while rat snakes kept at room temperature and fed every 1–2 weeks will defecate about every 1–2

weeks. Water snakes (if they are eating fish) will generally have looser more odoriferous stools than the rat snakes and hence will need to have their cages cleaned far more frequently. A snake on newspaper may create a wet mess by splashing water from the water bowl and then defecating, while one on indoor-outdoor carpet or artificial turf is not as likely to do so. High relative humidity in the cage will prevent the fecal material from drying rapidly, leading to more bacterial or fungal growth and making more frequent cleaning and disinfection a necessity.

Take special care to scrub the water bowl when the water is changed. Mineral deposits, bacteria, algae, or protozoan parasites can thrive in an infrequently cleaned (or infrequently disinfected) water bowl and these can lead to the demise of an otherwise healthy and well-adapted snake.

With regard to *Cryptosporidia*, a dreaded and presently untreatable protozoan parasite usually causing gastrointestinal damage and death in snakes, disinfection will not be accomplished with a sodium hypochlorite solution. Ten percent formalin, or glutaraldehyde, or 5% ammonia solutions are required instead.

Regardless of the disinfectant used, however, always isolate the sick individual from the

Table 2. Disinfectants Used in Snake Care

Agent	Bacteria	Spores	Viruses	Comments
Alcohol	+	−	−	Flammable
Ammonia	+	−(+)	−	Cheap, available, will kill coccidia
Bleach	+	−	−	Cheap, broad-spectrum
Chlorhexidine	+	−	−(+)	More expensive than bleach, some viruses killed
				Odor, toxicity, kills *Cryptosporidia*
Formalin	+	+	−(+)	
Glutaraldehyde	+	+	+	Odor, poor shelf life, kills *Cryptosporidia*
Iodophores (Betadine®)	+	−	−	Broad-spectrum, no odor, safe, may stain
Phenols (Lysol®)	+	−	−	Good cleaners, toxic, broad-spectrum
Quaternary ammonium chloride (Roccal®, Direct®)	+	−	−(+)	Good cleaner, deodorizer, broad-spectrum, some viruses killed, may leave toxic residues

+ = Agent will kill bacteria, spores, or viruses.
− = Agent will not kill bacteria, spores, or viruses.
(+) = Agent kills some types of viruses or spores.

others as much as possible and work with that animal last. Use Table 2 when deciding what disinfectant to use or not to use.

Temperature

Temperature is perhaps the most critically important physical parameter to be dealt with when maintaining and breeding snakes. To put it simply, every biological process that snakes (and indeed all animals) carry out, including respiration, ingestion, digestion, reproduction, circulation, immune response, and behavioral response, is directly or indirectly related to temperature. As ectotherms, snakes are extremely dependent on the environmental temperatures. In nature, however, they are not at the mercy of environmental temperatures. They can seek out different microenvironments and regulate their body temperatures very accurately by moving between sun and shade. In captivity, they are often offered the wrong temperatures or only one temperature. Temperatures that are too high or too low will not allow normal bodily functions to occur. The most obvious sign of this problem is vomiting, which often occurs when digestion cannot proceed due to a temperature drop after a big meal. Continued observation of snakes in both the wild and captivity reveals that they all have a

The largely nocturnal glossy snake is active over a wide range of temperatures, and seems particularly tolerant of cool temperatures. Nocturnal and arboreal snakes tend to be active over a wider temperature range, while many diurnal, terrestrial, and aquatic snakes seem to have narrower optimal temperature ranges. (photo by Patrick Briggs)

preferred temperature *range*. Early snake-keepers attempted to keep their snakes at one optimum temperature and were disappointed with the results. These snakes became ill, failed to reproduce, and eventually died. Later, it was observed that arranging enclosures with temperature gradients (a warm end and a cold end) frequently resulted in healthy breeding snakes (Table 3). The reason these snakes did well was because they were behaviorally thermoregulating by traveling back and forth in their cages to

Table 3. Body Temperatures of Active Individuals of Several Genera of Snakes in the Family Colubridae

Snake	10°C	20°C	30°C	40°C
Whipsnakes		O	+ O	
Racers		O	+	O
Rat snakes		O	+	O
Kingsnakes		O	+ O	
Gopher, bull, and pine snakes		O	+	O
Worm snakes		O	+	O
Green snakes		O +		O
Water snakes		O +		O
Ringneck snakes		O +		O
Garter snakes	O	+		O

Adapted from Brattstrom and Swenkmeyer 1965. Body Temperatures of Reptiles. *Am. Midland Nat.* 73:376–422.
Bars indicate temperature ranges; plus signs indicate average.

A yellow rat snake bloated after a large meal. Eating large meals places thermal demands on many snakes, and also increases their risk for predation. After eating, snakes will usually seek out secure places where they can hide and regulate their body temperature (stay warm). Small species of snakes and the young of larger species eat smaller meals that may be digested more quickly, however. Thus, their "down time" is less and their tolerance to foraging at cooler temperatures is probably greater. (photo by John Rossi)

adjust their temperatures up or down, just like in the wild. We now suspect they are choosing different temperatures for different functions, i.e., one temperature is best for digestion while another is best to enable the immune system to fight off an infection (Bels, 1989). Hence, the provision of a temperature gradient is essential in almost every cage. Those snakes that do well without a gradient usually have preferred temperature ranges similar to those experienced in the average household (i.e., room temperature with its usual daily fluctuations). Therefore, set up a gradient for all snakes, taking into account their preferred temperature ranges in the wild or ranges known to have worked well for previous herpetoculturists. Also consider the preferred habits of the snake in question. Is it terrestrial, arboreal, or fossorial? Set up the gradient in the following manner for each group.

Most Terrestrial Snakes (Including Water Snakes, Genus *Nerodia*)

If possible, select or build a rectangular cage rather than a square or octagonal one. Place a heating pad (set to low usually but check with a thermometer and determine the temperature at its surface at each setting after prolonged use) or other heating device under one end of the cage (outside of an aquarium but inside of a wooden cage right under the substrate). Heating cables and heat strips are also excellent ventral heat sources for snakes. Regardless of the heating device you are using, the temperature at the surface of the device, and more importantly at the surface of the substrate you have selected, should be near the upper level of the temperature range for that species. The other side of the cage should be unheated and preferably without any additional lighting.

For many snakes, an incandescent light alone may provide enough heat, but for the very active diurnal species like the racer or coachwhip, an ultraviolet (UV) light and ventral heat source are thought to be necessary in addition to the incandescent bulb. Many of the snakes the authors have worked with have done well for years with incandescent bulbs alone, adding more doubt to the necessity of UV light for many species of snakes. But see the section on lighting. A 15-, 25-, 40-, 60-, or 75-watt incandescent bulb works best under most conditions (check with a thermometer after the light has been on for several hours).

The hide box (see discussion under psychological factors) may be placed on the cool side of the cage, but this will not work for some very shy animals as they may hide in the box all the time and never venture to the warm side. For these animals, either place a box on each end of the cage (providing a warm and cool place to hide) or have a large hide box that is half off the heating pad. In either case, use dark-colored or thick hide boxes with small entrances so the light intensity within the box will not make it unacceptable to the snake.

Arboreal Snakes (Tree Dwellers)

Ultraviolet lights and incandescent bulbs should be placed in such a position as to provide an arboreal basking place (a warm spot among the branches or on a tree trunk). A heating pad beneath the substrate should also be provided for these species. Vine snakes, green snakes, and ribbon snakes, although extremely arboreal, may come to the ground and hide before shedding or laying eggs. Also remember that perch size and stability may be important in determining if and when a snake basks. You may have to experiment with different size branches and different arrangements.

Secretive, Nocturnal, or Fossorial (Burrowing) Snakes

Remember that, as a rule, these snakes burrow in order to reach cooler temperatures or search for food. Therefore, heat for these species should come primarily from above the substrate (an incandescent bulb is a good source). Thus, a heating pad may be contraindicated *under* the substrate. To our knowledge, no one has tried placing heating pads over the substrate, but we have used hot rocks as a surface heat source for some small fossorial snakes with a great deal of success. Some species are known to bask just below the surface of the substrate (e.g., *Tantilla* sp.) so some of the heat should probably come from a full-spectrum light. Both temperature and soil moisture gradients are critical for some fossorial snakes and can be controlled in the three-layer cage discussed in detail in the section on *Tantilla*. Both worm snakes and blackhead snakes have been maintained in captivity for over a year in these types of cages. Blind snakes may also do well in these cages.

Failure of the Snake to Thermoregulate

People often tell us they have two snakes living in the same cage. Both were eating, drinking, and defecating normally and suddenly one stops eating, shows respiratory and gastrointestinal signs, and goes downhill rapidly while the other one is just fine. The reason for this may be that one of these snakes does not thermoregulate. This snake is not able to "turn on" its digestive system or immune system because of the presence of the other snake. The dominant snake is using its captive environment fully and thereby stays healthy even though exposed to the same bacteria or parasites that are making the submissive snake ill. This observation clearly demonstrates the im-

portance of the captive environment and supports the contention that more than 90% of our captive reptile illnesses are related to an improper or overly stressful environment. The first step in treating these animals should always be to correct the environment, and in the case above, separate the snakes. Even if psychological factors are not an issue, isolation of a sick snake from a healthy one always makes good sense.

Other factors which contribute to a snake's failure to thermoregulate include stress not related to other snakes, such as too much handling or too many vibrations, and injury or severe illness, such as spinal damage, pneumonia, or severe infectious stomatitis (mouth rot). Treatment of these animals, aside from medications and supportive care, often requires giving them little choice in temperature and keeping them very warm (32–38°C; 90–100°F) for several weeks.

Acclimation Period

Snakes that have just been transported in the cold may die if abruptly placed in a high temperature. If they have been transported in the winter, allow them access to water and keep them at room temperature for several days before attempting to warm them. During the summer, snakes are usually acclimated to the warmth, but keeping them at room temperature, in a quiet place with access to water, is still a good idea. Obst et al. (1988) refer to this time as the acclimation period. As a general rule, avoid transporting snakes from southern temperature zones during the winter and consider brumating such animals at this time anyway (if they appear healthy).

Critical Periods

There appear to be certain periods of time during incubation or gestation when the proper temperatures are critical for normal development or survival. Many experienced herpetoculturists are all too familiar with the deformities caused by higher than normal incubation temperatures, but seem to forget that livebearing snakes may have similar problems.

Osgood (1970) showed that gravid salt marsh snakes cannot tolerate temperatures above 31°C (88°F) for periods during early gestation or embryonic death would occur.

Similarly, some of the higher temperatures tolerated by adults may result in dead or deformed neonates. A gravid western ribbon snake housed at higher temperatures during her gestation gave birth to several young with shortened kinked tails.

In addition to the damage caused to developing embryos, another more directly observable effect is possible. If the temperature rises sharply during the last week of gestation, a female may prematurely deliver her eggs or young. This is almost invariably fatal to the neonates.

See Table 3 for the body temperatures of active individuals of several genera of snakes in the family Colubridae.

The Thermal Environment in an Enclosure

Buy a thermometer. You have no idea of what may be going on in your enclosures unless you measure the temperature in them. There are some wonderfully accurate and inexpensive indoor-outdoor digital thermometers on the market. Once the thermometer or thermometers are in place, you will begin to develop an understanding of captive thermal gradients that you never had before. You will observe that there may be huge differences in temperature from one side of the cage to the other. There may even be significant differences from the top of the substrate to 1 inch below it; indeed, this is the way it is in nature. Different objects have physical properties that make them more or less likely to absorb or reflect long-wave solar radiation. Color, reflectance, and texture are three factors of importance in this regard.

Also, the position of an object relative to the incident angle of light will determine the temperature at its surface. For example, a rock with its broad side to the sun may be warmer than one with only one point facing the sun.

The same kinds of things may be said for objects in enclosures and their positions relative to an incandescent bulb. The color and

texture of the substrate, the position of cage accessories such as rocks and logs, and the wattage of the incandescent bulb will all have tremendous effects on the microthermal environment of an enclosure. So will the amount and kind of real or plastic vegetation.

Ventilation will be another critical factor in determining the temperature within an enclosure. Cages with poor ventilation and high wattage bulbs may turn into ovens in a short period of time. This can be avoided by carefully measuring the temperature at several locations within the enclosure 2–4 hours after the lights and other heating devices have come on and by making sure the cage is well ventilated. Good ventilation is important for other reasons as well.

Practical Solutions to Thermal Problems in the Home

In the average household, or perhaps in any small building, there are likely to be major differences in temperature from one room to another. Surprisingly, there are also major thermal gradients within the same room. We have noted that there may be as much as a 13°F difference between the floor and shoulder height during the winter in our main snake room. There may be another 4°F difference between shoulder height and the ceiling level in the summer. Thus, there may be huge temperature differences within a room of which the average snakekeeper may be totally unaware, even though it may have a major impact on the snakes in his/her care. Admittedly, thermal gradients in well-insulated homes may not be quite as dramatic, but they should be monitored by the serious keeper. Those who set their home thermostats at 24°C (75°F) and expect the temperatures on the floor of their home to be that temperature may be unpleasantly surprised if they are trying to maintain a subtropical reptile in a floor cage during the winter.

It is therefore important to arrange cages in such a manner as to take advantage of these gradients and avoid thermal errors. In large collections, snakes from more northern latitudes or higher altitudes may benefit by being placed lower than snakes from warmer climates. Conversely, those snakes from southern latitudes or lower altitudes may stay healthier at relatively higher positions in the room. Those snakes that are known to be diurnal and prefer higher temperatures such as coachwhips and racers would benefit from the placement of their cages at a greater height, while nocturnal or cool-adapted snakes such as Canadian garter snakes and rubber boas may benefit by the placement of their cages at lower positions in a room. Of course, at a more northern latitude the floor should be avoided for most snakes, while at a southern latitude the ceiling should probably be avoided. Nevertheless, these kinds of gradients may make it easier for snakekeepers to house snakes from areas with different climates in their homes. Once again, one should use a thermometer to make these kinds of decisions.

In addition to vertical temperature differences between floor and ceiling, there are often horizontal temperature differences. A cage positioned near an outside wall is likely to be exposed to a greater fluctuation of temperature than one against an indoor wall. In the summer, these may be warmer temperatures, while in the winter, these will be cooler temperatures. And most windows, even those with a high insulation value, often are the areas of greatest temperature fluctuation.

Temperature Control in Zoos and Other Institutions

Several of the modern zoological parks such as Chaffee Zoological Gardens of Fresno, California, and some professional snake breeders have installed climate-controlled enclosures in which a small computer is linked to a thermostat and actually mimics the daily and seasonal temperature fluctuations of a reptile's natural environment. These environmental chambers also control the light cycle, although humidity control is done by hand to allow for gradients. These enclosures along with the efforts of dedicated keepers can be superb for the maintenance of many snakes. They may even be programmed for winter cooldown and are hence particularly good for breeding many montane species of snakes. As one might imag-

ine, the expense of these chambers is somewhat prohibitive for the average individual.

However, several other reptile houses in zoos are divided into partitioned sections, each with its own temperature range. These can be duplicated by varying temperatures within different rooms within a house or other insulated structure.

Table 4 is an accumulation of temperature ranges reported by various authors for the captive maintenance of North American snakes.

Humidity and Water

Most reptiles, including most temperate zone snakes, will do well in a humidity range of 30–70%. The relative humidity in much of the United States and Canada is usually within this range except in the winter, when it may drop considerably (especially inside heated homes). Remember that as air is warmed, it is capable of carrying more moisture, hence the relative humidity drops very low inside our homes. This causes drying of skin and mucous membranes and leads to dysecdysis (difficult shedding) and respiratory infections, respectively. One can avoid extremely low humidity most of the time by using aquariums (as opposed to wood or wire cages) that contain large water bowls placed on the warm side of the enclosure and by *partially* covering your screen top with plexiglass or plastic wrap. This restricts ventilation and thereby increases the humidity because the evaporated water is trapped. Be extremely careful that you don't restrict ventilation too much, however, or the humidity will reach too high of a level. See the section on ventilation. Many professional herpetologists keep a humidifier running in their snake rooms throughout the winter (or all year) to avoid these low humidity problems.

Recently, herpetologists and reptile veterinarians have been stressing that the maintenance of high relative humidity should not be at the expense of reduced ventilation (which may lead to stagnant germ-laden air). This requires a humidifier to be hooked up directly to a cage via a PVC or metal pipe. An automatic timer will consistently control how long the humidi-

Table 4. Temperature Ranges for the Captive Maintenance of Snakes of the United States and Canada

Species	Day Temperature (°C)	Night Temperature (°C)	Brumation Temperature (°C)	Source
Baird's rat snake	25–30		10–15	M
Black rat snake	21–25			ME
Black swamp snake	23–27			ME
Blackhead snake	20–30			CL
Blackneck garter snake	25–30	26		T
Blacktail rattlesnake	23–27			ME
Blind snake	16–28			CL
Brazos water snake	27	18–21		CA
Brown snake	20–25		4–6	M
Bull-/Gopher snake	25–30		10–15	M
California mountain king	25–30		5–15	T
Cat-eyed snake	27			ME
Coachwhip	26–29			ME
Common garter snake	25–33	17–22	10	Z
Common kingsnake	24–30	20–22	15–20	M(Z)
Common rat snake	25–30		5–15	ME(M)
Copperhead	26			ME
Corn snake	22–28	18–20	5–15	Z
Eastern coral	22–24			ME
Eastern diamondback	23–27			ME
Eastern hognose snake	23–27			ME
Fox snake	20–25		5–15	M
Glossy snake	25–30	18–20		T
Gray-banded kingsnake	25–30		9–13	CR
Green rat snake	20–30		15–20	M
Green water snake	23–27			ME
Indigo snake	25–30		9–13	M
Lined snake	19–32			CL
Longnose snake	25–30		10–15	T
Lyre snake	24–26			ME
Mexican vine snake	25			T
Milk snake	25–30		10--5	T
Mountain patchnose snake	25–30			T
Mole kingsnake	23–28			Z(ME)
Mud snake	24–30	18–22	10–15	T
Night snake	22–28	18–20		T
Pine snake	25–30			M
Plainbelly water snake	20–28			T
Prairie kingsnake	23–28			ME(Z)
Pigmy rattlesnake	20–25			M
Queen snake	20–26		4–10	T
Racer	20–29	18–20		Z
Red diamond rattlesnake	23–27			ME
Ribbon snake	22–26			A
Ridgenose rattlesnake	24–29			A&M
Ringneck snake	22–26			T
Rock rattlesnake	20–35		10–19	S
Rosy boa	20–26		10–15	T

Table 4. Temperature Ranges for the Captive Maintenance of Snakes of the United States and Canada (continued)

Species	Day Temperature (°C)	Night Temperature (°C)	Brumation Temperature (°C)	Source
Rough green snake	23–25			ME
Scarlet snake	23–27			ME
Scarlet kingsnake	25–30		10–15	T
Sidewinder	25–30			M
Smooth green snake	25–27			T
Sonoran mountain kingsnake	25–27	18	5–15	T
Sonoran whipsnake	25–30			M
Southern water snake	20–28			T
Speckled racer	26–29			ME
Speckled rattlesnake	19–39			MO
Trans-Pecos rat snake	25–30			M
Twin-spotted rattlesnake	27			T
Western coral	22–24			ME
Western diamondback	25–30			M
Western hognose snake	23–27	18–20		T
Western rattlesnake	26–32			L&F
Western shovelnose snake	25–30			M
Worm snake	14–31			CL
Yellow rat snake	22–28		5–15	Z
Most snakes	27–30	22–25		J

Sources: A = Alderton (1986); A&M = Armstrong & Murphy (1979); CA = Carl (1981); CL = Clark (1968); CR = Cranston (1985); J = Jacobson (1987); L&F = Linder & Fichter (1977); M = Mattison (1988); ME = Mehrtens (1987); MO = Moore (1978); S = Swinford (1989); T = Trutnau (1981); Z = Zimmerman (1986).

Humidity box. The creation of an area of high humidity somewhere within an otherwise dry and well-ventilated cage has numerous uses and advantages. Even desert snakes may use these retreats at times to reduce water loss or assist in shedding their skin. Gravid females will often lay their eggs there as well. (photo by David G. Campbell)

fier operates each day. It may only need to operate 1–2 hours a day to achieve the desired humidity. Inexpensive humidity gauges can be purchased to measure the humidity.

Plastic sweater boxes stuffed with sphagnum moss that have small entrance holes (called "humidity boxes" by Steve Barten, DVM, of Chicago) are used by many snake keepers and are especially good for young snakes in the wintertime. We have found that many snakes, even desert-dwelling snakes, will use these high humidity areas at times when they may be beneficial, such as during ecdysis. See the housing discussion on the desert setup.

Drinking Water

In general, most snakes require that clean fresh water be available at all times. The bowl should not be tippable and generally should be large enough for the snake to immerse completely without spilling a drop on the substrate. Larger snakes, however, especially those from drier environments, will often do well with small water bowls such as those used to water cats. In fact, the majority of North American snakes will do well with water bowls ranging in size from that of a small ash tray to that of a large dog water bowl.

Scrub that water bowl when you change the water and change it about once per week. Algae, bacteria, and protozoans can easily grow in an infrequently changed water bowl and will even survive the water change if you don't scrub out that bottom! Mineral deposits can collect on the bottom of the bowl, making it look quite grim. As previously mentioned, table salt is very good for taking off mineral deposits. Bleach, at a concentration of 1–3 ounces per quart of water, is a cheap and effective disinfectant you can use after you scrub. We usually let some sit in the bowl for several minutes to hours before rinsing the bowl thoroughly and using it again. Also, try to keep the same water bowl in with the same snake to prevent the possible spread of infection. If paper towels are used to do the cleaning and disinfection, bowls do not need to be moved far from the cage for this process. We do not recommend washing all of the bowls in one sink and then returning the bowls to the cages at random since this is an excellent way to spread disease.

Some of the arboreal snakes, most notably the vine snake, rough green snake, and the ribbon snake, prefer to drink water from leaves and branches after a rain and may not drink from a water bowl. These snakes and rattlesnakes will also drink off themselves when drops of water form on their keeled scales. This may necessitate a light misting of the cage with water every other day, although this is not necessary for rattlesnakes. In fact, most rattlesnakes will drink from a dish and may do quite nicely if water is only offered every 1–4 weeks.

Recently, some herpetologists have been suggesting using additives in the drinking water to control bacteria. The two most well-known and successful additives are 4 N (normal) hydrochloric acid and good old sodium hypo-chlorite (bleach). If you are using the acid, add 1.5 ml to one liter (quart) of water. If you are using the bleach, use about 1 ml per liter (quart) of water.

More recently, some have suggested that phosphoric acid can be utilized to acidify drinking water for the purpose of suppressing the growth of two serious reptile pathogens, namely *Pseudomonas* and *Aeromonas* spp. (Frye, 1991). This acid, widely used in carbonated beverages, may not impart a disagreeable taste to the water as other additives may, although this is difficult to determine for snakes. The acid should be added until the measured pH of the solution reaches 5.0 to 5.5 (Frye, 1991).

Ventilation

The importance of good cage ventilation has been alluded to in other sections of this book, and it is a significant enough factor that it merits a brief discussion here. It has been our experience that poor ventilation of cages is the number one cause of disease among snakes cared for by experienced herpetoculturists. Even when all other aspects of the physical environment are satisfactory (including cleanliness), poor ventilation can result in the demise of a long-term captive snake.

As discussed in the section on humidity, poor enclosure ventilation tends to result in the elevation of cage humidity—which can rapidly reach unhealthy levels. This is often manifested in captive snakes by the onset of skin or respiratory infections. Particularly prone to these kinds of problems are juvenile snakes that are often housed in shoe box-sized containers that are stacked on top of each other. Even though numerous holes may be drilled in the sides of these boxes, the ventilation is poor enough that evaporated water from a water bowl can create a deadly level of germ-laden stagnant air. Infections spread more rapidly in juveniles, so that many are found dead by the time the keepers realize there is a problem. For this reason many large-scale breeders do not leave water available at all times, but rather place water in small containers only once per week.

A similar problem will occur in any housing

arrangement with a substrate that contains water, such as mulch or soil. In fact, one of the most common reasons small fossorial snakes die in captivity is septicemia (a massive infection) due to extremely high humidity in a poorly ventilated cage.

Similarly, some desert snakes appear to stop feeding or become ill in cages with water. This can usually be traced to poor ventilation resulting in the same cascade of events. Some of these snakes appear to be extremely sensitive to high humidity levels. See the section on the sidewinder in Part III.

Thus, ventilation is a critical factor in the care of snakes and one that is very likely to be overlooked by many snake keepers. Plastic shoe and sweater boxes, drawer-style cages, fiberglass cages with sliding glass fronts, many wooden cages, and aquariums with glass tops, full hoods, or even pegboard tops are all likely to be poorly ventilated and should be watched carefully. Water in these cages needs to be kept to a minimum, especially if an intense heat source such as an incandescent bulb is present and capable of causing rapid evaporation. In the case of many kingsnakes and rat snakes, these cages may be acceptable under conditions of gentle ventral heat applied at the end of the cage opposite to the water source, and in many cases if water is placed in the cage only intermittently.

It has been our experience that the cages with complete screen tops have the most satisfactory ventilation and the snakes within them seem to have the fewest problems related to ventilation. The screen top also gives the keeper much more leeway in providing either more water or more heat to the enclosure without fear of a dangerously high humidity or temperature level.

Lighting

Lighting is definitely important for diurnal species of reptiles and possibly even for some nocturnal or fossorial species. Both the quantity and quality of light are important for the continued successful captive maintenance and breeding of those species that require it. It appears, however, that most North American snakes do not have very demanding requirements when it comes to light. In fact, the majority seem to do well with filtered sunlight alone, or filtered sunlight combined with light produced by either fluorescent or incandescent bulbs for a period each day similar to that to which they are exposed in nature. We have maintained and bred the following species without any UV light sources: glossy snake, Trans-Pecos rat snake, rubber boa, Baird's rat snake, corn snake, gray rat snake, western hognose snake, eastern hognose snake, southern hognose snake, night snake, six species of kingsnake, rosy boa, western ribbon snake, smooth earth snake, rough earth snake, brown snake, and lined snake. We have maintained for more than 1 year but not bred the following species without UV light: banded sand snake, western shovelnose snake, racer, black-striped snake, Sonoran whipsnake, Brazos water snake, sharptail snake, ringneck snake, western hooknose snake, 4 species of whipsnake, gopher snake, 3 species of patchnose, ground snake, some *Tantilla*, 9 species of garter snakes, lyre snake, all 15 species of rattlesnake found within the United States and Canada, and 2 species of coral snake found within the United States.

Certain individuals representing a number of species, however, will not eat if they are not exposed to full-spectrum (natural) light for a sufficient length of time. Campbell (pers. comm., 1992) observed that certain anorectic individuals of otherwise very adaptable normally good-eating species such as gopher snakes may begin feeding after exposure to one of these lights, and others have observed this in rattlesnakes exposed to UV lights. Admittedly, these individuals represent a small fraction of the snakes (including other members of the same species) that have been maintained in captivity, but they do indeed appear to require full-spectrum light. For these few anorectic individuals, a Vitalite® (Durotest) or Reptisun® (Zoomed) may be useful. Snakes from temperate zones do best with 14–16 hours of light per day from one of these lamps (or other light source) followed by 8–10 hours of darkness (too much light can be very stressful also). Interestingly, some of these snakes will later continue to do well after the UV light is removed.

Because of the disparities in captive behavior listed above, we must question not only if these lights are necessary for most North American snakes, but also ask exactly what they are necessary for (i.e., what function they serve for these snakes). One theory suggests that snakes do not require full-spectrum light for the production of vitamins as in some lizards and tortoises (Moyle, 1989), but rather primarily to assist them in visualizing their prey. This is certainly a possibility for diurnal snakes such as whipsnakes and racers, but is unlikely for nocturnal or fossorial snakes. In fact, we have observed a number of these small snakes actively foraging under red lights or other low-light situations.

Since these fixtures produce heat as well as light, superior thermoregulation is another possible benefit of an additional artificial light in a small enclosure (whether it is a full-spectrum light or not). Perhaps then, all basking behavior in captive North American snakes is solely for the purpose of thermoregulation and not vitamin production as previously believed. This would help to explain why nocturnal snakes bask under red lights and fossorial snakes bask just *under* the substrate or surface objects. Indeed, improved thermoregulation alone could account for the observed increase in appetite in some difficult captives.

Therefore, for the majority of captive North American snakes it is probably safe to assume that a full-spectrum light is not a necessity if enclosures have adequate thermal gradients, although it may be beneficial for some. These benefits may include a better appetite secondary to improved visualization or improved thermoregulatory capability.

The use of sun lamps has also been recommended by some. Susan Barnard recommends that young snakes be exposed for 1–2 minutes under a sun lamp daily, while adult snakes be exposed for 2–4 minutes per day. This short period of intense light (heat?) apparently stimulates appetite, digestion, activity, and perhaps vitamin production (although once again the latter contribution is questionable for most snakes and the other observations can be explained by increased thermoregulatory capabilities).

Be careful with these lights, however, or you can cook a snake.

If the keeper chooses to provide full-spectrum light to a certain snake, remember that whatever your light source is, it should not be placed above glass or plexiglass as this will filter out some of the light necessary for the snake to make full use of that light and thereby defeat the purpose of purchasing it. Natural sunlight is also filtered by glass in this manner, and the risk of overheating via the greenhouse effect inside a glass terrarium is very great. Also remember that the intensity of light can be important, so the distance of the full-spectrum light from the snake may also be an important factor.

Recently, some experts warned that these full-spectrum lights should be replaced every 6 months even if they are still working, since they may stop emitting full-spectrum light at that time.

A timer is a very good investment that accomplishes the task of lighting very accurately and consistently every day. They are strongly recommended for the serious snake keeper and breeder.

Substrate (Flooring Material)

The last aspect of the physical environment, but perhaps one of the most important in terms of success, is the substrate (what is on the bottom of the cage). For most snakes, including water snakes, indoor-outdoor carpet or artificial turf (hereinafter referred to as artificial carpet/turf) are the antifungal substrates of choice. The little plastic fingers support the snake and allow air to circulate around and underneath it. This helps to avoid—and heal—skin infections. These substrates allow the snake to use serpentine locomotion effectively, as opposed to newspaper which does not. It has been our impression that snakes housed on carpet/turf are less likely to develop flaccid musculature or become egg-bound than snakes housed on newspaper, largely because of the increased level of exercise those on artificial carpet/turf receive. Another unexpected benefit of turf was discovered quite fortuitously with a clutch of young scarlet kingsnakes, *Lampropeltis triangulum elapsoides*. It was observed that those snakes from the clutch placed on artificial carpet/turf or mulch did fine while those placed on newspaper or in bare-bottomed containers suffered multiple spinal fractures. Presently, we believe that these very small, very excitable snakes suffered spontaneous fractures as they attempted to move rapidly in their enclosures without sufficient support (or traction).

The other major artificial substrate used by many snake keepers is newspaper. Aside from the potential drawbacks listed above, newspaper is an excellent substrate as it is easy to clean (or replace) and is parasite-free. This substrate is certainly a practical choice for those with large collections, but it is not as attractive as artificial carpet/turf.

Some snakes, however, require a more natural substrate and if not provided with it may not eat or will have problems shedding, defecating, mating, laying eggs, or having young. Cypress mulch and aspen shavings have worked very well as substrates for the majority of North American snakes in our care. We have found that a depth of 2.5–5.0 cm (1–2 inches) is satisfactory for most snakes. Peat moss and sphagnum moss or a mixture of these have been highly recommended by other workers. Those using these substrates recommend a depth of about one-third to one-quarter the length of the snake. Some have recommended stirring the mixture frequently to avoid the problem of moisture accumulating on the bottom, but we have found that small fossorial snakes actually use the moisture gradient found within these substrates to their benefit; we have had snakes do well for years in unstirred substrate. There may be other benefits derived from stirring the substrate, however. See the discussion on bioactive substrate below. Mixtures of mulch and peat moss also work well. Cedar mulch is to be avoided as it may contain toxins that are harmful to snakes. Untreated natural soil is also to be avoided because of the possibility of pathogenic bacteria or mites. If the soil is baked in a pan first you may use it, but be warned that the sandy component of many soils may cause intestinal impactions if the snake accidentally ingests it.

An alternative to baking the soil is to wash it. Soil that has been washed with large quantities of water has been used by many zoos and museums to create more natural looking environments. The soil is just placed over a fine screen and rinsed thoroughly. This "washed soil" usually works well, even though the sandy (nonorganic) portion is still present and is therefore potentially dangerous for the same reason listed above. Apparently, however, many fossorial snakes possess behavioral or physiological adaptations that either reduce the amount of soil ingested or allow it to pass through their gastrointestinal system without any harm. Certainly, sand-swimming snakes such as shovelnoses and banded sand snakes do extremely well with dry warm sand as a substrate, even though sand is not advisable for many other species or the average snake keeper under most circumstances. If sand is chosen, it must remain dry or many health problems are likely to occur in the captive snake. We have successfully used either white play sand or builder's sand for years, both of which are sold in many locations. WARNING: Be extremely careful about beach sand. It may contain large quantities of salt which will slowly dehydrate some small species of snake (e.g., crowned snakes, *Tantilla* sp.) if the keeper is unaware of its presence.

Avoid corncob litter for several reasons. First, if ingested it may cause stomatitis (a mouth infection) or an intestinal impaction (a blocked gut). Second, it is extremely drying, but if dampened it supports heavy bacterial growth that can predispose a snake to skin infections or respiratory infections. Never use kitty litter as it is even more drying than corncob litter and may also cause chemical irritation of the lungs.

Some species, unfortunately, must be maintained in water. If you have one of these (see the individual species accounts), the depth of the water, according to Barnard, should be about one-quarter the length of the snake. We have had a great deal of success using this guideline for water depth for adult snakes, but be careful with juvenile aquatic snakes, especially newborns, as we have had some drown in very shallow water. For them, a cypress mulch stew (a large amount of cypress mulch added to the swamp tea solution) or large quantities of real or plastic plants may be required.

Very recent advances in herpetoculture may revolutionize the way we keep snakes in captivity and think about their requirements. Dr. Philippe de Vosjoli discusses in detail the use of bioactive substrate systems (BSS)™ in his soon to be published book entitled *The Art of Keeping Snakes*. The basic theory behind these substrates is that they provide an environment where beneficial bacterial compete with pathogenic bacteria and fungi to support a healthly microhabitat for the captive. De Vosjoli indicates that stirring is the key. Stirring mixes the competitive bacteria in lower layers with fecal bacteria and others at the surface, thereby limiting their growth. Successful creation of the bioactive substrate requires that the substrate be at least 6.5 cm (2.5 inches) deep, and that it allow for good oxygenation and moisture retention. If the substrate dries out, it will not work. This is just a brief summary of what is needed for a bioactive substrate. The substrate developed by de Vosjoli will soon be available commercially. It has been tested on numerous species of snakes with great success. The reader is encouraged to learn more about this theory and associated product in de Vosjoli's book.

It should be noted that the moisture-containing substrate mentioned above probably has other benefits as well. Dr. Harvey Lillywhite and others have recently been commenting on the tremendous cutaneous water loss that captive snakes endure when they are placed in completely dry cages. This chronic water loss is suspected of being a major factor leading to the demise of these captive snakes; it may result in kidney damage. Thus, a moist substrate may create a microhabitat that protects a captive snake from both chronic dehydration and infection. Indeed, we have seen many small species do well in moist substrates, or where moist substrates are offered as one of the choices available to these snakes.

Check the individual species accounts to determine which substrate is best for the species under consideration.

Feeding

As mentioned in the introduction, we have learned a great deal about the feeding behavior of North American snakes in recent years. Our observations over the last several years have caused us to modify our views on captive feeding techniques for entire groups of snakes. In addition, we now believe that many species of snakes previously thought to be difficult to feed in captivity are no more difficult than those with which experienced herpeticulturists have become familiar, namely the rat snakes and kingsnakes. Indeed, the vast majority of the species we have studied have readily switched to feeding upon domestic mice or rats or some other captive-raised food item such as crickets or wax worms. This opens the door for large numbers of herpeticulturists to maintain, study, and breed these snakes in captivity, an undertaking that is desperately needed and long overdue.

Snakes eat other animals, specifically whole animals. In captivity, however, they do not necessarily eat live animals. This is a very important thing to remember when feeding a snake. Most snakes do not need to eat live animals since they rely heavily upon their sense of smell to locate, and determine the acceptability of, potential food items. Feeding live mice and rats to snakes is often unnecessary and is a risky business. It takes only one well-placed bite for a mouse to injure a snake's eye or the interior of its mouth. Admittedly, 999 out of 1000 times a snake will subdue and kill its prey with little damage to itself, but why take

Frozen food. Common food items can all be frozen. This allows for long-term storage, reduces somewhat the risk of parasitism, and allows the keeper to use methods that could not be accomplished when feeding live animals. (photo by David G. Campbell)

Scenting a prekilled pinky mouse with a spider. This procedure has been used with many food items in order to get the snake to take the common food, namely, the pinky mouse. Lizards and snakes are more commonly used for this purpose. (photo by David G. Campbell)

Sewing a prekilled lizard onto a prekilled pinky mouse. More stubborn feeders may require more devious means of trickery, as seen here. Note the lizard here is an introduced species, the Mediterranean gecko. (photo by David G. Campbell)

the risk with a snake that will eat dead rodents? Lizards will also bite and scratch and other snakes can bite and inflict severe wounds. In addition, all wild-caught prey items including invertebrates, fish, amphibians, reptiles, birds, and mammals may contain parasites harmful to a snake (Stoskopf and Hudson, 1982). Some of these can be eliminated by feeding dead items that have been frozen for several days and then thawed and warmed. Feeding dead animals also allows the keeper to persuade some snakes to eat items they would not eat otherwise. For example, a snake that eats only lizards may be induced to eat one lizard and several pinkies by suturing the pinkies to the lizard in a trainlike manner using sewing thread. These so-called "pinky trains" can eventually be switched to pinky/mouse trains for some individuals. Also, dead mice may be placed inside a shed skin for a snake that prefers to eat other snakes. Another method of getting snakes to eat more commonly available items includes rubbing the usual prey item on the intended food, e.g., rubbing toads or tadpoles on pinkies for young hognose snakes, or large salamanders on frogs for mud snakes. This is referred to by many as a scent transfer technique. You can keep the preferred item frozen in your freezer for years and just take it out as needed to spice up food. The majority of both garter snakes and water snakes will often rapidly switch to unscented mice after they have consumed scented ones for

a while, and even if they still prefer scented mice, it is a relatively easy process that spares native amphibians or fish and results in less odoriferous stools.

Small snakes may be induced to eat parts of usual or unusual prey items that are too large to eat in toto. Examples include feeding the frozen and thawed leg (with claws removed) of a large five-lined skink to a stubborn baby milk snake or a piece of a giant slug to a baby redbelly snake.

Recently, the invention of Snake Steak Sausages® by T-Rex (Ocean Nutrition Corporation, San Diego, California) has made it possible to feed some of the more difficult species. In fact, some juvenile snakes will accept these artificially flavored meals months before they consume pinkies. Since the sausages are sold frozen, and they come in many sizes, they are a very convenient food source for snakes. We have not had the opportunity to raise snakes solely on this food, so we cannot yet verify that they represent a completely balanced diet.

Some snakes will drink scrambled egg mixtures (with various things added) that appear to be relatively nutritionally complete, but these snakes may do so only if they are deprived of a regular source of drinking water. Of course, all of these methods of feeding treachery on your part may not result in a balanced diet for your snake. Therefore, use these methods to supplement the normal diet (to stretch a limited food supply) rather than as a substitute for it. For western North American snakes, this may be necessary only for leafnose snakes, *Phyllorhynchus* sp., and scarlet snakes, *Cemophora coccinea*, although hatchling milk snakes may drink an egg mixture voluntarily.

Several items or diets should be avoided. These include diets consisting primarily of obese rats and mice, diets consisting entirely of fresh fish, and diets consisting of only one species of insect such as crickets, wax worms, or mealworms. Feeding obese mice and rats regularly will result in steatitis (an inflammation of fat), heart disease, or obesity in a snake. Feeding only fresh fish may result in a vitamin B deficiency and result in neurologic signs. See under eastern ribbon snake for details. Feeding only one species of insect may easily result in a vitamin or mineral deficiency (crickets, wax worms, and mealworms are notoriously calcium-deficient), loss of interest and loss of appetite, or an intestinal impaction (blockage) because of the high level of indigestible chitin in the exoskeleton of some insects but especially mealworms (if not fed just after they have shed), large crickets, and some adult beetles.

Force-feeding should be attempted only under the following conditions:

1. There are no obvious physical signs of illness.
2. The snake is not eating and has not eaten for a considerable length of time *under the proper environmental conditions*. This length of time depends on the size of the snake and the type of prey being offered, but 2 months is a good time to start thinking about force-feeding.
3. You have offered a wide variety of food including the preferred food for that species in the wild.
4. The snake is housed separately.
5. A fecal examination has been performed by your veterinarian and the snake has been treated if worms or protozoans were found.
6. The snake has a place to hide and is not handled frequently.
7. It is not late summer or early fall with brumation (winter cooldown) being imminent.

Remember that many snakes will swallow small food items that are gently placed in their mouths, so try the following method before attempting anything more drastic. Gently pick up the snake; grab firmly right behind the head; insert a small, clean, smooth object into the mouth and slide it back to the angle of the jaws; put the food item in (and remove the prying device); then quickly and gently place the snake back in its cage. If the snake doesn't wipe it out of its mouth right away, it will usually swallow it. If this doesn't work one day, try it the next day with a different food item. If this doesn't work there are two alternatives. The first is to place the object in the mouth as mentioned above and gently push it down the throat with a smooth blunt-ended probe (lubricate the food item with water or egg white first). The second alternative is to use a liquid or semisolid diet. One semisolid food used by many veterinarians is called A/D (Hills Co.). The A/D is generally mixed with water at a ratio of 1:1 and tube-fed at a dose of 40 ml (total of A/D and water) per kilogram body weight once weekly until the snake begins to feed voluntarily again.

Another liquid diet is a mixture consisting of egg yolk, water, and a vitamin paste called Nutrical® (which most veterinarians carry) in a ratio of 1:0.5:1 (Fredrick Frye's [1979] formula consists of three parts strained meat, one part beaten whole egg, one-half part Nutrical®, and one part warm water) (Frye 1979, 1981). These mixtures can be fed via a small smooth stomach tube. An endotracheal tube size 7.5, 8.5, or 9.5 (Rosch Corporation) or size 18 French catheter/ stomach tube (Monoject Corporation) works well for some of the larger snakes, while a size 2.5 or 3.0 endotracheal tube or size 5 French catheter/feeding tube works well for some of the smaller snakes. The tube should be lubricated with water or egg white and very gently passed down the esophagus several inches. Never force the tube if it does not slide easily and always avoid placing it in the trachea (the glottis, which is constantly opening and closing as the snake breathes, is very far forward in snakes, and usually easy to see and avoid). The mixture you have selected should be placed in a large syringe, hooked up to the tube, and gently forced through it. Follow this with a little air in order to clear out the tube before you gently remove it from the snake. We usually pinch the tube while removing it in order to prevent any liquid that may remain in the tube from dribbling out in the snake's mouth and possibly being aspirated. Then place the snake down gently and do not disturb for as long as possible. A small amount of fluid may be regurgitated but this is usually nothing to worry about. If a large amount of fluid is regurgitated, you should be concerned that some of the fluid may have been aspirated into the lungs. If this happens, you should definitely see a reptile-oriented veterinarian.

A prepared liquid diet is available that contains one kilocalorie per ml (Vivonex®, Norwich Eaton Pharmaceuticals). Jarchow (1988) recommends 1–4 ml per 100 grams of body weight per day in divided doses as often as the snake would eat in nature. Another prepared liquid with an equal caloric density is Clinicare® (Abbott Laboratories).

In years past, the necessity of feeding "contaminated food" was one of the major problems of keeping nonrodent-eating snakes. Much of their food had to be collected in the great outdoors and there was no control over toxins, parasites, or potential bacterial pathogens. Freezing frogs, toads, salamanders, fish, worms, and insects for several days did reduce the parasite load in these animals, but there was still an increased risk and the food was still more difficult to procure. Recently, however, great strides have been made in the captive reproduction of numerous food mammals, amphibians, fish, and insects such that there are now many readily available substitute food items for most species of North American snakes. And as mentioned above, most of the natricine snakes (garter snakes and water snakes) that we have maintained have rapidly switched to scented and then unscented mice for long-term maintenance and breeding. (Within one summer, we had switched every large natricine maintained by us from fish and amphibians to mice. This was a dramatic change. We went from using nearly 500 fish and amphibians per month to none. These snakes gained weight, defecated less frequently, and in one case bred for the first time in years).

Some have suggested that microwaving food items may have some promise in eliminating parasites as well but this is as yet untested.

If food items must be collected, several precautions can be taken to help protect captive snakes. First, collect food items from areas that are not visibly polluted. This generally means the farther you are from a road, the better. In the area from which you collect, standing water should not have a visible oil film and theoretically there should be no trash there. Of course, stay away from industrial areas and sewage areas as animals collected there will be more likely to be contaminated by chemical or biological toxins. Paved roads are not good places to collect food as worms and frogs collected there often contain petroleum toxins, but if you wash them thoroughly before feeding they will probably not cause problems. Fresh road-killed amphibians are okay, however, as long as you wash them first and preferably also freeze them for at least several days. Finally, closely examine your potential prey item. It should look healthy (i.e., it should not be very thin or have lumps, bumps, mites, ticks, or unusual skin lesions). *If it does not look healthy, do not feed it to your snakes.* Rodent tumors, however, will not affect snakes.

In summary, breed your own mice, rats, fish, amphibians, birds, worms, or insects if possible, or purchase captive-raised animals as these will be less likely to be parasitized. Most species of North American snakes will readily accept these captive-bred animals as a substitute for their natural diet, and if not, most will readily take captive-bred food that has been scented with a preferred natural prey item. Furthermore, on the basis of the captive breeding success we have had, many of these artificial diets appear to be nutritionally complete. Hence, it is much safer and more practical to collect only those animals you need for scenting purposes and make every effort possible to switch most snakes to captive-bred animals. This is also a more environmentally sound practice as it spares native amphibians, reptiles, or fish.

If you are caring for a specimen that absolutely refuses anything but its natural prey, freeze the prey item for at least several days before thawing and feeding. It is rare indeed to find a snake that refuses its preferred food item just because it has been frozen. If a snake refuses to feed upon prekilled or frozen food items, remember that they should receive regular fecal exams and dewormings if necessary.

With regard to food preferences and items listed in the literature as the preferred food item for a particular species, remember that some of these snakes' ranges are vast and that food preferences may vary considerably from one area to another. Thus, avoid generalizing about the food limitations of an entire species, but rather be open-minded and willing to experiment a little if the snake in question is not eating what it is supposed to. For instance, sidewinders in certain areas of their range more readily consume mice, while many others prefer only lizards. Also, ringneck snakes from California are more likely to consume only slender salamanders and tadpoles or recently transformed treefrogs, *Hyla*, while those from the east may eat primarily earthworms. Graham's water snakes from some bodies of water may readily consume minnows, but those from other areas reportedly eat only crayfish. So keep an open mind when offering food to a snake. Observe the snake carefully for any signs of interest in unusual foods and remember that the snake's refusal to eat one time may be due to something aside from a lack of interest in the food item offered (see the list of possibilities in the prepurchase exam section). Remember that experimentation with a snake's diet should not be attempted with a long-term, good-eating

A regal ringneck eating a pinky. Many snakes have broad diets, and different food items are worth trying. (photo by John Rossi)

captive (as it may introduce parasites into the snake unnecessarily), but should be attempted with a recently captured animal that is refusing to eat a regular food item, even though the snake is set up properly.

One of the more unusual observations we have made with some North American snakes is that many will readily consume a number of food items with ranges that are not sympatric with theirs (their geographic regions do not overlap). Examples include the consumption of the ground skink, *Scincella lateralis*, by a number of western snakes including California mountain kingsnakes and Arizona coral snakes; squirrel tree frogs, *Hyla squirella*, by night snakes; Mediterranean geckos, *Hemidactylus turcicus*, by night snakes, lyre snakes, sidewinders, rosy boas, patchnose snakes, and gray-banded kingsnakes. Similarly, Florida wolf spiders appear to be readily consumed by western, desert, and Mexican hooknose snakes, and Florida centipedes are readily consumed by many blackhead snakes. This suggests that as far as most North American snakes are concerned, one lizard or arachnid may taste about as good as another. From a practical standpoint, this means that a snake keeper faced with a poorly feeding nonlocal snake may be able to find a suitable food substitute locally, and even an exotic (or introduced species) may serve as the main course. Certainly, feeding these animals may involve a definite risk, as they may harbor parasites not normal for the captive snake. However, freezing may help to reduce this risk.

Furthermore, the feeding of a widespread, urban-dwelling, introduced species such as the Mediterranean gecko, *Hemidactylus turcicus*, will have little impact on their numbers and no impact on the populations of native herptiles. The preservation of native herptiles should be a major concern to herpetoculturists who collect their food items from the wild rather than use captive-bred food items. Admittedly, over-collection of very prolific animals is unlikely, but combined with other factors such as pollution and habitat destruction, it could contribute to their demise. Of particular concern is the decline in numbers of many species of amphibians and their extinction in a number of areas.

Over the course of its lifetime, one captive garter snake may consume thousands of amphibians. Hence, switching it to captive-bred mice may save a tremendous number of these wild vertebrates.

Food Quality

It is commonly accepted that what you are feeding to your captive snakes is very important in determining feeding success (e.g., don't offer a worm to an adult rat snake). But successful maintenance of snakes, and more importantly, growth and reproduction, require more than just providing the appropriate food item.

The quality of the food must be controlled if possible. It is now known that both bacterial and parasitic infections can result from feeding mice or rats that have been raised under poor environmental conditions, and metabolic diseases can result from feeding mice or rats that have been fed poor diets. These low quality animals often appear in pet shops or are available through some wholesalers at very cheap prices. Reconsider the cost of feeding these poor quality animals in light of the medical problems they can cause for your captive snakes. We would strongly recommend buying your rodents from a consistent, clean, even and reputable source or, better, breeding them yourself. Breeding rodents is discussed in detail in other books and will not be discussed here. Never use wild rodents. In the absence of a clean source, killing and freezing the rodents for several days will eliminate many of the parasites (fleas, ticks, and mites as well as intestinal worms and those encysted in muscle may be killed) but not most of the bacteria and protozoans.

Some keepers have suggested microwaving dead animals for the same purpose. The exact technique and value of such treatment is still unknown at the time of this writing (you will have to experiment with the time and setting). Do not use the family microwave for this purpose and remember to slice open the belly (to allow gas to escape) before you place the animal in the microwave. No one knows if this will affect the nutritional value of the food

animals to the degree that it will negatively affect the snake. One would suspect that this treatment would improve the nutritional value of fish by destroying the enzyme thiaminase. *Do* remember to allow the animals to cool down sufficiently before feeding.

Psychological Factors

Psychological factors have only recently received a great deal of attention from herpetoculturists. As with other animals, many factors interact to produce the behaviors observed in snakes. Recent research has shown the tremendous complexity of behaviors in wild snakes (Seigel et al., 1987) and there is no reason to doubt complex behaviors are present in captive snakes (Gillingham, in Seigel et al., 1987), even though they may be drastically modified in captivity. Instinct and experience probably interact to produce the majority of behaviors we see in both wild and captive snakes.

In snakes, like other ectotherms, behavior is usually dependent upon daily and seasonal temperature fluctuations, as well as microenvironmental temperature gradients. And like all animals, physiological processes often underlie the behaviors observed. Therefore, in order to understand captive snake behavior, we must discuss both the environment and some physiology.

Perhaps the best discussion relating the captive environment to physiological and psychological factors is that of Cowan (1980). In this discussion, Cowan defined stress as the physiological responses to environmental variation, and related the process of acclimatization to an energy expenditure. In the high-stress environment, Cowan suggested that all of the available energy may be consumed maintaining internal stability rather than going to immunity, growth, and reproduction. Too much stress, or an environment too different from that with which the animal has evolved, may therefore result in a physical degeneration, loss of resistance leading to disease, and eventually death of the captive. Cowan referred to this process as "maladaptation syndrome" and it has come to be widely accepted by a number of well-respected herpetoculturists.

From our work with North American snakes, it also appears that those species that are extremely widespread, occupy a number of habitat types, and have broad diets may actually be preadapted to some extent for captive situations. Indeed, the very nature of these generalists gives them the ability to survive in conditions less than optimal and accept a wide variety of ambient temperatures and humidities, substrates, and food items. Those species with restricted ranges, habitat types, temperature requirements, and specialized diets may fare better than generalists in their particular habitat, or perhaps at finding and consuming their particular prey, but are no match for them in other habitat types as they do not appear to be very adaptable. Certainly, captivity may be considered a harsh and stressful environment, to which the captives must adapt or they will perish. Theoretically then, a habitat or dietary specialist must have certain aspects of its environment or diet re-created more accurately than a generalist, and even so may be under more stress than the generalist. Of course, a dietary specialist may not be a habitat specialist or vice versa, and this is why some specialists fare better than others in captivity.

How well a snake does in captivity then may depend upon a combination of inherited characteristics (the product of millions of years of tremendous evolutionary pressure), physical aspects of the environment it has been exposed to during its life (acclimation or acclimatization), and its experience (learned behaviors and social and environmental stimuli). Thus, a secretive burrowing snake must remain a secretive burrowing snake in captivity, and an arboreal snake will still seek to climb in captivity, but other behaviors may not be so genetically and phenotypically dictated. A cold-climate snake, although possessing a greater tolerance and preference for cooler temperatures than a warm-climate snake, may become acclimatized to a slightly warmer environment in time, and a lizard-eating snake, although having an innate preference for lizards, may adapt to eating mice in time. A snake born and raised in captivity may readily learn to accept domestic food items and may remain calm and be handleable, while one born in the wild may refuse to feed on domestic food items and remain nervous and irascible.

It would seem then, that there is a spectrum of adaptability to captivity for North American snakes. Those most likely to adapt would be captive-born individuals of the wide-ranging generalists, while those most likely to experience stress would be the adults of the habitat and dietary specialists. Exceptions may be found among those species with habitat or dietary specializations similar to those commonly offered in captivity (e.g., obligate rodent eaters, which prefer small dark areas in which to hide and rarely bask).

Some snakes are incapable of adjusting to captivity no matter how well they are cared for. These animals should be released exactly where they were collected if they do not adapt to captivity within a reasonable amount of time (1–2 months). They will nervously travel about the perimeter of the cage, day or night, traumatize their rostral scales, refuse to eat, and eventually wither away to skin and bones. There is no cure for this maladaptation syndrome; however, there are several things that can be done to prevent stress during the capture, transportation, and initial release into the cage that will help. See the sections entitled "Capturing a Snake" and "Transportation/Shipping" for details. Also, consider covering the cage with linen or construction paper into which very small holes have been placed so that you can see in but the snake can't see out. A black border placed on the outside of an aquarium around the bottom (5–16 cm or 2–6 inches high) may help to keep some snakes from running into the glass. Using a pegboard top instead of screen will also help. Make sure the animal receives the correct quantity and quality of light as mentioned earlier. Of course, an animal like this should always be housed singly and dead prey items should always be tried first.

These snakes should never be handled unless absolutely necessary. *Always* provide a hide box, crumpled newspaper, or the correct substrate if fossorial.

The hide box is without a doubt the most important and critical piece of cage equipment in any snake's cage. Some have suggested that the security they provide improves appetite, digestion, and breeding behavior; reduces the likelihood of vomiting or other illnesses; and may increase the life-span of a snake in captivity by years. The hide box may be made of cardboard, plastic, wood, metal, or even bark. Ceramic boxes are available commercially. We prefer the nonporous materials such as plastic. They can be easily cleaned and disinfected and they come in a variety of colors. The dark colors like brown, black, and green seem to work best for many of our native snakes as they seem to enjoy the reduced intensity of light within, although some have suggested that even a clear hide box would be acceptable to the snake as long as it was low enough to touch the snake's back (some of the security is provided when the snake feels something over it) (Radcliffe and Chiszar, 1983).

Snakes do learn. They learn to be fearful of particular prey animals (like mice) after they have been attacked by one. They learn to fear their cage when a branch or a rock collapses on them or when the cage is very unstable. They learn to be leery of people if they are always in a very busy room and are constantly disturbed or are always handled roughly. Too many vibrations from heavy traffic or an unstable cage location will also increase stress. Strangely, the height at which the cage is placed may make a difference. One kept lower (on the floor) may be thoroughly scared by an approaching person, while one on a shelf at waist or face level will not. This may be due to the vibrations or the different appearance of a person approaching when viewed from a low level.

Disoriented Behavior Syndrome

Many herpetologists have collected a snake, lizard, or turtle and seen it eat immediately after capture, sometimes even in the pillowcase on the way home. Male and female reptiles placed in the same cage immediately after capture may actually mate over and over again for several days. After several days they will never eat or mate again and will head rapidly downhill until they are released or die. What is happening with these reptiles? No one knows exactly, but we suspect that the environmental cues for feeding or mating were so strong at the time of capture that it may take several days for the animals to "realize" they have been captured. We don't know what physical factors or combination of physical factors we have changed. We don't know if hormones are involved. This phenomenon has been observed with numerous snakes, including the coral snake, eastern diamondback, numerous water snakes, some ringneck snakes, and others.

Upon seeing this behavior immediately after capture, realize what is going on and use it to your advantage. Feed heavily or allow mating if a mate is at hand. Feeding may buy some more time in which the snake can adjust to captivity, while mating may result in captive-born offspring (which may adapt to captivity very rapidly). Make sure to set up these animals in an ideal environment (see individual species sections) right away. Disturb as little as possible during this time and do not clean the cage unless absolutely necessary (see the section on breeding).

If your attempts at feeding fail after this initial period, consider releasing the animal where it was captured. If you collected the animal in the first place, you owe it to this animal to return it to exactly where it was caught or have someone else release it there for you. Only in some emergency situations should the snake be released in a similar habitat elsewhere within its natural range (state fish and game commissions will often not approve of this). *Do not release noticeably sick, parasitized, or very thin animals!* See the section on releasing snakes. If you have a female that you know or suspect has been bred, you may wish to keep her until she lays eggs or bears young and then for a short time afterward, during which time you should try to feed her. Remember that pregnancy is a common cause for inappetence, so feeding should always be attempted during this postpartum period before release.

Winter Cooldown (Brumation/Hibernation)

The act of "hibernating" our native snakes, sometimes called *brumation*, is one of the most important things serious snake keepers do. This cool inactive period, termed a winter cooldown by many herpetoculturists, is intricately tied to normal behavior, growth, feeding, and, of course, breeding of many reptiles.

Unfortunately, there is presently a great deal of disagreement as to the proper terminology for this cool winter period. The term *hibernation* is a term usually used only for mammals and has fallen into disfavor with many snake keepers lately. Likewise, the term *brumation*, although perhaps a more accurate term, technically speaking, has not been overwhelmingly received by herpetoculturists. Some started using the term, while others resisted the term on the grounds that the term *hibernation* had been so well accepted and widely utilized for so long that it is the phrase most often heard. Furthermore, they did not like the sound of the replacement term, saying it sounded much like the term *ruminate*, a digestive process carried out by cows, sheep, and goats. In addition, the American Federation of Herpetoculturists recently suggested the expansion of the term *hibernation* (addition of a definition) to include the semiactive state that reptiles undergo, rather than utilize a new term for the reasons discussed above. Nevertheless, some argue correctly that *hibernation* is a term that applies to a physiological process of mammals and is therefore inappropriate. Sean McKeown stated that using the term *hibernation* to describe this process in snakes is the equivalent of saying that a snake has beautiful plumage (a term used for birds). Many herpetoculturists have sought to avoid the dispute by using the term *winter cooldown*. Hence, we will use the term *brumation* or *winter cooldown* throughout the rest of this book.

We would strongly recommend either natural or artificial winter cooldown for all healthy, mature, temperate zone snakes. Some of the many techniques used are discussed in this section. Each method has advantages and disadvantages in terms of cost, labor, safety, and control.

Natural (Passive) Brumation (Winter Cooldown)

Generally, brumation may be accomplished by placing the snake in an area of cooler temperatures (10–15°C; 50–59°F for most North American snakes, but see the section on temperature for exceptions) with little or no *additional* light for 2–4 months (natural filtered light coming through a window or skylight is fine). The snake's own enclosure is the best thing to cool it in. Few changes are necessary in most cases if the snake is set up properly. Nothing needs to be added to the enclosure for larger snakes. However, slightly moistened cypress mulch or sphagnum moss may be a good addition for smaller snakes if they don't already have it, in order to keep them from becoming dehydrated.

In some southern areas of the United States, the average garage is an ideal location in which to naturally brumate snakes. These are generally dark or receive small amounts of natural light, and if uninsulated, as most are, the temperature will usually drop into the 4–15°C (40–59°F) range on even the coolest days. Another option is a corner room with an open window, window fan, and closed heat ducts. Similarly, house closets or basements work well in the northern United States and Canada or other cold-climate areas.

In these natural brumaculums, if the temperature rises for short periods, the snakes will become more active, wander about the cage, drink, and then return to their hiding places—presumably preparing for the next cold spell (one of the reasons the term brumation was proposed).

Buy and use a thermometer regularly to check on the snakes, especially during very cold weather, if using this method. The garage method of brumation probably closely approximates what the snakes are exposed to in their natural hiding places, so this is a very natural method of brumation. The benefits of this technique are twofold. The first benefit is minimal expense since no special equipment aside from a thermometer, fan, and electric heater may be needed. The second benefit is that lighting and temperature changes are generally very gradual and do not need to be regulated by the keeper. The disadvantage of this passive technique is that it cannot be regulated at will. The keeper and snakes do not have control over the climatic changes in their area and thus are slaves to them.

Artificial (Active) Brumation (Winter Cooldown)

Trutnau (1981) and others have recommended a somewhat more controlled artificial technique that involves placing the snakes in plastic containers that have been partly filled with crumpled newspaper or mulch and placing them in a refrigerator at 10°C (50°F). They suggest that small holes be placed in the boxes and that the refrigerator door be opened every 2–3 days to allow additional air in. Some have suggested that perlite or vermiculite may be used successfully in this manner, while others have reported accidental ingestion and stomatitis (mouth infection) when these are used. No light

Brumation boxes. The same plastic boxes useful as humidity boxes and egg-laying boxes may also be used as brumation boxes. One must monitor the snakes carefully for dehydration during this period since dehydration is the number one cause of death for brumating captive snakes (and probably wild snakes as well). (photo by David G. Campbell)

is necessary during this time, although small amounts of light will not harm the snakes. These snakes are kept under these conditions for the entire period of brumation (2–4 months) and then exposed to a 1-week period of limited quantities of light at room temperature before resuming a normal lighting and temperature regime. See Bruyndonckx (1984).

This artificial technique has been elevated to a science by a number of very serious snake breeders who have constructed very accurately controlled brumaculums. Finnegan (1984) described the construction of an excellent brumaculum and Applegate (1992) suggested that a wine chiller would work perfectly. The artificial approach does not leave the snakes and their keeper at the mercy of the weather. In some areas with warm climates, an especially warm winter may be disastrous for breeding.

Both natural and artificial methods are satisfactory but we have had more experience with the natural method, and since it requires less energy and allows the snakes to drink, we prefer this method. However, for northern or montane (mountain) species kept in the south (like fox snakes, rubber boas, some subspecies of the California mountain kingsnake, or Arizona mountain kingsnakes), the artificial method may be necessary, since some of these snakes seem unsatisfied with the milder southern temperatures and continue to waste energy wandering in their cages while refusing to eat or else simply failing to produce fertile eggs.

Sometimes the two methods can be combined. For example, chill the snake in a refrigerator for several weeks to months until cold weather arrives and then put it back into the seminatural environment of its enclosure.

Weighing a snake prior to brumation and comparing it with known weights of conspecific (individuals of the same species) healthy snakes of similar age, sex, and length would be a very valuable indicator of readiness for winter cooldown, although this type of comparison may be difficult in the absence of large numbers of captive animals, and it is not readily available in the literature for most species.

Generally speaking, however, one will rarely have problems if the guidelines below are followed. These guidelines are for temperate zone snakes only; never attempt to brumate a tropical boa or python like this. For those species, see Ross and Marzec (1990).

1. Never brumate a snake that does not appear completely healthy. *A sick snake may actually do well during the brumation period but will often die abruptly on removal from brumation.* The theory behind this is that upon warming, pathogenic organisms will multiply rapidly while the snake's immune response lags. Hence, it is critical that only healthy animals with low parasite loads be brumated.
2. Provide little or no extra light at this time for temperate zone snakes. Semitropical snakes like indigos, some rattlesnakes, black-striped snakes, and others do appear to require some light (or heat), and an incandescent bulb over the cage for 8–10 hours per day will allow them to bask during the day, even though exposed to cool temperatures at night; this approaches closely what tropical snake breeders do.
3. Maintain a high relative humidity (60–80%) by partly covering the cage (if it has a screen top) with a waterproof material or using some kind of mulch for smaller snakes. A humidifier may be advisable in some very dry situations. These humidity-increasing techniques are necessary only if the humidity in the room where the snakes are kept is very low. Otherwise, no covering or humidification will be required.
4. Keep clean water available throughout brumation (unless the snake sits in the water bowl frequently or you are using the artificial method of brumation).
5. Do not feed for 1–2 weeks prior to starting or during the actual brumation period in most cases. If using the natural method, offer food if the temperature rises sharply and is forecasted to stay high for a week or so. If it does go down abruptly, provide artificial heat for a short period to allow the snake to finish digesting its most recent meal. You can often judge by the snake's activity level whether it may be

interested in feeding or not. Remember, feeding snakes during these warm periods is almost always optional (and many will not eat anyway) and probably shouldn't be done if you don't have access to any artificial heat (heating pads).
6. Do not let the temperature of your brumaculum go below 3.5°C (38°F) for most snakes, 10°C (50°F) for southern snakes. For some snakes, like Texas indigos or coachwhips, you may want to always have supplemental heat available on one side of the cage. This is also a great idea for any snake that you are considering cooling down but do not know what temperatures to use. We have found this especially useful for subtropical snakes, snakes from extreme southern temperate areas, and snakes that arrive in the fall with an unknown health status.
7. Check your animals regularly for parasites or signs of infection. If you see this, warm them and treat or take to a reptile-oriented veterinarian immediately.
8. Brumate animals separately. This controls infectious diseases and helps when breeding time rolls around in the spring.
9. Disturb the cage as little as possible and do not clean just prior to breeding attempts.

Remember, the female snake with her shed skin should usually be placed with the male (not vice versa; see section on breeding) after 1 week of warming and a good meal for both snakes (although males may not eat until after mating). There may be some exceptions to this general scheme, and with certain species some have suggested that the male should be warmed several weeks prior to warming the female. Doug Finnegan, an experienced breeder of California mountain kingsnakes, believes that his breeding success with this species is much better when the snakes are treated in such a manner.

With regard to juveniles and hatchlings, be aware that many captive-born snakes and wild young captured prior to their first winter often do not need to be brumated their first year. Many breeders commonly skip brumation the first year in order to achieve rapid growth and early breeding after brumation the following year. Remember, however, that some snakes are "hard wired" for winter cooldown and the slightest drop in temperature or perceptible change in day length may send them into an anorectic state in preparation for cold weather.

It can be very frightening to a novice snake keeper when a highly prized snake stops eating about 2 months after purchase. Arizona mountain kingsnakes frequently demonstrate this kind of behavior. The answer to this problem is to work with nature and not against it: Cool down the snake and let it brumate. Admittedly, the thought of these small hatchlings not feeding for 2–4 months is somewhat disconcerting. However, it has been our experience that even a 5-gram blackhead snake can fast 5 months without ill effect if it is brumated properly. Therefore, a 15–20-gram neonate kingsnake should have no problem at all.

Last, consider the possibility of natural brumation outside for those snakes that are housed in outdoor enclosures. The construction of the enclosures and the outdoor brumaculum is discussed in some detail in the housing section.

Although some herpetoculturists dread this time of the year, we have found that it is beneficial for both the snakes and the keepers. It is a period when the time demands on the keeper are minimized. Use this extra time you have in the winter to catch up on your reading, holiday shopping, family, social life, and so forth, and prepare for the breeding season in the spring. Remember that in many cases, the length of the brumation period is just as important as the brumation temperature. Two months is thought to be a minimum.

Sexing

Techniques of sexing snakes may vary from the very simple and noninvasive to fairly complex, invasive, and sometimes expensive. These methods include the following: 1) observation of external characteristics (sexual dimorphism); 2) observation of reproductive behavior; 3) probing; 4) everting of "popping" the hemipenes; 5) saline injection; 6) cloacal swabs to examine

for presence of sperm; 7) hormone analysis; 8) ultrasonography; 9) fiberoptic endoscopy; and 10) exploratory surgery.

External Characteristics

Many of our native snakes can be sexed by external physical characteristics of the area around the vent (cloacal opening). Generally speaking, the tail of the male is longer and thicker than that of the female. This results in a more gradual tapering effect posterior to the vent. The females generally have shorter, thinner tails resulting in a pronounced tapering effect caudal to the vent. See the illustration below.

Of course, it is sometimes difficult to determine just how fast the tail tapers when you don't have a male and female next to each other for comparison. With smaller species, this may be the only practical method of sexing. It works extremely well for the vipers. Interestingly, another quick way the sex of a rattlesnake may be guessed at a glance is to count the number of tail stripes. Males generally have more tail stripes than conspecific females. Klauber (1972) stated this was too variable a characteristic to use as a definitive method of sexing, but we have found it to be useful in determining which individuals should be probed when looking for a certain sex. Also, among littermates, it may be an extremely accurate and quick method of sexing, even though there is too much variability to use it as a sexing method among all individuals of the species.

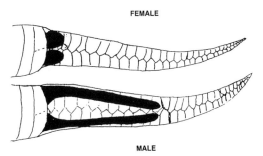

Ventral view of male and female snakes. (illustration by Roxanne Rossi, adapted from Laszlo, 1977)

Some field guides also list subcaudal scale rows (rows of scales under the tail behind the vent) as a method of distinguishing males and females, but there is often a considerable amount of overlap in these scale counts.

Observations of Behavior

Observation of various behaviors may provide a herpetoculturist with a great deal of information, not the least of which may be the sex of the animals in question. One very obvious observation is the deposition of eggs or young which of course indicates the snake is a female. It does not imply, however, that the cagemate is a male, since many female snakes are capable of storing sperm for long periods (Porter, 1972).

Other observations made when two animals are placed together may be equally as informative. The occurrence of copulation (mating) is not definitive, since pseudocopulation has been reported between snakes of the same sex. However, if one observes a hemipenis actually entering the cloaca of the partner, the probability that both sexes are present is very high.

Chasing and mounting are behaviors normally demonstrated by male snakes only, even though it has been observed occasionally in female snakes, and most commonly in female tortoises, lizards, and alligators. The snake being mounted may be of either sex, however.

Rhythmic jerking of the entire body, tail elevation, and crawling in reverse are all behaviors that have been associated with female snakes that are receptive to mating, while flight or tight coiling may be elicited in either a male or a nonreceptive female. Stewart (1989) warns that behaviors should be studied in one population at a time and the sex of animals demonstrating these behaviors should be confirmed with another method in order to classify that behavior as truly sex-specific behavior.

Probing

With the larger species, probing is a useful and practical alternative to observing the tail, but only in individuals large enough to perform this procedure. Basically, this involves inserting a clean, lubricated, smooth probe into one of the

Probing a snake. The most common method of sexing is probing. This involves inserting a smooth blunt probe toward the back of the tail. In general, if the probe inserts more than four scale rows, it is a male. If it enters less than this, it is a female. Observe an experienced prober before attempting this procedure or the snake may be injured. (photo by David G. Campbell)

inverted hemipenes just caudal (behind) the cloacal opening in the male. Insert the probe gently under the cloacal scale with the point toward the snake's head. Once inserted, gently reverse the direction of the probe so that the tip is now pointing toward the tip of the tail. Now gently advance the probe. If the probe doesn't insert more than 1–2 scales, you probably have a female (if greater than 3 or 4, a male). See the photos. *Warning!* If you have not seen this done before, do not attempt it or you may injure the snake. An experienced reptile veterinarian or snake breeder can demonstrate this technique for you.

In addition, using a dirty or nonlubricated probe may result in an infection of the cloaca (called cloacitis) resulting in the temporary or permanent sterility of that snake. Avoid doing this just prior to breeding unless it is absolutely necessary. According to Richard Fuhrman of Fuhrman Diversified Inc., the manufacturer of Furmont Reptile Probes®, the lubricant chosen for probing is also extremely important. Both KY Jelly® (Johnson and Johnson) and petrolatum are okay for probing, but are not recommended for adult snakes around breeding time, since both products contain chemicals that act as spermicides. Fuhrman Diversified

Inc. produces a probing lubricant called Lubi-fax® which, according to Fuhrman, can be used at any time, since it is not spermicidal. Many have used egg white quite successfully as a nonspermicidal lubricant. We also use gentocin ophthalmic ointment occasionally if we suspect there may already be a local infection. Most of these ointments also contain petrolatum, so they are spermicidal and should not be used just prior to breeding.

Many types of probes are acceptable as long as they have a smooth rounded end. Manufac-tured probes (Furmont Probes®), finely filed plastic paint brush handles, finely filed knitting needles, bobby pins, and even thick plastic filament have been used successfully for this purpose, as long as people remember to keep them clean and well lubricated with one of the lubricants described above. Robert Applegate, expert breeder, says a newborn rat snake or kingsnake can be probed with a single strand of copper wire, bent back on itself and twisted, but he recommends the Furmont Probe® for this purpose as well.

One last word is in order if one is contem-plating probing one of the smaller species. These snakes are usually wigglers and even an experienced snake prober can injure one if not extremely careful.

Eversion ("Popping") Technique

Applying gentle pressure to the bottom of the tail of young snakes may cause eversion of one or both hemipenes in most males. This proce-dure is known as "popping" and works nicely for young kingsnakes, rat snakes, patchnoses, glossy snakes, longnose snakes, garter snakes, many neonate rattlesnakes (restrained in a clear plexiglass tube), and others. It does not work well on adults of most of the larger species, but it may work well in adults of some of the smaller ones such as worm snakes. As you might imagine, this technique may require quite a bit of practice to achieve reproducible results and one must be very careful not to injure the snakes.

Occasionally, male snakes will spontane-ously evert their hemipenes briefly when they empty their anal glands at the time of capture.

Sexing a snake. Gentle pressure at the base of the tail of small snakes will often result in the eversion of one or both hemipenes. This is referred to as "popping" and is one method of sexing small snakes. (photo by David G. Campbell)

This may allow the herpetoculturist to identify a male immediately.

Injection of Sterile Solution

Another method of sexing, which is usually performed by experienced reptile veterinarians, is to insert a needle (the size varies depending upon the size of the snake; we usually use a 22 gauge) in the ventral tail about 12 scales behind the anal plate and inject a *sterile electrolyte solution* (like saline 0.9% or lactated Ringer's).

If probing does not give a definite answer, the injection of sterile isotonic fluids in the tail may result in the temporary protrusion of one hemipenis. Only temporary swelling will occur in the female. This should be attempted only by an experienced reptile veterinarian. (photo by David G. Campbell)

The temporary increase in pressure will cause the hemipene on the side injected to evert, making sexual identification more certain. If no eversion occurs, however, one cannot be certain the snake in question is a female, as some individuals have strong hemipene retractor muscles. Anesthesia may help in these cases. The fluid injected is absorbed and within 10–15 minutes the hemipene is back in its normal position.

Once again, do not try this unless you have seen it done, and definitely use the proper sterile solutions and sterile needles.

Cloacal Swab

Swabbing the cloaca of a snake and examining a smear of the swab under a microscope may reveal sperm. This may indicate that the swab was inserted in either a male or a recently mated female.

Ultrasonography, Fiberendoscopy, Laparotomy, Hormone Analysis

Ultrasonography, fiberendoscopy, exploratory laparotomy, and hormone analysis may have a place in herpetoculture, but they have not been widely used in snakes, especially North American snakes, because the previously discussed methods have worked so well and they are inexpensive and noninvasive.

Whatever method you are using, if you do it right, there is little chance for infection or injury.

Breeding

A great deal has been learned about breeding snakes in the last 5 years. Not only have a number of advances been made in the breeding of commonly kept snakes, but a number of North American species have been bred in captivity for the first time. From these observations, it appears that many species may be bred in captivity using the same basic techniques described for those that have been commonly bred, namely the kingsnakes and rat snakes. Apparently, high quality diets, parasite control, and proper thermal environment are important

factors for consistent breeding success that are common to all captive North American snakes. Indeed, most snakes will breed readily in captivity if prepared correctly. In fact, many species breed so readily that Bechtel (pers. comm., 1989) stated, "We don't make snakes breed. We just let them breed."

Age at Sexual Maturity

Mattison (1986) stated that reproduction may begin when snakes reach half of their eventual maximum size. The first brood or clutch will be very small but will increase gradually in size until the third or fourth season. He also mentions that sexual maturity is usually attained in 2 years but can occur at a younger age if the snakes are "pushed." Our observations agree with those of Seigel et al. (1987), indicating that the smaller species generally mature in less than 1 year in both nature and in captivity, while the larger North American species may reach sexual maturity in 3 or more years in the wild and in less than 2 years in captivity. Timmerman (pers. comm., 1989) believes that in the wild, most of these larger snakes do not reach sexual maturity until 4 or 5 years old, while W. S. Brown (1991, 1992) has collected evidence suggesting that it may take nearly 10 years for some snakes (e.g., wild female timber rattlesnakes) to reach sexual maturity. This discrepancy is discussed in more detail later in this section. It is interesting and important to note that in both the wild and in captivity males generally mature earlier than females.

Basic Guidelines

There are no hard and fast rules in breeding snakes. However, there are three very good guidelines for successfully breeding North American snakes. They are as follows:

1. Brumate your snakes.
2. Keep them separate until the time of mating.
3. Place them in a cage large enough so they can mate.

In the wild, temperate zone snakes usually mate in the spring, following winter cooldown.

North American snakes mate in both the spring and fall, while a few mate in winter. Here, two Brazos water snakes mate outside their hibernaculum before returning to the water to forage. (photo by John Rossi)

There are exceptions, however, and some snakes mate in the summer, fall, or winter (in the southern United States) and some may mate at any time. Apparently, normal gamete formation will not occur without a period of low temperatures, hence the reason for guideline number 1. If snakes of the opposite sex are kept together all year, they *may* lose interest and fail to mate, hence guideline number 2 (once again there are many exceptions, and snakes housed together may breed regularly). Physical impediment to mating may occur if the two snakes cannot stretch out or follow each other around the cage, hence guideline number 3.

Timing, Tips, and Tricks

Your success rate will be much higher if both the male and female have been warmed for about a week (after brumation) before placing the two snakes together.

Recently, however, some advanced snake breeders have been suggesting that the males should be removed from brumation (in the case of artificial brumation) 1–3 weeks prior to the females. Finnigan (pers. comm., 1992) suggests that this lag time allows the final maturation of sperm or has some other beneficial effect. He indicated that the number of infertile eggs produced by his montane kingsnakes dropped dramatically after he began this protocol. The actual benefit of this procedure is unknown but

Finnigan believes this mimics the earlier emergence of males from brumaculums in the wild.

It will also help if the female sheds before she is placed with the male. Remember, for maximum success, the female and her shed skin should usually be placed in with the male. It appears that the shed itself stimulates sexual behavior in some species. In these species the skin is suspected of containing pheromones, social hormones which in this case are thought to be chemical signals to the male snakes that the female is ready to breed. Some breeders enhance skin pheromones by making a paste out of the female's uric acid (white component of the excrement), which may also contain pheromones, and painting it on her back.

Placing the female in the cage with the male is not absolutely necessary but it probably more closely mimics the natural situation. Males of many species of snakes appear to wait for females to pass through their territory right after brumation. And since the males usually initiate mating, they are better off left in their own cages for this process.

Consider the fact that many snakes do appear to use pheromones as mentioned above to locate and communicate with potential mates. If this is true, cage cleaning may interfere with breeding. In addition to eliminating important odors, the actual disturbance of the snakes during the cleaning process may have a detrimental effect on potential breeders. Vic Morgan of Jacksonville, Florida, has successfully bred eastern diamondback rattlesnakes in captivity by placing the female in the male's cage for months (neither cleaning nor feeding). He says the cage should have a "snaky" smell and look (several shed skins lying around). This "dirty spring cage" concept may have potential for helping to breed other difficult species or individuals, but remember the old adage "dirty enough to be happy but clean enough to be healthy." Indeed, the presence of humans has been associated with changes in the behavior of wild pit vipers (W. S. Brown, 1991), and therefore human presence may well interfere with the breeding process.

There are many other tricks professional snake breeders use to help achieve successful mating. Robert Applegate sometimes sprays his snakes with warm water when he places them together. He has also been known to get the snakes excited by placing them in a bag and running around the house. Others have recommended using ice water. In several instances, we sprayed our fox snakes with ice water and breeding occurred within minutes. Another trick is to place several males in a cage first and allow territorial disputes before placing the female in the cage. Monitor this carefully and remove the less dominant animal before any damage is done. This technique has also been used with great success with some noncolubrid North American snakes such as pit vipers and boids. If no mating activity occurs with the first male, a second male can also be added after the female has been placed in the cage. For some snakes, a group of several males and females may be needed to ensure mating. This is referred to as "communal breeding" and may be especially valuable when attempting to breed natricine snakes (garter and water snakes).

A successful mating is one that produces live offspring. Mating may occur within minutes of introducing the two snakes or days afterward. It may never occur. Look for the male to grasp the female in his jaws (this grasping does not occur with all species) and wrap his tail around hers with their vents in close apposition. It may occur only once or several times during the course of the day or night. Some nocturnal species do nothing during the day but mate readily at night when the lights are out or diminished. The actual mating may end in minutes or may take hours. Do not interfere with the snakes during this time. Make sure to note the time and date in your records as it may help determine if the mating you observed was the mating that produced the eggs or live young (since some female snakes may retain live sperm for several years, mating you observe, or suspect, may not be the one that produced the clutch or litter). Adult female snakes in captivity less than 1 year should always be suspected of using retained sperm or suspected of mating just prior to capture. Also, you may consider this possibility if a very low percentage of the eggs are fertile (suggesting that old sperm may have been used). On the other hand, very high fertility rates strongly suggest a successful mating occurred that year.

Care During Gestation

After breeding, female snakes will usually continue to eat well until about the middle to last third of their gestation (egg-carrying period), when they will usually abruptly stop eating. The posterior one-half to one-third of the female will swell and the scales will be noticeably separate as the skin between them becomes distended. These are normal occurrences and one should prepare for imminent egg deposition. The bulge is more noticeable in the middle of the body and, if truly gravid, the bulge in the female will show progressively more in the posterior third of the body, and will be especially prominent along the sides. In some cases a midbody bulge will not move down the body or get significantly larger and infertile ova may be the end result. These "grapelike" masses will typically be passed at a later date in place of fertilized eggs or live young, to the disappointment of the herpetoculturist.

Some females will not feed while they are gravid. It is important to note, however, that many females will eat small meals during gestation, even during the latter stages. For those who desire multiple clutches (see below), offering food at this time will be important. Applegate (1989) advises offering small favored food items right up until the last day before laying,

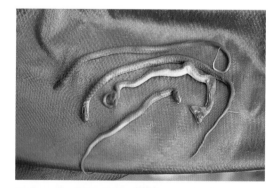

Embryonic deformities. These water snakes were born with fatal defects, possibly because the mother was exposed to teratogens or inappropriate temperatures during gestations. Defects might also be genetic. (photo by David G. Campbell)

and then immediately after laying. Indeed, we have found that some females will eat on the same day they lay their eggs.

Avoid deworming gravid snakes. Dead worms may lead to sepsis in a snake with poor gut motility and restricted circulation. Death of the mother and babies is a common sequela.

Egg Laying

The period of egg laying is very critical for both the eggs and the mother. Many breeders are now placing an "egg box" or an "egg-laying box" in the mother's cage when they think she is ready to lay her eggs. This consists of a plastic shoe box or sweater box into which damp sphagnum moss or some kind of mulch has been placed (much like a humidity box, mentioned under care of the young and humidity). This provides the mother with a safe place to lay the eggs and prevents her from wandering the cage for days in search of a suitable laying place. It also reduces the likelihood that she will become egg-bound and keeps the eggs from desiccating if you are not there to remove them right away. In the words of Dr. Bernard Bechtel, who has been breeding snakes since 1954, "Not using an egg box is cruel." Dystocia (egg binding) is discussed in the section on medical care. Also see Klingenberg (1991) and Rossi and Rossi (1996).

Most female colubrid snakes will shed just before they lay eggs, so add the box at this time. For most North American snakes, this will occur anywhere from 1–2.5 months after mating and 1–2 weeks before laying. In fact, this shed has been called the *prelaying shed* by some. Look for it.

Also remember that females carrying eggs need to drink regularly, so make sure that clean fresh water is always available. Infrequent handling and supplemental heat will also be helpful to the gravid snake (reducing the likelihood of egg binding). In addition, we have found that snakes housed on artificial carpet/turf appear less likely to become egg-bound than those housed on newspaper. We suspect this may be related to the support that carpet/turf provides, allowing the snakes to use serpentine locomotion, and helping them maintain better muscle tone. Furthermore, snakes of all sizes appear to be less likely to become egg-bound or unable to deliver young when housed on mulch or wood shavings. Again, we believe this is due to the muscle-toning nature of these natural substrates as opposed to newspaper, paper towels, etc. Perhaps cage accessories such as branches and rocks may also have a beneficial effect, much like the exercise wheels of caged rodents. This remains to be tested however.

Fred Antonio, experienced reptile curator, says, "There are no hard and fast rules for success in this young science." Different people have had success using different methods. In general, however, the best way to achieve successful mating is to keep the snakes healthy and well fed, especially when coming out of winter cooldown, provide them with a thermal gradient (a warm side and a cold side in their cage), and put them through winter cooldown (or at least a period of short day length). Their regular enclosure should be adequate to afford mating.

Last, the period after egg laying can be very risky for the female. She will often be very thin and dehydrated. Attempt to feed her straight away and very heavily in the weeks following the births/laying. Make sure that water is available. See the section on care of the eggs and care of the young. These thin snakes may not be able to breed the following year, but some captive female snakes, because of their lower activity level, higher plane of nutrition, and lack of parasites (when compared to their wild counterparts) can actually support two or more clutches every year. This is referred to by the pros as "double, triple, or quadruple clutching" and has been accomplished frequently with kingsnakes and rat snakes (Applegate, pers. comm., 1988; Michaels, 1989). Many vipers, on the other hand, may breed every 2 or 3 years in captivity. Some herpetoculturists feel that double clutching may affect the viability of the young and their breeding ability. Others say they have seen no problems with this after three generations, and presently it appears that keeping the snakes on a high nutritional plane will allow multiple clutching without deleterious effects. Robert Applegate says the decision of when to start breeding and whether to double clutch should be based on each individual female. Every animal is an individual.

Table 5 is a reproduction chart for all North American snake species, with breeding season, gestation/incubation period, and ranges of eggs or young produced. Refer to it as needed for each species.

Inbreeding

The danger of inbreeding is not as great in most reptiles as in mammals. One should definitely avoid mating siblings over several generations. If weak young are constantly raised to adulthood and bred, one *may* begin to observe signs of degeneration in that generation or their progeny. Also, pushing healthy young snakes through rapid growth and breeding early *may* result in reproductive problems in that generation or in ones to follow. Hence, it is *probably* best not to push snakes through rapid growth for early breeding or to double clutch (breed a female twice and have her produce two clutches in 1 year). See the discussion on double clutching under breeding. However, one must remember the purpose of the snakes being bred. If the purpose is to produce normal animals for release back into the wild, one should definitely avoid inbreeding, pushing, and double clutching. But, if breeding is primarily for the purpose of producing domesticated snakes, then what we are doing with these procedures is no different from what we have done with dogs, cattle, chickens, and horses. We are basically providing ideal conditions for the growth and reproduction of those animals we find appealing and/or economically rewarding. *Make no mistake, these animals will often not be very viable (nor could they reproduce well) in the wild.* But if they are strictly domesticated, is it really that terrible to produce these designer snakes? Their existence may actually reduce the pressure on native populations of snakes by reducing collecting. Genetic markers like albinism could serve to separate some wild-caught snakes from captive snakes, much to the relief of some state wildlife officials. On the other hand, we are now at the crossroads in the captive breeding of some kinds of snakes. The Burmese python, although an exotic, is a good

example. Thousands of normal pythons are being produced every year in captivity. But the number of albinos being produced is increasing dramatically. In 200 years will there be any normal Burmese pythons left? Probably, because as the normal type becomes less common, their value will increase, and they will be selectively bred. Hence, the breeding of mutants and hybrids is not necessarily bad and is unlikely to result in the complete disappearance of normal animals, but rather may increase that species' chances for survival into the next century.

We would still advise that breeders contact each other and trade potential mates every once in a while to bring new blood into their lines that will probably give more vigor to the young. Zoos generally keep very good records of the progeny of rare and endangered snakes in order to avoid inbreeding, and private individuals, through careful record keeping and cooperation with each other, can achieve the same results. The only reason for inbreeding is, of course, to produce valuable mutants, and although it is tempting economically, try not to invest all your energy in breeding mutants. Remember that the normal-appearing animals (geneticists call this the normal phenotype) are usually the most fit to be released back into the wild should the correct habitat be located. Honegger (1992) discussed the disturbing tendency of herpetoculturists to select mutants, hybrids, and other potentially unfit animals for breeding programs. To put it in Honegger's words, "They are keeping alive and breeding every sickly little snake they have." Ford and Seigel (1994) suggested that captivity often conditions snakes to eat only one thing (e.g., pinky mice) which may ultimately result in a captive population that would survive poorly, if at all, when released. Certainly, the medical problems of this group appear to be greater than in wild specimens (Funk, pers. comm., 1992), and interestingly, this closely mimics what has happened with many other domestic animals that are too highly inbred.

Indeed, the true success of captive maintenance can only be measured by continued successful breeding. If you have bred two successive generations, you're probably doing it right.

Table 5. Reproduction Chart for Snakes of the United States and Canada

Species	Mating Season	Incubation/Gestation (Days)[†]	Number of Eggs/Young	
Baird's rat snake	May–June	62–72	3–14	E
Banded sand snake	Spring?	?	3	E
Big Bend patchnose snake	Spring	90–125	5–10	E
Black-striped snake	Spring	40–54	1–10	E
Blackhead snake	April–May	59–65	1–4	E
Black swamp snake	Spring, Summer	?	2–14	Y
Blackneck garter snake	March–May	90–120	7–25	Y
Blacktail rattlesnake	Fall, Spring	140–180	3–7	Y
Brazos water snake	May–July	77–119	4–23	Y
Brown snake	March–May	105–113	3–18	Y
Brown water snake	March–May	90–120	10–58	Y
Bullsnake	April–May	52–85	2–24	E
Butler's garter snake	April	90–120	4–20	Y
California mountain king	April–May	48–87	3–9	E
Cat-eyed snake	Winter, Spring	79–90	2–12	E
Checkered garter snake	March–May	90	4–18	Y
Coachwhip	April–May	45–79	4–24	E
Common garter snake	March–July, Fall	87–116	3–85	Y
Common kingsnake	March–May	49–81	3–24	E
Concho water snake	May–June	77–119	4–23	Y
Copperhead	April–May, Sept.–Oct.	105–110	1–20	Y
Corn snake	March–May	51–83	3–30	E
Cottonmouth	Anytime	160	1–20	Y
Crowned snake	April–May	?	1–4	E
Desert hooknose snake	?	?	?	E
Diamondback water snake	April	90–120	8–62	Y
Eastern coral snake	Spring, Fall	70–90	2–13	E
Eastern diamondback	Spring, Fall*	200+	6–21	Y
Eastern hognose snake	April–May	50–65	4–61	E
Eastern rat snake	April–June	60–75	5–44	E
Eastern ribbon snake	May	85–120	3–26	Y
Flathead snake	April–May	59–65	1–4	E
Florida green water snake	April	90–120	7–101	Y
Fox snake	June–July	35–78	7–29	E
Giant garter snake	April–May?	90–120?	10–46	Y
Glossy snake	April–May	53–90	2–23	E
Glossy crayfish snake	April–May	?	8–16	Y
Gopher snake	April–May	52–85	2–24	E
Graham's crayfish snake	April–May#	?	4–39	Y
Gray-banded kingsnake	April–June	55–91	3–14	E
Green rat snake	May–July	77–88	3–7	E
Green water snake	April	90–120	9–19	Y
Ground snake	Spring, Fall	53–67	1–6	E
Indigo snake	Nov.–Jan.	73–102	5–12	E
Kirtland's snake	Spring, May	?	4–22	Y
Lined snake	Aug.–Sept.	335–365	2–13	Y
Longnose snake	March–May	65–83	4–11	E
Lyre snake	March–May?	77–79	2–20	E

(continued)

Table 5. Reproduction Chart for Snakes of the United States and Canada (continued)

Species	Mating Season	Incubation/Gestation (Days)[†]	Number of Eggs/Young	
Massasauga	Spring, Fall	84–120	3–19	Y
Mexican garter snake	Early Spring	90–120	4–25	Y
Mexican hooknose snake	?	?	?	E
Mexican vine snake	Early Spring	60–77	3–6	E
Milk snake	April–June	50–73	3–24	E
Mole kingsnake	April	45–78	3–16	E
Mojave rattlesnake	Spring, Fall	150–160	2–13	Y
Mountain patchnose snake	Spring	60–70	6–10	E
Mud snake	Late Spring	60–80	4–104	E
Narrowhead garter snake	Early Spring, Fall	?	2–51	Y
Night snake	Spring	47–82	2–6	E
Northern water snake	May–June	90–120	4–99	Y
Northwestern garter snake	March–May	90–120	3–20	Y
Pine snake	April–June	50–100	3–14	E
Pine woods snake	Early Spring	48–50	2–4	E
Plainbelly water snake	April–June	90–120	2–60	Y
Prairie kingsnake	Spring	45–78	5–21	E
Pigmy rattlesnake	Spring, Fall	120?	3–10	Y
Queen snake	Spring, Fall	120?	2–12	Y
Racer	April–June	43–65	2–31	E
Rainbow snake	Spring?	75–80	2–52	E
Red diamond rattlesnake	Feb.–April	141–190	3–20	Y
Redbelly snake	Spring, Fall	77	1–21	Y
Ridgenose rattlesnake	April–July*	390–480	1–9	Y
Ringneck snake	Spring, Fall	46–60	1–10	E
Rock rattlesnake	Spring, Fall*	312–362	1–8	Y
Rosy boa	April–June	103–362	1–12	Y
Rough earth snake	March–April	70	2–13	Y
Rough green snake	April–May, Fall	35–45	2–14	E
Rubber boa	April–May	90–150	1–8	Y
Saddled leafnose snake	Spring	60?	2–5	E
Santa Cruz garter snake	April	?	4–14	Y
Scarlet snake	Spring?	46–80	2–9	E
Scarlet kingsnake	April–May	50–70	3–24	E
Sharptail snake	Late Fall, Early Spring	?	2–9	E
Shorthead garter snake	April	90–120	5–10	Y
Short-tailed snake	?	?	?	E
Sidewinder	April–June	145–155	4–18	Y
Smooth earth snake	Spring, Fall	77–98	2–14	Y
Smooth green snake	May	4–23	3–13	E
Sonoran mountain king	May–June	58–81	1–9	E
Sonoran shovelnose snake	Spring?	?	3–6?	E
Sonoran whipsnake	April–May	59–68	6–13	E
Southern hognose snake	April–May	56–58	5–10	E
Southern water snake	Jan.–April	90–120	2–57	Y
Speckled racer	?	50–65	2–8	E
Speckled rattlesnake	Spring	140–145	2–11	Y
Spotted leafnose snake	Spring?	60?	2–4	E
Striped crayfish snake	Spring	?	4–12	Y

Table 5. Reproduction Chart for Snakes of the United States and Canada (continued)

Species	Mating Season	Incubation/Gestation (Days)[†]	Number of Eggs/Young	
Striped racer	April–May	60–95	6–11	E
Striped whipsnake	April–May	61–62	3–12	E
Texas blind snake	Winter?, Spring?	?	2–8	E
Texas rattlesnake	Spring	150?	1–6	Y
Timber rattlesnake	Spring, Fall/	200+	3–19	Y
Trans-Pecos rat snake	May–July	67–103	2–9	E
Twin-spotted rattlesnake	Summer*	?	3–9	Y
Two-striped garter snake	April–May	90–120	3–26	Y
Western aquatic garter	Spring	?	7–30	Y
Western blind snake	Winter?, Spring?	94?	2–8	E
Western coral snake	April–June	47–62	2–3	E
Western diamondback	March–May	100–150	2–25	Y
Western hognose snake	Spring, Fall	47–64	2–39	E
Western hooknose snake	Spring	?	1	E
Western patchnose snake	March–June	90–120	4–10	E
Western rattlesnake	April–May*	90–110 (240)	1–25	Y
Western ribbon snake	April–May	90–120	3–27	Y
Western shovelnose	Spring?	?	2–6	E
Western terrestrial garter	Spring	120–150	4–19	Y
Worm snake	Spring, Fall	18–60	1–8	E

Key: # Mates only in water. * May mate only every other year. [†] Numbers shown represent incubation period for eggs or gestation period for live bearers.

Captive Breeding as a Conservation Tool

Because of the incredible success herpetoculturists have been experiencing with captive breeding of snakes, it has great potential to become a valuable adjunct to conservation measures. Many biologists warn, however, that the captive environment and unnatural selection produces snakes that will not be releasable, especially after several generations. Furthermore, the concept of releasing snakes back into the wild is totally abhorrent to many biologists and the general public alike. This is discussed in the section on releasing snakes.

Care of the Eggs

The care of virtually all eggs of snakes is the same. They need to be maintained in a semi-moist medium (see below) protected from insects, desiccation, and accidental rotation. They do equally well if placed in a plastic, glass, or metal container, or even in a plastic bag, as long as the humidity within (preferably 90–100%) is maintained and fruit flies are kept out.

Temperature is also important; most do well around 25–30°C (74–86°F). Temperatures much higher or lower than this may result in physical defects, embryonic death, or developmentally damaged ("retarded") poor-feeding snakes. We have hatched the eggs of many species by just placing their containers on closet shelves and providing no additional heat. In fact, many caretakers provide an incubation environment that is far too warm and thereby increase the risk of damaging the embryos. Remember, these are not tropical snakes.

First-time snake egg hatchers also always overestimate the eggs' need for air. It is best if the containers are airtight. This keeps out the eggs' number one enemy—the fruit fly. Opening the container two or three times a week to let air in and check the eggs will usually be sufficient. But do not use a container much smaller than a shoe box, about 30 cm long × 16

Comparative egg sizes of some western North American snakes. From left to right are the eggs (2) of a California kingsnake, a Kansas glossy snake, a western hognose, and a spotted night snake. (photo by David G. Campbell)

cm wide × 10 cm high (12 inches long × 6 inches wide × 4 inches high), or sweater box, about 40 cm long × 15 cm high × 30 cm wide (16 inches long × 6 inches wide × 12 inches high), if you are using this technique or there *is* a chance an oxygen deficiency may occur. Even the largest eggs (bull-/gopher snake eggs) can be hatched easily using a container with the dimensions listed above, with only twice-weekly openings to allow air in.

Remember, do not change the position of an egg once it is laid. In other words, if an egg is laid with one end up, that end should remain up until hatching occurs. Recently, some research has shown that the eggs of some species may be rotated without deleterious effects, but as a general rule it is not advisable to allow this rotation to occur. If a rotated healthy egg during late incubation begins to "sweat," it may have been rotated to a point where venous congestion may be occurring in some of the egg membranes. This may lead to the death of the embryo as its circulatory system becomes compromised. Under these circumstances, you may wish to rotate the egg back to its original position if known, or guess and rotate the egg 90–180 degrees if the original position is unknown. Some breeders mark the top of each egg with a pencil just before moving them from the cage to the incubation box. This is not a bad idea for the reasons listed above but may not be necessary if you are very careful when moving

and setting up the eggs. If the eggs are dropped accidentally, or if two clutches are incubated in the same container and the hatchlings from the early clutch push around the eggs from the later clutch, one may wish the eggs were marked. The latter occurrence is the main reason we strongly suggest a one-clutch-per-box approach to incubating eggs.

If the eggs are stuck together, which occurs frequently, they need not be separated (but see below) and in fact, attempting to do so will probably cause some damage to many of the eggs. Just move all the eggs that are stuck together, as one clump, to the incubation box. Your hands should be thoroughly washed and dried so as not to contaminate the eggs with excessively large numbers of potentially pathogenic bacteria. Also, smokers may have minute quantities of tar and nicotine on their hands that can also contribute to an egg's demise. So smokers should wash especially thoroughly before handling snake eggs.

The actual process of picking up the eggs should be done as quickly and gently as possible. Avoid sliding your fingers along any of the eggs as this has been known to destroy the as yet undescribed antifungal properties of the surface of the eggs. Place the eggs gently into the substrate you have already prepared and place into the incubation box (see below for discussion on substrate). Then gently steep the incubation substrate around the eggs until each egg is only half exposed. Set the box or bag somewhere up high where it will not be disturbed and try not to move them around too much. If they must be moved, however, do it gently and remember the golden rule: Do not let those eggs rotate or shift position. We have moved two clutches long distances by car (900 and 1200 miles); in both cases the hatching rates were 100%, so it can be done. Incidentally, both of those clutches were in midincubation. Moving them earlier or later may be more difficult but this is unknown.

The substrate most commonly used now is vermiculite, a lightweight highly absorbent material sold in nurseries. Mixing vermiculite and water 50:50 by weight will usually produce suitable hatching medium. Test it by squeezing it with your hand. If it packs and retains its

The eggs of desert snakes often require an incubation substrate with a lower moisture level than for other snakes. (photo by David G. Campbell)

shape without dripping huge quantities of water, it is just right (it should be moist but not sopping wet). When squeezed, it should pack like snow. If estimating, add one-fourth to one-third cup of water to one cup of vermiculite.

Recently, a number of herpetoculturists have reported higher hatching rates with less water in the mixture. Hammack (1991) studied a group of Texas rat snake eggs and determined that hatchlings incubated in a mixture of 0.4:1 water to vermiculite were significantly longer and heavier than those incubated in a mixture of 1.1:1 water to vermiculite. Hammack also reported that more eggs died in the 1.1:1 water to vermiculite mixture than in the 0.4:1 mixture. In addition, hatchlings of the 0.4:1 group were more uniform in size than those from the 1.1:1 group.

Thus, the long recognized and accepted method of mixing water and vermiculite in equal amounts per weight appears to be somewhat faulty. Nevertheless, we still have a great deal to learn about incubating snake eggs.

Perlite is also an excellent hatching medium. Other combinations that have worked include mixtures of vermiculite and peat moss (50:50) or vermiculite and potting soil (50:50). Water is added to both of these mixtures until they are packing moist but not wet. People have also successfully used Spanish moss, sphagnum moss, various mulches, sand, and even moist paper towels. All of these will work but we

have had very good hatching rates with pure vermiculite, or perlite, most likely because they are cleaner and parasite-free. Some have stated that vermiculite will stick to the babies upon hatching, but we have not had a serious problem with this since it rinses off readily.

If you have mixed your vermiculite correctly and have an airtight container, the air humidity will usually take care of itself. You should expect to see some condensation on the sides and top of the container. But if your container and eggs are dripping wet, you will lose some eggs. All that is necessary in this case is to leave the top off a little while to increase ventilation and allow some evaporation to occur (usually it only takes a few minutes to a half-hour). Too much moisture will predispose to fungal growth. Sometimes it is wise to remove all of the eggs from a container that is too moist and transfer them to another immediately rather than wait for that particular container to lose water by evaporation. This is especially true if water was added in great quantities early in the incubation period to rehydrate dehydrated eggs. The eggs will recover from the dehydration but may either be attacked by a fungus during midincubation, or experience other problems, so switching them to a drier egg box is a good idea after the initial rehydration period.

It is normal for the eggs to change color slightly, swell, or wrinkle slightly during development; however, a rapidly appearing longitudinal wrinkle in early incubation usually indicates the humidity in the box is too low. Pour some lukewarm water in the vermiculite surrounding the eggs (*not directly on the eggs*), and make sure your box lid is tight enough. These wrinkles in early incubation, due to low humidity, will usually disappear within 2 days if the humidity is corrected. Wrinkles appearing in the eggs at this time may also be due to infertility, and if this is the case they will never disappear. Slight depressions appearing in late incubation are normal as the eggs become misshapen and swollen.

If fruit fly eggs or maggots do appear on your eggs, do not remove that egg at the expense of all of the adjacent ones. Remove it only if it detaches relatively easily from the others or is separate already (one good reason to separate the eggs initially, *if they come apart easily*). We have used two other methods successfully. The first method is to place a small strip of a no-pest strip (vapona-laden; see section on control of mites) in the egg box for several days. Then remove it for 2 weeks and put it back in for a few more days. The second method is to inject the affected egg with about 0.5 cc of ivermectin. Both methods will kill the larvae without affecting the eggs nearby. When using either method you must eliminate all of the adult flies and their source of entry at the same time.

Mold will rarely grow on healthy eggs that are maintained under the proper conditions. If it does, suspect that the eggs may have been dead to begin with or are presently dead. The other possibility is that they have not been set up properly and are usually too moist. We usually give them the benefit of the doubt by reducing humidity in the incubation box and allowing them to finish their normal incubation period, unless they are severely deformed and shrunken. Wiping off the mold with a paper towel moistened in a povidone-iodine solution may slow down the fungus but usually not stop it. Using a dilute povidone-iodine solution instead of water in the initial mixture with the vermiculite is something that may be worth trying to prevent fungal growth, but we have not had the opportunity to test this yet.

The keys to a good hatching rate then are as follows:

1. Start with a clean substrate (some substrates may be baked, but this is not necessary or possible with moss or vermiculite).
2. Maintain humidity between 90 and 100%.
3. Keep in an airtight container but open at least twice weekly.
4. Maintain temperature between 25 and 30°C (75 and 86°F).
5. Do not rotate eggs.

One last word about hatching: Do not place babies on wood or other porous surfaces immediately after hatching. The young snakes, still wet from the egg contents, will rest in one position, whereupon the ventral scales around the umbilicus will adhere to the wood. Later,

when the snakes move, the abdomen may be torn open leading to evisceration or peritonitis. Artificial carpet/turf is once again an ideal substrate to place baby snakes on immediately after hatching. Alternatively, babies may be left in the vermiculite of the egg box for several days.

Care of the Juveniles (Snake Pediatrics)

Young snakes may have specific environmental and dietary needs that differ in many cases from those of their parents. Neonates may also have medical problems that differ from those of their older conspecifics. Fortunately, as herpetoculture has become more advanced, observations on the care and medical problems of neonate snakes have increased dramatically, and from these experiences some recommendations can be made.

The care of juvenile snakes usually requires a bit more attention to detail than with adult snakes. Young snakes, of course, are generally smaller and will become emaciated or dehydrated much faster should they lack food or water, respectively. In addition, they require smaller food items that are often more difficult to find in sufficient quantity to keep the young snakes growing. The fact that they are growing means they have a higher caloric and nutrient requirement for their weight than an adult snake would and signs of these deficiencies

A vine snake hatchling is extremely thin. They shed and begin eating small lizards right away. (photo by John Rossi)

would appear more rapidly. Therefore, the need to feed whole animals whether they be earthworms or mammals is just as critical as the frequency of feeding.

Birth/Hatching

In general, all neonates are subject to injuries involving the umbilicus during the first several hours to days after live birth/hatching. In captivity, young snakes are particularly susceptible to evisceration if their umbilical cord becomes adhered to a smooth surface such as glass. This can happen as the snake rests. When the snake moves later, the dried umbilical cord may pull the yolk sac and other viscera through the umbilicus, resulting in sudden death or fatal peritonitis. For most of these neonates, artificial carpet/turf usually works well as a substrate until the umbilical cord dries out, which may take several days.

Feeding/Diet

After the initial period has passed, the young reptiles will usually refuse to feed until they have shed for the first time, digested the rest of the yolk they have internalized, or both. This may take several hours in the case of very small snakes (e.g., neonate lined, garter, ribbon, brown, or redbelly snakes), or weeks in the case of larger snakes (e.g., indigos, bull-/pine snakes).

As mentioned above, the diet of these young animals may be quite different from that of the adults. Most notable differences occur among the colubrids, especially kingsnakes, glossy snakes, longnose snakes, night snakes, crayfish snakes, and others. We are all too familiar with the juvenile gray-banded kingsnake that has no interest at all in pinky mice but will readily take lizards. The same can be said for most juveniles of the snakes mentioned above. Juvenile crayfish snakes appear to have a preference for dragonfly larvae and it has been hypothesized that they actually require these insects because they have a higher protein and calcium content than crayfish. Indeed, there may be numerous other subtle differences between the dietary preferences and requirements of neonate and adult snakes. Fortunately, the young of the

A hatchling Arizona coral snake. These snakes are difficult to keep in captivity because they prefer to eat primarily snakes and lizards. (photo by David G. Campbell)

most commonly maintained species of snakes, and even most of the uncommonly maintained snakes, will do well on a diet solely of domestic mice of varying sizes (although they may have to be scented with various things at first in order for them to be acceptable to many of these youngsters).

Smaller herps have a number of other problems related to foods and feeding. Generally, smaller animals have a higher metabolic rate and this is also true for ectothermic animals. Even though reptiles are considered to have indeterminate growth (they grow their entire lives), they grow most rapidly during their first several years. Furthermore, their small size often limits the size of the meals they can consume and their body fat reserves. They generally require more frequent feedings than adults if they are to grow or even just maintain themselves. Hence, young snakes should be fed very frequently, possibly every other day depending upon the species, the type of food item, and their size. For instance, a baby rat snake that just ate a fuzzy (1- to 3-week-old mouse) will take slightly more time to digest it than it would for a pinky (hairless mouse less than 1 week old). Worms seem to be digested much more rapidly than insects or vertebrates and, in general, fish and amphibians are digested more rapidly than mammals or birds.

Some authors suggest feeding baby snakes right after they defecate the remains of their last meal. This makes good sense but it is almost impossible to do with babies kept in one of the more natural substrates. Also, feeding this frequently may produce incredibly rapid growth resulting in early sexual maturity that may have long-term detrimental effects on some snakes or their progeny, even though this now appears unlikely. See the sections on breeding and inbreeding.

Vitamin Supplements: Food?

Vitamin supplements are considered a good idea for some baby snakes although many authors frown upon their use, since using whole animals theoretically provides a completely balanced diet and oversupplementing some nutrients may lead to problems. Insectivorous snakes, however, like ground snakes, shovelnose snakes, banded sand snakes, and green snakes, are definitely good candidates for calcium supplementation since their captive diet consists largely of pinhead (baby) crickets and mealworms, which are both notoriously calcium-deficient. There are two commonly used methods of calcium supplementation. The most common is called dusting the food. Dusting can be accomplished using the "shake and bake" system of placing the food item in a plastic bag with some of the calcium powder (e.g., Repti-cal®, calcium carbonate, dicalcium phosphate, etc.) and shaking several times.

For a long time it was believed that pinkies were calcium-deficient. Recently, however, some research has shown that pinkies do contain sufficient calcium in order to allow normal growth. Many young snakes have been raised on nothing but pinkies until they were large enough to consume fuzzies. Therefore, dusting pinkies with calcium powder is not considered necessary or even beneficial (Backner, 1990).

More recently, reptile researchers (Allen, 1989) have shown that dusting food items with calcium is not nearly as effective at raising the calcium level of that food as is feeding the animals a high-calcium diet for several days prior to feeding them to reptiles. Theoretically then, this treatment may make a difference in the growth rate and general health of young, insectivorous, captive snakes (although this has been tested in lizards only, not snakes) and hopefully will not reduce the palatability of the food items being fed to them (since the calcium will be inside, not outside, of the insect). This is called "gut-loading."

It should be pointed out that the value of this treatment for snakes is entirely unknown, and the possible benefits discussed above are pure speculation. Similarly, some authors have speculated that snakes evolved very different metabolic pathways from lizards, and that insectivorous snakes have minimal calcium and vitamin requirements which they can easily satisfy by consuming untreated insects. Indeed, many adult shovelnose snakes and ground snakes have been maintained for years being offered nothing but calcium-deficient, nonsupplemented, captive-raised crickets and apparently suffered no ill effects. However, how many of these same snakes have grown or reproduced regularly on this diet? The answer is that very few, if any, of these insectivorous snakes have carried out either process on a diet of solely bait shop crickets. Certainly, growth and reproduction are the two major criteria that must be met if a diet is to be considered balanced.

If one decides that calcium supplementation is needed, there are now several possible diets that appear to work well for fortifying the insects with calcium. Perhaps the simplest method is to feed them the diet recommended by Howard Lawler, Curator of Reptiles, Amphibians, and Invertebrates at the Arizona-Sonora Desert Museum in Tucson, Arizona. This diet consists of 85% rodent blocks and 15% calcium carbonate. Other successful diets include a homemade recipe listed below or the high-calcium diet produced by a feed manufacturer named Zeigler Brothers in Gardeners, Pennsylvania. The homemade diet is listed below and was provided courtesy of the Brookfield Zoo Herpetology Department in Chicago, Illinois.

Homemade High Calcium-Diet
48% ground wheat hulls (millings)
20% trout chow (#4 grade)
32% calcium mix (14 parts calcium gluconate,
                 7 parts dicalcium phosphate,
                 1 part ascorbic acid)

Fox snakes hatching. (photo by David G. Campbell)

Vitamin and Mineral Supplements: Water?

The use of calcium in the drinking water has also been shown to be beneficial to some reptiles (Zwart et al., 1989). This method is more widely used in Europe than America. Four grams of calcium lactate added per liter (roughly 1 quart) of water will definitely help a growing lizard and there is no reason to doubt it would help a growing snake. Zwart has also added aqueous vitamin D_3 to calcium-enriched drinking water and had satisfactory results. He determined that after 48 hours 83% of the vitamin D_3 was still available. We do not know if any or all of the vitamin D_3 required could be provided this way, but this kind of supplementation may be very valuable in borderline cases. You may want to use both UV lighting and vitamin D_3-"spiked" water for young insectivorous snakes or gravid snakes. We would advise avoiding doing this for most captive snakes, especially aged or normal adult snakes. Too much vitamin D_3 will cause calcification of various tissues and is just as harmful as not having enough.

Once again, there is no evidence yet indicating this kind of supplementation is necessary or helpful to snakes, but it is mentioned here for the keeper who may discover a need for such supplementation with one of the species discussed.

Lighting for Juvenile Snakes

Ultraviolet light sources may be extremely important for some diurnal juvenile snakes for the same reasons mentioned above. However, none of the diurnal juvenile snakes we maintained over the last 4 years were exposed to any UV light, and all appeared to grow and feed equally as well as the crepuscular (dawn/dusk active) or the nocturnal species. Hence, we strongly suspect that the majority of North American snakes (both juvenile and adults) do not require UV light, even though we cannot completely rule out the necessity of UV light for all North American snakes. Certainly, UV light may have nonessential but beneficial effects for many species. This is discussed in more detail in the section on lighting.

If a species of snake is discovered to require UV light for one function or another, remember that the intensity of UV light may also be very important to that species. Be aware that the intensity of light is inversely related to the distance from the cage, so one UV light on the ceiling will probably not be sufficient. A light over each cage would be advisable where they are required. Also remember that some authors believe many full-spectrum lights, including Vitalites® or Reptisun® lights, lose part of their spectrum after about 6 months (depending on amount of daily use), so replace them about this often even if they are still working. In addition, be aware that Gro Lights® and other plant lights do not produce the full spectrum of light needed and hence are not satisfactory substitutes.

As mentioned in this section and elsewhere, the necessity of full-spectrum light for snakes is controversial, but may have some beneficial effects. See the section on lighting.

Water

Catering to the water requirements of juvenile snakes means providing an easy access water dish. This usually means a *shallow water dish* with a low lip like a plastic jar lid, ashtray, plastic butter container, or coffee can lid. The problem with these containers is that the water in them will usually evaporate rapidly, therefore, check them frequently. Some advocate leaving water available at all times. Some keepers, however, only place the water dish in with the babies every 2–3 days, and then only

Many of the natricine snakes are viviparous (live bearers). This is a brown snake neonate less than 5 minutes old at its mother's side. They will usually break through the birth membranes in several minutes, and shed their skin within minutes to days. (photo by David G. Campbell)

for a short time, in order to avoid too much moisture in small cages that may eventually lead to skin or respiratory problems. This also helps to avoid intestinal problems related to soiled water (amebic and bacterial enteritis). We prefer to provide water at all times if the ventilation is good and the water is changed frequently. For large-scale breeding operations, intermittent water provision is probably safer and more practical.

Alternatively, a tight-fitting lid may be used over the water container—in which a suitably sized hole has been cut—as suggested by Applegate (1992). This restricts evaporation of the water and thereby reduces the humidity in the cage. In addition, this reduces the likelihood that water will be spilled if the snake knocks the water bowl over. The snake may enter the hole in the top in order to get a drink.

Humidity

Neonate (newborn) and juvenile snakes that are not brumated are often exposed to extremely low relative humidity and frequently experience problems shedding. This can be avoided by providing humidity boxes for them. A humidity box is a small plastic box with sphagnum moss packed inside into which the snake can retreat. The high humidity within the box aids in normal shedding and may even be a

good place to feed a shy snake, but will usually not cause skin or respiratory infections. These boxes are especially useful in the dry heated homes of the northern climates during the winter.

Hide Box

Juvenile snakes, like adults, do best when they are given a hide box (see section on psychological factors), a temperature gradient in the cage, and a clean environment. The hide box may do double duty if it is also used as the humidity box, but you may want to provide snakes with a dry place to hide as well.

Housing Young Snakes Together?

Like adults, juveniles of all species of North American snake seem to do best when reared alone. Placing two or more snakes in a cage leads to competition for food and possibly for space or warm spots needed for proper thermoregulation, increases the risk of cannibalism, and increases the likelihood for disease by increasing stress and exposure to pathogenic bacteria. Even species and individuals that you would never suspect of posing a threat to each other may surprise you unpleasantly. Neonate rock rattlesnakes, cottonmouths, garter snakes, and others may consume their siblings soon after birth. *So stick with one snake per cage.* See the discussion on thermoregulation in the temperature section and in the psychological factors section. Nevertheless, some neonates appear to have a "mutual affinity" for each other and have been found together in the wild for long periods of time. The benefits of this behavior are unknown at this time. Is some sort of socialization occurring or is this merely a "schooling" type of behavior? Will housing these animals separately have any negative effects? We don't know at this time.

Substrate

The substrate for baby snakes is critical for success. Artificial carpet/turf works well for rat snakes, kingsnakes (including milk snakes most of the time), indigos, garters, ribbons, water, hognose, racers, coachwhips, green snakes, and bull-/gopher snakes. The smaller snake babies, like the adults of those species, usually require some burrowing substrate such as cypress mulch, peat moss, sphagnum moss, or some other moisture-retaining mixture. These include sharptail snakes, worm snakes, brown snakes, redbelly snakes, earth snakes, ringnecks, blackhead snakes, crowned snakes, and lined snakes. We have had a tremendous amount of success with a horizontal moisture gradient, using cypress mulch on the dry side and moist soil on the wet side. See the individual species accounts for more suggestions.

Many breeders keep baby snakes in plastic shoe boxes with a piece of paper towel as the only cage accessory. Small holes are drilled around the upper sides of these boxes and they are stacked upon each other. Water is offered for only a short time every 2 or 3 days (as is food). This prevents infection, saves room, and is time-saving when maintaining large numbers of snakes, but many feel this is somehow not fair to the snakes. We do not favor keeping snakes this way, but it does seem to work. There is no evidence that snakes require more environmental stimulation than this, but we would prefer to add at least a small hide box and a plastic plant to this otherwise bleak enclosure. Also, some authors have reported "cage complacency syndrome" in habitat-deprived snakes. This does not make snakes too much more difficult to observe and will not make it more difficult for them to find their food. The reduction in stress may well be worth it.

Physical Environment

Smaller animals also possess a higher surface-to-volume ratio than larger animals. This means they are more prone to desiccation and overheating than their larger parents. Areas of high humidity and lower temperature within their cages are sometimes beneficial. A humidity box is such an area. Humidity boxes are plastic shoe boxes that have a moisture-containing medium such as sphagnum moss placed in them and one or two entrance holes cut in the sides or top. Aside from preventing desiccation, these boxes are also very useful in preventing

dysecdysis in young and old herps alike. These high-humidity retreats have also been found to be very important for adults of the smaller snake species (Rossi, 1992).

Summary

All the other commonly accepted basics of herpetoculture, including cleanliness, temperature gradient, clean water, good ventilation, proper substrate, and provision of some kind of retreat still apply, although modifications due to the smaller size of the neonates may be necessary.

Handling

How frequently should you handle a captive snake? The answer depends on the snake. Very small or very nervous snakes should be handled only as often as necessary for cleaning the cage or treating a medical problem. These include most members of the following species: ringneck snakes, most garter snakes and water snakes, ribbon snakes, banded sand snakes, both shovelnoses, black-striped snakes, sharptail snakes, all hooknose snakes, both leafnose snakes, young patchnose snakes, ground snakes, brown snakes, redbelly snakes, racers, Graham's crayfish snakes, crowned snakes, blackhead

The incorrect method of handling. Firm restraint about the middle of a snake's body will often cause wild gyrations as the snake attempts to escape and could result in the handler being bitten or defecated on. (photo by David G. Campbell)

The correct method of handling. No restraint at all is needed for most snakes if they are not being treated or examined. Just provide support and allow the snake to glide over your arms as it wishes. This technique should be used only for snakes with a friendly disposition. (photo by David G. Campbell)

The correct method of restraint. Hold the snake firmly but gently behind the head. Make sure the rest of the body is supported. Release the snake if it struggles violently this way or it may break its neck. This technique is not recommended for venomous snakes, however. (photo by David G. Campbell)

snakes, speckled races, cat-eyed snakes, lyre snakes, vine snakes, and, of course, all of the substantially venomous species. Individual snakes do have different personalities and we have seen very calm members of many of these species do well even when handled frequently.

Larger or calmer snakes can usually be handled several times weekly with no problem, but once again this depends upon the individual animal. Snakes that fall into this category include: most kingsnakes, most rat snakes, long-term captive hognose snakes, long-term captive patchnoses, glossy snakes, adult night snakes, rubber boas, rosy boas, many pine snakes, and indigo snakes. But once again there are individuals among this group that behave far more erratically than some from the first group. Many milk snakes are nervous animals. The same can be said for most green rat snakes.

Furthermore, the young of most species are generally much more nervous than the adults. Juvenile snakes have good reason to be nervous. In nature, when something picks up a juvenile snake, it is about to become a meal, not just be examined or purchased. Hence, many juveniles appear more aggressive and seem to resist handling more than adults.

Handling too frequently will predispose a snake to vomiting, loss of appetite, or maladaptation syndrome and may certainly result in

failure to breed. In addition, we have associated multiple spinal fractures with handling and measuring hatchlings of some of the very small species. Therefore, the decision to handle may be based on an individual's size, age, and behavior as well as species.

Basically, if a snake is a long-term captive that has been eating and shedding regularly, without excessive wandering, you can probably handle it fairly frequently. But if you see any of the signs mentioned above, temporarily stop handling the snake altogether.

The actual technique of handling a snake depends on the size and type of snake and its personality. If you are dealing with a friendly snake, you can allow it to slide over your hands without any restraint of the head, allowing it to explore your clothes, etc. A very nervous snake or one that must be treated is usually restrained by grasping it just behind the head and firmly holding part of the body. In either case, you must provide support for the snake's body. Remember that some very nervous snakes may struggle so violently when grasped behind the head that they may break their necks. In these instances one should release the head and prepare to get bitten or try to restrain the body more firmly until the snake tires. The two biggest mistakes in handling snakes are first, moving too fast, which makes the snake very nervous and more likely to bite, and second, grasping the snake firmly in the middle of the body without controlling the head, which also results in unnecessary struggling and potential biting. If a snake does bite you, try to avoid pulling back too vigorously as this may injure the snake and also worsen your bite wound. Remember that a bite from a small non-venomous snake is relatively harmless if cleaned properly afterward with soap and water. Infections under these circumstances are fairly rare. To be thorough and reduce the odds of infection, flush the wound with hydrogen peroxide and then wash with povidone-iodine solution. This combination will kill most pathogens (harmful bacteria). Also, make sure you have been vaccinated for tetanus within the last 5 years.

Some snake keepers like to take their favorite snake outside in the backyard. This is fine if all the precautions for transportation (see the section on transportation/shipping) are taken and the snake's personality allows it. There are several hazards to be aware of when walking a snake, however. There is a possibility that the snake will escape. The snake may get lucky and catch a bird, mouse, or frog, any one of which may be parasitized. And even though an unlikely possibility, the snake may be dragged off by a roaming dog, cat, or other predator before you can stop it. Last but not least, many snakes may think they are free again when placed outside temporarily. Some have struggled violently or viciously bitten their owner after only a few minutes of freedom when the owner tries to pick them up. This is discussed in the section on psychological factors.

Responsible handling does not include taking a snake anywhere the general public is unless it is a show where the general public is expecting to see a snake. Otherwise, such behavior by the owner may lead to local ordinances banning the keeping of snakes and other reptiles.

Venomous Snakes

Venomous snakes should never be handled except as necessary to treat. There are now two commonly used methods of restraint when

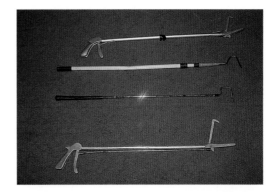

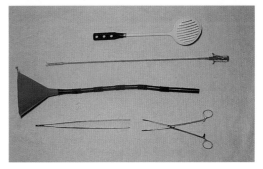

Snake hooks and tongs, if used carefully, are invaluable in handling venomous snakes. If not used properly, they are also a common source of injury to these animals. Long funnels, forceps, and flexible mechanics ''pick up'' devices are excellent for venomous snake work also. The funnels can be used to add water to the cage safely and the other devices may be used to add or remove food from a safe distance. (photos by David G. Campbell)

handling these dangerous animals is necessary. The old method of pinning the snake's head and grasping behind the angle of the jaw is now considered unjustifiably dangerous in light of these two newer procedures. Furthermore, this technique is potentially harmful to the snake as well as the handler.

The first method is to allow the snake to partially enter a clear plastic tube placed along a wall with a board placed against the other side. Then hold the tube in one hand and the snake and tube in the other while the veterinary work is being done. This is the method preferred by zoos. However, this technique has its drawbacks. Anyone who has ever tried to guide a large western diamondback rattlesnake into one of these tubes repeatedly knows exactly what we mean. The first several times it may go smoothly. Eventually, the snake learns to avoid entering the tube even if they are covered and made to appear as dark retreats. Furthermore, coral snakes and smaller rattlesnakes are more difficult to control in these tubes as some of them may be able to turn around in even a small tube. Hence, we feel this technique is an acceptable alternative for handling venomous snakes, but we feel more comfortable with the next technique.

Another safe, simple, and nontraumatic method of venomous snake restraint, and the one we use regularly when it becomes necessary to treat one of these snakes, is the use of a foam rubber pad and clear plexiglass shield. The snake is placed gently upon the pad with snake tongs or stick and pressed firmly into it by the person holding the shield. The snake is visible at all times and must first work loose and then strike over the top of the shield in order to bite the restrainer. And since the snake is never out of sight, this is an unlikely occurrence. We have used this technique hundreds of times and found it to be especially useful for measuring, sexing, or treating rattlesnakes, especially neonates and small species of rattlesnakes.

We definitely do not recommend the old technique of using snake sticks to pin down the head of the snake and then grasping it behind the head in light of the newer, safer, and less traumatizing methods.

Records

It is very important to record your observations of your snakes. Not only can you collect invaluable information, but it provides you with information you need to make important daily management decisions. Record when and what you feed or if the snake refuses food, when the snake sheds and the condition of the shed, behavior, reproductive activities, and medical problems like vomiting, etc. Weight and length should be recorded periodically. More detailed observations can be recorded if you have the time or desire and this may contribute tremendously to our knowledge of certain species. Herpetoculturists are constantly discovering important and previously unknown facts about the animals in their care. Your reptile veterinarian will also find these records tremendously valuable in making treatment decisions should the snake become ill.

Sample feeding chart.

Species:		Sex:		Card #
		Antivenin Type:		
Obtained from:		Date Born/Collected:		
		Date Obtained:		
Location/Cage #		Identification Marks:		

ST. AUGUSTINE ALLIGATOR FARM, REPTILE DEPARTMENT, SPECIMEN FOOD CHART

DATE	OBSERVATIONS/MEDICAL	Food	Accepted	Refused	Shed

Sample record sheet—St. Augustine Alligator Farm.

Neil Ford, a biologist and snake expert, enthusiastically encourages weighing prey items taken by snakes as well as weighing a female snake before and after egg laying. He also recommends weighing the eggs and neonates. Only in this way can we compare what happens in captivity with what happens in the wild. In general, we believe that captive snakes eat far more than do wild snakes and that they produce larger clutches earlier than do wild snakes.

There are several ways to keep records. Many people use index cards of varying sizes (see the copy included). When the card is full they file it and start a new one. Others use printed sheets made specifically for this purpose and place the sheets in a folder when they are finished (see the sample sheet from the St. Augustine Alligator Farm). Regardless of the type of information sheet you use, always try to include the following basic information on top:

1. Species (use the scientific name and common name).
2. Identification marks.
3. Geographic origin as specifically as possible.
4. Date of capture.
5. Sex, if known.

If the snake is captive-born and bred, also record the parents' names or identification numbers. This will help to avoid breeding mistakes later.

In summary, record keeping is well worth the effort and even poor records are far better than no records. When you check your records, you will be surprised how much you have forgotten, and then you will realize their value. Besides, it is far better to have recorded information and not need it than to have not recorded it and need it.

Warning Signs

How can you tell if you are doing something wrong? With all snakes, the number one sign is loss of appetite. Failure to feed is not necessarily a sign that something is wrong, but it

A rough green snake in a hollow on the ground. This snake died several hours later. Often, a snake acting abnormally (e.g., a nocturnal snake active diurnally or vice versa, or an arboreal snake spending a lot of time on the ground) has a medical problem. This snake was heavily parasitized with an unidentified flagellated protozoan. (photo by John Rossi)

certainly is a good sign that *something is happening*. (See the section on feeding or the table below for possible reasons.) Excessive wandering is another common problem and often indicates that the cage is not large enough or that there is no acceptable hiding place. These snakes often end up with rostral (nose) abrasions, leading to mouth infections. Sudden active wandering on the part of a male may also mean that a female in a nearby enclosure is cycling and the two snakes should be put together for mating. Failure to shed the outer layer of skin in one piece may be related to low relative humidity (e.g., heated homes in the winter time), new or old wounds, or no access to water. Open-mouth breathing, bubbles from the mouth, or puffing of the throat calls for immediate veterinary attention. This usually signifies respiratory infections, often associated with low environmental temperatures combined with inadequate cleanliness. Lumps, bumps, blisters, or sores on the skin may indicate parasites or tumors, but most frequently they indicate abscesses or superficial bacterial infections associated with unclean cages (which are usually too moist and often too cool). Sometimes they are secondary to burns from hot rocks or heating pads. Vomiting or diarrhea almost always indicate a major problem al-

though the most common reason for these signs can include handling a snake too soon after eating or keeping the snake at too low a temperature. Incidentally, the regurgitation of water when a snake is handled or just too excited is not usually a problem but should serve as a warning to the owner to handle the snake less frequently or reduce stress by covering more of the cage. This usually occurs when a snake ingests a large quantity of water right after a big meal. Retained eye shields (spectacles) are often associated with low relative humidity or no suitable object on which the snake can rub (rock, branch, etc.). Hognose snakes and indigo snakes seem especially prone to retaining the spectacles.

In summary, the overwhelming majority of medical problems of snakes may be related to improper management of their captive environment. Most snakes maintained correctly will rarely get sick and those that do may recover fairly rapidly with no treatment or just supplemental heat. In addition, the world's best and most current antibiotics will not save a reptile when its environment is not corrected. Your reptile veterinarian will make suggestions for environmental correction, many of which are summarized in Table 6 and elsewhere in this book.

First Aid and Medical Care

The purpose of this section is not to create reptile veterinarians, but rather to elucidate some of the more common problems experienced by captive snakes and discuss some of the more common solutions. There are a number of things you can do to head off medical problems before they get too serious. The first step in the treatment of any captive reptile is to examine the environment and correct it if necessary. After this you may attempt home treatment. For a more detailed discussion on home medical care of snakes, see Rossi and Rossi (1996).

Infections

Most skin and mouth lesions in snakes are caused by bacteria, although some may be

Table 6. Treatments for Various Problems

Problem	Probable Cause	Correction
Inappetance	1. Temperature too low	1. Increase temperature
	2. Too much stress	2. Decrease amount of handling
	3. Overcrowding	3. House singly
	4. Psychological problem	4. Add hiding places
	5. Parasites	5. See vet
	6. Bacterial infection (intestinal)	6. See vet
	7. Respiratory infection	7. See vet
	8. Stomatitis (mouth infection)	8. See vet or see first aid section
	9. Hibernation	9. Warm up or preferably hibernate if possible
	10. Gravid	10. See vet
	11. Tumor	11. See vet
	12. Disinterest in same food (or seasonal change of preference)	12. Offer new food forms
	13. Just prior to mating	13. Mate or wait
Excessive wandering	1. Cage is too small	1. Increase size of cage
	2. Hide box is inappropriate or too small	2. Try darker color, lower roof, or smaller opening in hide box
	3. Cage is too hot	3. Provide temperature and gradient and cool off
	4. Hunger	4. Feed
	5. Thirst	5. Give water
	6. Searching for mate	6. Mate or wait
	Also use visual barrier and pegboard top instead of screen	
Bumps, lumps, blisters, or sores	1. Cage is too moist	1. Use indoor/outdoor carpet for most, and keep dry
	2. Cage is too dirty	2. Disinfect frequently and use non-tippable water bowl
	3. Parasites	3. See vet or see first aid section
	4. Abscesses	4. See vet or see first aid section
	5. Burns	5. Check heat source, see vet
	All may have a secondary bacterial infection	
Difficult shedding	1. Relative humidity is too low	1. Use a humidifier and glass aquariums with somewhat restricted ventilation instead of wooden or wire cages
	2. Water not available or level is too low	2. Keep water available and deep enough for snake to immerse completely
	3. Mites or ticks	3. See vet or see first aid section
	4. New or old injuries	4. Assisting with shedding by placing in moist pillowcase
Vomiting	1. Too much handling	1. Stop handling
	2. Increased stress	2. Cover cage and house singly (isolate)
	3. Temperature is too low	3. Raise temperature (use a heating pad)

(continued)

Table 6. Treatments for Various Problems (continued)

Problem	Probable Cause	Correction
Vomiting (continued)	4. Parasitic or bacterial infection	4. See vet
	5. Foreign body obstruction	5. See vet
	6. Tumor	6. See vet
Diarrhea	1. Parasitic or bacterial infection	1. See vet
	2. Temperature is too low	2. Increase temperature
Open-mouth breathing, blowing bubbles, sneezing, puffing throat	1. Respiratory infection	1. Increase temperature and see vet
	2. Allergic reaction to substrate or cleanser	2. Change substrate, clean and rinse cage, and see vet
	3. Allergic or irritant reaction to cigarette smoke	3. Stop smoking near snake
Retained eye shield (spectacle)	1. Relative humidity is too low	1. Increase room humidity by using humidifier. If it occurs, soak snake in moist pillowcase for 2 hours and try to remove spectacle with a Q-Tip® by gently rubbing. If not sure, *see vet*
	2. Parasitic (mites) or bacterial infection	2. Treat for mites (see vet or first aid section)
	3. Old injury to eye	3. Assist shedding as for 1
Seizures, tremors, star gazing, weakness, or paralysis	1. Vitamine B$_1$ deficiency	1. Increase temperature and *see vet*
	2. Septicemia (massive infection and death may be imminent)	2. Increase temperature and *see vet*
	3. Encephalitis	3. Increase temperature and *see vet*
	4. Toxicity	4. Increase temperature and *see vet*
	5. Parasite migration	5. Increase temperature and *see vet*
Unusual swelling	1. Steatitis (inflammation of fat)	1. See vet
	2. Cellulitis (inflammation of tissue usually of bacterial origin)	2. See vet
	3. Tumor	3. See vet
Cloudy (blue) eyes	1. Normal just prior to shedding	2. Observe for several days if snake has been doing well prior to bluing. If not, see vet
	3. Possible early eye infection	1. See vet
Failure to lay eggs	1. Not gravid	1. Wait till next year or place in with male again
	2. Mated later than you thought	2. Check records
	3. Egg-bound	3. Increase heat and humidity in cage. Make sure plenty of water is available. See vet
	4. Eggs resorbed due to stress or other problem	4. Feed more, reduce stress, check for parasites, hibernate at higher or lower temperature. See vet
	5. Male snake	5. Probe again

caused by fungal, metazoan (worm), mycoplasmal, or viral invaders. Both bacterial and fungal lesions will respond to warmth, dryness, and daily applications of povidone-iodine (Betadine®) solution or ointment. Silvadene® cream has also worked well on many of these lesions. Creams and ointments will generally stay on the lesions longer than solutions, but both are effective and readily available at most pharmacies. Polysporin® ointment works well if you are dealing with a strictly bacterial infection, and Tinactin® or a miconazole-containing ointment works well on primarily fungal infections. Of course, without doing cultures, it can be difficult to distinguish between the two, so povidone-iodine is a good choice. Both types of infections may take over a month of daily applications to heal. Sometimes topical or systemic vitamin supplementation (especially vitamin A or C) may help. As with any infection in snakes, supplemental heat is a good idea, but remember this will increase evaporation so the snake must have access to water at all times. Also remember that the use of artificial carpet/turf is therapeutic for many skin lesions as it allows fresh air to circulate under the snake. In addition, make sure the cage is well ventilated.

Early respiratory signs like sneezing or mild hissing noises may respond to increased heat alone. If not, don't wait too long before getting the snake to a reptile-oriented veterinarian. Other signs of a respiratory infection include increased mucous in the mouth, puffing throat, blowing bubbles, and persistent elevation of the head. As with most other reptilian infections, the cause is usually bacterial; however, a virus may be responsible. Whatever the cause, it may respond to increased environmental heat as this will stimulate the snake's immune system. More serious infections will usually require antibiotic therapy, usually administered by injection to most reptiles.

There are some viruses, like paramyxovirus, that are deadly and for which prompt and aggressive veterinary care is essential if the snake is to have a fighting chance. Even with such care, most snakes with such viruses die.

If you have a strong stomach, superficial abscesses may be treated at home by slicing them open and flushing them with a povidone--

Snake injection. Most antibiotic injections are given to snakes in the front third of the body, usually in the muscle as pictured here. (photo by David G. Campbell)

iodine solution. But remember, reptile pus is usually solid, not liquid, so make sure you remove the pus manually (don't expect it to drain by itself). You may do this by applying pressure to the sides of the abscess and then using curettage (scraping out the inside of the abscess with a small spoonlike instrument) after you have expressed the majority of the pus through the slice you have made. Also, remember there is probably a reason those abscesses formed, so check the environment. (Is it warm enough, dry enough, and clean enough?) If you slice open a lump and find a parasite, wash your hands immediately and take your snake to a reptile-oriented veterinarian. This is called sparganosis (tapeworm embedded in the muscle or just under the skin) and is more of a problem than the average snake keeper can handle since the worms are usually distributed throughout the snake and not just in one lump.

Shedding Problems

Shedding problems may be avoided by correcting the environment (again!) but for a snake that needs help right away, place it in a warm wet pillowcase for 30 minutes to 1 hour. Don't forget to tie the top! *WARNING*: Do not place the pillowcase anywhere that water will overflow and cover the bag!! Also, do not place the pillowcase in an area where the snake can fall or get stepped on. After the prescribed time you can remove the snake and usually (if the snake is truly ready to shed) assist it shedding all of its old skin (including the eye shields-spectacles). The spectacles should be removed only with a wet cotton-tipped applicator if they don't come off with the skin. Apply a gentle circular motion for 15 minutes. If you don't succeed during this time, quit and repeat the whole process again in a few days, or quit and see a reptile-oriented veterinarian. If you force a spectacle off before it is ready you could expose the cornea and the snake could lose an eye.

Dehydration and Starvation (Inanition)

If a snake, particularly a small one, is very thin or appears dry (the skin has wrinkles which return very slowly or not at all to their original position if gently pulled away from the body—called poor skin turgor by veterinarians), get the snake to a veterinarian right away. It may need emergency fluids or tube-feeding. If you can't get it to a veterinarian right away, administer an electrolyte solution like Gatorade® or Pedialyte® via a stomach tube (about 2–3 ml of the chosen solution per 100 grams of body weight per day for several days or until seen by the veterinarian). These solutions are best diluted with water 50:50 prior to use however. Keep the snake warm but remember that increased temperatures will increase the rate of dehydration. See the section on force-feeding and Table 6 under inappetence.

Overheating

If a snake is frantically moving about its cage with its mouth open after being exposed to direct sunlight or coming out of a pillowcase after traveling on a hot day, immediately get it out of the sun and immerse it in cool running water (except for the head, of course). This has saved many a snake. Make an effort to avoid this by using proper transportation procedures (see the section on transportation/shipping). The presence of a large bowl of water in the cage is the snake's first line of defense if the cage gets too hot. This is the other common reason (aside from mites and preparation for shedding) that snakes sit in their water bowls for long periods of time. If you see this, check to make sure the cage is not too hot and is well ventilated. The sunlight may be hitting the cage when you are not around or a heating pad may have been turned up by accident (or be malfunctioning).

Vomiting and Diarrhea

Vomiting or diarrhea should be treated only by a reptile-oriented veterinarian, who will perform fecal exams to check for intestinal parasites, then treat with an appropriate parasiticide and antibiotic if needed. He/she will also replace fluid losses and provide supportive care as necessary. Sometimes vomiting and diarrhea will respond to increased environmental temperature alone. Do not handle at all until after the vomiting stops, except as necessary to treat. Indeed, the two most common reasons for vomiting are ambient temperatures that are too low or excessive handling after eating.

External Parasites

External parasites, most notably mites and ticks, can also cause problems shedding, aid in the spread of bacterial infections, and consume blood and cellular fluids. They are also suspected of transmitting fungal, viral, and blood parasite infections. Therefore, you must make every effort to keep them out of your collection and must eliminate them if they get started. They can be treated at home, but remember that your veterinarian has the ultimate weapon against these pests (see below). Consult him or her immediately if you have a severe infestation of one specimen or if you have a large collection at risk. If you have just a few snakes or the outbreak isn't too severe, you can usually attempt treatment and control yourself. The snake itself will often try to drown numerous parasites by soaking in the water dish for days on end. This behavior should alert you to the possibility of mites. The problem with the snake's attempt is that many of the mites will escape by migrating to the head, which the snake, of course, needs to keep out of the water in order to breathe. The old treatment for mites made use of this behavior. This would include soaking the snake in water and painting the head with various oils (like olive or corn oil, not petroleum-based oils) while at the same time disinfecting the cage thoroughly. Dilute sodium hypochlorite solution (bleach at a concentration of 1–3 ounces per quart of water) works well in the cage. You may wish to use a pyrethrin-based spray in the cage but allow it to dry completely before putting the snake back in.

Untreated wooden cages with large numbers of cracks and crevices are notoriously difficult to rid of mites, and one almost has to repaint or reseal the wood or get rid of the cage. All of the items in the cage should be soaked in the bleach solution, baked at 149°C (350°F) for 15 minutes, or thrown away. Do this for all of the cages in the same room.

Another technique is to place a no-pest strip segment in or over the cage. Some have used flea collars. The recommended method is to cut about 1 inch of the strip for each 10 gallons of aquarium space (or approximately 40,000 cm^3 = 40 liters). Set the piece on top of the aquarium screen. You can also put this piece in a small box in which holes have been punched and place it directly in the cage. It is best to leave it in or on the cage for 5 days (remove the water during this time), then remove it and put the water back in. Two weeks later remove the water again and put the strip back into action for another 5 days. When finished, wrap up the strip and save it for another time.

Be careful with this technique, however. Using vapona in a poorly ventilated cage has occasionally been associated with toxicity appearing as neurological signs or death.

Stay away from most organophosphate mammalian flea powders or sprays as many of these have proven very toxic to reptiles. Some veterinarians have had tremendous success with microencapsulated pyrethrin sprays or water-based (not alcohol-based) pyrethrin sprays, but others have had some snakes die when using these, so exercise some caution when using these.

Others have successfully used 5% sevin dust in a pillowcase for mite control. They just place the snake in the bag (which has been previously dusted with the aforementioned powder for 15–20 minutes) and then remove the snake and

rinse it off. The entire cage can be dusted with this product overnight, after which the powder may be vacuumed. The entire treatment should be repeated in 2 weeks.

New drugs such as Proheart® (moxidectin) may hold some promise for eliminating snake mites, but this drug and others have not been used on many species of snakes, so check with your veterinarian first.

Your veterinarian can administer an injection of ivermectin (Ivomec®) that will kill 100% of the mites and ticks (and many internal parasites as well) with just two doses 2 weeks apart. See the section on commonly used drugs. *Make sure to clean out that cage, however!* In fact, if you can't disinfect something thoroughly (like a log), throw it away and replace it. But remember that anything you bring in from outside should be thoroughly disinfected or baked. Failure to do this is probably what resulted in the first outbreak of mites you experienced.

Recently, a new topical for fleas named Advantage® (Bayer) has been used safely and successfully to eliminate snake mites. One application usually works. We usually place the snake in a pillowcase until the substance dries. The mites die within 4 days. This was surprising since this drug theoretically doesn't work on ticks and mites. Top Spot® has also been used successfully on some snakes but it must be used with some caution. None of these topicals is approved for use with reptiles by the FDA.

Internal Parasites and the Most Common Drug Treatments

Snakes can and do get worms, usually from ingesting food items that act as intermediate hosts for these parasites (although some can penetrate their skin or may be ingested with soil in infrequently cleaned enclosures). They can also be infected by protozoan parasites. Most of the worms and many of the protozoan pests can now be treated very safely, provided they are detected and treated early enough. Basically, snakes get the same kinds of worms (not exactly the same, but very similar in the kinds of damage they do, their life history, and even appearance of their eggs) as dogs and cats: hookworms, whipworms, roundworms, and

Table 7. Most Commonly Used Drugs in Snakes

Problem	Drug	Dose
Bacterial infection	Amikacin	2.5 mg/kg IM every 72 hrs. Load. Dose 5 mg/kg.
	Enrofloxacin	5 mg every 48 hrs IM. Load. Dose 10 mg/kg.
	Chloramphenicol	50 mg/kg SC every 24 hrs
	Ceftazidime	20 mg/kg IM every 72 hrs
	Carbenicillin	400 mg/kg IM every 72 hrs
	Ciprofloxacin	10 mg/kg PO every 48 hrs
	Pipracillin	100 mg/kg IM every 48 hrs
	Trimethoprim sulfa	30 mg/kg SC every 48 hrs ## Difficult to get. See below. (*Cryptosporidia*.)
	Amoxicillin	50 mg/kg PO every 24 hrs
Intestinal parasitism		
Amoebiasis	Metronidazole	60–125 mg/kg* PO +
Coccidiosis	Sulfadimethoxine	90 mg/kg 1st day PO then 45 mg/kg for 4 days
Nematodes (hooks, whips, rounds)	Ivermectin 10 mg/ml	0.01 ml/pound PO, SC, IM +
	Fenbendazole 100 mg/ml	50–100 mg/kg PO + (23–36 mg/lb)
Cestodes and Trematodes (tapes and flukes)	Praziquantel 56.8 mg/ml	7.5–30 mg/kg IM, occasionally PO + (3–14 mg/lb)
Cryptosporidia	None effective (limited success with trimethoprim and Humatin at 60 mg/kg once per day for 2 months)	Formalin and Glutaraldehyde okay as disinfectants
External parasitism		
Acariasis (mites and ticks)	Ivermectin 10 mg/ml	0.01 ml/lb PO, SC, IM +
	DDVP pest strips (VAPONA)	1 inch square/10 gallons for 5 days. Place on top of screen. +
	0.2% Neguvon powder	Dust pillowcase and put snake in for several hours. See text.
	5% Sevin dust	Dust cage overnight. Put snake in pillowcase for several hours. See text.
Hyperthyroidism	Methimazole	1 mg/kg PO every 24 hrs @

Key to symbols

Three to five treatments usually.

Six to 30 treatments (bone infections may require long-term treatment, as may *Cryptosporidia*).

* *Lampropeltis* and *Drymarchon* species (king snakes and indigos) should not be given more than 100 mg/kg; 40 mg/kg has been effective.

+ Repeat in 2 weeks.

@ Treat for 3 weeks.

PO = by mouth; IM = intramuscular injection; SC = subcutaneous injection.

tapeworms. It is not surprising, then, to find that many of these worms respond to the same medications used for treating their counterparts in dogs and cats. The two safest and most effective drugs used for treating worms in snakes today are ivermectin (Ivomec®) and praziquantel (Droncit®). Ivermectin will kill ophidian rounds, whips, and hooks. Praziquantel will kill tapes and trematodes (flukes). Fenbendazole (Panacur®) is an extremely useful and safe agent for eliminating rounds, whips, hooks, and probably many tapeworms, and some recent work indicates it may be more effective than ivermectin in eliminating some parasites. We have found it especially useful in small snakes where ivermectin can be very dangerous or in very heavily parasitized snakes (like those recently captured) where ivermectin can also be risky. You may choose to dose the snakes with fenbendazole first and follow up with ivermectin later.

The most common protozoan parasites to infect snakes are amoeba and coccidia. Amoeba can be treated with metronidazole (Flagyl®) while coccidia can be treated with sulfadimethoxine (Albon®, Bactrovet®). The doses for all of these drugs are listed in Table 7. Although one should make every effort to identify the parasites present by microscopic examination of the feces before treating the snakes (which is unnecessary if they have no worms), it is not a bad idea to combine a routine deworming of new snakes with a quarantine period before admitting them into a room with an established collection. The routine deworming should include the use of both ivermectin and praziquantel for those snakes likely to have tapeworms (those that consume fish, amphibians, or reptiles, like water snakes, hognose snakes, indigo snakes, or kingsnakes). Fenbendazole alone is also a suitable candidate for routine deworming, but it will probably not get all of the tapeworms, so reserve it for relatively clean snakes or very small snakes. If you want to be sure, bring a fecal sample to a reptile-oriented veterinarian and ask him or her to do a worm check for you. Any worms can be identified (at least into a major category) and protozoans may be detected. The veterinarian can then advise you on which medications to use and the

correct doses, or treat them properly and safely for you. Most veterinarians will recommend that the snake be examined and carefully weighed before dispensing or administering any medications (and this is the way it should be done in most cases). See Table 7 for the most commonly used drugs in snakes. Frank (1979) and Klingenberg (1993) have detailed discussions of snake parasite control.

Remember, there are some parasites in snakes for which there is no effective treatment (at the time of this writing). **This means the only way to protect your snakes from these parasites is by using good quarantine procedures, controlling food quality, and keeping cages clean.** These parasites include pentastomids, an unusual parasite that is mitelike as a juvenile and wormlike as an adult, and *Cryptosporidia*, a highly pathogenic protozoan. Both are also potentially dangerous to people as well if personal hygiene is not maintained (just like some of the parasites infecting dogs, cats, birds, horses, turtles, or any other animal). So thoroughly wash those hands with a good antibacterial soap (povidone-iodine scrub works well again) each and every time you handle a snake. We will often use dilute bleach on our hands if we are dealing with a particularly sick snake, but only formalin, ammonia, or glutaraldehyde may kill *Cryptosporidia*. However, neither formalin or glutaraldehyde should be used topically, since they are both carcinogens.

Releasing Snakes (How, Why, and When Not To)

Recently a great deal has been written about the various severely contagious viral or chlamydial diseases of certain reptiles. It is now believed that at least one of these diseases has become established in wild populations of reptiles (i.e., upper respiratory disease syndrome in tortoises) and that its source was most likely a released captive. Hence, the release of captive reptiles, whether they be tortoises, lizards, or snakes, may represent a very serious threat to native populations. Add to this the fact that some authors believe that some species may act as reservoirs or carriers of disease for other species, and the release of any animals, even those that appear healthy, becomes a questionable activity.

There is a great deal of concern among biologists that animals from one area will genetically contaminate populations if they are released in areas too far away from their original source or the area where their parents originated. Indeed, this is a valid concern. In one instance with mammals, hybrids could not survive in the habitat of either parent. However, anyone who has studied evolution must be aware of the positive survival value of gene flow and the degeneration that occurs in small populations without any gene flow. Thus, from a genetic standpoint, releasing a healthy captive snake that has been kept well isolated from snakes from other areas in an area fairly close to where it was captured may not be so bad. Franz (pers. comm., 1992) determined that some snakes (e.g., corn snakes) may naturally travel as many as 17 km in a straight line over a fairly short period of time. Therefore, 17 km may be a safe release radius (from a genetic standpoint) for some of the larger species (assuming a snake is healthy, its release anywhere within an area circumscribed by that radius from its point of origin will not expose the existing population to any genes they wouldn't naturally be exposed to). Future telemetry studies may indicate safe release radii for a number of larger species by revealing how much an average member of that species travels over its lifetime. The same information may be determined in small snakes by using radioactive wire implants. Once again, this entire discussion on the safeness of releasing a snake from a genetic standpoint is academic in light of the potential danger from an epidemiological standpoint (an introduced disease). Only healthy isolated snakes should be released.

Once the decision is made, several things need to be taken into consideration. To date, no one knows how well snakes that have been raised (or even just maintained for a short while) in captivity adjust to living in the wild again. Theoretically, since most of their behaviors are instinctive rather than learned (at least

at first), there should be few problems for healthy snakes to readjust. However, finding food and appropriate shelter, and avoiding predators, especially during the initial period after release, may be a problem. Captive snakes are often only fed one item (e.g., white mice) which may be prekilled and/or are placed in a confined space for capture and ingestion. Wild snakes usually will eat more than one kind of food, probably are rarely lucky enough to find them freshly killed, and may have to pursue their prey or prowl extensively, although many are sit-and-wait predators. Once they have captured their prey they must subdue it without being injured, a skill many captive snakes have not been able to practice.

Furthermore, many keepers have noted that some snakes seem to lose muscle tone when they have been maintained in captivity for some time. Their cages are often small, the substrate is often too smooth, and there may be few cage accessories for them to exercise on. Hence, there is ample reason for them to be out of shape and overweight!

With this in mind there are several things one can do prior to releasing a snake that may help speed its adjustment to a wild situation. First, start feeding live prey. If the snake won't take live prey you may want to reconsider releasing that specimen. Second, if the snake has a broad diet, try to capture and feed some of those items (like lizards, frogs, or fish). Third, allow the snake to lose some weight if it is excessively fat by feeding less frequently, or feed more frequently to put on weight if it is excessively thin. Fourth, deworm the snake prior to release. This will prolong the amount of time the snake can go without food and give it more time to adjust to the wild.

Release the snake in a suitable habitat at or near where it was caught. Also try to ascertain ahead of time the fate of the land upon which you are releasing the snake. Is the land slated for development in the near future? If so, you would, of course, not want to release the snake there.

Some areas, notably areas near water and areas with large amounts of vegetative cover, are better potential release sites. Remember that snakes are in the middle of most food chains (i.e., they eat many smaller animals but are in turn food for many animals) and as such they must have both food and hiding places or they will not survive in an area. Check the chosen habitat for both. An important factor to consider when choosing an area in which to release a snake is whether you have observed other members of that species there before. This at least indicates the habitat is suitable for that species although it doesn't tell you if that area can support more snakes of that species (that area may have already reached its carrying capacity—the maximum number of snakes it can support).

The first choice and perhaps the safest and most logical place to release baby snakes is where their parents were captured. Basically all you are doing is restocking the area you have depleted by the removal of the parents. Many argue that these babies will not survive, and indeed many will not. Perhaps none will survive, but this is not known. No one has studied the survivability of captive-bred baby snakes versus wild-bred baby snakes.

Furthermore, does "head starting" improve the survival of the young as it does with other reptiles, or does it harm these young snakes by conditioning them improperly? We just don't know. This would be an excellent area for research.

Once again, however, some would argue that any release of a one-time captive is a terrible idea and doesn't help the animal or the population into which it is released (Retes, in Hardy, 1992). Indeed, the release of one-time captives is an incredibly complicated issue. Teams of biologists like those of the I.U.C.N. (International Union for the Conservation of Nature) often study animal populations for years before making any recommendations for releasing animals, and then they may release animals only into areas where that species no longer exists (but did at one time). This protects existing populations from disease or genetic flooding (McLain, pers. comm., 1993).

It should be noted that it is absolutely illegal to release any captive reptile in a number of states. If you live in one of these states and need to give up some excess reptiles, give your animals to a friend or a herp society that will help to find them suitable homes. Check your local regulations (Levell, 1992).

****NEVER *release exotics, mutants, or sick or parasitized individuals. They may be very harmful to native populations.****

Summary/ General Guidelines

What do snakes need (in general)?

1. Correct size cage with smooth sides: aquariums, fiberglass, or wooden cages (with smooth treated wood) of at least the same length as the snake to be kept and one-half as wide as it is long. Large-scale breeders give their snakes smaller areas, but this is the ideal minimum cage size. Legal cage sizes in some states require that cages have a perimeter larger than the length of the snake to be housed (for minimum cage size). Check laws in your area.

2. Lock-on screen or pegboard tops. Snakes are excellent escape artists and pegboard is a nonabrasive alternative to screen for snakes that rub on screen a lot. Be careful with pegboard, however, as it may restrict ventilation to the point that the humidity in the cage increases to an unhealthy level. Screen or plastic-coated hardware cloth (for larger snakes) provides excellent ventilation, and this is very important in most cases. The newer fiberglass cages have a sliding front that eliminates the problem of searching for a tight-fitting top. Remember that screen may be very abrasive and should be avoided for some snakes.

3. Correct substrate—artificial carpet/turf looks great, reduces skin infections, and is super easy to clean. Some snakes do better on mulch, sand, or wood chips, but this should be researched first or discussed with your veterinarian. Newspaper is also an acceptable alternative as are paper towels, but see the chapter on the species in question for the most appropriate substrate.

4. Hide box. Plastic flowerpots or other items with a small hole cut in the side provide refuge, add years to the life of most snakes, and stimulate appetite, digestion, and normal shedding. Be careful the snakes don't get stuck in the drain holes in flowerpots, however! There are now excellent plastic hide boxes manufactured specifically for this purpose.

5. Water bowl. Shallow and weighted bowls are the best, but they must be deep enough for most species to soak in. They should not overflow when a snake enters it. Change the water frequently. Applegate (1992) and others have recommended the use of small plastic containers with lids into which a small hole has been placed. This prevents the water from being spilled and also reduces the evaporation from the water bowl, both of which are desirable goals. See the discussion on humidity and drinking water, however, as well as the discussion on ventilation.

6. Heat source. Heating pads (or any of the new cables or tapes) turned on low and placed under one end of the cage (aquarium) can be used to create a temperature gradient. Do not use hot rocks except for very small to medium-sized snakes. They cannot evenly heat large snakes and can cause burns. Warmth is critical for digestion and immunity.

7. Lighting. Vitalites® or other ultraviolet lights are probably not necessary for the majority of North American snakes. Some *diurnal* snakes may be exceptions, however, when it comes to long-term captive maintenance and breeding.

8. Food. Each species of snake has its own preferences, but in general mammal-eating snakes should be offered their food dead in order to prevent injuries to the snake. Rats and mice may be humanely killed by placing them in a small jar with an airtight lid for several minutes. Alternative methods involve placing a rat in a pillowcase and slamming it against a hard surface or picking up a mouse by the tail to perform the same task. Frog- and fish-eating snakes are best fed freshly frozen and thawed items (as freezing is known to kill some but not all parasites). Some snakes have very unusual food requirements that should be researched before attempting to keep that snake.

9. Books. Numerous books on snake care are available in almost all pet stores. Many, especially older titles, will not prove helpful. Choose carefully. Advanced Vivarium

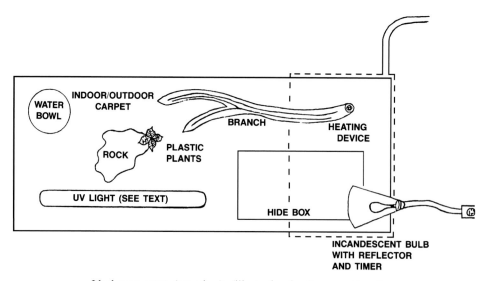

Ideal cage setup (top view). (illustration by Roxanne Rossi)

System books are very good. Ask your local herpetological society which authors they recommend. Well-written books are all good investments as are subscriptions to herpetocultural magazines, most notably *Reptiles* and copies of Captive Breeding Symposium volumes which can sometimes be purchased from reptile book dealers.

10. Veterinary care. Regular visits to a veterinarian for check-ups and fecal exams are important for a long healthy life.
11. Cleanliness. Bleach 1:30 (bleach:water) is a great disinfectant and should be used frequently. Cleaning and disinfection are discussed in more detail in the sections with those headings.

PART II

NONVENOMOUS SNAKES
NATURAL HISTORY AND CARE IN CAPTIVITY

Arizona elegans
Glossy Snake

The glossy snake is a medium-sized, 66–178 cm (26–70 inches), tan to pale gray-colored snake with very smooth shiny scales (hence the name), and a variably pointed snout. It has an inset lower jaw (i.e., the lower jaw fits inside the upper jaw when closed), which quite readily helps to distinguish it from bull-/gopher snakes or corn snakes.

Glossy snakes are voracious, reptile-loving, nocturnal prowlers over much of their range and throughout most of their active season. Preferred foods of wild specimens are numerous lizards including whiptails and race-runners, *Cnemidophorus* sp., spiny lizards, *Sceloporus* sp. (Tennant, 1985), side-blotched lizards, *Uta stansburiana*, desert iguanas, *Dipsosaurus dorsalis* (Van Denburgh, 1922), horned lizards, *Phrynosoma* sp. (Shaw and Campbell, 1974; Wright and Wright, 1957); and wild mice, including *Dipodomys ordi* and *Perognathus hispidus* (Ball, 1990; Stebbins, 1985; Tennant, 1985; Wright and Wright, 1957); small rats (Wright and Wright, 1957); small birds (Wright and Wright, 1957); and snakes (Shaw and Campbell, 1974). They are much like king-snakes in that they appear to have a preference for reptiles but will often consume mammals both in the wild and in captivity.

The preferred habitat of this species appears to be open sandy grasslands and desert shrublands (Wright and Wright, 1957; Stebbins, 1972; Tennant, 1984; Collins, 1993; Degenhardt et al., 1996). They also enter chaparral and open woodlands in some areas (Stebbins, 1972; Brown, 1997).

Consisting of nine subspecies altogether, the glossy snake occupies a huge range in the southwestern and central part of the United States and down into Mexico. The six subspecies found within the United States vary considerably in color and size, tail length, and

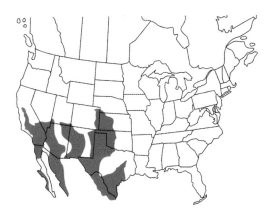

Arizona elegans

number of dorsal blotches. They include from westernmost to easternmost the following: California glossy, *A. e. occidentalis*, Mojave glossy, *A. e. candida*, desert glossy, *A. e. eburnata*, Arizona glossy, *A. e. noctivaga*, painted desert glossy, *A. e. philipi*, and the large eastern form (and nominate race), the Kansas glossy *A. e. elegans*. One subspecies is found in southern Baja California, which is referred to as the peninsula glossy. Their distinguishing coloration and scale counts are discussed in detail in Stebbins (1985) and will not be repeated here, since the care of all subspecies is very similar.

Some now consider the glossy snake to be two separate species, the eastern and the western. The eastern subspecies consists of the

Texas Glossy Snake, *Arizona elegans arenicola* (photo by David G. Campbell)

Kansas glossy, the Texas glossy, and the painted desert glossy snake.

Mating is believed to occur primarily in April or May and results in the production of 3–23 eggs (avg. = 8.5) about 1 month later. These eggs hatch in 57–90 days (Cowles and Bogert, 1944; Ball, 1990; Anderson, 1992; personal observations) into hatchlings measuring 22–28 cm (8.7–11.0 inches).

Predators of the glossy snake are thought to include owls and predatory mammals including skunks, coyotes, and bobcats. Ophiophagous snakes, such as kingsnakes and longnose snakes, may consume them as well.

Glossy snakes are rarely active on the surface at temperatures below 19°C (66.2°F) or above 35°C (Cowles and Bogert, 1944). These authors determined that the average critical thermal maximum for glossy snakes was 41.8°C (107.2°F). They are known to bask in the winter even though they generally avoid light, and one wild gravid female was observed basking at 38°C (100.4°F).

The glossy snake generally makes an excellent captive if it is started off properly. Most failures to maintain this snake in captivity are associated with overcrowding and poor husbandry (improper temperatures, very moist or filthy cages, or insufficient hiding areas) in the initial stages of their captivity. In addition, they are usually offered mice right away, and although many will take these readily under the proper conditions, they may not do so at first. The trick then for doing well with these snakes is to set them up properly, disturb them as little as possible, and consider offering them lizards or prekilled mice initially. Also remember that these snakes are largely nocturnal, and that feeding success will usually be higher if the food items are offered at night. Furthermore, they have absolutely no problems accepting prekilled prey.

Ball (1990) studied the captive maintenance and reproduction of the Kansas glossy snake in some detail and found the males from his site in Oklahoma were quite fastidious, often refusing domestic mice, while the females were consistent domestic mouse eaters. We have had a similar experience with the male Kansas glossy snakes we have collected in the Big Bend area of Texas. Nevertheless, we have found that most males will eventually accept fuzzy domestic mice quite consistently. Ball also found that gerbils and two species of wild rodents (*Dipodomys ordi* and *Perognathus hispidus*) are readily accepted by male Kansas glossy snakes. This disparity between male and female feeding behavior in captive snakes has been observed in a number of other species (e.g., the green rat snake), and some possible reasons are

Kansas Glossy Snake, *Arizona elegans elegans* (photo by David G. Campbell)

Desert Glossy Snake, *Arizona elegans eburnata* (photo by David G. Campbell)

discussed in the general care section under feeding.

In summary, lizards and smaller snakes do appear to be the preferred food, but most specimens will take either prekilled mice (especially fuzzies) or those that have been scented with lizard fairly soon, if they are set up properly. Feldner (pers. comm., 1992) found this to be true for the four subspecies he worked with in captivity. Some snakes, however, may refuse mice indefinitely, and one should consider releasing these where they were captured and trying with another. See the section on releasing snakes. Some specimens feed voraciously on any size mouse, while others will take only fuzzies. Furthermore, some will take only live fuzzies, while some will take only dead.

The basic (ideal) cage setup works well for these snakes, and no special modifications are necessary. Make sure to provide them with a dark secure hide box or they will get under the artificial carpet/turf or newspaper. A heavy water bowl is usually preferred for this species as they seem quite adept at knocking them over. Ventral heat is also very important for long-

term success with these snakes. Ball (1990) advises maintaining these snakes at 22–28°C (70–82°F) which agrees closely with Mehrten's (1987) range of 23–28°C (73–82°F). Cowles and Bogert (1944) reported that this species is active at temperatures of 20–27°C (68–81°F) and they considered it a very "cold-tolerant" species.

Brumation is essential for most of these snakes as they are prone to long periods of inappetence during the fall and winter months. This may be accomplished in the same cage and no modifications are necessary. See the section on brumation. We have used the natural brumation technique described in the general care section (as did Ball, 1990) in which the snakes were exposed to temperatures of 3–13°C (37–55°F) for 4–5 months.

Captive breeding has not been frequently accomplished with this species, but should not present a problem with healthy brumated individuals. Ball (1990) reported that the snakes in his care ovulated and mated consistently in May, even though they emerged from brumation in March. This is consistent with the

---

SPECIES: *Arizona elegans*, Glossy Snake
MAINTENANCE DIFFICULTY INDEX: 2 (1 = easiest, 5 = most difficult)
AVERAGE SIZE: 66–178 cm (26–70 inches)
FOOD: Lizards, smaller snakes, mice
CAGE SIZE: 10–20-gallon long aquarium
SUBSTRATE: Indoor-outdoor carpet, artificial turf, cypress mulch, pine bark mulch, or newspaper
VENTRAL HEAT: Not essential but helpful
UV LIGHT: Not essential but helpful
TEMPERATURE RANGE: 20–27°C (68–81°F)
SPECIAL CONSIDERATIONS: Often prefer lizards initially. Usually switch to mice fairly rapidly.

---

snakes in our care. Those matings reported by Ball resulted in oviposition in mid-July, while those we observed consistently resulted in oviposition in mid-June. Furthermore, our incubation period averaged 57 days at fluctuating temperatures of 26–33°C (79–91°F) compared to the 90-day incubation period reported by Ball at incubation temperatures of 25–32°C (77–90°F) and the 68-day incubation period (incubation temperature unknown) reported by Trutnau (1981). Eggs have been incubated and hatched in the usual manner using a wide variety of incubation mediums. See the general care section on care of the eggs and the reproduction chart (Table 5). Clutch size may reach 23, but the average is 7–9 eggs (Fitch, 1985).

A pair of Kansas glossy snakes in our care mated 3 successive years. Matings were ob-

served in May. Successive clutches were laid on 10 June, 21 June, and 6 June. Hatching dates for the 3 clutches were 9 August, 21 August, and 10 August, and incubation periods were 60, 61, and 65 days for the respective clutches. Clutch sizes were 5, 6, and 10 for the 3 consecutive years. One egg from the first year's clutch did not hatch, but 100% hatched in subsequent years. The sex ratio was 1:1, 1:2, and 1:1.5 males to females with the average total length (TL) of the young in successive years being 26, 29, and 29 cm (10.2, 11.4, 11.4 inches).

The hatchlings, ranging 22–29 cm (8.7–11.4 inches) in length, are very similar to their parents in coloration, although quite a bit lighter. We have found them to be robust aggressive feeders, with more than 91% consuming live unscented pinky mice fairly soon after their first shed. This is not consistent with those observations made by Ball (1990) in which fewer than one-half of his hatchlings consumed unscented pinkies immediately. Many switched over to them fairly soon afterwards, however, when they were scented with lizard for a while. The babies certainly seem to prefer lizards but will usually take pinkies before too long. These discrepancies may be nothing more than geographic variation or may be caused by differences in the ambient temperatures at which the snakes were maintained or at which the eggs were incubated. Indeed, Ball reported his snakes hatched in September or October (in Oklahoma) and they were immediately placed

California Glossy Snake, *Arizona elegans occidentalis* (photo by John C. Murphy)

in brumation, while our snakes hatched in August (in Florida) and did not refuse food until October (if they were exposed to cooler temperatures).

Ball reported a growth rate of 171 mm (6.7 inches) per year for the first 3 years of life for a male and female Kansas glossy snake. This growth rate was slower than two species of rat snakes, the common kingsnake, and the northern pine snake, and suggests that females may take 4 years to reach sexual maturity.

Overall, this is a very good-natured pretty snake that makes a good, although shy, captive. Adults will rarely attempt to bite a human, although they may do so accidentally if food is involved. Adult females and those snakes raised in captivity are very easy to maintain and may even make excellent first "pet" snakes,

while recently captured adult males may be quite fastidious and juveniles may actually be nervous enough to bite (juvenile hyperdefensive responses; many young snakes may snap in self-defense, but they will grow out of this in time and become excellent and handleable captives in most cases).

They may be quite long-lived in captivity. Snider and Bowler (1992) report one specimen that lived for more than 19 years in captivity. We have found them to be no more difficult to maintain in captivity than corn snakes once the feeding idiosyncrasies of certain individuals are learned and catered to. This beautiful, largely underrated, captive snake is now considered threatened in Kansas and may soon be so elsewhere, due largely to agricultural practices (Ball, 1990).

Bogertophis rosaliae
Baja California Rat Snake

In Baja California, along the eastern side of the long north to south ridge which enters Imperial County, California, lives a close relative of the Trans-Pecos rat snake. The Baja California rat snake, as it is usually called, is a medium-sized 85–145 cm (34–58 inches) olive or reddish brown snake that is still very poorly known. In overall appearance, it looks very much like a unicolored Trans-Pecos rat snake, for the head is well set off from the neck, and the eyes are very large. Furthermore, the body shape and scalation of the two species are similar. Indeed, in both species the head has no markings and there is a single row of scales under each eye.

Stebbins (1985) defines the habitat as hills, slopes, and arroyos near springs, seeps, and streams. In fact, other individuals who have captured these snakes refer to them as "oasis snakes" because they are most frequently found near water. Jim Kane is a herpetoculturist in Arizona and one of the leading breeders of this species. According to Kane (pers. comm., 1998), in California these snakes are found primarily in areas where there are large rocks with deep fissures, and they are generally found

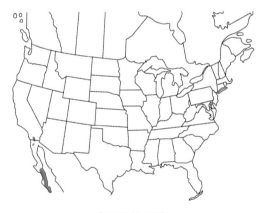

Bogertophis rosaliae

at elevations of 2000–3000 feet. Palm stands are often nearby. The most common snakes in these areas are speckled rattlesnakes, *C. mitchellii*, and rosy boas, *Lichanura trivirgata*, and the most common lizard inhabitant is the granite night lizard, *Xantusia henshawi*. Geckos of the genus *Phyllodactylus* are also found in this area. Interestingly, Kane believes that the population in southern California has been isolated

Baja California Rat Snake, *Bogertrophis rosaliae* (photo by Patrick Briggs)

for some time from the population in Baja California. Historically, the habitat may have been contiguous, but recent environmental changes have led to the development of coastal desert chaparral in northern Baja California, a habitat which Kane believes is not suitable for these snakes.

Virtually nothing is known of the wild diet of these snakes. Presumably, they may consume lizards and small wild rodents as juveniles, and switch to a diet composed almost entirely of rodents as adults. They are believed to forage at night, as most specimens have been found at night. As primarily nocturnal animals, they are probably preyed upon by nocturnal carnivores.

Reproductive data on wild snakes are scarce. Captive snakes generally mate in April and lay eggs in early June, and these eggs hatch in early September after about a 90-day incubation period. Hatching dates produced by Kane for several recent clutches are 2, 4, 5, 6, and 6 September. Eggs were incubated in a 1:1 vermiculite to water mixture (by weight) in closed plastic containers at 27.2°C (81°F). The average clutch size for captive snakes has been 10 eggs, and most young are around 38.1 cm (15 inches). The neonates have a faded brownish red to olive background color with numerous narrow

wavy yellow to whitish yellow bands dorsally and laterally (Staszko and Walls, 1994; Kane, pers. comm., 1998).

In captivity, the Baja California rat snake does fairly well in a basic arrangement. Kane uses plastic sweater boxes with aspen bedding, a hide box, and a water bowl. He also provides a strong thermal gradient in each box ranging from 23.8 to 37.7°C (75 to 100°F) by using ventral heat. The cages are well ventilated.

Under these conditions, Kane strongly recommends that these snakes not be overfed. Feeding an adult one mouse every 5 days is sufficient; any more frequent feeding may result in "regurgitation syndrome," as seen in some Trans-Pecos rat snakes. In fact, he stated that 10–15% were likely to develop this problem. As far as feeding is concerned, they are very aggressive, and domestic mice are readily taken. Even with good feeders, growth is fairly slow, and sexual maturity is usually not reached in captivity until the age of 4 or 5 years. Some have had captive-born young reach sexual maturity in 3 years, however.

Hatchlings are also aggressive feeders. Kane stated that all of his neonates took domestic pinkies right away. He added that he never had a single neonate refuse to feed and never had to

SPECIES: *Bogertophis rosaliae*, Baja California Rat Snake,
MAINTENANCE DIFFICULTY INDEX: Captive born, 2; wild caught 3 (1 = easiest, 5 = most difficult)
AVERAGE SIZE: 85–145 cm (34–58 inches)
FOOD: Domestic mice, wild mice, birds
CAGE SIZE: 20 gallon long aquarium to display case
SUBSTRATE: Indoor-outdoor carpet, artificial turf, or mulch
VENTRAL HEAT: Yes, to 100°F in one spot
UV LIGHT: Unknown
TEMPERATURE RANGE: 25.8–32.2°C (75–90°F)
SPECIAL CONSIDERATIONS: Brumation tricky. Some difficult to feed. See text. Prone to vomiting.

scent with anything else. To us, this would suggest that rodents, not lizards, are likely to be the primary prey of these snakes, but this is pure speculation.

As mentioned above, captive mating has generally occurred in April, right after the first shed of the season. Egg laying has generally occurred 9 days after the second shed, which is usually during the first 2 weeks in June. The usual clutch size is 10 eggs. An unusual observation made by Kane was that the eggshells produced by his females in captivity appear very thick. In fact, the hatchlings are sometimes not able to penetrate these shells. Hence, Kane watches for the first one to slit the egg, and then he carefully incises the shells of all of the others. The pathophysiology of this process is not understood at this time. Perhaps something in the soils where these eggs are naturally deposited helps to break down the shells, as has been seen with some turtle eggs. Or perhaps the incubation medium is being kept too moist. The eggs are nonadherent.

Based upon the observations made by Kane and our limited experience with this species, it appears that the Baja California rat snake will do fairly well in captivity, and pairs will breed in captivity if they are set up properly. Certainly, they appear to be similar to the Trans-Pecos rat snake in both appearance and care in captivity, as well as growth rate and reproduction. They are much more likely to succeed in captivity at this time than are green rat snakes, *Senticolis triaspis*. Wild-caught specimens can be problematic, however, and some of these have been found to be positive for *Cryptosporidia*, a protozoan that may cause gastric hypertrophy and result in chronic vomiting and, ultimately, death. This has not been a major problem with captive-born neonates. The authors would like to thank Jim Kane immensely for taking the time to share his extensive knowledge of this species with us.

Captive longevity has exceeded 6 years with this species, and that individual is still alive at the time of this writing.

Bogertophis subocularis
Trans-Pecos Rat Snake

The Trans-Pecos rat snake is a medium-sized snake 90–137 cm or 36–54 inches long, with a confirmed record of 167.6 cm or 66 inches (Conant and Collins, 1991) and one recent report of 228.6 cm (90 inches) (Van Devender, pers. comm., 1993). They range from southern New Mexico through western Texas and southward into north central Mexico. Most are relatively easily recognized by the H-shaped blotches found dorsally and the unmarked heads with relatively large eyes. Professional herpetologists will also examine the area under each eye to make sure there is a row of small scales there called suboculars, from which the snake receives its scientific name.

This nocturnal desert-dwelling snake prefers rocky areas of the Chihuahuan Desert. With regard to the preferred habitat, plant cover and proximity to water do not appear to be that

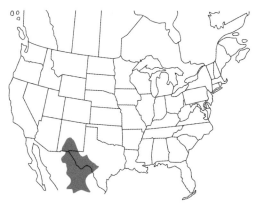

Bogertophis subocularis

important to these snakes; however, deep retreats or crevices in the rock are very important (Degenhardt and Degenhardt, 1965; Degenhardt et al., 1996). Food items listed as prey for this species in the wild include rodents (deer mice, *Peromyscus* sp., domestic mice and rats, *Mus* sp. and *Rattus* sp.), bats, kangaroo rats, *Dipodomys* sp., small birds (including cliff swallows and young chicks), and lizards (sideblotched, *Uta stansburiana*, crevice spiny, *Sceloporus poinsettii*, canyon, *S. merriami*, and earless, *Cophosaurus texanus*) (Shaw and Campbell, 1974; Trutnau, 1981; Tennant, 1984; Mattison, 1988; Stebbins, 1985; Mehrtens, 1987; Conant and Collins, 1991; Cranston, 1993; Degenhardt et al., 1996).

Predators of this species are suspected to include owls, predatory mammals, and possibly other snakes. It is now known that captive gray-banded kingsnakes will readily consume appropriately sized Trans-Pecos rat snakes, and presumably this occurs in the wild as well (Salmon, pers. comm., 1995). This may be one of the reasons that Trans-Pecos rat snakes breed so late in the year. See the discussion on breeding.

Trans-Pecos Rat Snake, *Bogertrophis subocularis* (photo by David G. Campbell)

This beautiful and popular captive snake is not at all difficult to keep in captivity (but there are exceptions). They are generally good eaters, fast growers, and good breeders. In fact, they have become so popular and they breed so readily that their numbers have skyrocketed in captivity and their price has dropped dramatically in recent years. And since they have been found to be fairly common over the last several years, the state of Texas has removed them from the threatened list, resulting in large numbers of both captive-born and wild-caught specimens being available for captive maintenance.

They come in a variety of color morphs, with the "blond" morph (a hypomelanistic snake, i.e., an individual with a very reduced amount of black pigment) being the most popular and expensive. Even the normal phase, however, with its well-defined H pattern and yellow-tan background color, is an extremely attractive animal. Perhaps the most outstanding external feature, and that which has endeared this snake to so many, are its big "bug" eyes, which presumably help this nocturnal snake locate food at night.

These snakes are also unique genetically, having 40 chromosomes, four more than most other North American snakes (Shaw and Campbell, 1974). In fact, this observation and others led to its removal from the genus *Elaphe* and placement in the genus *Bogertophis* (desert rat snakes) with the Baja California rat snake, *B. rosaliae*. Incidentally, the name *Bogertophis* is in honor of the great American herpetologist Charles Bogert, who died in 1992. There is presently some debate about the status of this genus (Van Devender and Bradley, 1994).

These snakes do well in the basic (ideal) cage setup, although they seem to do well in even simpler arrangements or much more complex arrangements. Many substrates will be tolerated by this species as well. These have ranged from gravel (Switak, 1984), which we do not recommend because of the danger of ingestion, to wood chips, which are usually satisfactory. We have never had a problem with those kept on artificial carpet/turf and provided with a heat source, and a good hiding place.

Cranston (1993) warned that some keepers of this snake have had difficulties maintaining them for any length of time if they were provided with water. He stated that regurgitation and poor muscle tone were possible sequelae. In our experience, the provision of water to members of this species has never been associated with a problem. We suspect that those individuals experiencing difficulties were using poorly ventilated enclosures, resulting in unhealthy, moist, bacteria-laden air. For a more detailed discussion, see the section on ventilation. Indeed, a common reason these snakes are presented for medical care is pneumonia, and they often have a history of being housed in plastic shoe box-style cages with water bowls. Hence, the use of screen tops or other well-ventilated arrangements will allow water to be provided free choice in most cases.

These snakes will usually feed readily on domestic mice, although recently captured individuals may be fastidious at first. Tennant (1984) mentioned that reptile curator Johnny Binder found that some of these snakes from very dry areas around Langtry, Texas, will often eat nothing but lizards. We suspect that even these animals could be switched to mice fairly rapidly using scent transfer techniques, however.

These snakes should be carefully checked for both internal and external parasites immediately after capture. Eliminating these parasites will often stimulate the snake's appetite and eventually improve breeding success. We observed several nematodes in the stool of those snakes we examined and Frye (1981) reported filarial worms in the eye of one of these snakes.

Interestingly, these snakes have their own species of tick, *Apomonna elaphensis* (Degenhardt and Degenhardt, 1965; Shaw and Campbell, 1974), and this tick is often responsible for damaging their tails. In fact, shortened or scarred tails should be a clue that an animal is wild-caught and not captive-born.

Temperatures reported as suitable for maintaining this snake in captivity are 25–30°C (77–86°F) during the active part of the year (Mattison, 1988), although we have successfully maintained these snakes at temperatures fluctuating through a much higher or lower range. The high temperature range was 27–

SPECIES: *Bogertophis subocularis*, Trans-Pecos Rat Snake,
MAINTENANCE DIFFICULTY INDEX: 2 (1 = easiest, 5 = most difficult)
AVERAGE SIZE: 90–137 cm (36–54 inches)
FOOD: Lizards, small birds, bats, rats, mice
CAGE SIZE: 10–20-gallon long aquarium
SUBSTRATE: Indoor-outdoor carpet, artificial turf, or cypress mulch
VENTRAL HEAT: Not essential but helpful
UV LIGHT: Not essential but helpful
TEMPERATURE RANGE: 25–35°C (77–95°F)
SPECIAL CONSIDERATIONS: May be heavily parasitized if wild-caught. Breeds in
  summer. Lays eggs in fall.

35°C (80–95°F) with no apparent ill effects. The low temperature range during brumation, which lasted for 4–5 months, was 3–18°C (38–65°F), quite a bit lower than that reported by Mattison (1990) of 15–20°C (59–68°F) or Cranston (1993) of 10–14°C (50–61°F).

As mentioned above, these snakes have been bred repeatedly in captivity. However, they tend to breed later in the year than many other snakes, with mating often occurring in mid-summer and egg laying in September or October. Nevertheless, spring mating may be attempted and achieved as early as May (Campbell, 1972). Females will usually lay 2–9 (up to 11) eggs 1–1.5 months later (McIntyre, 1977), which take 2.5–3.5 months to hatch if incubated in the standard manner. Incubation periods of up to 103 days have been reported, although Tryon (1976) listed an incubation period of 73 days at a constant temperature of 28°C (82°F).

Our observations of the captive breeding of this species agree with others that have found them to be summer breeders with fall egg laying and winter hatching. Two specimens were housed under identical conditions to a pair of corn snakes, *Elaphe guttata*, rat snakes, *E. obsoleta*, fox snakes, *E. vulpina*, mole kingsnakes, *Lampropeltis calligaster*, common kingsnakes, *L. getula*, scarlet kingsnakes, *L. triangulum elapsoides*, night snakes, *Hypsiglena torquata*, glossy snakes, *Arizona elegans*, western hognose snakes, *Heterodon nasicus*, eastern hognose snakes, *H. platirhinos*, and southern hognose snakes, *H. simus*, for 2 years. Every species listed mated in April or May except for the Trans-Pecos rat snakes, which showed no interest in mating until 20–28 July, when they mated regularly. Eggs were laid in early September, long after most of the others' eggs had hatched. Their eggs hatched in December, from 92 to 110 days later at temperatures fluctuating from 5 to 33°C (41 to 91°F).

A pair from Big Bend, Texas, produced clutches 3 consecutive years. They produced eggs annually in September which hatched in late November to late December. The ecological significance of these observations remains unknown. Do Trans-Pecos rat snakes in the wild really mate in May or July or in both months? We are unaware of "double clutching" in this species. Furthermore, are eggs laid in September going to hatch roughly 80 days later (as they might under constantly high temperatures) or much later? Will they hatch in December and, if so, what adaptive significance does this have? Perhaps the hatchlings experience reduced predation or parasitism by hatching during the winter. Interestingly, the last clutch we hatched was incubated at temperatures fluctuating down to 5°C (41°F) with no ill effects. The large healthy hatchlings pipped and emerged from the eggs at an ambient temperature of 5°C (41°F)!

The young snakes, approximately 28–38 cm (11–15 inches) at hatching (Campbell, 1972; Tennant, 1985; Mattison, 1988; Cranston, 1993), are colored similarly to the adults. For 3 successive years with the same pair, our hatchlings averaged 31.3 cm (12.3 inches), 35.4 cm (13.9 inches), and 36.3 cm (14.3 inches) TL, which falls well within the range reported.

These young snakes are usually very good eaters after shedding for the first time (approximately 20–21 days after hatching). Some individuals may have a large amount of yolk, however, and may not eat for months. We suspect many of these snakes may enter brumation immediately after hatching, if necessary, in the wild state, but this is unknown.

These snakes may reach sexual maturity in 2–3 years in captivity. Certainly, we have observed a 2-year-old male mate, and this mating resulted in fertile eggs. Captive longevity has been reported at more than 23 years by Tennant (1984).

Carphophis amoenus and *Carphophis vermis*
Eastern and Western Worm Snakes

The worm snakes are widely distributed in the eastern half of North America. There are two species, the eastern worm snake *Carphophis amoenus*, with two subspecies, *C. a. amoenus* and *C. a. helenae*, and the western worm snake, *Carphophis vermis*. All of these snakes are similar in color, being tan to dark brown above with a pink ventral surface, but they differ in meristic (scalation) characters that are covered in detail elsewhere. The eastern worm snake ranges from Massachusetts and southern New York southward through South Carolina, Georgia, and Alabama, and westward to Illinois, eastern Arkansas, and eastern Louisiana. The western worm snake ranges from western Illinois west to eastern Nebraska and south to northern Louisiana and eastern Texas.

The preferred habitat of the worm snakes appears to be woodlands with fairly moist soils

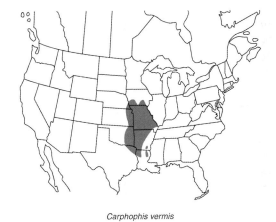

Carphophis vermis

(Minton, 1972; Mount, 1975; Linzey and Clifford, 1981; Collins, 1993; Klemens, 1993; Mitchell, 1994). In fact, Clark (1967) determined that worm snakes from Kansas selected soil moisture levels of 21–30%. They are often found under sun-warmed rocks, logs, and other surface debris. Body temperatures of active individuals in the wild have been found to range between 10 and 31.7°C (50 and 89.1°F) with a preferred temperature of 23°C (73.4°F) (Clark, 1967, 1970; Fitch, 1956). One was found brumating at 3.5°C (38.3°F) (Fitch, 1956).

The worm snakes have been reported to eat primarily earthworms, although a small ringneck snake and a salamander have been reported (Ernst and Barbour, 1989). Wright and Wright (1957) also listed snails and slugs as potential food items. Fly larvae have been

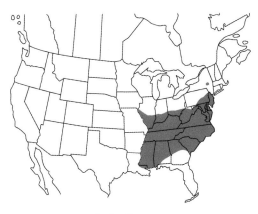

Carphophis amoenus

Midwest Worm Snake, *Carphophis amoenus helenae* (photo by David G. Campbell)

reported in the stomachs of two specimens (Linzey and Clifford, 1981).

Suspected predators of this species include shrews, toads, opossums, ophiophagous snakes, owls, and hawks. Known predators include copperheads, black racers, and domestic cats (Mitchell, 1994) as well as moles (Collins, 1993).

These snakes are thought to reach sexual maturity by their first year (Clark, 1970). Mating may occur in the fall or spring with up to 8 eggs (usually 3–5) being laid in June or July (Clark, 1970; Allen, 1992). These eggs usually hatch in 42–60 days into snakes measuring approximately 11.5–14.0 cm (4.6–5.6 inches) in length (Minton, 1972; Ernst and Barbour, 1989; Allen, 1992).

Fitch (1999) summarized 50 years' worth of observations on the western worm snake. The habitat of the western worm snake in Kansas has been described as open woodland or woodland edge with clay-loam soil, where they prefer to hide under flat rocks. The snakes in this study were active over a wide range of temperatures ranging from 19 to 31.7°C (66.2 to 89.1°F) with an average temperature of 25.7°C (78.3°F). Worm snakes apparently became less common when livestock were removed from an area and brush which shaded the substrate was

invaded (Fitch, 1999). The density of these snakes was estimated by Clark (1970) to range from 55 to 119 per acre. As with the eastern worm snake, earthworms were the preferred food and, strangely, an introduced European worm appears to be the most important food source. Mating has been reported in both fall and spring, with an average of 2.5 eggs laid per year (Clark, 1970). In that study the gestation period averaged 37 days, with an incubation period of 50 days. Longevity of two wild snakes was estimated based upon their size to be 9 and 10 years!

The worm snake requires a burrowing medium in order to survive successfully in captivity. This snake is often found under sun-warmed objects lying over primarily clay-sandy soils. Like the crowned snakes, they come up to the surface for warmth and dryness, and they also need some sort of surface cover for protection. Unlike the crowned snakes, however, their food is more frequently found below the ground rather than on the surface, and this is why worm snakes are rarely observed eating in captivity. Even when they come into contact with a small worm on the surface, they seem afraid and almost confused about how to attack it, even though it is obvious that they are interested in it because of increased tongue flicks and nudging. One worm snake, having attacked a worm on the surface, released the worm and fled from the scene after the worm began to struggle and hit the snake on the neck with one end. It is for this reason and the possibility of accidental ingestion of mulch (with resultant intestinal obstruction and death) that a cage of cypress mulch alone is not recommended. We believe the cage of choice is a three-layer cage (a modified crowned snake cage—see the picture). The lowest layer is about an inch of aquarium gravel. The middle layer is a clay-sandy soil mixture which has been baked at 300°F for 15 minutes. The top layer is a thin coat of cypress mulch with a flat stone or a piece of bark on top. A water dish should be partly submerged into the substrate and clean water should be provided at all times. Mist the substrate occasionally (once every week or two) and add water to at least keep the soil near the gravel moist. Change the cage substrates every 3 months to reduce the likelihood of infection. Provide heat from above in the form of a 40–75-watt incandescent bulb usually in an aluminum clip-on reflector lamp. Like the crowned snake cage, this setup will provide a thermal and moisture gradient from top to bottom similar to natural worm snake habitat: warmer and drier on the top and cooler and more moist the deeper it goes. Some source of UV light is recommended, as these little snakes appear to bask occasionally, but UV's contribution to the snake's health is unknown. As with

the brown snake, a "hot rock" may be useful as the snakes may approach it from underneath, much as they would a sun-warmed object if they were in the wild.

A simple but apparently effective alternative habitat (especially for the young) is made by putting mulch on one side of the cage and moist soil with worms on the other. Mist the soil every day. This creates a horizontal instead of vertical gradient. One may also cover the soil in the cage with a plastic lid or piece of glass. This will help retain the soil moisture and reduce the need for spraying to about once per week.

As mentioned previously, the preferred food of the worm snakes is the earthworm, although slugs, snails, salamanders, and even small snakes have been reported in the literature. Medium-sized worms are added twice-weekly to the soil, and they are consumed as they are found, which may be days later. In this, the worm snakes are much like the ringneck. One of these little snakes was maintained for over a year, offered nothing but two worms twice weekly, and was only observed eating once the whole year! This makes keeping a feeding record almost impossible. If the snake is kept separately, however, one may monitor feeding success to some extent by the frequency of shedding and the appearance of the shed. Weighing and measuring the snake would be more accurate, but weighing this species accurately requires a gram scale! Actually, we can get a rough idea of the weight of these little

---

SPECIES: *Carphophis amoenus* and *Carphophis vermis*, Eastern and Western Worm Snakes
MAINTENANCE DIFFICULTY INDEX: 4 (1 = easiest, 5 = most difficult)
AVERAGE SIZE: 19–28 cm (7½–11 inches)
FOOD: Earthworms
CAGE SIZE: 10-gallon aquarium
SUBSTRATE: A three-layer cage is preferred, but they will survive for some time in mulch-soil
VENTRAL HEAT: No, BUT some heat from above very helpful. See text.
UV LIGHT: Yes?
TEMPERATURE RANGE: 20–29°C ??
SPECIAL CONSIDERATIONS: These snakes are difficult to observe eating, breeding, etc. because of their burrowing. They will develop skin lesions if kept too moist.

snakes by using a dieter's scale that is marked in grams and a small plastic container. Just place the snake in the container and weigh both, then remove the snake and weigh the container. The Mars Corporation produces several excellent electronic gram scales.

To our knowledge breeding has not been accomplished in captivity, but it should be attempted as described in the general care section. One female in our care deposited 5 eggs on 6 June. The 4 fertile eggs averaged 2.12 × 0.58 cm while the infertile egg was 1.5 × 0.5 cm. These 4 eggs hatched on 20 July, an incubation period of 44 days at incubation temperatures varying from 25.5 to 28°C (78 to

82°F). The hatchlings were similar in coloration to the mother and averaged 9.0 cm TL. The sex ratio was 1:1. These babies were aggressive earthworm feeders. Worm snakes are more likely to breed in the fall, but may also breed in the spring, according to the literature. The eggs can be incubated as for other snakes. The problem is finding the eggs in the substrate before they are damaged. See the reproduction chart (Table 5) for more details.

A 10-gallon aquarium is usually a sufficient size cage for this species. One specimen we received as a juvenile survived 3 years and 2 months in captivity before it died of unknown causes.

Cemophora coccinea
Scarlet Snake

The scarlet snake is a beautiful and locally common snake which ranges over much of the southeastern United States. It is basically a tan-colored snake with numerous red saddles bordered by black. In some areas, the tan color becomes very yellowish, so that when viewed

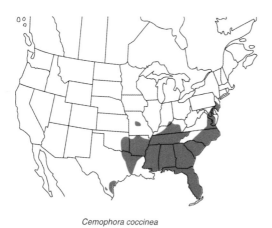

Cemophora coccinea

from above the snake appears similar in color to a scarlet kingsnake. However, one may rapidly identify the scarlet snake by the fact that the ventral surface is pure white rather than banded as in the scarlet kingsnake. The head is usually red and a black band generally runs directly behind the eyes. The venomous coral

snake, *Micrurus fulvius*, has a black head and complete red and yellow bands which touch each other.

There are three subspecies—the northern scarlet snake, *C. c. copei*, the Florida scarlet snake, *C. c. coccinea*, and the Texas scarlet snake, *C. c. lineri*. These subspecies may be distinguished by scalation differences, with the northern subspecies having the black band close to the eyes and the Florida subspecies having the black band separated by a greater distance. The Texas subspecies is distinguished by the lack of black bands below the third scale row (Behler and King, 1979; Conant and Collins, 1991). See Ernst and Barbour (1989) for more details on distinguishing the subspecies.

These secretive snakes seem to prefer habitats with sandy soil, often near water (Mount, 1975; Linzey and Clifford, 1981) although they have been found on dry rocky hillsides in Indiana (Minton, 1972). Mitchell (1994) also states they occur "where the vegetation is dominated by pine trees." They burrow quite readily using a side-to-side motion. They are often found under rotten logs or other surface debris, but are frequently collected crossing roads at night in areas where they are common.

There are no reports of the body temperatures of active individuals in the wild; however,

Northern Scarlet Snake, *Cemophora coccinea copei* (photo by David G. Campbell)

they have been found to be active at a wide range of environmental temperatures (Nelson and Gibbons, 1972).

The preferred food of the scarlet snake in the wild appears to be the eggs of other reptiles, although lizards, small snakes, small mice, insects, and small frogs have been reported by some authors (Ditmars, 1936; Hamilton and Pollack, 1956; Brode and Allison, 1958; Minton, 1972; Mount, 1975; Ashton and Ashton, 1981; Linzey and Clifford, 1981). Several different feeding methods have been reported, with small eggs reportedly consumed whole and larger eggs being chewed upon until the shell is perforated, whereupon the snake squeezes out the contents with a loop of its body and drinks it. See the picture below. Interestingly, Linzey and Clifford (1981) stated that these snakes did well in captivity and would eat skinks primarily!

On those rare occasions when a scarlet snake eats live prey, the prey item is usually constricted (Willard, 1977; pers. obs.).

Known predators of this species include southern toads (Brown, 1979), and Guthrie (1932) reported predation by a loggerhead shrike. Other predators may include ophiophagous snakes and mammals, and Ditmars (1936) reported that they eat their own eggs in captivity. Perhaps this behavior also occurs in the wild.

Mating has rarely been observed in the wild, although Mara (1994a) observed a recently captured pair mating in captivity in the summer. From 2 to 9 eggs are laid from June to mid-August and most hatch in September (Ditmars, 1931; Palmer and Tregembo, 1970; Martof et al., 1980). The incubation period is usually 70–80 days (Ernst and Barbour, 1989), although incubation periods as short as 46–48 days have been reported (Palmer and Braswell, 1995; Stengel, 1998). Hatchlings are approximately 17–19 cm (6.7–7.5 inches) in length.

The scarlet snake is undoubtedly the toughest of all eastern North American snakes to keep in captivity, and definitely represents a challenge in captive snake maintenance. Although it has been reported to eat lizards, small snakes, small frogs, and small mice in the wild, it is notoriously difficult to get it to start feeding in captivity. Apparently, its favorite food in the wild and the one which it can usually not resist even in captivity is the eggs of other snakes. As you might imagine, these are difficult to obtain on a regular basis and even if one has them, you usually do not want to use them for this purpose. Therefore, several methods have been devised to keep these snakes eating in captivity. The first is to keep them in cages without water. Water should probably be offered every 2 weeks to 1 month or during the day if a snake, especially a juvenile, is abnormally active. Offer a chicken egg/water mixture (50:50 to 25:75) in a shallow plate twice a week *at night*. This technique was initially discovered at the Savannah River Ecology Lab and reported by Trutnau (1981). It was also used successfully by Mara (1994a, b) and Stengel (1998). For juveniles, you may need to do this more frequently, perhaps every other night. Reptivite® or some other soluble vitamins are a good idea, but Reptical® will not often mix well with this mixture and sometimes seems to reduce palatability, since consumption is lower. Some adults will eat only once a month this way but they seem to do quite well, growing and shedding every 1–2 months. Another approach utilizes the same food but offers it in perhaps a more appetizing way for the snake. If a scarlet snake comes upon a snake egg too large to swallow whole, it slices the egg open with its teeth. You can therefore refill and reuse some of the larger snake eggs with the mixture mentioned above. Just keep the empty eggs frozen until needed.

These snakes are nocturnal and very shy so you may never see them eat, although you can if you are patient and don't mind watching under a 25-watt red light or some other very dim lighting. You can monitor eating by measuring the yolk mixture before and after feeding or less accurately by holding the snake up to a bright light the following day. The yolk is usually visible in the stomach. Tony Mills of the Savannah River Ecology Lab warns that snakes fed egg mixtures should be washed off regularly after eating (the next morning), since dried egg may adhere to their skin and lead to skin infections or dysecdysis (shedding difficulties). This tends to be less of a problem for snakes kept in mulch or vermiculite than it is for snakes kept on artificial (non-burrowing) substrates. We have a great deal more to learn about keeping this particular snake in captivity. Although these "tricks" work, there must be some other food item that these snakes relish. But perhaps in the south, reptile eggs are available during much of the year, and these snakes may truly be dietary specialists as their behavior and dentition suggest. In our experience, we have never had them consistently feed on anything aside from the egg mixture, although pinkies and skinks have been accepted occasionally. Some have even reported that earthworms have been consumed, but we have never observed this with the snakes in our care.

Recently, we noted that "slugs" (the infertile eggs of corn and rat snakes) will be readily devoured by captive scarlet snakes. Thus, large-scale snake breeders may be able to maintain and possibly breed this species using an otherwise wasted food source. The infertile eggs of iguanas will also be consumed. We

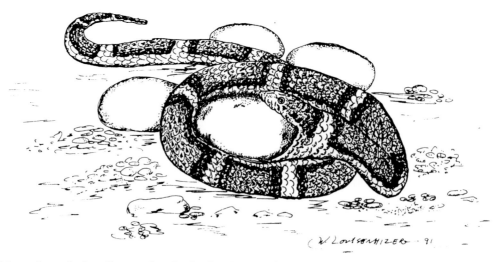

This scarlet snake has discovered a clutch of snake eggs in a subterranean cavity and is attempting to swallow one of them. If the egg is too large to swallow, it will wrap one coil around one end and chew on the other, thereby "milking" the egg of its contents.

SPECIES: *Cemophora coccinea*, Scarlet Snake
MAINTENANCE DIFFICULTY INDEX: 5+ (1 = easiest, 5 = most difficult)
AVERAGE SIZE: 36–51 cm (14–20 inches)
FOOD: Egg/water mix (50:50), snake or lizard eggs, rarely small lizards or pinkies
CAGE SIZE: 10-gallon aquarium
SUBSTRATE: Cypress mulch or pine mulch
VENTRAL HEAT: Yes, in fall or spring, but not necessary if good heat source from above
UV LIGHT: Not considered essential
TEMPERATURE RANGE: 23–27°C; 27–32°C for southern specimens (73–81°F; 81–90°F
   for southern specimens)
SPECIAL CONSIDERATIONS: Nocturnal. Needs vitamin supplements occasionally. May
   need to wash egg off.

have offered neonates and eggs, but those we tested showed no interest—other insects such as waxworms may be worth trying.

As mentioned above, the substrate that has worked the best for us with this species is clean cypress or pine mulch. You can collect this yourself from an old stump and bake it, or buy it and bake it. Put 5–10 cm (2–4) inches in a 10–20-gallon aquarium and lay some bark on top. Plastic plants and a rock make nice additions. Mist the mulch occasionally, once every week or two, since this stimulates activity, shedding, or feeding. Change the substrate every 3–4 months. Mara (1994a, b) reported that newspaper or paper towels also worked well. Stengel (1998) had a great deal of success with semimoist vermiculite covered with a layer of sphagnum moss.

Use a *weighted* screen top. Like the scarlet king and rough green snakes, scarlet snakes are great escape artists, and they will check the cage frequently to make sure you haven't put the top on loosely.

Special lighting does not seem to be necessary for this species, although a UV light source for several hours per day may be of some value. Keep the room temperature at 27–32°C (80–90°F) during the day and 21–27°C (70–80°F) at night. A heat lamp above or ventral heat is important in helping these snakes digest their egg mixture, but watch out for dehydration. A 25-watt bulb may be all that is necessary over a 10-gallon aquarium. (See the section on temperature.)

Brumate in the cage as you would for other snakes. Offer water at this time, but do not feed!

Captive breeding has been a real rarity. It has been accomplished several times but is by no means an easy and consistently repeatable process. See Mara (1994a).

Captive longevity has been reported for this species at 4 years and 10 months (Snider and Bowler, 1992), although Stengel (1998) reported one specimen still very healthy after 6 years in captivity.

Charina (*Lichanura*) *bottae*
Rubber Boa

The rubber boa has a geographically large range, but occurs only where environmental conditions are suitable for its existence. Short and stocky, the record length for this relative of the heaviest snake in the world (the anaconda) is only 83 cm (33 inches). Most individuals average around 61 cm (24 inches), with males being 51–56 cm (20–22 inches) and females being 61–66 cm (24–26 inches) in length. They range from southwestern Canada (British Co-

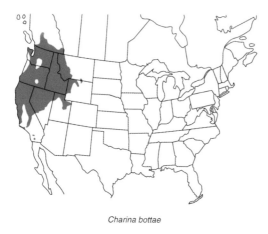

Charina bottae

ined (Stewart, 1988). Stewart states that the southern subspecies is generally smaller and tan-colored, with a fairly straight posterior border of the frontal scale, while the Pacific rubber boa is usually larger, greenish in color, and with an angular or distinctly convex posterior border of the frontal scale.

They occupy a wide variety of habitats within this huge range including grasslands, woodlands, and forests. They are fairly secretive and are frequently found hiding beneath some form of ground cover.

They are fascinating snakes. Not only are they one of the most northern boas in the world, but they are one of the most cold-tolerant of all snakes. There are stories of these snakes escaping into snowbanks (Wright and Wright, 1957; Shaw and Campbell, 1974). Then there is the peculiar blunt tail and its use as a decoy to lure the snake's enemies away from its head. Finally, this species is amazingly adaptable. These snakes appear equally at home in or near the water, in the trees, and underground.

lumbia) southward into the Sierras in central California, with isolated populations occurring in southern California. Toward the east they range into western Montana, Wyoming, and northern Utah. There is presently some discussion on the number of subspecies, but there are probably two, the Pacific rubber boa, *C. b. bottae*, and the southern rubber boa, *C. b. umbratica*. This distinction is based primarily on the shape of the frontal scale (large scale on top of the head), number of rows of scales, color, and average size of the individuals exam-

Rubber boas are certainly well named. They do look and feel like they are made of rubber. They are fairly variable in coloration with most individuals being brown or green above and having tan to yellow color below. Stebbins

Rubber Boa, *Charina bottae* (photo by Sean McKeown)

(1985) describes some individuals that have brown, orange, or black flecks ventrally, however. The dorsal scales are very small, giving the snake a shiny appearance, but the scales on top of the head are large.

In the wild, the rubber boa is also a dietary generalist. Literature reports of this snake's diet have included insects, rodents, shrews, birds, lizards, *Sceloporus* sp., snakes (including garter snakes and rattlesnakes), and amphibians (e.g., salamanders) (Wright and Wright, 1957; Shaw and Campbell, 1974; Stebbins, 1985; Stewart, 1988; Ross and Marzec, 1990).

Predators of this snake are believed to include other snakes, such as whipsnakes and kingsnakes, predatory birds such as hawks and owls, and mammals including skunks, badgers, bears, bobcats, and lynx, as well as foxes and wolves.

The rubber boa generally can do well in captivity and does so in a wide variety of captive environments. The basic cage setup using artificial carpet/turf or newspaper as the substrate, a hide box, and a water bowl will generally work although it may not be the most acceptable captive environment to these snakes. Some of these snakes may have difficulty finding water, and enjoy burrowing, so a humidity box may be substituted in place of an empty hide box and a burrowing medium may be preferable to newspaper or carpet/turf. Ross and Marzec (1990) and Hoyer and Storm (1991) recommend frequent soakings (once every 7–10 days in 1–2 inches of water for 10–30 minutes) for some of these boas in order to avoid dehydration, but many have not found this to be necessary for their individual snakes. Cypress mulch, pine mulch, aspen shavings, orchid mix, and others have all been used successfully as the substrate for this species. Hoyer and Storm (1991) used medium-fine Douglas fir sawdust. Avoid cedar shavings because of their aromatic nature. Cage accessories such as plastic plants, stable rocks, or treated logs will tremendously stimulate the appetite of rubber boas by increasing their sense of security.

Ventral heat on one side of the enclosure or preferably heat from above in the form of an incandescent bulb is advisable for these snakes, even though they are generally considered to be extremely cold-tolerant. (They still need to thermoregulate, even if they can withstand very cold temperatures and even though many have done well for years without a heat source in their cage.) This is especially true if captive reproduction is desired. Hence, even though these snakes have been reported to be active at temperatures down to 10–15°C (50–59°F) (Wright and Wright, 1957; Shaw and Campbell, 1974), they will do well at temperatures around 21–24°C (70–76°F) (Mehrtens, 1987) or up to 31°C (88°F) (Vitt, 1974). We have successfully maintained members of this species at temperatures that fluctuated daily from 27 to 35°C (80 to 95°F) during the summer months. This upper temperature is fairly close to the critical thermal maximum (temperature at which a snake

---

SPECIES: *Charina bottae*, Rubber Boa
MAINTENANCE DIFFICULTY INDEX: 2 (1 = easiest, 5 = most difficult)
AVERAGE SIZE: 51–66 cm (20–26 inches)
FOOD: Lizards, shrews, birds, snakes, rodents
CAGE SIZE: 5–10-gallon aquarium
SUBSTRATE: Indoor-outdoor carpet, artificial turf, or newspaper
VENTRAL HEAT: Yes
UV LIGHT: Not essential but helpful
TEMPERATURE RANGE: 21–35°C (70–95°F)
SPECIAL CONSIDERATIONS: Burrowing substrate works best. Shy. Cold-adapted. Need very cold brumation temperature of 5°C (41°F).

shows signs of stress and intolerance) reported by Shaw and Campbell (1974) for this species of 38°C (100°F). These snakes showed no signs of discomfort except occasionally soaking in their water bowls. In addition, they fed regularly and did not vomit their meals, suggesting they had acclimated to some extent to higher temperatures.

We certainly do not mean to suggest that these snakes be maintained at very high temperatures, only that they are fairly adaptable. We believe that rubber boas maintained at room temperature (as described above) with an incandescent bulb providing a warm spot during the day, will do well and be quite able to feed, grow, and breed in captivity.

At night the air temperature may safely drop to 10–15°C (50–59°F) or even lower under most circumstances. In the winter, temperatures down to just above freezing will be tolerated by these snakes. See below.

Full-spectrum lighting does not appear to be necessary for this species.

Feeding most members of this species in captivity generally does not present much of a problem. Even though some may stubbornly refuse anything but lizards or wild rodents, most will readily accept domestic mice of varying sizes. They will usually accept them prekilled as well, which is safer for the snake and allows for long-term storage of the mice via freezing and the use of scent transfer techniques from wild rodents or lizards.

Winter cooldown (brumation) is strongly recommended for these snakes if breeding is to be attempted. Two to 4 months at temperatures of 1–7°C (33–45°F) should be satisfactory. This may be accomplished either in their regular cage without any modifications or else in a plastic container with mulch that is placed in a refrigerator kept at those temperatures. See the discussion on brumation in the general care section.

Captive breeding has occurred hundreds of times using the techniques described in the general care section. Generally, the female should be placed with the male following brumation. Mating usually occurs in April or May (Hoyer and Storm, 1991). Successful mating will result in the birth of 1–8 (usually 4–5)

pinkish to light brown young 3–5 months later. In the wild, this generally occurs from the end of July until early November, with a peak in late August and September (Fitch, 1970; Stebbins, 1985; Hoyer and Storm, 1991). Spring brooding may also occur (Nussbaum et al., 1983).

The babies are usually only 15.2–22.9 cm (6–9 inches) long, with an average length of 18 cm (7 inches), but they seem quite prepared to fast throughout the winter. If kept warm, however, they will often begin feeding on pinkies. We have found that babies will often refuse prekilled pinkies, especially if they are offered during the day, but will readily consume live pinkies offered at night. Those that don't may be enticed to feed by offering small lizards (or pinkies of wild mice) initially and gradually switching over to lizard-scented or wild mouse-scented domestic pinkies. Otherwise they must be brumated or force-fed. If not, they will waste their valuable energy reserves and starve in midwinter. Remember the Q 10 rule. This rule states that for every 10°C drop in ambient temperature, the rate at which biological processes occur is halved. Therefore, a drop from 20 to 1°C will allow the snake to survive up to 4 times longer on the same amount of fat without eating anything.

Sexual maturity is usually reached in 2–3 years in captive specimens, 3–5 years in wild specimens according to Hoyer and Storm (1991). The same authors also stated that these snakes may breed only every 2–3 years in the wild. Annual breeding may occur in captivity but this may result in a dropping fecundity (number of young) every year until a break is given. Hoyer (in Ross and Marzec, 1990) mentioned that 20-year-old females continued to be fertile.

Interestingly, many snake breeders have observed breeding activity in captive specimens less than 1 year old. These matings are unlikely to result in the production of live offspring.

One of these snakes survived 20 years and 5 months in captivity (Slavens and Slavens, 1990; Snider and Bowler, 1992).

Although rubber boas are not considered beautiful by a number of individuals (some of the bright green ones actually are quite attractive), they do make hardy and interesting captives. They have increased tremendously in popularity among herpetoculturists in recent years despite the statement made by one well-respected herpetoculturist that "The drab colors and secretive nature of rubber boas are not conducive to their captive maintenance as pets" (Mehrtens, 1987). We would like to point out that most snakes are secretive and that drab color has nothing to do with our ability to maintain the animal or its quality as a captive.

Chilomeniscus cinctus
Banded Sand Snake

The banded sand snake is a fascinating and colorful snake of the southwestern desert. The background color is usually whitish or yellow, although most have quite a bit of orange dorsally. Variable numbers of broad black or dark brown bands distinctly mark the dorsal surface. The ventral color is usually pale yellow or white as in most desert snakes. They range from central Arizona southward into mainland Mexico and Baja California. They are relatively small, usually 15–25 cm (6–10 inches) in length (Wright and Wright, 1957; Stebbins, 1985).

Chilomeniscus cinctus

These secretive little snakes are the epitome of the sand swimmers, being extremely specialized for a life in and under the great western sea of sand. Their skin is extremely smooth and the small tight-fitting scales have been described by a number of authors as being varnished. They also have a deeply inset lower jaw, nasal valves, and small, inset, upturned eyes. From the side, they have a distinctly flattened head with a very pointed nose, presumably to aid them in moving through the sand. Indeed, their closest relatives in the United States are the two shovelnose snakes, which are similar in a number of ways to these little burrowers and are discussed in the next two sections.

The preferred habitat of this species appears to be loose sand to loamy-soiled areas of open desert with mesquite and creosote- or thorn scrub-dominated areas (Stebbins, 1985). Stebbins also states that they may be found in arroyos in rocky uplands associated with paloverde and saguaro as the dominant plants.

These snakes appear to prey almost exclusively on invertebrates, with sand roaches, centipedes, and ant larvae having been reported as food items in the stomachs of wild specimens (Fowlie, 1965; Stebbins, 1985).

Predators of this snake are unknown, but suspected predators include ophiophagous snakes such as kingsnakes, coral snakes, long-nose snakes, and glossy snakes, as well as predatory mammals and possibly owls.

Mating is believed to occur in the spring with up to 3 eggs being laid in the summer.

Like the shovelnoses, these snakes may be maintained very satisfactorily in relatively small enclosures (like 5–10-gallon aquariums) with *dry* loose sand as the substrate (approximately 5 cm or 2 inches of sand is acceptable for most). Remember that these cages must be well ventilated or the high humidity in the cage will rapidly lead to the snake's demise. This problem is discussed in more detail in the section on the sidewinder. Plastic cacti, stable rocks, and a small water bowl will complete the cage. Some keepers will not provide a water

Banded Sand Snake, *Chilomeniscus cinctus* (photo by David G. Campbell)

bowl, choosing instead to mist the rocks occasionally at night so the snake may drink. An intense heat source like a 40- or 60-watt incandescent bulb (lower wattage for a 5-gallon aquarium) above the screen top will ensure that the humidity stays low and that the snake will be able to thermoregulate properly during the day, digesting the food consumed the night before and regulating its immune system. Air temperatures suitable for this species appear similar to those of many other nocturnal desert dwellers, i.e., 25–30°C (77–86°F), although we have exposed these snakes to temperatures exceeding 35°C (95°F) for short periods on a regular basis throughout the summer. In fact, the temperature gradient in one cage during the hottest part of the day was 35–45.5°C (95–114°F) on the surface of the sand. The snake in this cage stayed submerged in the coolest part of the cage during this time, and we suspect this snake was dangerously close to lethal temperatures.

One very useful addition to such a cage may be a humidity box. This high humidity retreat will be used regularly by the snake to assist with shedding, to avoid desiccation, or to lay eggs. This high humidity area may seem unhealthy in light of the discussion above, but there is a major difference between a well-ventilated cage with a humid retreat and a poorly ventilated cage with inescapable stagnant air and high humidity throughout.

The diet of the banded sand snake appears to be strictly arthropods, however, so few observations have been made in captivity that other food items are possible. They appear specialized on sand roaches but have also been known to take other insects as well as centipedes. Fowlie (1965) thought that ant larvae represented the principal diet, but also found roaches and centipedes in the stomachs of those he examined. They will take small to medium-sized crickets in captivity and other kinds of roaches that may be captive-raised. Remember, however, that captive-raised insects can be notoriously calcium-deficient, so it is advisable to treat the insects as discussed in the general care section in order to avoid a deficiency of this critical nutrient in the snake. Two feedings (of 4–5 crickets approximately one-eighth to one-half inch in length) per week has successfully maintained those in our care and will probably be sufficient.

As with the shovelnoses, brumation is strongly advisable. These snakes may be brumated in their regular cages without any special modifications. Two to 4 months in the 10–15°C (50–59°F) range is appropriate, although we

---

SPECIES: *Chilomeniscus cinctus*, Banded Sand Snake
MAINTENANCE DIFFICULTY INDEX: 2 (1 = easiest, 5 = most difficult)
AVERAGE SIZE: 15–25 cm (6–10 inches)
FOOD: Centipedes, sand roaches, crickets
CAGE SIZE: 5–10-gallon aquarium
SUBSTRATE: Dry loose sand
VENTRAL HEAT: Not essential
UV LIGHT: Not essential
TEMPERATURE RANGE: 25–30°C (77–86°F)
SPECIAL CONSIDERATIONS: Must have dry loose sand as substrate in a well-ventilated
    cage. Eats small crickets. See text.

---

have exposed these snakes to temperatures fluctuating from 5 to 18°C (41 to 65°F) during this time. The wattage of the incandescent bulb used at this time may be reduced to 7.5 or 15 watts, or a light may be omitted completely at this time if the temperature of the room in which the cage is kept is allowed to drop. We have not tried artificial brumation (i.e., in a refrigerator) with this species yet, although it should be possible. The snakes will remain buried under the surface of the sand for months during this time.

To our knowledge, captive breeding of this snake has not occurred at the time of this writing. One female gravid at the time of capture in late July contained 3 large eggs (Stebbins, 1985). In the absence of any other information, we would suggest placing the female in with the male right after brumation as suggested in the general care section.

One of these snakes survived more than 4 years in captivity at the Arizona-Sonora Desert Museum (Bowler, 1977).

We have found banded sand snakes to be incredibly interesting captives. It is truly remarkable how they move through the sand, surfacing or submerging almost instantly. Feeding will rarely be observed with this species, as many individuals appear quite timid and they are nocturnal as well. A 25-watt red bulb may be helpful in observing these snakes at night. Shovelnose snakes appear to be much more aggressive feeders and will regularly eat during the day as well as at night.

Chionactis occipitalis
Western Shovelnose Snake

The western shovelnose is another sand-swimming snake found throughout much of the three western deserts (Sonoran, Colorado, and Mojave). Four subspecies range from southern Nevada through much of southeastern California and western Arizona, and down into northern Baja California and mainland Mexico: the Colorado desert shovelnose (*C. o. annulata*), the Mojave shovelnose (*C. o. occipitalis*), the Tucson shovelnose (*C. o. klauberi*), and the Nevada shovelnose (*C. o. talpina*). The subspecies vary considerably in coloration (number of bands and colors of the bands), but all can be identified as shovelnoses by the fact that they have 15 rows of dorsal scales rather than 13 as in the banded sand snake.

The preferred habitat of this species appears to be areas of fine loose sand with sparse vegetation (Fowlie, 1965). Stebbins (1972) further characterized the habitat by stating that this species was restricted to desert; washes, dunes, sandy flats, alluvium, or rocky hillsides where

Chionactis occiptalis

there are sandy gullies or pockets of sand among the rocks, from below sea level to 1430 meters (4700 feet), are suitable areas.

Food items reported for this nocturnal snake include spiders, scorpions, centipedes, moth pupae, and small lizards (Wright and Wright, 1957; Stebbins, 1972; Switak, 1984).

Suspected predators include ophiophagous snakes, predatory mammals, and owls. Many are killed by cars as they attempt to cross roads in the evenings.

Mating is believed to occur in the spring with 2–6 eggs laid in the summer (Wright and Wright, 1957).

The body temperature of active individuals in the wild has ranged from 20 to 34°C (68 to 93.2°F) but the highest voluntary temperature accepted in cages was 31°C (87.8°F) (Cowles and Bogert, 1944). In the same study, the CTM (critical thermal maximum) was 37°C (98.6°F).

These small, sometimes outrageously beautiful sand swimmers are very easy to maintain in captivity. They have not been very popular with herpetoculturists to date primarily because of their small size and insectivorous diets. In addition, they are largely nocturnal and do not make good display animals when they are housed as they should be, which is in loose dry sand. They tend to hide under the sand most of the day and are rarely seen by visitors to zoos and other educational institutions that choose to display them. Furthermore, their personality leaves something to be desired as they are extremely nervous snakes that disappear rapidly under the sand if given the chance, or coil

up, vibrate the tail, hiss, and strike if cornered. They usually strike with closed mouths, so bites rarely occur, but to the uninitiated they may be quite intimidating. When picked up these snakes usually writhe frantically and rotate until they are released. Hence, the reasons for their unpopularity abound in spite of their immensely beautiful color pattern. In fact, one of the subspecies, the Colorado desert shovelnose, is so brightly colored with yellow, black, and orange it puts some of the tricolored kings to shame. Furthermore, the scales are small, smooth, and closely woven, making the snake very shiny. The combination of the bright colors and the shiny skin make it hard to believe the snake is real. In fact, one young visitor to our home called one of these snakes a "candy cane snake."

Still, the western shovelnose is indeed an easy snake to maintain in captivity. They rarely exceed 24 cm (11 inches) and therefore will have ample room in a 10-gallon aquarium or similarly sized enclosure. In fact, some have suggested a 5-gallon would be more appropriate since these snakes seem to have a difficult time catching their prey (Switak, 1984). We believe either size will work and have not observed them experience much difficulty catching their food in the larger sized enclosure. In fact, they have several unusual behaviors useful for catching insects in open spaces. This is discussed in more detail below.

As mentioned above, the substrate of choice

Tuscon Shovelnose Snake, *Chionactis occipitalis klauberi* (photo by David G. Campbell)

Colorado Desert Shovelnose Snake, *Chionactis occipitalis annulata* (photo by David G. Campbell)

is dry loose sand. A depth of 2.5–5 cm (1–2 inches) will usually suffice. To this add flat stable rocks, plastic cacti, and a small water bowl (optional) and the artificial desert is complete. Good ventilation resulting in *dry* sand and a heat source from *above* in the form of an incandescent bulb during the day are essential for long-term maintenance. Remember, high humidity and sand as a substrate for desert reptiles do not mix, so keep their cages dry and warm. Air temperatures suitable for these snakes are very similar to those of the more commonly maintained snakes (25–30°C or 77–85°F) (Trutnau, 1981; Mattison, 1990), although we have maintained these snakes at temperatures much higher than this (27–35°C or 80–95°F) during the day, and much lower at night (18–21°C or 65–70°F).

As mentioned above, western shovelnose snakes are primarily insectivores, although there are literature reports of them consuming lizards occasionally (Trutnau, 1981; Switak, 1984). Switak stated that the desert night lizard, *Xantusia vigilis*, would be consumed by these snakes. Crickets, mealworms, and waxworms have been consumed by these snakes in captivity, although those in our care seem to have a marked preference for medium-sized crickets. It is fascinating to watch these snakes hunt. Upon seeing a cricket, they will rapidly chase it; when they get close, they will either strike rapidly, capturing the cricket, or use a loop of their body to herd the cricket into striking range. If a cricket doesn't move, or in a situation where numerous crickets are trapped in a small space, the snake will pin the insect(s) down with the coils of its body and then retrieve them with its mouth one at a time. Other food items taken in captivity have included spiders, centipedes, and scorpions, although they do not seem as fond of these as they are of insects. Frozen and thawed items will also be taken, which may make storage easier, but they seem to prefer live food. We usually place 4–6 crickets (half-inch to adult crickets will be readily taken by most) in the cage twice per week during the late afternoon, and the snakes will consume them as they are found. Waxworms may be alternated with crickets, but remember that crickets will eat waxworms, so try to make sure the cage is clear of crickets before adding the waxworms.

As with most insectivores, there is a possibility that a calcium deficiency may occur if only captive-raised crickets are fed. Remedies for this situation have been discussed in the general care section, but here are a few more tips. Howard Lawler, curator of reptiles, amphibians, and invertebrates at the Arizona-Sonora Desert Museum, says this can be

SPECIES: *Chionactis occipitalis*, Western Shovelnose Snake
MAINTENANCE DIFFICULTY INDEX: 2 (1 = easiest, 5 = most difficult)
AVERAGE SIZE: 25–35 cm (10–13 inches)
FOOD: Crickets, mealworms, waxworms
CAGE SIZE: 10-gallon aquarium
SUBSTRATE: Sand
VENTRAL HEAT: No
UV LIGHT: No, but an incandescent bulb is strongly advisable
TEMPERATURE RANGE: 25–30°C (77–86°F)
SPECIAL CONSIDERATIONS: Must have dry, loose sand as substrate and well-ventilated
  cage. Aggressive insect feeding.

avoided by feeding the crickets a diet of 85% rodent blocks and 15% calcium carbonate for several days prior to feeding them to your reptiles. In addition, there may be some benefit to using a full-spectrum light such as a Vitalite® or a Reptisun® 5.0 for these snakes, but this is unknown.

Western shovelnose snakes will drink from a water bowl if one is placed in the cage, but remember that using a water bowl should be attempted only if the ventilation is good. Otherwise, evaporation from the bowl will lead to trapped water vapor in the cage, resulting in possible bacterial growth and infection of the snake. Mattison (1988) suggested that spraying a flat rock during the evening would suffice to provide drinking water, since the snake would drink from the droplets forming on the rock. This will indeed work, but good ventilation still must be maintained in the cage so that it dries out completely fairly soon.

Brumation may be carried out in the usual manner in the same cage. No cage changes are necessary. Air temperatures of 10–15°C (50–59°F) for 3–4 months have worked well for some authors (Trutnau, 1981), but those in our care experienced temperatures dropping down to 4°C (41°F) on a regular basis during a 5-month brumation period without showing any ill effects.

Captive breeding has not been reported in the literature (but see below), and should be attempted as described in the general care section. It is known that females deposit 2–6 eggs

(possibly up to 9) in the early summer (Wright and Wright, 1957). An egg-laying box similar to that described in the general care section should be partially submerged in the sand during this time. The eggs can then be retrieved and incubated in the usual manner.

One pair of these snakes from southern California was supposedly maintained on a diet of crickets only and bred at least twice in captivity, but stopped producing eggs after this even though they continued to thrive in captivity. Although we could not confirm the accuracy of this report (this was second-hand word-of-mouth information), we suspect that if this was true, a marginal diet may have been responsible (i.e., a diet of crickets only may be too low in fat and calcium to allow repeated egg laying, but this is purely speculation on our part). It is possible that a seasonal fluctuation of the diet fed to the crickets intended for use as food, or a substitution of other food items, may prevent this potential problem.

The young, which are approximately 10–13 cm (4–5 inches), feed readily on small insects.

It has been our experience that western shovelnose snakes do extremely well in captivity, surviving many years just as described above. Eventually, they will calm down some, but they will never be very handleable. They are beautiful and interesting animals, however, and they are fascinating to observe as they swim through the loose sand or capture insects on the surface of their small desert terrariums. Some will even take crickets from your hand

(Ross, pers. comm., 1993). Make sure to have a tight-fitting lid on the cage, though. They are good climbers and are very strong as well, which makes them excellent escape artists.

There are no captive longevity records available, but these snakes may be quite long-lived in captivity. Howard Lawler reported they had maintained one of these snakes for more than 8 years on a diet of crickets (fed with rodent blocks and calcium carbonate as mentioned above) occasionally supplemented with centipedes and scorpions.

One last note is in order regarding this species. Occasionally, one of these snakes will temporarily tie itself in a knot during the shedding process. Interestingly, this behavior has also been observed in the yellowbelly sea snake, *Pelamis platurus*. Apparently, this maneuver helps snakes shed in environments where there is little to push against, whether it be a true sea or a sea of loose sand. It also points out the value of captive observation as an important learning tool for biologists working with snakes. This behavior may have been nearly impossible to observe in wild snakes, even if it occurred regularly.

Chionactis palarostris
Sonoran Shovelnose Snake

The Sonoran shovelnose is another beautiful insectivorous sand swimmer of the southwest. Its range is extremely restricted in the United States, however, being primarily within the boundaries of the Organ Pipe Cactus National Monument in extreme southwestern Arizona. They range in size from 25 to 42 cm (10 to 17 inches) (Stebbins, 1985) and are differentiated from the western shovelnose snake by their more rounded head and a relatively straight-fronted dark band from eye to eye (as opposed to concave in *C. occipitalis*). The orange-red bands are also much wider in this snake, making it an even better mimic of the western coral snake (to humans). Like the western shovelnose, these are extremely attractive snakes, competing with the tricolored kingsnakes in the intensity of their color and luster.

The preferred habitat of the Sonoran shovelnose is upland desert, with the vegetation usually dominated by paloverde, saguaro, creosote bush, and mesquite in very rocky areas (Fowlie, 1965; Stebbins, 1985).

The diet of this species is thought to consist primarily of centipedes, scorpions, spiders, and insects, although small vertebrates such as lizards may be consumed.

Predators probably include ophiophagous snakes such as coral snakes, kingsnakes, longnose snakes, and glossy snakes, predatory birds

Chionactis palarostris

such as owls, and mammals including coyotes, skunks, wild pigs, and others. Indeed, this species appears to closely mimic the sympatric Arizona coral snake, and hence may derive some selective advantage from its aposematic (warning) colors, but this is unknown.

Mating is believed to occur in the spring based upon seasonal surface activity patterns. This results in the production of perhaps 3–6 eggs in the summer.

These snakes are generally found on the surface when temperatures are above 20°C (68°F) in the early evenings. They are presently considered crepuscular, being active primarily at dusk, but possibly also at dawn.

Organ Pipe Shovelnose Snake, *Chionactis palarostris organica* (photo by David G. Campbell)

These snakes can apparently be cared for exactly as the western shovelnose snake. Basically, several inches of sand in a well-ventilated cage will suffice; however, the keeper may select a much more elaborate enclosure making use of stable rocks and plastic cacti as well. A 10-gallon aquarium provides a suitable enclosure for this species. A water bowl may be provided in the cage if ventilation is very good (a screen top) and humidity is kept to a minimum. Otherwise, the snakes may develop superficial dermatitis or blister disease, respiratory infections, or anorexia (see the discussion in the section on the sidewinder). An alternative to leaving water in the cage is to mist a rock every several days at night so the snake may drink from the droplets forming there.

The Sonoran shovelnose is an aggressive feeder in captivity and will readily take scorpions, small centipedes, and insects. Randy Babb, biologist with the Arizona Game and Fish Department, says these snakes are quite a bit more aggressive at feeding time than the

---

SPECIES: *Chionactis palarostris*, Sonoran Shovelnose Snake
MAINTENANCE DIFFICULTY INDEX: 2 (1 = easiest, 5 = most difficult)
AVERAGE SIZE: 25–42 cm (10–17 inches)
FOOD: Small lizards, crickets, waxworms, mealworms
CAGE SIZE: 10-gallon aquarium
SUBSTRATE: Sand
VENTRAL HEAT: No? Incandescent bulb above helpful.
UV LIGHT: No
TEMPERATURE RANGE: Unknown, 25–30°C (77–86°F)
SPECIAL CONSIDERATIONS: Care and breeding are probably similar to western
   shovelnose. They are reportedly more aggressive feeders.

---

western shovelnose snakes. He says they are much more likely to consume small lizards than the latter species. If they come upon a lizard too large to swallow, they may attack it anyway and end up swallowing the tail. They will also readily consume captive-bred insects in most cases, such as crickets, waxworms, and mealworms. Thus, these snakes are apparently not hard to provide for in captivity. See the section on the western shovelnose for more details that may be helpful in working with this species.

In our quest to study the parasites and captive maintenance of this species, our request (which consisted of a six-page research proposal) to collect two specimens inside of the Organ Pipe Cactus National Monument was denied. Said the park director, "Your research is nonessential."

To our knowledge these snakes have not been bred in captivity. Temperature preferences, parasite information, reproductive data, and other behavioral data are completely lacking for this species. In fact, Seigel et al. (1987) did not list a single fact on this species in their monumental work on the ecology and evolutionary biology of snakes. Furthermore, neither Slavens and Slavens (1990, 1991) nor Snider and Bowler (1992) reported any captive specimens or longevity records, so it is clear how "nonessential" our research efforts were.

Chionactis saxatilis
Mountain Shovelnose Snake

High above the typical sandy desert home of the other shovelnose snakes lives the mountain shovelnose. Or perhaps it is safer to say that it once lived there. In fact, none have been found for decades, however, not many have looked for them. In order to be complete, we will discuss what little is known about this species. It is very similar in many ways to the western shovelnose, *C. occipitalis*, and yet there are some interesting differences. Like most members of the genus, the mountain shovelnose is an attractive little snake with very smooth small scales, and multiple dark bands and saddles on a light background. These black bands are interspersed with orange saddles, except between the first and second black bands, and the third and fourth black bands. In these areas, the orange saddles are absent. The pointed head always has the crescent-shaped marking. These appear to be the smallest members of the genus, with the largest individual measuring 34.8 cm (13.7 inches) TL.

The mountain shovelnose is indeed found at higher elevations, in the rocky areas of the Gila Mountain range of southwestern Arizona. But the range of this small snake is fairly restricted. They are known only from three peaks in the Gila Mountains of Arizona. These peaks are all

Chionactis saxatilis

about 1 mile from each other and approximately 5–6 air miles south of Telegraph Pass on U.S. Highway 80. They have been collected between 1800 and 2400 feet above sea level (Funk, 1967). The habitat of these snakes appears to be barren rocky slopes with very little vegetation. Funk described the plants in their habitat and listed mesquite, creosote bush, elephant tree, teddy bear cholla, buckhorn cholla, ocotillo, brittle bush, and a number of cacti, including the saguaro cactus, along with other plants.

This snake appears to be more nocturnal than its closest relative, the western shovelnose,

Pattern of *Chionactis saxatilis*, based on the holotype (MCZ 77039).

sp., small scorpions, *Vacjovis* sp. and *Hadrurus* sp., moths, centipedes, and immature roaches, *Arenivega* sp. (Funk, 1967). One hatchling in Funk's care consumed the tail of a tiger whiptail lizard, *Cnemidophorus tigris*. These snakes consistently refused mealworms according to Dr. Funk.

There are no known predators of this species but suspected predators would include kingsnakes, night snakes, and predatory mammals and birds.

The mountain shovelnose has been reported to lay 3–6 eggs near the end of March (22–25 March) which hatch toward the end of June under captive conditions (an incubation period of 94–99 days) (Funk, 1967). The young, patterned similar to the adults, measured 11.2–12.0 cm TL (average 11.7 cm, 4.6 inches), and shed 7–9 days after hatching. The incubation mediums used successfully were dampened sand, dampened peat moss, and dampened tissue paper.

As mentioned above, captive snakes maintained their nocturnal activity pattern, appearing on the surface after 2130 hrs and remaining active until 0300 hrs. The western shovelnoses maintained in the same cages usually appeared on the surface earlier, usually around 2000 hrs and disappeared around 2200 hrs.

The senior author had the opportunity to visit the Gila Mountains during the spring of 1997 and searched the exact location where these snakes have been reported. No specimens were found at that time, although it would be quite

which is thought to be active primarily just after dusk and into the early evening. Funk found wild snakes on the surface from 2048 to 0245 hrs, and noted that captive snakes maintain a similar cycle. The food of mountain shovelnoses is not well known, but captive specimens have consumed spiders, *Latrodectis*

SPECIES: *Chionactis saxatilis*, Mountain Shovelnose Snake
MAINTENANCE DIFFICULTY INDEX: 2 (1 = easiest, 5 = most difficult)
AVERAGE SIZE: 25–42 cm (10–17 inches)
FOOD: Small lizards, crickets, waxworms, mealworms
CAGE SIZE: 10-gallon aquarium
SUBSTRATE: Sand
VENTRAL HEAT: No? Incandescent bulb above helpful.
UV LIGHT: No
TEMPERATURE RANGE: 25–30°C (77–86°F)
SPECIAL CONSIDERATIONS: Care and breeding are probably similar to Sonoran shovelnose

easy for inactive snakes to hide in such a rocky environment. Other snakes found there included speckled rattlesnake, *Crotalus mitchellii*, and a lyre snake, *Trimorphodon biscutatus*.

Being fortunate enough to speak with the species' discoverer, Dr. Richard Funk (who 30 years later also happens to be one of the most well-known reptile veterinarians in the country), we learned that in captivity these snakes seemed to stay in contact with the rocks in their cages, much as might be expected from their preferred habitat. Furthermore, they almost always remain submerged, emerging only to feed. Dr. Funk stated that at first, he really didn't think that these snakes were that different from the western shovelnose except in coloration. However, based upon continued observation of the habitat and behavior in captivity, he changed his mind. Indeed, they are a distinctly different population, completely isolated from the western shovelnose by habitat differences, and therefore are considered a separate species. Had Dr. Funk not been as observant, he would never have discovered this new species. How exciting to think that new species may still be waiting to be discovered, even in the United States, where snakes have been so well studied. Young herpetologists should take note.

Unfortunately, it is unknown if this species still survives. Only time will tell.

Clonophis kirtlandii
Kirtland's Snake

Kirtland's snake is a small, heavy-bodied, brownish to rust brown snake with large black blotches dorsally, and keeled scales. The keeled scales give it a "dull" appearance, not shiny as is often observed in snakes with smooth scales. The head is usually brown to black, but the lips are cream to yellowish. This color extends onto the throat. The belly is pinkish red with a double row of black spots running down the lateral aspects of the abdominal scales, much like the abdominal coloration of the Brazos water snake, *Nerodia harteri*. These are fairly small snakes, with the average adult ranging 36–45.7 cm (14–18 inches) in length and the record being 62.2 cm (24.5 inches) (Conant and Collins, 1991).

The preferred habitat of this snake appears to be fields near water and other open grassy areas like marshes or moist pastures (Wright and Wright, 1957; Minton, 1972; Ernst and Barbour, 1989; Harding, 1997). They seem to thrive near urban areas (Minton, 1972) and we have seen them in littered vacant lots where earthworms are found, even when there is little surface water. Others have also found them in grassy areas without standing water nearby (Harbsmeier, pers. comm., 1995). Recent laboratory studies have indicated that these snakes will not burrow much, and instead choose to sit on the surface of soil placed in their enclosures or to enter artificial burrows when they are available (Tucker, 1977). It was suggested that the presence of water, and hence, crayfish and their burrows, would be important for the species to survive in many areas (Tucker, 1994; Harding, 1997). Certainly, it is possible that the discrepancies in these observations may be related to variation among populations of this species.

As alluded to above, the earthworms are an important part of the diet of this species (Wright and Wright, 1957; Minton, 1972), but slugs, fish, and leeches have been reported as potential food for wild specimens since they have been consumed by captives (Tucker, 1977). Amphibians have been refused by captives, however (Conant, 1943; Tucker, 1977), although Allen (1992) states that wild individuals will also consume salamanders as well as worms and slugs. Harbsmeier (pers. comm., 1998) maintained and bred several of these animals and feels that this species is very unlikely to consume any vertebrate prey in most cases, even though an occasional captive may consume such an item. There is apparently one specimen at the Louisville Zoo that is feeding on pinky mice that have been scented

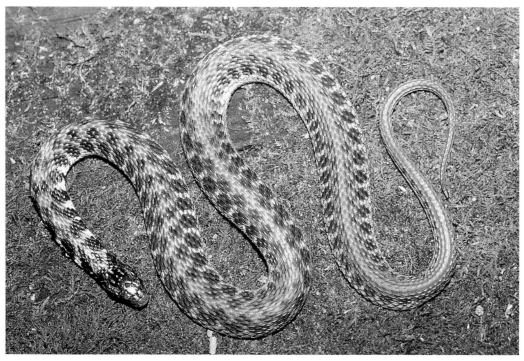

Kirtland's Snake, *Clonophis kirtlandii* (photo by Steve Barten)

with earthworms, and she has been doing so for over 3 years.

A black kingsnake found in Indiana had eaten a *Clonophis* (Minton, 1972). Probably predatory mammals and some birds also eat this snake. Harding (1997) listed probable predators to include milk snakes, shrews, weasels, cats, foxes, raccoons, skunks, as well as hawks, owls, and unappreciative humans. Habitat destruction is a huge factor affecting all species of snakes, but this species appears to be hit particularly hard by urbanization of its former habitat. Even though populations may survive for years in isolated "islands" of suitable habitat near cities, they are being destroyed as these areas are developed.

Mating is known to occur in the spring and has been observed during the first week in May (Smith, 1961; Minton, 1972). This results in the birth of 4–22 young from late July through September (Wright and Wright, 1957; Fitch, 1970). These young range 11–17 cm (4.3–6.7 inches) in length (Ernst and Barbour, 1989; Conant and Collins, 1991).

Kirtland's snake will do fairly well in captiv-

ity if provided with the basic cage setup. Although some herpetologists have had a difficult time maintaining this species in captivity, others have experienced a great deal of success and consider them relatively easy to maintain. Remember that even though these snakes used to be considered water snakes because they often live near water, they must be housed in a dry cage or they will develop skin lesions. A number of substrates will work, including soil, cypress mulch, or a combination such as seen in a wet/dry cage, and newspaper. A hide box is very important, as is a water bowl. These snakes eat and defecate frequently, so a simpler cage arrangement will be easier to keep clean. Ultraviolet light does not appear to be necessary at this time; however, it may yet prove beneficial to these animals. An enclosure the size of a 10-gallon aquarium should provide plenty of room for these snakes, although they have been maintained in plastic shoe boxes for long periods of time.

Although other food items have been listed, the preferred food (and perhaps the only food) of most Kirtland's snakes is the earthworm. Bill

Allen of Pennsylvania and Curt Harbsmeier of Orlando, Florida, have both maintained multiple members of this species on a diet solely of earthworms for periods exceeding 1 and 3 years respectively, and we have also maintained a specimen on earthworms only for over a year. A diet of earthworms alone has been shown to be a balanced diet for smooth earth snakes (Rossi and Rossi, 1993c), and is probably also balanced for this species. See the data from Harbsmeier below. Because earthworms may also serve as intermediate hosts for parasites, these snakes should be dewormed initially and checked for worms regularly thereafter. Panacur® at a dose of 50–100 mg is probably the safest drug for this purpose.

Brumation and breeding may be accomplished as described in the general care section, although this has not occurred commonly in captivity, probably from lack of interest. The general pattern is spring breeding resulting in late summer or early fall live birth.

A number of neonates have been born in captivity and captive breeding has occurred several times. We are indebted to Curt Harbsmeier for the following information.

A female collected in Indianapolis in June 1992 delivered 4 young and 3 egg masses on 6 September of that year. The young snakes ranged 11.2–14.1 cm (4.4–5.5 inches) in length with an average TL of 12.85 cm (5.1 inches). The birth weights ranged from 1.27 to 1.52 grams, with an average weight of 1.4 grams. These young fed voraciously in captivity, eat-

ing half an earthworm twice weekly. By 24 July 1993, they had reached an average weight of 5.33 grams.

The same adult female that produced this litter mated in April 1994 with a male that had been collected at the same locality. This resulted in the delivery of 3 live young and 3 egg masses on 2 August 1994. The young measured 13.2, 14.0, and 14.4 cm, and weighed 1.44, 1.49, and 1.56 grams respectively, with an average TL of 13.9 cm (5.5 inches), and an average weight of 1.49 grams. The estimated gestation period in this instance was approximately 110 days.

Harbsmeier indicated that these adults were exposed to temperatures fluctuating between 2 and 22°C (35.6 and 71.6°F) during the period from November 1993 to February 1994, and believed that this was not sufficiently cold or else not a long enough period of cold for these snakes to be fully fertile.

During the warm active part of the year, the snakes were kept in plastic shoe boxes and fed 2–3 worms weekly. A basking area was available for the female at 38°C (100.4°F). The snakes were housed in a similar manner during the winter, except that they were offered only one worm every 10 days.

We did not feed the Kirtland's snake in our care during the winter and it did fairly well.

The young snakes are voracious eaters; it is best to raise them in separate containers or they may be lost in fights over food, or the submissive snake's appetite may be inhibited in the

---

SPECIES: *Clonophis kirtlandii*, Kirtland's Snake
MAINTENANCE DIFFICULTY INDEX: 3 (1 = easiest, 5 = most difficult)
AVERAGE SIZE: 36–46 cm (14–18 inches)
FOOD: Earthworms, leeches, small fish
CAGE SIZE: 10–20-gallon aquarium
SUBSTRATE: Indoor-outdoor carpet or mulch
VENTRAL HEAT: Not essential but may be helpful
UV LIGHT: Yes?
TEMPERATURE RANGE: 20–25°C (68–77°F)
SPECIAL CONSIDERATIONS: Likely to be parasitized. Prone to skin lesions if kept too
   moist.

---

presence of the dominant one. Like juvenile brown snakes and earth snakes, Kirtland's juveniles are prone to desiccation and will benefit by having a high moisture retreat in an otherwise dry cage. It is believed that they reach sexual maturity in 2 years.

Although the range of this snake initially included part of western Pennsylvania, it is now considered nearly extinct in that state and is becoming rarer throughout much of its range. They are good candidates for more captive breeding efforts. More work is needed on the captive requirements of this species. Thanks to the efforts of herpetoculturists like Curt Harbsmeier, some of the missing information on the reproductive cycle, growth rate, and care of the young is now available.

One specimen has survived in captivity for nearly 3 years at the Louisville Zoo, and the pair in the care of Curt Harbsmeier were col-

Clonophis kirtlandii

lected as adults in June 1992, making them captives for 4 years, and since they were adults at the time of capture, they are likely to be at least 1–2 years older than that.

Coluber constrictor
Racer

This medium to large, fast-moving snake occupies a huge range in North and Central America. It is found in suitable habitats from coast to coast, from southern Canada (Ontario, British Columbia, and Saskatchewan) through much of

Coluber constrictor

the United States, and down the eastern side of Mexico into Guatemala.

There are 11 subspecies that vary considerably in size, color, preferred foods, reproductive strategy, etc. These include the western yellow-belly racer (*C. c. mormon*), the eastern yellow-belly racer (*C. c. flaviventris*), the blue racer (*C. c. foxii*), the Mexican racer (*C. c. oaxaca*), the buttermilk racer (*C. c. anthicus*), the northern black racer (*C. c. constrictor*), the brown chin racer (*C. c. helvigularis*), the blackmask racer (*C. c. latrunculus*), the tan racer (*C. c. ethridgei*), the southern black racer (*C. c. priapus*), and the Everglades racer (*C. c. paludicola*). Hence, it is somewhat difficult to generalize about the important aspects of natural history and draw from them in order to assist with captive maintenance of the specimens in hand. Yet, we must review and summarize some of this information very briefly in order to gain a better understanding of this animal and what it may require in captivity. This is especially important for this species because even though

Eastern Yellowbelly Racer, *Coluber constrictor flaviventris* (photo by David G. Campbell)

it is very common, very few herpetoculturists have ever successfully maintained one of these snakes in captivity and even fewer have successfully bred these snakes in captivity. In addition, it appears that the care of most subspecies is basically the same, even though there may be some variations in thermal preferences, brumation times, breeding times, etc.

The racer is one of the most nervous, irascible snakes of North America and one of the few snakes that has been reported to attack people in the wild (Ernst and Barbour, 1989). They occupy a wide variety of open habitats including grasslands, prairies, and open woodlands that are usually near water, and they hunt a wide variety of prey as mentioned below. They can reach more than 183 cm (6 feet) in length (record 185.4 cm, 73 inches), although most individuals average 76–127 cm (30–50

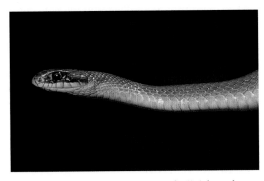

Blue Racer, *Coluber constrictor foxii* (photo by John Murphy)

inches). They are different from many other North American snakes in that they are distinctly diurnal, very visually oriented, and have a higher preferred body temperature than most (Bogert and Cowles, 1947; Brattstrom, 1965; Ernst and Barbour, 1989). Cloacal temperatures of active racers have usually ranged from 25 to 38°C (77 to 100 °F), and most activity in the wild has been observed when air temperatures exceeded 32°C (90°F). Brumation (hibernation) temperatures and activity of these snakes in the winter is described by Brown and Parker, 1976.

A list of food items by species would occupy many pages. This species has one of the most diverse diets of all North American snakes. Food items include grasshoppers, crickets, caterpillars, moths, cicadas, tree frogs, small toads, salamanders, lizards (including spiny lizards), anoles, legless lizards, skinks, worm snakes, garter snakes, ringneck snakes, green snakes, water snakes, birds and their eggs, fish and their eggs, mice, rats, and moles, among many other food items (Ernst and Barbour, 1989).

Known predators of this species include the coral snake, *Micrurus fulvius*, timber rattlesnake, *Crotalus horridus*, copperhead, *Agkistrodon contortrix*, rat snake, *Elaphe obsoleta*, prairie kingsnake, *Lampropeltis calligaster*, common kingsnake, *L. getulus*, and other racers, *Coluber constrictor* (Fitch, 1963; Jackson, 1971). Fitch (1963) found remains of one in a slender glass lizard, *Ophisaurus attenuatus*.

Western Yellowbelly Racer (neonate), *Coluber constrictor mormon*. Some have proposed that this is a separate species called the Western Racer, *Coluber mormon* (photo by John Rossi)

Hawks, barn owls, crows, roadrunners, foxes, dogs, cats, opossums, raccoons, and skunks probably eat them also. Owens (1949) reported that a tarantula ate hatchling racers.

Breeding season is usually from April to June over much of North America, even though they may breed earlier in the southern part of their range or possibly in the fall (Wright and Wright, 1957). Clutches of 2–31 eggs have been reported by most authors (Fitch, 1963; Stebbins, 1985; Ernst and Barbour, 1989); however, up to 50 eggs have been reported (Wright and Wright, 1957). Most clutches are between 3 and 12 eggs (Fitch, 1963; Stebbins 1985), and they vary considerably with the size of the female and the geographic origin (in the wild) (Fitch, 1970). Eggs are generally laid from June through August but may be as early as March in the south (Gillingham, 1976). The incubation period has been reported as ranging from 43 to 65 days with an average around 50 days (Ernst and Barbour, 1989). Two clutches we incubated hatched around the 50-day mark.

In the wild, their broad diet and quickness make them a successful denizen of numerous habitats. Unfortunately, these qualities are of little benefit to them in captivity, where nervous energy and high speed result in collisions with the enclosure walls and trauma, and white mice are the only item on the menu. In addition to these problems, keepers do not commonly provide these snakes with their preferred high temperature range of 25–37°C (77–99°F), which results in improper digestion and immune system function. Furthermore, since these snakes have very broad diets, they usually come into captivity with quite a number of internal and external parasites and these are usually not treated. The combination of the above factors is the real reason most authors writing on their care say racers "make poor captives."

Parasites are a major concern with racers. All of the racers we have examined have been parasitized. The most common intestinal parasites observed are hookworms, *Kallicephalus*, and rhabditiform larvae, possibly of the genus *Strongyloides*. One very thin and weak wild specimen from central Florida was observed to have a heavy infestation of trombiculid mites.

Actually, they can do very well in captivity but they require special care, which can be inferred from the discussion above. Success with most racers will depend on catering to their nervous personality and temperature requirements. A gentle capture, smooth transportation, and slow release into the cage (see the discussion on transportation) will really help them adjust to captivity. A good *stable* dark-

Mexican Racer, *Coluber constrictor oaxaca*
(photo by David G. Campbell)

Southern Black Racer, *Coluber constrictor priapus* (photo by David G. Campbell)

colored hide box with a narrow opening is absolutely essential in most cases. *Always house these snakes singly.*

Housing is not difficult as racers do well in relatively small cages (for their size). In fact, some believe that too large a cage will lead to increased nervousness. A 10-gallon cage is satisfactory for most juveniles, while a 30- or 40-gallon long aquarium or larger is more appropriate for an adult. The basic cage design mentioned in the general care section (including artificial carpet/turf, rock, sturdy branch, hide box, water bowl, and ventral heat) will work fine. Cages must have smooth sides and high tops or many of these snakes will rub their rostral areas (noses) raw. A hatch in the top is nice as it allows food to be dropped in without disturbing the snake. The front of the cage can be covered prior to feeding, or, if the snake is very nervous, most of the time. In addition, the cage should be placed at eye level, not on the floor. This should reduce vibrations, reduce cool drafts, and reduce the snake's stress when someone approaches the cage.

Then, thermal considerations and ventilation need to be considered. Remember, racers are diurnal. They like it bright, hot, and dry (as long as they have access to water). A 40-, 60-, or 75-watt incandescent bulb will create an area beneath it of over 38°C (100°F), and a screen top will keep the cage healthfully dry.

Brumation and breeding should be attempted as for most other snakes as discussed in the general care section. See Table 5 for more specific information.

Feeding the racer once it has adapted to captivity is no problem for any age snake because of their tremendously broad range of acceptable food items. Ernst and Barbour (1989) listed 15 species of frogs, nine species of

---

SPECIES: *Coluber constrictor*, Racer
MAINTENANCE DIFFICULTY INDEX: 3 (1 = easiest, 5 = most difficult)
AVERAGE SIZE: 76–152 cm (30–60 inches)
FOOD: Lizards, frogs, mice
CAGE SIZE: 30–40-gallon long aquarium
SUBSTRATE: Artificial turf, indoor-outdoor carpet, or newspaper
VENTRAL HEAT: Yes
UV LIGHT: No, but an incandescent bulb is useful
TEMPERATURE RANGE: 25–38°C (77–100°F)
SPECIAL CONSIDERATIONS: Usually very nervous. Young snakes usually refuse pinkies
    but will eventually switch over to them.

lizards, 21 species of snakes, and ten species of mice, as well as other items. Even hatchlings and juveniles are voracious eaters and seem to be very fond of lizards (primarily anoles and small skinks) and tree frogs, *Hyla* sp. Pinkies (and mice for the adult snakes), of course, are better for the snakes and the keepers because of their availability and absence of parasites (usually), but they are often refused by young racers. If some of your young racers must have lizards, frogs, or other snakes, try frozen and thawed items first, and if that doesn't work use live ones temporarily. Soon you will be able to switch to dead lizards or frogs. Tree frog-scented pinkies or lizard-scented pinkies are ideal for hatchlings, and we have used this trick regularly. They may also take fish (bait shop minnows and pet store goldfish have been consumed by many captive racers). Contrary to popular belief, a baby started on lizards, frogs, or fish can be switched to plain unscented pinkies and eventually mice using one of the tricks mentioned in the feeding section or just plain old persistence (many snakes change their food preferences with age or size).

Racers raised from hatchlings can be surprisingly calm in captivity and will often take food readily from your hand. Some of them even seem comfortable with frequent handling, but the decision to handle should be made on an individual basis with consideration given to the time of year (breeding season, laying season, or brumation time) and the proximity to shedding or feeding.

These snakes will probably survive 10–20 years in captivity, although longevity records are few. We maintained one adult female for 3 years in captivity, and since it was a large adult when captured, we suspect it must have been at least 6 years old when released.

Coniophanes imperialis
Black-striped Snake

The black-striped snake is a relatively small (31–51 cm, 12–20 inches), secretive, rear-fanged snake. It is beautifully marked with a tan-gold background color, three jet black to purplish black stripes dorsally, and a pinkish salmon to orange belly. They reportedly wave their brightly colored tails in the air when threatened, which Tennant (1985) suggested was a threatening gesture. However, on the basis of the number of specimens observed with incomplete tails, and the observation by Brown (1937) in Wright and Wright (1957) that their tails "seem to break off easily," we believe they use their tails as a lure, which when grasped will occupy a predator's attention long enough for them to make their escape. This behavior is similar to that of many lizards, even though one researcher has shown this not to be the case for other species (Gelbach, 1981). The head appears somewhat flattened with a square jaw and is very distinctly marked with light-colored eye stripes.

They range from extreme southern Texas, primarily in Cameron and Hidalgo counties, southward through Mexico into Guatemala.

The preferred habitat of the black-striped snake has not been well characterized in the literature to date, but it appears to prefer low areas with lush vegetation and heavy ground cover. They are nocturnal or crepuscular (dawn and dusk active) foragers that definitely have a

Coniophanes imperialis

broad diet, including small frogs and toads, small lizards, snakes, and young mice (Wright and Wright, 1957; Tennant, 1984, 1985; Conant and Collins, 1991). Tennant (1984) reported that the Rio Grande chirping frog, *Syrrhophus cystignathoides*, is an especially favored food item.

Predators of the black-striped snake are believed to include domestic cats and dogs, skunks, raccoons, birds such as crows, shrikes, and jays, as well as ophiophagous snakes such as kingsnakes and coral snakes.

The black-striped snake is a rear-fanged snake that possesses a venom capable of causing a mild reaction at the site of the bite, on those rare occasions when it does bite. The bite apparently feels like a bee sting and is associated with some swelling and possibly some increased bleeding from the bite wound, since the snake's venom possesses an anticoagulant (Brown 1939; Tennant, 1984).

Captive care is relatively simple, with the basic cage setup working excellently. A 10-gallon aquarium is a suitably sized enclosure for just about any member of this species, as they rarely exceed 46 cm (18 inches) TL. These secretive snakes will spend almost all of their time hidden in their hide boxes during the day, emerging at night to hunt, drink, shed, etc.

As mentioned above, they are not dietary specialists, with just about anything they can swallow becoming a part of their diet. They will consume small frogs and toads, lizards, snakes, and mammals in captivity, but of course, young mice (which may be scented with a small frog the first few times if necessary) are the preferred food for the keeper, since they are easier to obtain and are parasite-free. Parasites are a major problem for wild-caught members of this species, with as many as 3–4 different kinds of intestinal worms found in some individuals. Thus, an initial fecal exam and deworming, with subsequent exams and dewormings, are strongly recommended. Interestingly, one recently captured juvenile, fed nothing but captive-born pinkies during its stay in captivity, had negative fecal exams for 3 months and then tested positive for stomach worms (spiurids), rhabditiform larvae, and coccidia. Fenbendazole at a dose of 50 mg/kg repeated 2 weeks later was safely used to treat this snake. The coccidia was not treated.

A short period of slightly cooler temperatures is strongly recommended for this snake in order to facilitate breeding. Maintaining them at 13–18°C (55–65°F) for 1–3 months will probably suffice for breeding purposes but this is unknown. We have successfully brumated

Tamaulipan Black-striped Snake, *Coniophanes imperialis imperialis* (photo by David G. Campbell)

SPECIES: *Coniophanes imperialis*, Black-striped Snake
MAINTENANCE DIFFICULTY INDEX: 2 (1 = easiest, 5 = most difficult)
AVERAGE SIZE: 31–50 cm (12–20 inches)
FOOD: Small frogs and toads, small lizards, snakes, small mice
CAGE SIZE: 10-gallon aquarium
SUBSTRATE: Indoor-outdoor carpet, artificial turf, or newspaper
VENTRAL HEAT: Yes
UV LIGHT: No
TEMPERATURE RANGE: 25–30°C (77–80°F)
SPECIAL CONSIDERATIONS: Very likely to be parasitized. Are prone to dysecdysis
   (difficult shedding) in winter.

members of this species for 4–5 months at air temperatures fluctuating from 3 to 18°C (39 to 65°F). Like most other tropical snakes, however, a ventral heat source is advisable during this time and was available to ours. One of the problems we have experienced with these snakes during brumation is dysecdysis (difficult shedding). This is related to low humidity at this time and may be corrected by using a humidity box. Once it occurs, it may be treated by soaking the snake in a wet pillowcase for 30–60 minutes and then manually removing the softened skin. Interestingly, snakes manipulated in this manner have never offered to bite either of us.

The black-striped snake is an egg layer, usually laying 3–5 (maximum of 10) eggs in May or June (Wright and Wright, 1957; Fitch, 1970; Tennant, 1984, 1985). The incubation period has been reported at about 40 days (Fitch, 1970), but techniques of incubation and the incubation temperature were not reported. The time from mating to egg laying (gestation) is also unknown. As a subtropical snake, it is quite possible that this species does not follow the typical spring breeding pattern but may instead mate in winter, very early spring, or even the previous fall, but this is unknown. Other members of this genus are known to have breeding seasons that coincide with the rainy season and reach sexual maturity at 2–3 years of age (Zug et al., 1979).

On 16 May, a pair of *C. i. imperialis* was collected under a board in a suburban area of Brownsville, Texas, after a heavy rain. The pair was separated soon afterward and they were housed in separate enclosures. The female shed on 8 June, and laid 3 smooth slightly adherent eggs on 23 June. This would suggest a gestation period of at least 37 days. The eggs were laid in pine bark mulch instead of the very moist sphagnum moss present in an egg-laying box.

These 3 eggs measured 3 cm, 3.25 cm, and 3.25 cm (1.2, 1.3, and 1.3 inches) in length × 1 cm (0.4 inches) in width. The average weight of these eggs was 1.3 grams, with the clutch having a total weight of 4 grams. The female weighed 11 grams immediately after laying, which represented a maternal investment of 26% of her body weight. The female measured 40.64 cm (16 inches) TL and 29.2 cm (11.5 inches) SVL.

At incubation temperatures ranging from 25 to 30°c (77 to 86°F), the eggs hatched on 15 August, an incubation period of 53 days. The neonates were colored similarly to the adults, except that they were much paler. All 3 neonates measured 15.24 cm (6 inches) TL and 9.9 cm (4.5 inches) SVL. There was no sexual dimorphism in the length of the tails, however the one male did have a markedly thicker tail than either female, and this could be double-checked using the "popping" technique.

It was interesting to note that the babies displayed the characteristic "tail waving" display seen in the adults of the species, and they all had remarkably long tails relative to the length of their body. The neonates weighed 1.3 grams each.

The 3 neonates mentioned above refused

pinkies initially, instead preferring greenhouse frogs *Eleutherodactylus planirostris*. They would also consume small leopard frogs, *Rana utricularia*. One consumed a small Mediterranean gecko, *Hemidactylus turcicus*. Scented pinky parts and small pinkies would eventually be consumed, and soon afterward, plain pinkies.

The following year, the adults were brumated together from November until April in an air-conditioned room with temperatures ranging from 3.3 to 15°C (38 to 60°F). The female laid 2 fertile eggs on 7 June and these eggs were incubated in a manner similar to those above. One of the eggs shriveled in midincubation. The other hatched on 26 July, an incubation period of 49 days. The neonate measured 15.24 cm (6 inches) TL and 9.9 cm (4.5 inches) SVL. It weighed approximately 1.2 grams.

Within 24 hours of this egg hatching, the female laid another clutch of 3 eggs. The clutch weighed 7 grams, and the eggs measured 3.5, 3.5, and 3.8 cm (1.4, 1.4, and 1.5 inches) in length and approximately 1 cm (0.4 inches) in width. They had not yet hatched at the time of this writing. Of course, this raises several questions. Do well-fed captive black-striped snakes double clutch as do so many other colubrids, even though they might not do so in the wild? Or is this semitropical snake following the tropical pattern of reproducing throughout the year, as do many tropical snakes? Only time and further observation will tell.

Because they have a very restricted range within the United States and are limited to the very southern tip of Texas, they are protected and cannot be legally possessed without a permit. This is somewhat unfortunate since they are extremely adaptable snakes that do well in captivity and are probably easily bred. Still, this is unknown.

On the bright side, they do fairly well around human habitation and may not be as negatively affected as other species that are less well adapted to survive in disturbed habitats.

It is attractive enough and easy enough to care for that it might even become popular with professional and amateur snake breeders, thus enhancing its survival into the next century.

There are no listings for captive longevity in the recent literature; however, Wright and Wright (1957) quoted Brown (1937) as stating that several specimens "lived in captivity over 12 months." We maintained one male for 5 years and 8 months.

The keeper would be well advised not to grasp the tail of these snakes when moving them. More than one herpetologist has been surprised by the readily dropped tail. However, Gus Rentfro of Brownsville, Texas, regularly picks these snakes up by the tail and they usually do not break. Perhaps tail release requires a little more force than casual handling of a specimen. A frightened wild snake being grasped forcefully by the tail may well lose it.

The authors are indebted to Gus Rentfro for his assistance in acquiring the specimens above and a number of other snakes from southern Texas. He has published a number of articles on the snakes of southern Texas, and is a wealth of knowledge on these animals. We would also like to thank the Texas Parks and Wildlife Department for granting us a permit to conduct this research.

Contia tenuis
Sharptail Snake

The sharptail snake is in the minority. It is one of the few species of snakes in the United States whose range may be expanding due to the activities of man (Shaw and Campbell, 1974). One of these activities was to introduce a species of slug, *Arion* sp., which has become a favored food item. As the slug spreads, occupying areas around human habitation, so does this secretive little snake.

As one might expect from an animal specialized to feed on slugs, the sharptail snake's preferred habitat is any moist area. These in-

Contia tenuis

gous snakes including kingsnakes, whipsnakes, and western terrestrial garter snakes.

Mating is believed to occur in late fall or early spring. This results in the production of 2–5 eggs in late June or early July (Nussbaum et al., 1983). Clutches of 8 and 9 eggs have been found but are believed to have been deposited by two or more females. These eggs hatch from late summer to October. Hatchlings measure 8.9–10.4 cm (3.5–4.1 inches) and weigh 0.4–0.6 gram (Nussbaum et al., 1983).

The sharptail ranges from central California northward through coastal Oregon, with several isolated populations in Washington and on Vancouver Island, B.C. This snake ranges 20–47.5 cm (8–19 inches) in length and is generally reddish brown dorsally. It usually possesses a black mask on the face and a faint, light-colored, longitudinal stripe along each side. The sharptail's ventral surface is uniquely and distinctly marked by black crossbars on a light background. And of course, it possesses a sharp spine at the tip of the tail from which it receives its common name. The spine is harmless to people, but may startle one unfamiliar with the tail-pushing behavior of these snakes into

clude open hardwood or coniferous forests or fields and many habitats in between, anywhere moist soil may be found up to 1700 meters of elevation (Wright and Wright, 1957; Stebbins, 1985; Nussbaum et al., 1983). Within these areas, they usually seek the cover of a log or rock (Basey, 1976).

Known predators of sharptail snakes include Steller's jays and other birds (Basey, 1976). Suspected predators include domestic cats and dogs, weasels, skunks, badgers, and ophiopha-

Sharptail Snake, *Contia tenuis* (photo by Patrick Briggs)

SPECIES: *Contia tenuis*, Sharptail Snake
MAINTENANCE DIFFICULTY INDEX: 4 (1 = easiest, 5 = most difficult)
AVERAGE SIZE: 20–47.5 cm (8–19 inches)
FOOD: Slugs
CAGE SIZE: 10-gallon aquarium
SUBSTRATE: Cypress mulch or pine mulch on one side and soil on the other
VENTRAL HEAT: No, but heat from above, but do not overdo it. Hot rock would not hurt.
UV LIGHT: No, but an incandescent bulb is useful
TEMPERATURE RANGE: 11–26°C (52–79°F)
SPECIAL CONSIDERATIONS: Diet of slugs is often difficult to procure. Moist retreats and
    cooler temperatures are necessary. Some eat earthworms.

thinking they have been bitten, thereby resulting in the snake being dropped. Perhaps this has saved numbers of these snakes from other predatory animals and this may be the primary function of their sharp tail. Another proposed function of the spine is to anchor this snake when it is struggling with a prey slug (Basey, 1976).

These snakes will generally do very well in captivity in the wet/dry cage. Numerous hiding areas on both the wet and dry sides are advisable for this secretive snake. A 10-gallon aquarium is a suitable enclosure for even the largest member of this species. Ultraviolet lighting is probably not necessary but this is not known at this time. Ventral heat is probably not indicated for this species, but a hot rock over the substrate or an incandescent bulb (25 watts) may be a satisfactory source of dorsal heat. (Remember that fossorial snakes probably come to the surface to warm up and burrow to cool off or reach more moisture.)

It is important to note that this snake is active at very low temperatures (much like the rubber boa). Shaw and Campbell (1974) reported cloacal temperatures from a number of these snakes active in the wild ranging from 11 to 26°C (52 to 61°F). Some of these snakes had recently eaten. This temperature range may not be the preferred optimum temperature range, but it may be close, and temperatures much above room temperature may be detrimental to these snakes. With this in mind, air temperatures of 11–16°C (52–79°F) are probably suitable for these snakes in captivity, although we have

exposed them to temperatures ranging upward of 32°C (90°F) without any apparent ill effects.

As mentioned above, the preferred food of this species is slugs. A number of different types may be taken, even though the introduced European species, *Arion* sp., is considered the favorite. Fortunately, slugs can be bred in captivity (Frye, 1991). They may be added to the moist side of the cage twice weekly in order to allow the snake to feed free choice. We have had limited success offering earthworms to the snakes in our care, with one female eating only earthworms for nearly 1 year. Some may consume other invertebrates (e.g., *Bipalium* sp.).

The use of slugs as food for these snakes is not without some time-consuming drawbacks. Live slugs leave slime trails over the substrate, which may appear quite grimy if not cleaned occasionally. The actual swallowing process itself is very unusual indeed. Upon approaching a slug, these snakes very slowly (as if they were trying not to disturb the slug) open their mouths, grasp the slug, and then literally appear to suck the slug down their throats. During the swallowing process, the average slug barely moves, much less struggles with a sharptail snake, which leads one to believe that the main function of the sharptail's spine is not for use as an anchor, but rather for defense, as suggested above. In fact, there is so little of a struggle that a keeper must look carefully to make sure the snake is actually eating. The slug appears to almost cooperate in the whole process!

Even though they appear quite gregarious in nature, with many of these snakes being found in one area, we would advise housing them singly in order to avoid competition for food in a small enclosure.

Brumation is strongly advisable for this species in captivity and may be accomplished in the regular cage setup, since no modifications will be necessary. Make sure to provide high humidity retreats (like humidity boxes) at this time in order to avoid dehydration if the soil side (wet side) of the cage is not partially covered to retain some moisture. Good ventilation in all of these cages is absolutely essential. Those in our care have successfully withstood fluctuations ranging from 3 to 18°C (38 to 65°F) for 4–5 months. Since this species is so cold-adapted, however, they probably could withstand (and benefit by) 3–4 months at 3–7°C (38–45°F).

Captive reproduction is rare, probably mostly due to a lack of interest. In nature, mating occurs primarily in the spring, with 2–5 eggs being laid in the summer, which hatch approximately 2 months later. The babies prefer baby slugs (not surprisingly) and may be housed exactly as the adults.

There are no records for captive longevity of this species published. One in our care survived over 1 year when it died of intestinal parasitism (*Strongyloides*). In fact, Slavens and Slavens (1990, 1991) did not list a single captive specimen anywhere in the United States or Canada.

Recently, Richard Hoyer, a well-known herpetologist from Oregon, has noticed that there are two different "kinds" of sharptail snakes.

After studying scores of specimens preserved in collections as well as live specimens, he is certain that these represent two different species. While the description is not yet published, he has proposed that the new species, while outwardly similar in appearance to *C. tenuis*, has a distinctly longer tail, with a larger number of subcaudal scales. These scale counts do not overlap. This long tailed species (or subspecies?) seems to be more common in damp forested regions. Therefore, he has proposed the common name of forest sharptail, and expects to propose the scientific name *Contia longicauda*. This snake not only eats slugs, but also eats slender salamanders *Batrachoseps* sp. This "new" species ranges from Santa Clara County, California northward into three counties in southwestern Oregon: Curry, Coos, and Douglas Counties. He describes the distribution as a narrow coastal strip. He also stated that the two species overlap in several areas such as Sonoma County and Santa Clara County. Hoyer has maintained one of these forest sharptail snakes for 2 years and 2 months in captivity, and this female is still alive at the time of this writing. The official description has not yet been published, so this "species" has not yet been accepted by the scientific community. However, we felt we should include it since Mr. Hoyer has amassed a great deal of data supporting its existence. We would like to commend Mr. Hoyer for his careful observations on both this species and the rubber boa. He has been a major contributor to our understanding of northwestern snakes.

Diadophis punctatus
Ringneck Snake

Like the racer, the ringneck is a common and wide-ranging species, with a large number of subspecies. These subspecies (12 within the United States and Canada) vary tremendously in their size, color, activity patterns, habitats, and diet. Therefore, it is once again nearly impossible to generalize on the diet and temperature preferences of this adaptable little snake. Indeed, how can we generalize about the

food or thermal preferences of an animal that ranges from the northern mountains, forests, and plains through the southern swamps and deserts? Yet, we must briefly examine some of the natural history of this intensively studied snake in order to gain some idea of what may be required in captivity. Certainly, the common kingsnake and the milk snake have extensive ranges, yet the majority of subspecies are cared

Diadophis punctatus

for much the same, taking into account some variations in thermal preferences, reproductive parameters, and diet.

The ringneck snake receives its name from the ring around the neck, a very distinctive trait among North American snakes. Only the redbelly snake and the sharptail snake may be confused with this species over parts of its range, and they are fairly easy to distinguish from the ringneck upon closer examination. The ringneck has smooth scales, which readily distinguishes it from the redbelly, while the sharptail has the characteristic spine from which it receives its name. Some ringnecks do lack a distinct neck ring, but they are still fairly easily recognizable with a good field guide in hand.

The ringneck is a relatively small (20–84 cm or 8–33 inches) slender snake with a slate gray to olive brown dorsal color and yellow or orange belly. Melanistic (uniformly dark) individuals have also been observed. Its range is a huge geographic area that extends from southern Quebec and Ontario southward to Florida and westward to California, Oregon, and Washington, but excluding much of the western plains area. In general, it is secretive in nature and prefers moist areas with some cover, which includes such varied habitats as forests, fields, farms, and swamps. These moist areas are necessary to help it avoid desiccation (Clark,

1967). In Kansas, the preferred habitat of this species appears to be the forest grassland interface, where estimates of over 1000 per hectare have been made (Fitch, 1999). The snakes in this study had body temperatures of 25–29°C (77–84°F).

The 12 subspecies include the Key ringneck snake, *D. p. acricus*, the Pacific ringneck snake, *D. p. amabilus*, the prairie ringneck snake, *D. p. arnyi*, the northern ringneck snake, *D. p. edwardsii*, the San Bernardino ringneck snake, *D. p. modestus*, the northwestern ringneck snake, *D. p. occidentalis*, the coralbelly ringneck snake, *D. p. pulchellus*, the southern ringneck snake, *D. p. punctatus*, the regal ringneck snake, *D. p. regalis*, the San Diego ringneck snake, *D. p. similis*, the Mississippi ringneck snake, *D. p. stictogenys*, and the Monterey ringneck snake, *D. p. vandenburgii* (Collins, 1997). The ranges and detailed descriptions of each subspecies may be found in Ernst and Barbour (1989) and Conant and Collins (1991).

The diet of this species is very catholic (broad), although some populations seem to have strong preferences for one item or another. Western subspecies seem to have a preference for lizards and snakes while those in the central plains and eastern woodlands prefer worms and salamanders (Gehlbach, 1974; Henderson, 1970; Fitch, 1975; Ernst and Barbour, 1989; Rossi, 1992). The diet of this species has included earthworms, including an introduced species (Fitch, 1975), salamanders and their eggs, small frogs, including treefrogs and their tadpoles, slugs, insects, lizards, and snakes (Stebbins, 1985; Ernst and Barbour, 1989; Christiansen and Bailey, 1990). More specifically, western ringnecks have been reported to consume small snakes such as Chihuahuan blackhead snakes, *Tantilla wilcoxi* (Van Denburgh, 1922), earth snakes, *Virginia*, ground snakes, *Sonora* (Gelbach, 1974), and hatchling snakes (Tennant, 1985), small glass lizards, *Ophisaurus attenuatus* (Fitch, 1975), night snakes, *Hypsiglena torquata* (Babb, pers. comm., 1993), "small lizards" (Wright and Wright, 1957; Basey, 1976; Stebbins, 1985), treefrogs and their tadpoles (Van Denburgh, 1922; Wright and Wright, 1957; Basey, 1976; Stebbins, 1985; Hudson, 1985), salamanders such as slender salaman-

Northern Ringneck Snake, *Diadophis punctatus edwardsi* (photo by David G. Campbell)

ders, *Batrachoseps*, and others (Wright and Wright, 1957; Basey, 1976; Stebbins, 1985), insects (Wright and Wright, 1957; Fitch, 1975; Basey, 1976; Stebbins, 1985), and earthworms. Fitch (1975) found that an introduced European earthworm, *Allolobophora caliginosa*, was the preferred food of the prairie ringneck snake, *D. p. arnyi*, in Kansas and thought that the worm's introduction may have been largely responsible for a population explosion of ringnecks there. Tennant (1985) believes that Texas populations of the same subspecies and also the regal ringneck, *D. p. regalis*, feed almost exclusively on reptiles, particularly snakes. McKeown (pers. comm., 1992) stated that the majority of ringneck snakes in California seem to prefer slender salamanders, *Batrachoseps* sp., and will also take Pacific treefrogs, *Hyla* (= *Pseudacris*) *regilla*, tadpoles and subadults. They generally refuse earthworms, even though they will take smaller snakes. One Monterey ringneck, *D. p. vandenburgii*, in our care consistently refused to eat earthworms.

On the basis of the work of Henderson (1970) and his own observations, Fitch (1970) suggested that the average prairie ringneck snake will eat a worm every 8 days on the average or approximately 27 worms during a normal growing season.

Moving from preferred diet to preferred environmental factors, we must again offer the same warning. It is difficult or impossible to generalize about such a widespread variable species. However, in order to provide some information that may be used to assist the herpetoculturist, we have summarized some of the research here. Fitch (1975) determined that body temperatures of wild prairie ringnecks under cover averaged 26.1°C (79°F), while those out in the open averaged 26.6°C (80°F). The highest body temperature recorded was 34.4°C (94°F), and this was in a gravid female. Thus, behavioral temperature control (behavioral thermoregulation) appeared very precise.

As mentioned above, the ringneck generally prefers a habitat with moist soils. Clark (1968) studied the soil moisture preferences of this same subspecies and determined that these snakes prefer not to burrow, but rather remain active on the surface (under cover) over soil with an average soil moisture of 22%. Interestingly, Clark's study also revealed that these captive ringnecks chose temperatures of 21.2–31.1°C (70–88°F) with an average temperature of 26.5°C (79.7°F), which is remarkably similar to the body temperature of wild specimens.

Known predators of this species include coral snakes, copperheads, racers, kingsnakes, milksnakes, trout, bullfrogs, hawks, owls, and small mammals. A carabid beetle was observed to attack a ringneck (Barber, in Myers, 1965). On a roadside in Pasco County, Florida, we observed a boat-tailed grackle pick one up in its beak and fly off with it.

Mating season is generally in the spring, although mating may occur in the fall. This results in clutches of 1–10 eggs in June or July that hatch in 46–60 days, although there have been several cases reported of females bearing live young in captivity (Peterson, 1956). Females in the south may lay 2 clutches per year. One southern ringneck in our care laid 4 eggs on 17 June, 3 of which hatched on 24 July, an incubation period of 35 days.

The hatchlings mentioned above all measured 11 cm (4.3 inches) in length and were darker than the adults. Young are 9–13.5 cm (3.5–5.3 inches) in length at hatching and will grow rapidly to reach sexual maturity in 2 or 3 years. In Kansas, females reached sexual maturity at about 23 cm (by their third year) and lay clutches with an average size of 3.9 (Fitch, 1999). Clutch sizes did vary depending upon food supply. Fitch showed that these small snakes had no definite homes but tended to wander 1–3 meters per day during the active part of the year.

This species is not difficult to maintain in captivity, although some individuals can be very fastidious, refusing to eat for months. Their diet in captivity consists of worms (preferably), small salamanders, lizards, or snakes. Be aware that cannibalism is very likely with this species (Fitch, 1975; Mitchell, 1986) as are fights (over food?), so they should probably be housed singly, even if they appear gregarious.

As mentioned above, some individuals have a marked preference for one item or another, with worms or salamanders being the most popular for snakes from central and eastern populations, while slender salamanders, treefrog tadpoles and subadults, as well as small snakes are preferred by western populations. As might be expected, the salamander lovers can often be tricked into taking earthworms that have been rubbed with a salamander or salamander tail.

One large regal ringneck snake in the care of Randy Babb, a biologist with the Arizona Game and Fish Department, survived on pinkies for over 2 years and is still alive at the time of this writing. The snake was trained to

Southern Ringneck Snake, *Diadophis punctatus punctatus* (photo by David G. Campbell)

SPECIES: *Diadophis punctatus*, Ringneck Snake
MAINTENANCE DIFFICULTY INDEX: 2–5 (1 = easiest, 5 = most difficult)
AVERAGE SIZE: 20–84 cm (8–33 inches)
FOOD: Earthworms, salamanders and their eggs, small frogs, tadpoles, slugs, insects, lizards, snakes
CAGE SIZE: 10–20-gallon long aquarium
SUBSTRATE: Peatmoss-potting soil mixture upon which bark strips have been laid
VENTRAL HEAT: No, but heat from above, and do not overdo it. Hot rock would not hurt.
UV LIGHT: No, but an incandescent bulb is useful
TEMPERATURE RANGE: 18–32°C (65–90°F)
SPECIAL CONSIDERATIONS: Tremendous variation in size and food preferences from population to population. House singly. Cannibalistic.

accept pinkies by scenting them with a night snake that had been vomited by this snake soon after its capture. After scenting for some time, this snake began consuming plain unscented pinkies. Interestingly, Babb reported this did not result in an extremely obese snake.

A 10–20-gallon aquarium is a suitably sized enclosure for most members of this species. Once again, house singly to avoid feeding time battles and cannibalism and to make record keeping easier.

The substrate of choice is a peat moss-potting soil mixture on which bark strips or flat stones are laid in order to form surface refuges. The substrate should be no deeper than one-quarter the length of the snake but 2.5–5 cm (1–2 inches) deep is satisfactory for most snakes. It should be misted occasionally. Change the substrate every 5–6 months. The wet/dry cage setup will also work fairly well as long as there is some kind of cover over part of the wet side (i.e., glass, plastic, or a rock, piece of wood, or a water bowl). A moderately sized shallow water bowl is well used by these snakes.

Remember that with a moist substrate, good ventilation is absolutely critical for successful maintenance. Therefore, a screen top is advisable.

A branch and some small plastic plants are both aesthetic and practical as these little snakes will often climb and bask. This is one species that does very well with potted plants as it is not large enough to damage them and can be maintained in a very natural terrarium.

Ventral heat is not considered necessary or appropriate for this species. Remember this is a secretive, surface-burrowing snake that is used to getting its heat from above, so an incandescent bulb above one side of the cage is advisable. This bulb will provide the thermal gradient necessary for the precise temperature regulation discussed above, even though acceptable air temperatures in the terrarium may range from 18 to 32°C (65 to 90°F), for most subspecies. McKeown warns that Pacific ringnecks prefer cooler temperatures, however, and Trutnau (1981) reports that a daytime temperature range of 22–26°C (72–79°F) worked well for those in his care.

Brumation is strongly advisable for ringnecks and may be accomplished in their regular cage, provided it is set up as described above. Four months at temperatures of 6–10°C (43–50°F) has been recommended by Trutnau, but temperatures down to 3°C (38°F) are well tolerated by some ringnecks (Fitch, 1975).

Mating has occurred in captivity when the snakes have been treated as mentioned in the breeding section of general care. The female will usually deposit 3–7 eggs (up to 10) somewhere in the substrate. Once again, the problem with small fossorial snakes appears to be finding the eggs before they are damaged. The incubation time is relatively short (usually less than 50 days in captivity) and the young snakes are ready to eat almost immediately. They may be offered tubifex worms (obtainable at your local pet shop), very small earthworms, or very small salamanders. They do not seem to like dead prey (nor do the adults).

A specimen at the Jacksonville Museum of Science and History was maintained as described above for 4 years. Snider and Bowler (1992) report that one of these snakes survived more than 6 years in captivity. Fitch (1999) estimated the age of one snake in his Kansas study site to be approximately 20 years old!

Don't handle ringnecks much as they appear to have a fairly nervous disposition. In fact, you may have to cover the cage or stay perfectly still during a feeding attempt. Misting the cage will stimulate surface activity and you may offer food at that time.

In addition, the nervous nature of these snakes may take its toll in another way. As mentioned for smooth earth snakes, *Virginia valeriae* (Rossi, 1992), handling females during their gestation may be detrimental to their health and to the young they may be carrying.

In the case of the smooth earth snake, handling may result in the premature delivery of young. In the case of the ringneck snake and possibly the worm snake, *Carphophis*, handling or confinement just prior to egg laying may bring about the premature deposition of unshelled eggs. Fitch (1975) observed this in the ringnecks he studied, while Clark (1970) noticed this in the worm snakes in his care. This premature egg deposition has also been observed in other secretive snakes that are quite different from those mentioned here. Ross and Marzec (1990) mention that ball pythons captured and shipped during gestation are also likely to deposit thin-shelled premature eggs that usually fail to hatch. Cowan (1980) suggested that stress could result in a rapid release of steroids in reptiles, just as happens in mammals and birds. Could these very secretive snakes, when stressed, secrete even higher levels of steroids resulting in premature delivery, much as might happen in a mammal?

Drymarchon couperi and *Drymarchon corais erebennus*
Eastern and Texas Indigo Snakes

Glossy iridescents black snake, the indigo snakes are the largest nonvenomous serpents in the United States and Canada. The iridescent bluish black color gives them their common name. These snakes are also distinguished from large black racers and black rat snakes by the red markings on the chin and side of the face in some specimens.

As mentioned above, these are large snakes in length 152–213 cm (60–84 inches) with a record of 263 cm (103.5 inches) (Conant and Collins, 1991). The Texas indigo ranges 152–198 cm (60–70 inches) in length according to Conant and Collins (1991). However, Vermersch and Kuntz (1986) reported a record length specimen of 287 cm (113 inches = 9 feet 5 inches!). Heavy-bodied powerful snakes, they usually overpower their prey using a strong bite and a body coil rather than by constricting it as do so many other snakes.

The geographical range of the eastern spe-

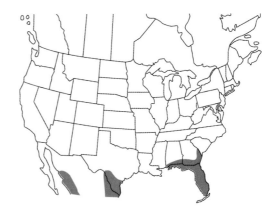

Drymarchon corais

cies includes all of Florida, southern Georgia, and historically, southern Alabama, with small populations in extreme southeastern South Carolina and introduced populations in extreme southeastern Mississippi. The Texas species is found only in southern Texas and adjacent

Eastern Indigo Snake, *Drymarchon couperi* (photo by David G. Campbell)

Mexico. The preferred habitat of the eastern indigo is high and dry areas near water, especially areas dominated by pine and oak. Not surprisingly, the Texas indigo occurs most frequently in the thorn woodland near water (Tennant, 1984).

These snakes are not specialized feeders. They have been reported to feed on a wide variety of prey items including fish, amphibians (including toads), and reptiles (small turtles, glass lizards, numerous snakes, including venomous snakes, and reptile eggs) (Carson, 1945; Wright and Wright, 1957; Mount, 1975; Ashton and Ashton, 1981; Ernst and Barbour, 1989). We observed a dead on road (DOR) indigo in Marion County, Florida, whose head was approximately 2 cm from a dead glass lizard. We suspect that the snake had been chasing the lizard onto the road when both were killed. Juvenile eastern indigos have also been observed to consume large slugs (Rossi and Lewis, 1994).

Werler and Dixon (2000) also reported a wide variety of food items for the Texas indigo, including snapping turtles, hatchling Texas tortoises, Mexican burrowing toads, and rattlesnakes. They also seem especially fond of bird eggs.

Small indigo snakes are probably preyed upon by ophiophagous snakes, birds of prey, and predatory mammals. Neill (in Moulis,

1976) reported an alligator feeding on an adult. Young indigos are believed to occupy a different habitat from adults (along stream banks) in order to avoid being preyed upon by them.

Mating is believed to occur primarily in the winter and early spring over much of these snakes' range. This results in the deposition of 3–12 large, rough-surfaced, nonadherent eggs. The rough surface comes from calcified "patches" similar to those seen in racer and whipsnake eggs. The eggs vary considerably in size, but are usually 5.0–10.0 cm (2–4 inches) in length and 2.7–5.0 cm (1.1–2 inches) in width. These eggs hatch in 73–102 days (Ernst and Barbour, 1989) and the speckled hatchlings measure 34–61 cm (13.4–24 inches) in length (Ernst and Barbour, 1989; Conant and Collins, 1991).

Breeding of the eastern indigo snake has been described in some detail by O'Connor (1991). He successfully bred this snake five times in a row using a technique originally described by Laslow (1979, 1983) in which the animals are exposed to an average nighttime low temperature of 16°C (60°F) with a 1:2 light to dark photoperiod. The snakes still receive heat from above in the form of an incandescent bulb (75-watt) during a brief 8-hour period every day. This technique resulted in breeding between October and February with eggs being produced in May. Hence, the gestation period reported by O'Connor varied from 126 to 176 days. These eggs, measuring 6.4 × 4.6 cm (2.5 × 1.8 inches), hatched in 71–103 days at temperatures ranging from 24 to 28.9°C (76–84°F). O'Connor recommended an incubation temperature of 27.8–28.9°C (82 to 84°F) as temperatures below this were associated with the longer incubation periods and temperatures 4 or 5 degrees above this may be associated with deformities or premature hatching. One of O'Connor's fascinating discoveries was the production of a postcopulatory plug, which is released approximately 6 weeks after the first mating of the year. Keepers may look for this plug as an indication that successful mating has occurred, and gain some idea of when by finding this plug in the cage.

O'Connor also observed high infertility or high full-term egg mortality with one of his females. The cause of this problem was not discussed in his article, but it appears that this is a major problem for many who attempt to breed indigo snakes, since Mattison (1988) also commented on this problem, as have others in our conversations with them. At this time we do not know why this occurs, but as Mattison noted, UV lights and vitamin supplementation of these snakes may help. However, O'Connor's observations may have narrowed down

the problem to the female snakes in this particular instance, since the same male—when mated with another female treated in the same manner—produced high percentages of fertile eggs every time. Did this female have a parasitic, fungal, or bacterial infection that interfered with the normal development of the eggs? Or was she simply more closely related to the male in question? Certainly, we have seen a female Texas indigo snake that had not produced viable eggs for over 10 years suddenly produce a viable clutch after she was treated for trematodes with several injections of praziquantel at the dose of 20 mg/kg IM.

It is unfortunate that in Florida and Texas, where light cycles, light intensity, and temperature ranges would be ideal for captive breeding, permits to maintain indigos are very difficult to obtain. Herpetoculturists in these areas would be able to contribute greatly to our knowledge if they were allowed to participate in captive breeding efforts. And in states where massive habitat destruction leaves hundreds or thousands of these snakes homeless every year, it only makes sense to allow captive breeding. The argument given by the state authorities is that permittees would go out into the wild and replace any legal captives which they might lose with wild-caught snakes. This is becoming

Texas Indigo Snake, *Drymarchon corais erebennus* (photo by David G. Campbell)

SPECIES: *Drymarchon couperi* and *D. corais erebennus*, Eastern and Texas Indigo Snakes
MAINTENANCE DIFFICULTY INDEX: 2 (1 = easiest, 5 = most difficult)
AVERAGE SIZE: 152–213 cm (60–84 inches)
FOOD: Mice, chicks, rats, frogs and toads, fish, snakes
CAGE SIZE: Display case (6–8′ long by 2′ wide) for adults. Ten-gallon aquarium for
   hatchlings.
SUBSTRATE: Artificial turf, indoor-outdoor carpet, or newspaper but cypress mulch is best
VENTRAL HEAT: Yes
UV LIGHT: Yes?
TEMPERATURE RANGE: 25–30°C (77–86°F); 15–20°C (59–68°F) hibernation (brumation)
SPECIAL CONSIDERATIONS: Must house singly or they will fight. Mates in winter or
   early spring. Sensitive to some medicines. Need a permit in most states. Messy!

---

less and less likely to happen as wild indigo snakes become harder and harder to find. Poaching is not a problem in Alabama because native populations are now considered virtually extinct (Mount, 1975). Indeed, once a marking system for these animals is approved allowing the recognition of individual snakes, captive breeding should be permitted, in our opinion. Recently, the state of Florida approved a captive breeding project.

Some individuals have commented that our support of captive breeding as an answer to the plight of this species' decline is naive. On the contrary, we believe that those who think that this species can be saved over most of its home range are naive. Certainly, preservation of these snakes in the wild will be the best possible outcome. However, this is very unlikely given the size of their home ranges and the rapid rate of land development (habitat destruction) in the state of Florida. Yes, these snakes may survive in the wild in parks and large preserves, but their survival elsewhere in the state through the next 3 decades is doubtful. Captive breeding efforts might ultimately result in many thousands of these snakes in captivity, which may be a major and extremely valuable resource for their survival in the future, both in captivity and in the wild.

While the indigo snakes (both species) are not difficult snakes to keep in captivity, they are very messy and require a great deal of work. Several suggestions for successful maintenance may be helpful. First, never keep two or more

indigos in the same cage. They will invariably fight, eventually if not immediately, and feeding time will rapidly become a disaster. They need good-sized cages as adults (see the Housing section), but you can start the hatchlings in small cages such as 10-gallon aquariums and work your way up. A heating pad under one side of the cage is absolutely essential, as is a hide box. Water bowls should be weighted or they will be knocked over or pushed around, and live plants should be avoided or they will be flattened. Artificial carpet/turf works well as a substrate for these species, but cypress mulch will also work well. Ultraviolet light sources are considered helpful for these species.

Most indigo snakes will eat readily in captivity, but there are exceptions. As with many other snakes, hatchlings often wait until after shedding before they begin eating, but they should be offered food and water almost immediately after hatching, just in case they are ready. They may refuse pinkies and take only minnows or small snakes at this time. Bait shop minnows are the most easily obtained and readily accepted food by neonates of both species. Always try pinkies first, but if you must use snakes, fish, or frogs, freeze them first. (See the section on feeding.) Eventually, the young snakes will take pinkies, then mice, chicks, and rats. Chicks are calcium-deficient, and the legs may present a problem to the young snake's digestive tract, causing an obstruction, so use them cautiously. Some keepers actually cut the legs off the pre-killed chicks before feeding in order to avoid this problem. Adult snakes recently captured (this shouldn't happen without a permit, by the way) may fast for long periods of time. Spadefoot toads, *Scaphiopus holbrooki*, are excellent appetizers to get an indigo to start feeding in captivity, but remember that they may be parasitized. (But then again so is a newly captured indigo.) Other food items listed by Ernst and Barbour that wild specimens are known to consume, and that might be worth trying on a recently captured adult, include lizards and small turtles, but turtles are to be avoided if at all possible. Road-killed juvenile rat snakes are also difficult for indigo snakes to resist.

Once they begin eating, one should expect shedding to occur frequently, up to once a month in the younger ones kept at the right temperature. Keep a close eye on these species at shedding time as they are prone to retaining their eye shields (spectacles) and tail tips. The Jacksonville Zoo prefers to keep indigos on cypress mulch misted frequently, as this high moisture substrate helps to avoid these problems. Humidity boxes are always advisable for indigos.

If all goes well, these snakes usually reach sexual maturity at 3 years of age. Mating usually occurs in winter or early spring. Attempt breeding as described in the general care section. Watch the snakes carefully. Biting is not thought to be a part of normal breeding activity, although nudging and light nipping

are. If breeding is successful, eggs are usually laid in May. Do not disturb the female during egg laying, or she may stop laying for a considerable length of time. The eggs should be set up in the usual manner around 27.7°C (82°F).

A pair of Texas indigos in our care mated in January and the female deposited 6 fertile (and 1 infertile) eggs on 11 April. The 6 fertile eggs averaged 6.42 × 2.63 cm (2.5 × 1.04 inches). The infertile egg measured 7 cm (2.75 inches) in length, but was only 1.5 cm (0.59 inches) in width. The 6 fertile eggs began hatching on 27 June, an incubation period of 76 days at temperatures fluctuating from 23.8 to 28.8°C (78 to 84°F). The speckled neonates ranged 33–38 cm (13–15 inches) in TL, an average of 36.6 cm (14.4 inches).

They are very likely to be parasitized. Flukes and roundworms are very common in wild-caught animals. Manual removal of visible flukes is advisable, along with the use of broad-spectrum deworming agents, such as fenbendazole at 100 mg/kg, repeated 3 times at 2-week intervals. Repeated fecal exams are also strongly advisable.

Remember that these snakes are very sensitive to some medications (like some kingsnakes) and will often require only half the dose that other species require. (See the drug chart in Table 7 and check with your veterinarian.)

One of these snakes survived nearly 26 years in captivity (Snider and Bowler, 1992).

Drymobius margaritiferus
Speckled Racer

The speckled racer is perhaps one of the rarest snakes in the United States, being found only in or near the few remaining old growth palm stands along the Rio Grande in the very southern tip of Texas. They are not very large snakes, with the average individual measuring 76–102 cm (30–40 inches) with a maximum 132 cm (52 inches), but they are rather attractively marked. The dorsal scales are black with blue bases and each has one yellow spot in its center.

The blue and yellow give this fast-moving snake a greenish appearance overall.

As mentioned above, one of the preferred habitats of the speckled racer in Texas is palm groves. These areas generally have a great deal of ground cover and are fairly moist. Hence, they are havens for a great deal of amphibian life, which forms the bulk of this snake's diet. Food items listed in the literature have included frogs and toads (Trutnau, 1981; Seib, 1984;

Drymobus margartiferus

Tennant, 1984, 1985; Mehrtens, 1987; Conant and Collins, 1991), lizards, mice, and birds (Trutnau, 1981; Seib, 1984; Mehrtens, 1987). They are active, fast-moving, visually oriented snakes, much like the racer, *Coluber constrictor*, although they appear largely crepuscular in southern Texas. Trutnau (1981) stated that these snakes were reputed to be nocturnal and his observations of captive specimens supported this.

The predators of this species are not well-known. Suspected predators include birds such as crows, jays, and hawks, and predatory mammals including opossums (which we have actually seen foraging in the vicinity of a speckled racer in south Texas), as well as raccoons, skunks, and small cats.

Mating is believed to occur in late winter to early spring in Texas. This results in the deposition of 7–8 adhesive smooth-shelled eggs from April to August.

The speckled racer will do fairly well in captivity if several things are taken into consideration. The first and most important thing to remember is that these snakes are tropical frog-eating animals that are usually loaded with parasites (Burchfield, pers. comm., 1992), much like many other frog-eating snakes. They must be dewormed immediately and checked for worms regularly thereafter. Aside from this, one should make every effort to control the parasite load by either feeding frozen and thawed frogs or switching the diet to mice as soon as possible. Captive snakes can usually be switched to small mice without too much difficulty using scent-transfer techniques. Mice are often taken immediately by captive specimens

Northern Speckled Racer, *Drymobius margaritiferus margaritiferus* (photo by David G. Campbell)

SPECIES: *Drymobius margaritiferus*, Speckled Racer
MAINTENANCE DIFFICULTY INDEX: 3 (1 = easiest, 5 = most difficult)
AVERAGE SIZE: 76–102 cm (30–40 inches)
FOOD: Frogs, toads, lizards, mice and birds
CAGE SIZE: 20–30-gallon long aquarium
SUBSTRATE: Artificial turf, indoor-outdoor carpet, or newspaper
VENTRAL HEAT: Yes
UV LIGHT: No, but an incandescent bulb is useful
TEMPERATURE RANGE: 25–30°C (77–86°F)
SPECIAL CONSIDERATIONS: Likely to be heavily parasitized. Sensitive to cold.

---

without any scenting at all (Ross, pers. comm., 1993); this is not surprising considering the work of Seib (1984) showing that these snakes were dietary generalists. Small chicks have also reportedly been taken by captives (Trutnau, 1981). If feeding prekilled, Mehrtens (1987) advises it may be necessary to move the food item in order to attract the snake's attention and elicit a strike.

Housing this species is not particularly difficult since they will usually do well in the basic cage arrangement discussed in the general care section. Artificial carpet/turf works excellently as the substrate, but cypress mulch will also work well. A stable hide box is strongly advisable for these nervous snakes and clean water should be available at all times. A stable branch and plastic plants will also help to reduce stress and will beautify the cage. A 20- or 30-gallon long aquarium is a suitable enclosure for this snake.

Ventral heat is strongly recommended for this tropical snake, as is an incandescent bulb over the cage that provides additional heat and light during the day. The air temperature should remain fairly constant at 25–30°C (77–86°F) during the day with slightly lower temperatures at night. A short period (2–3 months) of slightly cooler nighttime low temperatures (18–22°C or 65–72°F) during the winter may be beneficial for captive breeding purposes but this is unknown. Be aware that these snakes may be particularly sensitive to low humidity in heated indoor enclosures during the winter. Improper shedding and respiratory problems are likely sequelae.

Captive breeding of speckled racers has not been accomplished at the time of this writing. In fact, Slavens and Slavens (1990, 1991) listed no captive specimens at all. It is known that females will deposit clutches of 2–8 eggs from midspring to midsummer that will hatch in 50–60 days. It is important to note that the 50-day incubation period reported in Wright and Wright (1957), which has been frequently cited by other authors, resulted in the birth of 2 deformed babies that died several days later. These spinal deformities may have been the result of too high incubation temperatures, which may also have artificially shortened the incubation period to 50 days.

The young snakes range 15–28 cm (6–11 inches) in length (Conant and Collins, 1991) at hatching and will probably do best if fed frog-scented pinkies right from the start. One neonate in our care refused pinkies and lizards initially, but readily consumed small fish. This neonate had apparently fed several times before it was captured, since a fecal exam revealed both protozoan and metazoan parasites (rhabditiform larvae).

We were shocked and dismayed at the near total devastation of habitat in southern Texas. The habitat of this species was no exception. We believe this species illustrates well the necessity of captive breeding as a method of conservation. And yet, because it is a protected species, Slavens and Slavens (1991) could not list a single live specimen in captivity at the time of this writing. Are we really protecting the existence of the animals in the wild when we cannot protect the wild in which they exist? The answer is an undeniable "no." In our opinion, the Texas Department of Parks and Wildlife Department and many other Fish and Game Commissions around the United States and Canada need to start thinking seriously about legalizing the organized captive breeding of this and numerous other threatened or endangered animals before it is too late. This species is experiencing legislative extinction in the United States along with the indigo snake, montane rattlesnakes, cat-eyed snake, and a number of others. The fact that they are still plentiful in Mexico does not eliminate the responsibility for their preservation within the United States.

The purpose of captive breeding projects would be primarily to restock those areas of suitable habitat, either remaining or re-created, within the historic range of these species. Indeed, a species which exists only in captivity is biologically dead. Artificial selection and genetic drift will occur in captive populations, further reducing the likelihood for successful reintroduction as more time passes.

Snider and Bowler (1992) reported that one of these snakes survived more than 4 years and 4 months in captivity.

Elaphe bairdi
Baird's Rat Snake

Baird's rat snake, formerly considered to be a subspecies of *Elaphe obsoleta*, is a prime example of a captive breeding success story. This snake has a limited range in western and central Texas on the Edwards Plateau and does not appear extremely common within that range (Wright and Wright, 1957; Tennant, 1985; Mattison, 1988). But thanks to the efforts of many herpetoculturists and the fact that these snakes are relatively easy to care for, there are now thousands of them being maintained and bred in captivity, thereby reducing collecting pressures on wild populations.

A sparsely distributed resident of rocky canyons; Tennant (1985) describes these canyons as Cretaceous limestone canyons of the Edwards Plateau. . Baird's rat snake is a medium to large snake. Adults are usually 84–137 cm (33–54 inches) long with a record length of 157.5 cm (62 inches) reported (Conant and Collins, 1991). Wild members of this species have been known to consume a wide variety of foods including lizards, mice, rats, and birds and their eggs (Tennant, 1985). According to Tennant (1984), the natural diet of wild Baird's rat snakes is strongly oriented toward lizards, and includes tree lizards, *Urosaurus* sp., and crevice spiny lizards, *Sceloporus poinsetti*.

Suspected predators of this species include

Elaphe bairdi

predatory birds such as hawks and owls, carnivorous mammals (including skunks and coyotes), and ophiophagous snakes such as kingsnakes.

Mating generally occurs in April, May, and June, which results in the deposition of 3–14 eggs approximately 7 weeks later in midsummer (Brecke et al., 1976; Tennant, 1985; Mattison, 1988). These eggs hatch 62–83 days later, depending on the incubation temperatures into 28–40 cm (11–16 inch) long young (Tennant, 1985; Mattison, 1991). In the wild, sexual maturity is probably reached in 3 years.

These snakes will do very well in the basic

Baird's Rat Snake, *Elaphe bairdi* (photo by David G. Campbell)

(ideal) cage setup discussed in the general care section. This includes the standard cage amenities such as a hide box, water bowl, and proper substrate (artificial carpet/turf or newspaper). Rocks, plastic plants, and a branch are also nice options. Many of these snakes have done well with far less, however, and a number of breeders maintain them in drawer-style enclosures or large plastic boxes.

Ventral heat is a good idea for long-term maintenance, although many specimens seem to do fine without it. A heat lamp above is almost considered optional for this nocturnal snake. Air temperatures considered suitable for their maintenance have ranged from 25 to 30°C (77 to 86°F) (Mattison, 1988) to 27 to 34°C (80 to 93°F) (Brecke et al., 1976). We have maintained those in our care at temperatures slightly higher than this with no apparent problems, but we would not advise exceeding the upper limit by much more.

Feeding this snake is not a problem as all stages will readily consume domestic mice of the appropriate size. In fact, representatives of this species are probably among the most consistent feeders of all North American snakes. They will take mice dead or alive, which allows the keeper to store food for months by freezing it until needed.

The only time that feeding becomes inconsistent in a healthy snake is during the winter and spring when brumation and breeding, respectively, take precedence. Brumation is definitely recommended at 7–15°C (45–59°F) for about 3–4 months. This may be carried out in the same cage without any special modifications, although some keepers will not brumate first year snakes in order to push them for rapid growth and breeding at less than 2 years of age.

As mentioned above, this snake has been bred many times in captivity, and this may be accomplished simply by placing the female in with the male a week or so after the brumation period ends. See the section on breeding in the general care section. If successful, she will lay 3–14 eggs in about 1.5 months, which will hatch in 9–12 weeks into juveniles that look nothing like the adults. In fact, juveniles are steely blue-gray with small brown saddles (see photo), a pattern that will slowly fade (even though many herpetoculturists have wished it wouldn't) into the tan and striped pattern of the adult by about 2 years of age.

A pair in our care mated on 9 May and 13

SPECIES: *Elaphe bairdi*, Baird's Rat Snake
MAINTENANCE DIFFICULTY INDEX: 1 (1 = easiest, 5 = most difficult)
AVERAGE SIZE: 84–137 (33–54 inches)
FOOD: Mice
CAGE SIZE: 20–30-gallon long aquariums
SUBSTRATE: Artificial turf, indoor-outdoor carpet, or newspaper
VENTRAL HEAT: Yes
UV LIGHT: No
TEMPERATURE RANGE: 25–30°C (77–86°F)
SPECIAL CONSIDERATIONS: Beautiful and adaptable captives. Eat and breed readily in
    captivity. Good first snake.

May and the female laid 7 eggs on 19 June. Five of these eggs were fertile and hatched on 21 August, an incubation period of 63–64 days at an average temperature of 28°C (82°F). The neonates ranged 37–39 cm (14.6–15.3 inches) in TL with an average TL of 38.6 cm (15.2 inches). The two males and three females shed between 30 August and 1 September and ate pinky mice immediately thereafter. It is interesting to note that all 5 of these healthy eggs were completely covered by a fungus during their incubation but showed no negative effects.

The following year, the same pair mated repeatedly in May and this resulted in 10 eggs being laid on 6 June. These eggs hatched on 9 August, again an incubation period of 64 days. The 10 neonates ranged 37–42 cm (14.6–16.5 inches) in TL. The average TL of this clutch was 38.95 cm (15.3 inches). The sex ratio was 1:1. None of this clutch developed mold growth.

Overall, Baird's rat snake does well in captivity, and makes an excellent pet as well. They are usually mild tempered and rarely bite. Most don't seem to mind being held and they are vora-

Baird's Rat Snake, *Elaphe bairdi* (photo by David G. Campbell)

cious eaters. They have a subtle beauty some herpetoculturists do not appreciate, but take one out into the sunlight and you will. The brilliant orange wash between the highly iridescent yellow-gray scales is very characteristic of adults.

Captive longevity for this species has exceeded 15 years (Slavens and Slavens, 1991); hence it is presently considered one of the most long-lived North American snakes (in captivity). We have found them to be very rewarding low maintenance snakes that are very likely to breed and very unlikely to have problems. They are not nearly as prone to rubbing their rostral areas (noses) raw on cages and tops in efforts to escape as are members of the common rat snake group, *E. obsoleta.*

Elaphe gloydi and *Elaphe vulpina*
Eastern and Western Fox Snakes

The fox snakes are the northernmost rat snakes in North America. They are tan to yellowish snakes with large brown or black blotches along the back, and a heavily spotted ventral surface. It is believed that they received their name because of the strong odor of their anal gland secretion, which they release when frightened.

Formerly, these two snakes were considered to be the same species, and much of the literature summarizes the natural history of both. However, it appears obvious at this time that they are indeed two distinct species. They are geographically isolated, occupy different habitats, and demonstrate morphological differences in size and pattern. The two closely related species are discussed together here for comparison and for the convenience of the reader. Generally speaking, the western fox snake is a stouter darker snake with a larger number of smaller blotches. See Table 8.

Elaphe gloydi
Eastern Fox Snake

The eastern fox snake ranges from southwestern Ontario and eastern Michigan to northern Ohio, closely associated with the shorelines of the three easternmost Great Lakes: Huron, Erie, and Ontario. Their preferred habitat appears to be marshland or grassy open areas near

Table 8. Fox Snake Comparison

	Elaphe gloydi Eastern Fox Snake	*Elaphe vulpina* Western Fox Snake
Dorsal scale rows	23–25	25–27
Dorsal blotches	28–43 ($\bar{x}$ = 34)	32–52 ($\bar{x}$ = 41)
Color	Lighter background	Darker background
Size		
Adults	90–170.5 cm (35.4–67 inches)	90–155 cm (35.4–61 inches)
Hatchlings	26–31 cm (10.2–12.2 inches)	23–31 cm (9–12.2 inches)
Clutch size	6–29	7–27
Habitat	Shoreline marshes and open areas nearby	Open woodlands in north, prairies and pastures in south
Prey	Mostly mice and voles	East mice but also chipmunks, ground squirrels, rabbits, birds, and eggs
Behavior	Good swimmer, enters water. May brumate under water. Rarely climbs into bushes.	More terrestrial, but may also brumate under water. Climbs more frequently.

water (Wright and Wright, 1957), although they may also occupy adjacent fields, pastures, and open woodlands as well as rocky areas on islands (Harding, 1997). They are primarily terrestrial snakes, only occasionally climbing into shrubs or bushes. They do make use of old abandoned buildings, trash piles, and other human creations. They spend a great deal of time under things or in burrows during the day, even though they are considered to be primarily diurnal snakes. Like other snakes, they may move on warm nights also, particularly if it is raining.

Elaphe gloydii

These are medium to large snakes, ranging 90–155 cm (35.4–61 inches) in TL as adults (Harding, 1997). They have a yellowish to light brown background color with 28–43 (average 34) dark brown to black dorsal blotches (Ernst and Barbour, 1989). Count along the back on the body only; do not include the blotches on the tail. The head is usually plain light brown to coppery red in adults, although the heads of juveniles possess a dark brown stripe between the eyes which extends backward from the eyes to the angle of the jaw on each side. There are usually 23–25 scale rows at midbody and the anal scute is divided. The belly has irregular rows of dark spots on a lighter background.

Small mammals make up the majority of this snake's diet, with meadow voles, *Microtus*, and deer mice, *Peromyscus*, representing the largest percentage (Harding, 1997). Other food items may include birds, eggs, and other small mammals such as chipmunks, squirrels, and young rabbits. Young fox snakes may include ectothermic prey such as frogs, small snakes, and earthworms in their diet, since this has been observed in the closely related western fox snake.

Suspected predators of this species include ophiophagous snakes, birds of prey, such as egrets, herons, and hawks, as well as predatory

Eastern Fox Snake, *Elaphe gloydi* (photo by David G. Campbell)

SPECIES: *Elaphe gloydii*, Eastern Fox Snake
MAINTENANCE DIFFICULTY INDEX: 2 (1 = easiest, 5 = most difficult)
AVERAGE SIZE: 91–170.5 cm (36–67 inches)
FOOD: Mice, rats, other small mammals
CAGE SIZE: 20–30-gallon aquarium
SUBSTRATE: Artificial turf, indoor-outdoor carpet, or newspaper
VENTRAL HEAT: Not essential but helpful
UV LIGHT: Not essential but helpful
TEMPERATURE RANGE: 20–25°C (68–77°F)
SPECIAL CONSIDERATIONS: Good eaters, so stick with "clean" food. Gentle. May rub
    noses raw. Prone to periods of inappetence. NEED TO BE BRUMATED (HIBERNATED).

mammals such as foxes, raccoons, mink, shrews, weasels, and rodents. Prairie deer mice have reportedly been responsible for the destruction of fox snake eggs in Ontario (Evans and Roecker, 1951). Habitat destruction for waterfront development is considered a major threat to this species, which still remains common in some areas but is now absent in many of the areas where it was once found.

Mating is believed to occur primarily in the spring, often in April or early May, but may not be until June or early July in some cases. This results in the deposition of 6–29 eggs approximately 6 weeks later, in June or July, which usually hatch in 35–78 days (Wright and Wright, 1957; Keogh, pers. obs., 1992). The neonates generally measure 20–33 cm (8–13 inches). Growth rates and the age at sexual maturity of wild snakes are unknown, but it is believed that these snakes reach sexual maturity in 3–5 years.

The eastern fox snake will do very well in captivity under most circumstances. The basic cage design works extremely well for their maintenance and breeding. We have also had success maintaining these snakes in an outdoor enclosure. Like their closest relatives, the common rat snake, they have a tendency to rub their rostral areas (noses) on screen tops until they are raw. So watch carefully for this, and consider using smooth-sided cages and tops. A good hide box will help reduce this behavior, as will a larger and taller cage. Make sure to have clean water available at all times.

Ventral heat is strongly advisable. A UV light source is not considered necessary, but the eastern fox snakes in our care seemed to enjoy basking for a good portion of the day, so UV and incandescent lights may be beneficial.

Feeding is not a problem, since these snakes usually eat extremely well in captivity. Indeed, rodents are their favorite food and domestic rodents are usually readily consumed. Like most snakes, they have no problem taking dead rodents either. However, Mehrtens (1987) noted that these snakes are prone to long periods of inappetence, even if they are kept at higher temperatures, and we agree. These periods of anorexia are poorly understood by most keepers and may be partly responsible for a "bad reputation" among some that this snake does not do well in captivity. In fact, these periods of anorexia usually occur in the fall, frequently after one of these snakes has been exposed to a slight temperature drop. Under these circumstances, anorexia may be considered a normal self-protective behavior. Consider what would happen if a cold-climate snake ate a meal right before a cold front moved through. Unable to digest the meal, it would literally putrefy in the snake's stomach, possibly resulting in bloating, gastroenteritis, toxicity, and sometimes death. Hence, one should expect that anorexia may occur in the fall and consider cooling the snake down for winter. Remember that brumation or a winter cooldown may be accomplished in the regular cage, but that these snakes do not seem satisfied with slightly cooler temperatures. They appear to like it very cold. Those in our care over-wintered in plastic boxes filled with mulch that were set in the bottom of a refrigerator at temperatures fluctuating from 2 to 7°C (36 to 45°F) for 12 weeks. These boxes were very well ventilated and the snakes were monitored frequently for dehydration. Keogh (1992) also found that temperatures of 4–7°C (40–45°F) were suitable for this species. Interestingly, our snakes did wander in these containers, even at these low temperatures, until they were placed in with each other, at which time they became inactive. Perhaps the body contact was important. See the section on winter cooldown (brumation/hibernation).

Captive breeding has been accomplished numerous times, though not as frequently as with the other members of this genus. A pair from Ohio in our care mated on 12 April 1992 and the female laid 6 eggs on 21 May. All of these eggs hatched on 3 July, an incubation period of 43 days at an average incubation temperature of 28°C (82°F). These neonates ranged 30–33 cm (11.8–12.9 inches) in TL. The sex ratio was 1:1. These same snakes mated again on 10 and 11 April 1994, and the female laid eggs on 15 May. All of these eggs hatched on 29 June, an incubation period of 44 days at an average incubation temperature of 28°C (82°F). The sex ratio was 5:6 males to females (0.83:1). The gestation period was 39 days in 1992 and 35 days in 1994. The second clutch of neonates ranged 28–32 cm (11–12.6 inches) in TL, which averaged slightly smaller than the neonates from the first clutch.

Our incubation period was consistently shorter than the incubation period reported by Keogh (1992) of 50–65 days. However, all of these hatchlings appeared healthy, coordinated, and alert, and they ate readily. Perhaps our incubation temperatures were slightly higher than those which he used.

The eastern fox snake is not aggressive toward humans. They rarely bite and they do well in captivity. One captive survived over 7 years and 5 months (Snider and Bowler, 1992); however, they can probably survive much longer since other members of this genus have exceeded 4 times this age.

Elaphe vulpina
Western Fox Snake

The western fox snake ranges from the northern peninsula of Michigan and western Indiana westward through Wisconsin, Illinois, and Iowa as well as eastern Minnesota, South Dakota, and Nebraska. The preferred habitat of this species appears to be open woodlands in the northern part of the range and prairies, fields, marshes, and dunes in the southern part (Johnson, 1980; Holman et al., 1990; Harding, 1997). In Minnesota, the preferred habitat has been described as river bottom forests, upland hardwoods, pine barrens, and prairies (Oldfield and Moriarty, 1994), while in Iowa, the habitat has been described as woodland edges throughout the state (Christiansen and Bailey, 1990).

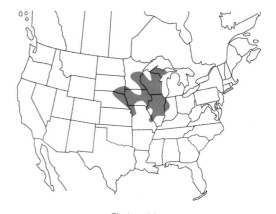

Elaphe vulpina

The latter authors have noted that these snakes seem to be more adapted to woodland than bullsnakes and appear less abundant where bullsnakes occur. We have observed this to be true in the sand prairie remnant in northern Illinois as well; where bullsnakes are abundant, fox snakes appear to be much less common. Yet fox snakes do occupy open areas in the southern part of their range. In Missouri, the fox snake is found near large natural marshes (Johnson, 1980). In fact, we found a dead juvenile on a road traversing a large marsh in northwestern Missouri, on 4 October 1998, on one of the last warm days of the fall.

The diet of this species is known to include mice, rats, chipmunks, ground squirrels, young

Western Fox Snake, *Elaphe vulpina* (photo by Steve Barten)

rabbits, birds, eggs, and nestling birds (Vogt, 1981; Ernst and Barbour, 1989). Duck eggs have been consumed by this species (Wheeler, 1984). Juvenile western fox snakes are believed to primarily eat nestling rodents in the wild; however, there have been reports of them consuming ectothermic prey including insects, earthworms, and small frogs (Oldfield and Moriarty, 1994). Even small snakes may be consumed, since one captive ate a smooth green snake (Markezich, 1962).

Predators of this snake are believed to include ophiophagous snakes such as milk and kingsnakes, birds of prey such as egrets, herons, and hawks, as well as predatory mammals including foxes, raccoons, mink, shrews, weasels, and rodents (Harding, 1997). Large fish and snapping turtles are also believed to prey upon young fox snakes. Many are killed by cars as they attempt to cross roads, but as with many other snakes, habitat destruction is the major threat to their continued survival.

Collection of these snakes for the pet trade may also have taken its toll, but in our experience over the last 30 years, these snakes are not as highly sought after as other rat snakes or kingsnakes, and hence are not as common in the pet trade as those snakes. Because of their large size however, they cannot remain inconspicuous like so many of the other wet prairie species such as Kirtland's snake or the lined snake, hence, many are killed by people mistaking them for rattlesnakes or copperheads. Indeed, like those species, many are surviving on small remnants of suitable habitat surrounded by development. The senior author and Chris Lechowitz found a juvenile western fox snake on a 5-hectare "island" of prairie surrounded by urban development near Chicago. Other species observed on the same land were brown snakes, *Storeria dekayi*, Kirtland's snakes, *Clonophis kirtlandii*, Chicago garter snakes, *Thamnophis sirtalis*, and smooth green snakes, *Opheodrys* (*Liochlorophis*) *vernalis*.

These snakes are believed to emerge from brumation in late April over much of their range. Mating occurs soon afterward with 7–27 eggs being laid approximately 30 days later

SPECIES: *Elaphe vulpina*, Western Fox Snake
MAINTENANCE DIFFICULTY INDEX: 2 (1 = easiest, 5 = most difficult)
AVERAGE SIZE: 91–155 cm (36–61 inches)
FOOD: Mice, rats, other small mammals
CAGE SIZE: 20–30-gallon aquarium
SUBSTRATE: Artificial turf, indoor-outdoor carpet, or newspaper
VENTRAL HEAT: Not essential but helpful
UV LIGHT: Not essential but helpful
TEMPERATURE RANGE: 20–25°C (68–77°F)
SPECIAL CONSIDERATIONS: Good eaters, so stick with "clean" food. Gentle. May rub
   noses raw. Prone to periods of inappetence. NEED TO BE BRUMATED (HIBERNATED).

(Zehr, 1969; Vogt, 1981). Mating has been described in great detail by Gillingham (1974). Interestingly, male western fox snakes have been observed to engage in "ritualized" combat, as seen in rattlesnakes and black rat snakes, and the males are often larger than the females.

Generally, the eggs hatch after 50–55 days of incubation, however ranges of 35–78 days have been reported for this species (Minton, 1972; Wright and Wright, 1957). Hatchlings range 23–31 cm (9–12.2 inches) in length and are patterned similarly to the adults except that the background color is much darker (gray) and the head has a distinct pattern. As in the eastern fox snakes, this pattern fades with age. It includes a dark bar across the top of the head which slants down to the angle of the jaw behind each eye.

In captivity, the western fox snake does very well when housed in the basic cage arrangement. Indoor/outdoor carpet has worked well; however, the authors prefer cypress mulch for this species. Ventral heat is very helpful, as is a good stable hiding area. Like the eastern fox snake and other members of this genus, these snakes are prone to damaging their rostral areas on screen tops or abrasive wood sides in their cages. Therefore, smooth-sided tall enclosures are recommended. Plastic sweater boxes with multiple holes drilled or burned in the sides and top have been used successfully for this species; however, it is critical that these cages are well ventilated. If not, these snakes are susceptible to dermatitis. Water should be provided at all times. A flat rock may be utilized as a basking area if the cage has an incandescent light above it. A stable branch may also be added to the cage.

Domestic mice and rats are readily accepted by most western fox snakes in captivity, so feeding is generally not a problem. These snakes have voracious appetites throughout the summer but they may stop eating altogether in the late summer or early fall. As discussed with eastern fox snakes and some of the montane kingsnakes, this is probably a self-protective behavior rather than a pathological condition. See those sections for more discussion on this behavior.

Breeding has been accomplished numerous times in captivity, when the snakes are healthy and well fed. Generally, the snakes mate immediately following brumation (within 2–3 weeks of warming). Remember that brumation temperatures for these snakes should be fairly low. Temperatures of 4–7°C (40–45°F) for 12 weeks should be suitable; and since brumation is often communal with this species, cooling down more than one animal per container may also be suitable.

The smooth, elongated, adherent eggs are laid a little over a month after mating is observed, and usually hatch in 35–50 days, although some clutches have taken longer. The babies are aggressive feeders and usually consume domestic mice pinkies immediately. Those babies that do not do so may still have sufficient yolk supplies or may be preparing for brumation. Do not panic if one does not eat right away.

Generally speaking, these are good natured serpents. The adults rarely bite, however, recently captured specimens will void their anal glands and writhe in an attempt to escape. Eventually they will calm down, but that tell-tale scent will appear again whenever they are frightened or handled roughly. As mentioned previously, the scent is believed to be the origin of their name. The odor is strong, pungent, and somewhat sweet, reminding some of the odor produced by a fox. Perhaps the reddish head of some adults contributed to this name. To us, the smell is very much like that produced by weasels, but we promise we will not propose a name change to the weasel snake! In any case, the longer they remain in captivity and the more they are handled, the less likely they are to release their anal glands. They usually do well in captivity as long as one is prepared for their fall/winter anorexia and cools them down appropriately. One captive specimen survived over 6 years (Harding, 1997), but they probably can survive much longer. Other members of this genus have survived past 30 years!

Elaphe guttata
Corn Snake

The corn snake is a variably colored medium-sized snake, with adults ranging 76–122 cm (30–48 inches) in length and a record of 183 cm (72 inches) (Conant and Collins, 1991). There are two widespread subspecies within the U.S., the corn snake, *E. g. guttata*, and the Great Plains rat snake, *E. g. emoryi*. A third subspecies, *E. g. meahllmorum*, was recently described (Smith et al., 1994) but will not be discussed due to the paucity of information available. All subspecies have large dorsal blotches, usually surrounded by black, and ventral surfaces with checkerboard patterns. The background color varies from tan to orange in the eastern subspecies and grayish to greenish in the western subspecies. The dorsal blotches are usually red or orange in eastern populations and brown or olive green in the western populations. Hence, the eastern snakes have an orangish appearance overall, while the western snakes are generally brownish. The adaptive significance of the orange color is unknown, while the pattern of those snakes in the west is thought to be mimicry of the western rattlesnake.

The eastern subspecies, the corn snake, ranges from southern New Jersey southward to Florida and westward to Tennessee, Mississippi, and eastern Louisiana, with isolated populations in Kentucky. The widespread western subspecies, the Great Plains rat snake, is found from southern Illinois southward through western Louisiana where the two subspecies intergrade, and westward to include much of southern Missouri and almost all of Texas and Oklahoma, as well as eastern Colorado and New Mexico. It also ranges southward into Mexico and there is a large isolated population on the Colorado-Utah border.

As might be expected from such a widely distributed species, these snakes occupy a vari-

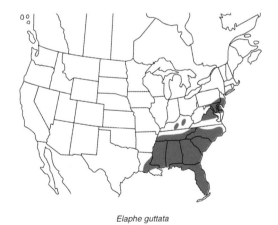

Elaphe guttata

ety of habitats. They seem to be especially numerous in open areas, whether they be grasslands or woodlands. Habitat types have been characterized as pine barrens, deciduous woodlands, brush fields, abandoned farms, woodland edge, corn fields, and junkyards (Vermersch and Kuntz, 1986; Mount, 1975; Ashton and

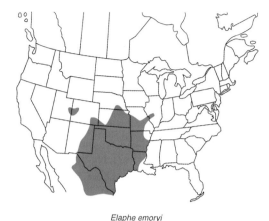

Elaphe emoryi

Ashton, 1981; Linzey and Clifford, 1981; Ernst and Barbour, 1989; Collins, 1993). Degenhardt et al. (1996) stated that two important components of the southwestern environment for this species were a permanent source of water and good cover.

The preferred food of the corn snake appears to be small mammals (including mice, rats, moles, and bats) and birds, but lizards, tree frogs, and insects have also been reported as food for this species, especially the juveniles (Wright and Wright, 1957; Mount, 1975; Mc-Coy, 1975; Behler and King, 1979; Ashton and Ashton, 1981; Ernst and Barbour, 1989). Other food items reported with some regularity have been other snakes including other corn snakes

(Ippoliti, 1980; Mitchell, 1986; Ernst and Barbour, 1989).

Known predators of this species include opossums, coyotes, bobcats, foxes, skunks, weasels, raccoons, hawks, owls, and ophiophagous snakes (Ernst and Barbour, 1989).

Mating generally occurs in late winter to late spring, with up to 30 eggs being laid approximately 35–68 days later (Ernst and Barbour, 1989). These eggs hatch in 50–80 days into neonates measuring 20–37 cm (8.0–14.6 inches). The hatchlings are patterned similarly to the adults although their colors are more subdued.

Interestingly, Great Plains rat snakes from Kansas lay much smaller clutches, averaging 6.43 ± 1.09 (Clark, 1953; Fitch, 1999). This is discussed below.

The Great Plains rat snake is now believed by many to be a separate species from the corn snake. Indeed, they occupy a different habitat, differ physically, and are geographically isolated from each other. The Great Plains rat snake occupies open areas, which are often rocky and may be dominated by grasses, while the corn snake often occupies forested areas. Adult Great Plains rat snakes average much longer and heavier than corn snakes, but produce smaller clutches (Fitch, 1999).

Werler and Dixon (2000) have also concluded that the variety of Great Plains rat snake found in southern Texas is different enough

Northern Plains Rat Snake, *Elaphe emoryi emoryi* (photo by David G. Campbell)

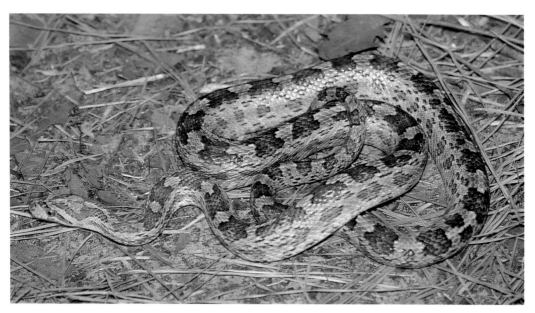

Southern Plains Rat Snake, *Elaphe emoryi meahllmorum* (photo by David G. Campbell)

from more northern animals to be considered a separate subspecies. They have also proposed a new common name for this subspecies, the southwestern rat snake. Drs. Werler and Dixon also expressed some concern that there was little data published on this subspecies; almost all reproduction information is from more northern locations. Thus, we have incorporated some of our own observations on a pair of southwestern rat snakes from extreme southern Texas (just east of Brownsville). A 3-year-old male and a 20-month-old female were placed in the same cage in mid-April. Mating was not observed but the female laid 6 large eggs on 7 June. Five of these eggs pipped on 22 August, an incubation period of 76 days at temperatures fluctuating from 22.2 to 30.5°C (72 to 87 °F). The neonates ranged 25.4–30.5 cm (10–12 inches) in TL, and their weight ranged from 8 to 10 grams. The average TL was 31.9 cm (12.55 inches) and the average weight was 9.4 grams. The neonates looked exactly like their parents, except they were slightly darker and had a pinkish tinge. These snakes all possessed the butterfly-shaped blotches found in many snakes of this subspecies from extreme southern Texas. The authors would like to express their gratitude to Gus Rentfro for helping them

acquire these snakes and sharing his knowledge of southern Texas snakes.

If the Great Plains rat snake is a separate species, the scientific name would become *Elaphe emoryi*. Collins (1997) has indeed elevated the Great Plains rat snake to *E. emoryi* and listed two subspecies, the northern plains rat snake, *E. e. emoryi*, and the southern plains rat snake, *E. e. meahllmorum*. The southern plains rat snake occurs in southern Texas south of San Antonio, where a broad area of intergradation occurs with the northern plains rat snake (Vaughan et al., 1996). The ecology of this snake is virtually unknown, but it may lay larger clutches than those from farther north.

The corn snake is an outrageously beautiful and popular snake. Even the western varieties have an attractive pattern, albeit not as bright as the eastern subspecies. Corn snakes come in a variety of colors and patterns including albinos (snow corns), anerytheristic (lacking red), amelanistic (lacking black), striped, blood red, combinations of the above, and the various geographic varieties (i.e., Ocetee corns, south Florida corns, etc.). See Bechtel and Bechtel, 1978, and McEachern, 1991. It is a wonderful eater at all ages except possibly the hatchling stage. At this tender age some are fond of

Corn Snake, *Elaphe guttata* (photo by David G. Campbell)

anoles, *Anolis* sp., and other small lizards, but most of them will take pinkies. Almost all of them will take their food prekilled, and of course this is strongly recommended for the snake's safety (if feeding adult or subadult mice). Both mice and lizards can be frozen and thawed as needed, but stay away from feeding lizards if you can, as they may be parasitized.

Literature reports on wild snakes also include the following as food items: bats, birds, eggs, small frogs, and even insects, but these are to be avoided also. Chicks may be good for a change every now and then, but they are considered by many to be calcium-deficient and the legs may lead to intestinal impactions as well. (See the discussion on feeding in the general care sec-

SPECIES: *Elaphe guttata*, Corn Snake
MAINTENANCE DIFFICULTY INDEX: 1 (1 = easiest, 5 = most difficult)
AVERAGE SIZE: 76–122 cm (30–48 inches)
FOOD: Mice, lizards (for very young) or occasional treefrog (for very young)
CAGE SIZE: 20–30-gallon aquarium
SUBSTRATE: Artificial turf, indoor-outdoor carpet, or newspaper
VENTRAL HEAT: Not essential but helpful (especially for young)
UV LIGHT: Not essential
TEMPERATURE RANGE: 22–28°C (72–82°F) day, 18–20°C (64–68°F) night, 5–15°C (41–59°F) brum.
SPECIAL CONSIDERATIONS: An ideal pet snake. Perfect as a first snake, although babies may bite. They calm down, eat well, are clean, and can be handled often.

tion and also the description of *Elaphe obsoleta*, yellow, gray and black rat snakes.) With very small or stubborn specimens, force-feeding can be accomplished with pinky legs or Pinky Pump. (See the discussion on force-feeding.)

In addition to being beautiful and good eaters, they are very hardy snakes that rarely become ill even if conditions are suboptimal. In fact, this snake often does so well in captivity, one often wonders if its natural habitat doesn't include aquariums, wooden or plastic cages, and artificial lights! We do not mean to imply that this snake should be housed in an incorrect manner, only that it will rarely become ill. Housing should be as described in the general care section for most terrestrial snakes, i.e., hide box, artificial carpet/turf), water bowl, ventral heat, etc.

Although less likely to be heavily parasitized than snakes which eat strictly amphibians or fish, wild-caught specimens are commonly parasitized with reptile hookworms and whipworms and should be dewormed. (See the section on parasites.)

The red rat snake is far less likely to wander around its cage and injure its nose than its cousins in the *E. obsoleta* groups. In fact, if given a hide box, most will happily sit in it at all times unless hungry, thirsty, shedding, looking for a mate, or defecating. A good keeper will notice these changes in activity and provide food, water, or a mate, or prepare to clean the cage at these times.

Breeding this species is very easy and has been accomplished perhaps thousands of times in captivity. Utilize the same techniques described in the general care section discussion on breeding. Care for the eggs as described in the general care section.

The following account may provide some insight into corn snake reproduction and feeding.

One pair of corn snakes was captured under a box spring in Duval County, Florida, on 6 March 1987. The male was approximately 150 cm (5 ft) and the female was 122 cm (4 ft) TL. The female began feeding on 11 March and consumed 14 mice until 10 May. She laid 14 eggs on 23 May, which hatched on 20 July, a 58-day incubation period. The adult male and female, along with all hatchlings except one female, were released.

This female refused pinky mice but consumed 18 lizards (anoles and ground skinks) before it started eating pinky mice on 11 October 1987. See Table 9. The first meal (an anole) was eaten on 26 July, 6 days after hatching. This snake consumed one fuzzy mouse per week until 6 December, at which point feeding ceased until mid-March 1988. It then resumed feeding at that rate until the fall of that year, when it refused mice in November, December, and much of January. From 28 January 1989 until 8 December 1989, it consumed 32 mice or small rats (approximately 50 grams each). Beginning on 3 January 1990 until 30 May 1990, this same female consumed 15 mice.

After egg laying on 6 June 1990, the female resumed eating on 9 June 1990 and consumed 19 mice until feeding ceased after 3 December 1990. Feeding resumed on 19 February 1991 and she ate 17 mice until 21 April 1991. Egg laying occurred on 26 May 1991 and feeding resumed

Table 9. Feeding and Reproductive Data for One Female Corn Snake, *Elaphe guttata*, from Duval County, Florida

Calendar Year	Fall Food Consumption	Spring Food Consumption	Number of Eggs	Average Neonate Size
1987–1988	19 Lizards, 12 Pinkies	16 Fuzzies	0	—
1988–1989	16 Fuzzies	16 Jumpers	0	—
1989–1990	16 Mice	15 Mice	13	?
1990–1991	19 Mice	17 Mice	25	?
1991–1992	16 Mice	11 Mice	25	26.8 cm
1992–1993	24 Mice	4 Mice	25	24.9 cm
1993–1994	22 Mice	7 Mice	25	27.1 cm

on 30 May 1991 and she ate 16 mice or small rats until 26 September 1991, after which feeding stopped until 17 February 1992. Feeding resumed then and the female consumed 11 mice until 23 April 1992. The female resumed feeding on 11 June 1992 and ate 24 mice until 9 October 1992. She resumed feeding on 3 March and ate only 3 mice and 1 rat until 11 May 1993, the year in which she produced the smallest neonates, and also the lowest number of viable eggs since her first year. This clutch was laid on 12 June 1993, which was also the latest clutch date. She resumed feeding on 21 June 1993 and consumed 22 mice until 1 November 1993. Feeding resumed on 7 March 1994 and the female consumed 7 mice until 27 May 1994.

After mating with a small male of 62 cm (24 inches) TL on 5 March 1990, this female laid 13 eggs on 6 June 1990 (at approximately 23 months of age). These eggs hatched on 1 August 1990, an incubation period of 55 days. Subsequent clutches were laid as follows:

1. 26 May 1991, 25 eggs, hatched 23 July 1991, an incubation period of 58 days. No further matings were attempted, but the female laid 12 infertile eggs on 12 July 1991.
2. 3 June 1992, 25 eggs, hatched 29 July 1992, an incubation period of 56 days. Neonates ranged 25–28.5 cm (9.8–11.2 inches) TL. The average TL was 26.8 cm (10.6 inches). The sex ratio was 1.27:1 males to females.
3. 12 June 1993, 25 eggs and 1 infertile egg, 22 hatched 9–12 August 1993, an incubation period of 58–61 days. The neonates

ranged 22–26 cm (8.7–10.2 inches) TL. The average TL was 24.9 cm (9.8 inches). The sex ratio was 8 males to 14 females.
4. 30 May 1994, 25 eggs, hatched on 1 August 1994, an incubation period of 61 days. The sex ratio was 12 males to 13 females. Neonates ranged 26–28 cm (10.2–11 inches) TL and the average TL was 27.1 cm (10.7 inches).

Attempt brumation in the usual manner as described in the general care section. Babies do not need to be brumated and some would argue that adults do not need to be either, but we disagree as a short cool period will improve breeding success. Since sexual maturity is usually reached at 2 years of age, a baby born in August will not need to be brumated until the following winter, about 15 months after it is hatched, in preparation for mating in spring.

The corn snake's personality varies and some can be snappy, but most calm down under the right conditions. Older snakes can be handled fairly frequently with no ill effects, but that depends on the individual snake's personality. As mentioned elsewhere, do not handle for about a day or two after they have eaten.

Overall, this snake makes an ideal captive and is perhaps the easiest of all eastern North American snakes to maintain and breed. Hence, it is a great snake for beginners. It is also fairly long-lived. In fact, many species of snake are being found to be long-lived, now that we are learning how to care for them and treat their ailments better. The Jacksonville Museum of Science and History had one in captivity for nearly 32 years, when it died from renal tumors!

Elaphe obsoleta
Common Rat Snake

A large extremely variably colored species, the common rat snake is one of the most well known of all American snakes. There are five subspecies: the black rat snake, *E. o. obsoleta*, the gray rat snake, *E. o. spiloides*, the yellow rat snake, *E. o. quadrivittata*, the Texas rat snake, *E. o. lindheimerii*, and the Everglades rat snake,

E. o. rossalleni. The black rat snake has the largest geographical distribution, ranging from western Massachusetts southward to Georgia and westward through southern Ontario, southern Michigan, southern Wisconsin, southward through Iowa and eastern Nebraska to northeastern Texas and all areas in between, except

Elaphe obsoleta

Black Rat Snake, *Elaphe obsoleta obsoleta*
(photo by David G. Campbell)

for the Mississippi Valley as far north as Indiana. It is the largest of the subspecies and is appropriately named, with adults being primarily black even though there is quite a bit of variation. The gray rat snake is found from the Mississippi Valley southward to northern and eastern Florida (recently some specimens have been found in western Duval County to Jacksonville, Florida, area, and they appear to be spreading eastward and southward). Fitch (1999) states that the geographic range of this species corresponds with the deciduous forest biome of the eastern United States, except that it extends farther west into the great plains. In Kansas,

Gray Rat Snake, *Elaphe obsoleta spiloides* (photo by David G. Campbell)

Yellow Rat Snake, *Elaphe obsoleta quadrivittata* (photo by David G. Campbell)

like many other areas, these snakes seem to prefer open rocky woodlands. These snakes retain their juvenile pattern throughout life, staying dark to silvery gray with dark gray dorsal blotches. The yellow rat snake is a coastal subspecies found from southeastern North Carolina through much of eastern South Carolina and eastern Georgia as well as much of peninsular Florida. Yellow rat snakes are pale yellow to brownish yellow with four longitudinal stripes running down the body. The Texas rat snake ranges from eastern Louisiana westward throughout eastern and central Texas. It is reddish tan with dark brown or black dorsal blotches. This species is well known for its feisty disposition and naturally occurring leucistic (white with black or blue eyes) morph. The Everglades rat snake is found only in extreme southern Florida and the Florida Keys. It is generally orange or orangish yellow with reduced gray longitudinal stripes.

As mentioned above, habitats occupied by this species include a variety of woodlands and shrublands, especially near water or deserted human habitation. Mitchell (1994) lists agricultural areas and hardwood forests as does Harding (1997) for rat snakes in Virginia and the midwest respectively. Both hardwood and pine forests are used in the south (Tennant, 1997).

The list of species consumed by this snake is immense. There appears to be a marked preference for mammals and birds, including moles, shrews, mice, rats, and squirrels, as well as over two dozen species of birds (Ernst and Barbour, 1989). Bruce Jayne and the senior author once witnessed a gray squirrel drop 40 feet from an oak tree into the Hillsborough River in Tampa, Florida, immediately followed by a large yellow rat snake. Amphibians, particularly treefrogs, *Hyla* sp., and anoles, *Anolis carolinensis*, are known to be particularly favored by juvenile common rat snakes. Less commonly, snakes and other species of lizards, as well as their eggs, have been reported as food for this species (Wright and Wright, 1957; Kennedy, 1964; Minton, 1972; Behler and King, 1979; Ernst and Barbour, 1989). Cannibalism has also been reported for captive members of this species (Mitchell, 1986).

Young rat snakes are preyed upon by ophiophagous snakes, hawks, egrets, owls, herons, wood storks, bobcats, cats, dogs, opossums, skunks, foxes, weasels, otters, and raccoons. Adult rat snakes have few natural predators except for alligators and indigo snakes (Ernst and Barbour, 1989).

Mating generally occurs in the spring, with 5–44 eggs being laid after a gestation period of 37–51 days (Fitch, 1970; Ernst and Barbour, 1989). These adherent eggs usually hatch in 55–75 days into hatchlings that are 29–38 cm (11.4–15 inches) in length. Mating behavior has been described in detail by Gillingham (1979).

Interestingly, the eggs of this species in Fitch's study (1999) would hatch on almost any medium at temperatures ranging 0–40°C (32–104°F). These young are believed to reach sexual maturity in 4 years. Rat snakes, like copperheads, were heavily parasitized by flukes in that Kansas study site, presumably from eating tree frogs.

The yellow rat snake usually does very well in captivity; however, it can be the most difficult of the eastern rat snakes to maintain. This is due to the fact that these snakes are more arboreal than the red rat snake and seem more delicate than the more northern and western subspecies, the gray, black, and Texas rat snakes. They will wander the cage and rub their snouts on objects far more often than the other rat snakes. This usually leads to a raw infected rostral area; the infection eventually spreads, enters the mouth, and if left untreated, the respiratory tract. The snake will invariably stop eating and succumb to infection or starvation. The best way to prevent this is with a large tall cage of glass or other smooth material with a pegboard top. A screen top is acceptable if the snake does not rub too much. Neodesha® cages work very well for this entire genus. A branch should be provided. As with many other snakes, artificial carpet/turf, a frequently cleaned water dish, and a hide box are all recommended. A UV light source and bottom heat will improve your success.

Fortunately, all of our rat snakes will eat both anoles and pinkies as babies and grow rapidly until they are eating strictly mice, rats, and chicks. Many will also eat chicken eggs; warm them up and rub them with a chick if you get them from the grocery store.

Brumate the breed in the usual manner as described in the general care section.

In summary, the yellow rat snake is an attractive and easy to care for snake, but not as easy to maintain as the other rat snakes. If you provide a slightly larger cage than called for in the general care section, you will probably have better success. In addition, captive-born and -raised specimens and all long-term captives will behave much more like red rat snakes, making them excellent pets.

The gray rat snake is also a very arboreal snake, although some of these snakes get so heavy-bodied, they may climb very little. Provide a sturdy branch regardless of size. Care for

---

SPECIES: *Elaphe obsoleta*, Common Rat Snake
MAINTENANCE DIFFICULTY INDEX: 1 (1 = easiest, 5 = most difficult)
AVERAGE SIZE: 107–183 cm (42–72 inches)
FOOD: Mice, rats, for very young, lizards or occasional treefrogs
CAGE SIZE: 20–30-gallon aquarium
SUBSTRATE: Artificial turf, indoor-outdoor carpet, or newspaper
VENTRAL HEAT: Not essential but helpful (especially for young)
UV LIGHT: Not essential
TEMPERATURE RANGE: 21–28°C (70–82°F); 5–15°C (41–59°F) brumation
SPECIAL CONSIDERATIONS: Ideal pet snakes, but can wander their cages a bit more than
   corn snakes. Can also be snappy but will calm down. Handling okay.

---

these snakes exactly as for the yellow rat snakes. Attempt brumation and breeding in the same manner also. It has been our experience that this subspecies is far less likely to traumatize its nose and go off feed than the yellow rat.

The black rat snake has, in our opinion, been the easiest of the three eastern subspecies to maintain in captivity, although still more difficult than the red rat, *E. guttata*. Set them up correctly and they will thrive. Treat exactly as the yellow or gray rat snakes. Texas rat snakes and Everglades rat snakes are also similarly easy to maintain.

Texas rat snakes are voracious feeders in captivity, but have a well-deserved reputation for being very aggressive animals. When threatened, an adult will raise its head and advance toward its "tormenter," striking repeatedly. Some captives lose this aggression eventually, but other remain that way for life.

In general, the *E. obsoleta* group is susceptible to problems including difficult shedding in the winter if the relative humidity is too low. They may have loss of appetite in the winter and should be brumated if healthy. Watch for problems with the nose and mouth. If they rub the cage frequently, increase the size of the cage and use pegboard tops or switch to a plastic cage with a sliding front. Rat snakes also seem prone to intestinal disorders like bacterial and protozoal enteritis. Keep the water clean and have fecal exams performed yearly. The babies can be picky about what they eat. Some individuals do prefer lizards, particularly as

hatchlings. If you are releasing some of the clutch back into the wild, we would suggest placing pinkies in with the entire group of baby snakes right after they shed the first time. Watch them carefully and choose the "keepers" from the ones that will immediately eat pinkies. Some of those that don't eat may just not be ready, but others may be lizard lovers. Most of these will eventually eat pinkies, but are best released because obtaining lizards will be time-consuming for the keeper and increases the risk of parasitism in a collection. Tony Mills of Savannah River Ecology Lab advises trying treefrogs, *Hyla* sp., on any young rat snake that you want to keep that refuses both lizards and pinkies, but these are also parasitized. Force-feeding is also an option. (See the section on force-feeding.) If you wish to keep a young snake that shows interest in lizards only, try to switch it over to pinkies as soon as possible using some of the tricks listed in the general care section (see under feeding and care of young.) Remember that freezing and thawing a lizard will usually not reduce its palatability and may eliminate some parasites.

These snakes will breed readily at about 2 years of age but can be "pushed" into breeding early by overfeeding. There is a tremendous controversy over whether this will have serious consequences for the mother or her babies. (See the section on breeding and inbreeding.) The eggs are hatched in the usual manner.

One of the snakes described by Snider and Bowler (1992) survived 23 years in captivity.

Farancia abacura
Mud Snake

A chunky glossy black snake with a pink-banded belly, the mud snake is one of our larger harmless snakes. The mud snake ranges from Virginia southward through Florida and westward in the coastal plains to eastern Texas and extreme southeastern Oklahoma. Presently, two species are recognized: the eastern mud snake, *F. a. abacura*, and the western mud snake, *F. a. reinwardtii*.

As mentioned above, the mud snake is fairly large. Adults generally range in size from 100 to 137 cm (40 to 54 inches) but they may reach 206 cm (81 inches) in length (Conant and Collins, 1991). Because of their large size and smooth black scales, they are frequently mistaken for indigo snakes until one gets close enough to see the lateral pink bands or the yellow chin so characteristic of the mud snake.

Farancia abacura

The preferred habitat of the mud snake includes swamps, marshes, bogs, creeks, and ditches or any other body of water with a soft muddy bottom (Wright and Wright, 1957; Minton, 1972; Mount, 1975; Ashton and Ashton, 1981; Linzey and Clifford, 1981; Tennant, 1984; Ernst and Barbour, 1989; Mitchell, 1994; Palmer and Braswell, 1995). They do emerge from the water and burrow into soft soil at its edge occasionally and perhaps this is a daily occurrence (Neill, 1948). Like the rainbow snake, these snakes are believed to be primarily nocturnal.

Mud snakes appear to be dietary specialists. Large aquatic salamanders such as amphiumas and sirens are their primary food items, but they have been known to consume other amphibians and eels. The young appear particularly fond of tadpoles of many different species (Wright and Wright, 1957; Minton, 1972; Linzey and Clifford, 1981; Mount, 1975; Tennant, 1984; Conant and Collins, 1991; personal observations).

Suspected predators of this species include ophiophagous snakes (such as cottonmouths), alligators, wading birds, and carnivorous mammals.

Mating is believed to occur in the spring, with 6–104 eggs being laid several months later (Palmer and Braswell, 1995). These eggs hatch in 60–80 days and the neonates measure 15.9–27 cm (6.3–10.6 inches) in length (Palmer and Braswell, 1995; Conant and Collins, 1991). Females generally wrap around these eggs, possibly protecting them against predators and controlling egg moisture levels.

One mud snake was collected as it was traveling through a pine flatwoods on a hot afternoon in early July in Duval County, Florida. She was approximately 0.5 km from the nearest water, which was a drainage ditch. The female snake shed on 14 July and laid 26 eggs on 24 July in a plastic egg laying box filled with moistened sphagnum moss. Sixteen of these eggs hatched on 16–17 September, an incubation period of 54 days. The neonates' weights

Eastern Mud Snake, *Farancia abacura abacura* (photo by David G. Campbell)

A number of snakes such as this mud snake make use of both cryptic and aposematic (warning) coloration. Snakes with bright undersides often expose them when threatened, possibly mimicking a brightly colored coral snake. (photo by Roxanne Rossi)

ranged from 2 to 5 grams with an average weight of 3.4 grams. The neonates ranged 19–22.2 cm (7.48–8.74 inches) TL, with an average TL of 20.6 cm (8.1 inches). The SVL ranged 17.1–19.7 cm (6.75–7.75 inches) and the average SVL was 18.3 cm. There were 5 males and 11 females—a sex ratio of 2.2:1 females:males. There was a distinct sexual dimorphism in the tail length, with males having a tail length of 3.18 cm (1.25 inches) and females having a tail length of 1.9 cm (0.75 inches). The males also had thicker tails.

The eggs were left with the mother for the first month at a temperature of approximately 23°C (73°F). She coiled around the eggs during this period and came out only to shed and drink. The eggs began to develop brown spots and several died, apparently from a fungal infection, so the rest of the eggs were transferrred to vermiculite mixed with water at a 1:1 ratio by weight, and incubated a temperatures fluctuating from 25 to 27.7°C (77 to 82°F). Interestingly, the mother had left the eggs at this point. Perhaps she sensed that they would not hatch if these conditions persisted. The eggs were nonadherent, so they were easily separated. The low temperatures to which the eggs

were exposed during the first month may have prolonged the incubation period.

The mud snake can be a very difficult snake to maintain in captivity because its food is very difficult to obtain. In addition, the ideal cage arrangement for this species has not yet been determined. There are several tricks and suggestions that have helped considerably, however. Mehrtens suggests using moist mulch 5–7.5 cm (2–3) inches deep as the substrate and laying bark on the surface. Others experienced in keeping mud snakes have suggested that artificial carpet/turf and crumpled newspaper will work. We prefer cypress or pine mulch as these snakes will wander considerably in their cages and damage their snouts unless they are in a dark secure place. Hide boxes, especially plastic ones, will usually be thrown about the cage unless they are well secured or very heavy, and some snakes will not use them. The same is true for water bowls. Therefore, mulch is apparently the substrate of choice for these snakes. Mist it well once per week, stir it every few weeks, and change it every 3–4 months. Large cages can be set up as "aqua-terrariums" with a divider separating the land (mulch) from the water, while small cages can include a shallow water bowl embedded in the mulch. The snakes will burrow in the mulch and rest comfortably most of the day and emerge at night for a swim, presumably to look for food. They will also enter the water during the day occasionally. Some keepers do not have water in the regular cage, but take the snakes to another aquarium once weekly for feeding or for a drink. Either method is acceptable. The former method is perhaps a little less stressful, and hence good for recently captured specimens; the latter makes it easier to keep the cage clean and works well with long-term captives.

The regular food of the adults includes amphiumas and sirens, but some (very few) individuals will take frogs or fish. Eels may also be consumed. Two tricks have been devised to feed these snakes if one does not have unlimited access to these large aquatic salamanders. The first involves rubbing a frozen amphiuma or siren on a freshly thawed amphibian or fish or even on pinkies or fuzzies. The second involves placing the intended food object in a small aquarium with a live amphiuma or siren for 1–2 hours before offering it to the snake. The snakes definitely seem to prefer to take their food in the water but will take it occasionally when they are on "dry land." This is not such a great idea if you are using mulch because of the possibility of accidental ingestion of that substrate.

Recently, some unexpected food items have been taken with apparently great relish by some captive specimens. Winchester Seyle of the U.S. Army Corps of Engineers has had a number of these snakes consume marbled salamanders, *Ambystoma opacum*. A specimen in our care has eaten several dusky salamanders, *Desmognathus fuscus*. There are probably many other terrestrial species of salamander that these snakes will consume, but more work is needed. It is not known if these animals represent a balanced diet for this snake or if they are parasitized. Interestingly, Seyle has noticed, as have we, that slimy salamanders, *Plethodon glutinosis*, are not consumed by these snakes. Slimy salamanders are known to produce a secretion which is very distasteful, so this is not surprising.

Many terrestrial amphibians may be threatened with extinction from environmental destruction or pollution so their use as food is not a suitable and practical approach to long-term captive maintenance and breeding and is not recommended. However, these observations, combined with the judicious use of the more common amphibians, may help us to develop a practical feeding strategy which is not so dependent on wild-caught amphibians in the future, when they may be very rare.

If salamanders of any kind are in very short supply, there are two more tricks which have been used with great success recently. The first, courtesy of Mr. Seyle, involves slicing open a siren or amphiuma and stuffing it with mice. This will really provide a super meal that lasts a long time. We have had success cutting off pieces of a dead siren and sewing them onto the lead fuzzy in a "fuzzy train." This is one way to really stretch the number of meals per siren. Once again, the nutritive value of a fuzzy train to a mud snake is unknown, but when sirens are in short supply, this meal seems to keep both the snake and the keeper happy. Incidentally, most mud snakes will gladly accept frozen and thawed sirens, so storage and parasite control are not as big a problem as previously thought. However, do not become overly confident with the freezing technique as a method of total parasite control. Metazoan eggs are indeed distorted and ruptured by the process, but protozoans and bacteria are probably often unharmed. A fecal exam performed on a greater siren, *Siren lacertina*, that had been frozen for 6 months revealed numerous live ciliates and other protozoans.

Mr. Seyle has developed an interesting variation of feeding this snake in a separate aquarium. He places the snake and intended food in a 5-gallon bucket with about 3–4 inches of water,

---

SPECIES: *Farancia abacura*, Mud Snake

MAINTENANCE DIFFICULTY INDEX: 5 (1 = easiest, 5 = most difficult)

AVERAGE SIZE: 102–137 cm (40–54 inches)

FOOD: Amphiumas, sirens, or fish or frogs scented with these. Young eat tadpoles of many different frogs.

CAGE SIZE: 30–40-gallon aquarium

SUBSTRATE: Cypress mulch

VENTRAL HEAT: No, but heated water is helpful, tea may be useful. See Striped Crayfish Snake.

UV LIGHT: Yes?

TEMPERATURE RANGE: 24–30°C (75–86°F) day; 18–22°C (64–72°F) night; 10–15°C (50–59°F) brumation.

SPECIAL CONSIDERATIONS: Snakes usually eat under water. Food is difficult to obtain. Feed in separate aquarium.

snaps on the lid, and leaves them together overnight. We have used this technique recently ourselves. It works fantastically. The full snake can just be gently placed back in its cage the following morning.

The mud snake has been bred in captivity but special care if any was not reported (Trutnau, 1981). In the absence of any specific information, one should attempt breeding as reported in the general care section. (See also Table 5.) The eggs will be deposited in the mulch and the female may coil around them. It is not known at this time if the female is guarding the eggs, incubating them, or performing some other function, but very high hatching rates have been achieved by removing the eggs from the mother and incubating them as described in the general care section.

The care of the young is similar to that of the adults except that the babies will feed voraciously on tadpoles. Their favorites include most species of *Rana*, but *Hyla* and *Bufo* (true frogs, treefrogs, and toads respectively) tadpoles are also taken. Like the adults, the babies should be fed in shallow water. We have observed the infamous spine on the tip of the tail "popping" large tadpoles, so even a small snake can eat a medium to large tadpole. Young amphiumas and sirens as well as dwarf sirens will also be consumed, of course. Some specimens will take frozen and thawed tadpoles while others seem to cue in on the motion and so will not take dead items. Remember that these snakes are largely nocturnal, so if you are having feeding problems, try feeding at night. House these snakes individually as they will fight over food. They will also fight with young rainbow snakes over tadpoles.

A 10-gallon aquarium is a sufficient size cage for a baby, while a 40-gallon should be large enough for most adults.

Brumation should be carried out in the same cage using the same kind of substrate, cypress mulch. See the section on winter cooldown (brumation and hibernation).

Remember the problem with most amphibian and/or fish eaters is the potential for parasitism. Therefore, one should have a fecal exam performed every 6 months to a year and treat if needed. Nematodes (roundworms) and other parasites have been found in these snakes.

In the wild, moisture and temperature levels determine the availability of food for young mud snakes. Semlitsch et al. (1988) determined that when tadpoles are scarce because of little or no precipitation, these snakes delay hatching or brumate until spring. The captive breeder had better take this into consideration when caring for the newly hatched young in the fall. If the tadpole supply is very short, you should probably put the babies into brumation right away in order to conserve their limited fat reserves. If you have access to a large number of tadpoles, you can feed them heavily before brumation or skip brumation completely the first year. Most hatchling mud snakes seem well prepared to go months in brumation without eating first.

Ernst and Barbour reported that one mud snake survived over 18 years at the Philadelphia Zoo (Ernst and Barbour, 1989; Snider and Bowler, 1992).

One last word is in order. Some of these snakes will not adapt to captivity and refuse to eat no matter what tricks are used. If the snake is still healthy, consider releasing it where it was found, but see the section on releasing snakes for further warnings.

Farancia erytrogramma
Rainbow Snake

One of our most beautiful native snakes, the rainbow snake is also one of the most difficult to maintain in captivity. The rainbow snake ranges from southern Maryland southward to Florida and westward to southeastern Louisiana. It is a large snake, with adults ranging 69–122 cm (27–48 inches) in length up to 168 cm (66 inches) (Conant and Collins, 1991). They are basically black with longitudinal red stripes dorsally, and yellow with rows of black spots ventrally. The smooth scales give the snake a lustrous iridescent appearance. Indeed the head and neck region are intricately patterned and extremely attractive. Like the mud snake, its closest relative, the rainbow snake possesses a terminal spine which it sometimes presses into the skin of a person trying to handle it. Presumably the purpose of this behavior may be to startle a predator for an instant into letting go of the snake.

The rainbow snake's habitat has been characterized as waterways surrounded by sandy soil (Ernst and Barbour, 1989) or streams in cypress swamps (Wright and Wright, 1957; Mount, 1975;

Farancia erytrogramma

Linzey and Clifford, 1981; Conant and Collins, 1991). Certainly, we have seen them in very large rivers and small creeks, as well as swamps.

Virtually nothing is known of the thermal preferences of this species, although it is believed that they are nocturnal. Those in the northern part of the range may brumate, while those in the south are believed to be active all year (Gibbon et al., 1977).

Wild adults are known to feed primarily on eels, *Anguilla rostrata*, but large aquatic salamanders and other amphibians are occasionally taken. Rothman (1961) observed captive juveniles eat red-backed salamanders, *Plethodon cinereus*, two-lined salamanders, *Eurycea bislineata*, and dusky salamanders, *Desmognathus* sp. We have observed the hatchlings regularly consume tadpoles of many different species.

Known predators of this species include hawks (Richmond, 1945), wading birds, raccoons, kingsnakes, coral snakes, and alligators are also likely predators. An indigo snake disgorged an adult rainbow snake (Neill, 1964).

The mating season is thought to be primarily in the spring, with up to 52 eggs being laid from June through August (Linzey and Clifford, 1981). These eggs usually hatch in 70–80 days into young measuring 20–26 cm (7.8–10.2 inches) (Ernst and Barbour, 1989).

These snakes are known to be heavily parasitized in some areas (Richmond, 1945).

The behavior of wild individuals gives a very good clue as to possible captive maintenance arrangements. These snakes are known to emerge from the water during the day and enter subterranean cavities or burrow into soil. At dusk they return to the water (Neill, 1964). They have also been observed to brumate out of the water (Gibbon et al., 1977).

The rainbow snake, one of the most beautiful snakes in the world, is best kept exactly like the mud snake, but its favorite food appears to be eels instead of sirens. Fortunately, eels can be obtained commercially in many areas. Like the mud snake, the rainbow snake will accept large aquatic salamanders (amphiumas and sirens) and almost anything flavored by them. Juvenile rainbow snakes, like the mud snakes we have worked with, have also been observed to eat terrestrial salamanders of the genera *Eurycea*, *Desmognathus*, and *Plethodon* in captivity (Rothman, 1961). They do prefer to eat underwater but will readily swallow food on land after they have seized it in the water. Some will take food on land. (See the section on feeding mud snakes.) Like the mud snakes, the ideal feeding arrangement appears to be a separate aquarium with shallow water into which the intended prey has been placed. Remember that these snakes are largely crepuscular (dawn and dusk feeders) and that partial darkness may contribute to your feeding success. Adults will usually take items which have been previously frozen and thawed.

Like the mud snakes, the young are voracious tadpole eaters, but will also take dwarf sirens, juvenile lesser and greater sirens, and the terrestrial salamanders mentioned above;

Common Rainbow Snake, *Farancia erytrogramma erytrogramma* (photo by R. D. Bartlett)

however, they are definitely far less likely to take dead prey than the mud snake juveniles are. Interestingly, once the tadpoles undergo metamorphosis and lose their tails, these snakes seem to lose all interest in them. Although frogs have been reported as an occasional food item in wild specimens, the captives which we maintained from northern Florida seemed to show no interest in them.

Fighting will occur over food so it is best to house and feed these snakes singly.

Housing, brumation, and breeding should be attempted as for the mud snake, although there is little known about the details of breeding in captivity. Like the female mud snake, the rainbow snake may coil about her eggs, but in cap-

tivity the eggs should be removed and incubated in the usual manner. (See the section on care of the eggs, the mud snake discussion, and rainbow snake in the reproduction chart [Table 5].)

Rainbow snakes are prone to parasitism because of their diet. Roundworms have been reported but there are probably numerous others; therefore, they should be dewormed initially and be checked for worms regularly afterward. These snakes are also prone to skin infections if kept in neutral or slightly basic water (i.e., with a pH around 7–7.4 like most tap water) that is not heated at all, and not kept clean. The specimens in our care seemed to be quite comfortable at water temperatures above 90°F, eating well and shedding frequently.

SPECIES: *Farancia erytrogramma*, Rainbow Snake
MAINTENANCE DIFFICULTY INDEX: 5 (1 = easiest, 5 = most difficult)
AVERAGE SIZE: 91–122 cm (36–48 inches)
FOOD: Eels, sirens, amphiumas, and fish and frogs with the scent of the first three items
CAGE SIZE: 30–40-gallon aquarium
SUBSTRATE: Cypress mulch
VENTRAL HEAT: No, but heated water is helpful, tea may be useful. See Striped Crayfish Snake.
UV LIGHT: Yes?
TEMPERATURE RANGE: 24–30°C (75–86°F)
SPECIAL CONSIDERATIONS: Snakes usually eat under water. Food is difficult to obtain. Feed in separate aquarium.

Ficimia streckeri
Mexican Hooknose Snake

The Mexican hooknose is a small 14–28-cm (5.5–11-inch) snake with a recorded maximum length of 48.3 cm (19 inches). They are chunky little snakes, generally gray to dull brown, with unmarked heads and numerous dark (olive green to dark brown) blotches dorsally. Of course, they have a sharply upturned rostral scale (nose area) from which they get their name. The entire hooknose group looks very much like small hognose snakes, but they can be readily identified because they have smooth scales, not keeled as in the hognoses. Also, the area behind the point of the nose is flat or slightly indented in the hooknoses, while it is ridged (keeled) in the hognoses. Furthermore, all hooknose snakes have fewer than 20 rows of dorsal scales, while all hognoses have more than 20.

The Mexican hooknose ranges from southern Texas southward into Mexico along the east coast. Its preferred habitat appears to be thornbush or thornthicket woodlands near water

Ficimia streckeri

(Tennant, 1984, 1985; Stebbins, 1985). They are fossorial (burrowing) snakes that generally hide submerged in the soil by day and emerge at night to hunt for spiders, centipedes, and possibly scorpions.

Suspected predators of this species include ophiophagous snakes and carnivorous mammals.

Little is known of their reproduction aside from the fact that they are egg layers (Wright and Wright, 1957; Behler and King, 1979; Tennant, 1984, 1985; Stebbins, 1985). No clutch size or incubation times have been reported and the mating and laying seasons are unknown, although the closely related western hooknose has been reported to lay one egg in early July (Tennant, 1985), presumably having mated in the springtime.

In addition to the lack of information about reproduction, there is also a lack of information available about the behavioral ecology of this species. No body temperatures have been recorded (and reported) from active snakes of this species in the wild.

In captivity, the Mexican hooknose snake will do well if kept in a similar manner to its more widespread relative, the western hooknose. A burrowing substrate such as sand will work well for this snake and may be necessary in order to provide them with a sense of security so they will eat. Sand will stick to food items, however, and will be ingested by these snakes as they attempt to feed. For this reason, we recommend that one part of the sand layer be covered with medium-sized gravel and that this area be used for feeding prekilled items.

In addition to the gravel area, a moist retreat may be necessary. We noticed these snakes were particularly sensitive to desiccation and dysecdysis (difficult shedding). We successfully used partially submerged humidity boxes (plastic boxes with some semimoist sphagnum moss inside) to treat and prevent this problem.

Stable rocks placed in such a manner as to provide hiding places above and below the sand are considered very beneficial and will provide trapping areas if live prey are used. Plastic cacti are nice additions to the terrarium that will not injure the snake or harbor pathogens, which is possible if a live plant is used.

An incandescent bulb (25 or 40 watts) in a reflector lamp placed approximately 30 cm (12

Mexican Hooknose Snake, *Ficimia streckeri* (photo by David G. Campbell)

inches) above the substrate will help to provide a thermal gradient in the cage during the day. Air temperatures of 25–30°C (77–86°F) have proven satisfactory for these nocturnal snakes.

Water should be provided in a small bowl, but remember that good ventilation is imperative if water is left in the cage permanently. Therefore, a screen top is strongly advisable.

Most specimens of this small snake will do well in a 5-gallon aquarium, although a 10-gallon can be used.

Feeding this snake may present a real problem. Not only are its preferred prey (spiders) somewhat difficult to procure, but so are the backups, scorpions and centipedes. Tennant (1984) reported that one long-maintained captive regularly ate a variety of small spiders, although it had difficulty capturing them. Fortunately, they will take spiders frozen and thawed, which makes food storage and parasite control more feasible, as well as making them easier for the snake to capture. One specimen in our care consumed frozen and thawed wolf spiders (family Lycosidae). See the section on the western hooknose for more details on capturing food items.

Insects are generally refused, although one specimen in Tennant's care refused both spiders and centipedes but ate cave crickets (Tennant, 1984).

Another trick that has occasionally worked for the western hooknose will work with this species as well. Rub a small pinky vigorously with a frozen and thawed spider. Some snakes may thus be tricked into taking the pinky.

Depending on the temperature and size of the food items offered, these snakes may be expected to eat every 1–5 days during the summer and every 3–4 weeks in the winter if they eat at all during this time.

Captive brumation for this and other desert invertebrate eaters is still poorly understood. It is known that when these snakes are exposed to temperature fluctuations, they will eat occasionally during the warm periods. We would therefore advise using the seminatural approach to brumation discussed in the general care section and continuing to provide heat from above in the form of an incandescent bulb daily for at least 5 or 6 hours for all but a very short period during the coldest part of winter. During that 1–2 month period, the light over the cage may be left off and the snake should not be disturbed. It may emerge on warmer days and drink, but will probably not eat during this extremely cool period. Fluctuating temperatures down into the 40s Fahrenheit may be well tolerated by this species in the winter, although 10–15°C (50–59°F) will probably be suitable for this snake as well.

As mentioned above, nearly nothing is known about the reproductive cycle of this snake. Its

SPECIES: *Ficimia streckeri*, Mexican Hooknose Snake
MAINTENANCE DIFFICULTY INDEX: 4 (1 = easiest, 5 = most difficult)
AVERAGE SIZE: 14–28 cm (5.5–11 inches)
FOOD: Spiders, centipedes, scorpions
CAGE SIZE: 5–10-gallon aquarium
SUBSTRATE: Sand, loose soil
VENTRAL HEAT: No
UV LIGHT: No, but an incandescent bulb is useful
TEMPERATURE RANGE: 25–30°C (77–86°F)
SPECIAL CONSIDERATIONS: Diet difficult to procure unless crickets are taken. Likely to
  be parasitized. Secretive, nocturnal.

closest relative in the United States, the western hooknose, is known to lay small clutches of eggs during the early summer, and we suspect this species may be similar. In the absence of any specific information, breeding and incubation should be attempted as described for most other snakes in the general care section.

These snakes may be extremely heavily parasitized and this may often result in their demise in captive situations. One specimen examined by us contained rhabditiform larvae and a coccidian. This particular specimen also contained *Entamoeba*, which we believe it contracted during its passage through a crowded pet facility.

Another important observation about these snakes is that they appear somewhat nervous.

Like the western hooknose, these snakes will engage in an extremely animated writhing if molested. This may be followed by the snake assuming a viperlike stance according to Tennant (1985).

Slavens and Slavens (1990, 1991) did not list a single specimen of this snake in captivity, and neither they nor Snider and Bowler (1992) listed a captive longevity. As mentioned above, Tennant (1984) mentioned a "long-maintained captive," but unfortunately did not mention how long. We have had a difficult time procuring these snakes until recently and cannot offer much information along the lines of longevity. One specimen survived 9 months, when it died from a protozoal gastroenteritis.

Gyalopion canum
Western Hooknose Snake

The most widespread of the hooknoses, the western hooknose ranges from southeastern Arizona through southern New Mexico, to western and central Texas and southward into central Mexico. They are slightly shorter and perhaps not quite as heavy-bodied as the Mexican hooknose, with most specimens recorded so far being 14–38 cm (5.5–12.5 inches), with a recorded maximum of 38.4 cm (15.1 inches) (Conant and Collins, 1991).

This snake is apparently a habitat generalist, as it is found in a wide variety of habitats from

low creosote and mesquite deserts (Wright and Wright, 1957; Stebbins, 1985; Conant and Collins, 1991) to short grass prairies (Tennant, 1984, 1985; Stebbins, 1985) and up into low mountains (elevation 5000 feet) (Wright and Wright, 1957). In New Mexico, it has been found most often in grass-covered foothills at intermediate elevations (Degenhardt et al., 1996).

As with all of the hooknoses, the preferred food of this species is spiders. Other items reported in the literature include centipedes and

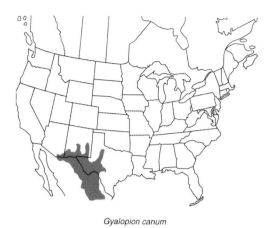

Gyalopion canum

scorpions (Kauffield, 1948; Wright and Wright, 1957; Tennant, 1984, 1985; Stebbins, 1985; Conant and Collins, 1991), but Stebbins (1985) also listed small snakes. Kauffield (1948) tried a number of other food items including millipedes, lizards, small snakes, frogs, and pinky mice but these were all refused. However, see below. Also, a large specimen collected in Chihuahua, Mexico, readily consumed pinky mice, and one from Texas ate rat legs, lizard legs, and strips of beef (Degenhardt et al., 1996).

This snake possesses an unusual behavioral repertoire. If disturbed it may writhe as if in pain and then may evert its cloaca, which produces a clicking sound.

Known predators of this species include mottled rock rattlesnakes, Texas coral snakes, and spotted skunks (Tennant, 1984). Degenhardt et al. (1996) reported that ringneck snakes may also eat them, since a larger ringneck was once found with a smaller hooknose in its jaws. Interestingly, the hooknose also had the ringneck in its jaws and Vaeth (1980) reported that a captive western hooknose ate a ringneck almost as long as itself.

As with the other hooknose snakes, reproductive information is virtually nonexistent. Tennant (1985) reported on one female that laid one egg 2.9 cm (1.15 inches) long in early July.

The western hooknose has had a very bad reputation as a captive snake, but it is not that impossible to maintain in captivity after all. It is true that the hooknose specializes on food items that do not sound too savory to us, namely spiders, scorpions, and centipedes (particularly the first two). And it is true that these items are not always easy to provide in great quantity.[1] However, we have devised some tricks to make the task of feeding these handsome little snakes much easier. First, both spiders and scorpions that have been frozen and thawed will be greedily consumed by the hooknose if they are placed in the cage just before dusk when these little snakes come to the surface. Furthermore, since these snakes are extremely scent-oriented, they will consume prekilled pinkies that have been rubbed with spiders or scorpions. The latter observation has made a tremendous difference in the ease of keeping this species in captivity as a frozen spider can be used to rub the dead pinkies. It is important to note, however, that there are certain times of the year when these snakes are more accepting of such trickery, namely late spring and early summer, and that the average spider seems to run out of flavor after three or four scentings. Some of these snakes will readily consume live crickets, so they are always worth trying.

If spiders are used, a 10-gram snake will probably consume quite a few every year. One specimen in our care consumed 60 spiders, 9 scorpions, and 6 pinkies one year, and 91 spiders, 3 scorpions, and 2 pinkies during its second full year in captivity. A wide variety of

---

[1] Although collecting spiders and scorpions may be somewhat time-consuming, herpetologists may easily collect the necessary items when they are out in the field for other purposes. Road cruising will provide the greatest number of spiders just as it does snakes. Typically, very small blue-green eyeshine indicates a spider. Upon sighting, the spider may be captured alive by placing a top-sealing plastic bag over it (this is more easily done at night) or collected for freezing by swatting it quickly with the hand. This technique may either stun or kill the spider depending on how hard one swats. One may wish to use a glove for this purpose, but this is not necessary with most wolf spiders. Although we have not tested it, we would suspect that SCORPIONS MAY NOT BE COLLECTED IN THIS MANNER. Instead, one may use a pair of forceps to grasp the scorpion near the stinger and place it in a suitable container.

Using the above methods, one may collect dozens of spiders in one night, and these may all be frozen for future use.

Western Hooknose Snake, *Gyalopion canum* (photo by David G. Campbell)

spiders will be accepted, but wolf spiders (family Lycosidae) appear to be the favorites. Fishing spiders, *Dolomedes* sp., from Florida were also consumed, suggesting these snakes are not very picky (these are aquatic spiders that are not likely to be common in the natural range of this snake). Interestingly, jumping spiders (family Salticidae) *from Florida* were usually refused by those snakes we maintained. The scorpions consumed were of the genus *Centruroides*, probably *C. vittatus*, a species not found in the range of the western hooknose but closely related to those found in that region.

The captive environment we have found that works best for these snakes appears to be nothing more than a desert (sand) setup, just as one would provide for a shovelnose snake. Generally, an area with several large stable rocks is advisable as these provide hiding places and are excellent areas in which to serve frozen and thawed spiders. Placing items on a rock will often avoid having it become coated with sand prior to consumption by the snake. A water bowl may be provided as long as the ventilation in the cage is good. A heat source in the form of an incandescent bulb over the

---

SPECIES: *Gyalopion canum*, Western Hooknose Snake
MAINTENANCE DIFFICULTY INDEX: 4 (1 = easiest, 5 = most difficult)
AVERAGE SIZE: 14–38 cm (5.5–12.5 inches)
FOOD: Spiders, centipedes, scorpions, scented pinky, crickets
CAGE SIZE: 5–10-gallon aquarium
SUBSTRATE: Sand
VENTRAL HEAT: No
UV LIGHT: No, but an incandescent bulb is useful
TEMPERATURE RANGE: 25–30°C (77–86°F)
SPECIAL CONSIDERATIONS: Diet often difficult to procure. Secretive, nocturnal.

---

screen top is required. A 25–40-watt bulb will work in most cases. Air temperatures fluctuating between 19 and 35°C (66 and 95°F) during the active season have been well tolerated by specimens in our care, although 25–30°C (77–86°F) would probably be acceptable.

Interestingly, one specimen housed in the basic cage setup (artificial carpet/turf, a hide box, etc.) refused to eat until it was placed in a more natural arrangement.

These snakes will shed every 3 weeks during the summer and every 2 months during the spring and fall. We have not seen any shedding problems with those in our care.

With regard to parasites and other medical problems, we have not found these snakes to be heavily parasitized by metazoans (worms), although we have found several with protozoans, namely coccidia. These were cleared with a dose of sulfadimethoxine (Albon®) given at a dose of 90 mg/kg every other day for three treatments. The dose was injected into the thorax of a frozen and thawed spider that was then offered to the snake as food.

One specimen housed in a poorly ventilated shoe box succumbed to a fungal pneumonia (branching nonseptate fungal hyphae were observed upon necropsy of this snake). Another specimen housed in a crowded cage as a food snake died from amoebiasis shortly after we acquired it.

Brumation may be accomplished in the regular cage and no special modifications are necessary. Fluctuating temperatures ranging from 3 to 18°C (38 to 65°F) during the winter have been well tolerated by the specimens in our care.

To our knowledge, this snake has not yet been bred in captivity. However, it is very likely to have a spring breeding and summer laying cycle and hence we would advise attempting captive breeding and egg incubation in the usual manner as discussed in the general care section.

Slavens and Slavens (1990, 1991) did not list a single specimen in captivity and no captive longevity has been reported. One specimen in our care survived 2 years and 11 months, and we have heard unconfirmed reports of one specimen surviving in captivity for 5 years.

In general, these are very adaptable and alert little snakes that are usually good eaters and a real pleasure to observe. One specimen yawned after a meal and displayed excellent control (independent movement) over the enlarged rear teeth of its upper jaw. In fact, it looked much like a rattlesnake adjusting its fangs after a big meal. Careful observation in captivity may reveal many more interesting facts about these tough little snakes.

Gyalopion quadrangulare
Desert Hooknose Snake

The desert hooknose (previously known as the thornscrub hooknose, then desert, etc.) is an attractively marked animal. Dark black saddles and reddish bands of variable thickness and intensity running down the sides, combined with a cream or yellow background color, give this snake a very striking appearance. Perhaps this snake is in the process of evolving a color pattern to mimic the largely sympatric (having overlapping geographic ranges) western coral snake. Rare within the United States, this small snake (usually 15–33 cm, 6–13 inches) had been found only in extreme southeastern Arizona in Santa Cruz County until recently, when

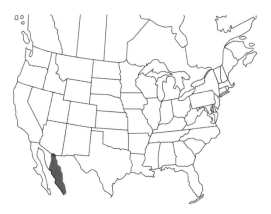

Gyalopion quadrangulare

Desert Hooknose Snake, *Gyalopion quadrangulare* (photo by David G. Campbell)

one specimen was found in Pima County, west of Tucson (Trescott, pers. comm., 1993).

The preferred habitat of this species within the United States is in loose soil near the base of grassy rolling hills, and this might be expected because spiders, its favorite food, are common there also. Other food items taken by these snakes in the wild include scorpions and centipedes (Behler and King, 1979; Stebbins, 1985). They appear to be strictly nocturnal since they have rarely been found on the surface during the day. Virtually nothing is known about reproduction in these snakes.

Predators are also unknown. One was found in a road-killed coral snake on Ruby Road near Pina Blanca Lake in southern Arizona (Finnegan, pers. comm., 1992).

Trescott observed and videotaped a fascinating behavior in one member of this species. Upon being cornered, this snake raised its head and vertically compressed its anterior quarter, appearing quite cobralike.

In captivity, the desert hooknose snake may be kept in a similar manner to its more widespread relatives, the Mexican and western hooknoses. A burrowing substrate such as loose humus soil or sand will work well for this snake and may be necessary in order to provide them with a sense of security so they will eat.

Stable rocks placed in such a manner as to provide hiding places above and below the soil are considered very beneficial and will provide trapping areas if live prey are used. Plastic cacti are nice additions to the terrarium that will not injure the snake or harbor pathogens, which is possible if a live plant is used.

As with other fossorial snakes, an incandescent bulb (15–25 watts is suitable) in a reflector lamp placed approximately 30 cm (12 inches) above the substrate will help to provide a thermal gradient in the cage during the day.

Water should be provided in a small bowl, but remember that good ventilation is imperative if water is left in the cage permanently. Therefore, a screen top is strongly advisable. Randy Babb, biologist with the Arizona Game and Fish Department, suggests that the water bowl be allowed to overflow on occasion in order to provide a small moist area, even though the rest of the cage is kept dry. We have successfully used a plastic box stuffed with sphagnum moss to provide a high-humidity retreat.

A 5–10-gallon aquarium should be a suitably sized enclosure for most members of this species.

Remember that like the other hooknoses, this snake feeds on spiders, scorpions, and centipedes. Fortunately, they will take spiders and centipedes frozen and thawed, which should

SPECIES: *Gyalopion quadrangulare*, Desert Hooknose Snake
MAINTENANCE DIFFICULTY INDEX: 4 (1 = easiest, 5 = most difficult)
AVERAGE SIZE: 15–33 cm (6–13 inches)
FOOD: Spiders, centipedes, scorpions, and crickets
CAGE SIZE: 5–10-gallon aquarium
SUBSTRATE: Sand, loose soil
VENTRAL HEAT: No
UV LIGHT: No, but an incandescent bulb is useful
TEMPERATURE RANGE: 25–30°C (77–86°F)
SPECIAL CONSIDERATIONS: Diet often difficult to procure. Secretive, nocturnal.

make food storage and parasite control more feasible. See the section on the western hooknose for more details on capturing food items. Scenting pinky mice with spiders may also be of some value as discussed in the last two hooknose sections. At least some will also readily consume crickets (Babb, pers. comm., 1993; Trescott, pers. comm., 1993; personal observation).

Captive brumation for this and other desert invertebrate eaters is still poorly understood. Once again, the reader is referred to the discussion on brumation in the section on western and Mexican hooknoses.

As mentioned above, nearly nothing is known about the reproductive cycle of this snake. Its closest relative in the United States, the western hooknose, is known to lay small clutches of eggs during the early summer and we suspect this species may be similar. In the absence of any specific information, breeding and incubation should be attempted as described for most other snakes in the general care section.

These snakes may be more fastidious in captivity than the other members of this genus. One herpetoculturist having experience with both this species and a western hooknose said that the desert hooknose did not eat well under the same conditions and being offered the same food as the western hooknoses. On the other hand, William Woodin noted in Fowlie (1965) that this species would feed readily on spiders in captivity, and Babb had one feed regularly on spiders, scorpions, and crickets for 1 year and 6 months. We have also had one of these snakes feed extremely well in captivity. Not enough specimens have been studied in captivity to draw any conclusions on whether or not they are actually more difficult to maintain in captivity than the western hooknose.

Slavens and Slavens (1990, 1991) did not list a single specimen of this snake in captivity, and no longevity record was given. As mentioned above, one specimen was maintained for 1 year and 6 months. One in our care survived 4 years and 5 months.

Heterodon nasicus
Western Hognose Snake

The western hognose is perhaps one of the first noncolubrine and nonboid North American snakes to become popular as a captive. One of the reasons is because their diet in captivity regularly includes mice and the young readily consume pinkies. This has allowed good qual-

ity control of the diet, resulting in parasite-free captives that can then be bred. Compare this with the other members of the genus, the eastern and southern hognose, that are infrequently kept because of their dietary preferences or because they succumb to parasitism and die after a short period in captivity—or survive but fail to thrive and breed. This is not a necessary outcome for the latter two species as the western hognose demonstrates.

The western hognose occupies a huge geographic area in North America. It ranges from southeastern Alberta through southern Saskatchewan and southwestern Manitoba southward through many of the central plains states into northern Mexico, with isolated populations in Illinois, Minnesota, Iowa, and Missouri. There are three subspecies: the plains hognose snake, *H. n. nasicus*, the dusty hognose, *H. n. gloydi*, and the Mexican hognose, *H. n. kennerlyi*. These subspecies may be distinguished from each other by either counting the dorsal blotches (the plains has more dorsal blotches, 35+ in males, 40+ in females, compared with 32− and 37− in male and female dusty hognoses) or by the scales on the head (the Mexican hognose has six or fewer scales behind the rostral-nose scale, while the other two subspecies have nine (Stebbins, 1985; Conant and

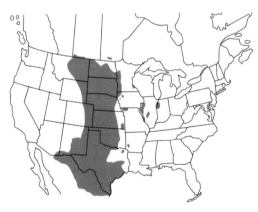

Heterodon nasicus

Collins, 1991). The preferred habitat of this species appears to be sandy-soiled grass-dominated areas, namely prairies, although in south Texas the Mexican hognose occurs in thorn woodland (Tennant, 1985) and in Arizona it occurs in canyons, farmlands, desert scrub, and along streams, rivers, and woodlands (Lowe et al., 1986). The species' presence in grasslands, but also in other very widely differing habitat types, has also been observed in New Mexico (Degenhardt et al., 1996).

These diurnal (daytime active) wide-ranging, adaptable snakes have a very broad diet in the wild. Food items mentioned in the literature for this species have included toads (*Bufo* and *Scaphiopus*), leopard frogs and tadpoles, tiger salamanders, lizards, lizard eggs, snakes and snake eggs, turtle eggs, birds and their eggs (including pheasant and quail eggs), mice, and shrews (Wright and Wright, 1957; Platt, 1969; Pendlebury 1976; Barten, 1980; Iverson, 1990). Preston (1982) reported that western hognoses from Manitoba would also consume treefrogs, *Hyla* sp., Canadian toads, and minnows.

Body (cloacal) temperatures of active free-ranging western hognoses in Kansas were 21.4–36.2°C (70–97°F) (Platt, 1969).

Known predators of this species include Swainson's hawk, buteo hawks, ferruginous hawks, coyotes, crows, and eastern hognose snakes (Platt, 1969; Blair and Schitoskey, 1982). Iverson (1975) reported a case of attempted cannibalism. Greene and Oliver (1965) reported seeing a western massasauga eat a road-killed western hognose snake.

The reproductive cycle of this species is similar to many other North American snakes. Breeding generally occurs in the spring but has been reported in the fall as well (Platt, 1969). Egg laying occurs from June to August but peaks around early July. Recorded clutch sizes have varied from 2 to 28 (Wright and Wright, 1957; Sabath and Worthington, 1959; Mattison, 1991) with 39 and 61 eggs listed as the largest clutches on record (Fitch, 1970; Shaw and Campbell, 1974). Clutches are usually 8–12, however, and these eggs generally hatch in 47–64 days (Preston, 1982; Tennant, 1985).

Generally, the western hognose will thrive in captivity if given the basic (ideal) cage arrangement described in the general care section. Artificial carpet/turf works well and in fact seems to help avoid muscle atrophy that is all too common in long-term captives of the sedentary species by giving them a rougher more natural substrate than newspaper. Many specimens will try to get under it and some will succeed, but the same can be said for newspaper. Most specimens will stay on it rather than under it if it is cut to fit flush with the cage sides and they are given a hide box that is dark

Western Hognose Snake, *Heterodon nasicus* (photo by David G. Campbell)

and secure. Cypress mulch, aspen shavings, or pine mulch may also be used successfully for some specimens and is readily accepted by these burrowing snakes. A nontippable bowl of clean water should always be available. Plastic plants are a nice addition.

Ventral heat is probably not necessary if the air temperature is maintained at 25–30°C (77–86°F), although several authors have reported that slightly lower temperatures, e.g., 23–27°C (73–81°F) daytime, 18–20°C (64–68°F) at night (Trutnau, 1981; Mehrtens, 1987), will be satisfactory for this species. Based on the body temperatures of active wild specimens, however, ventral heat would seem very advisable and may be helpful for long-term maintenance and especially for breeding purposes. Remember the benefits of providing a thermal gradient (see the general care section).

A UV light source is not considered essential for this species as it has been bred in captivity for numerous generations without access to this kind of light.

As mentioned above, adults will readily consume prekilled adult mice and juveniles will usually take pinkies; thus, there is never any reason to feed amphibians, although these will be greedily devoured. Rarely, a hatchling may need to be assisted in feeding (have the pinky or mouse tail placed in its mouth) until it starts on its own. One somewhat humorous feeding trick we discovered was that hatchlings engaged in the act of playing dead and lying upside down with their mouths open will consistently take pinky mice that are placed in their open mouths. Furthermore, some may partially swallow the pinky while lying upside down. In addition, hatchlings that resist consuming pinkies initially will often take prekilled Mediterranean geckos, like many other western snakes.

Like all hognoses, they can consume objects even larger than an experienced herpetoculturist would expect for many other species, and this is useful when feeding time rolls around (hatchlings will eat pinkies, then fuzzies, very quickly, while many yearlings have no problems swallowing an adult mouse).

Winter cooldown is strongly recommended for this species, especially for those from the northern part of the range. This can be carried out in the regular cage since no special modifications seem necessary. Do not bother to offer food at this time as many will refuse to feed and this may predispose to vomiting or other problems. See the section on brumation. Temperatures of 5–10°C (41–50°F) for 4–5 months are appropriate brumation temperatures. Those in our care showed no ill effects when exposed to temperature fluctuations from 3 to 18°C (38 to 65°F) during the winter months.

Breeding has not presented a problem and has been accomplished numerous times in captivity. Treat the snakes as mentioned in the general care section on breeding.

The female usually will deposit the eggs about 1–2 months after breeding. These eggs may be incubated in the usual manner and hatch in about 50–60 days.

One fascinating observation was that one female flared her neck and turned sideways in order to scoop and pack nesting material against her eggs. We had previously only observed the neck-flaring behavior as a defensive response.

Feeding once to twice a week, these young snakes will grow rapidly. Females approach sexual maturity at about 2 years of age, while males may breed as early as 8 months. One 8-month-old male in our care totally amazed us when he mated with a 2-year-old female more than twice his size! Her first clutch of 11 eggs was laid 60 days after her 10 April mating (11 June) and 10 of these eggs hatched from 3 to 5 August (an incubation period of 55–57 days at an average temperature of 82°C).

Double clutching is quite possible in captive specimens. One 3-year-old female in our care laid 16 eggs on 1 June and another 10 eggs on 18 July. Fifteen of the first clutch hatched from 24 July to 27 July, and all of the second clutch hatched on 6 September. Hence, the incubation period of the first clutch was 53–56 days, and the incubation period of the second clutch was 50–51 days.

The young take their time leaving the eggs after the first slit is made (called pipping), sometimes taking more than 2 days. The babies are usually about 15–20 cm (6–8 inches) long at hatching and after shedding (about 1–2 weeks later) will usually aggressively feed on pinkies.

The young snakes may be housed exactly the same as the adults, but humidity boxes may be extremely helpful for them since they seem to dry out and may have difficulties shedding at times, although not to the extent that is seen in the two eastern species of hognoses. See the discussion on humidity in the general care section.

Overall, this is a very easy snake to maintain and breed in captivity. They are fairly attractive (some, including us, consider their pudgy appearance and upturned noses "cute"). They are unlikely to bite, even though they may not particularly like human contact at times. Perhaps a word of warning is in order, however. Even though they can rarely be induced to bite

---

SPECIES: *Heterodon nasicus*, Western Hognose Snake
MAINTENANCE DIFFICULTY INDEX: 1 (1 = easiest, 5 = most difficult)
AVERAGE SIZE: 40–90 cm (16–36 inches)
FOOD: Mice, frogs
CAGE SIZE: 10–20-gallon long aquarium
SUBSTRATE: Artificial turf, indoor-outdoor carpet, or newspaper
VENTRAL HEAT: Not essential, but helpful
UV LIGHT: No
TEMPERATURE RANGE: 25–30°C (77–86°F)
SPECIAL CONSIDERATIONS: Captive-born animals have few problems. Wild-caught animals are likely to be heavily parasitized. Rarely bite.

and can be treated as nonvenomous for all intents and purposes, they do possess a venom that can cause swelling and pain in humans (Bragg, 1960). One such bite resulted in 3 days in a hospital and permanent scarring for one individual (Veverka, pers. comm., 1992), so care should be taken when handling these snakes.

Snakes that are not handled frequently will continue to hiss loudly, flatten out, and strike with closed mouths. This is somewhat distressing to young snakekeepers and their parents.

An even more displeasing habit sometimes encountered with captives of this species is the regurgitation of foul-smelling largely digested stomach contents onto the holder when picked up (McKeown, pers. comm., 1993). Frequent handling may overcome these defensive behaviors and many of these snakes will become very handleable.

Captive longevity for this species has been reported at 19 years and 10 months (Slavens and Slavens, 1991; Snider and Bowler, 1992).

Heterodon platirhinos
Eastern Hognose Snake

Named for its upturned rostral (nose) scale, the eastern hognose is the largest of the three North American hognoses. They are heavy-bodied medium length snakes that are extremely variably colored.

Eastern hognose snakes range 51–84 cm (20–33 inches) in length, with a record length of 116 cm (45.5 inches) (Conant and Collins, 1991). The color varies from solid black to brown, gray, greenish, yellow, or pink with a variable pattern. The geographical distribution of these snakes is extensive. They range from southern New Hampshire and Vermont southward through Florida, and westward to Minnesota, South Dakota, Colorado, and most of Texas.

The habitat of the eastern hognose appears to vary considerably from place to place, as might be expected from a snake with such a large geographic range. However, it appears that habitats with loose, well-drained, sandy, upland soils are preferred (Wright and Wright, 1957; Platt, 1969; Mount, 1975; Ashton and Ashton, 1981; Linzey and Clifford, 1981; Tennant, 1984; Holman et al., 1990; Dundee and Rossman, 1989; Ernst and Barbour, 1989; Klemens, 1993; Collins, 1993; Mitchell, 1994). Vegetation on such areas has been described as fields, broken habitat, open forests, pine flatwoods, wooded hillsides, longleaf pine-turkey oak-dominated areas and xeric hammocks. The senior author found many in the hilly sandy-soiled pine bush

Heterodon platirhinos

area of Albany, New York. Palmer and Braswell (1995) reported that these snakes were most common in and around fallow and cultivated fields in North Carolina.

Limited studies on the thermal ecology of this species indicate that they have a voluntary temperature range (preferred optimum temperature range?) of 22–37°C (71.6–98.6°F) (Platt, 1969; Kitchell, 1969; Jones, 1976).

The preferred food of this species appears to be amphibians, particularly toads of the genera *Bufo* and *Scaphiopus*, but numerous other food items have been reported. These include fish, lizards, small snakes, reptile eggs, hatchling turtles, mice, chipmunks, earthworms, and insects (Wright and Wright, 1957; Platt, 1969; Ernst and Barbour, 1989). Other amphibians

Eastern Hognose Snake, *Heterodon platirhinos* (photo by David G. Campbell)

taken include spotted salamander, *Ambystoma maculatum*, and others, newts, *Notophthalmus* sp., and treefrogs, *Hyla* sp. (Wright and Wright, 1957; Platt, 1969; Edgren, 1955; Klemens, 1993; personal observations). The senior author once disturbed a wild hognose in Putnam County, New York, and it regurgitated a large red salamander, *Pseudotriton ruber*.

Known predators of this species include cottonmouths, kingsnakes, coachwhips, racers, black rat snakes, barred owls, and red-tailed hawks (Platt, 1969). A captive tarantula was reported by Owens (1949) to have eaten a hatchling.

Mating is known to occur primarily in the spring, usually from March to May. Up to 61 eggs are laid from May through July (Platt, 1969). These eggs usually hatch in 48–60 days, but the incubation period may vary from 31 to 88 days (Platt, 1969; Ernst and Barbour, 1989). The neonates measure 15–25 cm (5.9–9.8 inches) in length (Conant and Collins, 1991).

The eastern hognose snake is not a difficult snake to maintain in captivity. It will do well in the typical cage setup described in the general care section. Ventral heat does not appear to be necessary but has been used with no ill effects under the artificial carpet/turf. Since this snake does not climb well, branches are usually not

necessary. The water bowl should be shallow but untippable because they often will try to get underneath it. A Vitalite® or some other UV light source is strongly recommended as is a hide box.

The eastern hognose snake preys most frequently on amphibians in captivity; unless tricked or trained it will eat only frogs, toads, and salamanders. This presents two major problems—availability of food and parasitism. In fact, these snakes, like water snakes, are almost invariably parasitized and should probably be dewormed by a veterinarian at the time of capture and twice per year afterward. There are several tricks which can be utilized to "stretch" your food supply and reduce parasitism. The first one is to freeze your food. This will allow you to store amphibians for months, taking advantage of seasonal availability and also killing some of the parasites they might otherwise give to your snake. Trutnau has recommended tying a piece of a frog to a fish or some meat. This is, as he states, a good way to "stretch" your food supply, but we don't know how much you can do this before the diet becomes deficient. We would prefer to do this with pinkies or fuzzies. Even 1-day-old pinkies have a fairly high calcium content and would theoretically be more nutritionally complete than a piece of meat. In addition, you can also rub frogs, toads, or tadpoles on dead pinkies or fuzzies. Some snakes, particularly young ones, will find this very acceptable. Even most adults can eventually be tricked into taking prekilled mice which have been rubbed with frogs or toads. Many of these snakes will rapidly learn to take unflavored mice while others never will. Remember that if you are feeding amphibians, you will probably need to feed twice a week, while mouse eaters do well on a weekly feeding schedule.

Brumation should be accomplished in the usual manner. Brumation is not only good for the snakes, allowing gamete maturation and increasing the likelihood of successful breeding, but is easier on the keeper since frogs and toads may be running low in midwinter.

Very little is known about breeding this snake in captivity, so you should make every attempt to breed them and report your techniques to your local herpetological society and the closest professional herpetologist so that he or she can work with you in publishing this information. Observing hognose snakes mating does not always translate into the laying of fertile eggs, or for that matter any eggs. It is our impression that most failures in captive breeding with this species are associated with the stress of captivity and untreated parasitism combined. Healthy males are quite willing to mate and copulation has been observed numerous times, but underfed, parasitized, stressed, or unbrumated females will often produce slugs or resorb their eggs and produce nothing. Com-

pare this with the success that breeders are having with the mouse-eating western hognose snake. Given the ease with which the babies can be trained to take pinkies, fuzzies, and eventually mice, and with an understanding of the importance of parasite elimination in recently captured breeding stock, captive breeding of these snakes should eventually become almost as common as in the western hognose snake.

Eastern hognose snakes in our care mated several times from 7 to 9 April, and the female deposited 31 eggs on 23 May. Twenty-nine of these eggs hatched on 13 July. Interestingly, on that very night the same female deposited another large clutch (21) of fertile eggs! Although it is not unusual for healthy females to lay 2 clutches in 1 year, it was surprising that this particular snake laid such a large healthy clutch without any additional mating that season. Furthermore, she never missed a single meal prior to either egg deposition.

Speaking of hognose eggs, they can be incubated in the usual manner (see the general care section and Table 5 on reproduction), but take heed: the external appearance of these eggs is not a very good indicator of what is going on within. Infertile eggs may not change color or shrivel until the fertile eggs in the same clutch are just about to hatch, and fertile eggs with healthy embryos may look terrible until they hatch. Healthy hognose eggs will usually develop a stippled appearance (small wavy lines appear).

SPECIES: *Heterodon platirhinos*, Eastern Hognose Snake
MAINTENANCE DIFFICULTY INDEX: 3 (1 = easiest, 5 = most difficult)
AVERAGE SIZE: 51–84 cm (20–33 inches)
FOOD: Toads, frogs, salamanders, tadpoles, and mice scented with those items. Can train to eat unscented dead mice.
CAGE SIZE: 20-gallon aquarium
SUBSTRATE: Artificial turf, indoor-outdoor carpet, or newspaper
VENTRAL HEAT: Not essential but helpful
UV LIGHT: Yes?
TEMPERATURE RANGE: 23–27°C (73–81°F)
SPECIAL CONSIDERATIONS: Availability of food may be a problem. Very likely to be parasitized. Occasionally has difficulty shedding skin between eyes and nose.

As exemplified above (and also see the reproduction chart), this species is quite fecund, and therefore capable of "earning its keep" for the average snake breeder.

For care of the young, see the section on baby southern hognose snakes.

Captive longevity has been reported at over 11 years (Cochran, 1994), but as with many other infrequently kept or heavily parasitized snakes, we suspect they are capable of living quite a bit longer with improved care and quality control of the diet.

Heterodon simus
Southern Hognose Snake

The southern hognose is a small pudgy snake. Adults range 36–51 cm (14–20 inches) in length with a record of 61 cm (24 inches) (Conant and Collins, 1991). It is the smallest and most poorly known member of the genus. It looks very much like the western hognose, *H. nasicus*, with its sharply upturned rostral scale and gray-brown background color. The dorsal surface, however, has large squarish blotches with varying shades of orange in between rather than smaller, more numerous, circular blotches without any orange between them. Neill (1963) suggested that this snake was a mimic of the pygmy rattlesnake, *Sistrurus miliarius*.

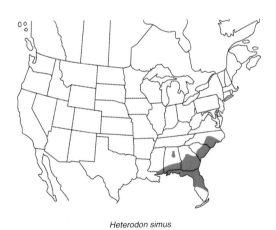

Heterodon simus

The southern hognose ranges from southeastern North Carolina south to central Florida and west to southern Mississippi. Their preferred habitat includes dry sandy areas such as pine and wire grass flatwoods, or longleaf pine-turkey oak "sand hill" forests (Wright and

Wright, 1957; Mount, 1975; Behler and King, 1979; Ashton and Ashton, 1981; Rossi and Rossi, 1991, 1992a; Palmer and Braswell, 1995).

The prey of this stout snake appears to be almost exclusively amphibians in the wild, which the snake may dig out with its sharply upturned rostral scale (Goin, 1947). Prey items have included the oak toad, *Bufo quercicus*, southern toad, *Bufo terrestris*, eastern spadefoot toad, *Scaphiopus holbrooki* (Deckert, 1918; Goin, 1947; Wright and Wright, 1957; Mount, 1975; Ashton and Ashton, 1981; Palmer and Braswell, 1995), and various tree frogs, *Hyla* sp. (Ashton and Ashton, 1981). Lizards (Van Duyn, 1937) and small mammals (Martof et al., 1980) have also been found in the stomach contents of wild specimens.

Known predators of this species include eastern kingsnakes (Palmer and Braswell, 1995). However, cottonmouths, coachwhips, racers, black rat snakes, owls, hawks, and carnivorous mammals may prey on them as well. One neonate in northern Florida was observed being picked up by a grackle and flown to a nearby birdbath, where we found this snake's remains.

Mating observations in the wild are rare. Neill (1951) observed a trio mating on 23 May, and another mating on 29 May. Other breeding pairs in the wild have been observed on 4 May and 28 May (Palmer and Braswell, 1995). This small hognose is oviparous but very few observations have been made of either wild or captive egg deposition. Females gravid at the time of capture have laid 6–10 eggs (Price and Carr, 1943; Edgren, 1955; Ashton and Ashton, 1981). Captive matings have produced 7–10 eggs (Rossi and Rossi, 1991, 1992a). Based upon our

Southern Hognose Snake, *Heterodon simus* (photo by David G. Campbell)

captive observations, the gestation period is believed to be approximately 56 days, and the incubation period has varied from 56 to 64 days. Neonates range in size from 15.2 to 18.0 cm (6 to 7.1 inches).

The care of the southern hognose snake is very similar to that of the eastern hognose. Adults are generally good eaters, given the proper-sized food and the correct environment. They seem to have a marked preference for spadefoot toads, *Scaphiopus* sp., although they will take southern toads, American toads, *Bufo terrestris* and *americanus*, and probably many other toads from this genus. Some adults in our care would even eat young giant toads, *Bufo marinus*. Ernst and Barbour (1989) also list treefrogs, lizards, and small mammals as part of the diet of wild specimens. Young snakes will eat cricket frogs, *Acris gryllus*, newly meta-morphosed toads (all *Bufo* and *Scaphiopus*) as well as the slimy salamander, *Plethodon glutinosus*, and probably many other salamanders. Slimy salamanders and others can be collected much more easily by most people than cricket frogs, and one average-sized salamander is a much larger meal than a cricket frog. Some snakes refusing salamanders initially may be enticed to eat them by rubbing cricket frogs on

them. However, if one chooses to use this technique, *you might as well spare our native amphibians and rub the cricket frog (or spade-foot toad) on a pinky*, as these snakes will usually take them just as quickly. This has several advantages: it is much easier to get pinkies and, theoretically, if you use a frozen cricket frog or a frozen spadefoot toad, or even a frozen tadpole to do the rubbing, there will be little chance for parasitism. Some southern hognoses, especially those born in captivity, will readily consume plain unscented pinkies and never need to be offered amphibians. Adults raised this way may eat full-grown prekilled mice that have never been flavored (just like eastern hognoses). If you are feeding young snakes any unfrozen amphibians at all, you should expect that they will be parasitized. It is not uncommon for young members of this species, even those born in captivity, to get very sick and die from this. You will usually notice a steady loss of appetite, and often restlessness, as well as loose stools. Therefore, as with the eastern hognose and other amphib-ian eaters, it is strongly recommended that the items to be fed be frozen for at least 2–3 days prior to thawing and feeding. Neither juveniles nor adults in our care have ever refused a meal

---

SPECIES: *Heterodon simus*, Southern Hognose Snake
MAINTENANCE DIFFICULTY INDEX: 3 (1 = easiest, 5 = most difficult)
AVERAGE SIZE: 36–51 cm (14–20 inches)
FOOD: Toads, salamanders; can try mice scented with the first two items, eventually unscented mice.
CAGE SIZE: 10-gallon aquarium
SUBSTRATE: Artificial turf, indoor-outdoor carpet, or newspaper
VENTRAL HEAT: Not essential but helpful
UV LIGHT: Yes?
TEMPERATURE RANGE: 25–30°C (77–86°F)
SPECIAL CONSIDERATIONS: Availability of food can be a problem. Very likely to be parasitized. Sometimes have difficulty shedding skin between eyes and nose.

---

just because it had been previously frozen. Even if you are feeding frozen items, it is not a bad idea to have a fecal sample examined every 6 months to a year. Your veterinarian may detect and treat parasites long before there are any signs of illness in your snake. Newly captured specimens should also have a fecal exam performed. It has been our experience that many wild-caught snakes of this species are not as heavily parasitized (either in numbers or types of worms) as their larger relative, the eastern hognose snake. Perhaps this is due to the fact that they feed largely on the spadefoot toad which breeds in temporary pools of water and has a very short larval stage, thereby possibly being less parasitized than other frogs and toads.

WARNING: DO NOT RUB YOUR EYES OR EAT WITHOUT WASHING YOUR HANDS AFTER HANDLING TOADS OR FROGS, AS YOU MAY EXPOSE YOURSELF TO TOXINS OR PARASITES. Also food collected on the road should be washed prior to feeding to your snake. Some snakes have been poisoned by road pollutants and died, according to some authors.

Housing should be exactly as described for the eastern hognose snake. (See the section on the eastern hognose and the general care section.) House separately.

Brumation should also be carried out as for the eastern hognose. See the section on winter cooldown (brumation/hibernation) under general care.

Breeding this snake in captivity has apparently been a real problem for herpetoculturists, although females recently captured have laid eggs which have been incubated and hatched in the usual manner. As with the eastern hognose, healthy captive males will mate readily in the spring, but that does not always result in eggs being laid, as the females may resorb them. A healthy parasite-free female (which has been brumated) in our care mated on 14 April, 9 May and 28 May and laid 9 eggs (8 of which were fertile) on 13 July. All 8 eggs hatched 56–58 days later.

There is still a great deal to learn about the captive reproduction of this snake. If you observe captive breeding, try to publish the information in some herpetological journal or newsletter.

Please remember that these short stout snakes climb to some extent, so resist the temptation to keep them in a tall cage without a lid.

These snakes have very shy dispositions and can rarely be induced to bite, but like the eastern hognose, a bite could be potentially serious. Scott Cushnir, a young herpetoculturist, was bitten on the hand by one specimen and experienced mild swelling around the bite that lasted approximately 12 hours. The keeper would be advised to make sure to wash the hands before handling if he or she has recently handled toads.

One specimen in our care survived over 8 years and 1 month at which time it was released. This snake was acquired as an adult.

One last note is in order. Some of the snakes will not eat in the late fall or winter, no matter what temperature they are kept at, so they really are best brumated.

Hypsiglena torquata
Night Snake

Occupying a huge range from southern British Columbia southward through Washington, Idaho, Nevada, Utah, California, Arizona, New Mexico, Colorado, Kansas, Oklahoma, and most of Texas, as well as all of Mexico, is this small 30–60 cm (12–26 inches) but incredibly adaptable nocturnal snake. They can be readily identified by the elliptical pupils (cat eyes) and big black spots on the neck.

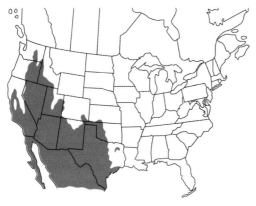

Hypsiglena torquata

The night snake, with its four subspecies in the United States and Canada (at last count), occupies nearly every habitat available from low desert to mountain meadows and forests. It is also a generalist when it comes to feeding. Items reported to have been consumed by wild snakes have included lizards, e.g., *Uta* and *Sceloporus*, and their eggs, small snakes, e.g., blind snakes, *Leptotyphlops* sp., frogs, spadefoot toads and salamanders, arthropods, centipedes, and insects (Wright and Wright, 1957; Webb, 1970; Stebbins, 1985; Degenhardt et al., 1996). Small ringnecks and ground snakes are suspected prey also. One night snake was observed eating a plains blackhead snake (Miller, 1987).

Suspected predators of this species include ophiophagous snakes, carnivorous mammals, and birds of prey. One wild-caught Sonoran coral snake regurgitated a juvenile night snake. Cannibalism in captivity has been observed.

Reproduction in the wild is characterized by spring mating, egg laying in April through June, with hatching occurring in July or August (Stebbins, 1985; Tennant, 1986). Two to 9 (usually 4–6) eggs are laid, which are reported to hatch in 50–60 days (Fitch, 1970; Clark and Lieb, 1973; Trutnau, 1981; Tennant, 1984, 1985).

The night snake is actually an extremely adaptable fascinating little snake. It adjusts readily to captivity if given a place to hide, the standard basic cage arrangement, and the proper food.

Daytime air temperatures during the summer may range 22–35°C (72–95°F), with acceptable nighttime low temperatures of 18–27°C (65–80°F). A ventral heat source is advisable but not a necessity if the above air temperatures are used. Ultraviolet light is not necessary for this species.

The night snakes in our care did very well on artificial carpet/turf or cypress mulch with a typical plastic hide box. Being largely nocturnal, they spend most of the day securely hidden away in their hide box, but at night they come alive, like so many other western snakes. Their

Desert Night Snake, *Hypsiglena torquata deserticola* (photo by John Rossi)

Spotted Night Snake, *Hypsiglena torquata ochrorhyncha* (photo by David G. Campbell)

nocturnal nature is, of course, obvious just by looking at them, as their pupils are elliptical. Like a cat stalking a mouse, they cautiously approach food items placed in their cage at dusk. Upon reaching the appropriate distance they strike, embedding their fangs into the intended prey item and injecting what has been described as a mild venom. Perhaps it is mild to humans, but we're unlikely to ever know as these inoffensive snakes are not known to make serious attempts at biting humans, and their small size would make it difficult for them to embed their fangs. They can probably be treated as nonvenomous snakes just as ring-necks, pine woods, ground, hooknose, and other small rear-fanged snakes, even though some states require they be treated as venomous (kept in locked cages, etc.). Live prey do succumb fairly quickly to their venom.

The diet of this species has been reported to be quite catholic in the wild with specimens consuming insects, centipedes, scorpions, frogs, and toads, but their favorite food appears to be other reptiles and their eggs. Small snakes and especially the Texas banded gecko and their eggs are preferred. Ringneck snakes and young racers have been consumed by night snakes in our care. Small night snakes in our care would

take squirrel treefrogs, *Hyla squirella*. Others have reported chorus frogs, *Pseudacris* sp., as regular food for captives, but reported toxic signs in captives after attempted consumption of a narrowmouth toad, *Gastrophryne* (Degenhardt et al., 1996). However, the food item of choice for captive specimens was discovered out of our desperation and is not, in fact, a native species. It is a relative of the favored banded gecko, the Mediterranean gecko, *Hemidactylus turcicus* (Rossi and Rossi, 1992c). This species is widespread and continuing to spread rapidly throughout the southern United States, is found in high densities around human habitations, and is easily captured. As we have stated elsewhere, it makes sense to use this and other introduced urban-loving species as food sources in captive husbandry efforts with native snakes. These snakes also fairly readily consume pinkies and fuzzies after they have been rubbed with Mediterranean geckos, and will soon be eating unflavored pinkies. In addition, these snakes will take dead food, which allows good quality control of their diet since potential prey items may be frozen for several days, thereby killing many metazoan parasites (worms). Be sure to allow the food item to thaw thoroughly prior to feeding.

SPECIES: *Hypsiglena torquata*, Night Snake
MAINTENANCE DIFFICULTY INDEX: 2 (1 = easiest, 5 = most difficult)
AVERAGE SIZE: 30–60 cm (12–26 inches)
FOOD: Lizards, scented pinky
CAGE SIZE: 5–10-gallon aquarium
SUBSTRATE: Indoor-outdoor carpet, artificial turf, or newspaper
VENTRAL HEAT: Not essential but helpful
UV LIGHT: No
TEMPERATURE RANGE: 22–35°C (72–95°F)
SPECIAL CONSIDERATIONS: Usually prefer lizards or small snakes initially but eventually
switch to mice. Often heavily parasitized.

Both external and internal parasites have been found on or in these snakes. Ticks and mites are common and coccidia (protozoan parasites that may cause gastroenteritis) have also been found. Three treatments of sulfadimethioxine at 90 mg/kg given every other day in small food items has been curative.

These snakes are definitely prone to long periods of inappetence during the fall and winter and should therefore be brumated. This can be accomplished in their regular cage. Temperatures fluctuating from 3 to 18°C (38 to 65°F) during the winter months have been well tolerated by those in our care. Because of their small size, they should be well fed in the months prior to brumation or they may have a difficult time making it through this period. Make sure to have a well-ventilated cage with a good hiding place and clean water available at all times.

Breeding has not been commonly attempted in captivity, but there have been reports of females gravid at the time of capture laying eggs, which have been hatched in the usual manner. We have maintained one pair captured in the Big Bend area of Texas for several years. Fertile clutches of 3 eggs have been produced every year that they have been in captivity.

On 29 March 1991 at 2300 hours, copulation was observed. The ambient temperature at this time was 28.4°C (83.1°F). On 19 June, the female laid 3 elongate eggs approximately 4.1 cm long × 2 cm wide (1.6 inches × 0.8 inches). These young pipped and emerged from these thin eggs within a 12-hour period on 5 and 6 August.

On 8 April 1992, mating was observed again.

Ambient temperature at the time of this mating was 25.3°C (77.5°F) and the humidity was 62%. Presumably, this mating was responsible for the production of 3 more fertile eggs of the same dimensions on 22 June 1992. These eggs pipped and the young emerged on 13 and 14 August.

Thus, the gestation periods (mating to laying time) were 82 and 75 days respectively, with an average of 78.5 days (11 weeks), while the incubation periods were 47 and 52 days respectively, with an average of 49.5 days (7 weeks). The following year and subsequent years, this female laid 4 eggs, except for one year when geckos were in short supply, when she dropped back down to 3 eggs. The longest incubation period during this time was 56 days.

The young snakes are patterned exactly like the adults, although possibly a bit paler in coloration. The individuals hatched in our care were remarkably similar in size at 17 cm (6.7 inches), with a SVL of 14 cm (5.5 inches) in the males and 14.5 cm (5.7 inches) in the females. Sexing may be accomplished by applying gentle pressure to the base of the tail, thus everting one or both hemipenes in the male (referred to as "popping") as discussed in the general care section under sexing.

The hatchlings are apparently full of yolk at the time they emerge from their eggs and may not eat for 1–2 months or even during winter without any problems, should they be exposed to cool temperatures soon after hatching. Some hatchlings in our care ate heavily starting in September and early October (one ground skink, *Scincella lateralis*, every 2–5 days) until feeding stopped in mid-October and did not resume until March. Others just refused to eat at all prior to brumation. Other food items consumed by hatchling night snakes included young Mediterranean geckos and anoles. Pre-killed and lizard-scented pinkies were first consumed at approximately 9 months of age (the same age as many hatchling gray-banded kingsnakes when they start eating pinkies voluntarily). It is quite possible that they may consume scented mouse tails earlier than this, but we have not yet tested this. Adults will readily consume pinky and fuzzy mice.

Night snakes have not been popular with herpetoculturists because of their small size and failure to eat pinkies right away after capture. But given their preferred food initially, they adapt readily and make wonderful little captives. They are attractively marked and some specimens can be quite stout. They are relatively slow-moving and do not seem to mind being handled. They will take food right from your hand (if you are that brave). Their personality is usually quite mellow, but they are distinctly curious and will explore your fingers, pockets, or furniture thoroughly, and therefore are very interesting to watch. In fact, this is one of our favorite snakes and can be highly recommended as a captive.

Captive longevity has been reported at more than 9 years and 3 months (Snider and Bowler, 1992). One pair collected by the authors as adults in Big Bend, Texas, in 1989 has bred regularly in captivity and is still thriving 10 years and 2 months later.

Lampropeltis alterna
Gray-banded Kingsnake

The gray-banded kingsnake is a medium-sized nocturnal snake of rocky areas in the Chihuahuan desert. It receives its name from the variable, wide, irregularly shaped gray bands which extend the length of the snake. Within the United States, the range of the gray-banded kingsnake is almost entirely within the state of Texas. Recently, several have been found in southwestern New Mexico. In Texas, it occurs in the western panhandle (Trans-Pecos region) and southward into north central Mexico.

As mentioned above, rocky areas constitute the preferred habitat of this species. These areas are dominated by Chihuahuan Desert plants such as sotol, mesquite, several species of cacti, ocotillo, acacia, and creosote bush (Degenhardt et al., 1996).

The food of this rock crevice dweller in the wild consists of the following items: Eastern fence lizard, *Sceloporus undulatus*, crevice spiny lizard, *S. poinsetti*, canyon spiny lizard, *S. merriami*, whiptail lizards, *Cnemidophorus* sp., lizard eggs, canyon treefrogs, *Hyla arenicolor*, and juvenile pocket mice (Wright and Wright, 1957; Miller, 1979; Tennant, 1984, 1985; Switak, 1984; Cranston, 1991). Small snakes have also been listed as a food item by a number of authors (Behler and King, 1979;

Lampropeltis alterna

Tennant, 1981; Mehrtens, 1987) but this has not been widely confirmed. Tennant (1985) stated that this "was the only nonsnake-eating member of the kingsnake family." It is now known, however, that captive gray-banded kingsnakes will consume other snakes. Both juvenile Trans-Pecos rat snakes and night snakes were readily consumed by captives (Salmon, pers. comm., 1995). In captivity, many other species of lizards have been consumed. See below.

Suspected predators of this species include carnivorous mammals and ophiophagous snakes such as the desert kingsnake. One herpetocul-

Gray-banded Kingsnake, *Lampropeltis alterna* (photo by David G. Campbell)

turist who has asked to remain anonymous accidentally placed his highly prized female gray-banded kingsnake in with his male Florida kingsnake. The commotion he heard was believed to be mating activity, but instead was feeding activity, as the Florida kingsnake consumed the smaller snake. When the keeper checked the cage later expecting to find a mating pair, he realized that he had placed his female gray-banded kingsnake in with the wrong male!

Observations of mating behavior in the wild have been rare. Noncaptive mating has been observed in late spring and early summer (Tennant, 1985; Cranston, 1991) that results in the deposition of eggs 1–2 months later (Trutnau, 1981; Mattison, 1988). These eggs, which may number 3–14 (Tennant, 1985; Mattison, 1988; Cranston, 1991) will generally hatch after an incubation period of 55–91 days (Mattison, 1988; Trutnau, 1981) at temperatures of 22–30°C (72–86°F) into young looking very similar to the adults but ranging in size from 17.7 to 30.5 cm (7 to 12 inches).

This is one of the most highly sought after North American snakes in the world. Herpetoculturists seem to lose their minds when it comes to this species. "Alternas," as they are affectionately called by the hard-core herpers, have become so popular that to many they have become an obsession. Their worship has become almost cultish. So heavily are these snakes collected and bred that some people can even tell you exactly where another person has found a particular specimen! This has led to subcults espousing the beauty of their preferred locality types above all others. For instance, the hot item at the time of this writing appears to be the "Langtry *alterna*" (a specimen collected at Langtry, Texas, or bred from stock collected at or near that area). Others are enthralled with the "River Road *alternas*." To make matters slightly more confusing, there are two color morphs that are referred to as "blairs" and "alternas." Blairs morph has broad orange bands or saddles while the alterna morph has narrow orange saddles.[1] The amount of orange within the saddles is also very variable. Dark morph blairs have almost no orange within the saddles while light morph blairs may have a

[1]Saddle = goes part way around body.
Band = goes all the way around body.

great deal of orange. Similarly, the alterna morph may have little or no orange in the saddles. Now, add to this that you can have anything in between the two morphs, and you begin to understand why no one understands the lingo of the gray-banded kingsnake at first.

Seriously, the gray-banded is a beautiful snake in all of its variable color patterns. It does very well in captivity in the most basic (simplest) of cages and attains a size of 51–90 cm (20–36 inches), average 81.3 cm (32 inches), with a record of 147.1 cm (57¾ inches) (Conant and Collins, 1991). Adults are usually not a problem to feed but hatchlings can be a real challenge.

The basic cage design discussed in the general care section will work very well for this species. The substrates that have worked well include artificial carpet/turf, newspaper, aspen and cypress chips, and others. Rocks, numerous hiding places (such as PVC pipes, small hide boxes, etc.), and a water bowl seem to be all that are required to complete the cage for this species. One alternative that has worked exceedingly well but does not appear necessary is the use of false bottoms, under which the snakes may hide. Plastic plants are a nice addition for the more decorative cages. Some keep these snakes in drawer-style cages with nothing but newspaper, however, and they seem to do fine. As with most other snakes, ventral heat is advisable. No special lighting is required. Air temperature may fluctuate quite a bit, but 25–30°C (77–86°F) during the daytime with a drop at night will work well.

Feeding is not a problem for the adults as they will usually readily accept small prekilled mice. Recently captured specimens may have a marked preference for lizards though and may have to be trained to take mice using scent-transfer techniques. Hatchlings on the other hand are notoriously difficult to get switched to pinkies. Some estimate that up to 50% of the babies will not consume anything but lizards voluntarily. Lizards of the following genera have been reported by various authors as food for captive juveniles and adults of this species: *Sceloporus*, spiny lizards, *Cnemidophorus*, racerunners and whiptails, *Eumeces*, skinks, *Holbrookia* and *Cophosaurus*, earless lizards, and *Uta*, the side-blotched lizard (Wright and Wright, 1957; Assetto, 1978; Miller, 1979; Ten-

nant, 1984). In our struggles with babies that refuse pinkies, we have discovered they are particularly fond of two other species of lizards, one of which was a tremendous surprise. The first, and not so unexpected, was the ground skink, *Scincella lateralis*. (Why not? Every other kingsnake in the country seems to relish them, and their ranges do overlap some.) The second lizard, the Mediterranean gecko, *Hemidactylus turcicus*, was a bit more of a surprise initially. In fact, four out of five hatchlings that had refused pinkies (one of which had refused other lizards), consumed these geckos immediately. After some time (up to 9 months in most cases) they were easily switched to plain pinkies (unscented). Some individuals, however, consumed gecko-scented pinkies immediately.

One individual consumed one brown anole, *Anolis sagrei*, another introduced species, but did not consume another; indeed, most North American snakes do not seem to relish eating this species.

With regard to feeding pinkies to the young snakes, a plethora of methods have been devised to make them more acceptable to the snakes. Washing the pinky off and scenting it with a lizard is the first alternative. A recent modification of this technique involves slicing open the abdomen of a dead lizard and dipping the head of the pinky inside (Feldner, pers. comm., 1992). After this comes the proven method of slicing open the head of a dead pinky (called "brain splitting" by the experts) before offering it to the young snakes. Admittedly, these tricks seem a bit strange to the average person; this is one of the reasons juveniles of this species are not recommended for the beginner. Only well-started animals are appropriate for those just starting out in snake keeping.

Two commonly used alternative methods for very young snakes are pinky pumping and mouse tail assist-feeding. The pinky pump is a mechanical device that macerates dead pinkies and forces them into the snake. It has been used with great success over the last several years to feed many young snakes that will not eat otherwise. The other very common method is to gently slide a mouse tail partially down the throat of one of these snakes. They will usually swallow it voluntarily at that point.

Brumation is considered necessary for breed-

SPECIES: *Lampropeltis alterna*, Gray-banded Kingsnake
MAINTENANCE DIFFICULTY INDEX: Adults 1, Hatchlings 4 (1 = easiest, 5 = most difficult)
AVERAGE SIZE: 51–90 cm (20–36 inches)
FOOD: Lizards, mice
CAGE SIZE: 10–20-gallon long aquarium
SUBSTRATE: Indoor-outdoor carpet, artificial turf, or newspaper
VENTRAL HEAT: Yes
UV LIGHT: No
TEMPERATURE RANGE: 25–30°C (77–86°F)
SPECIAL CONSIDERATIONS: Although some hatchlings readily take pinkies, most prefer lizards for 6 months. Once started, they are beautiful, good-eating snakes.

ing purposes, although not necessarily for general maintenance since this southern kingsnake may eat throughout the winter if it is not cooled down. The regular cage will not usually need modifications for this purpose; therefore, it is one of the best things to brumate many snakes in and gray-banded kings are no exception. Four months at temperatures of 15–20°C (50–59°F) have worked well for many authors, and temperatures below this have been well tolerated by those in our care (3.3°C, 38°F for several days during this time produced no ill effects). See the general care section on brumation.

As can be inferred from the breeding data listed above, captive breeding of this snake has become common. This can be accomplished in the usual manner (i.e., placing the female in the male's cage) right after brumation ends.

A pair of 19-month-old snakes in our care mated on 26 May through 28 May and the female laid 4 eggs on 5 July, 38–40 days later. These eggs hatched on 29 August, a 55-day incubation which is well within the reported range. These snakes bred regularly in May for many years.

In summary, the gray-banded kingsnake is an attractive and generally mild-natured serpent that is relatively easy to maintain and breed. Hatchlings, on the other hand, may be extremely difficult to get to start feeding and are not advisable for beginners, especially in light of their relatively high price.

It is a shame so many herpetologists and herpetoculturists have become so involved with this species that they have apparently lost interest in most other species of snakes. There are so many other colorful and fascinating North American snakes that need to be studied.

Captive longevity for this species has been listed by Snider and Bowler (1992) at 15 years and 2 months and Slavens and Slavens (1992) at 15 years and 6 months, but Cranston (1991) believes they will survive more than 20 years in captivity.

Lampropeltis calligaster
Prairie and Mole Kingsnakes

The prairie kingsnake, consisting of three subspecies, ranges from western Maryland southward to Florida and westward to extreme southeastern Nebraska to eastern Texas. The three subspecies are the prairie kingsnake, *L. c. calli-* *gaster*, the mole kingsnake, *L. c. rhombomaculata*, and the rare south Florida mole kingsnake, *L. c. occipitolineata*. The prairie kingsnake is the westernmost subspecies, with the range of this subspecies extending from western Ken-

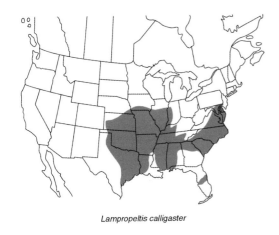

Lampropeltis calligaster

than 71 in mole kings). Other characteristic features used to separate the two main subspecies are the number of dorsal midbody scale rows: there are 25–27 rows in the prairie kingsnake and 21–23 rows in the mole kingsnake.

Like the prairie kingsnake, the mole kingsnake survives in a wide variety of habitats that have been categorized as yards, fields, old farmland, and woodlands (pine and oak) in the Atlantic coastal plain (Wright and Wright, 1957; Mount, 1975; Ernst and Barbour, 1989; Conant and Collins, 1991; Mitchell, 1994). Means (1992) indicated the seeming preference for fallow fields and said more research was needed to understand the original native habitat. This snake is largely fossorial and spends a great deal of time beneath the ground. Blanchard in Wright and Wright (1957) described the soil type as "light soil, sandy loam, near water." Palmer and Braswell (1995) stated that hydric environments were generally avoided by this species.

tucky through western Louisiana and then westward through southeastern Nebraska, most of Kansas, Oklahoma, and eastern Texas. The mole kingsnake is found from Maryland to northern Florida and westward to Tennessee, Mississippi, and eastern Louisiana. The third subspecies, the south Florida mole kingsnake, is rare and poorly known, and found only in disjunct populations in peninsular Florida. They are categorized as retaining the juvenile color pattern and having more than 75 dark blotches along the back and tail (Tennant, 1997) (vs. fewer than 60 in prairie kings and fewer

Nothing is known of the thermal ecology of the mole kingsnake.

The diet of the mole kingsnake in the wild has been reported to include lizards, small snakes, mice, and birds and their eggs (Wright and Wright, 1957; Mount, 1975; Brown, 1979).

Prairie Kingsnake, *Lampropeltis calligaster calligaster* (photo by David G. Campbell)

Mole Kingsnake, *Lampropeltis calligaster rhombomaculata* (photo by David G. Campbell)

Young mole kingsnakes apparently have a greater tendency to eat reptiles, but will also feed on small frogs and toads (Linzey and Clifford, 1981).

Known predators of this species include hawks, raccoons, skunks, opossums, adult ground squirrels, foxes, and eastern kingsnakes (Knable, 1970; Minton, 1972; Brown, 1979; Linzey and Clifford, 1981; Black, 1983).

Mating is known to occur in the spring, which results in the deposition of 3–16 eggs (Carpenter, 1985; E. E. Brown, 1992; Palmer and Braswell, 1995) approximately 47 days later (personal observations–see below). In the wild, egg laying generally occurs in late June to early July (Ernst et al., 1985; Palmer and Braswell, 1995). The hatchlings range 19.3–23.6 cm (7.6–9.3 inches) in TL (Ernst et al., 1985; Carpenter, 1985).

In captivity, mole kings generally do very well, although some may resist feeding. The basic cage setup as described in the general care section usually will work. Artificial carpet/turf, newspaper, and various types of wood chips have all been used with success. Once again, stay away from cedar as it contains aromatic compounds which may irritate the snake's skin or respiratory tract. A good hide box is critical for these secretive snakes. A piece of PVC pipe is an excellent hiding place, especially when partially buried in cypress mulch or some other burrowing substrate. A nontippable water bowl is also a good idea with this species since they are very strong and quite easily flip their water bowls over. Plastic plants and one or two stable rocks are nice cage additions.

Air temperatures of 23–28°C (74–83°F) have been recommended as suitable for these snakes, although at these temperatures a ventral heat source would be strongly advisable to allow the snake to reach higher temperatures. Remember that body temperatures of active prairie kingsnakes in the wild were measured at more than 30°C (86°F), so it only makes sense to offer this option to captive mole kingsnakes.

Brumation for 3–5 months at 10–15°C (50–59°F) has been used successfully for this species, allowing normal breeding. As with most other snakes, it may be carried out in the snake's own cage. No modifications are necessary. Those in our care repeatedly experienced temperatures as low as 2.7°C (37°F) for short periods of time with no ill effects.

Captive breeding of the mole king has been accomplished, but far less commonly than with the western subspecies. The techniques for allowing breeding as described in the general care section have worked very well. Basically, this involves placing the female in with the male soon after brumation ends. Eggs will usually be deposited 43–55 days later (Mattison, 1988).

Mole kingsnakes in our care mated and produced fertile eggs for 3 consecutive years. It is interesting to note that in all 3 years, mating did not occur until daytime high temperatures exceeded 27°C (80°F). That data is summarized below. In 1992, mating occurred on 10 and 11 April. This resulted in the deposition of 8 eggs on 27 May, 7 of which hatched on 15 July. The sex ratio was 0.75:1 males to females and the young snakes averaged 21.1 cm (8.3 inches) TL. In 1993, mating occurred on 14 April. This resulted in the deposition of 11 eggs on 1 June, 9 of which hatched on 23 July. The sex ratio was 0.5:1 males to females and these hatchlings averaged 20.5 cm (8.1 inches). In 1994, mating occurred on 23 March. This resulted in the deposition of 10 eggs on 9 May, all 10 of which hatched on 14 July. The sex ratio was 0.66:1 males to females and these hatchlings had an average TL of 25.5 cm (10.04 inches). Hence, the gestation periods were 47 days, 48 days, and 47 days and the incubation periods were 49 days, 52 days, and 64 days. Standard incubation techniques discussed in the general care section were used.

Snider and Bowler (1992) reported that one of these snakes lived for more than 14 years and 11 months in captivity.

The prairie kingsnake is a medium-sized kingsnake ranging 76–107 cm (30–42 inches) in TL, with a record of 147.6 cm (58.1 inches) (Conant and Collins, 1991; Tennant, 1985). They are characterized by a gray to brown background color, with a variable number of dark brown to brick red blotches dorsally, although there is tremendous variability in color pattern with some individuals being solid brown, longitudinally striped, or even black (Wright and Wright, 1957; Hudson, 1985; Tennant, 1985; Markel, 1990). The belly is usually marked with squarish brown to black blotches on a yellowish to grayish background. Like most kingsnakes, the scales are smooth and the anal plate is single, which differentiates this snake from the commonly confused Great Plains rat snake, *Elaphe guttata emoryi*, in which the anal plate is divided and the dorsal scales are weakly keeled.

This snake is both a habitat and dietary generalist. It has been found in tall grass prairies, marsh borders, pastures, cultivated fields, roadsides, open woodlands, mixed pine and hardwood forests, and in many places where debris is littering the ground (Wright and Wright, 1957; Tennant, 1985; Ernst and Barbour, 1989; Dundee and Rossman, 1989). Food items taken by specimens in the wild have

---

SPECIES: *Lampropeltis calligaster*, Prairie Kingsnake
MAINTENANCE DIFFICULTY INDEX: 1 (1 = easiest, 5 = most difficult)
AVERAGE SIZE: 76–107 cm (30–42 inches)
FOOD: Mice, rats, lizards, other snakes
CAGE SIZE: 10–20-gallon long aquarium
SUBSTRATE: Indoor-outdoor carpet, artificial turf, or newspaper
VENTRAL HEAT: Not essential but helpful
UV LIGHT: No, but an incandescent bulb is useful
TEMPERATURE RANGE: 23–28°C (74–83°F)
SPECIAL CONSIDERATIONS: Provide numerous hiding places. Likely to be parasitized. Cannibalistic.

included mice, rats, moles, ground squirrels, gophers, small rabbits, birds and eggs, fence lizards, (*Sceloporus* species), skinks, *Eumeces* sp., racerunners, *Cnemidophorus* sp., other snakes (including members of their own species), toads, frogs, and fish (Wright and Wright, 1957; Klimstra, 1959; Smith, 1961; Fitch, 1978; Tennant, 1985; Mitchell, 1986; Ernst and Barbour, 1989).

Very little is known about the temperature relations of these snakes in the wild. Fitch (1956) recorded body temperatures of two active individuals in Kansas at 30.4 and 33°C (86.7 and 91.4°F).

Mating has been observed to occur in the spring, usually early in the spring right after brumation (Tryon and Carl, 1980). This results in the laying of 7–21 eggs in late June to early July (Wright and Wright, 1957; Fitch, 1970, 1985; Ernst et al., 1985; Tennant, 1984). These eggs hatch in 45–78 days at variable incubation temperatures, usually 50–60 days at 28°C (82°F) (Carpenter, 1985; Mattison, 1988). Hatchlings are 24.4–30.5 cm (9.6–12 inches) long and usually have a much lighter and more distinct pattern.

Fitch (1999) estimated a density of 1–4 prairie kingsnakes per hectare. In Kansas, as elsewhere, the preferred habitat appears to be open grassland. Prairie kingsnakes in that study consumed a variety of lizards, snakes, and rodents, as well as shrews and quail eggs. In Kansas, mating occurred in May and egg laying occurred in June. Most clutches apparently hatch in August. One clutch in Fitch's study hatched in 62 days in the lab.

In captivity, prairie kings generally do very well, although some may resist feeding. The basic cage setup as described in the general care section usually will work. Artificial carpet/turf, newspaper, and various types of wood chips have all been used with success. Once again, stay away from cedar as it contains aromatic compounds that may irritate the snake's skin or respiratory tract. A good stable hide box is critical for these secretive snakes. A piece of PVC pipe is an excellent hiding place, especially when partially buried in cypress mulch or other burrowing substrate. A nontippable water bowl is also a good idea with this species since they are very strong and quite easily flip their water bowls over. Plastic plants and one or two stable rocks are nice cage additions.

Air temperatures of 23–28°C (74–83°F) have been recommended as suitable for these snakes, although at these temperatures a ventral heat source would be strongly advisable to allow the snake to reach higher temperatures. Remember that body temperatures of active snakes in the wild were measured at more than 30°C (86°F), so it only makes sense to offer this option to captives.

Brumation for 3–5 months at 10–15°C (50–59°F) has been used successfully for this species, allowing normal breeding. As with most other snakes, it may be carried out in the snake's own cage. No modifications are necessary.

Captive breeding has been accomplished hundreds of times using the techniques mentioned in the general care section. Basically, this will involve placing the female in with the male soon after brumation ends. Eggs will usually be deposited 43–55 days later (Mattison, 1988), and these can be incubated in the normal manner.

In summary, both common subspecies make excellent captives in most cases. There are individuals that may very stubbornly refuse to feed in captivity, just as there are some common kingsnakes that refuse to eat well, but these tend to be a small minority. Those in our care ate, shed, and bred regularly and were perhaps the least demanding of our captive North American snakes.

Their personalities may vary tremendously, however, with some individuals being vicious while others can hardly be induced to bite and are quite handleable. Most specimens appear to be of the latter variety, and even some of the aggressive ones may calm down in time. Juveniles, especially hatchlings, may be very nervous and aggressively bite their handlers, but this behavior usually fades quickly in captivity. See the discussion on aggression in the general care section.

Both Slavens and Slavens (1991) and Snider and Bowler (1992) reported one of these snakes lived for more than 23 years and 8 months in captivity.

Lampropeltis getula
Common Kingsnake

This species rivals the milk snake, *L. triangulum*, in geographic range and number of subspecies within the United States. Like that species, it has also been intensively studied, both in captivity and in the wild. Their large size, highly variable color pattern, and adaptability to captivity have made them one of the most popular pet snakes in North America.

All common kingsnakes possess patterns of coal black to dark brown interspersed with variable amounts of white or yellow. The white or yellow may be nearly completely absent as in the two subspecies of black kingsnake or dominant as in some California kingsnakes (e.g., the banana morph). Most subspecies fall in the middle with highly contrasting white or yellow spots, bands, or stripes, on a largely brown or black background (e.g., speckled kingsnakes, desert kingsnakes, most California kingsnakes, chain kingsnakes, and Florida kingsnakes).

Compared to the milk snakes, however, kingsnakes are much more uniform in size, disposition, handleability, and adaptability to captivity. Hence, all seven currently recognized subspecies in the United States and Canada can generally be cared for about the same, taking into consideration variations in breeding times, brumation times, thermal preferences, and preferred foods between populations. The natural history of the group is briefly summarized below.

The common kingsnake is a transcontinental species, with a range extending from southern New Jersey south through Florida and westward to Oregon and California and into a good portion of northern Mexico. The subspecies found in the area covered by this book include the California kingsnake, *L. g. californiae*, the desert black kingsnake, *L. g. nigrita*, the desert kingsnake, *L. g. splendida*, the black kingsnake, *L. g. nigra*, the speckled kingsnake, *L. g. holbrooki*, the eastern kingsnake, *L. g. getula*, and the Florida kingsnake, *L. g. floridana*.

Lampropeltis getula

These snakes have fairly characteristic color patterns so that merely knowing the geographic origin usually makes identification easy. Intergrades (animals with some characteristics of two or more subspecies) commonly occur in areas near the edge of subspecies' ranges and can be quite confusing, so consult a field guide if there is any question. Additionally, naturally occurring variable patterns are found in parts of its range.

As might be expected, the habitat of this species is incredibly variable, with some of the eastern species dwelling near swamps in pine forests and some in the west living in the driest of deserts. Others can be found in almost every habitat in between including along streams in moist woods, chaparral, canyon bottoms, open prairies, roadsides, or just about any kind of habitat near water (Wright and Wright, 1957; Fowlie, 1965; Basey, 1976; Tennant, 1985; Stebbins, 1985; Dundee and Rossman, 1989; Means, 1992).

The diet of this snake in the wild is also incredibly varied, even though certain populations and individuals seem to have preferences for one item or another. Fowlie (1965) reported that California kingsnakes in northern and western Arizona consumed whipsnakes, bullsnakes, rattlesnakes, quail eggs, rodents, and

California Kingsnake (striped morph), *Lampropeltis getula californiae* (photo by David G. Campbell)

Florida Kingsnake, *Lampropeltis getula floridana* (photo by David G. Campbell)

Eastern Kingsnake, *Lampropeltis getula getula* (photo by David G. Campbell)

pocket gophers, while desert kingsnakes from southeastern Arizona consumed frogs, ground snakes, and bird eggs among other foods. In Louisiana, Clark (1949) found their most common prey to be mice, followed in decreasing frequency by rats, water snakes, coachwhips, eastern hognose snakes, copperheads, birds, unidentified snakes, cottonmouths, rough green snakes, eastern garter snakes, timber rattlesnakes, and eastern coral snakes (in Dundee and Rossman, 1989). Most of the snakes mentioned as foods for the Louisiana kingsnakes are not even found in the range of the California kingsnakes. Furthermore, lizards, a common food item for kingsnakes from other areas, were not listed in this study on Louisiana speckled kingsnakes, while in another Louisiana study they were. Lizards listed as food for the common kingsnake in Georgia include racerunners, *Cnemidophorus*, skinks, *Eumeces* and *Scincella*, spiny lizards, *Sceloporus*, and glass lizards, *Ophisaurus*. Anoles, *Anolis* sp. (Hamilton and Pollack, 1956), and members of these same genera will be taken by this species in the western part of its range. Brown (1979) reported that kingsnakes from North Carolina have consumed glass lizards, rough green snakes, *Opheodrys aestivus*, ringneck snakes,

Diadophis punctatus, mole kingsnakes, *L. calligaster*, and birds, while Grout (pers. comm., 1993) reported an area in Maryland where smooth earth snakes, *Virginia valeriae*, and eastern worm snakes, *Carphophis amoenus*, seemed to be preferred food items. Other items reported as food for this species have included reptile eggs (snake, turtle, and lizard), salamanders, and insects. It is important to note there have been numerous incidents of cannibalism reported for this species (Mitchell, 1986). Thus, it is safe to say this snake is truly a dietary generalist.

The body temperatures of wild active common kingsnakes were studied by Brattstrom (1965) and found to range from 18.0 to 31.4°C (64.4 to 88.5°F) with an average body temperature of 28°C (82.4°F). This study also revealed that the critical thermal minimum for these snakes is −2°C (28°F) and the critical thermal maximum is 42°C (107.6°F). Once again, this species is so widespread, it is likely there will be considerable variation in the preferred optimum temperature ranges and possibly critical thermal minimums and maximums from one area to another. However, these data may be used as a general guideline in determining a thermal gradient to offer these snakes in captivity.

Speckled Kingsnake, *Lampropeltis getula holbrooki* (photo by David G. Campbell)

As far as predators are concerned, larger kingsnakes eat smaller ones. But hawks, raccoons, skunks, and opossums are probably the most serious predators on the adults (Ernst and Barbour, 1989). Bullfrogs may prey on small kingsnakes (Palmer and Braswell, 1995). They also reported that a large black racer consumed one 56 cm (22 inches) long. Fire ants may be consuming their eggs in Florida.

Reproduction has been observed numerous times in both wild and captive specimens. Breeding generally occurs from April to June, which results in the laying of 3–21 eggs (usually around 9–10 eggs) between 31 and 73 days later (Fitch, 1970; E. E. Brown, 1992; Mitchell, 1994). As with most species studied, the number and size of the eggs increase with the size of the mother. However, the larger the number of eggs, the smaller each egg tends to be. Some subspecies tend to lay larger numbers of smaller eggs (speckled kingsnakes and black kingsnakes lay up to 21 eggs), while others tend to lay smaller clutches with larger eggs (California kingsnake, desert black kingsnake, and desert kingsnake lay 4–12 eggs). Clutch size also tends to decrease as one moves from northern to southern populations (Zweifel, 1980; Fitch, 1985).

Incubation time varies from 47 to 81 days (Fitch, 1970; Mattison, 1988; Ernst and Barbour, 1989) depending on incubation temperature. The young vary from 20.2 to 33.0 cm (8 to 13 inches) long and weigh 5–13 grams (Mattison, 1988; Ernst and Barbour, 1989; Mitchell, 1994; Palmer and Braswell, 1995).

Common kingsnakes make almost perfect captives. They generally adapt so well to captivity that one may consider them the standard of ease against which all other North American species may be compared. They generally eat well and breed regularly; they have been bred in captivity for many generations (Zweifel, 1980). This is not to say that some individuals may not present a problem in captive situations. Certainly, we have encountered a small number of this species that steadfastly refused to eat in captivity and appeared to be suffering from maladaptation syndrome. See the discussion on this problem in the general care section. These individuals are best released where they were captured and replaced with other animals if possible.

Generally speaking, however, these animals do fantastically well in the basic cage arrangement discussed in the general care section. A 20–30-gallon long aquarium will be an acceptable size enclosure for most. Artificial carpet/turf or newspaper will work fine as a substrate, although wood shavings of various kinds (not cedar) have seen a great deal of success. A water bowl, rock, plastic plants, and branch are excellent cage accessories and a hide box is very advisable for this secretive species. Many of these snakes have done well for years in much simpler cages, however.

Air temperatures of 25–30°C (77–86°F) have been recommended as a suitable range for this species although summer temperatures fluctuating up to 35°C (95°F) have been toler-

Black Kingsnake, *Lampropeltis getula nigra* (photo by David G. Campbell)

Desert Kingsnake, *Lampropeltis getula splendida*
(photo by David G. Campbell)

ated well by common kingsnakes in our care and that of Zweifel (1980). If air temperatures do not fluctuate above 30°C (86°F), it is a very good idea to use a ventral heat source under one side of the cage to allow the snakes to thermoregulate. Nighttime temperatures may be allowed to drop to 18–20°C (64.4–68°F) without any problem. Interestingly, Zweifel (1980) used this temperature range for brumation and was repeatedly successful in captive breeding. Those in our care were exposed to temperatures ranging from 3 to 18°C (38 to 64.4°F) during the winter with no ill effects and were also bred repeatedly. Most authors recommend the standard 10–15°C (50–59°F) for 4–5 months as being appropriate for brumation of this species.

As mentioned above, captive breeding has occurred numerous times and is easily accomplished in the usual manner. Generally, mating will occur faster if the female is placed in the male's cage rather than vice versa, since the male is usually the one that initiates breeding and may instead seek to escape a new enclosure if placed in one. Mating usually occurs early in the spring, often within several weeks of emergence from brumation.

The eggs can be incubated in the usual manner (vermiculite and water) at temperatures ranging from 21 to 31°C (70 to 88°F).

Hatchlings are usually very good eaters right after they shed, usually 1–3 weeks after hatching. Pinkies are the usual fare for the first meal, but some individuals will refuse these. If so, a number of tricks can be used and these are mentioned in the general care section under feeding. These young will grow rapidly, usually shedding once a month, and may reach sexual maturity in 2 years if fed heavily (otherwise 3 or 4 years).

One feeding method that has worked well for stubbornly nonfeeding members of this species is to offer one newborn garter snake to them on a garter snake-scented pinky. They will usually eat that and often anything else that follows. After one such feeding they will readily take plain pinkies or at least scented pinkies.

Housing the young snakes has not been a problem. Many professional breeders have successfully kept hatchlings of this species in plastic shoe boxes for months or longer with no ill effects. One must make sure the ventilation of these shoe boxes is adequate, however. This can be accomplished in most cases by drilling

---

SPECIES: *Lampropeltis getula*, Common Kingsnake
MAINTENANCE DIFFICULTY INDEX: 1 (1 = easiest, 5 = most difficult)
AVERAGE SIZE: 75–208 cm (30–82 inches)
FOOD: Mice, rats, other snakes
CAGE SIZE: 20–30-gallon long aquarium for most
SUBSTRATE: Indoor-outdoor carpet, artificial turf, or newspaper
VENTRAL HEAT: Not essential but helpful
UV LIGHT: No, but an incandescent bulb is useful
TEMPERATURE RANGE: 25–30°C (77–86°F)
SPECIAL CONSIDERATIONS: Cannibalistic. Babies can be a problem to get started
    feeding. If pinkies are refused, try baby garter snakes. May stop eating for long periods.

or burning numerous small holes in the upper sides of the box. This way they can also be stacked on top of each other without interfering with ventilation. See the discussion on ventilation in the general care section.

Because of their diets, these snakes may be very heavily parasitized (either if they are wild-caught or captive-born but fed wild-caught items as food). In our experience, the largely snake-eating speckled kingsnake may be the worst subspecies for parasites, although all kingsnakes are likely to contain some parasites. We have found large numbers of rhabditiform larvae in all wild-caught specimens examined from South Carolina, Georgia, and northern Florida, hence, they should be checked for intestinal worms initially and regularly thereafter.

In summary, these snakes generally make ideal captives. Most have a reasonably calm disposition after a short period in captivity, even though some can be quite snappy. Albinos are often more aggressive than normal snakes.

They can be recommended highly as pets to someone who has little time to care for them and are also excellent pets for beginners. Most of these snakes become very handleable eventually. WARNING: Do not handle other animals prior to handling these snakes!

In our experience, once-weekly feedings have been sufficient.

One member of this species, a California kingsnake, was reported to have survived 33 years and 4 months in captivity and was still living at the time of this writing (Snider and Bowler, 1992). As such, it holds the captive longevity record for all North American snakes.

Lampropeltis pyromelana
Sonoran Mountain Kingsnake

The Sonoran mountain kingsnake is in our opinion one of the most beautiful and easily maintained of North American kingsnakes. This snake may reach 104 cm (41 inches) in length (Wright and Wright, 1957; Behler and King, 1979; Stebbins, 1985) and is beautifully ringed in red, black, and white. The bright colors and small smooth scales give this large mountain kingsnake a glistening appearance, which is no doubt partly responsible for its allure to herpetoculturists. Its distinguishing characteristic is the snout, which is usually white or pale yellow as opposed to black (as in the California mountain kingsnake). There are three subspecies in the United States: the Arizona mountain kingsnake, *L. p. pyromelana*, the Utah mountain kingsnake, *L. p. infralabialis*, and the Huachuca mountain kingsnake, *L. p. woodini*. The Utah subspecies (which is located in south central Utah with two isolated populations in Nevada and northern Arizona) has nine lower labials (lip scales), while the other two subspecies (which are found in north central and southern Arizona, southwestern New Mexico, and south into Mexico) have ten. The Huachuca subspecies has fewer than 42 triads (red rings bordered by two black rings). All are equally beautiful.

The preferred habitat of these snakes in the wild is primarily pine and fir forests and pinion juniper woodlands, particularly rocky slopes near streams, elevation above 850 m (2800 feet) (Wright and Wright, 1957; Fowlie, 1965; Shaw and Campbell, 1974; Stebbins, 1985; Degenhardt et al., 1996). They are also found in

Lampropeltis pyromelana

Arizona Mountain Kingsnake, *Lampropeltis pyromelana pyromelana* (photo by David G. Campbell)

chaparral areas dominated by manzanita and on rocky slopes near streams. They are frequently encountered on the surface during the day, at which times they appear to be basking (Fowlie, 1965; Degenhardt et al., 1996; personal observation), but they are also active at night when presumably they do most of their feeding.

In the wild, these snakes have been known to consume a wide variety of food items, including lizards, small mammals, nestling birds, and possibly other snakes (Shaw and Campbell, 1974; Stebbins, 1985).

Suspected predators of this species include carnivorous mammals, ophiophagous snakes, and birds of prey.

Mating has rarely been observed in the wild but is believed to occur early in the spring followed by egg laying in early summer, with the eggs (usually 3–6) hatching approximately 2 months later. A pair was observed mating on 5 May in southeastern Arizona. See below.

Virtually nothing is known of the thermal ecology of this species in the wild, but as mentioned above, they have been observed "basking" by numerous herpetologists, including us.

In captivity, they do well in a wide variety of cage designs ranging from the more natural arrangements to very barren or highly artificial arrangements. The basic cage design discussed in the general care section will work well,

Huachuca Mountain Kingsnake, *Lampropeltis pyromelana woodini* (photo by Steve Barten)

SPECIES: *Lampropeltis pyromelana*, Sonoran Mountain Kingsnake
MAINTENANCE DIFFICULTY INDEX: 2 (1 = easiest, 5 = most difficult)
AVERAGE SIZE: 45–104 cm (18–41 inches)
FOOD: Lizards, small mammals, and birds
CAGE SIZE: 10–20-gallon long aquarium
SUBSTRATE: Indoor-outdoor carpet, artificial turf, or newspaper
VENTRAL HEAT: Yes
UV LIGHT: No
TEMPERATURE RANGE: 25–30°C (77–86°F)
SPECIAL CONSIDERATIONS: Young must be fed heavily while they are eating before
    brumation. Often stop feeding in August. Parasitism likely in wild-caught specimens.

---

however. This includes artificial carpet/turf or newspaper as well as a variety of wood chips, although we do not prefer the latter substrate for this species. Ventral heat is considered very important, although lighting does not appear to be. Those in our care did very well with only indirect natural filtered light. Air temperatures of 25–30°C (77–86°F) during the active season have been recommended by several authors (Trutnau, 1981; Mattison, 1990), but those in our care and others appear to tolerate temperatures up to 35°C (95°F) fairly well (Zweifel, 1980). Nighttime low temperatures down to 18°C (64°F) have also worked well for this species (Zweifel, 1980; Trutnau, 1981).

Winter cooldown is strongly recommended since these snakes will almost invariably stop eating during the winter months regardless of the temperature at which they are maintained. Furthermore, this cool period is considered essential if breeding is desired. Temperatures ranging from 10 to 15°C (50 to 59°F) or even lower (Trutnau, 1981, suggested 5°C or 41°F) for 2–4 months have worked well for numerous herpetoculturists, even though Zweifel (1980) reported nine successful breedings when a pair of these snakes was maintained at winter temperatures around 18°C (64°F). No cage changes are necessary during brumation; it can be carried out in the regular cage. See the discussion on brumation in the general care section.

Sonoran mountain kingsnakes will usually readily take small mice, which may be offered prekilled. Even the hatchlings are usually voracious eaters of pinkies, unlike many of the

hatchlings of their nearest relative, the California mountain kingsnake. There are exceptions to this, however, and some juveniles must initially be fed lizard-scented pinkies (Mills, 1989).

These snakes breed well in captivity and have been bred frequently. Countless different and unusual techniques have been used to stimulate mating activity in this species. These include misting the snakes with water, placing in extra males, placing in extra females, bagging the snakes and shaking them up, and smearing some of the female's first uric acid deposits of the spring on her back before placing her in with the male. Most of the time, however, just placing the female with her shed skin in with the male a week or so after brumation will result in mating activity.

If successful, the female will usually deposit 1–9 eggs 4–8 weeks later (32–59 days) (Mattison, 1988), and these can be incubated in the usual manner. The incubation period is approximately 2 months (58–81 days depending on the incubation temperature, usually around 65 days at 28°C (82°F) (Zweifel, 1980; Trutnau, 1981; Mattison, 1990).

As mentioned above, the hatchlings, which are relatively large (23–29 cm, 9–11.4 inches) are good eaters. One must feed them heavily after hatching, though, because they will soon stop eating for their winter rest. Some of those in our care stopped eating as early as August, even though warm weather continued until October. This observation was also made by Applegate (1987). Applegate also noted that females are more likely to stop eating first, and after checking our records we must agree. This appetite loss (in either sex) can be very disconcerting to the inexperienced herpetoculturist who has just paid a fairly large sum for such a tiny snake. But if you have fed them well and cool them down for several months, you will rarely have problems. Under certain circumstances, however, especially when the young are born very late in the year, they may refuse to eat altogether (even if lizards are offered). Stay calm and prepare to brumate these snakes after their yolk appears completely gone. A 10–15-gram snake can easily go 2–3 months or more without eating if dropped down to 5–15°C (41–59°F).

The young will usually reach sexual maturity in 2 or 3 years if they are fed properly.

Parasites may be a problem for recently captured animals. They should have a fecal exam performed initially and regularly thereafter if wild-caught reptiles form part of their captive diet. Remember that freezing such food items prior to feeding them to your snakes kills some parasites, but also remember that a number of parasites will not be killed by the freezing process. Applegate (1987) reported that *Trichomonas* was a major problem for the Sonoran mountain kingsnakes in his care when they were fed wild-caught lizards. We believe these parasites will not be killed by the freezing process, even if the lizards were frozen for 6 months. Interestingly, the drug most commonly used to treat these protozoans (metronidazole) may be very toxic to tricolored kingsnakes at the old recommended dose. Applegate (1987) reported neurological signs developed at a dose of 125 mg/kg and that one female twitched for 2 years afterward. The recommended dose for these snakes is now 40 mg/kg.

Captive longevity has been reported to exceed 22 years and 5 months (Snider and Bowler, 1992).

In our experience, these snakes make ideal pets. Aside from being beautiful and good eaters most of the time, they really do not seem to mind being handled quite as much as some of the other kingsnakes. Once again, though, the decision to handle must be based on each individual animal.

Lampropeltis triangulum
Milk Snake

The milk snake is an incredibly variable and wide-ranging species. In fact, it has one of the largest ranges of any snake in the world, occupying most of the United States east of the Rocky Mountains and southern Ontario and Quebec, as well as most of Mexico, all of Central America, and northern South America. There are 25 subspecies recognized at the time of this writing, nine of which occur in the United States and Canada. The seven western and midwestern subspecies include the following: red milk snake, *L. t. syspila*, Louisiana milk snake, *L. t. amaura*, pale milk snake, *L. t. multistriata*, Central Plains milk snake, *L. t. gentilis*, Mexican milk snake, *L. t. annulata*, New Mexico milk snake, *L. t. celaenops*, and Utah milk snake, *L. t. taylori*. The two eastern subspecies are the eastern milk snake, *L. t. triangulum*, and the scarlet kingsnake, *L. t. elapsoides*. Over most of its range within the western United States, the milk snake is the only tricolored snake and hence is readily recognizable. In those areas where they do overlap with other tricolored snakes (mountain kingsnakes in Utah, Arizona, and New Mexico), they can be generally recognized by the widening of the white bands toward the belly. In some areas of Texas, Louisiana, Arkansas, and Oklahoma where they co-occur with the scarlet snake, that species may be recognized by the plain white belly. A good field guide should be consulted for the exact identification of the species in hand.

As we attempt to describe the natural history of this wide-ranging variably sized species in order to assist with captive maintenance efforts,

Lampropeltis triangulum

we must realize we are facing the same problem we have faced with the racer, ringneck, common kingsnake, and other transcontinental species. That is, it is hard to generalize on the care of such a species. Indeed, entire books have been written about this very species (Williams, 1988). Yet, we have successfully maintained and bred individuals of many such widespread species using the same basic approach, but taking into consideration minor differences between the subspecies in terms of thermal

preferences, breeding time, clutch sizes, incubation times and temperatures, as well as brumation times and temperatures. Indeed, the captive maintenance requirements of the milk snakes found within the United States appear much more uniform than those of several other wide-ranging species such as the ringneck, in which there are major dietary differences. Certainly, this is evidenced by examining the care sections of numerous books on snake care. For example, Markel (1990) successfully summarized the care and breeding of every species of kingsnake and milk snake in only eight pages of his beautifully illustrated book. Future works will undoubtedly provide more detail as more data become available, but the fact remains that most species of kingsnake, including all the subspecies of the milk snake, have been maintained and bred in a very similar manner. This is discussed in some detail below.

The milk snake is a small to medium-sized snake in the United States and Canada, ranging 13.0–114 cm (5–45 inches) in TL. Most of the western populations are smaller than those found in the northeast, and their maximum sizes are as follows, according to Williams

Mexican Milk Snake, *Lampropeltis triangulum annulata* (photo by David G. Campbell)

Scarlet Kingsnake, *Lampropeltis triangulum elapsoides* (photo by David G. Campbell)

(1988): red milk snake, 98.7 cm (38.8 inches); pale milk snake, 85.0 cm (33.5 inches); Central Plains milk snake, 80.7 cm (32 inches); Utah milk snake, 71.9 cm (28.3 inches); Louisiana milk snake, 64.9 cm (25.5 inches); and New Mexico milk snake, 63.0 cm (24.8 inches). An apparent exception, the Mexican milk snake may rival the eastern milk snake in size. The maximum for this subspecies recorded by Williams (1988) was 104.4 cm (41.1 inches). The ecological reasons for this size difference are controversial at this time.

The preferred habitat of these snakes appears to be also quite varied. They have been found in prairies, farmlands, broadleaf and coniferous forests, hilly and mountainous areas, suburbs, and either near water (rivers, streams, or near the coast) or far removed from it. Webb (1970) summarized the preferred habitat of the red milk snake in Oklahoma as "interior highlands," the Central Plains milk snake as "grassland and oak woodland," and the Mexican milk snake as "coastal plain." The preferred habitat of the pale milk snake has been characterized by Baxter and Stone (1985) as "scarp woodlands of the plains zone and in the foothills zone, at elevations below 6000 feet."

The habitat of the New Mexico milk snake appears to be primarily montane woodlands (Tennant, 1984; Williams, 1988), although Degenhardt et al. (1996) advise that many habitat types may be utilized.

The list of foods accepted by this species as a whole is phenomenal. However, it appears that lizards of many types are the preferred food, followed by small snakes and small mammals. Other items listed as food for the species include birds and their eggs, small frogs, small fish, earthworms, slugs, and insects (Williams, 1988), but these are not thought to represent common food items for the western subspecies. The types of lizards included as food items for the western subspecies have included spiny lizards, *Sceloporus* sp., skinks, *Eumeces* and *Scincella* sp., and anoles, *Anolis carolinensis*. Tennant (1984) also indicated that side-blotched lizards, *Uta stansburiana*, and whiptails, *Cnemidophorus* sp., would be taken by the New Mexico milk snake.

Small snakes that have topped the list of food items taken by the western subspecies have included blind snakes, *Leptotyphlops* sp., ringneck, *Diadophis punctatus*, worm snakes, *Carphophis* sp., rough earth snake, *Virginia stria-*

Central Plains Milk Snake, *Lampropeltis triangulum gentilis* (photo by David G. Campbell)

tula, smooth green snake, *Opheodrys vernalis*, garter snakes, *Thamnophis* sp., and blackhead snakes, *Tantilla* sp. (Webb, 1970; Williams, 1988). Cannibalism is also known to be extremely common in this species (Mitchell, 1986). Small rodents, particularly nestlings, are known to be an important food source and may represent a greater percentage of the diet in northern and eastern populations (Dundee and Rossman, 1989), although they have been reported as a food source for all subspecies studied. Tryon and Murphy (1982) may have summed up the overall feeding strategy of both wild and captive milk snakes when they described their observations of a captive-raised clutch of Louisiana milk snakes. They stated that newborns eat lizards and gradually shift to mice.

Body temperatures of active wild Central Plains milk snakes in Kansas ranged from 22.3 to 31.7°C (72.1 to 89.1°F) (Fitch and Fleet, 1970), while the same subspecies hiding under rocks in Oklahoma on a cool April day had body temperatures ranging from 18 to 21°C (64 to 70°F).

All subspecies appear to mate in the spring, although the actual time of mating may vary considerably from north to south.

The eastern milk snake is the largest milk snake north of Mexico and the only subspecies that is not distinctly tricolored. Adults range 61–90 cm (24–36 inches) in length with a record of 132.1 cm (52 inches) (Conant and Collins, 1991), and they generally have tan to gray background color with a series of brown to reddish black-bordered blotches running along the back and sides. The dorsal blotches are much larger than those along the sides. Many, but not all, have a Y or a V on the head and this is thought to be the origin of the scientific name, which means "triangle." Of course, the common name "milk snake" comes from the old false belief that these snakes would drink milk from cows. This richly colored snake ranges from southern Maine southward to Alabama in mountainous regions and westward through southern Ontario and Quebec to Minnesota, eastern Iowa, northern Illinois, and Indiana. To the south, they intergrade with the scarlet kingsnake, forming the "coastal plains milk snake." To the west, they intergrade with the red milk snake.

The preferred habitat of the eastern milk snake appears to be fields and open woodlands, but a wide variety of habitats are utilized including old buildings, rocky hillsides, marshy areas, bogs, and areas around streams and rivers (Wright and Wright, 1957; Minton, 1972; Williams, 1988; Holman et al., 1990; Hunter et al., 1992; Klemens, 1993). We have found specimens in open deciduous woodlands near lakes on Long Island, rocky hillsides and fields in upstate New York, and rockpiles near marshes in southern Wisconsin. In nearly every reference, some sort of surface cover was considered to be critical for these snakes and is often where they are found during the day. Minton (1972) commented on the importance of moisture for these snakes.

The diet of the eastern milk snake has been reported to include mice, small rats, moles, shrews, birds, lizards, snakes, fish, insects, and slugs (Wright and Wright, 1957; Minton, 1972; Williams, 1988; Ernst and Barbour, 1992; Mitchell, 1994; Palmer and Braswell, 1995). More specifically, mammalian genera have included *Mus*, *Peromyscus*, *Microtus*, *Zapus*, and *Blarina*. Lizard genera have included *Eumeces*, *Scincella*, and *Sceloporus*. Snake genera have included *Agkistrodon*, *Crotalus*, *Carphophis*, *Diadophis*, *Nerodia*, *Regina*, *Storeria*, *Thamnophis*, and *Virginia* (Williams, 1988).

Body temperatures on wild eastern milk snakes in Wisconsin ranged from 13 to 30°C (55.4 to 86°F) (Henderson et al., 1980).

Known predators of this species include bullfrogs (Hensley, 1962), brown thrashers (Flanigan, 1971), and other milk snakes (Skehan, 1960). However, predatory mammals and birds of prey probably eat them as well.

Mating of the eastern milk snake is known to occur in the spring with 6–24 eggs being laid 30–40 days later (Wright and Wright, 1957; Williams, 1988). These eggs hatch in 50–70 days (Ernst and Barbour, 1989) into neonates

Pale Milk Snake, *Lampropeltis triangulum multistriata* (photo by David G. Campbell)

measuring 17–26 cm (7–10 inches) in length (Fitch and Fleet, 1970; Williams, 1988).

The scarlet kingsnake is a much smaller, albeit more colorful, subspecies. It ranges 36–51 cm (14–20 inches) in length with a record of 68.6 cm (27 inches) (Conant and Collins, 1991). It ranges from southeastern Virginia southward through Florida and westward to eastern Louisiana and western Tennessee.

The relationship between the scarlet kingsnake and the eastern milk snake is very interesting. In the east, they intergrade with each other, while in the western part of their range, they do not. We suspect this may be similar to other situations in which species have evolved around mountain ranges. As the distance from the original populations increases, so does the difference between them. Finally, by the time the two populations overlap again on the other side of whatever physical boundary they were circling, they are so different that they do not interbreed, and in fact, may be two distinct species.

The natural habitat of the scarlet kingsnake has not been as clearly defined in the literature as it has for a number of other species. In our experience, they seem to have a preference for pinewoods, although sandy-soiled mixed pine and scrub oaks also harbor many. Williams (1988) and Palmer and Braswell (1995) also characterized their primary habitat type as pine woods. Water is often found nearby. Large numbers have been found in stumps or under pieces of wood or bark in such habitats, particularly in winter or early spring. We have found several crossing roads at night, several under surface debris, and one under a very large clump of grass. Others have plowed these snakes up in fields (Wright and Wright, 1957).

Foods reported to be consumed by scarlet kingsnakes have included numerous lizards, small snakes, mice, fish, insects, and worms (Wright and Wright, 1957; Mount, 1957; Williams, 1988). Williams (1988) lists the smooth green snake, *Opheodrys vernalis*, the common garter snake, *Thamnophis sirtalis*, the rough earth snake, *Virginia striatula*, and the brown snake, *Storeria dekayi*, as species previously reported in the literature. Palmer and Braswell (1995) also reported the southeastern crowned

Eastern Milk Snake, *Lampropeltis triangulum triangulum* (photo by David G. Campbell)

snake, *Tantilla coronata*, and the eastern worm snake, *Carphophis amoenus*, as food items. Lizards, particularly ground skinks, *Scincella lateralis*, and five-lined skinks, *Eumeces* sp., as well as anoles, *Anolis carolinensis*, are considered to be the most important part of the diet for wild adults, with the other items listed being relatively unimportant for this subspecies.

Mating is believed to occur primarily in the spring, with up to 9 eggs being laid approximately 40 days later. The incubation period for these eggs ranges 49–65 days (Barten, 1981; personal observation). The neonates range 8.6–20.3 cm (4.9–8 inches) in length (personal observations; Groves and Sachs, 1973; Williams, 1988; Palmer and Braswell, 1995).

In captivity, both eastern milk snakes and scarlet kingsnakes generally do very well if they are given secure and numerous hiding places in their cages. Otherwise, the basic cage design as mentioned in the general care section usually works fine for these snakes. A 10-gallon aquarium or similarly sized cage is suitable for either subspecies, although a large eastern milk snake may fare better in a larger cage. A locking or weighted screen top is considered essential if aquariums are used as both subspecies, and indeed all of the milk snakes, are incredibly muscular, and hence are fantastic escape artists. NOTE: WARNING. THESE SNAKES ARE THE BEST ESCAPE ARTISTS OF ALL NORTH AMERICAN SNAKES. BE PREPARED. In fact, the authors have not yet met a herpetologist who has never had a scarlet kingsnake or milk snake escape! For this rea-

son, fiberglass cages with sliding glass fronts and tight-fitting drawer-style cages have become popular with herpetoculturists working with this species.

Scarlet kingsnakes (from Duval County, Florida) in our care mated regularly in late March or early April and produced fertile eggs annually. The data is summarized here. In 1992, 7 eggs were laid on 26 May, which hatched on 15 July. The neonates ranged 12.5–15.3 cm (4.9–6.0 inches) in TL, with an average TL of 13.8 cm (5.44 inches). The sex ratio was 1.3:1 males to females.

In 1993, the same pair mated again and the female laid 3 eggs on 15 June, 2 of which hatched on 9 August and a third was found dead full-term in the egg. The live neonates were 15 and 15.5 cm (5.9 and 6.1 inches) in TL, while the dead one, a female, was 14 cm (5.5 inches) long. The average TL was 14.8 cm (5.8 inches). The sex ratio was .5:1 males to females. On 30 July of the same year, the female laid 4 slugs and a fertile egg, which hatched on 23 September. The male hatchling was 17 cm (6.7 inches) in TL. In 1994, the same pair mated again and the female laid 5 eggs on 21 May, 4 of which hatched on 15 July, and the other was dead full-term in the egg. These neonates ranged 15–17 cm (5.9–6.7 inches) in TL with an average TL of 16 cm (6.3 inches). The sex ratio was 1.5:1 males to females.

Hence, the incubation periods were 49, 54, 55, and 54 days, and the hatchling size varied from 12.5 to 17 cm (4.9 to 6.7 inches) in length. Also note that the average size of the neonates increased in the 3 successive years.

The substrates that have been used successfully for this species have included artificial carpet/turf, newspaper, and a variety of wood chips (but not cedar).

Air temperatures reported as suitable for this species in captivity have ranged from 25 to 30°C (77 to 86°F) (Trutnau, 1981; Markel, 1990; Mattison, 1990; personal observation), although these snakes in our care have done well at temperatures fluctuating from 18 to 35°C (64 to 95°F) during the active part of the year. Brumation temperatures of 10–15°C (50–59°F) for 3 or 4 months have been recom-

---

SPECIES: *Lampropeltis triangulum*, Milk Snake
MAINTENANCE DIFFICULTY INDEX: 2, hatchlings 4 (1 = easiest, 5 = most difficult)
AVERAGE SIZE: 13–114 cm (5–45 inches)
FOOD: Lizards, small mammals, small snakes
CAGE SIZE: 10–20-gallon long aquarium
SUBSTRATE: Artifical turf, indoor-outdoor carpet, or newspaper
VENTRAL HEAT: Not essential but helpful
UV LIGHT: No, but an incandescent bulb is useful
TEMPERATURE RANGE: 25–30°C (77–86°F)
SPECIAL CONSIDERATIONS: Babies of many subspecies are very small and prefer lizards.
  Adults eat small mice.

---

mended by a number of authors, with some indicating that 10–12°C (50–54°F) is best for northern snakes or montane snakes and 13–15°C (56–59°F) for southern snakes (Mattison, 1990). We have observed that temperatures fluctuating from 3 to 18°C (37 to 65°F) over 4–5 months will result in successful breeding of this species.

Captive breeding has been accomplished numerous times with most of these western subspecies. Generally, mating can be accomplished in the usual manner, i.e., placing the female in the male's cage within several weeks after brumation ends. Four to 6 weeks later following a prelaying shed, the female will lay 3–12 eggs. (Generally, the larger the subspecies, the larger the average clutch size.) These eggs will usually hatch in 60–65 days, although they have been known to hatch in as few as 36 days (Fitch, 1970) or up to 73 days (Mattison, 1988). Incubation temperatures of 23–30°C (74–86°F) will be satisfactory.

The young of some of these subspecies are often incredibly challenging. Inexperienced herpetoculturists who are enamored of the attractive colors of the adults are often shocked and dismayed when they see the small size of the hatchlings. Because of their small size (Utah milk snake hatchlings are notoriously small), the majority are not capable of consuming pinky mice initially. Offering hatchling lizards or lizard-scented mouse tails is probably the best chance for inducing a feeding response in and thus rearing such babies. Eventually,

they may take unscented tails, then pinky mice. It may take as long as 6–10 months for these small milk snakes to reach a size where they can swallow a pinky, however. Mexican milk snakes and some eastern milk snakes are an exception, with most babies often readily taking pinkies right away.

Although beautiful, because of their secretive and nervous nature most of these snakes are not very handleable. Their jerky rapid motions are often discomforting to inexperienced herpetoculturists, even though both the snake and the snake keeper will improve with age. Because of their small size, they appear prone to injury if housed in nonburrowing substrates, since they may thrash violently if handled or approached. Hence, we discourage any handling up to 6 months of age for these snakes and encourage the use of a supportive burrowing substrate like cypress mulch. Avoid newspaper if possible for these snakes. Because of the risk of injury, the size and nervousness of the neonates, and the lack of handleability at almost any age, we do not recommend either of these species for beginners.

The longevity records for some of these subspecies are as follows: eastern milk snake, 21 years and 4 months; Louisiana milk snake, 20 years and 7 months; Mexican milk snake, 20 years and 2 months; New Mexico milk snake, 10 years and 11 months; Central Plains milk snake, 10 years and 5 months; red milk snake, 16 years and 6 months; and scarlet kingsnake, 16 years (Williams, 1988).

Lampropeltis zonata
California Mountain Kingsnake

The California mountain kingsnake is a medium-sized snake ranging from 51 to 114.3 cm (20 to 45 inches) long. They are indeed beautiful snakes with their glistening bands of red, white, and black. And even though their color patterns are variable from one subspecies to another and even within a subspecies, all seven are characterized by having a black-tipped nose and white bands that do not widen conspicuously on the lower sides.

There are five subspecies recognized within the United States, one in Baja California and one on an island off the coast of Baja California. The five United States subspecies are the St. Helena mountain kingsnake, *L. z. zonata*, Sierra mountain kingsnake, *L. z. multicincta*, Coast mountain kingsnake, *L. z. multifasciata*, San Bernardino mountain kingsnake, *L. z. parvirubra*, and the San Diego mountain kingsnake, *L. z. pulchra*. These five subspecies are distributed from extreme southern Washington to the southern border of California. Their range is discontinuous.

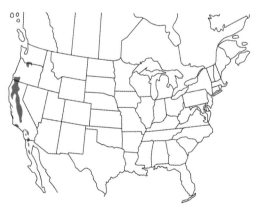

Lampropeltis zonata

The preferred habitat of this snake has been characterized as montane coniferous and mixed coniferous forests, with other habitats used by this species described as riparian woodlands, oak woodlands, and chaparral (McGurty, 1988).

The preferred microhabitat of this species appears to be south-facing rocky outcrops near streams in these plant associations. They may be found from sea level to over 2134 meters (7000 ft) (McGurty, 1988). The coast mountain kingsnake may live in stream canyons extending as low as a few hundred yards from the ocean itself. The Sierra mountain kingsnake is most abundant at midelevations in ecotone situations between pine and chaparral with abundant granite, although it occurs at much higher elevations as well (McKeown, pers. comm., 1993).

Food items taken by specimens in the wild have included western fence lizards, *Sceloporus occidentalis*, sagebrush lizards, *Sceloporus graciosus*, western skinks, *Eumeces skiltonianus*, lizard eggs, bird eggs, nestling birds, and mammals (Zweifel, 1980; McGurty, 1988). McKeown (pers. comm., 1993) is aware of white-footed mice and whiptails being consumed in the wild. Other items taken by captive specimens or reported in the literature as food items include side-blotched lizards, *Uta stansburiana*, garter snakes, *Thamnophis* sp., other small snakes, and domestic mice (Wright and Wright, 1957; Zweifel, 1980; Basey, 1976; Stebbins, 1985; McGurty, 1988; Low, 1993).

Suspected predators of this species include ophiophagous snakes, birds of prey, and carnivorous mammals.

Wild specimens usually emerge from brumation in April, mate in May, and lay 3–9 eggs in June or July. These eggs generally hatch in August or September (Stebbins, 1985; McGurty, 1988). Time from mating to egg laying reported for captives has been 34–56 days (Mattison, 1988). Incubation period in captivity has ranged 48–87 days depending upon the incubation temperature (23–29°C, 73.4–82.4°F). The young snakes measure 20–26.7 cm (7.9–10.5 inches) in length at hatching (Trutnau, 1981; Coote, 1984; Mattison, 1988; McGurty, 1988).

In general, this species does reasonably well in captivity, requiring the barest of cages and

California Mountain Kingsnake, *Lampropeltis zonata* (photo by David G. Campbell)

no special lighting. The basic cage design will work well for this species, i.e., artificial carpet/turf or newspaper, hide box, and water bowl. They must be managed properly, however, and cooldowns are essential. Other substrates such as aspen shavings or cypress mulch have also worked well. Plastic plants and a rock or two are nice additions to the enclosure. Ventral heat is advisable.

Air temperatures of 25–30°C (77–86°F) have been recommended by Trutnau (1981) and will probably work, although we have successfully maintained these snakes under daily temperatures fluctuating between 18 to 35°C (64 to 95°F) during the active part of the year. The Chaffee Zoological Gardens breeds them virtually every year and maintains them at 28°C (82°F), 21°C (70°F) night with a 3-month winter drop to 20–16°C (68–62°F), although they have been dropped several years past to 12°C (54°F).

Enclosure size is not critical. The hatchlings may be started in plastic shoe boxes with small holes drilled in the upper sides and tight-fitting lids, while older juveniles and adults do well in 10–20-gallon long aquariums or similarly sized cages. Drawer-type cages work well also. Be aware, hatchlings are excellent escape artists.

Feeding is usually not a problem for the adults. They will generally readily consume small mice. If not, they can be rapidly trained to consume mice by using scent-transfer techniques (rubbing a lizard on a pinky or small mouse). However, the hatchlings and juveniles almost invariably seem to prefer lizards to pinkies, which makes keeping them very difficult. Therefore, people in large cities or in northern states need to carefully plan how they are going to obtain these lizards. We have received a number of desperate calls from friends in the north asking for a care package of lizards. Admittedly, some individuals will take pinkies right away, but these seem to be in the minority. Others have to be force-fed pinkies with a Pinky Pump® for much of their early lives. At the Chaffee Zoological Gardens, hatchlings are typically pumped once weekly for 4–6 weeks. By that time, they will usually take a split-brained pinky off tongs. These snakes seem to do fine and eventually start taking pinkies on their own, but we prefer the more natural method of feeding. Once they have started feeding on pinkies, feeding is rarely a problem.

Interestingly, many lizards will be taken by these snakes, not just those from their natural range. Perhaps a most pleasant surprise was that these small snakes relish the ground skink, *Scincella lateralis*, a very common eastern lizard. As expected from the above observations, they will also consume small fence lizards, *Sceloporus* sp., side-blotched lizards, *Uta stansburiana*, western skinks, *Eumeces skiltonianus*, and brush and tree lizards, *Urosaurus* sp. We were also surprised to find out they would consume *Anolis sagrei*, the Cuban brown anole, even though irregularly. Other lizards may be consumed as well. One lizard that our specimens have not been particularly fond of is the Mediterranean gecko, which was surprising in light of their acceptance by night snakes, lyre snakes, and gray-banded kingsnakes, among others (Rossi and Rossi, 1992c).

Mike Clari of Smithtown, New York, said one of his juveniles greedily devoured a redback salamander, *Plethodon cinereus*, and indeed, many other amphibians may be consumed by these snakes. Remember that any wild-caught lizard or amphibian is potentially parasitized; therefore, they are best frozen for several days (3) before offering them to your young snake. Freezing will not kill most protozoans, however.

Winter cooldown is considered essential for this montane species, especially if breeding is desired. Temperatures used for adults have varied from 5 to 15°C (41 to 59°F). With regard to hatchlings, several expert breeders from the northeast United States use the "one meal rule." Basically, this means they believe that one good meal will be sufficient to get the hatchlings through their first winter cooldown. This is probably not necessary as most hatchlings probably have sufficient body mass to survive the winter without eating. Generally, it is advisable to offer these snakes food as long as they will take it, and this is especially true with hatchlings. Remember that hatchlings will not be bred the following spring, so they need not be brumated at all if they continue to eat. Therein lies the problem. Like most montane species, they often stop eating during the winter regardless of the temperatures at which they are kept. Therefore, cooldown is strongly recommended. This is also easier on the keeper since lizards may be in short supply at this time.

Brumation may be accomplished in their regular cages, providing that the room in which the cages are placed is sufficiently cold. No cage modifications are necessary. Like most other snakes during this time, they still require a source of drinking water. The duration of brumation may range from 2 to 4 months.

Be forewarned that several of the subspecies seem to require cooler temperatures in the winter than most other kingsnakes. Even the Arizona mountain kingsnake does not appear to require such cold temperatures in order to breed and produce fertile eggs as some of the northern subspecies of the California species. Successful breeding of the Arizona mountain kingsnake has occurred even when the winter temperatures to which they have been exposed did not drop below 18°C (65°F) (Zweifel, 1980), although lower temperatures are recommended for them also. Those who have had experience breeding most subspecies of this mountain kingsnake warn that consistently low temperatures in the 5–10°C (41–50°F) range are more appropriate for this species than most

---

SPECIES: *Lampropeltis zonata*, California Mountain Kingsnake
MAINTENANCE DIFFICULTY INDEX: 2 (1 = easiest, 5 = most difficult)
AVERAGE SIZE: 51–114.3 cm (20–45 inches)
FOOD: Lizards, mice, small snakes
CAGE SIZE: 10–20-gallon long aquarium
SUBSTRATE: Indoor-outdoor carpet, artificial turf, or newspaper
VENTRAL HEAT: Yes
UV LIGHT: No
TEMPERATURE RANGE: 25–30°C (77–86°F)
SPECIAL CONSIDERATIONS: Babies of many subspecies often prefer lizards. Need long cool brumation period for successful breeding.

others. For this reason, safe and effective bru-maculums are being developed by some herpe-tologists (Finnegan, 1984; pers. comm., 1992). At this time, these devices are still fairly expensive (even when homemade), so most individuals use the natural method of brumation. Hence, in warm years the fertility rate of these beautiful mountain kingsnakes will drop. Some have used wine chillers and refrigerators to avoid this problem. See the brumation section.

This species has reproduced many times in captivity. The basic technique of placing the female in the male's cage a week or so after brumation will usually result in mating. Females will then deposit up to 9 eggs 4–6 weeks later.

These eggs may be incubated in the usual manner and will hatch in about 2 months (see above).

The hatchlings are colored exactly as the adults. As mentioned earlier, they are very likely to prefer lizards to pinky mice.

The California mountain kingsnake is one of the most sought after American snakes (by herpetoculturists). They are popular because of their brilliant color pattern and the fact that they are relatively easy to maintain and breed. Check current state regulations before attempting to collect any of these snakes, however. One of these snakes was maintained 26 years and 4 months in captivity (Snider and Bowler, 1992).

Leptodeira septentrionalis
Northern Cat-eyed Snake

The northern cat-eyed snake *L. s. septentrionalis*, is a small snake ranging from 35.6 to 81.3 cm (14 to 32 inches) long, with a maximum recorded size of 98.4 cm (38.7 inches) (Tennant, 1984, 1985; Conant and Collins, 1991). It is another interestingly patterned rear-fanged snake that just barely makes it into the United States in the southern tip of Texas. Like several other snakes in this group, they have relatively broad heads and elliptical pupils (hence the name) and are secretive nocturnal snakes that are not particularly aggressive. This species has been reported to be somewhat arboreal. Combining this with the fact that their preferred habitat may be lush vegetation near water in areas of coastal thorn thickets (Wright and Wright, 1957; Tennant, 1984, 1985), it is not surprising these snakes are rarely seen unless they are searched for specifically. Even those who are looking for them (which should not occur without a permit since they are protected) see them infrequently. However, according to Gus Rentfro—who has studied the snakes in southern Texas for years—these snakes are not particularly arboreal and do not appear to be more common in areas with permanent water sources. Instead, the only unifying characteristic of the habitats where these snakes have been

Leptodeira septentrionalis

found has been sandy soil and open scrub-brush vegetation, such as commonly utilized by the Texas tortoise. Rentfro has never found these snakes in standing water or any vegetation. He stated that most of these snakes have been found at night, but they have also been found about in the daytime, particularly after rainfall. He warns that unlike the black-striped snake, *Coniophanes imperialis*, these snakes are intolerant of disturbed habitats and quickly leave or are extirpated. This includes farmlands.

The diet of these snakes in the wild is

Northern Cat-eyed Snake, *Leptodeira septentrionalis septentrionalis* (photo by R. D. Bartlett)

believed to be primarily frogs and their eggs and tadpoles, fish, salamanders, small lizards, small snakes, and small mice (Wright and Wright, 1957; Tennant, 1984, 1985; Burchfield, 1993). More specifically, frogs reported have included chorus frogs, *Pseudacris* sp., cricket frogs, *Acris* sp., tree frogs, *Hyla* sp., and leopard frogs, *Rana* sp. Lizards consumed have included spiny lizards, *Sceloporus* sp. (Burchfield, 1993). Snakes have included blackhead snakes, *Tantilla* sp., ground snakes, *Sonora semiannulata* (Tennant, 1984), and juvenile diamondback water snakes, *Nerodia rhombifer* (Burchfield, 1993). The following description of ophiophagy (snake eating) by a member of this species suggests that snakes may actually be one of the preferred prey items of this species.

The *Leptodeira* responded immediately by seizing the watersnake by the head. He then proceeded to rotate his body as if attempting to snap the neck of the prey. This physical abuse was used at the same time that the rear fangs were brought into play in an alternating and deliberate fashion to envenomate the prey. Determining whether the venom or the mechanical injury was the primary cause of death to the prey animal was impossible to ascertain, but death ensued within 10 minutes following the initial capture. Once the prey was dead, the cat-

eyed snake released its grip, then following a short head search behavior, it relocated the *Nerodia*'s rostrum and immediately began a very rapid side to side swallowing action, typical of most primarily ophiophagic species of snake. This method of swallowing is unmistakable. Once the act of swallowing was initiated, the entire snake was consumed within two or three minutes. (Burchfield, 1993).

Rentfro has also made several observations regarding the food items of wild cat-eyed

A cat-eyed snake consumes a juvenile diamondback water snake. These snakes are known to be primarily reptile and amphibian eaters, but will also take fish and small mice in captivity. (photo courtesy of Pat Burchfield)

snakes. One recently captured specimen defecated the remains of several large beetles, including dung beetles and Yucca beetles. We suspect that they may have been consumed by some amphibian eaten by a snake, however. Rentfro also observed a wild cat-eyed snake attempting to consume a spadefood toad, *Scaphiopus couchii*, and another attempting to consume a racerunner, *Cnemidophorus gularis* sp. Two DOR cat-eyed snakes found by Rentfro contained other snakes. One was a ribbon snake, *Thamnophis* sp., the other was a another cat-eyed snake. One cat-eyed snake consumed another of similar size when they were bagged together. These observations and those of Burchfield (mentioned above) strongly suggest that this species is a generalized opportunistic predator with a strong preference for ectothermic prey such as anurans, lizards, and snakes, even though large ones will also consume mice.

As noted above, this rear-fanged snake does produce what has been termed a mild venom. It produces a local anticoagulant effect in humans and may cause some minor pain and swelling; however, it does appear to be deadly to reptiles. Burchfield (1993) reported removing a live lizard from the mouth of one of these snakes after it had been in its grasp for several minutes. This lizard died within 7 minutes. There has also been a report of this species biting and killing larger snakes, namely a boa and hognose snake, with which they had been housed (Tennant, 1984).

Suspected predators include owls, indigo snakes, kingsnakes, and milk snakes, as well as predatory mammals like skunks, foxes, coyotes, and bobcats, as well as other cat-eyed snakes.

Reproduction in cat-eyed snakes has been poorly studied. Mating is thought to occur in the winter or very early spring as gravid females have been captured primarily in February, March, April, and May (Fitch, 1970). These eggs, numbering 6–12, have an incubation period of 79–90 days (Wright and Wright, 1957; Duellman, 1958; Fitch, 1970; Tennant, 1984, 1985). Hatchlings are 18–23 cm (7–9 inches) long and resemble the parents (Trutnau, 1981; Tennant, 1984, 1985).

The care of the cat-eyed snake is very much like that of one of its closest relatives in the United States, the lyre snake, *Trimorphodon biscutatus*, except that caging and food preferences differ slightly. Generally, the basic cage design discussed in the general care section will work extremely well. This includes artificial carpet/turf as the substrate, a secure hide box, and a water bowl. Add to this a number of sturdy branches (which have been previously baked at 149°C (300°F) for 15 minutes to kill parasites) and plastic plants and you have an ideal arrangement for a cat-eyed snake. Ultraviolet light is not believed to be necessary for this species, but this is still unknown. A number of specimens have been maintained for years without any UV, and certainly these are nocturnal snakes.

A 10-gallon aquarium is probably a suitable cage size for most; a 20-gallon high would be extremely roomy.

As semitropical snakes, these snakes do best when maintained at 25–30°C (77–86°F). Ven-

---

SPECIES: *Leptodeira septentrionalis*, Northern Cat-eyed Snake
MAINTENANCE DIFFICULTY INDEX: 3 (1 = easiest, 5 = most difficult)
AVERAGE SIZE: 35.6–81.3 cm (14–32 inches)
FOOD: Fish, lizards, small mice, smaller snakes
CAGE SIZE: 10–20-gallon high aquarium
SUBSTRATE: Indoor-outdoor carpet or artificial turf
VENTRAL HEAT: Yes
UV LIGHT: No
TEMPERATURE RANGE: 25–30°C (77–86°F)
SPECIAL CONSIDERATIONS: Prefers frogs and small snakes but will take mice. Likely to be heavily parasitized.

tral heat is very advisable throughout the year, even in the winter, and if it is provided, air temperatures can probably safely be dropped to 5–10°C (41–50°F). Without ventral heat, winter temperatures of no lower than 18°C (64°F) are probably safe. In either case, an incandescent bulb during the day is required to provide a hot spot in the cage throughout the year.

Burchfield warns that these snakes have thin skin and appear susceptible to skin problems if kept too moist. If maintained in too dry a cage, however, he states they are subject to dysecdysis (difficult shedding). Thus, a humidity box would be advisable for this species.

As mentioned above, their preferred food differs somewhat from the lyre snakes. Cat-eyed snakes prefer smooth-skinned frogs, and they have also been known to consume fish, lizards, small mice, and smaller snakes, including members of their own species, in captivity (Mitchell, 1986). Therefore, it is advisable to house them singly.

Rentfro and others have stated that these snakes adapt quickly and feed readily in captivity. Foods consumed by captives include lizards, frogs, and toads, their larvae, as well as fish and mice. The most readily accepted prey, according to Rentfro, has been the racerunner, *Cnemidophorus* sp. Frogs consumed included Rio Grande chirping frogs, *Syrrhophus cystignathoides*, Rio Grande leopard frogs, *Rana berlandieri*, small Gulf Coast toads, *Bufo valiceps*, Couch's spadefood toad, *Scaphiopus couchii*, and Mexican treefrogs, *Smilisca baudinii*. Fish consumed have included mosquito fish, *Gambusia* sp., and goldfish, and these are perhaps the most reliably taken items. Some steadily consume mice. Many lyre snakes can be switched to small prekilled mice using scent-transfer techniques. Thus, mice are the preferred food for long-term maintenance.

Interestingly, there appears to be some disagreement in the literature about periods of summer appetite loss in this species. Wright and Wright (1957), and Trutnau (1981) stated these snakes will stop eating for several weeks during the hottest part of the year. Tennant (1984) denied this occurs, stating "it eats well all year, undeterred by 90°F summertime temperatures." Certainly, there may be a good

explanation for this disagreement, but only time will tell as more specimens are maintained in captivity.

Although captive breeding is rare, a number of females gravid at the time of capture have laid eggs, which have been incubated in the usual manner. It should be noted that the incubation time reported was longer than that of most colubrids, 79–90 days (Duellman, 1958; Tennant, 1985). Clutch size ranges up to 12 eggs.

Another interesting fact is that this snake probably holds the world record for retaining viable sperm in the female's reproductive tract. One specimen laid 6 viable eggs after 5 years without a male! In light of recent observations, perhaps this snake is capable of parthenogenesis.

The 18–23-cm (7–9-inch) long hatchlings are similar to the adults in pattern but the colors are brighter. They may be difficult to provide for since they require smaller food items more frequently. In this respect, they once again are very similar to the lyre snake. See the discussion on lyre snake young.

Certainly, parasites are likely to be a major concern for this species since it is a semitropical frog eater. And these should be examined and controlled as discussed.

Once again, one is reminded of the lyre snake in terms of size, shape, venom, personality and behavior, caging, clutch size, hatchling size, and general care.

Rentfro and others have painted a relatively dismal picture of this snake's future survival in southern Texas. Rentfro describes isolated populations in Kenedy, Willacy, Hidalgo, Starr, and Jim Hogg Counties, with the possible extinction of these snakes in Cameron and Webb Counties. Areas known to have previously supported these snakes have not produced any since the late 1970s or early 1980s when major development occurred in these areas. More research on this species is needed. Captive breeding should be strongly encouraged to fill in the gaps in our knowledge, but to date there has been very little, if any, captive breeding.

Captive longevity has been reported to be more than 10 years and 11 months (Snider and Bowler, 1992).

Leptotyphlops dulcis and *Leptotyphlops humilis*
Texas and Western Blind Snakes

Although not attractive snakes, these little animals are absolutely fascinating. Their life histories and habits are truly amazing, and their scalation and skeletal structure are sufficiently unique to have allowed these snakes and their closest relatives to be placed in their own family, Leptotyphlopidae.

Within the United States, only two species are found, although the genus *Leptotyphlops*, the main genus in the family, contains at least 75 species of New World blind snakes. These two species are the Texas blind snake, *L. dulcis*, which has two subspecies, and the western blind snake, *L. humilis*, which has four subspecies. The two species are easily distinguished from one another by the scalation on the top of their heads. The Texas blind snake has three scales between the ocular scales (eye scales), while the western blind snake only has one scale between the ocular scales.

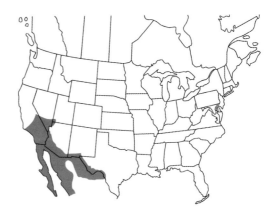

Leptoyphlops humilis

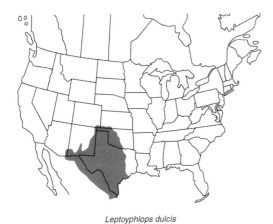

Leptoyphlops dulcis

The two species differ in a number of other ways. The western species reaches a slightly larger size, up to 41 cm (16 inches) (Stebbins, 1985), while the Texas blind snake usually does not exceed 27 cm (11 inches) (Tennant, 1985). The western blind snake is more of a surface dweller or shallow burrower, whereas the Texas species is considered a deep burrowing snake (Punzo, 1974). This is apparently related to

their different foraging strategies; the Texas blind snake appears to feed more heavily on ants and termites, while the western preys on a greater percentage of surface-dwelling insects, even though ants and termites are an important part of the diet of both species (Punzo, 1974). See Table 10 below, adapted from Punzo (1974).

The preferred habitat of blind snakes is any area of loose, damp soil. These snakes have been found from open desert areas to rocky

Table 10. Food Consumed by Western Blind Snake, *Leptotyphlops humilis*, and Texas Blind Snake, *L. dulcis*

Foods	Western, *L. humilis*	Texas, *L. dulcis*
Spiders	7.5%	2.3%
Beetles	11.1%	9.7%
Fly larvae	11.0%	9.3%
Ant larvae	30.1%	29.8%
Termites	24.1%	34.4%
Moth larvae	4.3%	5.6%
Ant lions	0%	2.0%
Crickets	9.6%	3.4%
Millipedes	1.5%	0.2%
Centipedes	0.4%	0%
Earwigs	0%	1.6%

Adapted from Punzo, 1974

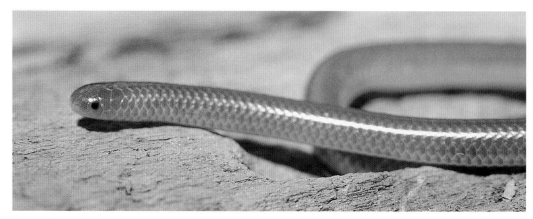

Texas Blind Snake, *Leptotyphlops dulcis* (photo by Ray Ashton)

hillsides, in stream beds, and even on beaches (Stebbins, 1985).

The members of this family are highly specialized for a burrowing way of life. Like some of the other burrowing groups, they have relatively nonflexible skulls, with short jaws and very small though well-developed eyes. Their scales are thick, very smooth and shiny, and very tightly overlapping. Furthermore, they have no gastrosteges (no large belly scales); rather, the scalation is uniform top and bottom. The solid skull presumably allows these snakes to burrow better, and the tightly arranged scales help protect these snakes from their prey's guardians—soldier ants or termites. That's where the small jaws come in. Blind snakes eat only soft-bodied insect larvae and eggs, primarily those of ants and termites. And often, the young insect is not even swallowed, but rather has its abdominal contents sucked out much like a spider might do. Most of the time, however, these species do swallow their prey items, even though they may try to break the worker ant's (or termite's) head off rather than swallow it.

Even more remarkably, these snakes use chemical signals to avoid being attacked by the ants, and then hide among the ants for protection from other snakes. And if this lifestyle isn't strange enough, it turns out they spray musk on themselves and change the angle of individual scales, thereby assuming a silvery color (Shaw and Campbell, 1974). Furthermore, at night under black lights, they glow a fluorescent pale

green color with a blue nose (Shaw and Campbell, 1974). There are probably many more things about these snakes we do not understand fully, and their care in captivity is but one of them.

Blind snakes probably have many predators. Perhaps their most important predators are other snakes. Sonoran coral snakes apparently prey heavily upon them, and night snakes have also been observed to eat blind snakes (Webb, 1970). Kingsnakes, milk snakes, and patchnose snakes will also eat them. Many birds and predatory mammals are likely predators.

As one might imagine from the above description, keeping these snakes requires a slightly different approach from that used with many of the other snakes we have discussed. But, if you remember the basics of snake care and modify them to accommodate a burrowing form, you will probably do well with these snakes. Clark (1967) studied these snakes (*L. dulcis*) in captivity and found they were the most fossorial of the five snakes he studied (Texas blind snakes, worm snakes, blackhead snakes, lined snakes, and ringneck snakes) and they sought out moister soils and cooler temperatures than all of the other species examined (18 individuals selected an average temperature of 20.6 ± 0.77°C, approximately 69°F). Furthermore, he concluded these snakes may avoid sand as a substrate, instead preferring clay-loam or clay-loam-sawdust mixes. This behavioral selection of high moisture/lower temperature areas may be related to water conservation in these desert-dwelling reptiles, since they are thought to have very permeable skin and thus may be very susceptible to desiccation (Stebbins, 1985; Retes, in Hardy, 1992).

As mentioned above, Punzo (1974) determined that the Texas blind snake, *L. dulcis*, appears to be even more fossorial than the western blind snake, *L. humilis*, and suggested this is related to their different food preferences in areas where both species occur together.

In light of the above discussion and based on the experiences of a number of individuals, it appears there may be several ways in which to successfully maintain these snakes. Regardless of the actual cage design, it is imperative that there be some semimoist burrowing substrate in the enclosure. Some have used sphagnum moss alone, others have used moist sand or loam-type soil, and others, including us, have used some combination of the above. Also, it is not entirely inconceivable that moist vermiculite or perlite would be suitable substrates. In addition, there must be drier areas, which are well ventilated, to which these snakes may retreat. Remember what happens to snakes housed in very moist, poorly ventilated enclosures, and how fast it may happen. See the sections on humidity and ventilation.

In addition to a moisture gradient, a thermal gradient is also advisable. Usually this can be provided by placing an incandescent bulb (15, 25, or 40 watts) over one side of the enclosure approximately 30 cm (12 inches) above the substrate.

Keeping these needs in mind, several arrangements can be devised. We have successfully used the following arrangement.

To a small aquarium (we have used 5 gallon or smaller but there is no reason why larger aquariums cannot be used), add 2–5 cm (1–2 inches) of sand. Place a small pile of sphagnum moss over the sand on one side and cover it with some flat impermeable object. We have used plastic containers cut in half, but there is no reason glass plates or flat rocks cannot be used for this purpose. Mist the sphagnum moss with water fairly heavily, and repeat every several weeks to maintain at least some moisture in that area of the cage. The water bowl may be placed over the flat object and allowed to overflow every several weeks in order to achieve the same effect. The incandescent bulb is best placed over the dry end of the cage in order to create a hot spot on the dry side, thereby reducing the rate of evaporation and

Western Blind Snake, *Leptotyphlops humilis* (photo by Steve Barten)

SPECIES: *Leptotyphlops dulcis*, Texas Blind Snake
MAINTENANCE DIFFICULTY INDEX: 4 (1 = easiest, 5 = most difficult)
AVERAGE SIZE: 13–27 cm (5–10.75 inches)
FOOD: Ants, termites, crickets??
CAGE SIZE: 5-gallon aquarium
SUBSTRATE: Sand, sphagnum moss
VENTRAL HEAT: No
UV LIGHT: No, but an incandescent bulb is strongly advisable
TEMPERATURE RANGE: 25–30°C (77–86°F)
SPECIAL CONSIDERATIONS: Food is often difficult to procure. Needs an area of
   semimoist burrowing substrate like sphagnum moss.

---

creating a horizontal temperature and moisture gradient.

Theoretically, the three-layer enclosure, originally designed for *Tantilla* sp., should also work well for these snakes. This includes a layer of gravel over which a layer of fine sand is placed, followed by mulch (on one side only) and strips of bark or rocks. The same heat source as recommended for the previous arrangement, namely an incandescent bulb, is placed directly above the setup. Set a shallow water bowl into the area with the mulch. Make sure to also add water to the gravel in order to create a vertical moisture gradient in the cage.

Recently, we have observed that these snakes are particularly fond of burrowing in rotted termite-eaten logs. One of these small logs (with a thriving termite colony) can be placed on the surface of the cage substrate and will provide both food and a variety of hiding places for these snakes.

Add ant larvae, termites, and (according to some) juvenile waxworms or crickets to the areas under the rock, bark, or water bowl, and the snake should be able to find them. As far as how many you will need to feed in order to maintain an adult, grow a juvenile, or build up a female for breeding and egg laying is unknown. The frequency of feeding is also problematic, but we have found that about 20 ant eggs or termites offered every 1–2 weeks during the spring, summer, and fall is sufficient for maintenance.

Other questions that need to be addressed soon are these: What kinds of parasites, if any,

do these snakes have? How well will they handle some of our newer antiparasitic drugs if they do have intestinal worms?

Western and Texas blind snakes have been long overlooked by herpetoculturists. Indeed, they are not very showy, they are rarely seen during the day, and their food is difficult to procure, but they are fascinating little animals that are very worthy of captive studies. Neither Slavens and Slavens (1991) nor Snider and Bowler (1992) listed any captive specimens or longevities. We have maintained two specimens of *L. humilis* for nearly a year, feeding primarily ant eggs and termites. Feeding may be observed if ant eggs are placed in a depression in the sphagnum moss right under the clear plastic or glass cover. It is fascinating to watch these little snakes' behavior as they approach their food supply. First, they appear to home in on their prey by using olfactory cues. The snake will move its head from side to side, occasionally touching it down, until it contacts the eggs. In the presence of worker or soldier ants, a rhythmic jerking may take place throughout the feeding. The purpose of this movement is unknown, but it is not unlike the rhythmic movements of larger snakes during breeding activities. Perhaps this motion sends a signal to the ants not to attack. In any case, the actual feeding process is incredible. Moving so quickly and deftly that the observer doubts his or her own eyes, the snake's head hovers over the mound of eggs and rapidly swallows one after another. The confirmation that the egg has been swallowed comes as the peristaltic waves carry a small ant egg-sized lump down the snake's neck into the abdominal region. One egg-sized lump may follow another down into the snake's stomach as often as every 10 seconds. As many as 15 eggs, but possibly more, have been consumed by one snake in a single feeding.

Brumation and breeding of these snakes in captivity is poorly known. We have brumated these snakes in their regular cages, providing no additional light or heat for 4–5 months and allowing the snakes to be exposed to naturally fluctuating temperatures in the Jacksonville, Florida, area. These temperatures ranged from 3.3°C (38°F) to 18.3°C (65°F). No food was offered during this time but the cages were misted occasionally. No mating activity has been observed by us at the time of this writing. However, an unusual period of surface activity occurred in early December, even though ambient temperatures at the time of the activity hovered between 10 and 15°C (50 and 60°F). Could these primitive snakes of tropical origin have a breeding season more like the tropical boas and subtropical indigo snakes? Indeed, once the eggs are laid (both species have clutch sizes ranging from 2 to 8 eggs), usually in early to midsummer (Fitch, 1970; Hibbard, 1964; Klauber, 1940), the females coil about their clutches very much like boas and pythons do. Whether they are protecting their eggs and from what is not known at this time, but protection against desiccation is a likely possibility. These eggs hatch in 1–3 months into juveniles measuring about one-third the maximum length of the adults (about 7.5 cm or 3 inches) (Klauber, 1940). Presumably, they may be cared for in a manner similar to the adults, taking into account the greater risk for desiccation.

In the absence of any specific information, breeding should be attempted as with other snakes. The eggs may be difficult to find, but in a properly maintained three-layer cage, they may incubate naturally.

Recent observations by Recchio revealed that incubation techniques similar to those used for colubrids would work for western blind snakes, *L. humilis*. One female captured on 5 June 1996 deposited 6 eggs on 9 June. The eggs were deposited on the surface of moistened vermiculite and the female coiled in the vermiculite immediately below her clutch. These eggs were 1.3–1.8 cm (0.5–0.7 inches) long at the time of laying. Four of those eggs were incubated at temperatures averaging 30°C (86°F) and hatched after 94 days (Recchio, 1998). Interestingly, the hatchlings appeared to be very pink initially, but became darker within the first hour after hatching. The total length of these neonates averaged 11.4 cm (4.5 inches).

Normal shedding should occur in one piece every 1–3 months. The shed may be difficult to find, however, since it may occur below the surface of the moist sand. Should numerous pieces of skin be found on the surface, it suggests that either the environment is too dry or else an old one-piece shed skin was recently unearthed by the burrowing action of the blind snake and crumbled on the surface.

In summary, there is a great deal to be

SPECIES: *Leptotyphlops humilis*, Western Blind Snake
MAINTENANCE DIFFICULTY INDEX: 4 (1 = easiest, 5 = most difficult)
AVERAGE SIZE: 18–41 cm (7–16 inches)
FOOD: Ants, termites, crickets
CAGE SIZE: 5-gallon aquarium
SUBSTRATE: Sand, sphagnum moss
VENTRAL HEAT: No
UV LIGHT: No, but an incandescent bulb is strongly advisable
TEMPERATURE RANGE: 25–30°C (77–86°F)
SPECIAL CONSIDERATIONS: Food is often difficult to procure. Needs an area of
    semimoist burrowing substrate like sphagnum moss.

---

learned about these fascinating little snakes. Until we learn more, one would be best advised to avoid using the term *primitive* when describing these animals. They appear to be extremely well adapted and highly evolved for a burrowing way of life. Even though they may have retained some of the skeletal characters that we consider primitive in snakes, one cannot fail to be impressed by the bewildering array of behavioral and morphological adaptations these snakes display that suggest they are anything but primitive.

Lichanura trivirgata
Rosy Boa

The rosy boa is an attractive small to medium-sized snake of rocky desert and scrubland in the southwestern United States and northern Mexico. They range from southern California southward throughout Baja California and eastward through southwestern Arizona and Sonora, Mexico. At the present time, most herpetologists agree there are three subspecies within the United States, although subspecies within Mexico have been the topic of a heated debate recently. Subspeciation of rosy boas is in a state of flux. However, the three subspecies traditionally recognized are the desert rosy boa, *L. t. gracia*, coastal rosy boa, *L. t. roseofusca*, and the Mexican rosy boa, *L. t. trivirgata*. Both Dave Spiteri and John Ottley, the two "experts," recognized other forms (see *The Vivarium* 5:3, 8:5).

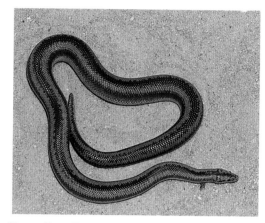

Desert Rosy Boa, *Lichanura trivirgata gracia* (photo by David G. Campbell)

Lichanura trivirgata

The desert rosy boa is best recognized by its relatively *smooth-edged* and distinct striping of reddish brown or orangish against a gray or tan background. This is the northernmost subspecies and the subspecies with the largest range in the United States. It occupies most of southeastern California and western Arizona. The coastal rosy boa may be recognized by three *uneven-edged* pink, reddish brown, or brown stripes on a gray or bluish background, often with a number of spots of the stripe color in the gray area. It occurs in extreme southwestern coastal California and into the northern part of Baja California. The Mexican rosy boa is the chocolate and cream snake (three dark brown stripes on a cream background—or is it four cream stripes on a brown background?). In the United States, they are usually found only in extreme southwestern Arizona. They do range into Sonora, Mexico, and southern Baja California, however. There is quite a bit of variation from location to location and intergradation is possible, which makes the situation a little more confusing, but for the purposes of this discussion, this description will be satisfactory. See Stebbins (1985) and Spitieri (1991, 1992, 1998) for more details.

The preferred habitat of the rosy boa appears to be dry rocky areas such as washes in desert canyons, and especially hillsides near permanent or intermittent streams (Fowlie, 1965; Stebbins, 1972, 1985). Large rocks appear to be present in most areas where these snakes have been found (Wright and Wright, 1957). Interestingly, Fowlie (1965) believed that the major competitor of these snakes were the "recent, efficient invaders from the southeast"—the rattlesnakes.

Predators are known to include whipsnakes, rattlesnakes, and birds of prey. Suspected predators include kingsnakes and predatory mammals. These snakes are also heavily collected because they are highly prized as captives.

As mentioned above, this is not a large snake. The record is 110 cm (44 inches), but most individuals are 61–91 cm (24–36 inches) in length. All have smooth small scales that give them a shiny appearance.

Like the rubber boa, their closest relative within the United States, rosy boas are not dietary specialists. Literature reports have included lizards, small mammals, small birds, and small snakes including venomous snakes (Wright and Wright, 1957; Shaw and Campbell, 1974; Switak, 1984; Stebbins, 1985). Shaw and Campbell (1974) mentioned that a juvenile sidewinder was consumed by a captive rosy boa at the San Diego Zoo. These snakes are powerful constrictors, again much like the rubber boa and indeed all boas. In fact, their close relationship to that species is evident not only by a number of morphological similarities (including small size, skeletal similarity, anal spurs in the males, small head relative to the neck, etc.), but also in feeding, mating, defensive behaviors, viviparity (birth of live young), and length of gestation. Consider, for example, the specialization on young rodents or birds, spring mating with live birth in the fall after 4–5 months gestation, and the practice of rolling into a ball and hiding the head when threatened. They are also both primarily crepuscular or nocturnal. There are many other similarities. One could even jokingly say they had the same initials (R.B.)! Yet the rosy boa has become extremely popular with herpetoculturists, while the rubber boa is considered undesirable by many, even though both adapt equally well to captivity.

In the wild, mating is thought to occur primarily in the spring and results in the birth of

Coastal Rosy Boa, *Lichanura trivirgata roseofusca* (photo by David G. Campbell)

live young approximately 120–150 days later. Neonates are often observed from September through November. The average litter size is 4–5 but litters as large as 19 have been reported (Fogel, 1997).

With regard to captive maintenance, *most* rosy boas will thrive in captivity in a wide variety of enclosures and cage arrangements. They will generally adapt better, however, if one caters to their secretive nature by providing a slightly more complex environment (Witwer, 1996). This is not to say that they *require* an extremely complex or natural arrangement, but that some individuals may adapt and start feeding better if housed with a more natural substrate and multiple hiding places. Spiess (1997) strongly recommends that hiding areas always be provided at both ends of the cage's thermal gradient. Indeed, one may consider this snake to be the "ball python" of North America. The ball python, *Python regius*, is a commonly imported African snake that is similar in many ways to the rosy boa. Some may be notoriously difficult to get to start feeding, but, like that species, they are quite prepared to go months without feeding. This is not conducive to the health and breeding success of the captive snakes, but it is something many individuals may go through initially. Many individuals are force-fed for some time before they adjust. Force-feeding can be avoided and the adjustment period shortened for some of these snakes if they are set up in a cage as described above and offered a variety of foods initially.

Thus, the standard enclosure for these secretive snakes should include numerous objects under which the snake may hide. People have had varying degrees of success with overturned clay pots, plastic flowerpots, curved bark, hollow logs, PVC pipe, commercially manufactured hide boxes, and combinations of the above. The substrate for these snakes may be smooth dry pea gravel or wood chips (cypress, pine, and aspen are okay) of about 2 inches deep or in the case of a good eater, newspaper or indoor/outdoor carpet (artificial turf). A stable branch, some stable rocks, and plastic plants all will help provide the snake with a sense of security and beautify the enclosure at the same time. A 10–20-gallon long aquarium is usually a sufficient size enclosure for this boa, but Switak (1984) suggested a larger enclosure and more hiding places if the snake tries to escape cages constantly. Spiess (1997) houses adults in cages that measure 1 × 0.66 × 0.66 meters (3 × 2 × 2 feet).

Water may be available at all times if the ventilation is adequate (screen top). Otherwise, it should be placed in the cage for a short period of time every week.

Ventral heat to maintain a "hot spot" of 29–34°C (85–93°F) is strongly advisable, especially for gravid females. Air temperatures of 20–29°C (68–85°F) during the day have worked well for a number of herpetoculturists. One must remember, however, that there may be a considerable variation in the preferred temperature range among members of this species depending upon the latitude and altitude of the place they originated. Nighttime temperatures may safely drop as low as 15–19°C (60–66°F) during their active feeding season or lower if ventral heat is provided. Brumation temperatures will be even lower. See below.

As mentioned above, most wild-caught adults will feed readily in captivity, but a number are extremely fastidious at first. Some will eat well if offered a certain size domestic mouse, but not another. Others will take mice only prekilled or only alive, or only at night, or only when offered in a paper bag, or under a log, etc. Some refuse domestic mice but prefer wild mice or prekilled domestic mice scented with these. Some captives have preferred nestling birds (finches, house sparrows, or quail). Indeed, a great deal of experimentation can and should be carried out with an anorectic rosy boa before one resorts to force-feeding. One individual in our care refused to eat voluntarily for more than a year until a pinky scented with Mediterranean gecko, *Hemidactylus turcicus*, was offered. Another experienced snake keeper who had difficulty getting numerous boas to eat insisted that the best trick to get them started was to place the snakes in a pillowcase and take them for a ride. Once the secret of each individual is discovered, offering its favorite food in the proper manner will result in a regularly feeding long-term captive.

Brumation for 2–4 months at 10–15°C (50–

SPECIES: *Lichanura trivirgata*, Rosy Boa
MAINTENANCE DIFFICULTY INDEX: 2 (1 = easiest, 5 = most difficult)
AVERAGE SIZE: 61–91 cm (24–36 inches)
FOOD: Mice, lizards, nestling birds
CAGE SIZE: 10–20-gallon long aquarium
SUBSTRATE: Woodchips (cypress, pine, aspen), pea gravel
VENTRAL HEAT: Yes
UV LIGHT: Not essential
TEMPERATURE RANGE: 20–29°C (68–85°F)
SPECIAL CONSIDERATIONS: Most eat readily, but some are very difficult to get started.
    Eat small mice.

59°F) is considered essential for captive reproduction. Those in our care showed no ill effects
when exposed to temperatures fluctuating from
3 to 18°C (38 to 65°F) during the winter,
however. Even if captive breeding will not be
attempted, brumation may be necessary because
some animals will stop eating every fall regardless of the temperatures at which they are kept.
Neonates are also notorious for this. These boas
may be brumated in their cages and no modifications of their cages are necessary during this
time. They may also be brumated artificially as
discussed in the general care section by using
plastic boxes with mulch that are placed in a
refrigerator maintained in the proper temperature range. See the section on brumation.

Captive breeding of this beautiful little constrictor has been accomplished numerous times.
Basically, there is no special trick to breeding
these snakes. Placing the female in with the
male a week or so after brumation will generally result in mating activity. If not, separate the
pair and try again at 1-week intervals until
mating activity is observed. Successful mating
will result in the birth of 1–12 young (usually 4
or 5) after a gestation period of 3.5–5 months
(103–134 days, usually) (Fitch, 1970; Shaw and
Campbell, 1974; Stebbins, 1985; Mattison,
1988; Ross and Marzec, 1990). The young are
generally 25–36 cm (10–14 inches) at birth and
may begin feeding on pinkies right away. Some
refuse to feed until after brumation, which
results in a fair amount of distress for the
inexperienced keeper and often unnecessary
force-feeding for the neonate born late in the

hatching season. A healthy looking neonate
should not be force-fed until all other options
including brumation have been exhausted.

Sexual maturity may be reached in 2–3 years
under normal captive conditions.

Aside from anorexia in the neonates and
recently captured adults, several other medical
problems are common in rosy boas. Parasitic
organisms occurring in wild-caught rosy boas
and commonly implicated in vomiting are the
protozoans, *Monocercomonas* (a flagellate) and
Cryptosporidium, and intestinal worms, namely
ascarids (Jarchow, 1992a). We have observed
rhabditiform larvae, probably *Strongyloides*, in
one Mexican rosy boa from southern Arizona.
Another parasite frequently found in these
snakes is *Entamoeba invadens*. This is not
something commonly seen in wild snakes (the
snakes are probably infected while in captivity). Thus, repeated fecal exams and dewormings are very important for wild-caught members of this species, or even long-term captives
that have just been purchased, especially when
they are about to enter a collection of snakes.
These snakes can be treated as discussed in the
general care section. This also points out the
value of a good quarantine procedure.

These are indeed beautiful and increasingly
popular snakes among herpetoculturists. They
are now being bred intensively and a tremendous number of "varieties" from different localities are available. These include the L.A.
Bay boa, San Gabriel mountain boa, hypomelanistic boa, and Morongo Valley boa, as
well as numerous others.

Mexican Rosy Boa, *Lichanura trivirgata trivirgata* (photo by David G. Campbell)

One must remember, however, that these snakes may be a bit trickier to maintain than some and probably do not represent good beginner snakes (even though some individuals might do extremely well in the hands of an inexperienced herpetoculturist). We would advise that beginners contemplating the acquisition of a rosy boa purchase a captive-bred snake that has been well started (an animal that has been eating on its own for some time). Even experienced snake keepers may have difficulties with these sometimes finicky feeders. On the other hand, many well-adapted rosy boas are very likely to bite because they are such aggressive feeders!

One of these snakes survived 18 years and 7 months in captivity (Snider and Bowler, 1992; Slavens and Slavens, 1990, 1991).

Masticophis bilineatus
Sonoran Whipsnake

The Sonoran whipsnake is the first of the whipsnake group to be discussed. This is a group of large, fast-moving, diurnal snakes that are generally high-strung and aggressive when cornered. All of them appear to be very visually oriented and, as might be expected from their diurnal nature, have higher temperature preferences than the vast majority of other North American snakes (Brattstrom, 1965). These factors need to be considered when establishing a captive environment and planning a feeding program for these snakes.

The Sonoran whipsnake is a large snake, ranging 60–170 cm (24–67 inches) in length (Wright and Wright, 1957; Stebbins, 1985). They are bluish gray in color and have two or three pale yellow or white stripes along each side. There are two subspecies, the Sonoran whipsnake, *M. b. bilineatus*, and the Ajo Mountain whipsnake, *M. b. lineolatus*. They can be readily distinguished because their ranges are disjunct and the Ajo Mountain whipsnake has a spotted chin. See a good field guide for further identification characteristics. The Ajo Moun-

Masticophis bilineatus

tain whipsnake is found only in one mountain range in Pima County, Arizona, while the Sonoran mountain whipsnake is found throughout southeastern Arizona and southwestern New Mexico, and south through much of western Mexico. The preferred habitat of these snakes appears to be open areas of brushy vegetation in foothills and lower mountain slopes, usually near streams (Wright and Wright, 1957; Stebbins, 1985).

The diet of this species appears quite catholic in nature as they have been known to consume lizards, small birds, and frogs in the wild (Wright and Wright, 1957; Fowlie, 1965; Shaw and Campbell, 1974; Stebbins, 1985) and they greedily consume domestic mice in captivity. There have also been several reports of cannibalism in other members of this genus in captivity (Mitchell, 1986), so small snakes will presumably be consumed as well. Juveniles may also eat invertebrates as well as lizards (Mattison, 1988). Other aspects of the natural history are lacking in the literature, probably because of this snake's restricted range within the United States. Certainly, it is the least known of the whipsnakes.

Suspected predators of this species include ophiophagous snakes, carnivorous mammals, and birds of prey.

Very little is known of the reproductive behavior of this snake in the wild. It is believed that they have a pattern of activity similar to that of other whipsnakes, with emergence from brumation in April or May. Mating probably occurs at that time as 6–13 eggs are laid in June

or July (Wright and Wright, 1957; Behler and King, 1979). These relatively large eggs, 37–52 mm (1.5–2 inches) long, hatch in approximately 2 months into miniature versions of the adults. One in our care laid 15 eggs (see below).

In captivity, the Sonoran whipsnake generally remains a nervous and challenging captive. They will survive for years if housed properly, however. Proper housing for this species and indeed all of the North American whipsnakes implies ample room, bright and warm lighting during the daytime, and great ventilation in the cage. Smooth-sided aquariums with screen tops will work; however, taller cages would probably be more appropriate since this would make it more difficult for the snakes to rub their noses on the screen.

The basic setup discussed in the general care section works well for these snakes, specifically artificial carpet/turf, a secure place to hide and a small water bowl. In our experience, carpet/turf is much more suitable than newspaper for this species since it provides much better traction. Wood chips have been used and seem to work very nicely, even though the snakes seem somewhat prone to ingest this material when rapidly striking and pinning their prey. Several secure rocks, a stable branch, and plastic plants will complete the artificial environment. To some extent, the more complex the environment, the more secure these snakes will be and the better they will eat and adapt. It is important, however, that the cage not be so crowded as to restrict their visibility to the point where they cannot find their food or catch it, especially recently captured specimens, since they often need to see, chase, and catch their food rather than just taking it prekilled. Long-term specimens will take their food prekilled, however.

One interesting observation with regard to housing whipsnakes was that there seemed to be some benefit to a mirror on one side of the cage. One snake demonstrated reduced wandering and a consistently good appetite when placed in this arrangement. Perhaps the mirror gave the impression that the cage was much larger, or perhaps it was just brighter. We were initially concerned that this arrangement would lead to some form of stress ("another" snake

Sonoran Whipsnake, *Masticophis bilineatus* (photo by David G. Campbell)

visible in the cage), but there was never any indication of this. Retes (1989) may have provided a good explanation for this. He suggested that a snake with a large territory like a whipsnake may feel more at home if it is allowed to see an open expanse of well-lit territory, while it is itself in a fairly small area that is densely packed with shelter and dark hiding places. Apparently, the mirrored side assisted with this illusion.

Other things that appear to reduce stress include placing the cage at face height as opposed to placing it on the floor and also possibly covering the front of the cage with an opaque substance. The first step will reduce vibrations and both steps will eliminate the view of a large animal approaching.

As mentioned above, there is little specific information regarding the thermal preferences of this snake. However, it is known that snakes from this group have higher preferred body temperatures than most snakes, hence, it is strongly recommended that their cages be kept very warm. Those in our care have been maintained successfully at temperatures fluctuating between 27 and 35°C (80 and 95°F) during the day and 18–27°C (65–80°F) at night during their active period of the year. Ventral heat was

provided at all times during the spring, summer, and fall and is considered a necessity. In addition, incandescent bulbs providing hot spots or basking areas within the cage are highly recommended during the day.

Brumation is strongly advisable for these snakes as many of them will stop eating in late summer or early fall regardless of the temperatures at which they are maintained. Those in our care consistently stopped eating in September. It is not known if brumation is necessary for captive reproduction in this species or, if so, what temperatures and durations are necessary. On the basis of observations of other North American snakes, we suspect it is necessary and therefore recommend it.

Brumation may be accomplished in their regular cage without any cage modifications. Air temperatures fluctuating between 3 and 18°C (38 and 65°F) have been well tolerated by those in our care. The ventral heat has been turned off during this time although this may not be necessary.

To our knowledge, captive reproduction has not occurred with this species. However, other members of the genus have been bred in the usual manner discussed in the general care section (place the female in with the male several weeks after brumation ends and once per week until mating is observed). Watch out for cannibalism at this time, as mentioned above.

A pair in our care mated in early May and the female deposited 15 eggs on 19 June. Only 5 of the eggs were fertile, however, which made us question whether the mating activity observed was that which produced these eggs (the female had been captured only several weeks prior to mating and may have retained sperm from a previous mating). The 10 infertile eggs averaged 2.82 × 1.91 cm (1.1 × 0.75 inches) and shriveled rapidly. The 5 fertile eggs, averaging 4.32 × 2.4 cm (1.7 × 0.94 inches), hatched on 25 August, an incubation period of 67 days at incubation temperatures of 28–30°C (82–86°F). These neonates were olive gray with brown snouts and measured 43–45 cm (16.9–17.7 inches). The sex ratio was 4:1 male to female, which was determined by the "popping" technique. All neonates shed within 7 days of hatching and consumed ground skinks as their first meal. This is consistent with what has been reported by others with regard to first feeding preferences.

The following year the same pair mated repeatedly in May, and the female deposited 7 eggs on 23 June. All eggs hatched on 2–3 September, an incubation period of 71 days. These neonates ranged 42–44 cm TL. There were three males and four females. Due to the high hatch rate, this was believed to be a true captive breeding.

Indeed, young whipsnakes of all species studied have a definite preference for lizards and insects, and may refuse pinkies initially. We have observed this to be the case for hatchling coachwhips and striped whipsnakes. In those species, lizards or lizard-scented pre-killed pinkies were readily accepted first meals. Unscented pinkies will usually be consumed within 6–8 months. Remember that meals are best offered during the day as feeding activity abruptly ends when the lights go out.

With regard to housing hatchlings, there are several words of warning. First, do not house these snakes in plastic shoe boxes. They require intense heat and excellent ventilation. In most cases, housing them in shoe boxes will result in anorectic snakes with respiratory problems; the snakes usually die before the keeper realizes how sick they are. Second, never house these babies with other snakes, even their own siblings, for any length of time. This is very likely to result in fights over food, cannibalism, or stress and disease in the long run. Instead, baby whipsnakes are best housed in 10-gallon aquariums set up exactly as described above.

One of the major medical problems of whipsnakes in general, and one that we have observed also with members of this species, is that they tend to rub their rostral areas (noses) raw in attempts to escape the cage (see also Jarchow, 1988). Infection may then start to spread into deeper tissues. This may often be recognized by a bubblelike appearance on the top of the head. The problem may be partially corrected by changing the environment of the

---

SPECIES: *Masticophis bilineatus*, Sonoran Whipsnake
MAINTENANCE DIFFICULTY INDEX: 4 (1 = easiest, 5 = most difficult)
AVERAGE SIZE: 60–170 cm (26–67 inches)
FOOD: Mice, lizards, small birds, small snakes
CAGE SIZE: 40-gallon long aquarium or display case
SUBSTRATE: Indoor-outdoor carpet or artificial turf
VENTRAL HEAT: Yes
UV LIGHT: Not essential but helpful. Incandescent bulb strongly advisable.
TEMPERATURE RANGE: 27–35°C (80–95°F)
SPECIAL CONSIDERATIONS: Nervous. Need large cages. Must be warm and bright.
   Aggressive initially. Prone to damage nose.

snake and possibly following the treatment for abscesses listed in the general care section. As usual, however, prevention is the best cure.

Parasites are possible in these snakes. The feces of one specimen from Sycamore Canyon, Arizona, contained acanthocephalan ova.

One of these snakes survived more than 2 years and 4 months in captivity (Slavens and Slavens, 1991; Snider and Bowler, 1992). One of the males in our care has surpassed this record by surviving 4 years and 1 week in captivity, at which time he was released.

Masticophis flagellum
Coachwhip

Over much of the southern and western United States, the coachwhip is a common and very visible snake. They are large, variably colored (usually tan or pink, sometimes black or grey or even striped), thin snakes, well-known for their speedy movements and aggressive tempers when cornered. They range 90–255 cm (36–102 inches) in length, although the western subspecies may not become quite as large as the eastern subspecies. There are seven subspecies in the United States, three of which just barely range into extreme southern New Mexico, Arizona, or California. The other four subspecies range from coast to coast (their combined ranges go from coast to coast), making this another transcontinental species.

As might be expected from such a broad-ranging species with so many subspecies, this snake varies considerably in habitat preferences, breeding times, color, and size. Hence, generalizing on the care, preferred diet, and temperature preferences is somewhat risky. Nevertheless, these adaptable broad-ranging species such as the racer, common kingsnake, and coachwhip do seem to have fairly uniform captive requirements compared to other transcontinental species such as the ringneck. A brief overview of the natural history is presented in order to assist the keeper in understanding the species a little better.

The preferred habitat of this species may be summarized as open areas. There doesn't appear to be any specific plant association as they have been found in deserts, open woodlands, prairies, dry uplands, and mountain foothills (Fitch, 1949; Clark, 1949; Wright and Wright, 1957; Tennant, 1984; Stebbins, 1985; Conant

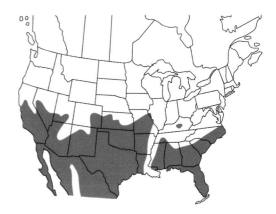

Masticophis flagellum

and Collins, 1991). Neither does soil type, the presence or absence of water, nor the slope of the land seem to inhibit their presence (Stebbins, 1985; Dundee and Rossman, 1989).

The diet of this snake is also broad. Literature reports of dietary items are numerous, and these include insects, frogs, snakes (including small rattlesnakes, racers, and smaller coachwhips), lizards (whiptails, *Cnemidophorus*, side-blotched lizards, *Uta stansburiana*, a variety of spiny lizards, *Sceloporus* sp., skinks, *Eumeces*, earless lizards, *Holbrookia*), small birds and their eggs, small turtles, mice, rats, shrews, bats, small rabbits, and carrion (Wright and Wright, 1957; Fowlie, 1965; Webb, 1970; Collins, 1974; Brown, 1979; Stebbins, 1985; Mitchell, 1986; Dundee and Rossman, 1989; Ernst and Barbour, 1992; personal observations). As mentioned above, these snakes are diurnal. They have been observed chasing many of these items during the day.

As diurnal snakes, they appear very adapted

Western Coachwhip, *Masticophis flagellum testaceus* (photo by David G. Campbell)

to higher temperatures. Body temperatures of wild active members of this species (two western subspecies) ranged from 24 to 37°C (75 to 99°F), while a separate study indicated the body temperature of an active individual was 32.6°C (91°F) (Brattstrom, 1965; Bogert and Cowles, 1947). Hammerson (1977) found that the coachwhips he studied had preferred body temperatures of 34°C (93°F), with a number of active individuals as high as 40°C (104°F). These snakes generally have a very high metabolic rate, one of the highest measured for reptiles (Ruben, 1976).

Suspected predators of this species include carnivorous mammals, hawks, roadrunners, and other snakes.

Mating generally occurs in the springtime, right after brumation. This results in the deposition of 4–24 eggs, which hatch in 45–79 days (Guidry, 1953; Wright and Wright, 1957). The hatchlings are 30–41 cm (12–16 inches) long

and have a blotched pattern similar to young rat snakes.

The coachwhip represents a tremendous challenge to most snake keepers. This large, extremely nervous, and alert snake requires several special modifications of its cage in order to do well in captivity.

First, the cage must be fairly large, and cages of 2.4 × 0.6 × 0.6 meters (8 × 2 × 2 feet) are not unreasonably large for an adult coachwhip (display cases work well). Second, ventral heat is absolutely necessary so plan on using a heating pad or several loops of a heating cable under one side of the cage. Third, an incandescent bulb should be used to produce a very warm and bright environment during the day (air temperature greater than 32°C (90°F) with a gradient on the surface from one side to the other (27–38°C, 80–100 °F). A hide box (large, dark, and heavy) on the cool side is also essential. Artificial carpet/turf works extremely well for this species. Plastic plants, a rock, and a nontippable small water bowl will complete the cage. Most snakes will do well if given this cage arrangement and are covered up in the cage for the first several days after a gentle capture and a slow release from the bag. Do not offer food for at least 1 week (2 weeks might be even better).

Ultraviolet light is not considered necessary for maintenance of these snakes in captivity, as a number have done well for years without it. Repeated breeding of a pair (or possibly several generations) in captivity without access to this kind of light would be substantial evidence that UV light may not be required at all. Some now believe that the only benefit a UV light provides to a captive snake is increased visualization of the prey, so it should be considered in the case of an anorectic snake.

Unfortunately, these snakes are extremely visually oriented and almost invariably (at first) take only moving prey. Fortunately, they will consume and seem to relish domestic mice. Therefore, you can control the quality of the food (by giving nonparasitized mice) even though you may be forced to feed live mice at first (and place the snake at greater risk of injury). Eventually, many of these snakes will learn to take dead mice, but in the meantime,

---

SPECIES: *Masticophis flagellum*, Coachwhip
MAINTENANCE DIFFICULTY INDEX: 4 (1 = easiest, 5 = most difficult)
AVERAGE SIZE: 107–152 cm (42–60 inches)
FOOD: Mice, lizards
CAGE SIZE: Display case or other large enclosure 6–8 feet long
SUBSTRATE: Artificial turf, indoor-outdoor carpet, or newspaper
VENTRAL HEAT: Yes
UV LIGHT: Not essential but helpful. Incandescent bulb strongly advisable.
TEMPERATURE RANGE: 27–35°C (80–95°F)
SPECIAL CONSIDERATIONS: Need large cage. Must be kept very warm. Many will not take prekilled mice or prekilled lizards. May be parasitized.

---

there are several things you can do to reduce the likelihood of injury to the snake. Keep the cage very warm when offering food and feed relatively small mice. Some of these snakes are very good at dispatching large mice, even though they are not constrictors, and so for them this technique may not be necessary. But however you feed, be consistent. Do not feed a dead mouse one time and the next a live mouse, and try to stick with one size mouse if you can.

The color of the mouse does not seem to matter to these snakes, although we have offered the more natural-colored ones (brown) first to reduce stress and stimulate the appetite, then switched to the typical albinos.

These snakes have a high metabolic rate (Ruben, 1976), so you must feed them frequently (2 times per week is usually adequate). Although these snakes are very fond of lizards, do not offer them because of the risk of mites, internal parasites, or potentially pathogenic bacteria unless an adult snake refuses mice for more than 1 month. Do so only after examining the cage environment, behavior, and status of the snake (gravid female or not).

House these snakes alone. These active roaming snakes are probably territorial and one will usually refuse to eat (in captivity) in the presence of another. Also see the discussion on thermoregulation in the general care section.

Brumation is strongly recommended since most will stop eating with the slightest drop in temperature and will waste their valuable fat reserves at middle temperatures of 16–24°C (60–75°F). Brumation will also contribute to breeding success as mentioned in the general care section. See that section for details on brumating snakes. This snake may be brumated in its regular cage without any special modifications.

It is fascinating to watch these snakes eat. A healthy coachwhip will almost fly out of its hidebox when it sees a mouse. If sufficiently warm, it moves like a guided missile toward its prey and adjusts its strike for a direct hit on the side of the neck even if the mouse moves at the last second. It then throws one loop over the mouse and suffocates it with the force of this loop plus its jaws. On artificial carpet/turf it sounds like a large fishing reel that has just been hit by a huge fish. If the snake acts indecisively or moves slowly, something is wrong. Check to see if it is warm enough in the cage. Check your records to see if it may be preparing to shed. If this snake is not completely interested in subduing and eating a mouse, it may be injured by it, so the mouse should be removed quickly.

Although these snakes will always remain nervous and never be a likely candidate for frequent (or any) handling, they are fascinating and challenging captives. Since they may be endangered in years to come because of habitat destruction (they are large snakes with large home ranges like the indigo snake), captive breeding of this species should be attempted.

It has been our experience that these are the least fragile of the whipsnakes in captivity. Certainly, the majority we have worked with have fed aggressively.

The Philadelphia Zoo maintained one of these snakes more than 18 years and 1 month in captivity (Snider and Bowler, 1992).

Masticophis lateralis
Striped Racer

The striped racer, formerly called the California whipsnake, is another speedy and nervous member of the whipsnake group. They are also fairly large snakes, ranging from 76 to 152 cm (30 to 60 inches) long (Wright and Wright, 1957; Basey, 1976; Stebbins, 1985). They are attractive snakes, with a rich dark brown or black dorsal surface and one solid pale yellow stripe running along each side of the back. Like most other whipsnakes (but not the Sonoran whipsnake), the belly is pinkish toward the tail.

The habitat of these snakes is, once again, open country. They have been found primarily in brushy foothill areas (chaparral) that are often rocky and have streams nearby. They

Masticophis lateralis

have also been found in open pine forests in the mountains (Wright and Wright, 1957; Basey, 1976; Behler and King, 1979; personal observations).

The list of foods consumed by this fast-moving diurnal snake is quite lengthy. Certainly, the whipsnakes are not dietary specialists, but lizards, especially fence lizards, *Sceloporus* sp., are preferred. Literature reports of foods taken by wild specimens include lizards, snakes (including rattlesnakes), birds and their eggs, small mammals, frogs, and insects (Van Denburgh, 1922; Wright and Wright, 1957; Basey, 1976; Stebbins, 1985). These snakes appear to

patrol areas actively, with their heads held high, looking for any movement.

Suspected predators of this species include carnivorous birds and mammals, and ophiophagous snakes.

Unlike the Sonoran whipsnake, numerous observations of mating behavior have been made and recorded. Mating season is known to occur primarily in April and May, right after the snakes emerge from brumation (Wright and Wright, 1957; Hammerson, 1978). Males apparently emerge 1–2 weeks prior to the females and engage in territorial disputes with other males in which biting may occur. Mating occurs as the females emerge (Hammerson, 1978). Six to 11 eggs are laid 47–57 days later, and these hatch in 60–94 days (Fitch, 1970; personal observations). These eggs are typical for whipsnakes and racers in that they are non-adherent and have numerous spicules on their surface. The young are patterned similarly to the adults.

It is interesting to note that one of these snakes was uncovered while brumating and the temperature reported at that location was 12.7°C (55°F) (Wright and Wright, 1957). Could this be the origin of the "magic" number "55" so commonly suggested as the standard brumation temperature for so many snakes?

In captivity, the striped racer faces all of the same problems as the other members of the whipsnake group. In small standard cages they will generally rub their noses on the screen tops or sides and end up traumatizing this area severely. This can be prevented, as suggested elsewhere, by using larger cages with smooth sides and a high top. The purpose of a high cage is to make it more difficult for the snake to reach the top. Screen or wire tops are still advisable, however, because of the good ventilation they provide. Plastic screening is quite a bit softer than metal, though, and may be less traumatic for these snakes. We have also found that pieces of smooth plastic sheeting, when inserted in the corners of the top, may help to

California Striped Racer, *Masticophis lateralis lateralis* (photo by David G. Campbell)

reduce the trauma, while these snakes adjust to their cages.

After this, it appears that the basic cage arrangement discussed in the general care section, with the modifications discussed in the chapter on the Sonoran whipsnake, will be satisfactory. Remember that these snakes require a secure hiding place and will benefit tremendously from placement in an area away from a great deal of human traffic. They should be housed alone except for breeding purposes.

Daytime air temperatures of 27–35°C (80–95°F) will be well tolerated by these snakes during the active part of their year. Nighttime lows dropping down to 18°C (65°F) will also have no ill effects on these snakes. Ventral heat is strongly advisable during the spring, summer, and fall, however. Also advisable for these heat-loving snakes is a hot spot created by an overhead incandescent bulb. This will provide an area of intense heat during the day that the snake may use. Temperatures measured at the surface of the substrate directly under these lights in our enclosures have reached as high as

45.5°C (114°F), which is very close to some of the ground temperatures that some of these snakes encounter while quickly skirting areas in their diurnal forays. Remember that the cage must have suitable retreats from these kinds of temperatures, however.

Brumation temperatures in the winter of 3–18°C (38–65°F) appeared suitable for those animals in our care.

Feeding these snakes in captivity has not been a problem when they have been set up properly. Most will readily consume prekilled domestic mice without hesitation. Those that refuse to eat are usually being maintained at too cool a temperature or in too small a cage, or else the snake has a medical problem. Gravid females will also refuse to eat.

To our knowledge, captive reproduction of this snake has occurred, but rarely, probably from a lack of interest. One well-publicized captive mating occurred at the San Diego Zoo (Shaw and Campbell, 1974).

However, much of the information above was gathered by Hammerson (1978), who

SPECIES: *Masticophis lateralis*, Striped Racer
MAINTENANCE DIFFICULTY INDEX: 4 (1 = easiest, 5 = most difficult)
AVERAGE SIZE: 76–152 cm (30–60 inches)
FOOD: Mice, lizards, snakes
CAGE SIZE: 40-gallon long aquarium or display case
SUBSTRATE: Indoor-outdoor carpet or artificial turf
VENTRAL HEAT: Yes
UV LIGHT: Not essential but helpful. Incandescent bulb strongly advisable.
TEMPERATURE RANGE: 27–35°C (80–95°F)
SPECIAL CONSIDERATIONS: Nervous. Need large cage. Must be warm and bright.
    Aggressive initially. Mate in trees and shrubs. Prone to damage noses.

placed these snakes in a large outdoor enclosure that incorporated some of their natural habitat. This enclosure was 3.5 × 3.5 meters (10.5 × 10.5 feet) and included four subterranean burrows, two rock piles and woody shrubs up to 1 meter (3 feet) in height. Indeed, breeding was accomplished in this arrangement. This is an idea that may have great value for future captive breeding efforts with this species and others. Also see the discussion on outdoor enclosures in the general care section, the queen snake discussion, and the Brazos water snake section.

If captive breeding is successful, the young will usually hatch in August, September, or October. These young snakes represent the biggest challenge to a snake keeper since they will not usually consume pinkies, preferring lizards instead. However, snakes as young as 1 month old will consume pinkies scented with a lizard or if it has a piece of the lizard on it. These hatchlings will eat prior to brumation if it is warm enough (Hammerson, 1978).

One of these snakes was maintained for more than 4 years and 11 months in captivity (Snider and Bowler, 1992).

Masticophis taeniatus
Striped Whipsnake

The striped whipsnake, like its congeners the Sonoran whipsnake, the striped racer, and the coachwhip, is a fast-moving, nervous, diurnal snake. They are challenging captives because of this nervous nature, and if not housed properly will generally do very poorly.

Once again, we will examine the natural history and draw from our own experiences in keeping these animals in order to form a plan for captive maintenance. Basically, it appears that the maintenance of this species is very similar to that of the other members of the genus.

The striped whipsnake has the greatest latitudinal distribution of any whipsnake in the United States. They range from central Washington southward through much of eastern Oregon, southwestern Idaho, eastern California, Nevada, Utah, northern Arizona, New Mexico, and western Texas, and down through much of Mexico. Once again, open brushy areas seem to define the preferred habitat, with various authors characterizing these areas as shrublands, grasslands, open desert, barren rocky areas, foothills, pinion/juniper woodlands, and open pine/oak forests (Wright and Wright, 1957; Fowlie, 1965; Tennant, 1984; Stebbins, 1985).

As their name implies, they are indeed striped snakes. Two or more solid or broken longitudinal stripes run the entire length of the body on each side. The background color is black, gray, olive, or blue, and the belly may

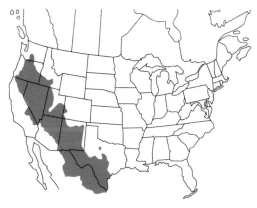

Masticophis taeniatus

vary from pink to yellow. Unlike all other members of the whipsnake group, they have 15 scale rows at midbody, not 17, and this is the most reliable method of identification if the snake is in hand.

There are four subspecies in the United States, only one of which, the desert striped whipsnake, *M.t. taeniatus*, occupies the entire range within the United States outside of Texas (even though it does enter the western portion of that state). The other three subspecies, found from north to south in Texas, are the Central Texas whipsnake, *M. t. girardi*, Schott's whipsnake, *M. t. schotti*, and Ruthven's whipsnake, *M. t. ruthveni*. A good field guide should be consulted for identification of specimens collected in Texas. Recently, Crother et al. (2000) proposed that Schott's and Ruthven's whipsnakes be elevated to the species level. They would become subspecies *M. schotti schotti* and *M. s. ruthveni*, respectively, if this change occurs.

The diet of all subspecies appears quite varied. Food items mentioned in the literature have included lizards (whiptails, *Cnemidophorus* sp., side-blotched lizards, *Uta stansburiana*, tree lizards, *Urosaurus ornatus*, spiny lizards, *Sceloporus* sp.), snakes (patchnoses, *Salvadora* sp., rattlesnakes, *Crotalus* sp., garter snakes, *Thamnophis* sp., racers, *Coluber constrictor*, gopher snakes, *Pituophis catenifer*, other whipsnakes), young birds (including house sparrows and eggs), and rodents (mice, rats), insects, and occasionally frogs (leopard frogs, *Rana* sp., green frogs, *Rana clamitans*) (Van Denburgh, 1922; Wright and Wright, 1957; Fowlie, 1965;

Brown and Parker, 1982; Tennant, 1984, 1985; Stebbins, 1985; Mitchell, 1986; Linder and Fichter, 1991).

As might be expected, this widespread member of the whipsnake family has a high preferred optimum temperature range. Body temperatures of active individuals in the wild were 18–37°C (65–98.6°F) (Hirth and King, 1969).

Suspected predators of this species include ophiophagous snakes, birds of prey, and carnivorous mammals.

Mating generally occurs in April and May over much of the range of this species, presumably right after the snakes emerge from brumation (which has been observed to occur in communal or den-type situations). This is followed by the deposition of 3–12 eggs in late May or early June that usually hatch approximately 2 months later (see below) in July and August (Wright and Wright, 1957; Bennion and Parker, 1976; Tennant, 1984; Linder and Fichter, 1991). The young are fairly long, ranging 35–43 cm (13.75–17 inches) in TL (Wright and Wright, 1957; Tennant, 1984). These snakes probably reach sexual maturity at 3 years of age in the wild.

Proper housing for this species means warm and dry housing. Ventral heat and heat from overhead lamps are both considered essential, and a UV light source may be helpful as it may aid in improved visualization of prey items. A

Schott's Whipsnake, *Masticophis taeniatus schotti* (photo by David G. Campbell)

Striped Whipsnake, *Masticophis taeniatus* (photo by David G. Campbell)

secure dark place to hide is another basic necessity. Additional visual barriers in front of the cage will also go a long way to helping this species adapt to captivity, especially at first. We usually use paper taped to the front of the cage for several weeks or months until the snake seems comfortable.

The cage size is also critical, and slightly larger cages than usual are strongly advisable. See Table 1 in the housing section.

Everything else used in the standard (ideal) cage setup will work well for this species. Artificial carpet/turf is an ideal substrate for these fast-moving snakes since it permits rapid serpentine locomotion, which facilitates the capture of live prey items added to the cage. See below on feeding.

A small nontippable water bowl should be provided at all times.

With regard to cage accessories, we believe this species does well in a slightly more complex environment. Rocks, plastic plants, and branches (all securely placed) will increase the snake's security, aid in locomotion, and improve appetite. Don't go too far overboard on the accessories, however, as this may limit the snake's visualization of prey items added to the cage and provide too many hiding places once the snake does see them and gives chase.

Good ventilation is a must in order to prevent stagnant, germ-laden, moist air from building up in the enclosure. These snakes, like many other desert snakes, are prone to respiratory infections if the humidity in their enclosure is too high.

Perhaps the one good thing about keeping these snakes in captivity is their diet. As mentioned above, they are not dietary specialists and wild specimens have been reported to consume smaller snakes, lizards, nestling birds, mice, and insects. Keepers will, of course, prefer to use captive-born and -raised mice because of their availability and absence of parasites. Unfortunately, like the coachwhip, this snake is very visually oriented and is attracted to its prey items primarily by their movements and not by their smell (although olfactory cues are important in the final stages of judging a food's acceptability). This means that recently captured members of this species will usually have to be offered live mice rather than prekilled ones and that there will be a slightly higher risk to the snake. That risk may be minimized by feeding smaller mice (fuzzies and jumpers) rather than adults. See under the discussion on the coachwhip, *Masticophis flagellum*, for more details. Also, being visually oriented, the color of the mouse may have an

SPECIES: *Masticophis taeniatus*, Striped Whipsnake
MAINTENANCE DIFFICULTY INDEX: 4 (1 = easiest, 5 = most difficult)
AVERAGE SIZE: 76–152 cm (30–60 inches)
FOOD: Mice, lizards, snakes
CAGE SIZE: 40-gallon long aquarium or display case
SUBSTRATE: Indoor-outdoor carpet or artificial turf
VENTRAL HEAT: Yes
UV LIGHT: Not essential but helpful. Incandescent bulb strongly advisable.
TEMPERATURE RANGE: 27–35°C (80–95°F)
SPECIAL CONSIDERATIONS: Nervous. Need large cage. Must be warm and bright.
  Aggressive initially. Prone to damage nose.

effect on whether or not it will be acceptable to these snakes. We always prefer to start a recently captured striped whipsnake on the more naturally colored brown mice rather than on the more common albinos. Eventually, many of these snakes will learn to accept prekilled mice, but some never do.

Brumation is strongly recommended as these snakes are very prone to a period of winter inappetence that will rapidly deplete them if they are maintained at high temperatures. Temperatures fluctuating from 3 to 18°C (38 to 65°F) for 4–5 months have been well tolerated by those in our care. Brumation may be carried out in the regular cage arrangement as no changes appear necessary.

To our knowledge, this snake has not been bred in captivity. Breeding should be attempted in the usual manner, placing the female in with the male several weeks after brumation ends and her spring shed has occurred. Three to 12 rough-surfaced eggs are laid that hatch in approximately 2 months. One clutch laid on 1 May hatched on 1 July when incubated in the usual manner at 28°C (82°F) indicating an incubation period of 61 days. This is similar to the artificial incubation period reported by Tennant (1984) of 62 days.

The hatchlings are similar to the adults in pattern although they may have slightly lighter colors. The young have a tremendous preference for small lizards right from the start, but have taken lizard-scented pinkies as their first meals.

Overall, this shy nervous snake represents a captive challenge, even though they are attractive and fascinating to watch. Being diurnal, they will be out basking when you are about, not hiding as do so many kingsnakes and rat snakes during the day. With time, their nervousness may decrease, but they will never enjoy being handled and may continue to bite. But then again, so do many kingsnakes. One member of this species survived more than 3 years and 11 months in captivity (Snider and Bowler, 1992). However, we suspect they may live much longer with parasite control and proper care (other whipsnakes have survived well into the teens in captivity).

Nerodia clarkii
Salt Marsh Snake

The salt marsh snake is a small, 38–76-cm (15–30-inch) long, variably colored water snake (Conant and Collins, 1991). The three subspecies range from the central Atlantic coast of Florida to the southern Gulf coast of Texas.

The most northeastern subspecies, the Atlantic salt marsh snake, *N. c. taeniata*, is striped anteriorly but blotched posteriorly. It is the smallest of the subspecies, averaging around 51 cm (20 inches) in length with a record of 60.3

Nerodia clarkii

cm (23.75 inches) (Conant and Collins, 1991). It is found only in Volusia County, Florida, and is considered threatened.

The mangrove salt marsh snake, *N. c. compressicauda*, ranges over much of the coastal area of southern peninsular Florida, extending from southern Volusia County on the eastern coast of Florida to Citrus County on the western coast. It is also found on several small islands and the northern coast of Cuba. It is tremendously variable in color, ranging from yellow, green, brown, gray, or nearly black, with or without bands dorsally. Adults of this subspecies are usually 38–76 cm (15–30 inches) in length with a record of 94 cm (37 inches) (Ashton and Ashton, 1981; Conant and Collins, 1991).

The Gulf salt marsh snake, *N. c. clarkii*, ranges from Citrus County in Florida northward along the coast all the way to the southeastern coast of Texas. It possesses longitudinal tan and dark brown stripes, and is the least variable of the subspecies. Adults are similar in size to the latter subspecies with a record of 91.4 cm (36 inches) in length.

The preferred habitat of this species appears to be brackish or saltwater mangrove swamps, meadows, estuaries, and marshes, although they may occasionally enter freshwater ponds near coastal areas, especially in the absence of larger water snakes, as in the Florida Keys (Ashton and Ashton, 1981; Ernst and Barbour, 1989; Rossi and Rossi, 1995a).

The natural prey of these small snakes is primarily small fish (*Fundulus*, *Poecilia*) and small crabs (Ashton and Ashton, 1981; Ernst and Barbour, 1989; Rossi and Rossi, 1995a) but frogs and toads have been reported (Neill, 1965; Tennant, 1984). Captive observations suggest that they are not specialists however, and other snakes and small mammals may also be taken by wild specimens.

Suspected predators of this species include cottonmouths, wading birds, hawks, and predatory mammals.

Mating season is thought to occur in early spring, varying with latitude. Those in the Florida Keys will mate in January and February (Swanson, 1948), while those farther north have

Gulf Salt Marsh Snake, *Nerodia clarkii clarkii* (photo by David G. Campbell)

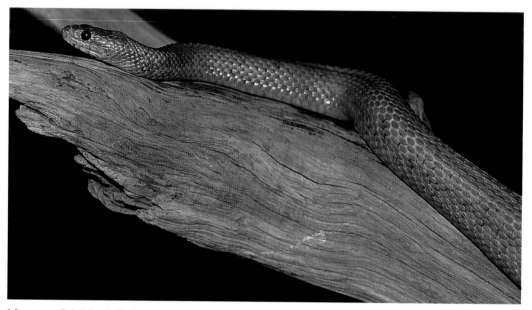

Mangrove Salt Marsh Snake, *Nerodia clarkii compressicauda* (photo by David G. Campbell)

been observed mating as late as March or April. Mating season may actually range from late autumn through early spring in some locations (Ashton and Ashton, 1981). Litters of 2–20 are born approximately 120 days after mating, usually in the middle of summer. Neonates usually range 14–24 cm (5.5–9.5 inches) in length.

The salt marsh snake may be cared for exactly like other water snakes. (See the general care section and the brown water snake section.) Although these snakes possess physiological and behavioral mechanisms for surviving in salt water (like not drinking sea water), they do not require exposure to it in order to do well in captivity (as do some exotic snakes). Therefore, the provision of artificial carpet/turf, hide box, a UV light source and a place to bask, ventral heat, and a small clean water bowl (with tap water) will usually keep these snakes healthy. Be aware that these snakes may not drink their water initially but its presence is absolutely necessary. If they get warm, they will reduce their rate of dehydration by getting into it temporarily, until their next meal comes along, which is their main source of water in the wild. But make no mistake. They will drink water after tasting it via numerous tongue flicks to make sure that it is indeed fresh water and

not sea water. One Gulf salt marsh snake in our care drank heavily within 2 minutes of being placed in her new cage.

Their diet includes fish, frogs, and salt water crustaceans such as small crabs, so feeding is not a problem, although parasitism is. Freezing their food and regular dewormings will help keep this problem under control. Incidentally, these snakes will consume freshwater fish with equal relish, and many in our care have switched readily to diets of small mice.

Brumation, or at least a short cooling off period, is strongly advisable if captive breeding is desired. We exposed those in our care to temperatures fluctuating from 3.3 to 18°C (38 to 65°F) for 5 months with no ill effect. These mangrove salt marsh snakes mated in the early spring, right after brumation.

A pair of mangrove salt marsh snakes in our care produced offspring in captivity 2 consecutive years and the data is summarized here. In 1993, copulation was not observed, but was suspected to have occurred during the last week in March since that is when the snakes were placed with each other. The female gave birth to 8 young on 23 July of that year. The young ranged 18–21 cm (7.1–8.3 inches) in length with an average TL of 18.9 cm (7.4 inches). The

SPECIES: *Nerodia clarkii*, Salt Marsh Snake
MAINTENANCE DIFFICULTY INDEX: 3 (1 = easiest, 5 = most difficult)
AVERAGE SIZE: 38–76 cm (15–30 inches)
FOOD: Fish, frogs, and salt water crustaceans
CAGE SIZE: 20–30-gallon long aquarium
SUBSTRATE: Artificial turf, indoor-outdoor carpet, or newspaper
VENTRAL HEAT: Yes
UV LIGHT: No, but an incandescent bulb is helpful
TEMPERATURE RANGE: 20–28°C (68–82°F)
SPECIAL CONSIDERATIONS: Likely to be parasitized. Skin lesions will occur if kept in
  moist cage. The Atlantic salt marsh snake is protected by law. Permit required

sex ratio was 1.6:1 males to females, and the ratio of light color morphs to dark color morphs was 1.6:1 light to dark, with 80% of the males being light and 30% of the females being light in color. In 1994, copulation was observed twice on 21 March and once on 22 March, but may have occurred afterward as well. This resulted in the birth of 11 young on 12 July. These neonates ranged 19–20 cm (7.5–7.9 inches) in length, with an average TL of 19.45 cm (7.7 inches). The sex ratio was 1.2:1 males to females and the ratio of light to dark color morphs was 4.5:1 light to dark, with 83% of the males being light-colored morphs and 80% of the females being light-colored morphs. Thus, the gestation period the first year was 124+ days, and the gestation period the second year was 113 days. There were no dead or defective neonates in either litter. The female that gave birth to these young was acquired as a neonate on 18 August 1991. Thus, she mated at approximately 19 months of age, and gave birth at 23 months of age.

The neonates were voracious eaters, readily taking feeder fish, and soon afterward, fish-scented pinkies. Fighting may occur over food items, so they should be separated from each other. The same is true for those Gulf salt marsh snakes that we have worked with.

The Atlantic salt marsh snake is an endangered or at least threatened subspecies, although there are some questions as to the validity of this subspecies (Kochman, 1992). With such a limited range and such habitat destruction occurring within that range, the status of this population would have to be considered as precarious. One hurricane, like that which struck Miami several years ago, could theoretically eliminate this subspecies. Captive populations might form a valuable reserve from which restocking or reintroduction attempts could be accomplished. Certainly, it would appear from our results with a closely related subspecies that they are raised and bred fairly easily in captivity.

One mangrove salt marsh snake in our care, captured as a yearling, survived over 7 years and 10 months in captivity.

Nerodia cyclopion
Mississippi Green Water Snake

This large, greenish or brownish, heavy-bodied water snake has an indistinct pattern and is most easily recognized by the presence of sub-ocular scales (a series of scales between the bottom of the eye and the scales of the upper lip). Unfortunately, these are not easily seen from more than a few feet away.

As mentioned above, these are fairly large snakes, ranging 76–114 cm (30–45 inches) in length (Conant and Collins, 1991). They range

Nerodia cyclopion

We have also observed them to be very common in open marshy areas in southern Louisiana brackish estuaries, as have others (Wright and Wright, 1957; Dundee and Rossman, 1989). In Texas, they have also been found in vegetation around rice field lakes and canals (Tennant, 1984).

Like most water snakes, these snakes' preferred food appears to be fish. However, they seem much more specialized on fish than some of the other water snakes, only rarely taking crayfish or amphibians (Mushinsky and Hebrard, 1977; Kofron, 1978). The previous studies found that the young prefer mosquito fish, *Gambusia affinis*, while the adults prefer sunfish, *Lepomis* sp., and bass, *Micropterus* sp. Texas specimens from some areas readily take amphibians however, with adults taking frogs and salamanders, and juveniles preying heavily upon tadpoles (Tennant, 1984).

from southern Illinois southward in the Mississippi Valley to coastal Louisiana, then westward to southern Texas and eastward to extreme western Florida where they may hybridize with the Florida green water snake.

The preferred habitat of this species appears to be slow-moving bodies of water, usually with thick vegetation (Wright and Wright, 1957; Ernst and Barbour, 1989; Conant and Collins, 1991) and many overhanging limbs.

Mating is known to occur in the spring, primarily in April (Wright and Wright, 1957; Tennant, 1984; Ernst and Barbour, 1989; Dundee and Rossman, 1989). The gestation period is thought to be between 90 and 120 days

Mississippi Green Water Snake, *Nerodia cyclopion* (photo by David G. Campbell)

A Mississippi green water snake showing its heavily pigmented ventral pattern. The belly of the Florida green water snake is usually plain. Sometimes differences between closely related species or subspecies go unnoticed for a long time. (photo by John Rossi)

(Meade, 1934; Ernst and Barbour, 1989), with 9–34 young being born in July, August, or September (Kofron, 1979; Dundee and Rossman, 1989). The young range 25–30.5 cm (9.8–12 inches) in length (Kofron, 1979; Dundee and Rossman, 1989).

Suspected predators of this species include cottonmouths, alligators, large aquatic birds, and carnivorous mammals.

Captive maintenance of the Mississippi green water snake is relatively straightforward. They may be maintained in the basic cage setup, utilizing all of the various cage accessories including hide box, water bowl, rock, and a basking branch. Other important features of the cage should include a ventral heat source and an appropriate substrate. The substrate which has worked the best for us has been artificial carpet/turf. The reason for this is that most wood chips will stick to fish that are placed in the cage and may be ingested by accident. Newspaper, on the other hand, will often get wet and fall apart. Neither of these latter two problems is likely to happen with the carpet/turf.

Remember that even though these are water snakes, they must not be maintained in a moist environment. If they are, they are very likely to suffer from "blister disease." Treatment will involve removing the snakes to a dry environment and possibly starting them on systemic (injectable) antibiotics as discussed in the general care section.

As mentioned above, the preferred food of the Mississippi green water snake is fish. Many are quite resistant to change in captivity and will often refuse anything but fish. This is especially true of males. Females and larger specimens, however, may take heavily scented mice if they are of a suitable size and this seems to assist them in their reproductive efforts in captivity.

As with other water snakes, the warnings about parasitism apply. These snakes are very likely to be parasitized by a wide variety of worms.

Captive breeding of this species should present few problems and has occurred in several labs and outdoor enclosures. However, Slavens and Slavens (1991) did not list a single specimen of this snake in captivity and they have not been popular captives for reasons discussed below.

It should be noted that the disposition of these snakes is usually somewhat pugnacious, although they may improve with time in captivity. Most herpetologists who have attempted to pick one up in the wild can attest to the propensity of this species to bite, but some chew if they make contact. In fact, one from

SPECIES: *Nerodia cyclopion*, Mississippi Green Water Snake
MAINTENANCE DIFFICULTY INDEX: 3 (1 = easiest, 5 = most difficult)
AVERAGE SIZE: 76–140 cm (30–55 inches)
FOOD: Fish (minnows, shiners), frogs
CAGE SIZE: 20–30-gallon long aquarium
SUBSTRATE: Artificial turf, indoor-outdoor carpet, or newspaper
VENTRAL HEAT: Yes
UV LIGHT: No, but an incandescent bulb is helpful
TEMPERATURE RANGE: 23–27°C (73–81°F)
SPECIAL CONSIDERATIONS: Likely to be parasitized. Skin lesions will occur if kept in
   moist cage. Nasty disposition. Remove young snakes right away

Cameron County, Louisiana, bit the senior author so hard that it took several minutes to dislodge the snake from his right hand. Incidentally, the area around the bite began to swell immediately, and led the authors to suspect that either a toxic secretion was present in the saliva or else we had witnessed an allergic reaction to the saliva. The swelling disappeared within several hours. Indeed, most water snakes seem to have very sharp teeth, which they use in slashing-type bites, so the prolonged biting and chewing may have been more than a coincidence.

Snider and Bowler (1992) did not list a captive longevity for this species, but it is suspected that they may live at least 10 years. One in our care survived for 2 years and 11 months, at which time it was released.

Nerodia erythrogaster
Plainbelly Water Snake

The plainbelly water snake is represented in the United States by 4 subspecies. These include the redbelly water snake, *N. e. erythrogaster*, the yellowbelly, *N. e. flavigaster*, the copperbelly, *N. e. neglecta*, and the blotched water snake, *N. e. transversa*. The first three subspecies have solid bluish gray or reddish gray dorsal (back) color and solid pinkish red, yellow, or coppery red bellies respectively. The latter subspecies has variably sized dark-colored blotches along the back. The background color varies considerably but is usually some shade of brown or gray. The belly of these snakes is usually yellowish to light orange. They range in size from 76 to 122 cm (30 to 48 inches) long with a record of 157.5 cm (62 inches) for the redbelly water snake (Conant and Collins, 1991). The record lengths for the other two subspecies are slightly smaller. The species ranges from southern Delaware and Maryland southward and westward through eastern Virginia, North and South Carolina, Georgia, and northern Florida and then west-

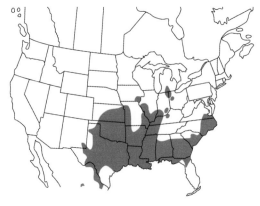

Nerodia erythrogaster

Redbelly Water Snake, *Nerodia erythrogaster erythrogaster* (photo by David G. Campbell)

ward through much of Texas and the Mississippi Valley. The redbelly is found in the eastern part of the range, intergrading with the yellowbelly in western Georgia, Alabama, and the Florida panhandle. The yellowbelly occupies the central part of the range and intergrades with the blotched water snake in southwestern Louisiana, eastern Texas and Oklahoma, and western Arkansas. The copperbelly is found in northern Kentucky, southern Illinois, Indiana, Ohio, and Michigan. The senior author and Chris Lechowitz had the opportunity to observe copperbelly water snakes in southern Illinois, where they appear in densely vegetated swamps along with cottonmouths.

The preferred habitat of the plainbelly water snake appears to be slow-moving acidic waters with muddy bottoms, in thickly wooded areas in the east (Ernst and Barbour, 1989; personal observations). In Florida, it has been reported to occur mostly in or near large rivers (Ashton and Ashton, 1981) while in Alabama and Louisiana it has been reported to occur in most kinds of permanently aquatic habitats (Mount, 1975; Dundee and Rossman, 1989). In the west, these snakes are known to occur in fast-moving clear streams (Tennant, 1984), but rivers and irrigation drains have been reported as habitat for this species in New Mexico (Degenhardt et al., 1996). These snakes appear to be primarily nocturnal (Mount, 1975).

Frogs are thought to be the preferred prey of adults (Mushinsky and Lotz, 1980), while fish are thought to be preferred by juveniles, although they have been reported to eat a wide variety of prey including fish, tadpoles, aquatic salamanders, crayfish, and aquatic invertebrates (Mount, 1975; Ashton and Ashton, 1981; Tennant, 1984; Dundee and Rossman, 1989). Fish are thought to be the primary food of this species in Texas (Tennant, 1984). Mushinsky et al. (1982) showed that these snakes shifted their diet from fish to frogs as they matured and reached sizes greater than 50 cm SVL.

Ernst and Barbour (1989) listed the following natural enemies: minks, skunks, otters, redtailed hawks, red-shouldered hawks, marsh hawks, turkey vultures, herons, egrets, American bitterns, clapper rails, herring gulls, cottonmouths, kingsnakes, racers, larger water snakes, snapping turtles, alligators, bullfrogs, bass, pickerel, pike, and catfish. Crabs may also be predators (Conant and Lazell, 1973).

We have found large numbers of these snakes in central Texas along the Brazos River during our studies on the Brazos water snake. Snakes 2 years old and under were extremely common and appeared to be occupying the niche once commonly occupied by young Brazos water snakes. The subspecies in this area is the blotched water snake, *Nerodia erythrogaster transversa*. When captured, these snakes often regurgitated red-finned shiners and minnows. Ten specimens captured in mid-July 1999 fell into a similar size range and were presumed to be approximately 11–12 months of age. They had an average weight of 39.3 grams and average SVL of 36.6 cm (14.4 inches). One specimen captured at the same time measured 53.3 cm (21 inches) SVL and weighed 126 grams. This was most likely a 2-year-old snake. Apparently, these snakes were foraging in shallow water nocturnally, and then retreated to sun-warmed rocks along the water's edge by morning. By midday, the heat under smaller rocks requires the snakes to move to areas under larger rocks or into vegetated areas. This is the same general behavior pattern observed by the young Brazos water snakes along the river and may suggest that competition is occurring (Rossi and Rossi, 1999a, b, c, 2000a, b, c).

All of these snakes we maintained in captivity readily ate both fish and fish-scented mice. They were notoriously aggressive feeders. Interestingly, these snakes were passing large numbers of *Entamoeba* sp. in their stool, suggesting that these organisms were not pathogenic for these snakes.

Mating is known to occur in the spring from April to June (Wright and Wright, 1957; Ernst and Barbour, 1989), which results in the birth of 2–32 young (Conant, 1965; Fitch, 1970; Minton, 1972; Dundee and Rossman, 1989) some 90–120 days later, usually in September. The neonates range in size from 19 to 28.3 cm (7.5 to 11.1 inches) (Ernst and Barbour, 1989).

Once again, these large water snakes will do best if treated in the same manner as described for other water snakes. All of these snakes seem to have a wonderful appetite in captivity and will rapidly be taking fish out of your hand or, if you are not that brave, right out of your feeding tongs. Frogs, toads, fish (including saltwater fish), salamanders (including aquatic salamanders) and tadpoles are all taken with great relish. These snakes are more like the southern water snakes in their adaptability to captivity than the brown water snakes are. Babies do extremely well. Incidentally, fish-scented pinkies for the babies and mice for the adults will also be heartily consumed by most of these snakes and may help to reduce the vitamin deficiencies of a diet consisting of only fish, or be a good substitute when your fish supply is low. Some of these snakes in captivity have eaten nothing but unscented mice for years.

The same warnings against parasites exist. In fact, parasitism combined with the stress of

Blotched Water Snake, *Nerodia erythrogaster transversa* (photo by David G. Campbell)

SPECIES: *Nerodia erythrogaster*, Plainbelly Water Snake
MAINTENANCE DIFFICULTY INDEX: 3 (1 = easiest, 5 = most difficult)
AVERAGE SIZE: 76–122 cm (30–48 inches)
FOOD: Fish (minnows, shiners), frogs and toads. May also take mice scented with these.
CAGE SIZE: 20–30-gallon long aquarium
SUBSTRATE: Artificial turf, indoor-outdoor carpet, or newspaper
VENTRAL HEAT: Yes
UV LIGHT: No, but an incandescent bulb is helpful
TEMPERATURE RANGE: 20–28°C (68–82°F)
SPECIAL CONSIDERATIONS: Likely to be parasitized. Skin lesions will occur if kept in
   moist cage. Very adaptable. Calms down and feeds very well.

---

capture and frequent disturbances are probably responsible for more water snake deaths in early captivity than anything else. So get them treated early. The longer you wait, the weaker they will get.

These snakes have been bred repeatedly in captivity using the basic techniques for brumation and breeding described in the general care section.

One last word about this species is in order.

With time, *individuals* of this species will mellow out considerably, and allow themselves to be handled without the usual water snake response of biting and defecating, and will almost seem to enjoy handling occasionally. Be gentle and move slowly and you should have few problems with these kinds of individuals.

One of these snakes survived over 14 years and 11 months in captivity (Snider and Bowler, 1992).

Nerodia fasciata
Southern Water Snake

The southern water snake is a large adaptable snake that seems to thrive in a variety of habitats. It is a medium to large snake, usually 61–106.7 cm (24–42 inches) in length, with a record of 152.4 cm (60 inches) (Conant and Collins, 1991). They are extremely variable in color, with some individuals being brightly banded while others are almost solid brown or black. There are three subspecies which range from eastern North Carolina southward through Florida and westward to include the Mississippi River Valley as far north as Illinois. They extend as far west as eastern Texas and southeastern Oklahoma. These three subspecies are the banded water snake, *N. f. fasciata*, the Florida water snake, *N. f. pictiventris*, and the broad-banded water snake, *N. f. confluens*. The broad-banded water snake occupies the west-

ernmost part of the range, extending as far east as Louisiana and western Alabama, while the Florida water snake is found in peninsular

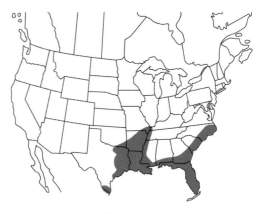

Nerodia fasciata

Broad-banded Water Snake, *Nerodia fasciata confluens* (photo by David G. Campbell)

Florida, and the banded water snake is found in those areas northward and eastward of the other two subspecies. Florida water snakes may also be found in southern Texas, where they have been introduced. We have seen a number of specimens there, so apparently the population is thriving.

The preferred habitat of the southern water snake appears to be any permanent or temporary body of water (Wright and Wright, 1957; Mount, 1975; Dundee and Rossman, 1989; Ernst and Barbour, 1989; Palmer and Braswell, 1995). They are nocturnal during the warm months and are known to move to temporary bodies of water to take advantage of temporary increases in amphibians (Mount, 1975). They bask frequently during the cooler times (Mount, 1975).

The body temperatures of active individuals in the wild have been measured in one study to range from 21.5 to 32°C (71 to 90°F) (Osgood, 1970).

Although they seem to prefer fish throughout their entire range, these snakes feed on a variety of other prey, including amphibians such as the green frog, *Rana clamitans*, bullfrog, *Rana*

catesbeiana, chorus frog, *Pseudacris triseriata*, green treefrog, *Hyla cinerea* (Dundee and Rossman, 1989), southern toad, *Bufo tonnostris*, gray treefrog, *Hyla chrysoscelis*, barking treefrog, *H. gratiosa* (Brown, 1974), carpenter frog, *Rana virgatipes*, pine woods treefrog, *Hyla femoralis*, spring peeper, *Pseudacris crucifer* (Palmer and Braswell, 1995), and dusky salamanders, *Desmognathus* sp. (Brown, 1979). Other reports have included small mammals and birds (Clark, 1949). Wright and Wright (1957) also reported several other food items. These include smaller reptiles, newts, and worms.

Suspected predators of this species include cottonmouths, large wading birds, birds of prey, alligators, and carnivorous mammals.

Mating season is in January through April, with January breeding reported in Florida and later breeding reported farther north (Fitch, 1970; Behler and King, 1979; Ernst and Barbour, 1989). This results in the production of 2–57 young (Ernst and Barbour, 1989) sometime from early June through mid-August. The contrastingly banded young range 20–25.5 cm (7.9–10 inches) in length (Dundee and Rossman, 1989; Ernst and Barbour, 1989).

This water snake is one of the most common snakes in the southeastern part of the continent. The "water bandit," as it is known in some areas, is incredibly easy to keep in captivity. All they require is a water bowl, artificial carpet/turf, and a hide box. Ventral heat is a nice addition.

They will thrive on a diet of bait shop minnows and shiners, frogs and toads, and sometimes mice (scent them with fish at first). Remember the problem with parasitism, and try to stick with frozen fish and occasional mice if possible, however. (See the section on brown water snakes or garter snakes for more warnings or feeding tips.) Of course, if you have a water snake that is taking dead mice, then you could feed it a diet entirely of these. One of these snakes survived 8 years eating nothing but prekilled mice. Remember that if the snake in question has been captured recently, it will probably need to be treated for worms and other parasites.

These snakes will take food right from your hand once they get used to you. If feeding strictly fish and amphibians, they will require more frequent feeding than mouse eaters (twice per week usually).

They are easy to breed if given a short brumation period and are kept separately until the time of breeding. (See the breeding section under general care. See the reproduction chart, Table 5.)

The young are born alive about 3–4 months after mating. They are usually about 20.3–25.5 cm (8–10 inches) long and can easily handle medium-sized bait shop minnows.

One last word of warning: feeding these snakes can be hazardous to their health if they are not fed separately or watched carefully. They are such frenzied feeders that two snakes will definitely kill each other in a fight over a tasty item. A larger snake may swallow a smaller one that is trying to eat the same food item, or if two equal-sized snakes are fighting, one will try to swallow the other and both will die in the process.

If raised from a baby or kept for some time, these snakes can be relatively calm, but one should always be wary and move slowly and

Florida Water Snake, *Nerodia fasciata pictiventris* (photo by David G. Campbell)

SPECIES: *Nerodia fasciata*, Southern Water Snake
MAINTENANCE DIFFICULTY INDEX: 3 (1 = easiest, 5 = most difficult)
AVERAGE SIZE: 56–107 cm (22–42 inches)
FOOD: Fish (minnows, shiners), frogs, toads, and mice scented with these
CAGE SIZE: 20–30-gallon long aquarium
SUBSTRATE: Artificial turf, indoor-outdoor carpet, or newspaper
VENTRAL HEAT: Yes
UV LIGHT: No, but an incandescent bulb is helpful
TEMPERATURE RANGE: 20–28°C (68–82°F)
SPECIAL CONSIDERATIONS: Excellent eaters but likely to be parasitized. Skin lesions will
    occur if kept in moist cage. Slightly messy.

handle gently to avoid being bitten. As with other water snakes that are being fed fish and amphibians, they will be defecating more frequently and the stool is a bit more odoriferous, so they are considered "messy" snakes and require a little more work to keep their cage clean. This is necessary, however, in order to maintain a healthy environment for both the snake and the keeper.

Thousands of these snakes and green water snakes were killed every year on Route 441 as it crosses through Payne's Prairie, just south of Gainesville, Florida. The state of Florida has just constructed under-road tunnels and roadside walls to end this massacre of snakes which apparently need to migrate.

One of these snakes, acquired as a neonate, survived 8 years and 1 month in captivity.

Nerodia floridana
Florida Green Water Snake

Like the latter species, these greenish or brownish heavy-bodied water snakes have an indistinct pattern and are most easily recognized by the presence of subocular scales. Unlike the latter species, most of the ventral surface is unspotted. They range 76–140 cm (30–55 inches) in size with a record of 188 cm (74 inches) (Conant and Collins, 1991). The Florida green water snake consists of two separate populations which include one in southeastern South Carolina and one in southern Georgia and all of Florida. It hybridizes with the Mississippi green water snake in the extreme western panhandle of Florida and Alabama.

The habitat of the Florida green water snake appears to be slow-moving waters, including swamps, ponds, sloughs, lakes, and marshes (Wright and Wright, 1957; Ernst and Barbour, 1989), although there is considerable disagree-

ment as to the difference in habitat preference between this and the latter species. Mount (1975) stated that the optimum habitat for the Mississippi green water snake was a wooded

Nerodia floridana

Florida Green Water Snake, *Nerodia floridana* (photo by David G. Campbell)

swamp, while that for the Florida green water snake was weed-choked marsh or wet prairie. We have seen each species in both of these habitats, however, with Florida green water snakes in wooded swamps in central Florida and Mississippi green water snakes in salt marshes or wet prairies in central and southern Louisiana.

The preferred food of the Florida green water snake is frogs, but fish, salamanders, tadpoles, small turtles, and invertebrates have also been taken by wild specimens (Van Hyning, 1932; Wright and Wright, 1957; Mount, 1975; Ashton and Ashton, 1981).

Suspected predators of this species are the same as the Mississippi green water snake, including cottonmouths, alligators, large aquatic birds, and carnivorous mammals. Large fish may eat the young.

Mating is thought to occur in the spring (Wright and Wright, 1957; Ernst and Barbour, 1989) resulting in the birth of 7–101 young some 90–120 days later (Wright and Wright, 1957). These young measured 22.2–26 cm (8.7–10.2 inches) in length (Van Hyning, 1931).

These huge and somewhat vicious water snakes do fairly well in captivity if given the basic cage setup as discussed in the general care section. Everything else is as described in the sections on the brown, southern, and northern water snakes. The same warnings apply

with regard to parasitism and skin infections due to excessive moisture in the cage. A small bowl of water is all they need.

These snakes are occasionally somewhat fastidious, but not half as bad as the brown water snakes can be. See the general care section under capture, transportation, maladaptation, feeding tricks, and again the brown water snake discussion for additional tips with this species. As mentioned above, green water snakes may be difficult to get started feeding in captivity but once they do, they will usually become voracious eaters. Their favorite food appears to be frogs, then fish, but Ashton and Ashton (1981) reported they will also eat tadpoles, salamanders, and small turtles. Long-term captives will take prekilled scented mice, however.

These snakes have been bred repeatedly in captivity using the basic techniques for breeding and brumation described in the general care section. WARNING: There have been reports of Florida green water snakes eating their young in captivity, so make sure you remove the babies from the mother's cage right away. We have also seen this with eastern garter snakes, so it is probably not a behavior that is restricted to this species, but rather many natricines. Watch many of your live-bearing snakes.

One of these snakes in our care survived over 2 years in captivity until we released it at the site where it was captured.

SPECIES: *Nerodia floridana*, Florida Green Water Snake
MAINTENANCE DIFFICULTY INDEX: 3 (1 = easiest, 5 = most difficult)
AVERAGE SIZE: 76–104 cm (30–55 inches)
FOOD: Fish (minnows, shiners), frogs
CAGE SIZE: 20–30-gallon long aquarium
SUBSTRATE: Artificial turf, indoor-outdoor carpet, or newspaper
VENTRAL HEAT: Yes
UV LIGHT: No, but an incandescent bulb is helpful
TEMPERATURE RANGE: 23–27°C (73–81°F)
SPECIAL CONSIDERATIONS: Likely to be parasitized. Skin lesions will occur if kept in
   moist cage. Nasty disposition. Remove young snakes right away.

Nerodia harteri and *Nerodia paucimaculata*
Brazos and Concho Water Snakes

Known only from two river systems in central Texas, both of these snakes are considered rare and are in some danger of extinction. Both species are protected in Texas and may not be collected without a permit. Although locally common in some areas, their stream habitat is being modified or destroyed by the construction of dams and other human activities. No other species on the continent is more exemplary of the very special plight of snakes.

Both species occur in the remaining upper rocky portions (rapid waters) of the rivers from which they are named. Both species have four rows of dark spots dorsally, although they are duller in the Concho water snake. Ventrally, the Brazos has a pinkish orange stripe down the center with a double row of spots bordering the outer edges of the scales (Conant and Collins [1991] compare this to the ventral color of the Kirtland's snake, saying it is very similar), while the Concho lacks the lateral spots in most cases.

These are not large snakes. Conant and Collins (1991) listed 51–76 cm (20–30 inches) with a maximum of 90.2 cm (35.5 inches) for the Brazos water snake and Dixon et al. (1991) reported maximum SVLs for male Concho water snakes as 61.5 cm (24 inches) and females as 82.0 cm (32.3 inches). However, two female Brazos water snakes in our care in an

Nerodia harteri

outside enclosure achieved TLs of 94 and 96.5 cm (37 and 38 inches). We also captured an adult female with a TL of 91.4 cm (36 inches) in the wild. Thus, the two species are similar in size (Tennant, 1985). In the wild, they are known to feed primarily on fish but may also take frogs since they have done so in captivity. Wright and Wright (1957) also reported the following food items: dusky salamanders, *Desmognathus fuscus*, two-lined salamanders, *Eurycea bislineata*, wood frogs, *Rana sylvatica*, green frogs, *R. clamitans*, bullfrogs, *R. catesbeiana*, and their tadpoles, and fresh- and saltwater fish (perch, smelts, and killifish). One specimen ate crayfish. Dixon et al. (1991) also

Nerodia paucimaculata

listed the red shiner, *Cyprinella lutrensis*, bull-head minnow, *Pimephales vigilax*, mosquitofish, *Gambusia affinis*, channel catfish, *Ictalurus punctatus*, flathead catfish, *Pylodictus olivarus*, gizzard shad, *Dorosoma cepedianum*, bigscale logperch, *Percina macrolepida*, and numerous species of sunfish, *Lepomis* sp., as food items for the Concho water snake.

Predators are known to include the western cottonmouth (Tennant, 1984). Suspected predators include large fish, birds of prey, and carnivorous mammals such as raccoons, which may forage in shallow water nocturnally, about the same time as the snakes do. On 13 August, we found one dead neonate floating down the river, which appeared to have had its belly torn open and liver removed. This has been described in garter snakes preyed upon by crows.

Mating occurs primarily in the spring, but also in the fall, with birth occurring sometime in late summer or fall. We found neonates in two widely separated areas of the Brazos River on 13 August. In the Brazos water snake, litter size has varied from 4 to 23 young, which are 18.4–22.9 cm (7.25–9 inches) long. However, see below. Litter size for the Concho water snake is very similar, with a range of 4–29 (average 10) reported (Dixon et al., 1991). In addition, they noted that the neonates grew an average of 7.0 cm (2.75 inches) prior to brumation.

The earliest report of the captive maintenance and breeding of the Brazos water snake was that of Carl (1981). It is summarized below.

These snakes were housed together in a 30 × 45 cm (12 × 18 inches, approximately the size of a 10-gallon aquarium) fiberglass cage with limestone rocks, a wood limb, plastic plants, and a large water bowl. Skylights were used to provide a natural photoperiod. Temperatures were maintained around 27°C (81°F) during much of the year but allowed to drop down to 18–21°C (64–70°F) during the winter. The snakes were fed live fish and defrosted frogs.

Carl observed breeding activity during the first 2 weeks in May for both years that breeding was observed. This resulted in the birth of live offspring on 25 July the first year and 5 September the second year (11- and 17-week gestation periods, which is similar to the 90–120-day gestation period observed in most other North American water snakes). Clutch sizes of these two captive breedings were 13 the first year and 4 the second year. The juveniles of these 2 litters plus another from the same female 4 years previously ranged 17.0–25.2 cm (6.69–9.92 inches) in TL. The average size of the young increased with the age (or size) of the female.

The young snakes were patterned similarly to their parents except they possessed slightly more vivid colors according to Carl. The males definitely had longer tails than the females in most cases, but the snakes could also be sexed by using the "popping" technique (Freedman and Catling, 1978; Gregory, 1983; personal observation); also see the general care section of this book under sexing. We found that judging juvenile snakes of this species by tail length was unreliable, and that "popping" was preferable. The young snakes ate small live fish.

A trio of Brazos water snakes in our care mated from 8 to 11 April 1998. Female number 1 mated with the male on 8 and 9 April, while female number 2 mated with the male on 10 and 11 April.

Female number 1 gave birth to 23 young on 24 August 1998. The 11 females and 12 males ranged 20.5–23 cm (8.1–9.1 inches) in TL with a range of 15–17 cm (5.9–6.7 inches) SVL. These neonates ranged 2.5–4 grams in body mass, with an average body mass of 3.08 grams and average TL of 21.6 cm (8.5 inches). This female measured 87 cm (34.25 inches) in TL with a SVL of 68.6 cm (27 inches).

Female number 2 gave birth to 17 live neonates and 1 dead severely kinked neonate on 25

Brazos Water Snake, *Nerodia harteri* (photo by David G. Campbell)

August 1998. Interestingly, this group consisted of only five males (one of which was the deformed individual mentioned above) and 13 females. This deviated strongly from the 1:1 sex ratio seen in the previous litter and most other snake litters reported. Is it possible that the male, after mating repeatedly with female number 1, had exhausted some of the male sperm. Indeed, the females were housed in a similar manner right next to each other, so other environmental factors were similar. These babies ranged 19.5–23 cm (7.6–9 inches) in TL, with an average TL of 18.2 cm (7.1 inches). Neonate body mass ranged 2.5–5 grams with an average body mass of 3.4 grams. This snake was 1 year younger than female number 1, and also slightly shorter than that female, at a TL of 84.8 cm (33.4 inches), with a SVL of 66 cm (26 inches).

It is interesting to note that the gestation periods of both snakes were exactly the same, offset by only 1 day (exactly the same as the offset in breeding dates), 138 days.

The females were 5 and 4 years old, the male was 4 years old. The male was 66.7 cm (26.25 inches) in TL, with a SVL of 48.3 cm (19 inches) at the time of breeding. All snakes were brumated for 4 months at temperatures fluctuating from 4.4 to 15°C (40 to 59°F). No breeding ac-

tivity had been observed in previous years when the snakes had been treated in the same manner.

The following year these same females gave birth again. This time the exact breeding dates were unknown, since the females had been housed in a large outdoor snake enclosure. Breeding activity was observed both immediately after shedding in late March and then again in late April and early May. These outdoor snakes had spent the winter outside and had hidden for months, thereby successfully surviving several freezes and many months without food. The snakes began to demonstrate posterior body swelling by late June and were very swollen by July. The became extremely secretive at this time and were very difficult to find. They were collected from the pen and brought inside by mid-July, and gave birth on 28 July and 1 August. Female number 1 gave birth to 36 babies (31 live), which is a record for this species. The clutch born on 1 August consisted of 13 males and 23 females, a sex ratio of 1.76:1 females to males. These snakes weighed 1.5–3 grams and their SVLs measured 14–17.78 cm (5.5–7 inches).

Their TLs ranged from 18.4 to 22.9 cm (7.25 to 9 inches). Female number 1 weighed 430 grams prior to birth and 192 grams afterward, representing a maternal investment of 55.3% of her body mass. Female number 2 gave birth to a more average size clutch of 16 (13 live). This clutch born on 28 July consisted of 9 males and 7 females. They weighed 1.8–4 grams and ranged 15.2–25.4 cm (6–10 inches) in TL. The SVLs of these snakes, including the 3 dead, ranged 10.2–17.8 cm (4–7 inches). The smallest live snake had a SVL of 14 cm (5.5 inches) and a TL of 17.8 cm (7 inches). Female number 2 weighed 394 grams prior to birth and 242 grams afterward, an investment of 26%. As might be expected, those neonates from the smaller clutch had a larger average weight and TL than those from the larger clutch. The neonates from the smaller clutch had an average weight of 3.10 grams and an average TL of 22.35 cm (8.8 inches), while those from the larger clutch averaged 2.29 grams and 20.83 cm (8.20 inches) TL. If we exclude those babies born dead, the differences are even greater. Most of the neonates from the 2 clutches were released back into the wild at the site where the parents were captured, and recolonized that site (Rossi and Rossi, 1999c, 2000a, c). See the discussion below.

The authors would like to thank the Texas Department of Parks and Wildlife for granting us a permit to collect the neonates and raise them for this project.

Thanks to these excellent observations by Carl and subsequent observations by many others, we have some idea of how to care for these snakes. We know both species will do well in the basic cage setup as described in the general care section and outdoor enclosures (Rossi and Rossi, 2000c).

Brazos water snakes in our care consumed fish and scented pinkies without much difficulty and bred with some ease in captivity, following a seminatural brumation period as described in the general care section. Like other North American water snakes, they are probably heavily parasitized; those in cages indoors and out harbored rhabditiform larvae and *Entamoeba* in their gut, as well as unidentified filarid worms subcutaneously. Wild snakes demonstrated only *Entamoeba* cysts (Rossi and Rossi, 2000b). Sexual maturity is probably reached in 1–2 years for males and 2–3 years for females (Dixon et al., 1991).

A captive longevity has not been reported. However, from Carl's paper, it is obvious that the female survived 5 years in captivity and was an adult at the time of capture. Therefore, she was probably at least 7 years old at the time the paper was published. One of our females is now 8 years old.

As stated above, these species are in trouble. Tennant (1985) estimated there were only 330–600 of the Concho water snakes left. Scott et al. (1989, 1993) say that Tennant's statistics are wrong and that he was "extremely pessimistic" about the history and future of these species. Yet, even Scott et al. use the term "precarious" to describe the future of these two species, and stated that it was too early to assess the effectiveness of measures taken.

For the Concho water snake, which is federally protected, these measures have included a

---

SPECIES: *Nerodia harteri*, Brazos Water Snake
MAINTENANCE DIFFICULTY INDEX: 3 (1 = easiest, 5 = most difficult)
AVERAGE SIZE: 51–76 cm (20–30 inches)
FOOD: Fish, frogs
CAGE SIZE: 10–20-gallon aquarium
SUBSTRATE: Artificial turf or indoor-outdoor carpet
VENTRAL HEAT: Yes
UV LIGHT: No, but an incandescent bulb is helpful
TEMPERATURE RANGE: 20–35°C (68–95°F)
SPECIAL CONSIDERATIONS: Protected species. Permit required for maintenance. Likely to
   be parasitized.

SPECIES: *Nerodia paucimaculata*, Concho Water Snake
MAINTENANCE DIFFICULTY INDEX: 3 (1 = easiest, 5 = most difficult)
AVERAGE SIZE: 51–76 cm (20–30 inches)
FOOD: Fish, frogs
CAGE SIZE: 10–20-gallon aquarium
SUBSTRATE: Artificial turf or indoor-outdoor carpet
VENTRAL HEAT: Yes
UV LIGHT: No, but an incandescent bulb is helpful
TEMPERATURE RANGE: 20–30°C (68–95°F)
SPECIAL CONSIDERATIONS: Protected species. Permit required for maintenance. Likely to
   be parasitized.

---

major effort to study and preserve this species in the wild by preserving and creating as much habitat as possible. A unique agreement between government agencies concerned with development and species preservation has been reached (Scott et al., 1989, 1993).

Unlike the Concho water snake, the Brazos water snake did not receive federal protection. It was known to occupy a greater distance of its respective riverine habitat, and was therefore believed to be somewhat more resistant to extinction. So while the Concho water snake received a great deal of attention, research, and government action, the Brazos water snake was largely ignored. It was by a purely serendipitous discovery that we determined that this species had been completely eliminated from a number of locations where it was once common, thus serving as a warning (Rossi and Rossi, 1999c, 2000a). In fact, the site where the species was first discovered back in 1941 was the first site determined to be free of Brazos water snakes in 1999. Since then, the snake was determined to be absent from several other sites. The suitability of the habitat and the complete absence of this species was confirmed by the release of 35 captive-born neonates (Rossi and Rossi, 2000c). Only these released snakes were found at the release site throughout 2000. In other words, no natural recruitment had occurred at this site for over 2 years, even though the habitat would support them. Local extinctions and the failure to repopulate these areas were predicted by Scott et al. (1989). We were just surprised that it would happen at the

site where the species was discovered. This happens to be one of the rockiest most stable habitats on the 35-mile stretch below the Morris Dam (Possum Kingdom Lake). It is nearly at the center of the best remaining stretch of habitat for this species, which is the 35 miles of the river below the dam. There are less than ten riffle areas in that entire distance, and these riffle areas are considered essential habitat for the survival of neonates. Outside of this region very little continuous habitat for this species exists.

As mentioned above, our discovery of this snake's plight was purely accidental. Eight years before any of this happened, we had received a permit to collect two pairs per year for 2 years for parasite studies and captive maintenance for earlier versions of this book. The snakes grew well and reproduced, and the babies became part of a study comparing the growth of siblings in an outdoor enclosure with those in cages indoors. After 10 months, it was determined that those housed outdoors had obtained 3 times the mass and were 33% longer than those raised inside (Rossi and Rossi, 2000b). When we went back to the Brazos River to measure and weigh similar age wild snakes for comparison, we found that there weren't any! Instead, there were large number of blotched water snakes, *N. erythrogaster transversa*, and diamondback water snakes, *N. rhombifer*. It was at that point that a strictly herpetocultural research project developed into a conservation project. Over the next year a total of 53 marked captive-born Brazos water snakes were released into the river at the site where the parents were captured, as well as another site just southeast of the latter site. Both sites now still show only these released snakes, with their recognizable branded belly scutes. If any of the released 1-year-olds survived, they will be reproducing at the time of this writing, and we are anticipating the discovery of wild-born young at the original site of release, the site where the species went extinct, and the site where the species was first discovered.

Meanwhile the study of the outdoor enclosure had been a huge success (Rossi and Rossi 2000b). Natural mating and reproduction had occurred and is still occurring. Growth rates were determined to be very similar to those snakes in the wild, and many more snakes are being produced for release. The U.S. Fish and Wildlife Service was contacted regarding this species and presented with our survey data. At the time of this writing, they are considering granting the Brazos water snake federal protection. Perhaps the species will survive after all.

The story above is interesting for several reasons. Firstly, it shows how precarious the existence of some species may be, and how rapidly they may disappear. Secondly, it shows how rapidly a habitat may change, and in ways that are not particularly obvious to us. Thirdly, when habitat does change, it shows how other species moving into that changing habitat may accelerate the elimination of the species in question. The plight of the Brazos water snake is not over by any means. Even now, there are plans in the works for another dam near Mineral Wells. This would probably destroy the remaining stretch of river described above. Theoretically, it would raise the water level 1.5 meters (5 feet) above its present level over much of that 35-mile stretch, there by wiping out most of the remaining riffle areas and inundating the site where the species was first discovered. We are hoping that this will not occur, and that the people of central Texas will consider preserving the last remnant of the upper Brazos River the way it used to be.

Nerodia rhombifer
Diamondback Water Snake

The diamondback water snake is a fairly large, stocky snake, usually ranging 76–122 cm (30–48 inches) in length, with a maximum length of 160 cm (63 inches) (Dundee and Rossman, 1989). They are named for the diamondlike pattern along their backs, areas of lighter background color outlined by a darker netlike pattern. The background color is basically tan with a greenish yellow tint in some specimens, while the netlike pattern is dark brown. The belly and chin are usually yellow to cream-colored.

These heavy-bodied snakes are widespread in the central part of the United States, ranging from central and western Alabama northward to southern Indiana, Illinois, and Iowa and then westward through much of Kansas, Oklahoma, and eastern Texas. These snakes also extend southward into eastern Mexico. The preferred habitat of the diamondback water snake appears to be permanent and slow-moving water

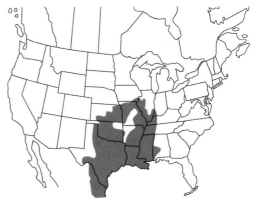

Nerodia rhombifer

such as ponds, lakes, swamps, bayous, large ditches, and large slow moving streams or rivers (Wright and Wright, 1957; Minton, 1972; Mount, 1975; Vermersch and Kuntz, 1986; Dundee and Rossman, 1989; Ernst and Bar-

Diamondback Water Snake, *Nerodia rhombifer rhombifer* (photo by David G. Campbell)

bour, 1989; Collins, 1993), although they have been found in fast-moving streams toward the western parts of their range (Collins, 1993). Tennant (1984) reports that a wide variety of habitats may be used. Overhanging vegetation appears to be an important factor (Vermersch and Kuntz, 1986). We have seen numerous diamondback water snakes along the Brazos River in north-central Texas. The juveniles are often found under flat rocks in the riffle areas; the adults are frequently found basking on overhanging vegetation or foraging in open water.

The preferred body temperatures of active individuals in the wild have been measured at approximately 24–29°C (75–84°F) (Brattstrom, 1965; Mushinsky et al., 1980), while the critical thermal maximum (high temperature that causes death) was around 40°C (104°F) (Jacobson and Whitford, 1970). These snakes tend to become nocturnal during the warmer parts of the year.

These snakes are not specialized feeders, although they seem to feed predominantly upon fish. Types of fish reported have included carp, catfish, sunfish, and suckers (Tennant, 1984; Ernst and Barbour, 1989), which have been described by Collins (1993) as slow-moving fish. Carrion, especially fish, is also thought to

be preferred. Other prey items reported include frogs (particularly bullfrogs, leopard frogs, and bronze frogs) and toads, snapping turtles, and birds as well as insects and crayfish (Clark, 1949; Dundee and Rossman, 1989). Tadpoles (bullfrog) apparently are also an important part of the diet of many (Tennant, 1984; Vermersch and Kuntz, 1986).

Suspected predators of this species include cottonmouths, alligators, large wading birds, snapping turtles, large fish, bullfrogs, and carnivorous mammals.

Mating occurs in the spring with 8–62 young born 3–4 months later, usually from August to October (Kofron, 1979). Fitch (1970) reported an average of 47.2 young per litter. The young range 21.1–33 cm (8.3–13 inches) in length (Tennant, 1984; Vermersch and Kuntz, 1986; Dundee and Rossman, 1989; Ernst and Barbour, 1989). Interestingly, one female had 6 young on 9 September and 24 more on 5 October (Fitch, 1970).

The care of the diamondback water snake in captivity is very similar to that of the other water snakes. It will feed much more readily than both the brown and green water snakes right from the start. The preferred foods are amphibians and fish but scented mice will also be taken. As with other water snakes, make

SPECIES: *Nerodia rhombifer*, Diamondback Water Snake
MAINTENANCE DIFFICULTY INDEX: 3 (1 = easiest, 5 = most difficult)
AVERAGE SIZE: 76–122 cm (30–48 inches)
FOOD: Fish (minnows, shiners), frogs and toads. May also take mice scented with these.
CAGE SIZE: 20–30-gallon long aquarium
SUBSTRATE: Artificial turf or indoor-outdoor carpet, or newspaper
VENTRAL HEAT: Yes
UV LIGHT: No, but an incandescent bulb is helpful
TEMPERATURE RANGE: 25–30°C (77–86°F)
SPECIAL CONSIDERATIONS: Likely to be parasitized. Skin lesions will occur if kept in
   moist cage. Generally are very good eaters.

sure that they are treated for parasites since they are very frequently parasitized. Treat initially and frequently thereafter. Every 6 months wouldn't be a bad idea, but try to avoid deworming just prior to brumation as the medications will often sit in an inactive gut and may be harmful. Also, in order to reduce stress, the risk of increased parasitism, and the likelihood of fights over food, never house them with any other species of water snake. In fact, all water snakes should be housed singly.

Housing requirements are exactly the same, and once again, a source of UV light is recommended for long-term maintenance and breeding. The basic cage arrangement for terrestrial snakes will work excellently. (See the discussion on brown water snakes and the general care section for specific information.)

Brumation and breeding may be accomplished as described for the other water snakes and indeed most snakes in the general care section.

Unlike the northern, plain belly, and southern (banded) water snakes, these seem to maintain a nasty disposition indefinitely. They are beautiful snakes, however, and they do breed well in captivity. (See Table 5, the reproduction chart.) It is surprising that some of these water snakes are not more popular with herpetoculturists.

Note that the beautiful color pattern may be hidden in a wild specimen. It is only after shedding, possibly several times, in a clean cage while receiving a good quality diet that their beautiful pattern will appear, although recently shed wild specimens may look great too.

One of these snakes survived 4 years and 11 months in captivity (Snider and Bowler, 1992).

Nerodia sipedon
Northern Water Snake

The northern water snake has the largest range of any water snake in North America. They range from central Maine through southern Quebec and southern Ontario to eastern Colorado and southward through Kansas, Oklahoma, and Arkansas to eastern Louisiana, Mississippi, and Alabama. In the east, they are absent from only southeastern North Carolina along the coastal plains through Florida. There are four subspecies, including the northern water snake, *N. s. sipedon*, the midland water snake, *N. s. pleuralis*, the Lake Erie water snake, *N. s. insularum*, and the Carolina salt marsh snake, *N. s. williamengelsi*. The midland water snake basically occupies the southern part of the range, particularly the Mississippi Valley and the area south of the Tennessee–Kentucky and Virginia–North Carolina bor-

Nerodia sipedon

described. Some of these descriptions include ponds, lakes, marshes, ditches, swamps, rivers, streams, bogs, meadows, tidal creeks, bayous, sloughs, bays, rain pools, and many others (Kelly et al., 1936; Wright and Wright, 1957; Minton, 1972; Mount, 1975; Linzey and Clifford, 1981; Hudson, 1985; Holman et al., 1990; Hunter et al., 1992; Collins, 1993; Klemens, 1993; Mitchell, 1994; Oldfield and Moriarty, 1994; Palmer and Braswell, 1995). They prefer slow-moving waters with open vegetation and do not tolerate badly polluted areas (Hunter et al., 1992). Palmer and Braswell (1995) report that in coastal areas where *N. sipedon* and *N. fasciata* coexist, *sipedon* occurs in brackish water, while *fasciata* is primarily found in fresh water.

ders. The two melanistic subspecies are found in only limited geographic areas, with one on the southern shore of Lake Erie and the other along coastal North Carolina. Both the northern and midland water snakes have tan to gray background colors with brown crossbands. Refer to a field guide to distinguish between these two subspecies.

These snakes may attain a fairly large size, averaging 56–102 cm (22–40 inches) with a record of 150 cm (59 inches) (Conant and Collins, 1991).

As might be expected from a snake with such an extensive range, it is difficult to generalize about the preferred habitat of this species. They certainly appear to occur around water, but scores of different habitat types have been

Reports of their daily activity pattern suggest that they are diurnal in the fall and spring, but nocturnal in the summer. They appear to have a preferred body temperature of 20–35°C (68–95°F), with most choosing temperatures between 24 and 28°C (75 and 82.5°F) (Brattstrom, 1965; Collins, 1993). Blem and Blem (1990) reported average body temperatures of wild and captive individuals of this species at 25.5°C and 25.6°C respectively. Brumating snakes have been measured with body temperatures of 7°C (44.6°F) (Carpenter, 1953).

The northern water snake will consume a wide variety of food items in the wild. These include many species of fish, eels, frogs, tad-

Northern Water Snake, *Nerodia sipedon sipedon* (photo by David G. Campbell)

Midland Water Snake, *Nerodia sipedon pleuralis*
(photo by John Rossi)

poles, toads, salamanders, lizards, snakes, small turtles, birds, mammals, earthworms, insects, and crayfish (Wright and Wright, 1957; Brown, 1979; Linzey and Clifford, 1981; Ernst and Barbour, 1989; Hunter et al., 1992; Klemens, 1993; Mitchell, 1994; Oldfield and Moriarty, 1994; Palmer and Braswell, 1995).

Suspected predators of this species include cottonmouths, hawks, large wading birds, bullfrogs, large fish, birds of prey, crabs, and carnivorous mammals.

Mating is known to occur in the spring, usually from April to June, resulting in the birth of 4–99 young some 90–120 days later, usually in late August to early October (Slevin, 1951; Fitch, 1970; Mitchell, 1994). Most litters range 15–30 (Fitch, 1970, 1985; Mount, 1975). The neonates range 14–24 cm (5.5–9.5 inches) in length and weigh around 5 grams at birth

(Wright and Wright, 1957; Ernst and Barbour, 1989).

Like the southern water snake, this snake is a very adaptable captive and generally feeds very well. The preferred foods are fish and amphibians, but snakes, lizards, worms, birds, and mammals will also be consumed according to Ernst and Barbour (1989). They will thrive in the basic cage design described for terrestrial snakes in the general care section. They are extremely aggressive feeders and should be housed individually. Even when they don't fight over food, one snake will become dominant and get most of the food placed in the cage and thereby grow much faster.

Remember that water snakes do not need any more water in their cages than do other snakes. In fact, they are very prone to skin lesions if they are kept too moist. Like the other water snakes, they need to be fed about twice per week and they run the risk of being parasitized. Therefore, you should try to feed these snakes frozen, thawed, and then heated fish as mentioned for the other water snakes and in the general care section. Plan on getting these snakes checked and dewormed every 6 months to a year. Much of this can be avoided if you can get these snakes switched over to captive-raised mice, initially scented with fish, but freezing your food will also go a long way in helping control parasites. Cutaneous lumps and bumps may be a warning that parasites are present. (See the first aid section under general care.) These snakes are also prone to serious

---

SPECIES: *Nerodia sipedon*, Northern Water Snake
MAINTENANCE DIFFICULTY INDEX: 3 (1 = easiest, 5 = most difficult)
AVERAGE SIZE: 56–107 cm (22–42 inches)
FOOD: Fish (minnows, shiners), frogs, toads, and mice scented with these
CAGE SIZE: 20–30-gallon long aquarium
SUBSTRATE: Artificial turf or indoor-outdoor carpet, or newspaper
VENTRAL HEAT: Yes
UV LIGHT: No, but an incandescent bulb is helpful
TEMPERATURE RANGE: 20–28°C (68–82°F)
SPECIAL CONSIDERATIONS: Excellent eaters but likely to be parasitized. Skin lesions will
   occur if kept in moist cage.

eye infections (called panophthalmitis by veterinarians if it involves the entire eye). The eye
affected will usually be cloudy white and very
puffed out. Take the snake to your veterinarian
immediately and he or she may be able to save
the eye with aggressive antibiotic therapy, but
sometimes it will have to be removed. One-
eyed snakes will continue to eat and will thrive
in captivity, but we can usually avoid this loss
by keeping the cage clean, warm, and dry right
from the start. Disinfect regularly with a dilute
mix of 1 ounce of bleach per quart of water. See
the general care section on cleaning. Also get
these snakes dewormed immediately upon capture or purchase.

Brumate and breed in the usual manner described in the general care section. (See the
reproduction chart, Table 5.)

The babies are born in the late summer and
are extremely aggressive feeders right away;
usually even before they shed they will tackle a
medium-sized minnow. House singly if you can
as they will fight over food and end up killing
each other when they accidentally (gluttonously?) try to swallow one of their siblings.

Certain individuals of this species can be
very attractive, and since they calm down eventually and even take food from your hand, they
make reasonable pets.

One of these snakes has survived over 9
years in captivity (Snider and Bowler, 1992),
but they can probably survive much longer.

Nerodia taxispilota
Brown Water Snake

The brown water snake is one of the largest and
heaviest of the water snakes, with the average
individual measuring 76–152 cm (30–60 inches)
in length and the record being 176.6 cm (69.5
inches) (Conant and Collins, 1991). They generally have a rich brown background color with
squarish "chocolate" brown blotches along
their backs and sides. The jaws are long and
narrow, giving the head a triangular appearance
which is common in aquatic fish-eating snakes.

These snakes are widely distributed in the
southeastern United States, from southeastern
Virginia southward through much of eastern
North Carolina, South Carolina, Georgia, southern Alabama, and all of Florida. Their preferred
habitat appears to be large bodies of water such
as large rivers, lakes, reservoirs, marshes
around bays, brackish estuaries, and cypress
swamps (Mount, 1975; Ashton and Ashton,
1981; Ernst and Barbour, 1989; Mitchell, 1994;
Palmer and Braswell, 1995), wherever there is
slow-moving water with much emergent vegetation. We have seen them in weed-choked
sloughs in central Florida, in floating mats of
introduced hyacinths. They appear to be quite
fond of basking in such vegetation. Certainly,
they are considered to be one of the most

Nerodia taxispilota

diurnal of the water snakes. One study reported
that these snakes maintained their body temperatures in the 20–37°C (68–99°F) range (Osgood, 1970) by moving into and out of the
water at different times of the day. In the same
study, gravid females were reported to maintain
their body temperatures in the 26–31°C (79–
88°F) range.

The preferred food of the brown water snake
appears to be fish, although frogs, other vertebrates, and invertebrates have reportedly been
consumed (Wright and Wright, 1957; Mount,

Brown Water Snake, *Nerodia taxispilota* (photo by David G. Campbell)

1975; Ashton and Ashton, 1981; Linzey and Clifford, 1981). We have observed two recently captured specimens from central Florida regurgitate a catfish and an unidentified sunfish. This is similar to what has been observed in North Carolina specimens (Palmer and Braswell, 1995).

Suspected predators of this species include cottonmouths, alligators, large wading birds, birds of prey, large fish, and carnivorous mammals.

Mating is known to occur primarily in the spring, but has also been reported to occur in the fall (Ashton and Ashton, 1981; Ernst and Barbour, 1989). Between 10 and 58 young, measuring 17.5–27 cm (6.8–10.6 inches) in length are born 90–120 days after mating, usually in the late summer or early fall (Wright and Wright, 1957; Ernst and Barbour, 1989), but possibly as early as mid-June (Fitch, 1970). Among 17 North Carolina females, the young vary in number from 9 to 61 and these neonates ranged 25.7–34.0 cm in TL with a mean TL of 29.3 cm (Palmer and Braswell, 1995). The young are colored exactly the same as the adults.

As Mitchell (1994) did in discussing the status of the species in Virginia, we must express some concern over the apparent reduction in the relative abundance of these snakes in Florida. Their habit of basking on overhanging branches makes them susceptible to being shot or collected by individuals in boats.

This large "chocolate" blotched water snake is one of the most difficult water snakes to keep in captivity. It is very fastidious and some of these snakes will never eat in captivity, although their diet (primarily fish) is relatively easy to provide. Providing a large cage with the standard "ideal" cage amenities may help. Especially important are a place to hide and a branch to bask on. These snakes should always be housed individually and certainly never with other water snakes or other aggressive feeders. Other water snakes seem to inhibit them from eating and southern water snakes (even babies) are incredibly aggressive when it comes to eating. We have seen southern water snakes steal fish from the mouths of brown water snakes that were much larger than themselves. Aside from housing singly, some sort of visual barrier like paper on the outside of the cage will prevent the snake from seeing the keeper or any other outside motion, and is an excellent idea for this species, particularly at first. In addition, this snake's adjustment to captivity may be related to the stress at the time of capture. Specimens captured quickly and bagged individually may adjust quickly while specimens that are chased, prodded, cornered, crowded, and left in the bag too long may never adjust to captivity.

Fish may be taken readily in the water by some specimens, so you may want to put live minnows or shiners in a wide shallow water dish the first few times you feed. Frogs are usually refused. Avoid goldfish as a regular food item because they contain too much fat. Remember that fish (including bait store fish) and amphibians may contain parasites which will infect these snakes. A large percentage of wild water snakes, greater than 90% (Acha and Szyfres, 1980), are parasitized because of their feeding habits, so they should be tested upon capture and regularly afterward and treated if necessary. Therefore, your goal will be to get these snakes to accept frozen and thawed fish.

Also remember that snakes fed exclusively frozen fish may have other problems. Fish contain an enzyme called thiaminase which destroys thiamin (vitamin B_1) and eventually leads the snake to develop a thiamin deficiency. This causes neurologic signs, including tremors and convulsions, and eventually death. These signs usually develop within 5–6 months after this diet begins. This can be avoided in several ways. Freeze the fish first, then thaw thoroughly and warm up to 80°C for 5 minutes. This will destroy the enzyme and hence control the problem. The freezing may destroy most of the parasites, but this may not work for northern parasites as they may be cold-adapted. Mehrtens recommends inserting a brewer's yeast tablet into the mouth of every fish. In an emergency, a veterinarian can administer a thiamin (vitamin B_1) injection which will often stop tremors or convulsions. You can always offer a variety of food (frozen first) to try and prevent a vitamin deficiency, although these snakes usually refuse anything but fish, if captured as adults. Neonates and juveniles may readily consume scented pinkies and fuzzies. Feeding live fish also seems to prevent the vitamin deficiency problem, even though it will increase the risk of parasitism.

Once they start eating, they will usually do well for years. One specimen in our care survived for 2 years and 6 months and then was released. You can attempt brumation and breeding for this species as mentioned in the general care section and Table 5.

In summary, a large clean cage with a branch, a UV light source, hiding place, etc., plus a diet of fish (primarily minnows and shiners) which have been treated as described above, and a regular check-up for parasites, will usually result in a long-lived, healthy, captive brown water snake. They are definitely one of the prettier water snakes but their personality is not the greatest, although they may mellow out some in captivity. Babies will definitely calm down, and are also fantastic eaters right from the start. When these snakes are raised in captivity they can be gorgeous and even-tempered.

SPECIES: *Nerodia taxispilota*, Brown Water Snake
MAINTENANCE DIFFICULTY INDEX: 4 (1 = easiest, 5 = most difficult)
AVERAGE SIZE: 76–152 cm (30–60 inches)
FOOD: Fish (minnows, shiners), scented mice?
CAGE SIZE: 20–30-gallon long aquarium
SUBSTRATE: Artificial turf, indoor-outdoor carpet, or newspaper
VENTRAL HEAT: Yes
UV LIGHT: No, but an incandescent bulb is helpful
TEMPERATURE RANGE: 25–30°C (77–86°F)
SPECIAL CONSIDERATIONS: Can be very difficult to get to start eating but once they do, they will do well. Likely to be parasitized. Skin lesions will occur if kept in moist cage.

Opheodrys aestivus
Rough Green Snake

The rough green snake is one of our most beautiful serpents. Solid lime green above and white with sulfur yellowish tinge below, they are commonly overlooked by many people passing close by. This incredible camouflage is nearly perfect for this, the most arboreal of the snakes in eastern North America. The rough green snake is not a heavy-bodied snake. The average snake ranges 56–81 cm (22–32 inches) in length (Conant and Collins, 1991) but is seldom thicker than 1–1.5 cm (0.39–0.59 inches) in diameter. The record length is 115.8 cm (45.6 inches). They range from southern New Jersey (and there have been unconfirmed reports of several specimens on Long Island) southward to include all of Florida and westward through southeastern Kansas, eastern Oklahoma, and central and eastern Texas. They range southward into eastern Mexico. There are 4 subspecies discussed in detail by Ernst and Barbour (1989).

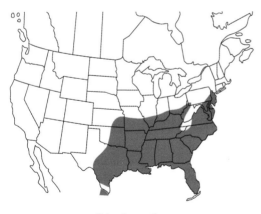

Opheodrys aestivus

As mentioned above, the green snake is very arboreal. Their preferred habitat appears to be bushes or trees near low moist areas or bodies of water such as lakes, marshes, streams, creeks, or swamps (Wright and Wright, 1957; Mount, 1975; Tennant, 1984; Vermersch and Kuntz, 1986; Ernst and Barbour, 1989; Dundee and Rossman, 1989; Allen, 1992; Collins, 1993).

Mitchell (1994) further categorizes the habitats in which these snakes are found as open deciduous forest, mixed hardwood/pine forest, old fields, myrtle thickets, and the wrack zone of barrier islands. Virtually all of their movement and feeding occurs during the day, suggesting that these animals are strictly diurnal (Plummer, 1981).

Although a great deal has been written about the habitat and dietary preferences of this snake, little has been written about its thermal preferences. Plummer (1993) reported that these snakes were active over a broad range of temperatures, with body temperatures of active individuals being 17.9–36.8°C (64.2–98.2°F), with a mean of 29.3°C (84.7°F). This correlates well with the appearance of active green snakes in the spring and their disappearance in the fall. Vermersch and Kuntz (1986) state that these snakes become active as soon as daytime temperatures are consistently above 21°C (70°F) and become inactive when average temperatures drop below 16°C (60°F). Generally speaking, basking is considered to be a rare behavior and thermoregulation is imprecise (Lillywhite and Henderson, 1993).

Brumation is believed to occur underground in leaf litter, ant mounds, or crayfish burrows, although we have seen specimens in northern Florida wedge themselves into hollow stumps during very cold weather. They may also coil inside stumps of grass or inside woodpiles. All three locations allow them to bask for brief periods and quickly retreat when temperatures drop below freezing in the evenings. They often remain in the bushes until temperatures drop close to freezing and then slowly retreat to ground cover.

Spiders, harvestmen, caterpillars of both moths and butterflies, grasshoppers, crickets, and moths appear to make up the greatest part of the diet of these snakes (Wright and Wright, 1957; Mount, 1975; Brown, 1979; Linzey and Clifford, 1981; Tennant, 1984; Vermersch and

Rough Green Snake, *Opheodrys aestivus* (photo by John Rossi)

Kuntz, 1986; Ernst and Barbour, 1989; Plummer, 1991; Allen, 1992; Collins, 1993). Other food items have been reported to include land snails, mantids, katydids, dragonfly larvae, wood roaches, and wasps (Uhler et al., 1939; Mitchell, 1994; Vermersch and Kuntz, 1986). Tennant (1984) stated that tiny treefrogs and hatchling anoles have also been reported as prey.

Known predators of this species include swallow-tailed kites and Mississippi kites (Tomkins, 1965; Guthrie, 1932). However, other birds, ophiophagous snakes, and predatory mammals may also prey on these snakes. Clark (1949) reported seeing an alligator gar attack a swimming *Opheodrys aestivus*. Little is known of neonate behavior in the wild but some have proposed that the young are far more terrestrial than the adults (Gritis, 1993). Perhaps this is used as a partial means to evade predators.

Mating is known to occur in the spring and fall (Richmond, 1956; Plummer, 1984; E. E. Brown, 1992). This results in the deposition of 2–14 eggs, usually 3–7, sometime in late spring or early summer. These eggs have a relatively short incubation period, hatching in 36–43 days (Plummer, 1984; E. E. Brown, 1992; personal observations). These hatchlings measure 17.9–21.1 cm (7–8.3 inches). See also Plummer (1983). One long incubation period, 81 days, was reported by Mitchell (1996). It was believed that the eggs were exposed to cooler temperatures.

The young grow fairly rapidly and may reach sexual maturity by their second year, although Plummer (1983) reported that 50% of the females do not reach sexual maturity until their third year.

There is a tremendous summary of the ecology and behavior of arboreal snakes by Lillywhite and Henderson, in Seigel et al. (1993).

Many herpetoculturists consider this a "junk" snake and the literature that is available suggests that it is difficult to maintain in captivity. However, this gentle-natured serpent is, in fact, one of our most beautiful native snakes and is actually quite easy to maintain in captivity. Furthermore, in our opinion, there is no such thing as a "junk" snake.

They are ferocious hunters of insects and spiders in the wild and once they adapt to captivity will happily feed on grasshoppers, crickets, moths, and caterpillars. The easiest way to obtain these insects is to sweep them up from around an outdoor light at night. Insects collected this way are called "sweepings" by herpetoculturists. Some will eat mealworms, but a word of warning is needed. The hard exoskeleton (external chitinous skeleton of insects) if consumed in quantity may cause an obstruction in the intestinal tract which could possibly lead to the death of the snake.

All insects, but especially crickets and mealworms, should be dusted with a calcium powder (e.g., Reptical®) just before feeding, or fed a high calcium diet for 2 days prior to being fed to the snake. (See the section on feeding for dusting technique and recipe for high-calcium insect diet.) The latest research has shown that the latter technique will provide the highest levels of calcium to your reptiles (Allen, 1989). Examples of such diets are Ziegler's Cricket Chow® and Pretty Pets Gut Loading Diet® for crickets. Feeding high-calcium greens such as turnip greens or collard greens to your crickets is also a good alternative.

Some of the literature available mentions that these snakes may also eat small lizards and frogs, and this may occur, but we have never had one in our care show any interest in these animals. Wax worms and an "occasional" pinky mouse have also been reported as food items for captive specimens by Wood (1994).

The green snake will do quite well in a 10–30-gallon aquarium (depending on the size of the snake) with numerous branches (baked or thoroughly scrubbed to remove mites first), plastic plants, and artificial carpet/turf or wood chips for a substrate. Do not make the plastic plants and branches too dense, however, or you may make it very difficult for this snake to find its food. A dark hide box is very important for this species, as they will stay inside their hide box for a week or so just prior to shedding or after a big meal and the security seems to aid their appetite. The cage should be misted every other day as these snakes will often refuse to drink from a water bowl, choosing instead to drink droplets off branches and leaves. Make sure the cage is well ventilated for this reason. You want it to dry out completely between mistings. This is another reason why the carpet/turf is ideal. Even if the floor gets wet the plastic fingers will hold the snake's body above the water and allow air to circulate underneath, thereby preventing skin infections if the snake is on the bottom for any length of time. Most of the time these snakes will bask in the upper branches of your terrarium. Vitalites® or some other UV light source are strongly recom-

No snake is more cryptically colored than the rough green snake. Not only is it ideally marked for its arboreal existence, its behavior contributes to its hiding ability. When approached, it often freezes, and when moving on a windy day, it often sways with the branches. (photo by John Rossi)

SPECIES: *Opheodrys aestivus*, Rough Green Snake
MAINTENANCE DIFFICULTY INDEX: 3 (1 = easiest, 5 = most difficult)
AVERAGE SIZE: 56–81 cm (22–32 inches)
FOOD: Moths, crickets, grasshoppers, caterpillars, spiders, mealworms
CAGE SIZE: 10–30-gallon high aquarium
SUBSTRATE: Artificial turf, indoor-outdoor carpet, or newspaper
VENTRAL HEAT: Yes
UV LIGHT: Yes?
TEMPERATURE RANGE: 23–25°C (73–77°F)
SPECIAL CONSIDERATIONS: May be slow to start feeding but once it starts, watch out.
   Feed a variety and feed frequently. Must mist cage regularly. Needs vitamins.

mended for this species! The snake will also use these high branches to attempt escape every once in a while, so make sure your screen is *tight-fitting and weighted down*. These snakes are second only to scarlet kingsnakes in their escaping abilities.

A short period of brumation (at least 1–2 months) is strongly recommended. For this small snake you may just place some cypress mulch in its regular hide box during this time to help avoid dehydration. Nothing else need be changed. (See the section on brumation under general care.) This short period of cooler temperatures and no feeding will be good for both the snake and the keeper. Temperatures fluctuating from 3.3 to 18.3°C (37 to 65°F) were well tolerated by those in our care during the winter.

Captive breeding of this species has occurred, although not commonly. Females in captivity have laid eggs which have been incubated and hatched. Attempt breeding in the usual manner described in the general care section, after brumation. Captive mating was described by Morris and Vail (1991).

The eggs can be incubated in the usual manner but the incubation time for this species is usually quite short, around 40 days. One female from Duval County, Florida, in our care deposited 6 eggs on 20 May, which hatched on 26 June, an incubation period of 37 days. The eggs were set up in the usual manner on vermiculite, and incubated at temperatures fluctuating from 26.1 to 29.4°C (79 to 85°F). The neonates ranged 17.8–19.0 cm (7.0–7.5 inches) in length with an average TL of 18.1 cm (7.13 inches). The sex ratio was 1:1.

Griswold (pers. comm., 1998) reported that a male captured in north central Florida in early spring was observed mating with a captive female on 16 April. This female laid 1 infertile egg on 16 May and 7 more (5 were viable) on 20 May. These eggs were incubated on moist vermiculite at 27.7–29.4°C (82–85°F) and 4 of this group hatched on 5 July, a 46-day incubation period. The fifth egg had a dead fully formed embryo with severe kyphoscoliosis.

A second clutch of eggs (6) was laid on 2 July, even though there were no additional matings. Four of these eggs were fertile and hatched on 17 August, also a 46-day incubation period. These neonates (five males, three females) had an average TL of 20.3 cm (8 inches).

Griswold housed the neonates in half-gallon plastic jars with aluminum screen lids. He provided sphagnum moss as the substrate as well as a small climbing branch. The moss was misted daily. Under these conditions, his neonates remained hidden under the moss until they shed, 5–7 days after hatching. Griswold stated that most of these neonates were eating 0.6-cm (0.25-inch) crickets by 10 days of age. One of the snakes that hatched on 5 July reached a TL of 30.5 cm (12 inches) by November of that year, a growth rate of approximately 2.5 cm (1 inch) per month for the first 4 months.

Baby crickets (0.25 inch in length), which can be ordered in bulk from biological supply houses or wholesalers, can form the mainstay of the diet, but young mealworms (see above), caterpillars, moths, and other young insects should be added.

The amount of food consumed by these snakes in captivity is startling. One adult snake may consume over 100 insects per month, eating three or more per day. Snakes may eat far less however, with some in our care apparently maintaining their body weight on as few as 10–20 insects per month. The presence of more than one snake in a cage may inhibit feeding by some snakes, however, and occasionally fights over food items have been observed, so housing these snakes singly is advisable. In one instance, two neonates died as they both attacked the same cricket, and one tried to swallow the other.

These snakes have been known to contain internal parasites including several species of coccidia. One specimen collected in Duval County, Florida, contained large numbers of flagellates. Snake mites, *Ophionyssys* sp., have been observed on this species, as have chiggers, *Trombicula* sp. Much more work is needed on this species.

One of these snakes survived 6 years and 8 months in captivity (Snider and Bowler, 1992).

Opheodrys (*Liochlorophis*) *vernalis*
Smooth Green Snake

The smooth green snake is a solid lime green above, with a yellowish white belly. Some midwestern specimens are solid brown above, however. The scales are smooth, not keeled. They are also slightly smaller than the more arboreal rough green snake, with most individuals measuring 31–51 cm (12–20 inches) in length, with the record being 66 cm (26 inches) (Conant and Collins, 1991). The smooth green snake has an unusual distribution, with many disjunct populations over much of the country. There are two subspecies, the eastern smooth green snake, *O. v. vernalis*, and the western smooth green snake, *O. v. blanchardi*. The eastern subspecies has seven upper labials (upper lip scales), while the western subspecies has six. The eastern smooth green snake ranges from Nova Scotia southward to the western mountains of Virginia and North Carolina and westward to northern Wisconsin, Minnesota, and southern Manitoba. The western smooth green snake is found from western Indiana and Ohio, westward to eastern Kansas and Nebraska and northward to southern Saskatchewan and Manitoba. There are numerous disjunct populations of this subspecies widely distributed in Wyoming, Utah, Colorado, New Mexico, and Texas.

The preferred habitat of this little snake appears to be areas of moist soil with thick low vegetation such as fields, prairies, meadows, marsh borders, and open hardwood woodlands

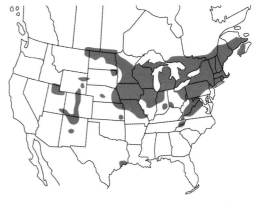

Opheodrys vernalis

(Wright and Wright, 1957; Minton, 1972; Linzey and Clifford, 1981; Tennant, 1984; Hudson, 1985; Holman et al., 1990; Allen, 1992; Hunter et al., 1992; Klemens, 1993). Perhaps a more accurate habitat description would be high elevation grassy fields (Mitchell, 1994; Degenhardt et al., 1996). In Maine, they have been known to frequent vacant lots and gardens in suburban areas (Hunter et al., 1992).

The body temperatures of active smooth green snakes have been reported at 18–31°C (64.4–88°F) (Brattstrom, 1965). They are usually active on the surface from late April through October over much of their range.

Brumation is often communal in this species, as is egg laying. Hibernacula have been observed in Manitoba (Criddle, 1937), Minnesota

Smooth Green Snake, *Opheodrys* (*Liochlorophis*) *vernalis* (photo by David G. Campbell)

(Lang, 1969), Virginia (Linzey and Clifford, 1981), and New Mexico (Degenhardt et al., 1996).

Numerous insects and other invertebrates have been reported as food for these snakes in the wild. These items include spiders, caterpillars, crickets, grasshoppers, moths, millipedes, centipedes, slugs, snails, and salamanders (Wright and Wright, 1957; Minton, 1972; Tennant, 1984; Ernst and Barbour, 1989; Hunter et al., 1992; Klemens, 1993). Spiders, moths, and hairless caterpillars appear to be favorites (Minton, 1972; personal observations). Logier (1958) suggested that "possibly" small salamanders and snakes may be eaten, but this would appear to be an exception if it does occur. Hammerson (1986) reported that a small crayfish had been consumed by one of these snakes.

Suspected predators of this species include birds, ophiophagous snakes, and carnivorous mammals. A black widow spider was reported by Neill (1948) to have preyed on one.

Mating is known to occur in the spring, summer, or fall, with 3–13 eggs being laid 4–10 weeks later, or the following summer, depending upon the environment. The presently held belief is that those snakes from cooler climates retain the eggs longer, which results in a shorter incubation period once they are laid, while those from warmer climates lay the eggs earlier, resulting in longer incubation periods. These eggs usually hatch in a relatively short period of 4–26 days (Blanchard, 1933; Fitch, 1970; Preston, 1982). The hatchlings, which are darker green than the adults, measure 8.4–16.5 cm (3.3–6.5 inches) in length (Conant and Collins, 1991), and reportedly are heavily laden with yolk and will refuse food for 2 weeks.

The smooth green snake will do well in captivity if it can be made comfortable enough to start feeding and if it is kept on a substrate that is not too moist. A 10-gallon aquarium is sufficiently large for most. The substrate of choice is cypress mulch and soil 50:50, although artificial carpet/turf has also worked well with certain modifications. If the carpet/turf is used, one should provide a little pile of mulch or a small humidity box to keep these little snakes from dehydrating rapidly. Flat rocks or pieces of bark can be placed on the surface to provide natural looking refuges, or small plastic hide boxes can be used. The snakes will accept both. Plastic plants are a very nice addition, as they beautify the enclosure and provide basking and hiding places. These plants are also easily cleaned and disinfected. A shallow bowl of clean fresh water should always be provided, but these snakes will also drink when the cage is misted and this should be done twice weekly. As with the rough green snake, the cage should be well ventilated so that it will dry out rapidly after a misting. A UV light source may be essential for this species and an incandescent bulb for heat will help, but be careful not to keep the cage too warm.

Feeding the smooth green snake is very similar to feeding the rough green snake, although this species can be quite a bit more fastidious at first. Refer to the previous section for information on collecting food and the treatment of the food prior to feeding. These snakes' favorite food appears to be hairless caterpillars, but crickets and mealworms as well as other insects will also be greedily devoured. Ernst and Barbour (1989) also list centipedes, millipedes, slugs, and snails as food items for wild members of this species. Trutnau (1981) stated that these snakes may consume salamanders as well, but none of the specimens in our care displayed any interest in slimy salamanders, *Plethodon glutinosis*; however, this is no surprise, and other salamanders may be taken. These snakes will fight each other viciously over an insect, so they must be housed singly for long-term maintenance.

Internal parasitism is a real threat to captive success with this species as amoebas, coccidia, trematodes (flukes), and stomach worms have been described in this species (Fantham and Porter, 1952). Treating them is no easy task because of the small size of the patient, but it can be done.

Brumation in mulch for 2 or more months is strongly recommended. This is beneficial prior to attempting breeding and is easier on the keeper as well, since insects may become more difficult to obtain in midwinter. Do not feed for at least 1 week prior to brumation. The greatest risk to these animals during brumation is desiccation, so a semimoist retreat must be present during this time. Humidity boxes work well. Because of their insect diet, these snakes are believed to be sensitive to insecticides, and some herpetologists suspect that they may have been eliminated from some areas where these chemicals have been used.

Although true captive breeding is rare, gravid females have deposited eggs in captivity. One should attempt breeding as described in the general care section, right after brumation. Mattison advises that gravid females, which are both thicker and longer than the males, will do best if removed from the usual cage for egg deposition. He also warns that females should not be offered food at this time (they may not eat anyway), since live crickets will destroy the eggs. Dr. Steve Barten warns that gravid females will die if they are not given a suitable nesting site because they will become egg-bound. (A plastic box with a moist medium like sphagnum moss is a good egg laying box.) If all goes well, one should expect eggs in the late spring or early summer with hatching in the late summer or early fall. (See Table 5.) The eggs should be incubated in the usual manner as

---

SPECIES: *Opheodrys* (*Liochlorophis*) *vernalis*, Smooth Green Snake
MAINTENANCE DIFFICULTY INDEX: 5 (1 = easiest, 5 = most difficult)
AVERAGE SIZE: 36–51 cm (14–20 inches)
FOOD: Hairless caterpillars, crickets, moths, grasshoppers
CAGE SIZE: 10-gallon aquarium
SUBSTRATE: Artificial turf, indoor-outdoor carpet, or cypress mulch and soil. Provide hiding
   places. See text.
VENTRAL HEAT: No, but heat from above, but don't overdo it. "Hot rock" wouldn't hurt.
UV LIGHT: Yes?
TEMPERATURE RANGE: 25–27°C (77–81°F)
SPECIAL CONSIDERATIONS: Can be very poor eater, but usually okay once it starts.
   Needs vitamins. Must mist cage regularly. Collecting food may be time-consuming. Feed
   frequently.

described in the general care section. The young can be cared for exactly as the adults, but they will, of course, require smaller food. If you are purchasing crickets, tell the distributor you need 0.25-inch crickets. Fly larvae (maggots) may also suffice in a pinch, but most people would rather not feed these to their snakes. Small wax worms may be taken as well. The technique of collecting "sweepings" may be used throughout the year in the south (see the rough green snake section). Babies should be housed and fed separately. Feeding of the young should be accomplished right away. Research on the closely related rough green snake indicates that the neonates have only about half a month's worth of body reserves, and that they probably need to eat heavily before brumation.

These snakes are perhaps one of the most mild-tempered and beautiful snakes in eastern North America. They make great captives once they start eating, and if you feed them a variety of foods, they will stay healthy.

They are by no means a low maintenance or "easy" animal to breed or raise, however. Housing singly and providing large quantities of food when it will be consumed are the keys to successful maintenance. We still do not have all the ingredients in the "recipe" for consistent captive growth and reproduction of this species. We suspect that a protected outdoor enclosure may provide the best solution for this species.

One of these snakes survived 6 years and 1 month in captivity (Snider and Bowler, 1992).

Oxybelis aeneus
Mexican Vine Snake

The Mexican vine snake is one of the rarest snakes in North America north of the Mexican border. It has been found in the United States in only two mountain ranges in southern Arizona. However, it is one of the most common snakes south of the border. There is no mistaking this extremely arboreal snake. It looks basically like a vine since it is extremely thin with a narrow pointed head and long (up to 1.9 meters or 6 feet) TL (Trutnau, 1981). The average size

Oxybelis aeneus

within the United States has been 90–152 cm (36–60 inches) (Wright and Wright, 1957; Stebbins, 1985; Lowe et al., 1986).

In fact, these snakes are so thin for their length that most individuals seeing them for the first time are quite surprised. Lowe et al. (1986) describe well just how thin these snakes are with a comparative statement. They say, "… at four feet, an average-girthed male Tropical Vine Snake weighs about 36 grams (1.27 ounces). It would take more than thirty four foot vine snakes to equal the weight of one four foot rattlesnake."

It is brown or gray in color dorsally and pale white ventrally, with a great deal of yellow toward the neck and chin. There is a black stripe running along each side of the head from the nasal opening through the eye and onto the neck.

As mentioned above, this snake is very arboreal. They spend most of their lives hunting among the trees and shrubs of their tropical habitats. In fact, it is probably safe to say this is the most arboreal North American snake. Certainly, they have been observed most often in trees and bushes, and their preferred habitat

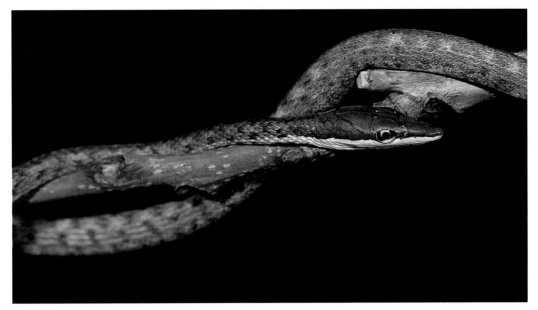

Mexican Vine Snake, *Oxybelis aenus* (photo by David G. Campbell)

appears to be open areas dominated by bushes and low trees, often near streams (Fowlie, 1965; Henderson, 1974; Trutnau, 1981; Mehrtens, 1987). Lowe et al. (1986) characterized their habitat as canyon riparian woodlands.

These snakes are diurnal and have been observed sleeping in a characteristic loose coil (with their head hanging down) at night (Henderson, 1974). In Belize, they are usually found at heights of 1.5 meters (4.5 feet) during the day and 2.9 meters (9 feet) at night, presumably climbing higher for increased safety, but possibly because their preferred prey items move in a similar manner (Henderson, 1974).

The primary prey of these snakes in the wild appears to be lizards, but insects, frogs, small birds, and small mammals have also been reported as food items (Shaw and Campbell, 1974; Henderson, 1974; Lowe et al., 1986). Slow stalking or ambush have been the primary methods of prey capture. A large specimen in our care attacked a smaller specimen three times. An adult male in our care consumed 27 lizards in an 11-month period, while an adult female in the same cage consumed 35 in the same time period. They might have eaten many more.

Very little is known about the temperature preferences of this species in the wild. Most

arboreal snakes do not appear to precisely thermoregulate and are active over a wide range of temperatures (Lillywhite and Henderson, 1993).

Suspected predators of this species include other snakes, jays, crows, hawks, and carnivorous mammals. One case of predation occurred immediately after capture when a large Mexican vine snake was placed in the same container with a green vine snake, *Oxybelis fulgidus*, and was immediately consumed by it.

Mating is thought to occur in early spring with egg laying in late spring or early summer. These eggs hatch in September (Lowe et al., 1986).

In captivity, remember this is an arboreal snake and as such will require all of the modifications discussed in the general care section for arboreal snakes. These include a tall cage, numerous sturdy branches, a basking site among the branches (an incandescent bulb above a screen top works well for this purpose), and frequent misting of the cage with water. The cage must be well ventilated. Plastic plants are also strongly recommended, as are all of the other amenities of the basic (or ideal) cage. These include a water bowl (even if you are misting the cage daily since we have observed one of these snakes drinking almost daily from such a bowl), sturdy hide box, and a suitable substrate. Artificial carpet/turf or mulch will work nicely. Remember that all branches that you intend to place into the cage should be baked first at 149°C (300°F) for about 15 minutes in order to destroy potential parasites they may be harboring. Also remember it is counterproductive to jam so many branches into the cage that the snakes cannot easily find their prey, and this will also make it more difficult to clean up after the snake or to remove it from the cage.

Although it is believed that healthy wild arboreal snakes rarely bask, we have noticed this species does appear to position itself such that it receives the "first light" of the morning. Perhaps this would give wild snakes an advantage or perhaps this is an artifact of captive tropical snakes housed in a temperate environment.

For this tropical snake, the temperature and humidity should not be allowed to fluctuate wildly; a constant temperature range of 25–30°C (77–86°F) has been recommended by Trutnau (1981). He stated that they "catch colds easily if subjected to fluctuations in warmth." Neither we nor Randy Babb, Arizona Game and Fish Commission biologist, found them to be very sensitive to temperature fluctuations, however.

A UV light source such as a Vitalite® is not considered essential but has been described as "beneficial" (Trutnau, 1981). Whether this light contributes at all to vitamin synthesis in this species is unknown. Ventral heat is also not considered a necessity for this snake, even though a hot spot (usually under the incandescent bulb mentioned above) among the branches is considered beneficial.

Feeding the Mexican vine snake may be a problem for those keepers in northern latitudes because, although literature reports of food items for this snake include small birds, small mammals, small frogs, and insects, it appears that most captives prefer lizards of the family Iguanidae or Teiidae. Furthermore, we and Randy Babb have observed that they usually will take only live lizards. Three specimens in his care have consumed lizards of the following genera: anoles, *Anolis*, spiny lizards, *Sceloporus*, side-blotched lizards, *Uta*, whiptails, *Cnemidophorus*, and tree lizards, *Urosaurus*. They "could care less what kind of lizard it is but it must be alive," Babb says. "Wiggling a dead lizard with a long pair of forceps just won't cut it," he added. "They seem to know the difference, even when the lizard is moved in a natural manner." We agree completely. Four specimens in our care regularly consumed live lizards including green anoles, *Anolis carolinensis*, brown anoles, *A. sagrei*, Mediterranean geckos, *Hemidactylus turcicus*, Indo-Pacific geckos, *H. garnotii*, ground skinks, *Scincella lateralis*, and a six-lined racerunner, *Cnemidophorus sexlineatus*. No dead lizard was ever consumed by one in our care. Indeed, this observation that movement is a very important factor in eliciting a strike by this species has been discussed by Seigel et al. (1987) and Lillywhite and Henderson (1993). This makes quality control of the food very difficult and predisposes captives to continual exposure to

---

SPECIES: *Oxybelis aeneus*, Mexican Vine Snake
MAINTENANCE DIFFICULTY INDEX: 4 (1 = easiest, 5 = most difficult)
AVERAGE SIZE: 90–152 cm (36–60 inches)
FOOD: Lizards (live)
CAGE SIZE: Display case
SUBSTRATE: Indoor-outdoor carpet or artificial turf
VENTRAL HEAT: No
UV LIGHT: Not essential but helpful. Incandescent bulb advisable.
TEMPERATURE RANGE: 25–30°C (77–86°F)
SPECIAL CONSIDERATIONS: Need tall cage with hot spot among branches. Require live lizards.

---

parasites; and as tropical snakes, they are very likely to be parasitized at the time of capture. Therefore, an initial deworming and regular dewormings afterward are probably in order for this species. Fenbendazole (Panacur®) at a dose of 50 mg/kg has been used as a broad-spectrum dewormer in this snake. Fortunately, they seem to adapt fairly well to captivity and rarely seem seriously affected by parasites. Still, captive reproduction of this species has been rarely reported and one must wonder if untreated parasitism is partly to blame.

Several specimens had numerous spangana (tapeworms) under the skin, which required manual removal.

Just prior to this volume going to press, one of the specimens in our care was offered a 1.5-cm pine woods treefrog, *Hyla femoralis*. The snake stalked, caught, and consumed the frog. Interestingly, the snake's approach to the frog was different from its approach to lizards. The approach was distinctly in a more cranial and dorsal fashion than the more direct angle usually used to approach lizards. Perhaps the snake was anticipating a potential leap by the anuran.

As mentioned above, this species has not been bred regularly in captivity. Perhaps, like other tropical snakes, they need a short period of slightly cooler temperatures and short day length. At this time we don't know.

It is known that females will lay 3–6 eggs, measuring 5–6.4 cm (2–2.5 inches) in length in late spring or early summer, which hatch in about 2 months (Fitch, 1970; Lowe et al., 1986). One female in our care laid 3 fertile eggs on 31 August 1994, approximately 10 weeks after being placed with a male. The eggs averaged 4.2 cm (1.6 inches) in length and had numerous spicules on their surface. Two of these eggs hatched on 13 November and 16 November, incubation periods of 74 and 77 days. The male was 41 cm (17.2 inches) TL with a 21 cm (8.2 inches) SVL, and the female was 44 cm (17.2 inches) TL with a 27 cm (10.5 inches) SVL. The snakes began eating young anoles within a week and they are both still alive at 3 years, 2 months, and 3 weeks of age at the time of this writing.

It should be noted that this is a rear-fanged snake that possesses a mild venom. Stebbins (1985) mentioned that one person bitten by one of these snakes reported a numbing sensation that lasted about 12 hours. Crimmins (1937) reported a slight redness, itching, and numbness that lasted for several hours at most, with a blister that lasted several days. Generally, however, this snake is not considered to be dangerous to humans, much like the lyre snake, black-striped snake, and other rear-fanged North American colubrids. The senior author was bitten by one of the juveniles as he attempted to extract a lizard from its mouth. A localized numbing sensation lasted about 45 minutes. They will often bluff, with mouth wide open and head reared back, but rarely bite. Being active during the day, and being arboreal, this snake is fascinating to observe as it climbs gracefully among the branches of its enclosure.

One of these snakes survived more than 11 years and 10 months in captivity (Snider and Bowler, 1992).

Phyllorhynchus browni
Saddled Leafnose Snake

The saddled leafnose snake is perhaps the "scarlet snake" of the west. It is notoriously difficult to keep in captivity as it appears to be a dietary specialist *and* refuses to eat in captivity. Still, they are very attractive snakes and many people have tried to keep them. Here are some of the facts.

The saddled leafnose snake is a small to medium-sized (30–50 cm, 12–20 inch) snake with a sharply upturned and elongated rostral scale with free edges. Both subspecies in the United States commonly referred to as the Pima leafnose, *P. b. browni*, and the Maricopa leafnose, *P. b. lucidus*, are characterized by having fewer than 17 dark brown (chocolate) dorsal saddles on a pink to cream background color.

The Maricopa leafnose may be distinguished from the Pima by having saddles that are about equal in width to the spaces between them. The Pima leafnose has saddles that are much wider than the spaces between them. Both are robust beautiful snakes. Both subspecies are found in a small area in south central Arizona. There has recently been a proposal to eliminate all subspecies of U.S. leafnose snakes. We await further developments before we eliminate such different-appearing subspecies.

In nature, this snake is known to live in a wide variety of desert habitats and soil types, but particularly those brushy areas dominated

Phyllorhynchus browni

by mesquite, saltbush, creosote, paloverde, and saguaro cactus (Wright and Wright, 1957; Stebbins, 1985). Like most desert snakes, it is nocturnal. Its preferred food appears to be the banded gecko, *Coleonyx variegatus*, and its eggs, but other lizards (side-blotched lizard, *Uta stansburiana*) and occasional insects (including mealworms?) have been reported. Randy Babb, biologist for the Arizona Game and Fish Commission, has dissected a number of these snakes seeking to determine their preferred foods and has invariably found empty stomachs. Perhaps only hungry snakes come to the surface. In any case, very little is known about this snake's diet, either in the wild or in captivity. Several authors have reported they will readily consume banded geckos, but this has not been borne out by the herpetologists that have tried. We suspect these snakes may be demonstrating reptile disorientation syndrome when they are first captured (they will eat or mate for a short time after capture because they are confused, but will stop eating shortly thereafter, and rarely eat in captivity again).

Virtually nothing is known about the thermal ecology of this snake. We observed one juvenile crossing a road when the air temperature was 20°C (68°F). The closely related *P. decurtatus* has a critical thermal maximum of 36°C (96.8°F).

Pima Leafnose Snake, *Phyllorhynchus browni browni* (photo by David G. Campbell)

Maricopa Leafnose Snake, *Phyllorhynchus browni lucidus* (photo by David G. Campbell)

The predators of this species are poorly known. Foxes, coyotes, wild pigs, raccoons, owls, and ophiophagous snakes are suspected predators. Many are killed by cars.

Many (including us) have tried numerous lizards on these snakes in captivity without any success. These have included banded geckos (live and frozen), anoles, ground skinks, and Mediterranean geckos. We have also tried insects (crickets and mealworms) and pinkies with similar results. Babb (pers. comm., 1992) indicated that some would feed on side-blotched lizards, *Uta stansburiana*, and small crickets with some regularity. Feldner (pers. comm., 1992) stated that one out of ten would consume "any random lizard." Interestingly, these snakes will swallow ground skinks, *Scincella lateralis*, frequently when they are gently placed in their mouths. Others have maintained these snakes only by force-feeding. Even hatchlings resist feeding in captivity, although Fowlie (1965) stated that "juveniles have been observed to live on insect larvae."

Recently, however, we made an exciting observation of one captive specimen. One large female consistently fed on eggs of the Mediterranean gecko, *Hemidactylus turcicus*, even though the geckos themselves were refused. Eggs placed in the cage at dusk were consumed fairly quickly. In fact, this snake nudged a prekilled gecko out of the way to get to the eggs. Just why this widespread introduced species and its eggs are so irresistible to native snakes is unknown, but extremely interesting and advantageous for snake keepers.

Nevertheless, we have a long way to go when it comes to feeding these snakes in captivity. Perhaps our captive environment is incorrect, but this is hard to judge when the snakes never eat.

Indeed, herpetoculturists look at feeding as a signal that the environment is close enough to keep the snake healthy and hungry. Therefore, we cannot say with a great deal of certainty what the proper caging should be. We have attempted to mimic desert habitats using sand, rocks, and plastic cacti with numerous hiding places. The snakes seem to stay healthy but still refuse to eat. We have tried smaller cages (down to the size of plastic shoe boxes) and different substrates (including artificial carpet/turf, sand, and cypress mulch) but they still refuse to eat. We have tried high humidity and low humidity and exposed them to a wide variety of temperatures, but they still refuse to eat. Indeed, this species and the closely related spotted leafnose appear to be the big challenge to herpetoculturists among western snakes.

One of the techniques we have tried that has met with some limited success has been the "food colony" approach. This is where one snake is housed in a colony of geckos or crickets. The geckos or crickets breed, then lay eggs and produce young, and the eggs or young serve as food for these snakes. Mixed food colonies may not work, however, as the crickets may eat the gecko eggs before the snakes do.

Some parasites have been observed in this species. They remain unidentified, but appeared to be some type of rhabditiform larvae, possibly *Strongyloides* sp. They were observed in the stool of a very young specimen that had been force-fed frozen and thawed ground skinks for 4 months. Thus, we are unsure if these parasites are naturally occurring or were an artifact of the captive environment. In either case, a fecal exam and regular dewormings may be in order for this species. Fenbendazole (Panacur®) is probably the drug of choice for this purpose.

Brumation is strongly recommended. Healthy specimens captured in the fall have been brumated in their cages for 4 months in the 10–15°C (50–59°F) range.

SPECIES: *Phyllorhynchus browni*, Saddled Leafnose Snake
MAINTENANCE DIFFICULTY INDEX: 5+ (1 = easiest, 5 = most difficult)
AVERAGE SIZE: 30–50 cm (12–20 inches)
FOOD: Gecko eggs?
CAGE SIZE: 10-gallon aquarium
SUBSTRATE: Sand?
VENTRAL HEAT: No?
UV LIGHT: No, but an incandescent bulb is helpful
TEMPERATURE RANGE: 18.8–34.7°C (66–94.5°F)
SPECIAL CONSIDERATIONS: Captive requirements still poorly understood. Diet difficult to
    provide. Serious snake keepers only. See text.

Captive reproduction of this species has not been reported and is unlikely until we can figure out how to get them to feed in captivity. In the absence of any other information, the standard approach of placing the female in with the male in early spring is advisable.

Females gravid at the time of capture have deposited 2–5 eggs in late spring or early summer, which have been incubated in the usual manner. The incubation period is approximately 2 months.

The young are 15–17 cm (6–7 inches) in length and appear to be just as much of a challenge to get to start feeding in captivity as the adults. Still, we believe that captive-born hatchlings hold more promise for getting started and surviving in captivity than the adults. Perhaps they will someday form the breeding stock for captive reproduction programs. On a scale of 1–5, with 5 being the most difficult to maintain, this snake has earned a score of 5+.

One will not find the captive longevity of this species listed in *Reptiles and Amphibians in Captivity Breeding Longevity and Inventory* (Slavens and Slavens, 1990) nor in Snider and Bowler (1992). Those who have tried to maintain this snake are few and far between, and even they may be too embarrassed to discuss the captive longevity of specimens in their care. One in our care has survived over 1 year and 4 months in captivity when it died from gastroenteritis secondary to untreated parasitism. Perhaps snake eggs would be better accepted. This snake still requires a great deal of research.

DO NOT COLLECT THIS SPECIES OR THE NEXT UNLESS YOU HAVE A GREAT DEAL OF TIME AND EFFORT TO INVEST IN TRYING TO MAINTAIN THEM. MAINTENANCE MAY REQUIRE RE-CREATION OF VERY NATURAL ENVIRONMENTS AND PROVISION OF DIFFICULT-TO-PROCURE FOOD ITEMS. BE ADVISED.

Phyllorhynchus decurtatus
Spotted Leafnose Snake

Like the saddled leafnose in size and structure, but more widespread within the United States, the spotted leafnose is another of our fascinating western species. And like that species, which is its closest relative, it is also a snake keeper's nightmare.

It is a small snake, usually 30–50 cm (12–20 inches) long (Stebbins, 1985) that is charac-terized by an enlarged rostral scale similar to that found in the saddled leafnose, but unlike that species it has more than 17 dark blotches on its back. The background color is pale tan.

The preferred habitat of this species appears to be primarily open sandy areas with some brush (Wright and Wright, 1957), but Stebbins (1972, 1985) pointed out that this species' range

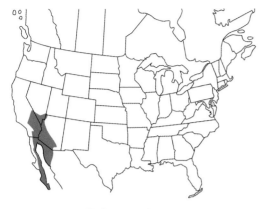

Phyllorhynchus decurtatus

largely corresponds with the distribution of the creosote bush. There are two subspecies within the United States, the western leafnose snake, *P. d. perkinsi*, and the clouded leafnose snake, *P. d. nubilis*. These subspecies may be distinguished by the number of spots on the back. Although there is some intergrading in the central Arizona area, the clouded leafnose has more than 42 blotches, while the western leafnose has fewer than 48. Some have proposed as many as five subspecies for this snake, while others have proposed that there are none. The western leafnose occupies the majority of the range of this species within the United States, ranging from southeastern California through southern Nevada to extreme southwestern Utah, and southward through western Arizona into Mexico. The clouded leafnose is found only in south central Arizona and adjacent Mexico.

The diet of this species in the wild has included primarily the eggs of the banded gecko, *Coleonyx variegatus*, but the geckos themselves and their tails, as well as insects, have also been reported (Wright and Wright, 1957). There is some indication there may be a seasonal variation in diet, with lizard eggs being reported in five out of 11 wild-caught specimens in May and insects or lizards being reported at other times. In fact, Fowlie (1965) stated that insect larvae were the principal food of these snakes, with geckos and other lizards being taken occasionally. Furthermore, the possibility of geographic or populational dietary variation exists.

Temperatures taken at the time individuals were found active on the surface have been measured at 18.8–34.7°C (66–94.5°F), with most at 31.1°C (88°F) (Klauber in Wright and Wright, 1957). Klauber later found nine specimens at temperatures of 28.3–30.0°C (83–86°F). Cowles and Bogert (1944) reported a critical thermal maximum for this species of 36°C (96.8°F). This low critical thermal maximum is fairly common among nocturnally active desert snakes. Indeed, they seem to wait until it cools off before becoming active. Klauber reported that most were collected between 2000 and 2100 hrs, even though he collected others between 1900 and 0029 hrs.

Two individuals were observed at a depth of 76 cm (30 inches) below the surface of a small sand dune and were presumed by Cowles to be brumating. The temperature he measured at a depth of 101 cm (40 inches) was 19.5°C (67.1°F).

Suspected predators of this species include carnivorous mammals, ophiophagous snakes, and birds of prey.

Mating has not been reported for snakes in the wild, although it is thought to occur in the spring. Up to 4 (2–4) relatively large eggs 1 cm wide × 3.5 cm long (0.4 inch wide × 1.4 inches long) are laid from April to August (mostly in June and July) (Klauber in Wright and Wright, 1957; Fitch, 1970; Stebbins, 1985). These eggs are believed to hatch in approximately 2 months into babies that range from 16.8 to 19.0 cm (6.6 to 7.5 inches) long.

Fitch (1970) believed that females of this species reached sexual maturity in 3 years in the wild.

Western Leafnose Snake, *Phyllorhynchus decurtatus perkinsi* (photo by David G. Campbell)

Clouded Leafnose Snake, *Phyllorhynchus decurtatus nubilis* (photo by David G. Campbell)

As mentioned above, the captive maintenance of this species has not proven easy. Certainly, it has been maintained, as have other small desert snakes, in relatively small cages (such as 10-gallon aquariums) and in relatively simple desert setups. However, even though the snakes appear to remain healthy, they usually refuse to eat in captivity and rapidly decline. The pattern that emerges when examining the literature and speaking to snake keepers is that they either refuse to eat entirely, or that they eat several times and then stop. This has certainly been our experience. Therefore, it is difficult to state with a great deal of certainty exactly what the proper diet or captive environment is for this species. See the discussion under saddled leafnose snakes.

At the present time, we believe that the desert setup discussed in the general care section is appropriate for this species, but we cannot be sure. Judging from the activity patterns of captives, they hide by day under rocks or other objects placed in the cage and emerge at night, just as wild members of this species do. This would at least suggest we are creating a reasonable captive environment. However, consistent feeding behavior has not been observed in this arrangement.

One arrangement that has worked slightly better is to set one of these snakes up in a colony of geckos. If there is some moist soil in the cage, the geckos will deposit their eggs, which the snakes then consume. It is interesting to note that the adult geckos in these cages respond to the approach of one of these snakes by waving the tail back and forth as if to attract the snake's attention, a behavior considered appropriate for the geckos. However, the snakes seem to ignore these geckos and often constantly patrol the perimeter of their cages apparently seeking only to escape. Perhaps a larger cage or a cage with a deeper layer of sand would be beneficial for these snakes, but this is unknown.

We have observed one of these snakes eating the egg of another lizard, namely that of a five-lined skink, *Eumeces fasciatus*. Also, like the saddled leafnose, a number of these snakes have voluntarily swallowed prekilled ground skinks, *Scincella lateralis*, but only when the small skinks have been gently placed in their mouths. Everything else we have offered up to the time of this writing has been refused. This has included spiny lizards, *Sceloporus*, anoles, *Anolis*, smaller snakes, *Tropidoclonion*, and insects (wax worms and crickets). Others have reported limited success with the side-blotched lizard, *Uta stansburiana*, or with crickets and mealworms.

SPECIES: *Phyllorhynchus decurtatus*, Spotted Leafnose Snake
MAINTENANCE DIFFICULTY INDEX: 5+ (1 = easiest, 5 = most difficult)
AVERAGE SIZE: 30–50 cm (12–20 inches)
FOOD: Gecko eggs?
CAGE SIZE: 10-gallon aquarium
SUBSTRATE: Sand?
VENTRAL HEAT: No?
UV LIGHT: No, but an incandescent bulb is helpful
TEMPERATURE RANGE: 18.8–34.7°C (66–94.5°F)
SPECIAL CONSIDERATIONS: Captive requirements still poorly understood. Diet difficult to
   provide. Serious snake keepers only. See text.

Spotted leafnose snakes have been compared to the scarlet snakes of the eastern United States. Indeed, their apparent preference for reptile eggs is similar. However, at this time it appears they are much less likely to eat in captivity than scarlet snakes. Some may drink scrambled chicken egg when it is placed in the cage.

To our knowledge, breeding has not yet been accomplished in captivity, although females gravid at the time of capture have deposited eggs.

Captive brumation has been successfully accomplished by maintaining these snakes in their regular cages and dropping the temperature down to 4–18°C (40–65°F).

As with the saddled leafnose, neither Slavens and Slavens (1991) nor Snider and Bowler (1992) listed a captive longevity or even a single specimen in captivity.

Pituophis catenifer
Gopher Snake and Bullsnake

This large widespread snake is one of the most familiar snakes in both the United States and Canada, not just to herpetoculturists but to the general public. It is to western snakes what the corn snake has been to eastern snakes: a popular and easily recognizable animal that is generally accepted as being a "good" snake because of its rodent-destroying ability. And do they ever destroy rodents! Even small captives of this species can put away eight mice per week, and larger ones even more. Van Denburgh (1922) mentioned one of these snakes containing 35 pink mice. Needless to say, these bold good-feeding snakes have also become favorites among herpetoculturists. Like the corn snakes in the east, their good appetites and adaptable nature make them great first snakes (even though some may be aggressive at first).

San Diego Gopher Snake, *Pituophis catenifer annectans* (photo by Sean McKeown)

The gopher snake is a large snake, ranging 90–275 cm (36–110 inches) in length. These snakes are tan to yellowish, sometimes reddish orange in background color with large blotches, usually of dark brown or reddish brown. The scales are strongly keeled.

There are six subspecies in the area covered by this book. These include the bullsnake, *P. c. sayi*, and the five gopher snakes: the Great Basin gopher snake, *P. c. deserticola*, the Sonoran gopher snake, *P. c. affinis*, the Pacific gopher snake, *P. c. catenifer*, the San Diego gopher snake, *P. c. annectens*, and the Santa Cruz gopher snake, *P. c. pumilis*. Together, these subspecies occupy a remarkably large geographic area, being found in every state west of the Mississippi (except for Louisiana, which is occupied by the closely related pine snake), and the southern part of Canada's three westernmost provinces. About 90% of this range is occupied by the bullsnake and the first two subspecies listed. The other three are found in California, Oregon, and Washington. This species also extends far into Mexico.

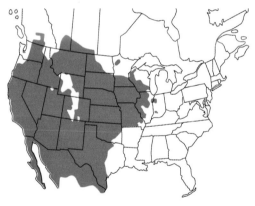

Pituophis catenifer

As might be expected from such a wide-ranging species, the habitats occupied, diet consumed, reproductive cycle, and thermal ecology vary considerably from area to area. Nevertheless, we will try to summarize some of the natural history of this intensively studied snake in order to assist the keeper in developing a rational approach to maintenance and breeding.

An adaptable snake, the gopher snake survives in a wide variety of habitats. It has been reported from plains, prairies, brushlands, forests, deserts, and even areas of intensive agriculture and human habitation (Wright and Wright, 1957; Fowlie, 1965; Linder and Fichter, 1977; Stebbins, 1985; Hudson, 1985; Baxter and Stone, 1985; Tennant, 1984, 1985; Conant and Collins, 1991; Degenhardt et al., 1996). Throughout their range, these snakes seem particularly common around agricultural areas, especially near old houses, barns, and junk piles. We have found then in old junk piles from Kankakee County, Illinois, to Hidalgo County, Texas.

The diet of this snake in the wild has included a wide variety of food items including mice, rats, pocket gophers, chipmunks, ground squirrels, bats, lizards, birds and their eggs, and occasionally turtle eggs and frogs. Lizards and insects are reported to be taken by wild juveniles (Wright and Wright, 1957; Fowlie, 1965; Webb, 1970; Linder and Fichter, 1977; Switak, 1984; Baxter and Stone, 1985; Hudson, 1985; Tennant, 1984, 1985; Stebbins, 1985; Conant and Collins, 1991; Collins, 1993). One study, however, found that adult gopher snakes from the northern Great Basin primarily ate side-blotched lizards, *Uta stansburiana* (Brown and Parker, 1982). Several apparent attempts at cannibalism have also been reported, but usually in situations where feeding on more normal food items may have just occurred (Mitchell, 1986). In general, these snakes are powerful constrictors with an apparent preference for warm-blooded prey.

Body temperatures measured in active individuals from Kansas were 19.5–32.4°C (67.1–90.3°F) with an average temperature of 28°C (82.4°F) (Fitch, 1956). Brattstrom (1965) reported an activity range of 16.4–34.6°C (61.5–94.2°F) with a critical thermal maximum of 40.5°C (105°F). This species is considered to be primarily diurnal, but it has been observed frequently at dusk and occasionally at night.

This is one of the few species of snakes where brumation temperatures of wild specimens have actually been measured. Schroder (1950) measured the temperature in an Indiana brumaculum containing five of these snakes and seven racers and found it to be 6.7°C (44.0°F).

Suspected predators of this species include

Sonoran Gopher Snake, *Pituophis catenifer affinis* (photo by David G. Campbell)

birds of prey and carnivorous mammals. Young may be preyed upon by ophiophagous snakes. We observed a caracara eating a bullsnake in a roadside ditch south of Hebronville, Texas, but were unable to determine if the bird had killed the snake or just scavenged a road kill.

Mating has been observed to occur primarily in April and May, with most clutches being laid in June, July, and August (Fitch, 1970; Linder and Fichter, 1977; Tennant, 1984, 1985; Baxter and Stone, 1985; Stebbins, 1985). Egg laying generally follows mating by 37–40 days, and

Great Basin Gopher Snake, *Pituophis catenifer deserticola* (photo by David G. Campbell)

Santa Cruz Island Gopher Snake, *Pituophis catenifer pumilus* (photo by Patrick Briggs)

the incubation period of these eggs has ranged from 52 to 85 days (Wright and Wright, 1957; Fitch, 1970; Mattison, 1988), usually 59 days at 28°C (82°F) (Mattison, 1988). Clutch size for the species ranges from 2 to 24 (Stebbins, 1985). Fitch (1985) noted that clutch size tended to be higher in central populations (bullsnakes) and lower toward each coast (gopher snakes and pine snakes). In addition, they tend to show a decrease in clutch size from north to south. Those from the Great Plains produced 5–22 eggs with an average of 12.9. Those from the Great Basin (Utah) produced 4–15 eggs with an average of 8.4, while those from the west coast produced 3–19 eggs with an average of 8.5. Pacific gopher snakes from northern California averaged 9.3 eggs per clutch while San Diego gopher snakes from southern California averaged 8.1 eggs per clutch. Mating and egg laying are thought to occur every year, but females may occasionally skip a year (Fitch, 1970).

Hatchlings range 26–45 cm (10.25–17.7 inches) in length, usually not quite as large as pine snake hatchlings (Wright and Wright, 1957). Wild snakes are thought to reach sexual maturity in 3 or 4 years (Fitch, 1970).

The basic cage setup will work well for this species. This, of course, includes artificial carpet/turf, a hide box, and a heat source. Heating pads, heat tapes, and strips work well; try to avoid the hot rocks for such a large stout-bodied snake. A heavy water bowl (or at least one that is not easily tippable) with clean fresh water should be provided at all times. Plastic plants and a heavy branch or a rock are nice cage accessories. An incandescent bulb is an excellent light (and additional heat) source. Ultraviolet light is not considered necessary for this largely diurnal snake, but see the discussion under lighting in the general care section as it may be helpful for a poorly eating snake.

Bullsnake, *Pituophis catenifer sayi* (photo by David G. Campbell)

SPECIES: *Pituophis catenifer*, Gopher Snake and Bullsnake
MAINTENANCE DIFFICULTY INDEX: 1 (1 = easiest, 5 = most difficult)
AVERAGE SIZE: 90–275 cm (36–110 inches)
FOOD: Mice, rats, pocket gophers, lizards
CAGE SIZE: 20-gallon long aquarium or display case
SUBSTRATE: Indoor-outdoor carpet or artificial turf
VENTRAL HEAT: Yes
UV LIGHT: Not essential but helpful. Incandescent bulb strongly advisable
TEMPERATURE RANGE: 25–30°C (77–86°F)
SPECIAL CONSIDERATIONS: Large size. Some may be aggressive. Likely to be parasitized
  if wild-caught. Otherwise excellent pet in many cases.

One anorectic Great Basin gopher snake began feeding immediately after a UV light source was added to its enclosure (Campbell, pers. comm., 1992).

Air temperatures of 25–30°C (77–86°F) have been reported as suitable for daytime temperatures during the active season; however, these snakes can tolerate a much wider fluctuation of temperatures, especially if they have access to a ventral heat source. Those in our care seemed to thrive at temperatures fluctuating from 27 to 35°C (80 to 95°F) daily during the summer. Brumation temperatures for those same snakes were 3–18°C (38–65°F) for 4–5 months.

We believe the minimum cage size for all but the hatchlings should be a 20-gallon long aquarium, with those over 5 feet being housed in display cases with the cage length either exceeding or closely approximating the snake's length. Hatchlings and small specimens will do well in 10-gallon aquariums but will rapidly outgrow them.

As mentioned above, these snakes are voracious mammalvores. In the wild, adults have been known to consume mice, rats, small rabbits, birds and their eggs, and occasionally lizards, but in captivity keepers should try to avoid feeding anything but captive-bred mice, rats, or chicks since parasitism may be controlled in this manner. Wild-caught members of this species are likely to be parasitized and the type of parasite may vary from place to place. Two specimens from Arizona that were examined by the authors contained an unidentified

tapeworm, while nematodes have been found in snakes from Texas. This means a fecal exam (or preferably repeated fecal exams) should be performed on recently captured specimens in order to determine the proper deworming agent or agents. In addition, these snakes will readily take prekilled mice and rats which makes food storage and quality control of the diet even easier.

Some specimens, however rare, may present a problem feeding in captivity. Patience will usually suffice in getting these animals to start feeding. However, Switak (1984) suggested offering white-footed deer mice, *Peromyscus* sp., or meadow voles, *Microtus* sp. As the snake is swallowing one of these, Switak advises guiding a prekilled domestic mouse into the snake's mouth right behind the wild rodent with a long pair of forceps. After this is done several times, the snake may accept the domestic mice regularly.

Brumation is strongly recommended for this species for the usual reasons: many stop eating anyway during the winter (some as early as August) and the cooler temperatures allow gamete maturation which improves breeding success. They can be easily brumated in their regular cages; no special modifications are necessary. Just make sure they have plenty of water available. See the general care section on brumation.

Like the corn snake, this species has been bred in captivity perhaps thousands of times. Mating usually occurs readily in the spring following brumation, when the female is placed in with the male for several days. The large eggs are usually laid 1–2 months later and these should be removed and incubated in the usual manner. See the section on the care of the eggs.

Captive-born hatchlings are usually voracious eaters of pinkies, however, an occasional snake will hold out for a lizard. Even these can be rapidly switched to pinkies using scent transfer techniques. They grow rapidly in captivity and some may reach sexual maturity in as few as 2 years, especially if brumation is skipped the first year.

Overall, these snakes are adaptable excellent captives that usually have a reasonably calm personality if they are raised in captivity. The young may be a bit nervous and nippy at first but generally calm down in time. In zoo settings they can be safely housed with rattlesnakes to show the difference.

The captive longevity for this species has been reported at 33 years and 10 months (Snider and Bowler, 1992). This record is held by a Great Basin gopher snake, but other members of the species have survived long times in captivity as well. The records for each subspecies are as follows: bullsnake, 22 years and 5 months; San Diego gopher snake, 20 years and 5 months; Pacific gopher snake, 17 years and 10 months; and Sonoran gopher snake, 15 years (Snider and Bowler, 1992).

Pituophis melanoleucus
Eastern Pine Snake

The eastern pine snake is one of the largest snakes in the eastern half of the United States, with the average adult measuring 122–168 cm (48–66 inches) and the record being 228.6 cm (90 inches) (Conant and Collins, 1991). There are four subspecies in the area covered by this book, and they vary considerably in color and pattern. These are the northern pine snake, *P. m. melanoleucus*, the Florida pine snake, *P. m. mugitus*, the black pine snake, *P. m. lodingi*, and the Louisiana pine snake, *P. m. ruthveni*. Collins (1997) and Crother et al. (2000) list this one as a separate species. The closely related bullsnake/gopher snake, *Pituophis catenifer*, extends as far eastward as Indiana.

The northern pine snake, which has the greatest contrast between the dark blotches and background color (the species' name translated means "black/white"), is found in widely separated populations in southern New Jersey, western central Virginia, Kentucky, Tennessee, North Carolina, South Carolina, northern Georgia, and central Alabama. The Florida pine snake is found from southern South Carolina through southern Georgia and almost all of Florida. In the panhandle of Florida, the Florida pine snakes get progressively darker as one travels west until they are nearly solid black.

Pituophis melanoleucus

The snakes in southern Alabama and Mississippi have been named accordingly, and have been described as a separate subspecies, *P. m. lodingi*. The Louisiana pine snake is found in western central Louisiana and eastern Texas, and is distinguished by the faded brownish blotches on the front half and sharply contrasting blotches on the back half. This is the smallest and rarest of the pine snakes.

All subspecies are found in dry, sandy-soiled, pine or oak dominated habitat (Kelly et al., 1936; Wright and Wright, 1957; Mount, 1975; Ashton and Ashton, 1981; Dundee and

Florida Pine Snake, *Pituophis melanoleucus mugitus* (photo by David G. Campbell)

Rossman, 1989). Those in western Virginia have been reported to occur in mountainous areas, however (Wright and Wright, 1957; Linzey and Clifford, 1981; Mitchell, 1994).

These snakes are thought to be primarily diurnal, and active pine snakes in New Jersey had cloacal temperatures measuring 22–34°C (71.6–93.2°F) (Zappalorti et al., 1983), however, some authors have reported quite a bit of nocturnal activity (Linzey and Clifford, 1981; Tennant, 1984).

The preferred food of the pine snake appears to be small mammals (particularly pocket gophers but also mice, rats, squirrels, moles, and rabbits), birds and their eggs, and occasionally lizards (Wright and Wright, 1957; Mount, 1975; Brown, 1979; Ashton and Ashton, 1981; Linzey and Clifford, 1981; Tennant, 1984; Palmer and Braswell, 1995), although Tennant (1984) reported three specimens which had the remains of amphibians in their stomachs.

Predators of this snake are known to include skunks, foxes, shrews, and humans (Burger et al., 1992). Suspected predators of this species include carnivorous mammals, birds of prey, and the young ophiophagous snakes.

Mating is known to occur in the early spring with 3–14 large eggs being laid in late June or July (Fitch, 1970; Zappalorti et al., 1983). These eggs have been reported to hatch within 64–79 days, although a range of 50–100 days is possible (Ernst and Barbour, 1989). The hatchlings are large, usually measuring 30–48 cm (12–19 inches) in length (Behler and King, 1979; personal observations), but we have observed several hatchling Florida pine snakes over 51 cm (20 inches) in TL.

The pine snake is actually a very easy snake to keep and breed in captivity, although the Florida pine may be a little trickier to breed at times. It can have a very nervous disposition at first (sometimes longer), however, which may prevent eating for a long time. Given time, a place to hide, and a large, warm, dry cage (the basic cage setup works excellently), they will readily adapt and begin eating. Mice, hamsters, rats, gerbils, and chicks are all taken readily. Some will even take chicken eggs if warmed up and rubbed with a chick. A small water dish will suffice, but it should be a heavy one so as not to be tipped over. Artificial carpet/turf or aspen, cypress, or pine mulch works very well.

A heating pad turned on low and placed under one side of the cage is an excellent idea, even in the winter when the snake is brumating. Many snakes seem to do quite well without ventral heat, but it is recommended. (See under heating and winter cooldown [brumation/hibernation] in the general care section for details.)

Keep only one snake per cage as a general rule to avoid disturbing their appetites, and handle the nervous ones as infrequently as possible.

As with most other eastern snakes, successful breeding is usually tied to brumation. Females from the northern part of the range should always be placed in with the male after warming and shedding, with the female's skin.

According to some authors, Florida pine snakes may breed in the winter (Ashton and Ashton, 1981). However, a pair of captive Florida pine snakes which we housed together for nearly 2 years under natural lighting in northern Florida mated on 16 and 17 May, and the female laid 5 huge eggs on 5 July. The eggs weighed approximately 100 grams and were just over 10 cm (4 inches) long! A wild female from the same area which was captured the same week also deposited 5 eggs. Pine snakes have been observed to lay eggs in late June or early July over much of their range from New Jersey through Virginia, North Carolina, and Florida (Zappalorti et al., 1983; Mitchell, 1994; Palmer and Braswell, 1995; personal observations).

The Jacksonville Zoological Park has had similar success with their Florida pine snakes. Dr. Jack Meyer, former Herpetological Curator at the park, reported that their pine snakes mated in late March and early April and laid eggs in May; hatching occurred in July. Clutch sizes ranged from 5 to 7 eggs. Interestingly, indigo snakes housed in the same facility under the same environmental conditions mated in December, January, and February. (They are true winter breeders. See the section on indigo snakes.)

A pair of fourth generation black pine snakes, the great grandparents of which were collected in extreme western Florida by Roger Conant, mated in April and the female laid 5 large eggs on 25 May. Four of these hatched on 14–15 August, an incubation period of 80 days. One of these eggs appeared to have heavy fungal growth over half of its surface. The neonate from this eggs weighed only 19 grams and was solid black. The other 3 neonates, the eggs of which were not infected with fungus, weighted 58, 59.5, and 63 grams. These 3 neonates had dark blotches on a lighter background; one had a very dark background (slate gray) with black blotches and the other two had tan backgrounds with dark brown blotches. The small solid black snake was a male, as was the largest and lightest-colored neonate. One female had a slate gray background and the black blotches, and the other female was tan-colored with brown blotches. Thus, the sex ratio was 1:1 and the color pattern did not appear to be sex-linked, based upon these few specimens. The TLs of these snakes were 35.6, 39.4, 46.4, and 47 cm (14, 15.5, 18.25, and 18.5 inches), with the smallest being the black one described above. The observation of the small neonate

---

SPECIES: *Pituophis melanoleucus*, Eastern Pine Snake
MAINTENANCE DIFFICULTY INDEX: 2 (1 = easiest, 5 = most difficult)
AVERAGE SIZE: 122–168 cm (48–66 inches)
FOOD: Mice, hamsters, gerbils, rats, and chicks
CAGE SIZE: Display case or homemade cage 5–8′ long
SUBSTRATE: Artificial turf, indoor-outdoor carpet, or newspaper
VENTRAL HEAT: Yes
UV LIGHT: Not essential but may be helpful
TEMPERATURE RANGE: 25–30°C (77–86°F)
SPECIAL CONSIDERATIONS: Can have nervous disposition. Often undergoes prolonged
    periods without eating. Babies may be tough to get started. Permit required in some states.

hatching from a severely fungal-infected egg is fascinating. It would suggest that the fungus was robbing nutrition from the embryo, since its egg was the same size as that of the other snakes and the snakes all hatched at the same time. It is not known whether the fungus affected the color pattern, although this has been reported in corn snakes (Love, pers. comm., 1998). It is important to note that the parents of these snakes were very dark but not solid black (some remnants of a pattern remained).

These observations suggest that the clutch size and the breeding times observed were not purely artifacts of the captive environment. Perhaps pine snakes from southern Florida start breeding a little earlier, because the spring starts earlier there but in our opinion they are still basically spring breeders.

Therefore, it is recommended that spring breeding be attempted for all captive pine snakes, even those from Florida (if you possess a permit).

The eggs are hatched in the usual manner (see under care of the eggs in the general care section) and the babies will usually feed on pinkies readily. Offer them food even before they shed for the first time; many will surprise you and eat right away. Remember to separate the babies and cater to their nervous dispositions.

The key to doing well with this species is to provide them with at least a short brumation period. Even the young, which are fairly large at birth, seem to lose their appetites in the winter and will do much better if given a short cool rest with no food.

Pine snakes seem to have very few problems in captivity, and since they breed readily, herpetologists should be encouraged to keep and breed this species. The Florida pine snake and the northern pine snake are protected by law in some states, however, and therefore cannot be kept without a permit in those states. As with the indigo snake, their habitat is being rapidly destroyed and the state agencies which are strictly prohibiting their captive propagation may be ensuring their extinction rather than their continued existence. We should strive to preserve them in the wild through conserving their natural habitat, but it would be prudent to also allow herpetoculturists to provide a "back-up" system.

These snakes are frequently parasitized. All four specimens that were examined from northern Florida contained reptile whipworms, *Capillaria* sp., and two of those examined contained roundworms, *Ophidascaris* sp., so they should be dewormed when first captured.

The disposition of these snakes in captivity is very variable. Some adapt fantastically, seem to enjoy handling, and never bite, while others remain extremely aggressive and irritable. Captive-born and -raised individuals tend to mellow out nicely. They also seen to be fairly neat snakes. Given a long cage, they will usually defecate in the same corner every time (the opposite side from where they spend most of their time).

One of these snakes was maintained in captivity over 20 years (Snider and Bowler, 1992).

Ramphotyphlops braminus
Brahminy Blind Snake

The Brahminy or island blind snake is a small dark brown to black-colored snake that looks at first glance like an earthworm. Upon closer examination, one can see the blunt head, scales, laterally located nares (nostrils), and of course, a flicking tongue. Eyes are difficult to visualize, as is a neck, in these very thin dark snakes. There are no scutes (or large belly scales), since all of the scales are small, both dorsally and ventrally, presumably due to the burrowing nature of this animal. Other features of this snake which are also seen in other burrowing snakes are a spine on the tip of the tail and a lower jaw that is deeply inset or countersunk.

This is North America's only established introduced snake species, most likely because it is small, adaptable, and parthenogenetic, i.e., an all-female species, where individuals reproduce

Ramphotyphlops braminus

Their preferred habitat appears to be in shaded areas with loose moist soil. They have also been found under surface objects such as rocks and logs. Ernst and Barbour (1989) summarized the ability of this snake to get into buildings and municipal water supplies through small cracks. They even mention reports of this snake attempting to get in the ears of people sleeping on the ground, and cite Daniel (1983).

The food of the Brahminy blind snake is known to include insects such as beetles, termites, ants and probably their eggs, small caterpillars, and possibly even small earthworms. This is the only snake known to engage in coprophagy, or the ingestion of feces; one was observed eating the feces of a caterpillar (Annandale, 1907).

by producing genetic duplicates of themselves. They appear to have been introduced into North America and many other areas around the world in potted plants.

Their range within the United States is known to include Dade and Monroe Counties in southeastern Florida, and Pinellas County in western (midpeninsular) Florida. However there may be populations elsewhere in the state of Florida, and other southern subtropical areas including southern Texas and southern California. In fact, this species was recently reported from Cameron County in southern Texas (Bartlett, 1998) and in southern Georgia near the town of Jesup (Jensen, 2000).

Reproduction of this species is poorly understood. These snakes are believed to lay clutches of 2–8 eggs, and they may do so at any time of the year. How many clutches they may lay per year is unknown. The only reported incubation period for these eggs is 38 days (Cagle, 1946). Cagle observed that a clutch of 3 eggs was laid on 21 April and 2 of these eggs hatched on 29 May. These hatchlings measured 5.3 and 6.2 cm (2.1 and 2.4 inches) in TL.

In captivity, this species may be maintained as other small woodland species in a wet/dry cage or a three-layer cage with soil instead of

Brahminy Blind Snake, *Ramphotyphlops braminus* (photo by Sean McKeown)

sand. Water should be added to the soil regularly in order to maintain its moisture level. Heat from above in the form of a small wattage incandescent bulb may be helpful. Of course, good ventilation of any cage with a moist substrate is absolutely critical, so a screen top is advisable. Termites and other insects may be added regularly or a colony may be maintained. Watch out for crickets; large crickets will not be consumed by this snake and may attack the snake.

Overall, this is a fascinating little snake and it will undoubtedly become the object of more study as it becomes more common in Florida and elsewhere.

Regina alleni
Striped Crayfish Snake

The striped crayfish snake is a dark brown snake above with one broad pale yellow stripe along each side. Closer examination reveals three darker brown stripes running longitudinally in the dark brown area along the sides and back. The scales are smooth, which gives the snake a glistening appearance. The belly is yellow to orangish pink and there may be pigmentation directly in the center of each ventral scute. These are not large snakes although they may be quite heavy-bodied, with the average individual measuring 33–51 cm (13–20 inches) and the record being 65.4 cm (25.7 inches) in length (Conant and Collins, 1991).

These snakes range over much of peninsular Florida and extreme southern Georgia. They

Regina alleni

seem to thrive in floating vegetation and hence are found in ditches, swamps, sloughs, marshes, ponds, lakes, and bogs. Water hyacinths appear especially favored (Godley, 1980; Ernst and Barbour, 1989; personal observations).

The preferred food of the striped crayfish snake is crayfish (Franz, 1977; Godley, 1980; Ashton and Ashton, 1981), although other food items are taken on occasion. Dragonfly larvae and freshwater shrimp are also readily taken by neonates and juveniles. We also observed, as did Van Hyning (1932), that some specimens will consume dwarf sirens, although not as consistently as crayfish. Crayfish were found in the stomachs of wild specimens at water temperatures of 15.5–27.4°C (60–81.3°F), suggesting that this might be the preferred temperature range (Godley, 1980).

Predators of this species are numerous. Juveniles are preyed upon by adult crayfish, and adults are known to be included in the diet of other snakes including kingsnakes and cottonmouths, birds including great blue herons and egrets, and mammals such as river otters and raccoons (Godley, 1982). Alligators are also suspected of being predators of this species.

Mating is thought to occur in the spring but this is still largely unknown. From 4 to 34 young are born sometime between May and September (Duellman and Schwartz, 1958; Fitch, 1970; Ashton and Ashton, 1981). The young measure 15.9–18 cm (6.25–7.0 inches) at birth (Conant and Collins, 1991).

The striped crayfish snake is to aquatic snakes what the scarlet snake is to terrestrial snakes—one of the most difficult eastern North American snakes to maintain in captivity. Both the captive environment and the preferred food are difficult to provide. In addition, they are extremely susceptible to skin infections ("blister disease") in captivity, and will not take their food dead, making quality control of the diet

A crayfish is captured with a quick strike and wrapped up in one or more coils to immobilize its powerful claws and tail. This striped crayfish snake will then swallow it tailfirst. The whole process may take 15–20 minutes and occurs entirely underwater.

difficult, with parasitism much more likely. They are fond of burrowing in regular aquarium gravel and may drown if this is used as an aquatic substrate. They will dehydrate rapidly and refuse to eat in a regular cage setup. In spite of all these problems, captive maintenance is possible as described below.

Before proceeding, read the section on the black swamp snake. As mentioned in that chapter, their natural environment and this snake's are very similar, and so are their problems in captivity.

The captive environment which has worked well for the authors is as follows:

1. Use no substrate.
2. Into an empty 10–20-gallon aquarium pour 3–6 gallons of swamp tea (see below).
3. Oxygenate the water.
4. Keep a heating pad turned on low under the aquarium, or a water heater in the aquarium to keep the base water temperature no lower than 27.7–28.8°C (82–84°F).
5. Put a 60-watt bulb in a reflector over the screen at the top of the aquarium and turn it on about 12 hours per day. This will raise the tea temperature into the mid 90s during the day.
6. Add some plastic plants and a piece of driftwood for the snake to hide among when it is in the water, or bask on when it is out.
7. Add 2.5–7.5 cm (1–3 inches) of cypress mulch to a wide plastic container and place it on the tea to form a floating cypress island. Add some plastic plants to the mulch.
8. Place one to two bricks lengthwise in one end to provide more cover for the snake and allow "cornering areas" where it can trap the crayfish.
9. Buy and install a thermometer to monitor the temperature.

(See the photograph of this setup.)

Directions for Swamp Tea

Six tea bags are placed in 1.5 quarts of water. Bring the water to a boil for about 3 minutes, then allow it to cool. Add to this solution enough water to bring the total to 3 gallons. This produces about a one-third strength tea solution with a pH of about 6.4 (depending upon the kind of tea and the acidity of your water) which very closely approximates the acidity of the swamps from which we have removed these snakes (around 6.2).

Striped Crayfish Snake, *Regina alleni* (photo by David G. Campbell)

Compare the acidity of this solution with normal tap water, which in most areas is around or above pH 7 (7.4 in our area). Thus, the tea solution is 10 times more acidic than tap water. The benefits of the tea solution are twofold. Not only does it help to control infection in these aquatic snakes, but it also provides them with a sense of security which reduces stress considerably. The only drawbacks so far have been reduced visibility (the keeper can't see the snake as well, just as the snake can't see the keeper) and some residue on the sides of the aquarium that will eventually come off. Change the swamp tea every 1–2 weeks or top off with tea solution as needed to maintain the acidity. *HIGH TEMPERATURES AND HIGH ACIDITY MUST BE STRICTLY CONTROLLED FOR THIS SPECIES OR THEY WILL GET SICK AND PERISH.*

The original idea to use tea as a medium for these snakes apparently came from that great herpetologist Ross Allen, but Florida Game and Fresh Water Fish Commission biologist Paul Moler uncovered this information and shared it with us. The concentration of tea used and the rest of the cage design came from trial and error.

An alternative to using no substrate and floating cypress islands is to use large smooth pebbles steeped up to form a dry area on one side, with a little pile of cypress mulch on top. But it has been our experience that this design does not work as well as the former design.

Once set up properly, the striped crayfish snake is a voracious eater of crayfish. As mentioned above, however, it will usually not take dead crayfish, which is a major drawback since food cannot be stored for long periods of time and parasite control becomes almost impossible. Of course, one could attempt to raise "clean" crayfish and maintain them alive until needed, but for most people this is not practical. Usually, procuring food means visiting your local swamps, streams, or drainage ditches, and this can be time-consuming. These snakes will usually eat twice per week. We use an oxygenated container to keep the crayfish in until they are needed. Other items are hardly ever taken in captivity by adults, although dwarf

SPECIES: *Regina alleni*, Striped Crayfish Snake
MAINTENANCE DIFFICULTY INDEX: 5 (1 = easiest, 5 = most difficult)
AVERAGE SIZE: 33–51 cm (13–20 inches)
FOOD: Crayfish, dragonfly larvae
CAGE SIZE: 10-gallon aquarium
SUBSTRATE: Swamp tea, floating cypress mulch islands. See text.
VENTRAL HEAT: Unknown but probably helpful. Water must be heated. Need light from above.
UV LIGHT: Yes?
TEMPERATURE RANGE: 27–35°C (81–95°F) day; 25–28°C (77–82°F) night
SPECIAL CONSIDERATIONS: Food availability can be a big problem. They prefer live food. Usually eat under water. Will develop skin lesions if kept too cool.

sirens and frogs may be consumed by wild specimens occasionally. The young have a marked preference for and apparently a need for dragonfly larvae, which can be just as difficult to procure as crayfish. Thus, even if the snake cooperates, feeding this animal is far from easy in terms of the difficulty of providing enough food.

It is unlikely that these snakes brumate; however, a short period of cooler temperatures would more closely resemble natural conditions and probably increase the chances for breeding success. As with other members of this genus, brumation, if attempted, should be carried out in a separate aquarium with cypress mulch. A small water dish should be provided with the tea solution in it as these snakes will drink frequently. Keep at 1–15°C (33–59°F) for 2 months. WARNING: All temperature adjusting should occur after the snake has been removed from its usual cage and placed in the brumation cage. Lowering the temperature to

less than room temperature can quickly result in blister formation if the snake remains in water (or tea). At the first sign of blister disease put the snake back into its regular cage setup.

Captive breeding has not been reported, but one should attempt it as described in the general care section under breeding, following brumation. These snakes bear live young, which should be separated and raised in a similar environment to the adults. Remember that they prefer dragonfly larvae, but will take small crayfish.

Overall, this snake is a very time-consuming and difficult, but not impossible, snake to maintain in captivity. (See the section on the glossy crayfish snake for more suggestions that may be applicable to this species.) We still have a great deal to learn about the captive maintenance and breeding of this snake, and there may be many other techniques that work as well or better than those discussed here. An outdoor enclosure may provide the best results.

Regina grahamii
Graham's Crayfish Snake

Graham's crayfish snake is for all intents and purposes a western version of the queen snake. They are similar in appearance, behavior, habitat preference, and diet. In the few areas where their ranges overlap, they may be distinguished

from the queen snake by the absence of four dark lines on their ventral surface (Graham's water snakes generally have plain yellowish tan ventral scales, while the queen snakes have the stripes). Dorsally, these snakes are olive brown

Regina grahamii

to dark brown with a black-bordered light brown stripe middorsally and thick yellow stripes laterally.

These are not large snakes, with the record being only around 119 cm (47 inches). Common locally, they occupy a huge range in the central part of the United States from northern Iowa and Illinois southward to much of eastern Texas and Louisiana.

The preferred habitat of this species appears to be slow-moving bodies of water with soft muddy bottoms and numerous hiding areas along the edges (Ernst and Barbour, 1989). The soft bottoms allow the snakes to burrow, and they may create a submerged hollow in which they place their entire body, protruding only the head to breathe (Kofron and Dixon, 1980). They also use crayfish burrows in which to hide and hibernate.

The preferred diet of this species in the wild (and in captivity) is crayfish, particularly soft-shelled or newly molted crayfish, but in some areas (where crayfish have been thought to be scarce) frogs (cricket frogs, *Acris* sp., and possibly others), fish, salamanders, or snails have been reported as food (Strecker, 1927; Liner, 1954; Wright and Wright, 1957; Hall, 1969; Tennant, 1984). Shrimp may also be consumed in coastal areas (Behler and King, 1979).

Predators are known to include cottonmouths, large wading birds such as egrets and herons, hawks, and raccoons.

Body temperatures of active wild individuals of this species are 22–27°C (71.6–80.6°F) with an average of 25.8°C (78.6°F) (Mushinsky et al., 1980).

Mating has been observed to occur in April and May, with 6–39 live young (17.8–24.1 cm or 7–9.5 inches in length) being born from late July through September (Wright and Wright, 1957; Tennant, 1984; Ernst and Barbour, 1989).

Graham's Crayfish Snake, *Regina grahamii* (photo by David G. Campbell)

SPECIES: *Regina grahamii*, Graham's Crayfish Snake
MAINTENANCE DIFFICULTY INDEX: 5 (1 = easiest, 5 = most difficult)
AVERAGE SIZE: 45.7–71 cm (18–28 inches)
FOOD: Crayfish
CAGE SIZE: 10–20-gallon aquarium
SUBSTRATE: Swamp tea. See striped crayfish snake text.
VENTRAL HEAT: Yes
UV LIGHT: No, but an incandescent bulb is useful
TEMPERATURE RANGE: 22–27°C (71.6–80.6°F)
SPECIAL CONSIDERATIONS: Acidic tea medium may be necessary. Diet difficult to
  procure. Captive requirements still poorly understood.

As might be expected for these aquatic snakes, mating occurs in the water and usually occurs at night (Strecker, 1926; Curtis, 1949; Hall, 1969). Numerous males are often involved in a swarming-type behavior described for many garter snakes, but individual pairs have been observed (Tennant, 1984).

The young are believed to reach sexual maturity in 2 (males) or 3 (females) years (Hall, 1969; Tennant, 1984; Ernst and Barbour, 1989).

As mentioned above, these are aquatic crayfish-eating snakes and hence represent the same captive challenge as the other members of this genus. Like the queen snake, however, these snakes appear to have a greater tolerance for temperature and pH fluctuation in their captive environment than the glossy crayfish and the striped crayfish snakes do. Therefore, the swamp tea setup, discussed in detail in the section on the striped crayfish snake, is the indoor setup of choice at this time. Generally, several inches of the tea in a 10- or 20-gallon aquarium will work well. Plastic plants placed in and out of the water will add security and provide necessary resting and hunting areas, while bricks in the corners will provide trapping areas where these snakes may corner escaping crayfish. Floating wide-mouthed plastic containers with several inches of cypress mulch will form floating cypress mulch islands that will be used by these snakes on occasion. Driftwood is also an excellent addition to the enclosure, as these snakes are known to bask at times. The provision of an underwater hiding place is also beneficial, and the use of mud is

not entirely without merit although it makes visualization of the snake and cage cleaning more of a challenge. Also, the addition of a humidity box with sphagnum moss is very helpful. The snakes will spend a great deal of time there and less in the water, making the use of tea less necessary.

These snakes will consume crayfish, especially soft-shelled crayfish, in captivity. However, most of those in our care (from Texas) have not been good eaters, even when sufficient food is provided. In this respect, they differ from the glossy crayfish snake and the striped crayfish snake, which have both been voracious feeders in our care. In addition to this somewhat fastidious nature (at least initially) their food is difficult to provide in sufficient quantity unless one happens to live near a good crayfish source. Furthermore, they will not usually take dead crayfish in captivity, which makes parasite control and food storage very difficult. At the present time, we believe the average-sized snake of this species will consume 2–4 crayfish per week.

Brumation may represent a real problem for the average snake keeper. The reason is that these snakes are prone to dehydration if they are artificially brumated in mulch. Furthermore, if they are maintained in swamp tea enclosures, they may rapidly succumb to blister disease dermatitis at these low temperatures. At the time of this writing, we have used the artificial technique of brumating, but have used humidity boxes with semimoist sphagnum moss to prevent desiccation. Those in our care have been exposed to temperatures fluctuating from 3 to 10°C (37 to 50°F) for 3 months and appeared to tolerate these temperatures fairly well.

To our knowledge, captive breeding of long-term captives has not been accomplished, although females gravid at the time of capture have delivered live young.

It is important to note that these snakes appear particularly sensitive to various medications. One injected with a standard dose of Gentocin® (2.5 mg/kg) died soon after the injection. Three others sprayed with a water-based microencapsulated pyrethrin spray as a treatment for mites showed neurologic signs for days afterward. All of these snakes recovered, however.

These are nervous snakes and they do not seem to appreciate handling at all. Many will defecate when handled. They are fascinating to observe in captivity, however, and as we continue to study their captive requirements, we may learn easier and better ways to maintain them. Presently, we consider outdoor enclosures to be the most practical and the easiest approach for captive maintenance of these snakes. Snider and Bowler (1992) did not list a captive longevity for one of these snakes. At the time of this writing, several of these snakes had been in our care for 6 months. One of the closely related queen snakes has been reported to have been maintained for 19 years and 3 months, however. We still have a great deal to learn about the captive maintenance of these snakes.

Regina rigida
Glossy Crayfish Snake

The glossy crayfish snake is a relatively small dark brown snake with faint darker stripes on its back. The belly is generally plain yellow to orangish yellow with two longitudinal rows of half-moons. There are three subspecies which appear to have relatively minor differences in coloration or scalation. These are discussed in detail in field guides. (See Behler and King, 1979, or Conant and Collins, 1991). Like the other members of the genus, it appears to have thick spectacles, giving it a "goggle-eyed" appearance. We suspect that this may be an adaptation to allow these snakes to see better underwater, perhaps helping them deal with the refractive index of that medium as they hunt their wholly aquatic prey, namely crayfish. Another possibility is that these thick spectacles may help protect the snakes' eyes from being injured by their hard-shelled prey. Certainly, their teeth are highly evolved for grasping hard-shelled prey since they have been shown to be hinged and chisel-like (Rojas and Godley, 1979).

As mentioned above, these interesting little snakes are fairly small. They range in size from 36 to 1 cm (14 to 24 inches) with a record of 79.7 cm (31.4 inches) (Conant and Collins, 1991). They are widely distributed in the southeastern United States, ranging from coastal North Carolina southward through much of northern Florida, and westward to include southern Arkansas, southeastern Oklahoma, and eastern Texas. There is (or was recently) an isolated population in southeastern Virginia (Linzey and Clifford, 1981). Ernst and Barbour (1989) thought that this population was now extinct, but in 1991 several specimens were found, confirming the continued presence of a

Regina rigida

Glossy Crayfish Snake, *Regina rigida rigida* (photo by R. D. Bartlett)

population in New Kent County, Virginia (Mitchell, 1994).

These snakes are usually found in swamps, marshes, bogs, ditches, sloughs, ponds, or lakes, as well as streams throughout their range, especially inland (Mount, 1975; Ashton and Ashton, 1981; Tennant, 1984; Dundee and Rossman, 1989; Ernst and Barbour, 1989). Tennant (1984) also reported their presence in inundated rice fields. In these areas they are usually found in floating vegetation or on branches overhanging streams. They have also been commonly found under objects near the water's edge, particularly during the day or during periods of cooler weather.

The preferred food of the glossy crayfish snake appears to be hard-shelled crayfish, for which they seem especially well adapted; however, other aquatic invertebrates such as dragonfly larvae, as well as fish, frogs, and small sirens have been reported to be consumed (Clark, 1949; Huheey, 1959; Kofron, 1978; Ashton and Ashton, 1981). Dragonfly larvae seem especially important in the diet of young snakes (Brown, 1978; Ashton and Ashton, 1981; personal observations).

Known predators of this species include kingsnakes and bullfrogs (Viosca, 1926; Hensley, 1962). Humans are also responsible for a large number of deaths as these snakes often attempt to cross roads after heavy rainfall, and they are one of the more frequently found road kills in northern and central Florida.

Mating is thought to occur in the spring (Ernst and Barbour, 1989), with 6–16 young being born during midsummer to early fall (Ashton and Ashton, 1981; Dundee and Rossman, 1989). The young generally measure 15–22.7 cm (5.9–9 inches) in length (Ernst and Barbour, 1989; Conant and Collins, 1991).

The glossy crayfish snake is an aggressive, alert, and voracious predator of crayfish (all stages) and dragonfly larvae. It can be kept in a manner similar to the striped crayfish snake if one has a steady supply of these items. Other prey animals are not well accepted in captivity, although there are reports of frogs, sirens, and fish being found in the stomachs of wild-caught specimens. Food will be taken only in the water, even if it is just a shallow puddle. These snakes will usually not take dead crayfish since they rely heavily upon motion to home in on them. This is unfortunate since freezing would aid in the storage of food and possibly in parasite control. Generally, a crayfish is actively pursued, cornered, and grasped in the

SPECIES: *Regina rigida*, Glossy Crayfish Snake
MAINTENANCE DIFFICULTY INDEX: 5 (1 = easiest, 5 = most difficult)
AVERAGE SIZE: 36–61 cm (14–24 inches)
FOOD: Crayfish, dragonfly larvae
CAGE SIZE: 10–20-gallon long
SUBSTRATE: Swamp tea, aquatic cage. Floating cypress mulch islands. See striped crayfish
  snake text.
VENTRAL HEAT: Unknown but probably helpful. Water needs to be heated.
UV LIGHT: Yes?
TEMPERATURE RANGE: 25–35°C (77–95°F) night/day
SPECIAL CONSIDERATIONS: Food availability can be a big problem. They prefer live
  food and usually eat under water. Prone to skin lesions if kept too cool.

jaws much as any terrestrial snake would do, but entirely underwater. The snake then tightly coils around the crayfish, as if it were constricting it, and proceeds to swallow, almost invariably from the tail end. Presently, we suspect that this coiling action is not intended to suffocate the crayfish, but simply to immobilize the powerful tail and claws to prevent escape or injury to the snake. The snake may not breathe during the entire process. The striped crayfish snake eats in a similar manner.

Just as for the striped crayfish snake, the swamp tea needs to be only about 5.1–10.2 cm (2–4 inches) deep. Plastic plants, both in and out of the water, seem to be appreciated, as well as a branch to climb on. A UV light is probably beneficial, but an incandescent bulb for heat and light is absolutely essential, as is a water heater or heating pad under the aquarium (10–20-gallon aquariums work well).

These snakes will spend a tremendous amount of time in the water (months on end), only surfacing to breathe, or for an occasional visit to the mulch, and if not kept in an acidic warm medium like the tea solution described in the section on the striped crayfish snake, they will rapidly develop "blister disease," a superficial infection which can become systemic, eventually leading to respiratory signs and death. The tea can be changed every two weeks if the pH is kept between 6.0 and 6.5 and the temperature is kept above 26.7°C (80°F) (greater than 32.2°C [90°F] daytime, greater than 26.7°C [80°F] night). Usually, the pH of the setup described in the striped crayfish snake section will rise slowly to almost neutral after several weeks.

Shedding should occur monthly under the proper conditions, and will usually occur completely underwater. As with land snakes, a one-piece shed is usually the sign of a relatively healthy snake.

Brumate as described for the striped crayfish snake, using a humidity box.

To our knowledge, captive breeding has not been reported with this species. In the absence of any specific information, one should attempt breeding as mentioned in the general care section. Mating will most likely occur in the water right after brumation. Females are known to bear live young which can be cared for just like the adults, except that dragonfly larvae are an important part of their diet. They will also eat small crayfish, but there is some question as to whether a diet of crayfish alone is high enough in calcium or protein to allow normal growth.

House and feed singly or drowning may occur in a fight over food.

In our opinion, these snakes are not as difficult to maintain as the striped crayfish snakes are. They appear to be more tolerant of changes in the acidity and temperature, less prone to skin infections, and a little more aggressive at feeding time than the latter species. Still, they represent a tremendous challenge and much more work is needed on the captive maintenance technique for this species.

(See also the section on the black swamp snake.)

Regina septemvittata
Queen Snake

The queen snake is a medium-sized, fairly slim, dull, dark brown snake that may or may not have thin dark brown stripes dorsally. The belly is pale yellow to tan with four dark brown stripes and the chin and throat are usually yellowish tan-colored. These snakes usually range 38–61 cm (20–30 inches) in length with a record of 96.1 cm (36.25 inches) (Conant and Collins, 1991). Their geographic range includes a huge area from southwestern Ontario southward through western New York and Pennsylvania to the Florida panhandle, and westward to Michigan and Illinois southward to Mississippi. There is also a disjunct population in southwestern Missouri and northwestern Arkansas.

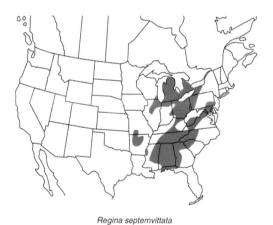

Regina septemvittata

The preferred habitat of the queen snake appears to be streams or brooks, although marshes, ponds, canals, and other open slow-moving bodies of water have been reported (Minton, 1972; Mount, 1975; Ashton and Ashton, 1981; Linzey and Clifford, 1981; Holman et al., 1990; Allen, 1992). Ernst and Barbour (1989) stress that clean unpolluted water is important. Most authors indicated that the presence of rocks and other hiding areas were important.

The preferred prey of the queen snake is newly molted crayfish, which they eat almost exclusively, although other items have been reported from wild specimens. These have included small hard-shelled crayfish, dragonfly larvae, fish, newts, toads, small frogs, and snails (Wood, 1949; Wright and Wright, 1957; Adler and Tilley, 1960; Minton, 1972; Branson and Baker, 1974; Linzey and Clifford, 1981).

Known predators include crayfish (juveniles), fish, hellbenders, other snakes such as black racers, and birds, e.g., the great blue heron (Minton, 1972; Branson and Baker, 1974; Palmer and Braswell, 1995). Suspected predators include rodents, raccoons, and otters (Branson and Baker, 1974).

Mating occurs primarily in the spring, but also in the fall, with up to 31 young (usually 10–20) being born in late summer or early fall (Fitch, 1970; Minton, 1972; Ashton and Ashton, 1981; Linzey and Clifford, 1981; Holman et al., 1990). The newborn snakes are 17.3–26.6 cm (6.8–10.5 inches) in length (Conant and Collins, 1991) and are more distinctly marked than the adults.

The queen snake represents another challenge in captive snake maintenance. This is not just because of the dietary specialization on soft-shelled crayfish, but also because of the tendency for this snake to develop skin lesions just like other members of this genus when kept improperly in captivity. In our experience, these have been the most fastidious difficult captives of the genus *Regina* and perhaps all eastern North American snakes.

The diet of this snake is actually not as strict as it is for other members of this genus. They will accept small fish, frogs, and even newts but apparently not as frequently as crayfish (Wright and Wright, 1957; Branson and Baker, 1974). As mentioned, their preferred food item is a newly molted (soft-shelled) crayfish. The food can be offered in one of two ways. First, live soft-shelled crayfish and minnows can be placed directly into the snake's cage, exactly as described for other crayfish snakes. Or second,

Queen Snake, *Regina septemvittata* (photo by David G. Campbell)

minnows can be placed in a shallow pan with an inch of water and several frozen (and thawed) soft-shelled crayfish. The pan can be placed into any cage arrangement, but works best when the snakes are housed in a dry cage (i.e., artificial carpet/turf and the basic cage amenities discussed in the general care section). This "standard" cage arrangement may help to prevent skin infections in the long run, if the snakes will accept it. We strongly recommend first trying the latter technique of using the pan for feeding and maintaining the snake in the typical cage arrangement. Use the other crayfish snake cage arrangement only with those individuals that refuse to eat from the pan. Fred Dulan of Indianapolis suggests that you not provide water to these snakes at all, except for that which they get in the feeding pan. He offers them the pan every 3 days. The latter technique also allows you to feed more of the common item, namely minnows, and less of the more difficult-to-find soft-shelled crayfish (which can be frozen). If using the other crayfish snake cage arrangement, you will probably need a larger supply of both soft-shelled crayfish and minnows. Also, more attention must be paid to the cleanliness of the water as well as the acidity and temperature. (See the discussion on this in the sections on the striped and glossy crayfish snakes.)

These snakes do bask and a UV light source and an incandescent bulb (for heat) are strongly recommended.

Brumation should be carried out in mulch exactly as described for the glossy and striped crayfish snakes, using humidity boxes with sphagnum moss. Do not offer food during this time. Do offer water.

To our knowledge, there is only one report of the queen snake being bred in captivity, and this was accomplished in an outdoor enclosure in England in the late 1800s. In the absence of any specific information, one should attempt breeding as discussed in the general care section, right after brumation. As with other members of this genus, the female bears live young, which can be cared for exactly as the adults, except that you may have to substitute feeder fish for minnows with the pan feeding technique. The babies should be offered the pan more frequently, as they are more likely to become dehydrated than the adults. Also remember that dragonfly larvae are considered an excellent food source for young members of this genus. Babies are at risk of drowning when first born and aquatic vegetation (real or artificial) is considered helpful in the aquarium at this time.

A 5–10-gallon aquarium is sufficient for the babies, while a 20 long or 30 long provides plenty of room for the adults. House individually. We still have a great deal to learn about captive maintenance of these snakes. John Murphy of Chicago says he has had a great deal of success with this species when boxes are provided for them to hide in. They spent much more time in these dry boxes and less in the water, which resulted in fewer skin problems.

We believe that the best enclosure for this species (and all members of this genus), however, is an outdoor enclosure with an artificial stream or waterfall. One pair of queen snakes was collected in late July in Cincinnati, Ohio. The female gave birth to 12 neonates the second week of August. The babies averaged 21.6 cm (8.5 inches) TL, with an average weight of 3 grams. These snakes were placed in a large outdoor enclosure with an artificial stream and overhanging branches (wax myrtles) on 14 August, 1998. Some of these snakes were collected periodically afterward. On 6 June, 1999, three males were collected and measured. Their weights were 11, 11.5, and 15 grams. Their lengths were 32.4, 34.3, and 40.6 cm (12.75, 13.5, and 16 inches). Their average TL was 35.8 cm (14.1 inches), and their average weight was 12.5 grams. One female found in early October 1999 weighed 36 grams and had a TL of 53.3

cm (21 inches). Another female captured on 2 November, 1999, weighed 23 grams and had a TL of 45.7 cm (18 inches) and a SVL of 35.6 cm (14 inches). This female had a stub tail, suggesting that she had survived a predation attempt, which was quite possible in an open snake enclosure. By 12 April, 2000, the latter two of the three males mentioned above weighed 18 and 27 grams respectively, and had TLs of 46.9 cm and 50.8 cm (18.5 and 20 inches) respectively. The female measured in October weighed 32 grams by 12 April, having lost 4 grams over the winter. At this time, her TL was exactly the same at it was in October—53.3 cm (21 inches). The female that was collected in November weighed 19 grams on 12 April, also having lost 4 grams during the winter, and also not demonstrating any change in length. The male that weighed 11.5 grams and measured 34.3 cm (13.5 inches) TL on 6 June was recaptured on 26 August. At that time he weighed 24 grams and measured 47.5 cm (18 inches) TL. When captured the following spring on 12 April, he weighed only 18 grams and measured 49.6 cm (18.5 inches) TL. He had lost 6 grams over the winter and had grown only 1.25 cm (0.5 inch). Thus, the snakes probably stopped feeding during the winter even though crayfish were available. One of these females gave birth to an undetermined number of neonates in June, 2001, suggesting that males and females reached sexual maturity by the beginning of their second year.

These snakes are extremely adept at hiding,

SPECIES: *Regina septemvittata*, Queen Snake
MAINTENANCE DIFFICULTY INDEX: 5 (1 = easiest, 5 = most difficult)
AVERAGE SIZE: 38–61 cm (15–24 inches)
FOOD: Soft-shelled crayfish, minnows, frogs(?). Crayfish must be soft-shelled (newly molted).
CAGE SIZE: 10-gallon aquarium
SUBSTRATE: Artificial turf, indoor-outdoor carpet (preferably), or aquatic setup. See striped crayfish snake text.
VENTRAL HEAT: Unknown but probably helpful
UV LIGHT: Yes?
TEMPERATURE RANGE: 20–26°C (68–79°F); 4–10°C (39–50°F) brumation.
SPECIAL CONSIDERATIONS: Food availability can be a big problem. Skin lesions are likely if water is too cool or dirty.

The remains of an adult queen snake that was eaten by a domestic "house" cat. Feral cats are extremely damaging to all small vertebrate populations, and should be controlled for both humane and ecological reasons. (photo by John Rossi)

and one of these snakes had remained hidden for 15 months before she was recaptured! From these observations, it appears that queen snakes may be successfully maintained in an outdoor snake enclosure, and grow at a rate that approximates that of wild specimens. Predation is a serious threat however. Our adults were killed by marauding house cats. This was prevented by screening in the top of the pen during July of 1999. Also, at least one juvenile was killed when it was sucked into the pump circulating the water for the stream. This was prevented by placing the pump in a mesh cage.

One of these snakes survived 19 years and 3 months in captivity at the Racine Zoo (Snider and Bowler, 1992).

Rhadinaea flavilata
Pine Woods Snake

The pine woods snake is a small orangish tan to brown-colored snake, with a darker head and a dark brown stripe running horizontally through the eye on each side. The belly and lip scales are plain white or yellow, which was the origin of the old species name, the yellow-lipped snake. They are smooth-scaled, which gives them a lustrous appearance.

As mentioned above, these are small snakes. They range 25–33 cm (10–13 inches) in length with a record of 40.3 cm (15.9 inches) (Conant and Collins, 1991). There are several disjunct populations ranging from the coastal plains of North Carolina southward to include much of Florida and westward to southern Alabama, Mississippi, and southeastern Louisiana. The

Rhadinaea flavilata

Pine Woods Snake, *Rhadinaea flavilata* (photo by David G. Campbell)

species appears to be locally abundant in suitable habitats and is found most frequently in areas classified as moist pine flatwoods (Mount, 1975; Ashton and Ashton, 1981; Dundee and Rossman, 1989; Conant and Collins, 1991; Palmer and Braswell, 1995). They are also occasionally found in hardwood hammocks in Florida and dry woodlands on coastal islands (Ashton and Ashton, 1981; Ernst and Barbour, 1989). These secretive semifossorial snakes usually spend most of their time under some cover such as leaf litter, fallen bark, logs, and recently, trash. In fact, we have never found a specimen on the surface or crossing a road in Florida, as we have so many other small species. Yet, they are commonly found around human habitation and populations apparently survive on very small patches of pine forest completely surrounded by development. The authors repeatedly collected adults and hatchlings on a 4-acre parcel of pine flatwoods that had been isolated by development in western Duval County for nearly 20 years. Some standing water with resident populations of anurans and ground skinks probably supported this population.

The preferred food of the pine woods snake has been reported to include treefrogs, *Hyla* sp., true frogs, *Rana* sp., cricket frogs, *Acris gryllus*, and ground skinks, *Scincella lateralis* (Myers, 1967; Mount, 1975) although sala-

manders have been reported (Myers, 1967; Ashton and Ashton, 1981). Wright and Wright (1957) even reported baby mice, but did not state whether this was a wild or captive feeding observation.

Palmer and Braswell (1995) list the dusky salamanders, *Desmognathus fuscus*, cricket frogs, *Acris gryllus*, pine woods treefrog, *Hyla femoralis*, squirrel treefrog, *Hyla squirella*, spadefoot toads, *Scaphiopus holbrooki* (recently transformed), green anole, *Anolis carolinensis*, ground skink, *Scincella lateralis*, and a small southeastern five-lined skink, *Eumeces inexpectatus*, as food items consumed by captive pine woods snakes from North Carolina.

Known predators of the pine woods snake are black racers (Palmer and Braswell, 1995; personal observation) and coral snakes, *Micrurus fulvius* (personal observation). Suspected predators include kingsnakes and predatory mammals.

Mating is believed to occur primarily in the spring with 2–4 eggs being laid 1–2 months later, usually from June through August (Myers, 1967; Fitch, 1970). These eggs hatch in approximately 50 days (personal observations, see below) into neonates measuring 11–16 cm (4.3–6.5 inches).

Another difficulty in breeding these nocturnal semifossorial snakes in captivity is detecting the time of mating activity. Hence, it is

A pine woods snake ingests a small treefrog that had been paralyzed by the snake's venom just a few minutes previously. This snake is harmless to man, however.

difficult to determine the gestation period. A pair acquired as subadults in August 1993 were housed together. On 3 June 1994, the female died in dystocia containing 2 eggs. Based upon the observations of temperature increases and the mating activities of other snakes in our care that year, we suspect that mating may have occurred in mid-March. Hence, we suspect that the gestation period is approximately 45–50 days. From this, we also believe that both sexes may reach sexual maturity at 10 months of age. These eggs were removed from the dead female, but they failed to hatch when set up in vermiculite and incubated in the usual manner.

Another female from Duval County, Florida (Jacksonville), in our care deposited 3 eggs on 12 June 1994. These eggs measured 2.6 × 0.7 cm, 2.8 × 0.7 cm and 3.2 × 0.7 cm (average 2.9 × 0.7 cm = 1.13 × 0.28 inches). Using the same incubation technique as above, hatching occurred on 30 July, an incubation period of 48 days at a relatively constant temperature fluctuating from 26.1 to 27.2°C (79 to 81°F). The neonates were lighter in color with a dark cap on the head, looking remarkably similar to

crowned snakes. They measured 11, 12, and 12.5 cm (4.3–4.9 inches) in length, and the sex ratio was 2:1 males to females.

The pine woods snake is actually easy to maintain in captivity if you can procure its favorite food (small frogs) and give it the security of a good substrate. Cypress mulch or pine mulch, which you have collected or purchased, and baked at 148°C (300°F) for 15 minutes, seem to work very well. Do not use cedar chips or shavings or pine shavings or other commercially treated products. They contain toxins which can harm the snakes and are usually the wrong consistency. Pine mulch with pieces of pine bark placed on top has worked well for us. If these snakes are not given mulch, they will usually refuse to eat and starve in the midst of plenty even if they have a hide box. Change the mulch every 3 months and mist it about once per week. Stir it occasionally (every 1–2 weeks should be enough). These snakes are nocturnal, so they will emerge only at night to feed. A 25-watt red light bulb is an excellent way to observe feeding. But you must be patient and remain very still, especially at first.

The snake will usually wait just under the surface of the mulch for a frog to pass by, whereupon it will ambush the hapless amphibian and hang on while it struggles. In a few minutes the frog will go limp and the snake will release the frog completely to search for the front end. Upon finding the frog's snout, it will swallow the frog in the usual manner. This observation supports the theory that this snake possesses a mild venom, although it is incapable of injecting this venom into a person because of its small size and nonaggressive nature. Frogs consumed include cricket frogs, *Acris gryllus*, green treefrogs, *Hyla cinerea*, squirrel treefrogs, *H. squirella*, small leopard frogs, *Rana utricularia*, and the pine woods treefrog, *H. femoralis*. Its favorite food appears to be the cricket frog. Some have reported that these snakes will eat small lizards, small snakes, and salamanders but none of the snakes in our care showed any interest in ground skinks, *Scincella lateralis*, or slimy salamanders, *Plethodon glutinosus*. Neither did they show any interest in dead frogs, but we would not rule out the possibility that they may eat dead frogs.

Two adult specimens from Duval County, Florida (Jacksonville), in our care each consumed a minimum of five to a maximum of 15 small frogs per month (almost entirely adult cricket frogs), but they might have consumed far greater numbers of smaller frogs, like little grass frogs or newly metamorphosed frogs, had they been available. It is interesting to note that envenomation of these animals rarely exceeded 5–15 minutes, while those reported by Neill (1954) were seldom held for less than 45 minutes. Perhaps there is a geographic variation in the toxicity of the venom as there is in members of the family Crotalidae (rattlesnakes), or possibly the food items we were offering were smaller than those offered by Neill.

Make sure to provide a water bowl that is partially submerged in the substrate. Change the water fairly frequently. These snakes will use the water bowl but also will drink and actively prowl when the cage is heavily misted just before lights out.

House separately, as two snakes will fight over the same frog and one may attempt to swallow the other. The presence of one snake may inhibit another from eating.

Brumation should be carried out in the same cage in which they live the rest of the year, just like the scarlet snake. No changes are necessary. Brumation temperatures of 3.3–18.3°C (38–65°F) have been utilized by these snakes in our care with no ill effects. Do not feed during this time. (See the section on brumation in the general care section.)

To our knowledge, breeding has not been

Pine Woods Snake (albino), *Rhadinaea flavilata* (photo by David G. Campbell)

SPECIES: *Rhadinaea flavilata*, Pine Woods Snake
MAINTENANCE DIFFICULTY INDEX: 4 (1 = easiest, 5 = most difficult)
AVERAGE SIZE: 25–33 cm (10–13 inches)
FOOD: Cricket frogs, treefrogs, small *Rana* sp. frogs, and ground skinks (reportedly)
CAGE SIZE: 10-gallon aquarium
SUBSTRATE: Cypress mulch or pine mulch
VENTRAL HEAT: No
UV LIGHT: No
TEMPERATURE RANGE: 27–32°C (80–90°F)
SPECIAL CONSIDERATIONS: Food availability may be a problem. Nocturnal. Can observe
    at night with red light.

---

accomplished in captivity yet. Part of the problem may lie in the difficulty in sexing these small snakes although the males do have longer thicker tails as discussed in the section on sexing, and the fact that few people have successfully maintained these snakes in captivity for long periods of time, much less had a pair together. They should actually be fairly easy to breed, if you have a pair and the patience to treat them as described in the general care section under breeding. The female will deposit the eggs in the mulch in the early summer; however, they prefer to use an egg-laying box if one is provided, and may die from dystocia if a suitable egg-laying place is not available. Try to get a rough idea of the time of laying by observing her girth and loss of appetite around this time. After a very thin but previously fat female begins eating again after a period of inappetence, she has probably just laid her eggs. Carefully search the cage and remove the eggs for incubation in the usual manner.

The young are voracious eaters also and will do well in the same habitat as the adults, shedding monthly and growing rapidly, if given newly metamorphosed frogs of the same species mentioned above.

This is another species for which we will have a very difficult time controlling the quality of the food. Not only do they consume anurans (frogs) but most will refuse dead ones, making it very difficult to rid them of many parasites by freezing. In addition, their small size makes them more difficult to deworm safely. Fortunately, they do not seem to be easily stressed and will usually stay very healthy if kept in the environment discussed above.

We have kept them at 27–35°C (80–95°F) during the day and 21.1–27°C (70–80°F) at night. No ventral heat is required but an incandescent bulb for heat may be useful, as some snakes seem to be basking just below the surface of the substrate. A 25-watt red bulb is very useful for observing these snakes at night.

One of these snakes in our care survived 1 year and 6 months in captivity.

Rhinocheilus lecontei
Longnose Snake

The longnose snake is a widespread, highly adaptable, attractive snake that occupies a huge geographic area from southwestern Kansas through western Oklahoma and Texas, westward through central and southern New Mexico and Arizona, western Utah, much of Nevada and central and southern California, with an isolated population in southwestern Idaho. They range southward extensively into Mexico as well. They are medium-sized snakes ranging 56–81 cm (22–32 inches) in length, with a record of 104 cm (41 inches). The longnose snake is generally marked with a large number of black saddles on the back and variably colored with red, orange, pink, yellow, or tan between the blotches. They often have dark flecks in the light areas and light flecks in the dark areas, but some specimens are more uniformly colored. There are two subspecies in the United States, the western longnose snake, *R. l. lecontei*, and the Texas longnose snake, *R. l. tessellatus*, with the western longnose being found (roughly) west of the Arizona-New Mexico border and the Texas longnose snake being found east of that border. The two subspecies

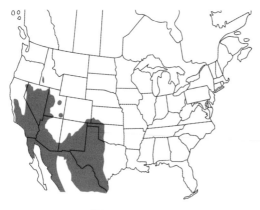

Rhinocheilus lecontei

are distinguishable by looking at their noses among other things. The Texas longnose snake has a more pointed and sharply upturned nose, while the western longnose has a more rounded-appearing nose. Many of these western long-noses lack the red coloration, thereby looking much like California kingsnakes in their overall appearance.

A quick method of distinguishing this species from all other species in its range is to examine the scales under the tail. It is the only nonvenomous snake in the area covered by this book that has a single row of scutes (large belly scales) behind (caudal to) the vent. The single scales do not extend all the way to the tip of the tail, but certainly do extend down much of the tail. Most nonvenomous snakes, including kingsnakes and rat snakes, have a double row posterior to the vent.

These snakes are found in a variety of habitats, but most frequently they are found in soft-

soiled lowlands, deserts, dry plains, coastal thorn forest and chaparral, and other brush areas, usually avoiding mountains (Wright and Wright, 1957; Fowlie, 1965; Webb, 1970; Tennant, 1984; Stebbins, 1985; Conant and Collins, 1991; Degenhardt et al., 1996). They are nocturnal most of the year, but have been observed basking in the mornings during the spring and fall (Webb, 1970; Jarchow et al., 1992). During the heat of the day, these snakes apparently burrow into several inches of soil or enter a rodent burrow for protection from the heat. They are also thought to burrow nocturnally in search of sleeping lizards or reptile eggs.

These snakes exhibit an unusual behavior when first captured. Females writhe from side to side and distend the anal area while hemorrhaging from the cloaca and possibly nasal area (McCoy and Gehlbach, 1967).

The diet of this species in the wild has been reported to include lizards (whiptails, *Cnemidophorus*, side-blotched lizards, *Uta stansburiana*, spiny lizards, *Sceloporus*, desert night lizards, *Xantusia vigilis*) and their eggs; small snakes and snake eggs, including those of their own species; rodents (mice, kangaroo rats, gophers), and insects (Wright and Wright, 1957; Shaw and Campbell, 1974; Behler and King, 1979; Tennant, 1984; Switak, 1984; Stebbins, 1972, 1985; Conant and Collins, 1991; Degenhardt et al., 1996). Linder and Fichter (1977) and Stebbins (1985) also mention that birds may be taken occasionally.

The temperature at which individuals have been found active (nocturnally) in the wild has ranged from 15 to 30.5 °C (59 to 87°F) (Wright and Wright, 1957; Shaw and Campbell, 1974). They are reported to be one of the most cold-tolerant of desert snakes, having been observed to be active at temperatures lower than most other snakes (Klauber, 1941; Cowles and Bogert, 1944; Wright and Wright, 1957; Shaw and Campbell, 1974; Tennant, 1984; personal observations). Specimens of this species have been uncovered underground during cold weather, presumably brumating, but the temperatures were not measured at these times.

Known predators include large desert centipedes (Tennent, 1984) but many animals are presumed to prey upon these snakes. These

Western Longnose Snake, *Rhinocheilus lecontei lecontei* (photo by Steve Barten)

include armadillos, skunks, foxes, coyotes, owls, and larger snakes (Tennant, 1984).

Mating is believed to occur in the early spring (March to May) over much of this snake's range. This generally results in the deposition of 4–11 eggs ranging from 3.1 to 3.7 cm long × 1.6 cm wide (roughly 1.3 × 0.6 inches) approximately 1–2 months later. Incubation periods reported for eggs of this species have ranged from 65 to 83 days at variable incubation temperatures of 23.9–33°C (75–91.4°F) (Lardie, 1965; Fitch, 1970; Kronen, 1980; Stebbins, 1985; Degenhardt et al., 1996).

Like the closely related kingsnakes, double clutching has been reported for this species (Fitch, 1970), or strongly suspected (Degenhardt et al., 1996), although some believe that some females may produce eggs only every other year.

The young range 17–28 cm (6.7–11 inches) in length at hatching and usually shed within 2 weeks (Wright and Wright, 1957; Kronen, 1980). These very attractive young snakes are patterned similarly to the adults in most cases,

but usually have duller colors (pink instead of red dorsally) and less speckling.

In captivity, the longnose snake will generally thrive if cared for in a manner similar to the kingsnakes. The basic cage setup described in the general care section will generally work excellently, taking into account the shy nature of this animal. Provide increased hiding places in the cage such as PVC pipe, an extra hide box, flat rock, or bark. However, because of the burrowing nature of this snake, wood chips or mulch are sometimes preferable to artificial carpet/turf or newspaper. In addition, a humidity box (basically a hide box stuffed with some lightly misted sphagnum moss) is an excellent idea for these snakes. Other cage accessories may include plastic plants and a few extra rocks, but these are not considered necessary. A small heavy water bowl is advisable, however, as long as the cage is well ventilated.

Air temperatures of 25–32°C (77–90°F) during the day have been reported as suitable daytime temperatures for members of this species by several authors (Trutnau, 1981; Switak,

Texas Longnose Snake, *Rhinocheilus lecontei tessellatus* (photo by David G. Campbell)

1984). Those in our care tolerated temperatures ranging up to 35°C (95°F) with no ill effects, however. Nighttime temperatures during the active season of 18–27°C (65–80°F) have also been well accepted by the snakes in our care. Indeed, we have observed some nocturnal foraging at temperatures lower than this with those captives we maintained.

Brumation temperatures reported for captive specimens have ranged from 10 to 15°C (50 to 59°F) for 2–3 months (Trutnau, 1981), but those in our care tolerated temperatures fluctuating from 3 to 18°C (38 to 65°F) for 4 months without ill effect. No cage changes are necessary at this time.

Captive breeding of this species has been exceedingly rare (or at least rarely reported), considering their apparent abundance and availability. We suspect this may be due in part to a lack of effort on the part of many skilled herpetologists, but also because many of the females maintained are either poorly fed (because of their smaller size, many are offered lizards but are not offered enough) or still have heavy parasite loads. Thus, captive mating does not always result in the production of eggs. We have observed poorly feeding females mating in captivity but never producing eggs, suggest-

ing they had not ovulated due to insufficient fat stores. Even females that are feeding heavily going into the fall may not feed readily in the spring, thereby depleting some of that fat stored the previous year and possibly reducing the number of eggs produced. Basically, however, captive breeding is accomplished as discussed in the general care section, i.e., place the female in with the male within several weeks of the end of brumation. A pair in our care mated on 24 April and the female deposited 7 eggs on 4 June. These eggs were fertile and all hatched on 10 August, an incubation period of 67 days. They averaged 3.79 cm (1.5 inches) in length by 2.0 cm (0.8 inch) in width. The neonates (four males and three females) measured 21–24 cm (8.3–9.5 inches) TL, 18–20 cm (7.25–8.0 inches) SVL.

Eggs produced have been incubated in the usual manner (see above), and this presents few problems. However, the hatchlings may be quite a challenge. These small snakes may be housed in plastic shoe box-sized enclosures or 5–10-gallon aquariums (with tight-fitting lids). They have a strong preference for small lizards, but most can be trained fairly rapidly to eat prekilled pinkies that have been scented with lizard. Others have reported that juvenile side-blotched lizards, *Uta* sp., are a well-accepted food item for these young, and we have found that ground skinks, *Scincella lateralis*, will be greedily consumed by most of these snakes.

Wild-caught adults often represent the biggest challenge with this species. Many are very shy and quite fastidious initially. This problem is compounded by the standard pet trade practices of overcrowding, mixing species, and lack of a suitable hiding place or thermal gradient. The inexperienced hobbyist then purchases this snake (which at this time usually has marginal dermatitis and pneumonia as well as untreated intestinal parasitism), offers it a live, large, white mouse in the middle of the day, and then wonders why it doesn't feed. The snake heads downhill rapidly, and often doesn't receive medical attention until it is either too late or never (because it is still common enough to be inexpensive and the owner does not consider a veterinary visit justifiable).

If the snakes survive, they may calm down within several weeks and begin feeding on small mice or else the keeper may have to offer lizards. Prekilled lizards, especially those offered at night, are the most likely to be consumed. If one species is not taken, try several others. One member of this species, having refused numerous other lizards for nearly a year (but having been force-fed several pinkies during that time), began feeding voraciously on Mediterranean geckos, *Hemidactylus turcicus*, and thereafter became a fantastic feeder on gecko-scented pinkies, and then unscented pinkies. This was initially quite a shock until

we found that numerous other snakes accepted this introduced lizard (Rossi and Rossi, 1992c). Other lizards well accepted by the recently captured adult longnoses in our care included the ground skink, *Scincella lateralis*, and the five-lined skink, *Eumeces fasciatus*. All of these lizards were excellent for scenting purposes as well.

Other food items mentioned in the literature have included small snakes. The ground snake, *Sonora semiannulata*, appeared particularly irresistible to the longnoses in our care. A word of caution is due regarding the ringneck snake, however. One western longnose snake was offered a medium-sized ringneck snake from Florida. It grasped the ringneck and swallowed it completely. The ringneck remained motionless until its head was inside the longnose snake's mouth, whereupon it opened its mouth and bit down on the inside of the longnose snake's lower jaw. After several hours in this position, the longnose released the ringneck and tried again, with the same result. The whole process was repeated again several hours later. Shockingly, after nearly 17 hours, the longnose snake died and the ringneck snake crawled away. This observation certainly lends some validity to the commonly held belief that ringneck snakes produce a venom. In addition, it may provide some new insight into the warning colors of the small snake. Indeed, this particular ringneck snake acted like it was well programmed to respond to this attack. Perhaps, the ringneck snakes found in the range of the longnose snake do not produce as powerful a

---

SPECIES: *Rhinocheilus lecontei*, Longnose Snake
MAINTENANCE DIFFICULTY INDEX: 2 (1 = easiest, 5 = most difficult)
AVERAGE SIZE: 56–81 cm (22–32 inches)
FOOD: Mice, lizards
CAGE SIZE: 10–20-gallon aquarium
SUBSTRATE: Indoor-outdoor carpet, artificial turf, wood chips, or mulch
VENTRAL HEAT: Not essential but helpful
UV LIGHT: Not essential, but an incandescent bulb is helpful
TEMPERATURE RANGE: 25–32°C (77–90°F)
SPECIAL CONSIDERATIONS: Prefer lizards and snakes initially but switch to mice fairly rapidly. Likely to be parasitized. Treat like kingsnakes.

venom, or perhaps the Florida ringnecks do not possess the proper warnings for a western longnose snake. In any case, this word of warning about ringneck snakes as food for longnose snakes is necessary. Be aware that prekilled snakes, lizards, and rodents are all usually well accepted by these snakes, and this may reduce the risks considerably. Freezing is considered to be a humane method of euthanizing small reptiles and may eliminate some, but not all, parasites.

As mentioned above, some of the longnose snakes in our care seem to forget they were regularly consuming mice the previous fall and would undergo long spring fasts following a winter cooldown. Certainly, a short fasting period has been reported for a number of colubrids, particularly males prior to breeding, but this fasting seems to have involved both males and females and seems quite prolonged (several months). Reoffering lizards at this time and quickly moving them back over to scented, then unscented mice may be the answer to this problem. Perhaps these snakes experience a strong seasonal food preference as suggested by Breen (1974).

In general, we have found these snakes to be very attractive, nonaggressive, regularly eating captives that may become very well adjusted to captivity, and do not seem to mind handling at all. Therefore, they make excellent pets. Set them up properly, house them singly, and have them checked and treated for intestinal parasites and they will do extremely well. They can be quite long-lived in captivity. Snider and Bowler (1992) reported that a Texas longnose survived more than 19 years and 10 months in captivity, and it was a wild-caught adult. Another snake, a western longnose, survived more than 18 years and 3 months in captivity.

Salvadora deserticola
Big Bend Patchnose Snake

The patchnose snakes are another group of speedy diurnal (or crepuscular) snakes. They are also relatively nervous animals, but are not particularly aggressive snakes (as are the whipsnakes and the racers). They possess an enlarged rostral (nose) scale that helps them uncover food items buried in the sandy soil and from which they receive their name.

This species was previously considered a subspecies of the western patchnose *S. hexalepis*. Therefore some of the data published on these two species are intermingled, and difficult to assign to one species or the other. We have tried to distinguish between the two, but realize there may be some overlap of information.

The Big Bend patchnose snake is a medium-sized snake, usually ranging 51–81 cm (20–32 inches) in length with a record of 101.6 cm (40 inches) (Tennant, 1984; Conant and Collins, 1991). Thus, it is a medium-sized patchnose as well, being larger than the mountain patchnose and slightly smaller than the Texas and western patchnoses. They are attractive snakes, charac-terized by tan-colored sides with a narrow dark stripe on the fourth scale row from the bottom. On the back, a wide tan to peach-colored area is set off by two narrow zigzag dark lines. They also possess two or three small scales between the posterior chin shields, but one should refer to a field guide for a diagram of this characteristic.

These snakes are found in the United States from the Big Bend area of Texas through southern and central New Mexico and southeastern Arizona. Their preferred habitat appears to be any dry and open natural areas, particularly creosote-dominated scrub desert and rolling grasslands at middle elevations, especially around washes or streams (Wright and Wright, 1957; Behler and King, 1979; Tennant, 1984; Conant and Collins, 1991). We observed large numbers in the rolling grasslands near Ruby Road in southeastern Arizona.

The diet of these snakes in the wild has been reported to include lizards (particularly geckos, *Coleonyx* sp., whiptails, *Chemidophorus* sp., spiny lizards, *Sceloporus* sp., and in captivity

Salvadora deserticola

anoles, *Anolis* sp.), smaller snakes, and the eggs of both lizards and snakes (including eggs of their own species occasionally), as well as small mammals (Fowlie, 1965; Shaw and Campbell, 1974; Behler and King, 1979; Tennant, 1984; Feldner, pers. comm., 1992; Degenhardt et al., 1996). They have been observed digging and removing eggs and lizards from under sandy soil.

Very few studies have been done on the thermal ecology of this particular species. One study on the closely related western patchnose

revealed a preferred temperature range of 30–35°C (86–95°F) with a critical thermal minimum of 7°C (44.6°F) and a critical thermal maximum of 44°C (111.2°F) (Jacobson and Whitford, 1971), suggesting that this snake is indeed adapted for activity during fairly high daytime temperatures as some have suggested. They have been observed to be active primarily at dawn and dusk during the midsummer, however (Tennant, 1984).

Suspected predators of this species include hawks, whipsnakes, longnose snakes, glass snakes, kingsnakes, and predatory mammals.

Mating is believed to occur in the spring, from late March to June, with 5–10 eggs being deposited about 1–2 months later. However, this species has not been well studied, and Fitch (1970) believes some patchnoses may double clutch in the wild. The incubation period of these eggs is thought to be similar to that of the Texas patchnose, and these have required an unusually long period of 90–125 days (Conant and Downs, 1940; Minton, 1959). Stebbins (1954) reported an incubation period of 85 days for the western patchnose, *S. hexalepsis*.

The hatchlings are known to be 23–28 cm

Big Bend Patchnose Snake, *Salvadora deserticola* (photo by David G. Campbell)

SPECIES: *Salvadora deserticola*, Big Bend Patchnose Snake
MAINTENANCE DIFFICULTY INDEX: 4, hatchlings 5 (1 = easiest, 5 = most difficult)
AVERAGE SIZE: 51–81 cm (20–32 inches)
FOOD: Mice, lizards
CAGE SIZE: 20–30-gallon long aquarium
SUBSTRATE: Indoor-outdoor carpet, artificial turf, or newspaper
VENTRAL HEAT: Yes
UV LIGHT: Not essential but helpful. Incandescent bulb strongly advisable.
TEMPERATURE RANGE: 27–35°C (80–95°F)
SPECIAL CONSIDERATIONS: Restless; frequently wander cage perimeter (even long-term captives). Juveniles often very difficult to start feeding. Like geckos.

(9–11 inches) long, and are colored similarly to the parents. Their first shed generally occurs between 11 and 16 days later. These small snakes have a definite preference for lizards, particularly geckos. They are believed to reach sexual maturity in 2–3 years. Goldberg (1995) found that males of this species and the western patchnose, *S. hexalepis*, produce sperm when they reach 46.8 cm SVL.

In captivity, the Big Bend patchnose snake will generally do well in the basic cage arrangement discussed in the general care section. This includes artificial carpet/turf or newspaper as the substrate, a stable dark-colored hide box, plastic plants, a stable rock or two, and a stable water bowl. Sand or wood chips have worked well for a number of snake keepers, however, and we have also successfully used cypress mulch. Good ventilation via the use of a screen top is a very good idea as is a slightly larger cage than usual. A 20-gallon long aquarium will probably be satisfactory for most snakes, but a 30-gallon long would be excellent. High-sided aquariums also are beneficial as the snakes will not be able to reach the top and rub their noses on it as easily as they would in a shorter aquarium. In our experience, this species is the most high-strung of the patchnoses and is far more likely to pace its cage nervously constantly seeking a way out than are the other two species. Even so, they are still far less likely to damage their noses than any of the whipsnakes and some of the rat snakes.

Even though they may pace their cages, most of these animals seem to adjust fairly well to

captivity and become regular feeders. The majority of the midsize and larger specimens will readily accept pinkies and feed twice per week.

The hatchlings and juveniles, however, may present quite a problem. They are usually more difficult to get to start feeding on pinkies than are hatchling whipsnakes. Even scented pinkies may be refused for months. In addition, even many lizards may be refused. One hatchling in our care refused ground skinks, *Scincella lateralis*, small five-lined skinks, *Eumeces fasciatus*, green anoles, *Anolis carolinensis*, and even a hatchling eastern fence lizard, *Sceloporus undulatus*. It did, however, regularly consume Mediterranean geckos, *Hemidactylus turcicus*, of the appropriate size.

Suitable captive temperatures have not been reported for this species in captivity. However, an acceptable range of temperatures have been reported by several authors for the closely related western patchnose and the mountain patchnose. Switak (1984) suggested a daytime air temperature of 27–29.4°C (80–85°F) and a nighttime temperature around 21°C (70°F) for the western patchnose. Trutnau (1981) suggested a temperature of 25–30°C (77–86°F) would work well as a daytime temperature for the mountain patchnose. Those in our care have been successfully maintained at daytime temperatures fluctuating from 27 to 35°C (80 to 95°F) during the active season of the year and nighttime temperatures of 18–28°C (65–80°F). We strongly recommend ventral heat, as do all other authors. In addition, a hot spot created by the use of an incandescent bulb during the day is also valuable for these heat-loving diurnal reptiles.

Brumation temperatures that have been well tolerated by those in our care have fluctuated between 3 and 18°C (38 and 65°F) for 4–5 months.

Captive breeding has not been reported for this species, although it may probably be bred in the usual manner. The western patchnose has been observed to breed in captivity. The eggs may be incubated in the usual manner.

Overall, these snakes adapt fairly readily to captivity and usually switch to small mice rapidly. They also calm down and remain fairly nonaggressive. Unfortunately, they seem to remain the most nervous and the least handleable of the patchnoses.

Snider and Bowler (1992) do not report a captive longevity for this species. One specimen was in our care for 7 years and 8 months when it was released.

Salvadora grahamiae
Mountain Patchnose Snake

Fast-moving, nervous, and racerlike are all terms that have been used to describe this snake. Good captive has not. Therein lies the fallacy. Although very nervous initially and quite a speedster, these richly colored good looking snakes make reasonably good captives since they will calm down nicely and feed well if set up properly.

The mountain patchnose actually consists of two quite different subspecies, the widespread, lowland-dwelling Texas patchnose, *S. g. lineata*, and the spottily distributed mountain-dwelling mountain patchnose, *S. g. grahamiae*. The Texas patchnose tends to be slightly larger, with adults ranging 66–102 cm (26–40 inches) in length , with a record of 119.4 cm (47 inches). The mountain patchnose ranges 56–76 cm (20–32 inches) in length with a record of 95.3 cm (37 inches) (Conant and Collins, 1991). Both are attractively marked, with the Texas patchnose having very broad dark dorsolateral stripes and a distinct narrow stripe below them on scale row 3. The mountain patchnose has narrower dorsolateral stripes and usually lacks a distinct stripe on the third scale row from the belly. This gives the Texas patchnose a very dark overall appearance (it looks much like a garter snake except it has smooth scales) and the mountain patchnose a very light appearance overall. Because of their smooth scales, both of these snakes—and indeed all of the patchnoses—have a glossy appearance. These two snakes have been placed together as one species largely because of the scale pattern under the chin. Both species have either none or one small scale between the posterior chin shields, while the Big Bend and western patchnose have two or more such scales. Once again, however, a field guide should be consulted to clarify this point and seek further clues with which to identify the species in hand.

The Texas patchnose ranges from north central Texas southward throughout southern Texas and into Mexico. Toward the Big Bend area it intergrades with the mountain patchnose which occurs from there westward through southern New Mexico and southeastern Arizona. Thus its range significantly overlaps that of the Big Bend patchnose.

The habitat of the two subspecies also differs. As mentioned above, the mountain patch-

Salvadora grahamiae

Mountain Patchnose Snake, *Salvadora grahamiae grahamiae* (photo by Steve Barten)

nose is found in higher elevations, usually above 4000 feet, often on the timbered slopes. On the other hand, the Texas patchnose has been found most commonly from sea level to 2000 feet in a wide variety of open habitat including grasslands, open woodlands, and farmlands (Wright and Wright, 1957; Tennant, 1984; Stebbins, 1985). We have found them on coastal sand dunes near Boca Chica, Texas, as well.

Both subspecies eat a wide variety of food items that have been reported to include lizards (spiny, *Sceloporus* sp., side-blotched, *Uta stansburiana*, geckos, *Coleonyx* sp., and whiptails, *Cnemidophorus* sp.), small snakes (ground snakes, *Sonora semiannulata*), reptile eggs, small rodents (deer mice), and frogs (Wright and Wright, 1957; Fowlie, 1965; Tennant, 1984).

Very few specific temperatures have been reported from wild individuals of this species; however, it is believed they have a higher preferred optimum temperature range than many other snakes, probably similar to that of the western patchnose (30–35°C or 86–95°F) (Jacobson and Whitford, 1971). These snakes also have a great tolerance for cool temperatures, becoming active early every morning during their active season.

Virtually nothing is known about natural predators of these snakes; however, hawks, whipsnakes, and predatory mammals are probably significant predators.

Mating is believed to occur primarily in the spring, as clutches of 6–10 eggs have been reported in April and May. It is important to note that the smaller clutch sizes have been reported from mountain patchnoses, while larger clutches are reported for Texas patchnoses. Also, those few dates of egg laying reported for the mountain patchnoses were in May or later, while the Texas patchnoses laid (their first clutch?) in April. Does this represent a delayed mating/laying season in mountain patchnoses associated with the higher altitudes at which they are found? Fitch (1970) believed these snakes may lay one clutch early and then another clutch later in the season. Reported size

Texas Patchnose Snake, *Salvadora grahamiae lineata* (photo by David G. Campbell)

of the white, adherent, rat snakelike eggs has ranged 2.4–3.2 cm (0.9–1.2 inches) in length and 1.3–1.5 cm (0.5–0.6 inches) in width (Wright and Wright, 1957; Tennant, 1984).

The hatchlings range from 22–29.3 cm (8.5–11.4 inches) (Wright and Wright, 1957; Behler and King, 1979; Tennant, 1984; Degenhardt et al., 1996) and are colored exactly the same as the parents. They usually shed within 2–3 weeks of hatching.

We prefer a larger-than-usual cage with smooth high sides for this species. Like certain other snakes, they are prone to eroding their rostral plates by constantly rubbing in efforts to escape, and this can be minimized by the cage modifications discussed above. Thirty- to 40-gallon long aquariums will work well for these medium-sized snakes, but 20-gallon long aquariums have worked fairly well also. Another technique we have used to help prevent this disfiguring activity is to place neatly folded plastic bags in the upper corners of the cage. The slippery bags prevent these snakes from destroying their most characteristic feature, their patchnose. Dr. Elliott Jacobson of the University of Florida advises the use of plastic screening instead of the more commonly used aluminum screening for many nervous snakes, and this may also be helpful with this species. It has been our experience that this is the calmest of the patchnoses and is less likely to traumatize its rostral scale than other members of the group. Long-term captives act much like rat snakes, spending most of their time in their hide boxes, and may only rarely pace their cages.

Other than the modifications mentioned above, the standard (ideal) cage setup discussed in the general care section will work well for this snake. A dark-colored secure hide box is absolutely essential. So is a good heat source. Incandescent bulbs (60 or 75 watts) in aluminum reflector lamps work well for this purpose. Ventral heat also appears to be used by these snakes. Artificial carpet/turf is a suitable substrate but wood chips will work also. Clean water should be available at all times. The cage may be completed by adding some rocks and plastic plants. Make sure the rocks are stable and will not collapse on the snake. An accessory that does not appear to be needed by this terrestrial snake is a branch, since they will rarely use it to bask and it will contribute to their rostral damage as they will use it to try to escape at night.

Feeding the mountain patchnose is not a problem since they will usually take prekilled pinkies, fuzzies, or small mice right away. If not, they may be induced to start feeding in captivity by either offering lizards (skinks, anoles, or geckos were preferred by those in our care and Tennant [1984] reported skinks, anoles, and Texas spiny lizards, *Sceloporus olivaceus*, were readily consumed by those he maintained) or by flavoring the mice with the lizards. This may be done by rubbing the lizard on the mouse or placing a piece of skin or tail tip from a frozen and thawed lizard into the dead mouse's mouth. Freezing the lizard will also reduce the risk of parasitism and injury that might occur if feeding live lizards. Indeed, our feeding success with this species has been much higher when prekilled food items have been used. Interestingly, this is another species of western snake that will readily consume prekilled Mediterranean geckos, *Hemidactylus turcicus*. Even hatchlings will readily consume these introduced lizards.

An unusual observation on the feeding behavior of these snakes in captivity has been made by Trutnau, and after seeing it ourselves numerous times, we feel it needs to be related to would-be keepers of this snake. This is the tendency of these diurnal snakes to wait until dusk before they feed in captivity, even if the food item is placed in the cage at midday. Perhaps this is related to crepuscular tendencies in

SPECIES: *Salvadora grahamiae*, Mountain Patchnose Snake
MAINTENANCE DIFFICULTY INDEX: 3 (1 = easiest, 5 = most difficult)
AVERAGE SIZE: 66–102 cm (26–40 inches)
FOOD: Lizards, mice
CAGE SIZE: 30–40-gallon long aquariums
SUBSTRATE: Indoor-outdoor carpet, artificial turf, or newspaper
VENTRAL HEAT: Yes
UV LIGHT: Not essential but helpful. Incandescent bulb strongly advisable.
TEMPERATURE RANGE: 30–35°C (86–95°F)
SPECIAL CONSIDERATIONS: Calmer than Big Bend patchnose, Texas patchnose is the
    larger, more handleable of the subspecies. Non-aggressive, good captives.

wild specimens during periods of hot weather. Whatever the case, it would be advisable not to place food in the cage early in the day for members of this species. We usually place the prekilled mice in the front of the hide box right at dusk, and they are generally consumed fairly soon afterwards. Once-a-week feedings will usually be sufficient, but twice-per-week feedings are preferable.

Parasitism is a major factor in captive failures with this species, and they should be suspected of being parasitized upon capture. A number of specimens we have examined have been harboring coccidia. Fecal exams should be performed initially and regularly thereafter, especially if they are receiving live wild-caught prey items like lizards. Treatment should be attempted with the standard deworming agents discussed in the general care section. *WARNING*: THESE SNAKES ARE PARTICULARLY SENSITIVE TO IVERMECTIN AND MET-RONIDAZOLE SO USE THE LOWER END OF THE DOSE RANGES IF THESE DRUGS ARE INDICATED BY THE FECAL EXAM. Panacur® and sulfadimethoxine appear to be well tolerated.

Brumation is strongly recommended since these relatively slender snakes will usually refuse to eat during the winter and will rapidly waste away. As with other snakes, this winter rest at cooler temperatures may be crucial for breeding success. No special modifications of the cage are necessary during this time. Make sure to provide plenty of water, however. A 3–5-month period at 10–15°C (50–59°F) is

recommended by Trutnau (1981) and should work well. However, we have exposed several of these snakes in our care to temperatures fluctuating from 3 to 18°C (38 to 65°F) for 4 months with no ill effects.

Very little has been written regarding the captive breeding of this snake and apparently very few have tried. It should not be difficult with healthy captives if one uses the standard approach discussed in the general care section under breeding. Females will lay 6–10 eggs in April or May, presumably after an early spring or previous fall mating. Many North American snakes breed in both the spring and fall.

The eggs may be incubated in the usual manner, and the incubation period under standard artificial conditions discussed in the general care section has ranged 3–4 months. The young, similar in pattern to the adults but slightly paler, will usually consume small lizards and eventually small pinkies, even though it may take months for unscented pinkies to be consumed.

One female in our care laid 6 eggs on 25 April. Five of these eggs hatched on 17 July, an incubation period of 83 days. These young measured 25–28 cm (10–11 inches) TL. Their first foods were ground skinks, *Scincella lateralis*, or young Mediterranean geckos, *Hemidactylus turcicus*. Young green anoles, *Anolis carolinensis*, were also taken. It is our impression that these hatchlings will be a major challenge for the average snake keeper. Not only do they prefer lizards for up to 6 months, but they are also extremely nervous, much more so than the adults. Once they make it through the first several months, however, they will generally adapt nicely and do very well.

In general, this species rarely bites and calms down soon after capture. The adults make far better pets than one would suspect from their initial nervous dispositions and wild reputations. The authors do not recommend frequent handling for any member of this genus, although some specimens seem to adapt very well to it. Others will vomit their last meal at the slightest disturbance. They are attractive serpents that frequently come out to bask during the day and feed regularly, hence, we believe they are actually quite suitable as pets. Treat each as an individual and you will rarely go wrong.

Captive longevity for this species has not been reported, but the closely related western patchnose has been maintained for more than 14 years in captivity. One snake in our care, captured as a subadult in Boca Chica, Texas, had been in captivity 5 years and 7 months, at which time it was released.

Salvadora hexalepis
Western Patchnose Snake

The western patchnose snake has been the most well studied of the patchnoses, yet it is still a relatively unknown animal to both field herpetologists and herpetoculturists. It is a widespread snake consisting of four subspecies, three of which are found within the United States. Together they range from northern Nevada south through much of southern California, eastward to southwestern Utah and much of western and central Arizona. The three subspecies within the United States are the desert patchnose snake, *S. h. hexalepis*, the Mojave patchnose snake, *S. h. mojavensis*, and the coast patchnose snake, *S. h. virgultea*. They are distinguishable by minor scalation and color characteristics described in more detail in a good field guide. Briefly, the Mojave patchnose does not have upper lip scales that contact the eye, while the other two subspecies do. To distinguish the coast patchnose from the desert patchnose, examine the head color and thickness of the central (median) back (dorsal) stripe. In the coast patchnose, the top of the head is brown and the dorsal stripe is narrower (two scale rows wide = 1 + 0.5 + 0.5 scale rows) as opposed to the desert patchnose which has a gray head and a dorsal stripe three scale rows wide (Stebbins, 1985).

These are not large snakes, with most ranging from 55 to 115 cm (20 to 45 inches) (Stebbins, 1985), but with a record of 122 cm (48 inches) (Wright and Wright, 1957).

As with other members of the genus, they appear to be snakes of open sandy areas and foothills, with the desert patchnose being aptly named as it is found in brushy, rocky, barren, and sandy deserts, while the other two subspecies are commonly seen in brushy foothills and chaparral (Wright and Wright, 1957).

The preferred food of the western patchnose in nature does not appear to differ significantly from those of the other patchnoses. Most authors list lizards as the preferred food, with reptile eggs a close second, followed by small or young snakes, small mammals (pocket mice), and birds (Wright and Wright, 1957; Fowlie, 1965, Stebbins, 1972, 1985; Shaw and Camp-

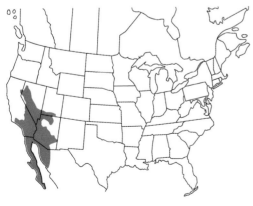

Salvadora hexalepis

Mojave Patchnose Snake, *Salvadora hexalepis mojavensis* (photo by David G. Campbell)

bell, 1974; Behler and King, 1979; Switak, 1984). These snakes may also be cannibalistic (Switak, 1984).

The preferred optimum temperature range for this species has been measured in one study to be 30–35°C (86–95°F) with a preferred body temperature of 33°C (91.4°F) with a critical thermal minimum of 7°C (44.6°F) and a critical thermal maximum of 44°C (111.2°F) (Jacobson and Whitford, 1971).

Virtually nothing is known about natural predators of these snakes; however, hawks, whipsnakes, longnose snakes, glass snakes, and predatory mammals are probably predators.

Mating is believed to occur from March to June, as eggs are deposited from late May through August. Clutches of 4–10 eggs have been reported (Wright and Wright, 1957; Behler and King, 1979; Stebbins, 1985). Fitch (1970) believed these snakes may produce 2 clutches per year (double clutch) in the wild but this is still unknown. The incubation period is 3–4 months.

Hatchlings may be fairly long. The smallest members of this species measured in August and September were 28–30 cm (11–12 inches), even though Wright and Wright (1957) thought these snakes were older than hatchlings.

In captivity, these snakes will generally do well in the basic cage setup as discussed in the general care section. See the discussion on the maintenance of the Big Bend patchnose and the mountain patchnose for details.

Remember that like the other patchnose snakes they are diurnal and need a warm, dry, well-ventilated environment. Therefore, it is advisable that an intense heat source such as an incandescent bulb be placed over a screen or wire-topped enclosure. Be aware also that these are somewhat high strung, energetic snakes that will pace their cages on occasion and may abrade their rostral areas if the screen top is too easily reached. Therefore, smooth-sided cages (aquariums) with high tops generally work well. Twenty-gallon long aquariums have worked well for adults, while juveniles and subadults have done well in 10-gallon aquariums. Thirty- or 40-gallon aquariums are considered ideal and very roomy enclosures for these snakes. This is not to say that patchnoses will not survive in smaller cages. Many have survived for some time in shoe box arrangements used commonly for kingsnakes and rat snakes. However, we do not believe this is the best method of maintaining or breeding these diurnal heat-loving snakes.

Ultraviolet light sources have been called exceptionally useful (Switak, 1984) in the maintenance of these snakes, however, they may not be necessary. Those in our care seemed to do well in their absence. It is important to note that we have not bred these snakes in captivity, however, and some need for UV light may be found later for these frequently basking snakes. Certainly, an anorectic patchnose snake might be expected to benefit by the addition of a UV light source to the enclosure for reasons discussed in the section on lighting.

Air temperatures reported for the successful maintenance of this species have been reported at 27–29.5°C (80–85°F) with a drop down to 21.1°C (70°F) at night (Switak, 1984). Those in our care seemed to feed and shed regularly at active season daytime temperatures fluctuating from 27 to 35°C (80 to 95°F), which is consistent with the preferred optimum temperature range reported above. Brumation temperatures successfully tolerated have fluctuated between 3 and 18°C (38 and 65°F) for 4 months. The tolerance of these lower temperatures than that reported as the critical thermal minimum above 7°C (45°F) suggests some acclimatization had occurred prior to these temperature drops. Possibly, however, the specimens we worked with had a more northern origin than those tested in the study above. Speaking of brumation, it may be carried out in the regular cage setup; no changes are required.

Feeding the western patchnose has not presented any particular problem in captivity, as most seem quite willing to consume pinkies.

Some specimens may need to be started on lizards initially, but then rapidly switch to the small mice. Once again, prekilled mice placed in the cage at dawn or dusk may be more readily accepted, while mice placed in the cage at midday may be ignored. Wild-caught adults from the more northern areas or higher altitudes may stop feeding as early as August, much to the concern of the keeper. As long as the snake in question looks healthy, it is probably just preparing for brumation. We believe this is a self-protective mechanism whereby snakes from these colder areas "play the odds," that is, expect cold weather and refuse to consume a meal that will not be able to be digested because of cold inactivation of their digestive enzymes. This meal may result in death if broken down by bacteria leading to gastroenteritis and peritonitis (an infection in the gut that spreads to the abdominal cavity). One unfortunate specimen in our care received an unnecessary force-feeding the first year this happened (anorexia occurred).

Captive breeding has occurred rarely with this species and may probably be carried out in the regular manner as discussed in the general care section. The female should probably be placed in the male's cage at weekly intervals starting in March until breeding activity is observed.

Eggs may be incubated in the usual manner as discussed in the general care section.

Overall, we have found this species to be less nervous and less likely to pace the cage than the Big Bend patchnose. However, those in our

---

SPECIES: *Salvadora hexalepis*, Western Patchnose Snake
MAINTENANCE DIFFICULTY INDEX: 3 (1 = easiest, 5 = most difficult)
AVERAGE SIZE: 55–115 cm (20–45 inches)
FOOD: Mice, lizards
CAGE SIZE: 30–40-gallon long aquarium
SUBSTRATE: Indoor-outdoor carpet, artificial turf, or newspaper
VENTRAL HEAT: Yes
UV LIGHT: Not essential but helpful. Incandescent bulb strongly advisable.
TEMPERATURE RANGE: 30–35°C (86–95°F)
SPECIAL CONSIDERATIONS: Usually adapt to captivity but shy. Specimens from Nevada
    often stop eating in August in preparation for brumation.

care have not been quite the aggressive feeders that the Texas patchnoses have been, giving the appearance of being slightly more shy and delicate than that species in captivity. Hence, they may not represent the easiest of snakes to maintain in captivity, but they are not terribly difficult either. In fact, we would not consider any of the patchnose snakes particularly difficult to maintain, and we believe most snake keepers have ignored this very attractive group for too long. Furthermore, most are not aggressive (rarely biting) after a short time in captivity, a characteristic that will endear them to many snake keepers.

One of these snakes was maintained more than 14 years and 3 months in captivity (Snider and Bowler, 1992). It is interesting to note that this snake was wild-caught as an adult.

Seminatrix pygaea
Black Swamp Snake

The black swamp snake is a small glossy black snake with a red belly. There are three subspecies which may be most easily differentiated by the amount of black on the ventral scales, and the ventral scale count. These subspecies include the Carolina swamp snake, which has a pair of black bars on each ventral scale and has 127 or more ventrals, the north Florida swamp snake, which has similar paired bars on a plain red belly and has 118–124 scale rows, and the south Florida swamp snake, which has paired dark triangular marks instead of bars and has 117 or fewer ventrals (Conant and Collins, 1991). The Carolina swamp snake, *S. p. paludis*, is found over much of the coastal plains in North and South Carolina. The north Florida swamp snake, *S. p. pygaea*, ranges over much of eastern Georgia and northern Florida. The south Florida swamp snake, *S. p. cyclas*, occupies the southern half of Florida. They range in size from 25 to 38 cm (10 to 15 inches) with a record of 48.9 cm (19.25 inches) (Conant and Collins, 1991; Palmer and Braswell, 1995).

These snakes are most commonly found in floating vegetation, such as water hyacinths, which are introduced, as well as a wide variety of other aquatic plants. These include water pennywort and sphagnum moss, among others (Wright and Wright, 1957; Mount, 1975; Palmer and Braswell, 1995). General habitat types for this species include cypress swamps, sloughs, bogs, swamps, wooded swamps, river swamps, canals, marshes (including brackish marshes), ponds, lakes, open lakes, and prairies (Wright and Wright, 1957; Mount, 1975; Ashton and Ashton, 1981; Ernst and Barbour, 1989). It appears extremely common right in the floating plants but has often been found under objects near the water's edge, and they are frequently seen cruising roads at night after heavy rains.

A wide variety of food items are taken by wild specimens. These have included earthworms, fish, amphibians (tadpoles, small frogs, and sirens, *Pseudobranchus*), and leeches (Ernst and Barbour, 1989). Palmer and Braswell (1995) also reported that captive specimens from North Carolina consumed a redback salamander, *Plethodon cinereus*, and several dusky salamanders, *Desmognathus* sp., in addition to earthworms and fish.

Predators are believed to include wading birds, large fish, and ophiophagous snakes (Ernst and Barbour, 1989).

Seminatrix pygaea

North Florida Swamp Snake, *Seminatrix pygaea pygaea* (photo by R. D. Bartlett)

Mating season is thought to occur in the spring with 2–14 young being born in midsummer to late fall (Dowling, 1950; Fitch, 1970; Palmer and Braswell, 1995). The young range 10.7–16.5 cm (4.5–6.5 inches) in length (Conant and Collins, 1991; Palmer and Braswell, 1995).

One female from Putnam County, Florida, delivered 4 young on 23 June. These snakes measured approximately 10.1 cm (4 inches) in TL. They shed within several days and shed thereafter approximately every 3 weeks until November of that year. First meals in captivity consisted of pieces of earthworms, but by 1 month of age they readily consumed small dwarf sirens, *Pseudobranchus* sp., and mosquito fish, *Gambusia* sp.

Hence, the black swamp snake, microterror of the southeastern waterways, is a very easy snake to maintain in captivity. It is not finicky when it comes to feeding time and its broad diet is a reflection of this. Captivity doesn't seem to slow them down a bit. Captives in our care have eaten all of the items mentioned above except leeches (because we haven't offered them). They are incredibly alert and will start searching for the food item almost immediately when it hits the water if they are in the water at the time. If there is no direct visualization of the food item, they appear to home in on it using olfaction and they have absolutely no reservations about taking frozen and thawed prey, which makes parasite control easier. They may fight over food so they should be housed singly.

They may be housed exactly the same way as the striped crayfish snake, which makes sense since they live in the same environment. If kept in plain tap water at room temperature, they will develop skin blisters initially, and may eventually die from this. But if kept warm and well fed, they will either recover from this or survive with blisters of varying severity; every time they shed they look better, but the blisters slowly return before the next shed. If they are placed in brackish water (we used 12.5% seawater produced by diluting Instant Ocean®), they will still get a few blisters, but not quite so many, and if placed in swamp tea (see the section on the striped crayfish snake) the blisters will usually disappear. What is probably happening is this: when the snakes are placed in a medium which is basic or neutral, they are

SPECIES: *Seminatrix pygaea*, Black Swamp Snake
MAINTENANCE DIFFICULTY INDEX: 4 (1 = easiest, 5 = most difficult)
AVERAGE SIZE: 25–38 cm (10–15 inches)
FOOD: Earthworms, fish, tadpoles, small amphibians
CAGE SIZE: 10-gallon aquarium
SUBSTRATE: 1–4 inches of acidic water (swamp tea) with dry area and hiding places. See text.
VENTRAL HEAT: Unknown but probably helpful. Water needs to be heated, light above will help.
UV LIGHT: Yes?
TEMPERATURE RANGE: 27–35°C (81–95°F) day; 10–15°C (50–59°F) brumation; 23–27°C (73–81°F) night.
SPECIAL CONSIDERATIONS: Likely to develop skin lesions if not kept in acidic water. Good eaters. Use swamp tea. See striped crayfish snake text.

exposed to bacterial pathogens which are different from those with which they have evolved (or at least the concentration of bacteria with which they have evolved). At room temperature, the snakes' immune systems are most likely either nonfunctional or severely impaired. Thus disease develops. But at higher temperatures and with a good food intake, their immune systems are fully functional even though the environment still favors the bacteria, and a less severe manifestation is observed. In brackish water, the concentration and types of bacteria are changed (probably reduced) and the snake gains an advantage, and thus improves. In warm tea, as described, the snake is exposed to bacteria similar to those with which it has evolved, and its immune system is functional if it is well fed and no disease occurs. These observations and our interpretation of them are strictly that. We have not run repeated trials with large numbers of animals nor run cultures on the different mediums mentioned. Nevertheless, these are valid observations and we would welcome different hypotheses to explain them or valid experimentation to refute our explanation.

What is being observed is a good example of what all herpetoculturists need to understand in order to be successful with any reptile. That is, given the proper environment, disease is far less likely to occur. But given the improper environment, one can reduce the likelihood of

disease in reptiles by catering to the reptile's immune system (keeping it warm and on a high nutritional plane), controlling parasites and maintaining cleanliness. To be successful with some reptiles, like most members of the genus *Regina* (crayfish snakes) and the black swamp snake, we must come as close as possible to re-creating the environment. Still, we do not believe that it is necessary to bring in swamp mud and plants (which may contain parasites), as some have suggested. The artificial environment described for these "swamp" species in the striped crayfish snake section is probably close enough for long-term maintenance, and we have had a great deal of success with it.

These snakes are considered nocturnal, but do bask occasionally in captivity, so you may want to add a UV light source in addition to an incandescent bulb in a reflector (40–60 watts). The base temperature should probably go no lower than about 28.3°C (83°F), and the heat from the incandescent bulb will usually raise the temperature into the low 90s during the day.

Brumation is recommended, but it should be in damp cypress mulch at 10–15.5°C (50–60°F), not in the regular cage environment. In fact, wild members of this species have been observed to leave the water at this time and burrow in the soft soil surrounding their "swamp." Remember what may happen in cooler temperatures in an aquatic environment. Do not feed at this time but provide access to water by placing a small pan of the tea solution in the mulch.

To our knowledge, breeding has not been reported for this species in captivity, although females gravid at the time of capture have given birth in captivity (see above). The new-born snakes shed almost immediately after birth and will usually eat within 2 days. They are best removed to a smaller shallower environment than the mother's, as we have had

some drown. Small worms, fish, and sirens will be consumed right from the start. These snakes grow very rapidly.

With these cage modifications, the black swamp snake may be kept by almost anyone, anywhere. Tea, plastic plants, fish, and worms can be purchased even in the heart of the "big city." They are indeed fascinating little crea-tures, and mastering their captive environment should soon lead to captive breeding.

Senticolis triaspis
Green Rat Snake

The green rat snake is a medium-sized, 60–158-cm (24–63-inch), relatively slender, montane rat snake. In fact, the species name is now officially the mountain rat snake, although the subspecies that occurs in the United States (in four mountain ranges in southern Arizona and one mountain range in southern New Mexico), *S. t. intermedia*, is still called the green rat snake. It has only recently been removed from the genus *Elaphe* (rat snakes) based on a num-ber of morphological (structural) and genetic differences from members of that group. It is a rare snake in the United States, both in the wild and in captivity, although this may change soon due to captive breeding efforts. It receives its common name from the light green to olive green dorsal color of most adults.

Very little is known of the natural history of

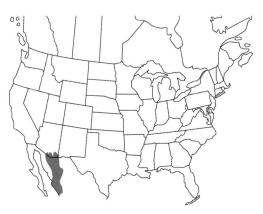

Senticolis triaspis

this snake. Some say it is arboreal, others say it is terrestrial. Some say it is diurnal, others say it is crepuscular. The preferred habitat of this species appears to be riparian woodlands in canyons in mountainous areas (Fowlie, 1965; Behler and King, 1979; Stebbins, 1985; Cran-ston, 1989a; Degenhardt et al., 1996).

The preferred food of wild specimens ap-pears to be small mammals including deer mice, *Peromyscus* sp., wood rats, *Neotoma* sp., and the domestic mouse, *Mus musculus* (Steb-bins, 1954; Cranston, 1989a). Lizards and birds have also been reported as food items (Steb-bins, 1985). So poorly known is this snake that just about everything available in the modern literature is the work of one herpetoculturist, Thurgess Cranston (1989a, b).

Suspected predators of this species include carnivorous mammals and birds of prey.

The times of mating and egg laying in the wild are still poorly known. Behler and King (1979) believe the eggs were laid in late sum-mer, as is the pattern for the Trans-Pecos rat snake. Indeed, Joleen Barry, who has main-tained and bred a pair of these snakes for years, says they are late breeders, usually breeding from late May to July. However, captive mating has occurred for others in the early spring with eggs being laid about 2 months later (June and July), so breeding may begin earlier, perhaps in response to different environmental conditions.

We captured one adult female on 25 April that laid 4 eggs on 4 July. These adherent eggs

Green Rat Snake, *Senticolis triaspis intermedia* (photo by David G. Campbell)

averaged 7.63 cm (3 inches) in length × 2.95 cm (1.2 inches) in width. Using the standard mixture of vermiculite (1:1 water to vermiculite by weight) and incubation temperatures of 27.2–30.5°C (81–86°F), 3 of these eggs died within several weeks. The fourth egg hatched on 14 September, an incubation period of 72 days. The hatchling appeared bright and alert and was normally colored (tan with darker spots), but had numerous kinks of the caudal spine and tail. In addition, a significant amount of yolk remained in the egg.

These observations confirmed Cranston's observation and raise several questions. Certainly, they confirm that the gestation period is long, at least 71 days in this instance, and that mating may occur in early spring. Second, they confirm that the incubation period is long, at least 72 days in this instance. Because of the low hatch rate, kinked spine, and large amount of remaining yolk, we suspect the incubation period was abnormally short, however. The primary cause of this incubation failure was thought to be excess moisture in the hatchling medium, much as suggested by Hammack

(1991). Certainly, the only egg to hatch was the only egg not in contact with the vermiculite. Another interesting observation was that the female laid her clutch on top of the egg-laying medium (sphagnum moss) not under it, as have so many of the other North American snakes we have bred, possibly suggesting the selection of a lower moisture area. Thus, the trend toward using less water in incubation mediums may be very important for many species and this desert species is definitely a prime candidate for such. The water to vermiculite ratio should probably not exceed 0.3:1 by weight. Although recounting these early experiences with this species is somewhat painful and embarrassing, we hope this discussion will help others avoid the same mistakes we have made.

Cranston painted a picture of this snake being a very sensitive nervous captive quite affected by stress. In addition, his work showed that wild-caught animals may be extremely heavily parasitized with intestinal parasites including nematodes, acanthocephalans, and protozoans (*Trichomonas* and coccidia) and blood parasites (hemogregarines and trypanosomes).

Drugs and doses recommended in Cranston (1989a) for the treatment of these parasites are in line with what has been reported in the general care section of this book. Blood parasites were not treated, and it is presently believed they may not be very harmful to the reptiles.

Cranston stated in no uncertain terms that it was vital to the survival of recently captured snakes that they be tested and treated for parasites within 1 month, as he had specimens die within 6 weeks of capture from untreated parasitism (coccidiosis). He also advised a prophylactic course of antibiotics based on a culture and sensitivity of newly captured specimens. Indeed, this may make sense for an easily stressed animal since its immune system may not function properly. Under such circumstances, normal bacterial commensals (bacteria that live in the gut and do not cause problems) may become pathogens (disease-causing organisms). In either case, it makes sense to work closely with your veterinarian if you are contemplating obtaining wild-caught specimens of this species.

The basic cage design discussed in the general care section will be suitable for this snake if several modifications are made that take their nervous nature into account. First, larger cages are preferable. Second, most who have maintained this snake successfully have provided numerous hiding places, and usually one of these is stuffed with moist sphagnum moss or vermiculite, thus creating a humidity box, which remains in the cage year round. Hide boxes at the top of the cage as well as the bottom are appropriate since they often like to hide up high at times. In fact, some of these snakes in captivity have been observed to climb a branch to their upper hide box during the day and climb down the branch to their ground hide box in the late afternoon or evening (a situation similar to that which has been reported in nature).

Artificial carpet/turf or mulch would be satisfactory as the substrate outside of the hide boxes. Cranston (1989b) reported that pine shavings were very acceptable to these snakes as well.

Drawer-style cages have worked very well if they are well ventilated. One of the specimens in our care developed a mixed bacterial/fungal

Green Rat Snake (immature), *Senticolis triaspis intermedia* (photo by David G. Campbell)

SPECIES: *Senticolis triaspis,* Green Rat Snake
MAINTENANCE DIFFICULTY INDEX: Captive-born and females 2; Males (wild-caught) 5
  (1 = easiest, 5 = most difficult)
AVERAGE SIZE: 60–158 cm (24–36 inches)
FOOD: Domestic mice, wild mice, birds
CAGE SIZE: 20-gallon long aquarium to display case
SUBSTRATE: Indoor-outdoor carpet, artificial turf, or mulch
VENTRAL HEAT: Yes
UV LIGHT: Unknown
TEMPERATURE RANGE: 20–27°C (68–80°F)
SPECIAL CONSIDERATIONS: Need large cages. Moist retreats necessry (humidity boxes).
  Brumation tricky. Some difficult to feed. See text.

dermatitis after it was placed in a poorly ventilated drawer-style cage with a continuously full water bowl. This infection, which appeared as multiple gray patches, was eliminated once the snake was placed back into a well-ventilated aquarium. If aquariums are used, a 10–20-gallon long aquarium is a sufficient size in which to house the younger members of this species; however, one may wish to partially cover the front or switch to a drawer-style cage if a specimen doesn't feed. Clean water should always be made available for this species if the cages are well ventilated. Ventral heat is also essential for this snake to do well and it must be provided all year, even during brumation, or Cranston warns they may become ataxic (unable to control their movement) in cooler temperatures. He used ventral heat to create a thermal gradient in the cage of 20–27°C (68–80°F). Barry noticed this incoordination as well. She stated it occurred at temperatures of 12.7°C (55°F) when no ventral heat was provided, thus supporting Cranston's observations. Her snakes recovered from the ataxia in 3 weeks with suitable warming, but she noticed these snakes failed to breed that year.

Thus, it appears that air temperatures lower than 16°C (60°F) may potentially cause ataxia and result in breeding failure as well if no ventral heat sources are provided. With ventral heat, air temperatures during brumation may drop lower, down to 9–13°C (48.2–55°F) for 2–3 months (Cranston, 1989b).

Feeding recently captured adults, particularly males, has been a real problem. While the females may consume domestic mice after they have settled down and feel secure, the males usually refuse them. Furthermore, the males may refuse to eat even wild mice adults, instead preferring barely weaned *Peromyscus* sp. and occasionally domestic mice scented with the wild rodent (Cranston, 1989a). Food items will be taken prekilled which is the preferred method.

Captive breeding of this snake has been accomplished several times and described by Cranston (1989b). As described above, the snakes were brumated for 3 months at 9–13°C (50–55°F), after which they were warmed for several weeks and the females were placed in with the males. Barry (pers. comm., 1993) brumated her green rat snakes from November to March at around 15°C (60°F).

Mating is similar to that described for many other colubrids except that Cranston observed that his captive males would not breed the same female more than once in a season, even though they would breed another female that had been bred by another male.

Females lay between 3 and 7 eggs roughly 50–80 days after mating, which hatch 77–88 days later at 26°C (78°F) (Cranston, 1989b). These eggs were incubated in a 50:50 combination of peat moss and sand mixed with some water to make it slightly damp. Vermiculite mixed as described in the general care section has also been used successfully. Interestingly, in these initial captive breedings with wild-caught animals reported by Cranston, egg fertility was very low (29%). Barry has reported 100% fertility with her two captive-bred animals for 3 years in a row. This suggests that green rat snakes are much like many other species of snakes in that the captive-born animal, well adjusted to captivity and lacking parasites, is far more likely to reproduce than short-term wild-caught animals. Perhaps as we learn more about this species' captive requirements and gain more experience incubating their eggs, captive breeding and high fertility rates will become a common occurrence.

The hatchlings are 28–35 cm (11–13.7 inches) long and are tan-colored with small dark brown saddles. They will usually take pinkies right away. If they do not, Cranston advises they be fed white-footed- or deer mice (*Peromyscus*), scented pinkies and switched to unscented pinkies in time. Barry insisted that scenting with wild mice was never needed for her hatchlings. Those fed three times per week doubled their weight in 6 months (Cranston, 1989b).

An interesting observation regarding the growth of this species was made by Barry. She observed that the young snakes grew very rapidly in length but didn't really "bulk out" until their third year.

Like many of the rat snakes, the juvenile pattern will fade and be replaced by the adult color pattern in about 2 years. One of Cranston's males mated at 31 months of age.

As one can infer from the details above, captive maintenance and breeding of this snake are not exactly easy. Fortunately, the care of the hatchlings is not very much different from the care of rat snake hatchlings (even the captive-born males feed with great regularity). And indeed, the captive-born juveniles hold the most promise for long-term captive breeding projects, as seen with the snakes in the care of Joleen Barry. Once larger numbers become available, they have the potential to become extremely popular snakes. The major drawback of this species is the fact that most are non-handleable nervous animals that may stop eating or fail to breed if they are handled. Hence,

the general rule is no handling except as necessary to clean the cage or treat the snake. In fact, if sufficient hiding places are available, most cleaning should be done without disturbing these snakes.

This snake is presently the subject of a number of strange rumors, some of which may have their basis in fact. Because they are sensitive animals and die frequently in captivity, some have sought to explain these deaths by blaming a virus. Furthermore, some believe it is a sexually transmitted virus. This is certainly possible; however, at this time no virus has been discovered. In addition, we are well aware that many dangerous organisms may be spread without sexual contact, be they bacteria, viruses, or protozoans. Just placing a wild-caught nonquarantined snake in with a long-term captive may result in the demise of the long-term captive. Indeed, Barry described one instance in which a long-term captive-born female died soon after breeding with a wild-caught male.

Another disturbing observation reported by several independent sources is that green rat snakes from different mountain ranges vary in their survivability in captivity. Those from the Chiricahuas die, according to these sources, while those from the other mountain ranges supposedly fare better in captivity. We do not know if this is true and we have no idea what the cause might be if it is true.

In our limited experience with these snakes, they appear to adapt fairly readily to captivity. Two juveniles and an adult female fed readily on domestic mice of the appropriate size (reportedly, the problem is feeding recently captured adult males). They remained nervous, however, and darted about in a jerky manner when handled. Repeated fecal exams of these wild-caught specimens failed to yield any parasites. Interestingly, these specimens were not captured in the Chiracahuas (where they are apparently heavily parasitized) suggesting there are different parasite loads in these widely separated populations, much as seen in other species.

Captive longevity for this snake has been listed at more than 19 years and 9 months (Snider and Bowler, 1992).

Sonora semiannulata
Ground Snake

The ground snake is perhaps one of the most common snakes of western North America. It ranges from southwestern Missouri, southern Kansas, and southeastern Colorado southward through much of Oklahoma and Texas, westward through southern New Mexico, Arizona, California, and Nevada, with isolated populations in Kansas, Colorado, Utah, Nevada, Idaho, and Washington (Stebbins, 1985; Conant and Collins, 1991). It is tremendously variable in coloration with some specimens being solid pink, brick red, orange, tan, brown, glossy black, or gray and others being ringed with black (rings or saddles numbering from 1–50) on a variable background color. Individuals from some areas may even have a broad middorsal stripe, and all of these forms may occur in the same area. Some are stunningly attractive. No matter what the pattern, however, all ground snakes can be identified by a dark spot on the front of each scale, a characteristic not found on any of the other small snakes in their range.

Ground Snake (red unicolor), *Sonora semiannulata* (photo by John Rossi)

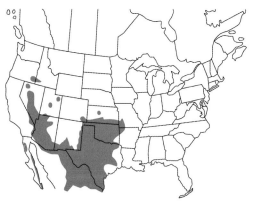

Sonora semiannulata

They are not large snakes; the average-sized ground snake ranges 20–30 cm (8–12 inches) in length, with a record length of 48 cm (18.9 inches) (Stebbins, 1985; Conant and Collins, 1991).

The preferred habitat of the ground snake appears to be any semiarid area with hiding places. Indeed, it appears quite variable, with some authors reporting wooded rocky terrain, deserts, prairies, limestone embankments, thorn scrub woodland, vacant lots, dumps, etc. Rocky hills with southern exposures are apparently very much to their liking (Kassing, 1961; Webb, 1970; Stebbins, 1972, 1985; Linder and Fichter, 1977; Behler and King, 1979; Nussbaum et al., 1983; Tennant, 1984; Hammerson, 1986; Conant and Collins, 1991; Degenhardt et al., 1996). The majority of what we know about these snakes comes from the classic study by Edith Force Kassing (1961), a study that is referred to heavily here.

As might be expected from such wide-ranging habitat generalists, they have a broad diet (of invertebrates) which has been reported to include in order of preference: spiders (family Lycosidae, wolf spiders) and their egg cases; centipedes, *Lithobius* sp., scorpions, family Buthidae; and insects (orders Lepidoptera—moths and butterflies, probably their larvae,

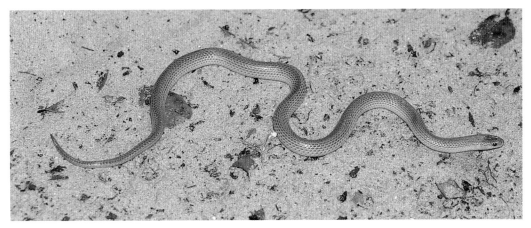

Ground Snake (dorsal stripe), *Sonora semiannulata* (photo by David G. Campbell)

Coleoptera—beetles, Hymenoptera—ants and wasps, Orthoptera—crickets) (Kassing, 1961). It is possible that some vertebrate prey may be taken; however, Degenhardt et al. (1996) reported finding one trying to eat a DOR gecko, *Coleonyx brevis*, in Big Bend National Park.

Known predators of this species include many larger snakes such as patchnoses, whipsnakes, longnose snakes, glossy snakes, king snakes, coral snakes, and night snakes (Tennant, 1984; Collins, 1993). Many mammals and birds also prey upon them, as well as collared lizards (Webb, 1970).

Mating has been observed to occur in wild or recently captured specimens in April, May, and June, and again in September. Mating behavior in these snakes appears every bit as complex as in some of the larger snakes, as many of the behaviors observed in the rat snakes and kingsnakes have also been observed in the ground snake. It is important to note that many of the attempted matings Kassing and others witnessed in captivity were just that—attempted matings. Apparently, some aspect of the timing or the environment was not correct in those cases. Perhaps a communal mating scheme is necessary; there was some evidence for this in Kassing's research. The temperature at the time of one of these captive matings was 31.6°C (89°F).

Egg laying occurs from the end of May through early July. Those in the south lay at the earlier end of this range, while those in more

Ground Snake (banded), *Sonora semiannulata* (photo by David G. Campbell)

northern localities lay their eggs later. In fact, there is one report of one of these snakes laying a clutch on 25 August (Staedeli, 1964). The time from mating to egg laying is thought to be around 3–6 weeks.

The incubation period of these eggs ranged 53–67 days with an average of 55 days at temperatures fluctuating from 27 to 32.2°C (80 to 90°F) (Kassing, 1961). This closely matches the observation of Staedeli (1964) of one clutch requiring a 56-day incubation period. It is important to note that only 15.4% of those eggs in Kassing's study hatched. It is difficult to say whether the temperature, humidity, fertility, or substrate was to blame. It is also known that stress may result in the premature deposition of eggs in some species, which could have been a factor in this case. See below. Degenhardt et al. (1996) report one female from New Mexico laid 5 eggs on 9 June, 4 of which hatched on 19 August, a 71-day incubation period.

The young snakes, which may also be variable in color (even from the same clutch), range from 7 to 12.5 cm (2.75 to 5 inches) long. Staedeli (1964) noticed that a monocolored gray hatchling developed a dorsal stripe within several weeks of hatching. These hatchlings feed on smaller versions of the same prey as their parents, which appear common in the fall. It is believed they grow rapidly and reach sexual maturity by their second spring (1.5 years old) at a length of 23–24 cm (9–9.5 inches) (Kassing, 1961).

One pair of ground snakes was collected in Palo Pinto County, Texas, on 28 March, 1999, within 100 meters of each other. The male (solid gray above) weighed 9 grams and measured 30 cm (11.8 inches) TL with a SVL of 24 cm (9.5 inches). The female (solid red above) weighed 7 grams and her TL was 26 cm (10.25 inches) and her SVL was 22 cm (8.7 inches). The pair was placed in an aquarium with numerous hiding areas and a water bowl, and offered crickets and wax worms as a staple diet. The pair mated in late April, and the female shed on 23 May and laid 4 eggs on 31 May. These nonadherent eggs ranged in length from 1.8 to 2.2 cm (0.7 to 0.9 inches) with an average length of 2.0 cm (0.8 inch). The width ranged from 0.6 to 0.8 cm (0.23 to 0.31 inches) with an average width of 0.65 cm (0.25 inches). All 4

A wide variety of snakes lay eggs, while others bear live young. The ground snake may produce the smallest eggs of all colubrid snakes, as shown here. (photo by David G. Campbell)

eggs weighed less than 2 grams. Incubation on a 50:50 mixture of vermiculite and water (by weight) at a temperature fluctuating from 22 to 31°C (72 to 88°F) with an average temperature of 27.2°C (81°F) resulted in hatching on 15 August, an incubation period of 75 days. The young snakes were all gray dorsally and pale white ventrally. They measured 9, 9.5, 9.5, and 10 cm (3.54, 3.7, 3.7, and 3.9 inches) TL. The SVLs were 7.5, 7, 7, and 8 cm (3.0, 2.8, 2.8, and 3.1 inches) respectively, with an average of 7.38 cm (2.9 inches) SVL and 9.5 cm (3.7) TL. The sex could not be easily determined, but there appeared to be three females and one male. All four snakes together weighed less than 1 gram! They shed within 10 days. First food offered was wingless fruit flies and 0.25-inch crickets, which were taken within several days. The cricket gutload diet was actually placed in the snake's cage. These small snakes seemed susceptible to dehydration and dysecdysis if kept without a moist substrate, and blister disease if kept too moist. Providing a moist area such as a humidity box over an otherwise dry substrate seemed to solve the problem. They also do not seem to climb very well, so a shallow easily accessible water bowl is necessary. These snakes could easily compete for the title of North America's smallest baby snakes, in close competition with the young of *Tantilla* species, worm snake, *Carphophis*, and earth snake, *Virginia*.

Color change has been reported to occur in these young snakes. This may occur over several weeks as reported elsewhere in this chapter, or over several months. A clutch may possess individuals with multiple color patterns, and the genetics of these variations have not yet been determined.

Ground snakes generally adapt readily to captivity and are easy to care for. They have not been popular with herpetoculturists, however, and very little has been written about their captive care. There are two reasons why this snake has not been commonly kept in captivity. The first is their small size. The second reason is their diet, which consists largely of invertebrates such as insects, spiders, and centipedes. We have also had success feeding these snakes

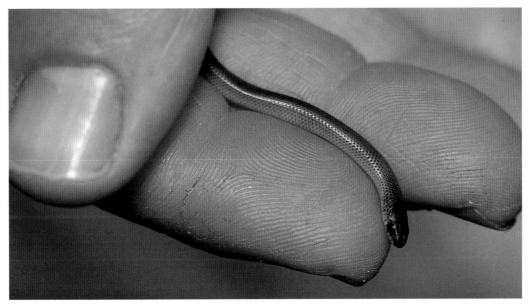

A newly hatched ground snake, measuring a whopping 8 cm (3 inches)! They readily consume small crickets (not pinheads). (photo by David G. Campbell)

crickets, ant eggs, and wax worms, although individuals vary in their preferences. Spiders are undoubtedly their favorite food, however.

Spiders may be collected in sufficient quantities by road cruising (look for blue-green eyeshine) or by using pit traps, two techniques well-known to herpetoculturists. They may also be collected while out rummaging through junk piles for herps. The fast-moving creatures may be batted with the bare hand such that they will be either killed or stunned but not flattened. They may then be picked up. Carry a zip-lock plastic bag to pop them into and you will always be ready. Centipedes may be collected with a small pair of metal forceps.

Fortunately, ground snakes rely heavily upon olfactory cues and readily consume frozen and thawed food items, which makes storage of their food much easier. Remember that insect- and invertebrate-eating snakes need to eat frequently, so plan on feeding at least 2–3 times a week during the active part of the year (spring, summer, fall). Remember also the warnings about calcium deficiencies in reptiles that eat only one species of insect. This can be overcome by feeding a variety and by feeding the

insects a high-calcium diet just prior to feeding them to your reptiles. See the general care section on feeding. Also be aware that these desert snakes, like most others, are largely nocturnal, so food is best accepted if offered at dusk. Specimens in our care have thrived solely on "gut-loaded" crickets for years.

Maintain these snakes in a desert terrarium as discussed in the general care section. Provide plenty of rocks or strips of bark. Make sure to provide clean fresh water at all times. Heat from above in the form of an incandescent light bulb (25–40 watts for a 5- or 10-gallon aquarium) is necessary and adequate. A 5- or 10-gallon aquarium is an excellent size enclosure for this species. Sometimes a smaller enclosure with just one hiding place makes it easier to feed the snake, since the keeper can just place the frozen and thawed item right in front of that spot rather than having to search the cage thoroughly or depend on the snake to find the food item in a large cage.

A humidity box is considered critical for all captive ground snakes, especially neonates and young animals.

Brumation is strongly recommended for this

SPECIES: *Sonora semiannulata*, Ground Snake
MAINTENANCE DIFFICULTY INDEX: 2 (1 = easiest, 5 = most difficult)
AVERAGE SIZE: 20–30 cm (8–12 inches)
FOOD: Crickets, ant eggs, waxworms, centipedes
CAGE SIZE: 5–10-gallon aquarium
SUBSTRATE: Sand
VENTRAL HEAT: No
UV LIGHT: No, but an incandescent bulb is useful
TEMPERATURE RANGE: 23–31°C (73.4–88°F)
SPECIAL CONSIDERATIONS: Insect and spider eaters. Generally do well in captivity.
    Provide moist retreat.

species, and it may be accomplished in the same cage without any modification. Winter temperatures that have been well tolerated by those in our care have fluctuated between 3 and 18°C (38 and 65°F).

Long-term maintenance and captive breeding of this species has not been accomplished at the time of this writing, although recently captured animals have been observed mating in the laboratory (Kassing, 1961). In addition, females captured when gravid have been known to deposit clutches of 4–6 eggs from June through August. These eggs have been incubated in the usual manner (and some in the not-so-usual manner) and hatched into young approximately 16 cm (4 inches) long (see above).

We have found these shy snakes to be adaptable little captives, eating almost anything they can swallow. Interestingly, if they cannot swallow an entire spider, they will swallow the abdomen and then press the thorax down and twist, presumably trying to separate the abdomen. This is unusual in that very few snakes have been known to consume parts of their natural prey items when the whole item is available. However, a similar behavior has been observed in a different family, the Leptotyphlopidae (blind snakes), when faced with a similar problem (eating termites that may be too large).

In many ways, these are delightful and fascinating snakes that are nonaggressive and easy to maintain. They do not appreciate handling, but this is a small flaw for an otherwise ideal terrarium snake. Snider and Bowler (1992)

failed to list a captive longevity for this species in captivity, but we have maintained a south Texas specimen collected as an adult for 4 years and 1 month.

Parasites have been observed in some of these snakes. One specimen from southern Texas had *Capillaria* eggs, while a specimen from west central Nevada was discovered to have filarial worms in the posterior vena cava (the major blood vessel returning blood to the heart). The latter snake had never done very well in captivity and these parasites, possible equivalents of heartworms in dogs, were suspected of hastening its demise.

The ground snake is the epitome of the "junk" snake in the minds of some people. They have a huge range and are very common within that range. In addition, a large part of their range falls within that area of the United States that is still not heavily developed, and may never be. Therefore, there is little desire to learn the captive requirements of these snakes and little fear that they will ever be in need of a captive breeding program. Perhaps most herpetoculturists are right in their lack of concern for this species, but remember the passenger pigeon. It is all too easy to eliminate a species about which we do not understand the requirements. Remember that habitat destruction and pollution are major causes of extinction, and both processes are occurring even in the middle of our most pristine deserts. No, the ground snake is not a junk snake. It is just a very common one right now.

Stilosoma extenuatum
Short-tailed Snake

The short-tailed snake is a rarely seen and poorly understood snake of the central Florida uplands. Even those who live within its range rarely see this snake, and certainly there are few in museum collections. Virtually nothing is known of its natural history, aside from its preferred habitat, which appears to be sandy-soiled, open, longleaf pine-turkey oak woods.

Literature reports of reproduction, behavior, natural food items, and predation are scarce and those of captive maintenance and reproduction are nonexistent. However, we have learned a great deal about this snake in recent years.

Short-tailed snakes have been found only in Florida so far. They range from southern Columbia and Suwannee Counties in northern Florida southward to Highlands County in south central Florida. They are small snakes, rarely exceeding 51 cm (20 inches), with a

Stilosoma extenuatum

record of 65.4 cm (26 inches) (Conant and Collins, 1991). They are also exceptionally thin snakes, with a large adult being no thicker than a child's soda straw. In fact, upon seeing these snakes for the first time most herpetologists are stunned by their slim form. The head, however, is short and blunt, looking remarkably like that of a kingsnake.

The color and pattern of these fossorial snakes is very similar to that of the pigmy rattlesnake, *Sistrurus miliarius*, and the southern hognose snake, *Heterodon simus*. Basically, they are light gray with black dorsal and lateral blotches. The dorsal blotches are frequently separated by areas of orange or reddish orange, again similar to the aforementioned species.

These snakes are thought to be primarily fossorial. They are rarely found on the surface except for the months of April and October. Presumably, they are searching for mates at these times, but not necessarily, since neonates and juveniles have been found at this time as well.

The natural prey of these incredibly thin snakes appears to be smaller snakes, particularly Florida crowned snakes, *Tantilla relicta* (Ashton and Ashton, 1981; Mushinsky, 1984), but Ditmars (1939) reported that they would also take brown snakes, *Storeria dekayi*, in captivity. We have observed a number of these snakes feed in captivity and have found them to take the following species: Florida crowned snake, *T. relicta*; two subspecies of brown snake, *S. dekayi*; two subspecies of redbelly snake, *S. occipitomaculata*; rough earth snake, *Virginia striatula*; ringneck snake, *Diadophis punctatus*; lined snake, *Tropidoclonion lineatum*; black swamp snake, *Seminatrix pygaea*; pine woods snake, *Rhadinaea flavilata*; rough green snake, *Opheodrys aestivus*; and the eastern glass lizard, *Ophisaurus ventralis* (Rossi and Rossi, 1993a, b; and more recent personal observations). Ground skinks, *Scincella lateralis*, have not been accepted by either the adults or juveniles in our care unless they are placed in the mouths of the specimens, in which case they will swallow them voluntarily. They will take snakes which have been frozen and thawed, even though movement appears important in eliciting the final strike.

Suspected predators of this species include ophiophagous snakes and carnivorous mammals.

Short-tailed Snake, *Stilosoma extenuatum* (photo by David G. Campbell)

Very little is known of this snake's reproduction. They are oviparous (Wright and Wright, 1957), but we do not know when mating season is, or the average clutch size, or the time of egg laying. The size of the neonates is unknown but we suspect that the neonates are smaller than 19 cm (7.5 inches), since one specimen of this size still had a very distinct umbilical scar. Juveniles also eat small snakes (Rossi and Rossi, 1993a).

Internal parasites have been reported from some of these snakes. Coccidia (Telford, pers. comm., 1992) and an unidentified nematode have been observed in the stool samples. Whether these organisms are harmful to this species or are just commensals is unknown at this time.

The short-tailed snake appears to be a very nervous and irritable snake. They seek cover when first discovered, but if trapped, they hiss, shake their tails, and may bite repeatedly. The bite is harmless to a human and most attempted bites will not make contact with or penetrate the skin. The bite may be associated with a

sneezelike hiss, which Conant and Collins (1991) compare with a milk snake's behavioral repertoire.

Captive maintenance of the short-tailed snake is similar to that of many other North American colubrids. The basic cage setup as described in the general care section, using artificial carpet/turf or cypress mulch as the substrate, appears to work very well for this species. They do seem to prefer mulch, as one might expect from their fossorial nature. A hide box will be well utilized by members of this species. A water bowl and other cage accessories such as a piece of rock, bark, or wood will complete the cage. Plastic plants are also a nice addition, and the snakes do occasionally climb into these plants.

It is important to note that several of these snakes in our care have done extremely well in the very simple plastic shoe box-type arrangement utilized by many breeders of other species.

A ventral heat source is considered helpful and an incandescent bulb of small to medium wattage (15–40 watts) will work excellently for these snakes. In most cases, those in our care

The mysterious short-tailed snake eating a Florida brown snake. For years, these snakes were believed to consume only Florida crowned snakes, *Tantilla relicta*. Our research has shown that they will consume at least eight species of small snakes and young legless lizards. Thus, they are specialized for an ophiophagous diet, but may not be as specialized as previously thought. (photo by John Rossi)

As mentioned above, the short-tailed snakes consume other snakes in captivity. The snakes consumed are usually smaller, and many of those we observed being consumed were neonates of the species listed above. The short-tailed snake is a constrictor, and it usually rapidly coils around the prey snake after grasping it. Its constricting abilities appear weak, however, and appear to function primarily in immobilizing the prey rather than killing it (Mushinsky, 1984; Rossi and Rossi, 1993a, b). This has been referred to as a more primitive type of constriction, which Greene and Burghardt (1978) refer to as being similar to the boid pattern of constriction. We have observed, as have others, that many prey snakes do escape from their coils. It must be remembered, however, that these observations are occurring above ground under highly artificial conditions. Escapes are probably rare in tight underground passageways where their prey may be found. Judging from the thin and elongate nature of these snakes, they are probably highly effective snake hunters, capable of pursuing their prey and capturing it in very small spaces.

did very well with only filtered natural light. Temperatures of 21–32°C (70–90°F) appear suitable during the active (feeding) time of the year, which ranges from March through October. Several months of lower temperatures during the winter are well tolerated by these snakes and may be important in captive breeding attempts. Temperatures of 10–18°C (50–65°F) have been well tolerated by those in our care.

There are no published reports of reproduction for this species. One adult female in our care was placed in with an adult male in early April and the male followed the female for a short period, while the female displayed rhythmic "jerking" type movement, but no copulation was observed and the behavior ceased in several minutes. No further observations have been made at the time of this writing. Sexing of

---

SPECIES: *Stilosoma extenuatum*, Short-tailed Snake
MAINTENANCE DIFFICULTY INDEX: 4 (1 = easiest, 5 = most difficult)
AVERAGE SIZE: 36–51 cm (14–20 inches)
FOOD: Crowned snakes (*Tantilla*); other small snakes
CAGE SIZE: 10–20-gallon long aquarium
SUBSTRATE: Dry loose sand (2–3 inches deep), cypress mulch
VENTRAL HEAT: Unknown if necessary, but a heat lamp above the sand probably is
UV LIGHT: No
TEMPERATURE RANGE: 27–32°C (81–90°F) day. Slightly cooler at night.
SPECIAL CONSIDERATIONS: Food availability is a real problem, but "tricks" may help.
  Permit is required to keep this species. Very little is known about it.

---

most individuals may be accomplished in most cases by using the "popping" technique to manually evert the hemipenes.

As can be seen from the above discussion, there is still a great deal to be learned about this species. We would like to thank the Florida Game and Fresh Water Fish Commission for granting us a permit to study these animals, and Gene Trescott for helping us acquire several specimens. See Trescott (1998).

We maintained one of these snakes for 1 year and 9 months.

This species is protected. A permit is required to collect or maintain this snake.

Storeria dekayi
Brown Snake

These are secretive small brown snakes which usually have one or two longitudinal rows of black spots along their backs. The dorsal color is extremely variable, however, and individuals may be pinkish, orangish, gray, or tan in color. The bellies are usually pink or cream-colored. They generally range 23–33 cm (9–13 inches) in length with a record of 52.7 cm (20.75 inches) (Conant and Collins, 1991).

There are eight subspecies in all, with five present in the United States and Canada. These include the northern brown snake, *S. d. dekayi*, the Florida brown snake, *S. d. victa*, the marsh brown snake, *S. d. limnetes*, the midland brown snake, *S. d. wrightorum*, and the Texas brown snake, *S. d. texana*. These subspecies are distinguished by minor variations in color pattern and scale count, as well as geographic origin, and they are discussed in detail in a number of field guides and other books (Behler and King, 1979; Ernst and Barbour, 1989; Conant and Collins, 1991). Some have proposed that the Florida brown snake is a separate species, *S. victa*. See Crother et al. (2000).

An extremely common snake in the eastern half of North America, the brown snake has one of the largest ranges of any snake species in the world. It ranges from southern Quebec, Ontario, and Maine southward to the Florida Keys, and westward to Minnesota and southeastern North Dakota to southeastern Mexico and all areas in between. As one might expect, the types of habitats occupied vary tremendously from one place to another, however, they all appear to have one thing in common, and that is the presence of earthworms and some sort of

Storeria dekayi

cover. Descriptions of habitats in which brown snakes have been found have included both dry and moist situations such as second growth woodlands, pine forests, hardwood forests, meadows, near ponds, lakes, marshes or swamps, and vacant lots (Wright and Wright, 1957; Mitchell, 1994; Palmer and Braswell, 1995; Harding, 1997). Within these habitats, it is thought to be largely secretive and nocturnal, often being found under a wide variety of objects by day, and abroad during the night. Mitchell (1994) described their microhabitat as the soil-humus layer. Wright and Wright (1957) sum up this species nicely with the statement: "It is a versatile, ubiquitous, urban and rural creature."

Earthworms are the preferred food; however, a number of other items have been reported in the diet of wild specimens. These include slugs, fish, amphibians and their eggs, as well as some insects and spiders (Wright and Wright, 1957;

Northern Brown Snake, *Storeria dekayi dekayi* (photo by David G. Campbell)

Minton, 1972; Mount, 1975; Brown, 1979; Dundee and Rossman, 1989; Mitchell, 1994). Brown snakes are also known to extract snails from their shells (Rossman and Myer, 1990).

Known predators of this snake include snakes such as racers, milksnakes, kingsnakes, cottonmouths, and pigmy rattlesnakes, birds such as hawks, shrikes, and robins, and mammals such as raccoons, skunks, and opossums (Palmer and Williamson, 1971; Ernst and Barbour, 1989).

Mating is known to occur in the wild during

Juvenile brown snake. This young brown snake from Ohio flattened out and performed a "tongue threat mimic," a behavior performed by threatened rattlesnakes. Many snakes behaviorally mimic venomous snakes. (photo by Roxanne Rossi)

Marsh Brown Snake, *Storeria dekayi limnetes* (photo by David G. Campbell)

1985). One report of 41 young exists (Morris, 1974)! The young range 7–11.7 cm (2.75–4.4 inches) in length at birth and are generally much darker than the adults (Ernst and Barbour, 1989; Conant and Collins, 1991). They also have a light collar in the neck region, which usually fades as they mature. The average weight of newborn brown snakes in North Carolina was 0.25 gram (E. E. Brown, 1992).

Fitch (1999) noted that in Kansas, as open pastures accumulated dense vegetation and woody plants, the number of brown snakes increased. Brown snakes in that study moved a great deal compared with other small snakes; daily movements of more than 30 meters were recorded! Fitch also commented on the early birth dates of these snakes (early August), which was presumably due to early activity associated with cold tolerance. Brown snakes in Kansas had a much lower population density than ringnecks, which Fitch estimated at less than 42 per hectare.

the spring, right after emergence from brumation (Clausen, 1936; Ashton and Ashton, 1981; Ernst and Barbour, 1989), but also in the fall (Collins, 1993). Females may retain viable sperm up to 4 months, however (Fox, 1956), and delayed ovulation the following spring may result in young being born fairly early the following year. Typically, spring mating will result in the birth of 3–31 young approximately 110 days later (105–113 days) (Fitch, 1970,

In captivity, brown snakes will do very well if kept in a 10- or 20-gallon aquarium with plain cypress mulch, or a mixture of mulch and soil, with strips of bark or flat rocks for hiding places and a clean water dish. The aquarium should be

Florida Brown Snake, *Storeria dekayi victa* (photo by David G. Campbell)

Midland Brown Snake, *Storeria dekayi wrightorum* (photo by John Rossi)

misted once or twice a week, and food should be offered twice a week in the summer, less in the spring and fall. No food should be offered during brumation, which can be accomplished in the usual manner as described in the general care section. The same cage arrangement can be used during this period; no changes are necessary. Make sure plenty of water is available during this time, and mist once in a while.

In the wild, adult brown snakes have been reported to eat worms, slugs, small salamanders, and soft-bodied insects. In captivity, earthworms are the preferred food (of both the snake and the keeper), and we suspect that worms alone represent a balanced diet (Rossi and Rossi, 1993c). With other animals, a balanced diet is considered one that is sufficient to allow growth and reproduction over two generations, and this would be a good way of defining a balanced diet for snakes as well. Some keepers have sprinkled the worms with Reptivite® just as they have done for ringneck snakes to tip the scale in their favor. This is probably not necessary.

These snakes do appear to bask on occasion, so provide an incandescent light source. Bottom heat does not appear necessary for this species. Incidentally, "hot rocks" may be useful for these very small snakes, as they may approach them from underneath, much as they would a sun-warmed object in the wild.

Immediately following brumation one should attempt breeding in the usual manner. Mating and live birth have been accomplished in captivity, but only rarely, probably from lack of interest. (See Table 5, the reproduction chart.)

The young are born alive in the late summer or fall and are usually 7.6–10.2 cm (3–4 inches) long at birth. If kept in the same manner as the adults (but in smaller enclosures so you can find them), and offered live tubifex worms or pieces of regular earthworms, they will do fairly well. You may have even better success with the babies by keeping moist soil with worms on one side and mulch on the other. This will provide a horizontal moisture gradient. House the young separately as they will fight over a worm. Some authors have reported that the babies will also eat fruit fly larvae, *Drosophila* sp. See the second to last paragraph in this section, however.

At this time it is not known if these snakes are parasitized frequently, but it is known that earthworms as an intermediate host for a number of parasites of other vertebrates, so we should be suspicious. Rhabditiform larvae (a type of nematode) have been reported in some brown snakes, so have fecal exams performed every once in a while, and treat if necessary.

The big problems for brown snakes in captivity are as follows: (1) skin infections leading rapidly to septicemia (bacteria in the bloodstream) and death. This is usually associated with too much moisture in the cage; (2) slow wasting if kept too warm. Theoretically, the higher temperatures cause certain vitamins to be utilized faster than the snake can replenish them, according to some herpetologists; and (3) dehydration, a common problem with this species if it is kept on artificial carpet/turf for any length of time, even if water is available.

In general, these are hardy, fascinating little snakes which are excellent feeders, even in a classroom situation with a bunch of children moving about. They put on quite a show when wrestling with a worm half their size. They rarely if ever bite, although they may musk or defecate when handled, so this is best left to the larger snakes.

Although generally considered easy to maintain in captivity, we have noticed that males

SPECIES: *Storeria dekayi*, Brown Snake
MAINTENANCE DIFFICULTY INDEX: 2 (1 = easiest, 5 = most difficult)
AVERAGE SIZE: 23–33 cm (9–13 inches)
FOOD: Earthworms, slugs, small salamanders
CAGE SIZE: 10-gallon aquarium
SUBSTRATE: Cypress mulch or mulch on one side and soil on the other. Bark or stones.
VENTRAL HEAT: No, but some heat source is recommended. (See text.)
UV LIGHT: No
TEMPERATURE RANGE: 20–25°C (68–77°F)
SPECIAL CONSIDERATIONS: Must mist substrate occasionally. Prone to dehydration if not
    kept in mulch mix, skin lesions if it is too moist, vitamin deficiency if too warm.

appear to be quite less aggressive at feeding. When housed together with other males or females, they sometimes refuse to feed.

Also, we have noticed a disturbing pattern with the males in our care. Following mating season in early spring, they tend to become anorectic and often die. Presently, we suspect a stress-related immune suppression is allowing a fatal septicemia (a massive infection) to occur.

In addition, neonates, while aggressive feeders, are also difficult to rear in numbers. They are very sensitive to humidity which is too high or low, and may die from desiccation or bacterial infection, respectively. They are often inhibited from eating by the presence of other young, and we have found them to be much more difficult to raise than either hatchling worm snakes or earth snakes. Hence, these snakes should not be thought of as being "easy" to breed in captivity, although wild-caught adults, especially females, appear to thrive for years.

One of these snakes survived 7 years in captivity (Snider and Bowler, 1992).

Storeria occipitomaculata
Redbelly Snake

Like the brown snake, which is its closest relative, the redbelly snake has a huge distribution in the eastern half of North America. They are seemingly ubiquitous where suitable habitat exists. From above, the redbelly looks very much like a brown snake; they may be brown or gray with darker markings and are very similar in size. However, closer examination will reveal several major differences. The bright red, yellow, or orange unmarked belly is the most outstanding feature from which the snake receives its common name. Also, the neck has three light-colored spots. These may look like the ring of a ringneck in some cases, especially when they fuse, as they do in northern Florida specimens.

There are three subspecies. The northern redbelly, *S. o. occipitomaculata*, has three well-defined spots on top of the neck. It occupies most of the range of the species.

The Florida redbelly, *S. o. obscura*, occupies northern Florida and much of the southeast from Georgia to eastern Texas. It may be recognized by the fusion of the neck spots into a solid band. The third subspecies is the Black Hills redbelly, *S. o. pahasapae*, which is found not only in the Black Hills region of western South Dakota, but intergrades over a wide range from Manitoba through Minnesota to northwestern Iowa. The spots on the neck of this subspecies are either absent or very reduced, and there is no spot on the fifth upper labial scale, as seen in

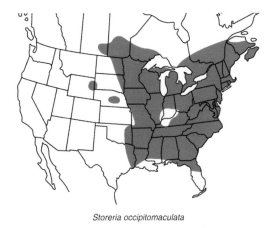

Storeria occipitomaculata

the other two subspecies (Conant and Collins, 1991).

As mentioned above, these are not large snakes. Adults range 20.3–40.6 cm (8–16 inches) in length (Conant and Collins, 1991; Allen, 1992). They are quite stocky for their length, however, and are often mistaken for venomous snakes by those who are not very familiar with snakes.

The preferred habitat of the redbelly snake is in moist woodlands, particularly near water in mountainous areas (Wright and Wright, 1957; Mount, 1975; Preston, 1982; Allen, 1992; Collins, 1993). Other habitats described include bogs, marshes, and swamps, usually under some object near the edge of such bodies of water (Preston, 1982), although Minton (1972) stated that most specimens in Indiana were found in dry forested areas. Like their close relatives the brown snakes, they appear to be crepuscular or nocturnal, emerging primarily at night to forage and hiding under surface objects or leaf litter by day. They are not strictly nocturnal, however, and they have been observed abroad during the day in the south (Dundee and Rossman, 1989; personal observations). Occasionally, these snakes do climb in low bushes (Smith, 1961).

Body temperatures of two wild specimens were measured at 24.3°C and 28.2°C (75.7°F and 82.8°F) by Brattstrom (1965).

The preferred food of the redbelly snake over most of its range appears to be slugs (Hamilton and Pollack, 1956; Wright and Wright, 1957; Brown, 1979; Ernst and Barbour, 1989) although

Mount (1975) and Preston (1982) mention insects (such as beetle larvae), snails, isopods, and other invertebrates (such as millipedes). Earthworms are also fairly commonly reported food items for wild specimens (Wright and Wright, 1957; Ernst and Barbour, 1989; Dundee and Rossman, 1989). Captive specimens from North Dakota in our collection readily consumed earthworms. Small frogs and salamanders have also been reported by two authors (Linzey and Clifford, 1981; Ashton and Ashton, 1981). Like brown snakes, redbelly snakes are capable of extracting snails from their shells (Rossman and Myer, 1990).

There are many natural predators of this species. These include kingsnakes (mole, common, milk), racers, and in Florida, captive short-tailed snakes (Ernst and Barbour, 1989; personal observations). Birds such as hawks, crows, and chickens are also known to consume them, as well as mammals, such as shrews and raccoons (Ernst and Barbour, 1989; Linzey and Clifford, 1981; Harding, 1997).

Mating is known to occur during the entire active season (from spring to fall) (Trapido, 1940; Wright and Wright, 1957; Fitch, 1970; Gregory, 1977; Ernst and Barbour, 1989). Birth of 1–21 young, usually 2–8, occurs from midsummer to late fall. These young usually measure 7–10 cm (2.75–4 inches) in length (Conant and Collins, 1991).

Florida Redbelly Snake, *Storeria occipitomaculata obscura* (photo by anonymous)

Northern Redbelly Snake, *Storeria occipitomaculata occipitomaculata* (photo by David G. Campbell)

Sexual maturity is believed to occur at 2 years of age at sizes that vary from population to population (Semlitsch and Moran, 1984). Sperm can be maintained in the oviducts of the female to allow fertilization in the spring (Fitch, 1970).

Interestingly, the redbelly snake is dimorphic over much of its range. The two morphs are referred to by most herpetologists as light morph and dark morph snakes. The percentage of each morph varies from population to population. In northern Florida, the dark morph appears much more common.

We have collected scores of these snakes crossing the roads that pass through swampy areas in pine-dominated forests in the Osceola National Forest. They actively cross roads late into the night (even on cool nights)—behavior that suggests that they may be truly nocturnal and not just crepuscular.

Two of the most comprehensive studies on redbelly snakes were those of Blanchard (1937) and Semlitsch and Moran (1984).

The redbelly snake should be set up in a captive environment exactly the same as the brown snake, with a 50:50 mixture of cypress mulch and potting soil as the substrate or plain cypress mulch on one side and soil on the other. It can be anywhere from 2 inches deep to one quarter the length of the snake. Maintain good ventilation and mist the substrate occasionally. Stir every 2–4 weeks and change about every 3 months. Place bark or flat stones on the surface to provide refuges. Plastic plants are a nice addition. A great alternative is to provide a humidity box, a plastic container which has a semimoist substrate such as sphagnum moss. This arrangement negates the need for soil elsewhere in the cage. Maintain a small bowl of clean water, partially submerged in the substrate. A 10-gallon aquarium will be sufficiently large for most adults. House individually.

Some of these snakes will consume earthworms, but most of the specimens we have maintained (mostly from northern Florida) will flatly refuse worms and eat only slugs. Furthermore, they seem to prefer smooth-skinned gray or tan slugs. Very large slugs, black slugs, and rough-textured slugs are usually ignored by redbellies, although northern specimens (from New York State) will tackle them. Live tubifex worms will be taken by some, but you will have better luck if you chop them into short pieces. If you have a snake that eats earthworms or

SPECIES: *Storeria occipitomaculata*, Redbelly Snake
MAINTENANCE DIFFICULTY INDEX: 3 (1 = easiest, 5 = most difficult)
AVERAGE SIZE: 20–25 cm (8–10 inches)
FOOD: Slugs, slugs, slugs but some eat earthworms, or tubifex worms
CAGE SIZE: 10-gallon aquarium
SUBSTRATE: Cypress mulch and potting soil mix (50:50) or just cypress mulch with soil on
   one side
VENTRAL HEAT: No
UV LIGHT: No
TEMPERATURE RANGE: 20–25°C (68–77°F)
SPECIAL CONSIDERATIONS: Food availability is a real problem, especially in cool
   weather. Can get skin lesions if too moist, but also dehydrate on carpet/turf.

tubifex worms, try to avoid feeding slugs at all, as some specimens we have done this with have refused to go back to worms afterward. One specimen which refused to eat anything but slugs did eat a piece of a giant slug that had been cut into suitably sized pieces. Slugs that have been frozen and thawed will also be taken, but the snake will have much more difficulty swallowing a dead slug, as the mechanics of swallowing a slug appear to involve the movement of the slug. Interestingly, southern redbelly snakes will gladly devour slugs captured in the northern states. Some have suggested that small amphibians will also be taken but we have never tried any.

Underground (ventral) heat does not seem necessary and neither does a UV light source. Brumation in the same cage is strongly recommended and is both better for the snake and easier on the keeper.

To our knowledge, successful breeding has not been accomplished in captivity. However, so few people have seriously tried to keep and breed these secretive snakes that we really don't know if they require more than just the standard approach to breeding. If you want a challenge, try to maintain a *Storeria* colony!

These snakes may be parasitized. One recently captured specimen from northern Florida was heavily infested with protozoans, specifically ciliates. *KEEP IN MIND, HOWEVER, THAT SOME CILIATES MAY BE NORMAL (COMMENSALS) FOR SOME OF THESE SMALL SNAKES AND TREATING MAY NOT BE INDICATED. UNLESS THE SNAKE IS SHOWING OTHER SIGNS OF ILLNESS SUCH AS LACK OF APPETITE, WEIGHT LOSS, OR FOUL-SMELLING LOOSE STOOL, WE WOULD ADVISE AGAINST TREATING.* Also remember that metronidazole, the drug of choice for treating most protozoan parasites in reptiles, is extremely difficult to dose accurately in these small snakes, and is toxic (producing seizures) if the dose is exceeded by too much. In these instances, the liquid form of metronidazole (5 mg/ml) is extremely useful.

One advantage of keeping this snake is that it bears live young. However, baby redbellies, like their parents, feed primarily on slugs—baby slugs!! And if you think it's difficult finding slugs, try finding baby slugs! On the bright side, breeding slugs in captivity may not be that difficult, but we haven't seen the procedure described. Other authors have reported that *Drosophila* larvae (fruit fly larvae) are also taken by babies, but the specimens we have worked with seem to want only one thing—slugs. Incidentally, they need about two feedings per week, so count on needing between 100 and 200 slugs per year (minimum) for an adult snake, possibly more smaller slugs for the babies.

So far, the longest record of this snake surviving in captivity has been only 4 years and 7 months (Snider and Bowler, 1972), but we suspect they can live much longer.

Tantilla sp.
Blackhead, Flathead, and Crowned Snakes

The genus *Tantilla* is a large group of small flatheaded snakes which, considering their huge range within the United States and Mexico, is extremely poorly known. They are normally 12.7–38.1 cm (5–15 inches) in length with a record of nearly 66 cm (26 inches) in one species, the blackhood snake (*Tantilla rubra*). They are usually tan to brown-colored animals with black or dark brown heads (with the exception of the flathead snake, *T. gracilis*, which does not have a black head in most cases). Many possess white collars. All of them possess 15 rows of smooth scales dorsally that usually do not have any black spots on them and ventral scales that are primarily pinkish, orange, or red in color (but white or yellowish in some), which are also unmarked by black spots. The ventral color (where present) usually does not extend all the way to the end of each ventral scale and therefore looks like a thick stripe running down the middle of the belly. This helps to distinguish members of this group from some of the other small snakes, namely ringnecks.

As mentioned above, the natural history of this entire group is very poorly known. The best

Southeastern Crowned Snake, *Tantilla coronata* (photo by R. W. Van Devender)

observations of their behavior have come from captive specimens, and since very few have been successfully maintained in captivity for any length of time, our knowledge of their behavior is very sketchy. Combining the observations made by field herpetologists and what has been observed in captive specimens, it appears that they prefer loose, usually sandy soils with a fairly high moisture content where there may be varying amounts of ground cover such as rocks, logs, etc. Their presence in an area, however, does not appear to be strongly correlated with a particular type of vegetation or assemblage of such, but many specimens have been collected in dry pine forests.

Open areas are preferred. Fitch (1999) observed two small colonies of flathead snakes disappear from south-facing limestone outcroppings as trees and brush invaded their habitat.

Most of them appear to be especially fond of centipedes, but different species will take other invertebrate prey in varying quantities. These include beetles, butterfly and moth larvae, spiders, termites, and, rarely, earthworms. Millipedes have been found in the stomach contents of some of these snakes, but none of the snakes in our care showed any interest in them.

Known predators of these snakes include other snakes, lizards, birds, and small mammals such as moles, shrews, skunks, armadillos, and raccoons (Tennant, 1984; Ernst and Barbour, 1989; Collins, 1993; Palmer and Braswell, 1995). In two separate instances, frogs were observed eating these snakes (Burt and Hoyle, 1935; McDiarmid, 1968).

From the few observations made by us and others, it appears these snakes may be largely crepuscular (dawn and dusk active) although many may be nocturnal. Certainly, they appear to be very secretive, almost always being found under a rock or other surface debris except for very brief periods of time.

Degenhardt et al. (1996) reported that they regularly found *Tantilla hobartsmithi* on the

Big Bend Blackhead Snake, *Tantilla cucullata*. Formerly known as the Devil's River Blackhead Snake or the Blackhood Snake, this snake is the largest and one of the rarest of the genus. (photo by Scott Cushnir)

road on evenings when temperatures were 15–25°C (59–77°F).

Our knowledge of reproduction, especially captive reproduction, is very limited. It is known that within the United States most species mate in the spring (April to May) and lay 1–4 eggs in late spring or early summer (usually in June). These snakes are also known to mate in the fall and females may retain the sperm until the following spring (Aldridge, 1992). Like the blind snake, females of this species have lost the left oviduct and this is considered to be an independently evolved ad-

aptation for a fossorial way of life. Another observation of interest is that *Tantilla* females usually ovulate far more eggs than the normal clutch size produced (3–4 times as many) and that most of these eggs appear to be reabsorbed (Fitch, 1970). Those eggs laid have an incubation period of approximately 2 months at which time the 8-cm (3-inch) long hatchlings emerge. The young grow rapidly and probably reach sexual maturity by 1 year of age. In Oklahoma, flathead snakes reach sexual maturity by their third year (Force, 1935).

There are 11 species within the United States (about 50 in the genus, which ranges all the way down to Argentina). Within the United States they are primarily southern snakes, but three species range far into the north. These are the southeastern crowned snake, *Tantilla coronata*, which ranges as far north as southern Indiana and Virginia; the flathead snake, *T. gracilis*, which ranges as far north as northern Kansas, central Missouri, and southern Illinois; and the plains blackhead snake, *T. nigriceps*, which ranges as far north as Nebraska and eastern Colorado. Most of the other species have extremely restricted ranges within the United States, such as the Mexican blackhead snake, *T. atriceps*, which is found only in southern Texas; the western blackhead snake (formerly known as the California blackhead snake), *T. planiceps*, which is found only in

Flathead Snake, *Tantilla gracilis* (photo by David G. Campbell)

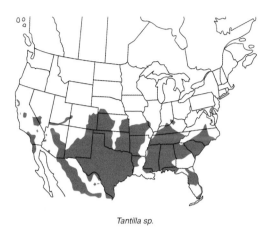

Tantilla sp.

ber that the geographic origins of the snakes in question is probably the most useful information in properly identifying many of these snakes.

Care

Fortunately, at the present time it appears that the care and maintenance of these mild-mannered secretive little snakes is the same for most members of the genus, taking into account minor variations in diet and perhaps preferred temperature range. It is important to note we still have many more questions than answers when it comes to maintaining and breeding members of this group, but we have had some success using the captive environment and diet discussed below.

Most books state that these snakes eat larval insects, live in sandy soil, and never do well in captivity. This is not entirely true or at least not that simple. These snakes will eat insect larvae and spiders, but they seem to prefer centipedes. They are burrowers, but not as much so as blind snakes and worm snakes (Clark, 1968). They live in sandy or other soil types (Clark, 1968), but they also bask partially submerged, just below the surface of the sand (or soil). They also come to the surface when it rains heavily. This suggests that they, like many other snakes, prefer to be warm, and if not completely dry at

central and southwestern California; the rim rock crowned snake, *T. oolitica*, which is found only in southeastern Florida; the Florida crowned snake, *T. relicta*, which is found only in central and northern Florida; the Big Bend blackhead snake, *T. rubra*, whose two subspecies, the blackhood snake, *T. r. cucullata*, and the Devil's River blackhead snake, *T. r. diabola*, are found only in a small area of western Texas; and the Chihuahuan and Yaqui blackhead snakes, *T. wilcoxi* and *T. yaquia*, respectively, which reach only into southeastern Arizona. The southwestern blackhead snake, *T. hobartsmithi*, is the only species in the far western United States to have a sizable range, and this includes southeastern California, much of Arizona and southern Utah, and a large portion of western Texas and adjacent Mexico.

Knowing where these snakes live is one thing, but identifying them, maintaining them, and breeding them in captivity is another. Even trained herpetologists have a difficult time identifying these snakes in areas where a number of species overlap. They frequently must resort to the use of meristic characters (scale counts) or internal morphology in order to make a positive identification. It is beyond the scope of this book to discuss these identification characters in detail; however, a brief summary of distinguishing characteristics is presented in Table 11 for completeness (captive breeding cannot be attempted without proper identification). See Conant and Collins (1991) and Stebbins (1985) for more details. Remem-

Plains Blackhead Snake, *Tantilla nigriceps* (photo by David G. Campbell)

Table 11. Quick Reference for Identification of Blackhead, Flathead, and Crowned Snakes, *Tantilla* sp.

Snake	Distinguishing Characteristics
Mexican* *T. atriceps*	Rear edge of cap straight. Stops at back of large scales on head (parietals). No white collar. 12.7–23.1 cm (5–9.1 inches). Only in southern Texas in United States.
Southeastern Crowned *T. coronata*	Only blackhead east of Mississippi River and north of Florida. Thick white collar and black on neck. 20.3–33 cm (8–13 inches).
Flathead *T. gracilis*	No black cap, but if present is concave at rear. 17.8–25.1 cm (7–9.9 inches).
Southwestern** *** *T. hobartsmithi*	No dark band or spots at rear edge of white collar. Cap does not go below angle of jaw. 17.8–38.1 cm (7–15 inches).
Plains* *T. nigriceps*	Head cap extends two or more scale rows past large scales on head and pointed or convex at rear edge. No white collar. 17.8–38.2 cm (7–15.1 inches).
Rim Rock Crowned *T. oolicta*	Cap solid from snout to neck in most. Only blackhead in extreme southeastern Florida. 17.8–29.2 cm (7–11.5 inches).
Western** *T. planiceps*	Dark band or spots at rear edge of white collar. Cap does not go below angle of jaw. Possible middorsal stripe. 12.7–39.4 cm (5–15.5 inches). Only in western California.
Florida Crowned *T. relicta*	Only blackhead in peninsular Florida. 17.8–22.9 cm (7–9 inches).
T. r. neilli	Black on head and neck continuous
T. r. relicta	Thick white collar, but very little white on head
T. r. pamlica	Thick white collar with a good deal of white on head
Big Bend *T. rubra*	
T. r. cucullata	Black cap extensive, covering both dorsal and ventral head and neck. If collar present, it is interrupted by black. 21.6–65.8 cm (8.5–25.9 inches). Only in western Texas.
T. r. diabola	Same as above, but usually has white collar that is not interrupted by black. 21.6–57.8 cm (8.5–22.75 inches). Only in western Texas.
Chihuahuan *T. wilcoxi*	Thick white collar crosses at back of large head scales (parietals). Cap extends to angle of jaw. 17.8–35.6 cm (7–14 inches). Only in southeastern Arizona.
Yaqui*** *T. yaquia*	Thick white collar crosses 2 to 4 scales behind large head scales (parietals). Often has dark spots at its posterior edge. Cap extends below angle of jaw. Whitish spot on side of head. 17.8–32.4 cm (7–12.75 inches). Only in southeastern Arizona.

*,**,*** Snakes that are most frequently confused with each other have the same number of asterisks.

least not entirely moist, although they may frequently visit moist areas to capture their prey and possibly to avoid desiccation. Snakes kept in moist sand never seem to do well because they develop skin infections or respiratory infections and die. As with most small snakes, these infections progress rapidly. Typically, the keeper notices blisters one day, labored breathing the next, and finds the snake dead the following day. Furthermore, veterinarians have an extremely difficult time treating the very small snakes as they are very hard to dose accurately. Therefore, the following arrange-

ment is proposed for keeping *Tantilla* warm and hopefully healthy for long periods of time. We have kept a number of specimens for long periods of time this way.

In a 5–10-gallon aquarium, place 2.5 cm (1 inch) of regular aquarium gravel. Then add water until it is just touching the top of the gravel. Then place 10 cm (4 inches) of sand from the place of capture (if this is not known, "silver" sand, beach sand, or even children's playbox sand may be used) over the gravel. Bake the sand first at 149°C (300°F) for 15 minutes. On top of this place several pieces of

Western Blackhead Snake, *Tantilla planiceps* (photo by Steve Barten)

bark (also baked) or flat rocks to provide surface refuge. Take a 25- or 40-watt incandescent bulb with a reflector and place it about 30 cm (1 foot) above the surface of the sand. Provide light for about 10–12 hours per day (shorter in the wintertime). Add water as needed to keep the water level stable. This arrangement will provide a vertical temperature and moisture gradient, with the bottom being the coolest and most moist. The snake can choose the temperature and humidity preferred. A small shallow water bowl should be set into the surface and filled frequently. Change the sand and wash the gravel every 3–4 months. House the snakes singly to avoid competition for food and possible spread of infection.

Florida Crowned Snake, *Tantilla relicta* (photo by David G. Campbell)

Centipedes should be added to the terrarium weekly (usually one medium to large size centipede per week will be sufficient). Recently, some amateur herpetologists reported that both wax worms, mealworms, and crickets have been consumed by captive specimens. The snakes in our care showed no interest in mealworms, but if most do, this could represent a major breakthrough in the captive maintenance of this species. Whether this will represent a balanced diet is also unknown. If mealworms are fed, the high-calcium diet mentioned in the feeding section under general care is recommended for them. Feeding grubs to crickets is also very healthful for the snakes that consume those crickets.

It is not known if brumation is necessary for these species, but as with most native species, it will probably increase your chances of successful mating. Cool down in the same cage, but with shorter periods of light and lower temperatures for 1–5 months. Do not feed during this time. See the section on brumation under general care.

As mentioned above, very little is known about reproduction except that breeding probably occurs in the spring as up to 4 eggs are laid in the late spring or early summer. One may attempt breeding as mentioned for other species in the general care section (i.e., the female is placed in with the male just after brumation).

Chihuahuan Blackhead Snake, *Tantilla wilcoxi* (photo by R. W. Van Devender)

See Table 5, the reproduction chart. As with other snakes kept this way, finding the eggs may be a big problem. Watch the female's activity pattern and girth for clues as to when to look for the eggs. Eggs may be clearly visible in the abdomen of these small snakes.

Fecal exams performed on these snakes have revealed rhabditiform larvae (a kind of nematode), two kinds of coccidia, and other parasites. These may be isolated occurrences or very common, and if common may help to explain why these voracious centipede eaters do poorly when placed under the normal stress of captivity. Deworming and treating these little snakes for coccidia is extremely difficult, however, because of their small size.

When maintained as mentioned above, these little snakes are fascinating to observe. They will remain submerged most of the day, often emerging at dawn or dusk to patrol their cages. Upon locating a centipede, they will strike rapidly (this is a pretty wild sight when the

Yaqui Blackhead Snake, *Tantilla yaquia* (photo by David G. Campbell)

SPECIES: *Tantilla* sp., Blackhead, Flathead, and Crowned Snakes
MAINTENANCE DIFFICULTY INDEX: 5 (1 = easiest, 5 = most difficult)
AVERAGE SIZE: 12–55 cm (5–22 inches)
FOOD: Centipedes, insect larvae
CAGE SIZE: 5–10-gallon aquarium
SUBSTRATE: Gravel, sand
VENTRAL HEAT: No
UV LIGHT: No, but an incandescent bulb strongly advisable
TEMPERATURE RANGE: 25–35°C (77–95°F)
SPECIAL CONSIDERATIONS: Most eat centipedes, which are often time-consuming to
    procure. See text.

snake emerges from just under the surface of the sand) and hang on while the centipede thrashes about violently. The snakes will often be bitten repeatedly, but seem oblivious to the centipede's bite (although one time we noted some exposed muscle tissue in one captive after it had been fighting with a centipede). After several minutes, the snake will begin chewing and working its way toward the centipede's head (and presumably injecting venom as it does since the centipede seems to become segmentally paralyzed, with all areas behind the snake's head paralyzed and those still to be chewed on thrashing occasionally), stopping only if the centipede begins thrashing wildly again. The centipede will usually go limp in 15–30 minutes and the snake will swallow it from the head end. The snake will submerge after a big meal and will not be seen again for 5–7 days (the same is true just prior to a shed). A 22.9-cm (9-inch) *Tantilla* will take centipedes up to 10.2 cm (4 inches) long and about the same girth as itself! Frozen centipedes will also be taken by many, and this may help with parasite control.

Overall, these snakes make fascinating captives, but because they are not large or flashy-colored snakes, few people have attempted to maintain them and little was known of their captive requirements until recently. With the advent of the three-layer cage described above, the first major obstacle has been cleared. This is not to say that this is the only cage setup that will work, but it is one. Other simpler environments providing moisture and thermal gradients may be suitable (e.g., the wet/dry cage for

A slide-magnifying loupe is ideal for identifying very small species alive in the field. It allows accurate head and labial scale counts for definite identification.

small fossorial snakes of the eastern United States and Canada).

Providing food is also difficult. Now, however, so many different types of insects are bred in captivity that this is also not the obstacle it once was. Wax worms, mealworms, and others, offered to provide a variety, may provide an alternative to wild-caught centipedes and insect larvae. But remember that frozen and thawed centipedes may be used as a supplement to this diet.

It is not surprising that Slavens and Slavens (1990, 1991) or Snider and Bowler (1992) did not list either a captive longevity or a single specimen in captivity for any of these snakes (11 species). Two specimens of *Tantilla relicta* in our care survived over 1 year and 1 month in captivity.

Introduction to the Garter Snakes

The garter snakes are a huge and diverse group of snakes that occupy a variety of habitats throughout North America. Including the two species of ribbon snakes, there are 16 species (at last count) of the genus *Thamnophis* in the United States and Canada, more species than any other genus. In addition, they occupy the largest geographic area and extend farther north than any other group of snakes. Thus, they are arguably the most successful and adaptable group of North American snakes.

Yet the group is indeed very diverse. Among its ranks are several relictual species, apparently specialized on one food item or another such as earthworms or slugs, and they are limited in size and geographic distribution by the limitations of that prey. Several other species are highly aquatic and apparently specialized on fish, while several are very terrestrial and will eat almost anything. It is this handful of terrestrial species, most notably the common garter snake, *T. sirtalis*, the plains garter snake, *T. radix*, the western terrestrial garter snake, *T. elegans*, the checkered garter snake, *T. marcianus*, and to some extent the western ribbon snake, *T. proximus*, which by their adaptable natures have occupied habitats as varied as subarctic boreal forests to desert oases and tropical thornforests. It is these terrestrial species that have occupied huge ranges across North America and have made the garter snakes a transcontinental group. And as stated elsewhere in this book, it is these highly adaptable wide-ranging species that also adapt readily to captivity. Common garter snakes, like common kingsnakes, eat domestic rodents readily in most cases. Indeed, it has been our experience and that of others that these regular-headed, normal-eyed, terrestrial garter snakes readily consume mice, while the long-headed (long-jawed) bug-eyed species resist feeding on mice unless heavily scented (these are aquatic fish-eating snakes in nature). The same

can be said for the short-headed (worm- or slug-eating) species; they also resist feeding upon rodents and are therefore considered somewhat more difficult to maintain in captivity. The long-jawed species (presumably an adaptation to assist in catching fish—sort of snake versions of gharials) include the western aquatic garter snake, *T. couchii*, the narrowhead garter snake, *T. rufipunctatus*, and the giant garter snake, *T. gigas*. The small-headed garter snakes include the northwestern garter snake, *T. ordinoides*, Butler's garter snake, *T. butleri*, and the shorthead garter snake, *T. brachystoma*.

Captivity

In general (regardless of the dietary preferences), most garter snakes have similar problems and requirements in captivity. The keeper needs to remember that the basic cage arrangement discussed in the general care section will work extremely well as long as the ventilation is adequate. Artificial carpet/turf works well as the substrate since it will not fall apart when it gets wet as do many other substrates. It will also dry out rapidly if it gets wet. A good stable place to hide, a small water bowl, and ventral heat or heat from above in the form of an incandescent bulb are all considered essential. It is certainly true that many garter snakes have done well for years in captivity without ventral heat or thermal gradients (much like some kingsnakes and rat snakes); however, we must remember that many of these snakes have preferred optimum temperature ranges near that which may be found in many homes. This does not lessen the importance of a thermal gradient for these species. It means only that they have been accidentally provided with them in some homes. *A thermal gradient is important!*

Other cage accessories that beautify the enclosure and may reduce the stress of captivity include plastic plants and stable rocks and branches (bake branches first at 149°C (300°F) for 15 minutes to kill mites).

As mentioned above, most garter snakes (but not all) prefer amphibians or fish. Some are specialized on worms and at least one species appears to prefer slugs. All of these food items are likely to be heavily parasitized and may serve as intermediate hosts for parasites that infect garter snakes. In addition, many garter snakes are likely to be heavily parasitized when they arrive in captivity. This means the herpetoculturist needs to do two things to keep these snakes healthy. The first is to have the snake checked for parasites and treated for them as necessary. The second is to reduce the intake of parasites by controlling the quality of food. This is discussed in detail in the general care section, but basically involves either feeding captive-bred food items (clean food items) such as mice, some fish, and worms or controlling the parasites in wild-caught food items. Many, but not all, of these parasites may be killed by freezing the food items for several days prior to feeding them to your garter snake.

Be aware that a diet of strictly frozen and thawed fish is also fraught with danger for the captive garter snake. Basically, this diet is likely to cause the snake to become deficient in thiamin (vitamin B$_1$) or vitamin E. A vitamin B$_1$ deficiency will cause neurologic signs, while a vitamin E deficiency will lead to inflammation of fat, also known as steatitis. These problems can be avoided by feeding a variety of foods (see below), using fresh captive-bred fish on occasion, and supplementing with both vitamins every 6 months. This is discussed in more detail in the general care section.

Remember also that many garter snakes are extremely scent-oriented and therefore initially may be easily tricked into consuming prekilled mice by using one of their preferred food items, be it amphibians, fish, worms, or in some cases slugs, in order to scent the mice. *After a variable amount of time, depending on the size, age, and species of garter snake, most will readily accept prekilled unscented mice as gluttonously as any rat snake.* In addition, most are too small to swallow scented pinkies initially and may need to be head started on worms, small fish, and fish-scented mouse tails or pinkie parts.

Perhaps the toughest garter snakes to maintain are the young garter snakes. Because of their small size they are prone to desiccation (dehydration) if kept too dry. Yet, if housed in a cage that is too moist or has poor ventilation, they will rapidly develop respiratory or skin infections. They will also fight over food, often swallowing each other in feeding frenzies. They are quick nervous snakes that will rapidly launch themselves from a container with low sides like a plastic shoe box.

Hence, they do not do well in the standard, poorly ventilated, shoe box-type arrangements so commonly used for kingsnakes and rat snakes. And like most snakes, they should always be housed alone. We have found that a 2.5- or 5-gallon aquarium with a screen top and numerous hiding places will work well in rearing very young garter snakes. The basic cage setup is all they seem to require. Feed frequently, perhaps 2–3 times per week.

Indeed, for such a widespread group of snakes, the literature on their captive reproduction is incredibly scanty. Several papers and books on garter snakes are listed in the reference section. Perhaps the most thorough and detailed reference on garter snakes is the recently published volume, *The Garter Snakes: Evolution and Ecology* (Rossman et al., 1996). This excellent book will serve as the standard reference on garter snake natural history for many years. While we have attempted to summarize the basic aspects of the natural history of each species, that reference contains much more of the detailed information that professional herpetologists need such as meristic data, museum specimen locations, and anatomical features, as well as many detailed natural history notes.

THE AUTHORS MUST ISSUE A STERN WARNING AGAINST HANDLING GARTER SNAKES IN A CAVALIER FASHION. There a numerous reports in the literature of serious garter snake bites. At the time of this writing, one of our employees is in a hospital emergency room after allowing a common garter snake from northern Florida to chew on her hand. Her entire arm became swollen and numb. In another incident this year, a local veterinarian experienced similar swelling in his arm after such a bite and ended up at the emergency room. Do not allow these snakes to chew on you if you pick them up! Attempt to remove them as soon as possible. Typically, releasing your grip on the snake in the initial phase of the bite will result in the snake releasing its hold on you.

Thamnophis atratus
Pacific Coast Aquatic (Santa Cruz) Garter Snake

It is fitting to begin the section on western garter snakes with this species. In the ever-changing world of garter snake taxonomy, this species and both subspecies (formerly three subspecies) lead the way in confusing herpetologists. This group of subspecies has been reassigned taxonomically so many times in the last century that much of the data available on this species are very hard to attach to the species we presently recognize. Once again, we must emphasize that detailed identification characteristics are not described here as these are available in numerous field guides. However, we have attempted to summarize the basic characteristics of each subspecies in order to reduce the confusion somewhat. In this section and throughout this book we are using common and scientific names as described by Collins (1997). Fortunately, the care of this species is similar to that of the majority of the garter snakes, and this is discussed in detail below.

The northern subspecies is the Oregon garter snake, *T. a. hydrophilus*. This subspecies is heavily blotched dorsally and often lacks a distinct vertebral stripe, which makes it very similar in appearance to the western aquatic garter snake, *T. couchii*. The Oregon garter may be distinguished from the western aquatic in most cases by the presence of 10 lower labials (lip scales) instead of 11 (Stebbins, 1985).

The other subspecies is fairly distinct from the other garter snakes. It possesses a yellow to orangish middorsal stripe and yellow throat. It is the first subspecies to be described by taxonomists, the Santa Cruz garter snake, *T. a. atratus*. In the northern part of its range, the Santa Cruz garter snake, which is found in areas just south of the Oregon garter and interbreeds with it, usually can be distinguished by its bright dorsal stripe, yellow chin, and gray eyes. In the southern part of its range, the Santa Cruz garter snake also has the yellow dorsal stripe and chin, but usually has very dark or black eyes. The presence of intergrades makes the situation

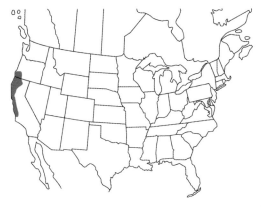

Thamnophis atratus

more complex than this, but the majority of the animals examined can be distinguished using the characteristics discussed here. See Stebbins (1985) for more details. Formerly, those Santa Cruz garter snakes in the northern part of the range were classified as a separate subspecies, named the aquatic garter snake, *T. a. aquaticus*, but many herpetologists no longer consider this a valid subspecies. A third subspecies has been proposed recently, *T. a. zaxanthus*, the Diablo Range garter snake (Boundy, 1999). This will undoubtedly add to the confusion.

The natural history of the Pacific Coast aquatic garter snake, as presently recognized, is somewhat difficult to extract from the literature available. However, we have attempted to summarize some of that information here in an attempt to assist snake keepers. Presently, it appears that these snakes are aquatic; they are more often than not found around bodies of standing or flowing water. It is believed that the Oregon garter snake is the more aquatic subspecies, being found most frequently in the vicinity of larger streams and being primarily a fish eater, while the Pacific Coast aquatic garter snake is less aquatic, being found around ponds and small streams and consuming primarily frogs and tadpoles, but other items as well (Wright and Wright, 1957). Salamanders, such

Santa Cruz Garter Snake, *Thamnophis atratus* (photo by David G. Campbell)

as the newt, *Taricha*, and a variety of plethodontids including arboreal salamanders, *Aneides*, *Ensatinas*, *Ensatina*, and slender salamanders, *Batrachoseps*, have also been consumed (Rossman et al., 1996).

These are not large snakes. The Oregon garter snake appears to be the larger subspecies, ranging 35.6–101.6 cm (14–40 inches) in length, while the Santa Cruz subspecies is smaller, ranging 38–61 cm (15–24 inches) in length (Stebbins, 1985; Boundy, 1990).

As alluded to above, the more aquatic subspecies, namely the Oregon garter snake, is primarily fish eating, but frogs and salamanders have also been reported as food (Wright and Wright, 1957). The food of the much less

Oregon Garter Snake, *Thamnophis atratus hydrophilus* (photo by David G. Campbell)

SPECIES: *Thamnophis atratus*, Pacific Coast Aquatic (Santa Cruz) Garter Snake
MAINTENANCE DIFFICULTY INDEX: 2 (1 = easiest, 5 = most difficult)
AVERAGE SIZE: 35.6–73.7 cm (14–29 inches)
FOOD: Fish, scented small mice
CAGE SIZE: 10–20-gallon aquarium
SUBSTRATE: Indoor-outdoor carpet or artificial turf
VENTRAL HEAT: Yes
UV LIGHT: No, but an incandescent bulb is useful
TEMPERATURE RANGE: 25–33°C (77–91.4°F)
SPECIAL CONSIDERATIONS: Rapidly switch to small prekilled mice. Likely to be
   parasitized.

---

aquatic Santa Cruz garter snake has included slugs, fish, tree frogs, salamanders, lizards, small snakes, birds, and rodents (Wright and Wright, 1957). Other items have been reported for this species by Nussbaum et al. (1983), but it is difficult to tell from their description if they are referring only to the Oregon garter snake or the group as a whole, before these confusing garter snakes were rearranged by taxonomists again. The food items listed by Nussbaum et al. (1983) included fish (sculpin and small trout), frogs and their tadpoles, *Rana boylii*, and salamander larvae, *Dicamptodon ensatus*.

Suspected predators of this species include raccoons, skunks, hawks, and other snakes.

Mating has been observed in the wild in April, and birth has been observed in late August (Fitch, 1940; Wright and Wright, 1957). Reported clutch size for the Pacific Coast aquatic garter snake is 3–14 babies, with averages of 6.4–8.4. Nussbaum et al. (1983) reported clutch sizes of 7–25 but once again it is difficult to determine which species they may be referring to. The newborns (for the group) range 18.6–24.9 cm (7.3–9.8 inches) in length.

The Santa Cruz garter snake, *T. a. atratus*, is a voracious feeder in captivity. They adapt extremely well and readily feed on unscented pinkies at a very young age. Adults in our care readily fed on small mice. Under these conditions, they grow rapidly and rarely have problems in captivity. Surprisingly, however, both young and old Oregon garter snakes in our care readily consumed unscented pinkies and fuzzies.

As mentioned in the introduction to the garter snakes, they can be housed in the basic cage setup quite nicely. Refer to that section and the general care section for more details. Also remember they are quite likely to be parasitized, so fecal exams are necessary.

Daytime air temperatures fluctuating between 25 and 33°C (77 and 91.4°F) have been well accepted by those in our care. Brumation temperatures fluctuating between 3 and 18°C (38 and 65°F) have been tolerated without ill effects by those in our care, and this has been accomplished in their regular cage.

Overall, we have found the Pacific Coast aquatic garter snake to be a very adaptable and easily maintainable captive. The northern subspecies is more aquatic and therefore may accept mice less readily. They will accept them, however. The trick is to use small, heavily fish-scented prekilled mice for those snakes that are stubborn. Sometimes offering a live or prekilled fish along with scented prekilled mice will result in a feeding frenzy type of behavior in which the fish and all of the mice offered will be consumed. Eventually, this or any form of scenting may become unnecessary.

Two *T. a. atratus* from the Nowell Creek area of Santa Cruz consumed pinky mice every 3–4 days from March to October every year, averaging about 52 mice per year. Almost all of these were plain unscented mice.

One specimen in our care, captured as a juvenile, survived 8 years and 1 month and was still alive at the time of this writing.

Thamnophis brachystoma
Shorthead Garter Snake

The shorthead garter snake is a small dark brown to black-colored snake with three longitudinal stripes running the length of the body. Unlike the common garter snake, however, this small species has a relatively small head and seems to feed almost entirely on earthworms. They range 36–45.7 cm (14–18 inches) in length with a record of 55.9 cm (22 inches) (Conant and Collins, 1991).

The shorthead garter snake has a very small geographic range, occupying extreme southwestern New York and northwestern Pennsylvania. The preferred habitat appears to be open areas near water such as fields, meadows, and marshes, although Allen (1992) further defines the preferred environment by stating that they are creatures of the "uplands, preferring dry meadows and hillsides."

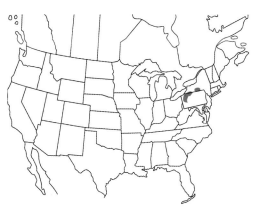

Thamnophis brachystoma

Body temperatures of wild individuals have been reported to average 30°C (86°F) during the active season (Asplund, 1963). The body temperatures of 13 brumating individuals in the wild ranged from 2.8 to 3.3°C (37 to 38°F) (Bothner, 1963).

As stated above, the preferred food of the shorthead garter snake is earthworms, which they seem to feed on almost exclusively (Asplund, 1963; Wozniak and Bothner, 1966; Ernst and Barbour, 1989; Allen, 1992). Several of these authors have mentioned insects, isopods, slugs, and small salamanders as other possible food items.

There are few known predators of this species but predatory birds, mammals, and reptiles are suspected (Swanson, 1952; Harding, 1997).

Mating is known to occur in the spring right after emergence from brumation (Pisani, 1967; Pisani and Bothner, 1970; Ernst and Barbour, 1989). This results in the birth of 5–14 young measuring 11.8–15.9 cm (4.6–6.25 inches) in length sometime from late July to early September (Swanson, 1952; Pisani and Bothner, 1970; Allen, 1992). One specimen collected in southwestern New York by Dave Campbell gave birth to 10 neonates on 26 July. These babies had an average TL of 14.5 cm (5.7 inches).

A gestation period of 90–120 days is likely. The young are patterned exactly as are the adults, although they may be a bit darker. Most captive babies begin feeding within a week of birth.

The shorthead garter snake may be maintained in a cage setup similar to that recommended for the common garter snake. See the section on the common garter snake for details. Artificial turf will suffice as a substrate, although a burrowing substrate such as a soil-wood chip mixture will be more readily accepted. A hide box and water bowl are the only other necessities, although cage accessories including flat rocks and plastic plants are helpful. Ventral heat or heat from an incandescent bulb placed above the cage is probably necessary, since active individuals in the wild maintain their body temperatures fairly high.

The preferred food of the shorthead garter is the earthworm, but they have been known to take slugs, small fish, and small amphibians, even though the latter three food items are rarely taken compared to earthworms. Calcium supplements should probably be used for these worm-eating snakes.

The following observations on the care of shorthead garter snakes were contributed by David Campbell of Clay County, Florida:

Shorthead Garter Snake, *Thamnophis brachystoma* (photo by David G. Campbell)

1. Shorthead garter snakes use a combination of sight (motion of the food item) and scent to locate and identify prey. Taste may also be important; juveniles occasionally strike a food item and then release it. If the taste of the same prey is changed, they will readily consume it.

2. Wigglers are an acceptable food for most shortheads. Reluctant feeders can be persuaded to take wigglers that have been scented by rubbing them on a nightcrawler. The wigglers used in these observations were farmed in southern Georgia, while the nightcrawlers, which were readily acceptable to these snakes, were from southern Canada, much closer to the shorthead's natural range.

3. The worms called red wigglers are not acceptable to shortheads. Young snakes would strike them and then let them go. No amount of scent transfer would make red wigglers palatable. Reportedly, these worms are toxic to some animals.

4. Juveniles and postpartum females should be fed every other day. Snakes can take prey up to one-half to two-thirds the length of the snake. Adults do well on one large worm every third day.

5. Ventral or dorsal heat is desirable. I have used a 40-watt lamp at one end of a 10-gallon aquarium for adults and a commercial heating pad set to the low setting under half of the container for juveniles.

Shorthead Garter Snake (immature), *Thamnophis brachystoma* (photo by David G. Campbell)

6. Maintaining the proper humidity in the cage can be a challenge. I have made hide boxes from broken clay pots which are misted with water every other day. In the wild the snakes seem to prefer moist soil beneath sandstone or shale rocks, so this seems to mimic the natural habitat. Humidity must be closely monitored. If it is too dry, dysecdysis (difficult shedding) occurs. If it is too moist, skin or respiratory problems can occur.

7. The hide box should be low enough to almost touch the snake when it is inside. When feeding, shortheads will back into the hide box to stretch the worm out, facilitating the swallowing of that worm. Snakes with

SPECIES: *Thamnophis brachystoma*, Shorthead Garter Snake
MAINTENANCE DIFFICULTY INDEX: 3 (1 = easiest, 5 = most difficult)
AVERAGE SIZE: 36–46 cm (14–18 inches)
FOOD: Earthworms, slugs, small amphibians
CAGE SIZE: 10-gallon aquarium
SUBSTRATE: Artificial turf, indoor-outdoor carpet, or newspaper
VENTRAL HEAT: Not essential but may be helpful
UV LIGHT: Yes?
TEMPERATURE RANGE: 20–25°C (68–77°F)
SPECIAL CONSIDERATIONS: Likely to be parasitized. Prone to skin lesions if kept too
  moist.

several crevices to use in this way are more successful feeders than snakes with one crevice or none.

8. The preferred substrate is rich soil with as little peat as possible. Peaty soils tend to clump on worms during feeding and make it harder for the snakes to keep their mouths and heads clean during and after a feeding attempt. Rich soils appear closer to the natural habitat observed and they appear to hold moisture more effectively.

9. Frequent feeding is necessary for juveniles. We saw little growth (although the snakes appeared healthy) on a twice-per-week feeding schedule. One extra feeding each week helped the growth rate noticeably. Supplemental heat is necessary for juveniles. We lost several juveniles during the first cold snap of the fall when the house temperature dropped to 18.8°C (66°F) for 2 days (i.e., the snakes had eaten recently).

Also, Asplund (1963) noted that this species did not feed well at temperatures less than 25°C (77°F).

As with other members of this genus, these snakes should be dewormed initially and have regular fecal exams performed thereafter. A fecal exam performed on four specimens from New York revealed rhabditiform larvae and an unidentified nematode in both. A fecal exam performed on another specimen from Warren County, Pennsylvania, revealed a coccidia, probably *Isospora*, and an unidentified embryonated orange-colored stronglye egg.

A 10-gallon aquarium is a sufficient size enclosure for this species. Excellent ventilation (i.e., a screen top) is considered a necessity.

Because of the restricted range and the habitat destruction within that range, an organized captive breeding (and restocking?) program would be a good idea for this species. A number of competent herpetologists have told us that these snakes are becoming much harder to find in the wild.

Ernst and Barbour (1989) report a captive longevity of more than 3 years for this species. One female captured as an adult in southwestern New York has been in captivity 3 years and 10 months and is still alive at the time of this writing.

Thamnophis butleri
Butler's Garter Snake

The closest relative of the shorthead garter snake is Butler's garter snake. Like that species, it is fairly small, with the average adult measuring 38–51 cm (15–20 inches) and the record being 69.2 cm (27.25 inches) (Conant and Collins, 1991). They are colored similarly to the shorthead garter, with three longitudinal stripes on an olive brown background color.

The lateral stripes are primarily on scale rows 2 and 3, but extend slightly onto scale row 4. As in the shorthead garter, the head is fairly small compared to a common or plains garter snake of a similar size.

These snakes are distributed over much of western Ohio, northeastern Indiana, Michigan, and extreme southwestern Ontario. There is also an isolated population in southeastern Wisconsin. The preferred habitat within this range appears to be open areas such as fields, marshes, prairie remnants, or vacant city lots, usually near water (Wright and Wright, 1957; Minton, 1972; Ernst and Barbour, 1989; Conant and Collins, 1991). Disturbed areas such as old

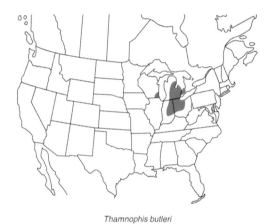

Thamnophis butleri

dumps and old house foundations in grassy areas are also heavily utilized (Rossman et al., 1996).

Like many snakes, this species is diurnal during cooler weather, and crepuscular during very warm weather. Most activity appears to occur in the morning (Ernst and Barbour, 1989). The body temperatures of active snakes in the wild have averaged 26.1°C (79°F) and these snakes actively thermoregulate to maintain temperatures in this range (Carpenter, 1956). These snakes are known to brumate in the winter at temperatures just above freezing.

The preferred food of Butler's garter snake is the earthworm, although leeches, small frogs, and fish have been reported (Catling and Freedman, 1980; Ernst and Barbour, 1989). Cricket frogs, *Acris* sp., chorus frogs, *Pseudacris* sp., and treefrogs, *Hyla* sp., as well as guppies, have been reported as being readily consumed by captives (Ernst and Barbour, 1989).

Known or suspected predators include predatory mammals such as skunks and raccoons, birds such as crows, owls, and hawks, and other snakes including kingsnakes, milk snakes, and racers (Harding, 1997). Cannibalism is believed to be rare in this species.

Mating occurs in the spring immediately following brumation (Finneran, 1949; Minton, 1972; Ford, 1982). This results in the birth of 4–

Butler's Garter Snake, *Thamnophis butleri* (photo by David G. Campbell)

SPECIES: *Thamnophis butleri*, Butler's Garter Snake
MAINTENANCE DIFFICULTY INDEX: 3 (1 = easiest, 5 = most difficult)
AVERAGE SIZE: 38–51 cm (15–20 inches)
FOOD: Earthworms, slugs, small fish, small amphibians
CAGE SIZE: 10-gallon aquarium
SUBSTRATE: Artificial turf, indoor-outdoor carpet, or newspaper
VENTRAL HEAT: Not essential but may be helpful
UV LIGHT: Yes?
TEMPERATURE RANGE: 20–25°C (68–77°F)
SPECIAL CONSIDERATIONS: Likely to be parasitized. Prone to skin infections if kept too
  moist. More likely to eat other foods than the shorthead garter.

20 similarly colored young sometime in August or September. These young measure 12.5–18.5 cm (5–7.3 inches) in length (Ernst and Barbour, 1989).

For all intents and purposes, this snake is the western version of the shorthead garter snake and may be maintained exactly the same way. In fact, most herpetologists believe that this and the former species were one and the same until they were separated by a glacier. This species is more likely to accept small fish and amphibians than is its eastern counterpart, however. Earthworms are definitely the preferred food, and calcium supplementation is believed to be helpful.

The warnings about parasitism in the other natricines apply to this species as well. Make sure they are checked for worms initially and regularly thereafter.

Brumation, breeding, and care of the young is exactly as described for the common garter snake.

A 10-gallon aquarium is definitely a large enough enclosure for this species.

The record for captive longevity of this species is just over 2 years (Snider and Bowler, 1992). This record probably reflects lack of interest, since so few people are trying to keep and breed these snakes.

Thamnophis couchii
Western Aquatic Garter Snake

Formerly, this species consisted of the giant garter snake (now *T. gigas*), the two-striped garter snake (now *T. hammondi*), the Sierra garter snake (still *T. couchii*, but the common name has been changed to the western aquatic garter), and the Pacific Coast aquatic garter snake (now *T. atratus*) with its two subspecies: the Oregon garter, *T. a. hydrophilus* and Santa Cruz garter, *T. a. atratus*. Please refer to Collins (1990, 1997). Hence, our discussion of the western garter snakes will make use of these names. The western aquatic garter snake, *T. couchii*, refers only to what was formerly known as the Sierra garter snake.

The western aquatic garter snake is a medium-sized snake, usually no longer than 120 cm (48 inches). They have a blotched pattern dorsally with a very faint dorsal stripe, if they have one at all. They are best distinguished from the other garter snakes within their range by looking at their internasal scales, however, which are longer than they are wide. Ventrally, black marks may be seen on the cranial (front) part of every scute. They range from north central California to south central California east of the great valley and into western Nevada. For a complete description see Rossman and Stewart (1987).

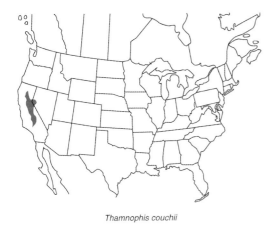

Thamnophis couchii

These snakes are usually found near permanent rivers and streams in a variety of plant associations from coniferous forests to grasslands and chaparral and, as might be expected, prefer food items from these riparian habitats (Wright and Wright, 1957). Various authors have reported food items including frogs, fish (trout, suckers, and mosquitofish), fish eggs, toads, salamanders, larval amphibians, earthworms, and leeches (Wright and Wright, 1957; Basey, 1976; Rossman et al., 1996).

The only known predators of adult western aquatic garter snakes are red-tailed hawks (Fitch, 1949) and humans. Predatory mammals, other birds, kingsnakes, and large fish are suspected of being potential predators, however.

Mating is thought to occur early in the spring, with up to 38 young being born in the late summer (Hansen and Tremper in Rossman et al., 1996). The young are usually around 12.7 cm (5 inches) long (Basey, 1976).

These snakes can be cared for the same as the other garter snakes. The basic cage setup that uses artificial carpet/turf or paper as a substrate, a good hide box, good ventilation, tight-fitting lid, and ventral heat source will generally work very well. Plastic plants, branches treated to prevent mites (by baking at 149°C [300°F] for 15 minutes), and stable rocks are all nice additions that, although not necessary, will help beautify the enclosure. A small bowl of clean water is a necessity for this species, however. A full-spectrum light source may be beneficial for this diurnal snake, but at the present time it is not known if one is necessary for this or any other diurnal snake.

Those in our care have done well at daytime

Western Aquatic Garter Snake (Sierra Garter Snake), *Thamnophis couchii* (photo by David G. Campbell)

SPECIES: *Thamnophis couchii*, Western Aquatic Garter Snake
MAINTENANCE DIFFICULTY INDEX: 3 (1 = easiest, 5 = most difficult)
AVERAGE SIZE: 46–120 cm (18–48 inches)
FOOD: Fish, scented small mice
CAGE SIZE: 10–20-gallon aquarium
SUBSTRATE: Artificial turf or indoor-outdoor carpet
VENTRAL HEAT: Yes
UV LIGHT: No, but an incandescent bulb is useful
TEMPERATURE RANGE: 27–33°C (80–92°F)
SPECIAL CONSIDERATIONS: Highly aquatic but can be housed similar to terrestrial
   snakes. Usually does well on fish-scented mice. Parasitism likely.

temperatures fluctuating from 27 to 33°C (80 to 92°F), although they probably would have done equally well at lower temperatures. These same specimens have been brumated in their own cages with nothing added at temperatures fluctuating from 3 to 18°C (38 to 65°F) for 4 months.

In captivity, these snakes will readily take fish and worms, but fish-scented mice may be taken by most. These snakes are not as likely as the western terrestrial garter or the plains garter to accept these, however. The best way to start them on pinky mice initially is to offer several fish first to start a feeding frenzy and then add the fish-scented prekilled pinkies.

Remember the problems that most natricine snakes have with parasites and vitamin deficiencies as discussed in detail in the general care section. The solution to most of these problems lies in a good parasite control program and quality control of the diet, which is also discussed in the same section of the general care section.

Captive reproduction of this snake is rare, probably from lack of interest. It would be advisable to place the female in with the male in the spring following brumation, much as discussed for the other garter snakes.

The young are born in late summer or early fall, and these may be cared for much as discussed for other young garter snakes.

Perhaps because it lacks a striking color pattern, this is one of the least commonly maintained garter snakes. We have uncovered no longevity records at all, and Slavens and Slavens (1991) listed only two individuals in captivity. One specimen in our care has been in captivity for 5 years and 11 months and is still alive at the time of this writing. It was captured as an adult at the south fork of the Stanislaus River.

Overall, these snakes seem to fare well in captivity, and we have had a great deal of success with them. Initially, fish are definitely a preferred item in the menu, but most will rapidly consume scented mice, even though unscented may be refused.

Thamnophis cyrtopsis
Blackneck Garter Snake

The blackneck garter snake is a medium-sized species, with most adults measuring 40–71 cm (16–28 inches) and a record of 114.4 cm (45 inches) (Tennant, 1984; Stebbins, 1985; Rossman et al., 1996). Possessing the typical striped pattern of the garter snakes, they are relatively slim-bodied (most of the time) and fast-moving snakes. They receive their name from the prominent paired black blotches on the neck. The other important characteristic that helps to distinguish this snake from the other garter snakes with which it is commonly confused is that it only has 19 scale rows, and the side stripes are on the second and third scale rows. This compares with the checkered garter snake (21 scale rows, stripe on row 3 only) and the Mexican garter snake (19 or 21 scale rows, stripe on rows 3 and 4 on front of body). See Stebbins (1985).

There are two subspecies within the United States, the eastern blackneck, *T. c. ocellatus*, and the western blackneck garter snake, *T. c. cyrtopsis*. The eastern form is found from central Texas to the Big Bend region. The western subspecies is found from southeastern Arizona, most of New Mexico, and western Texas into most of Mexico.

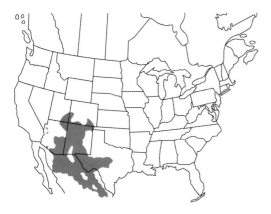

Thamnophis cyrtopsis

The preferred habitat of the blackneck garter is along streams at middle and higher elevations, even though they are often encountered on rocky slopes and grassy areas away from streams during cooler wetter weather (Wright and Wright, 1957; Fowlie, 1965; Behler and King, 1979; Tennant, 1984; Stebbins, 1985; Hammerson, 1986; Conant and Collins, 1991). The western subspecies is most commonly found in rocky canyons, while the eastern subspecies is usually found on rocky hillsides and in wooded ravines (Millstead, 1953).

The food items listed for wild members of this species have included a wide variety of amphibians, primarily frogs and toads (cliff chirping frog, *Syrrhophus marnockii*, treefrogs, *Hyla* sp., red-spotted toad, *Bufo punctatus*, Woodhouse's toad, *Bufo woodhousii*, spadefoot toads, *Scaphiopus* sp.), and tadpoles of these frogs, as well as slimy salamanders, *Plethodon glutinosus*, fish, crustaceans, *Triops* sp., and

Western Blackneck Garter Snake, *Thamnophis cyrtopsis cyrtopsis* (photo by David G. Campbell)

lizards (ground skinks, *Scincella lateralis*) (Foquette, 1954; Wright and Wright, 1957; Fowlie, 1965; Tennant, 1984; Stebbins, 1985; Hammerson, 1986).

The preferred temperature range of this species has been determined by one researcher to be 22–32°C (71.6–89.6°F) (Fleharty, 1967), and by another to be 22.5–35°C (72.5–95°F) with an average of 27.5°C (81.5°F) (Rosen, 1991).

No natural predators have been reported for this species, although the usual garter snake predators are suspects (e.g., raccoons, skunks, hawks, and other snakes).

Mating occurs from March to May with up to 22 young (average 19) having been reported in one brood (Jones, 1990). These young, which are usually born in late July to early September, range 20.3–27 cm (8–10.6 inches) long at birth (Wright and Wright, 1957; Fitch, 1970; Tennant, 1984).

The blackneck garter snake is one of the adaptable terrestrial garter snakes discussed in the introduction to the garter snakes. As such, it seems to demonstrate tendencies toward a broader diet and greater versatility with respect to habitats occupied. This makes this species one of the easier garter snakes to maintain in captivity, even though perhaps not quite as easy to care for as the common garter snake, the plains garter snake, or the checkered garter snake.

Generally, these snakes do extremely well in

Eastern Blackneck Garter Snake, *Thamnophis cyrtopsis occellatus* (photo by David G. Campbell)

the basic cage setup discussed in the general care section. A cage the size of a 10-gallon aquarium will work extremely well for all but the very largest of blacknecks. Artificial carpet/turf works very nicely as a substrate because it provides support for these snakes and allows them to use normal serpentine locomotion. A hide box, stable branch, plastic plants, and water bowl will complete the cage. Remember also the necessity of good ventilation (a screen top) for these snakes.

Ventral heat is strongly advisable. We have noticed a definite difference in the appetites of snakes housed with and without this heat, with those having the ventral heat feeding much more regularly than those without it. One might expect this Mexican snake to be heat loving.

An incandescent bulb (25 or 40 watts) placed above one spot in the cage to provide a hot spot is an excellent idea also, but may not be necessary with a ventral heat source. At the present time, UV light is not considered essential, although it may have some beneficial effect as yet unobserved in this species.

Daytime air temperatures that have proven suitable for members of this species in our care have fluctuated from 27 to 33°C (80 to 93°F) during their active season. Trutnau (1981) re-

ported that air temperatures of 20–30°C (68–86°F) were "comfortable" for those in his care, but advised ventral heat.

Brumation temperatures fluctuating between 3 and 18°C (38 and 65°F) have been well tolerated by this and many other species.

Feeding a captive blackneck garter has proven relatively easy. Those in our care were readily switched to scented prekilled pinkies and fuzzies. They would also consume unscented mice regularly thereafter. One specimen ate nearly 300 minnows its first full year in captivity, but was switched to fuzzy mice in its second year. It consumed 35 in the second year and 47 in the third year.

Captive reproduction has rarely been attempted with this species, although a number of wild-caught females have delivered young in captivity.

The young usually shed within several hours to days and are aggressive feeders right from the start, assuming you give them what they want—small frogs or frog-scented food. Tennant (1984) reported one litter cared for by Ray Meckel that refused worms, minnows, and fish slivers but fed ravenously on cricket frogs. These snakes reach 56.5 cm (22.25 inches) by 11 months of age. They will often consume

---

SPECIES: *Thamnophis cyrtopsis*, Blackneck Garter Snake
MAINTENANCE DIFFICULTY INDEX: 2 (1 = easiest, 5 = most difficult)
AVERAGE SIZE: 40–71 cm (16–28 inches)
FOOD: Fish, scented small mice
CAGE SIZE: 10–20-gallon aquarium
SUBSTRATE: Indoor-outdoor carpet or artificial turf
VENTRAL HEAT: Yes
UV LIGHT: No, but an incandescent bulb is useful
TEMPERATURE RANGE: 27–33°C (80–93°F)
SPECIAL CONSIDERATIONS: Rapidly switch to small prekilled mice. Likely to be
  parasitized.

---

pinky parts and pinkies fairly soon after birth if they are properly scented. They should be housed singly to avoid feeding accidents in which one juvenile may attempt to swallow another in a fight over food.

One western blackneck garter snake was maintained more than 6 years and 3 months in captivity (at which time it was released) (Slavens and Slavens, 1991; Snider and Bowler, 1992). One which we collected in Sycamore Canyon in Arizona has been in captivity 6 years and 10 months and is still alive at the time of this writing.

Overall, we have found the blackneck garter snake to be an interesting and fairly easily maintainable snake. They eat readily and calm down nicely. Some become handleable, but most do not seem to appreciate much handling. Even so, this snake rarely attempts to bite once it has been in captivity for some time.

Thamnophis elegans
Western Terrestrial Garter Snake

Consisting of six subspecies, five in the U.S. and Canada, the western terrestrial garter snake occupies an immense area from southwestern Canada throughout much of the western United States with numerous isolated populations surrounding the continuous range. These subspecies include the Arizona garter snake, *T. e. arizonae*, the mountain garter snake, *T. e. elegans*, the coast garter snake, *T. e. terrestris*, the wandering garter snake, *T. e. vagrans*, and the upper basin garter snake, *T. e. vascotanneri*. The sixth subspecies, *T. e. hueyi*, is restricted to a small mountainous area in Baja California.

As might be expected from a snake with this large a range, these snakes vary considerably in size, preferred habitat, color pattern, reproductive patterns, and dietary preferences. In fact, one experiment with this species showed that

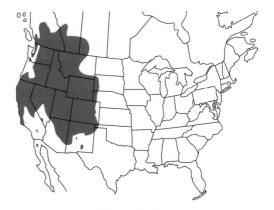

Thamnophis elegans

the babies from coastal regions ate slugs while those that lived inland did not (Arnold, 1977). Some subspecies are quite aquatic, others are very terrestrial. Nevertheless, we will attempt

Mountain Garter Snake, *Thamnophis elegans elegans* (photo by Sean McKeown)

to summarize the natural history of this well-studied snake and present it here in order to assist snake keepers in caring for this species a little better.

The western terrestrial garter snake is a medium-sized snake, ranging in size from 45 to 107 cm (18 to 43 inches), with the mountain garter snakes from south central Oregon being considered the largest and the most aquatic of the subspecies (Wright and Wright, 1957; Nussbaum et al., 1983; Stebbins, 1985).

As mentioned above, they occupy a wide variety of habitats that vary considerably in vegetation and proximity to water. The mountain garter snake, coast garter snake, and wandering garter snake are all fairly terrestrial. In any case, these snakes are usually found in moist situations near water, from damp meadows and open grasslands to forests (Wright and Wright, 1957; Webb, 1970; Basey, 1976; Behler and King, 1979; Nussbaum et al., 1983; Stebbins, 1985; Degenhardt et al., 1996).

The list of food items consumed by this species in the wild is phenomenal. It has included ants, spiders, beetles, slugs, snails, leeches, earthworms, lampreys, fish, salamanders, (especially tiger salamanders, *Ambystoma*

tigrinum), toads (spadefoot toads, *Scaphiopus* sp., Woodhouse's toad, *Bufo woodhousii*), chorus frogs (Pacific chorus frogs, *Pseudacris regilla*), western chorus frog, *Pseudacris triseriata*, true frogs (yellow-legged frogs, leopard frogs, *Rana* sp.), lizards (eastern fence lizard, *Sceloporus undulatus*), snakes (plains garter snakes, *T. radix*, other western terrestrial garter snakes), young birds, mice, shrews, and carrion (Wright and Wright, 1957; Fowlie, 1965; Basey, 1976; Nussbaum et al., 1983; Hudson, 1985; Stebbins, 1985; Hammerson, 1986; Mitchell, 1986; personal observations).

Surprisingly little has been written about the predators of such a wide-ranging snake. They probably have predators similar to those of the other species of garter snakes, e.g., hawks, raccoons, skunks, and other snakes.

The temperatures of active individuals of this species have been measured by several researchers and found to range from 20 to 36°C (68 to 97°F), with a preferred body temperature of 31°C (88°F) (Fleharty, 1967; Scott et al., 1982; Peterson, 1987). It is interesting to note this is one of the few species where it has been demonstrated that different temperatures allow different functions to occur more efficiently

(Stevenson et al., 1985). For example, swimming performance is superior at cooler temperatures, which may be beneficial to these snakes foraging in cool mountain streams. Body temperatures of 13°C (55.4°F) have been recorded for members of this species foraging in streams (Scott, 1978).

Mating occurs during the spring and usually 4–12 (record 19) young are born in late summer (July through September). The young range 12.7–27.6 cm (5–10.9 inches) in length (Wright and Wright, 1957; Fitch, 1970; Basey, 1976; Linder and Fichter, 1977; Behler and King, 1979; Nussbaum et al., 1983; Stebbins, 1985; Hammerson, 1986). Litter size tends to decrease as one goes from south to north in this species (Fitch, 1985).

The western terrestrial garter snake is probably the easiest of the garter snakes to maintain in captivity (Butler, 1985). The reason for this is that most have a natural preference for more terrestrial prey items, including mice. In the wild they have been known to consume a great variety of foods as listed above. However, there

is no doubt that in captivity most prefer reptilian or mammalian prey. This was demonstrated clearly to us the first time we placed a newborn of this species with a newborn western plains garter snake, *T. radix*. No sooner than they had been placed in the same bag did the young western terrestrial garter snake attack and try to swallow its fellow captive. In addition, both juveniles and adults in captivity are extremely fond of lizards, especially skinks. Ground skinks, *Scincella lateralis*, from the southeastern United States were readily consumed by a newborn in our care. Pinkies will also be taken readily by the juveniles, and both juveniles and adults will readily consume dead prey items (which allows freezing and storage of their food). Captive adults may be fed prekilled adult mice, which they consume with the voracity of a rat snake.

Hence, they are one of the easiest of the garters to raise and it is quite easy to maintain good quality control of the diet. Admittedly, the mountain garter snakes from Oregon, which are more aquatic in nature, are a little trickier to

Coast Garter Snake, *Thamnophis elegans terrestris* (photo by David G. Campbell)

Wandering Garter Snake, *Thamnophis elegans vagrans* (photo by David G. Campbell)

switch to pinkies, but even these snakes adapt fairly well to captivity and should accept fish-scented pinkies without too much resistance.

The basic (ideal) cage setup discussed under the general care section works well for this species. This includes the usual artificial carpet/turf, hide box, rock, water bowl, and heat source. Heating pads and heat tapes work well. Plastic plants are a nice addition. Ultraviolet lighting does not appear to be essential for this snake.

Air temperatures of 20–26°C (68–79°F) along with a ventral heat source have been suggested by Trutnau (1981) as suitable daytime temperatures during the active part of the year. Certainly, this temperature range should work (with supplemental heat from an incandescent bulb or ventral heat). However, those in our care have done well at daytime temperatures fluctuating from 27 to 35°C (80 to 95°F) without supplemental heat.

Remember that garter snakes are really not best kept in small plastic containers such as shoe boxes (like one might for kingsnakes or rat snakes). If nothing else, they are very quick nervous snakes that will rapidly jump out of their small low-walled enclosure. It is for this reason that we strongly advise against these types of enclosures for these snakes. A 10-gallon aquarium is a suitably sized enclosure that works well for most members of this species. They should definitely be housed singly since cannibalism is likely. In fact, there are more records of cannibalism among western

terrestrial garter snakes than any other species of garter snake (Mitchell, 1986).

As one might expect from their diet, parasitism is also a potential problem. Therefore, these snakes should be checked for worms initially and regularly thereafter.

Even though they are fantastic eaters and will usually eat well into the fall and early in the spring, a short period of brumation is strongly advisable. As discussed elsewhere, this short period of cooler temperatures allows the normal maturation of gametes and will assist in breeding. Those in our care have tolerated temperatures fluctuating from 3 to 18°C (38 to 65°F) for 4 months. This species has been bred in captivity, but not very commonly (Trutnau, 1981). Arnold (1980) had good success with captive breeding by brumating these snakes for 10 weeks at 5–10°C (40–50°F). The brumation temperature was then raised to 15°C (59°F) for one week and 28°C (82.4°F) the next week.

Four to 19 young are born in late summer or early fall (June to September) after a gestation period of 120–150 days. The babies shed within a week and eat voraciously. See above. They require no special care as compared with the adults, except perhaps that they require more frequent feedings. Two or three feedings per week are appropriate. They must be housed alone because of their tendencies toward cannibalism. Usually, these snakes will be consuming unscented pinky mice by the time they are 3–4 months old, although they may take mouse tails and pinky parts prior to this. Sexual maturity is usually reached in 2 years, although some males may mature in 1 year, and some females may take 3 years.

Snider and Bowler (1992) reported that one of these snakes had been maintained in captivity more than 6 years and 1 month. One wandering garter snake collected in Colorado as a neonate has survived 7 years and 6 months in captivity and is still alive at the time of this writing. Slavens and Slavens (1991) reported a coast garter snake that survived more than 12 years and 8 months in captivity. Obviously, garter snakes are not the fragile short-lived reptiles we once thought they were.

Overall, these alert active snakes are very

SPECIES: *Thamnophis elegans*, Western Terrestrial Garter Snake
MAINTENANCE DIFFICULTY INDEX: 2 (1 = easiest, 5 = most difficult)
AVERAGE SIZE: 45–107 cm (18–43 inches)
FOOD: Mice, lizards
CAGE SIZE: 10–20-gallon aquarium
SUBSTRATE: Indoor-outdoor carpet or artificial turf
VENTRAL HEAT: Yes
UV LIGHT: No, but an incandescent bulb is useful
TEMPERATURE RANGE: 20–26°C (68–79°F)
SPECIAL CONSIDERATIONS: Adults readily take mice. Hatchlings and juveniles prefer
    lizards or snakes. Parasitism likely.

hardy in captivity. They don't seem terribly aggressive once they adjust to captivity, and will soon lose the urge to bite and the urge to musk on their handler, even though they do not seem very fond of being handled. It is also important to note that members of this species have been reported to produce fairly serious bites, with quite a bit of pain and swelling around the bite wound (Vest, 1981). It is believed that this species, especially the more terrestrial subspecies, possess mildly toxic saliva and are capable of causing envenomation in humans, even though this is a relatively uncommon occurrence. We would urge handlers to exercise some caution when handling, but by no means are we suggesting this is a dangerous snake. If a bite occurs, remove the snake as soon as possible by placing the snake on the ground and releasing your hold of it, as suggested by Vest (1981).

Thamnophis eques
Mexican Garter Snake

The Mexican garter snake is one of the rarest species of garter snake in the United States and Canada. There are three subspecies, only one of which reaches the United States, *T. e. megalops*, the northern Mexican garter snake. They are now found only in southeastern and central Arizona, southwestern New Mexico, and southward into Mexico.

Recognition of this species is not terribly difficult because the lateral stripes are on the third and fourth scale rows along the front of the body, even though they are generally similar in pattern to the checkered and blackneck garters.

Their preferred habitat appears to be lowland waterways such as streams, ditches, ponds, or lakes in the desert and at the bases of mountains (Wright and Wright, 1957; Behler and King,

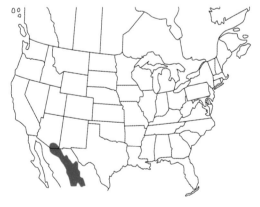

Thamnophis eques

1979; Sweeny, 1992), as long as it is permanent and vegetated (Rosen and Schwalbe, 1988). They are apparently becoming rarer throughout

Northern Mexican Garter Snake, *Thamnophis eques megalops* (photo by Cecil Schwalbe)

their range due to habitat destruction and perhaps the introduction of the bullfrog, *Rana catesbeiana*, which is believed to consume the juvenile snakes (Rosen and Schwalbe, 1988; Lawler, 1992).

Like the majority of other garter snakes, they are medium-sized snakes ranging 45–112 cm (18–44 inches) in length (Wright and Wright, 1957; Behler and King, 1979; Stebbins, 1985; Rosen and Schwalbe, 1988).

Literature reports of this rarely seen snake seem to indicate a preference for aquatic food items, namely frogs, fish, and leeches (Wright and Wright, 1957; Stebbins, 1985; Sweeny, 1992); however, small mice and lizards are readily taken by captives from some areas (Ewald, pers. comm., 1993). Indeed, there may be quite a bit of variation in the dietary preferences from one population to another, with those from the Chiracahuas preferring more terrestrial prey and those from the lowlands preferring the more typical garter snake prey. See below.

Nothing is known of the thermal ecology of this species; however, Ewald (pers. comm., 1993) believes these snakes are primarily nocturnal in the Chiricahuas.

Suspected predators of this species include hawks, raccoons, and other species of snakes.

Mating is believed to occur early in the spring but fall breeding may be possible, with up to 25 young being born in mid- to late summer (Wright and Wright, 1957). Rosen and Schwalbe (1988) determined the average clutch size in Arizona specimens to be 13.6. The average size of the neonates in two clutches they examined were 13.7 cm (5.4 inches) and 19.4 cm (7.6 inches).

In captivity these snakes will do extremely well if housed in the basic cage setup discussed in the general care section. Substrates that have worked well have included artificial carpet/turf, newspaper, or pine shavings, with the former being preferred by us for most garter snakes and the latter being preferred by others. Only a small water bowl is necessary.

Ventral heat is strongly advisable for this snake of the Mexican plateau but a full-spectrum light is probably not necessary. An incandescent bulb providing a hot spot in the cage during the day might be helpful as well, but is also probably not necessary. Most can be satisfactorily housed in a well-ventilated enclosure the size of a 10-gallon aquarium.

The preferred food of the Mexican garter snake is frogs, but many will readily take small live mice (fuzzies) and fish. Interestingly, Greg Ewald, who has maintained and bred this species in captivity, indicated that the adults in his care (collected in the Chiricahuas) preferred mice or lizards to fish (almost all refused fish) and stated that the captive-born babies refused fish, worms, or pinkies, instead eating only hatchling lizards or small frogs.

Conversely, Randy Babb, biologist with the Arizona Game and Fish Commission, has maintained some of these animals (from the San Bernardino Wildlife Refuge) for months feeding them goldfish and bullfrog tadpoles. He says they are typical garter snakes in captivity since they feed quite aggressively and present few problems.

One should remember to have them tested and treated for internal parasites, however. As semitropical amphibian eaters, they are very likely to be heavily parasitized. Ewald indicated that wild-caught individuals were quite prone to cestode infections. Also remember the problems experienced by snakes that are fed diets of entirely fish, namely a thiamin deficiency and a vitamin E deficiency, resulting in neurological signs or steatitis, respectively. These two problems can be avoided by feeding a varied and parasite-controlled diet as discussed in the general care section under feeding. As discussed elsewhere, however, mouse-eating garter snakes will thrive and breed on a diet of mice only, and since captive-bred mice are presumably parasite-free, a diet of 100%

mice appears to be the diet of choice for these captive animals.

Brumation is strongly advisable for this species if captive breeding is intended, and this may be accomplished in the regular cage. No modifications are necessary. Two to 4 months at 10–15°C (50–59°F) are probably suitable, although Ewald indicated that brumation should be "harsh and brief; 13°C (55°F) for 1 month is sufficient to maintain sperm survival."

Captive breeding has not been reported in the literature, and very little is known about reproduction of this snake in the wild. This species has been bred in captivity by Greg Ewald, however, who has produced several litters totaling more than 50 young. Litter sizes ranged from 4–8 young, and the babies ranged 11.7–15.9 cm (4.63–6.25 inches) in length and were very stout-bodied.

A recent communication from Cecil Schwalbe, Arizona herpetologist, indicated that these snakes are rapidly disappearing from Arizona. He believes that the major reason for their disappearance is the destruction of 90% of Arizona's wetlands. But Cecil stated that even in wetland preserves, the presence of the introduced bullfrog appears to be devastating to populations of this snake. "It is the last nail in the coffin for this species," he added. They have found old females, including a 10-year-old female, but young snakes are few and far between. In addition, some of the larger snakes have abscesses on their tails, which have been observed to be caused by bullfrog attacks. Some of the other snakes found have had

---

SPECIES: *Thamnophis eques*, Mexican Garter Snake
MAINTENANCE DIFFICULTY INDEX: 3 (1 = easiest, 5 = most difficult)
AVERAGE SIZE: 45–102 cm (18–40 inches)
FOOD: Fish, scented small mice, amphibians
CAGE SIZE: 10–20-gallon aquarium
SUBSTRATE: Indoor-outdoor carpet or artificial turf
VENTRAL HEAT: Yes
UV LIGHT: No, but an incandescent bulb is useful
TEMPERATURE RANGE: 27–33°C (80–93°F)
SPECIAL CONSIDERATIONS: Aggressive feeders (most will take either scented or unscented mice). Parasitism likely.

subcutaneous lumps, which have been associated with subcutaneous parasites.

The elimination of these snakes from the wild places a greater emphasis on their research in captivity. It serves as a prime example of how unforeseen forces can reach into pristine habitats, even wildlife preserves and parks, and eliminate animals rapidly. This can happen in spite of overzealous "protection" by some government agencies. In fact, by restricting all collection of specimens and their maintenance in captivity, they eliminate the possibility of collecting more sorely needed data on these species.

Unfortunately, there are very few of these snakes in captivity at the time of this writing. Slavens and Slavens (1991) did not list a single captive specimen in their inventory section. In addition, Snider and Bowler (1992) did not list a captive longevity for this species, although Greg Ewald maintained one female for 2 years and 3 months at which time it was released. As mentioned above, the longevity of this snake in the wild has been reported at just over 10 years.

It is also unfortunate that this is one of the handful of North American snakes we have been unable to work with. Even though granted a permit by the Arizona Game and Fish Commission, we were unable to collect any live specimens. Hence, we have little to add to the data collected by Wright and Wright nearly 40 years ago. However, thanks to concerned herpetologists like Greg Ewald, Cecil Schwalbe, Phil Rosen, and Randy Babb, we have something to report.

Thamnophis gigas
Giant Garter Snake

Like the California condor, the giant garter snake is a threatened species of days gone by. It is a victim of gross habitat destruction to California's Great Central Valley (San Joaquin Valley). As recently as 1952, this snake's habitat extended from the base of the Tehachapi Mountains south of Bakersfield well into the Sacramento Valley, 400 miles to the north in northern California. The San Joaquin Valley began being modified for irrigation shortly after the California gold rush in the early 1850s. The damming of the Kern River in 1952 sealed the fate of the giant garter snake in the remaining southern portion of its range. Its preferred habitat was muddy-bottomed, large, permanent, or seasonal bodies of warm water (shallow lakes and marshlands with tules, cattails, and willows). It is indeed a large snake, with a recorded length of 144.8 cm (4 feet 9 inches) (Wright and Wright, 1957; Shaw and Campbell, 1974; Hansen, pers. comm., 1992) up to 162.6 cm (64 inches) (Stebbins, 1985). There are naturalists alive today in the Central Valley who say they have measured specimens that approached 1.83 m (6 feet). One former museum vertebrate curator estimated the maximum length of specimens in what was then Buena Vista Lake, west of Bakersfield, as "over eight feet in total length and as thick around as a man's arm." Hence, this species is certainly the largest of the garter snakes and may have the potential to reach a larger size than that currently known. Its potentially large size needs to be taken into consideration when maintaining these snakes in captivity. This should not occur without a permit, however, since, as mentioned above, this is a threatened species. In fact, this species may

Thamnophis gigas

Giant Garter Snake, *Thamnophis gigas* (photo by Robert Hansen)

soon be in a situation similar to that of the Brazos and Concho water snakes since they have adapted somewhat to manmade habitats (ditches without concrete bottoms). Viable populations still exist in several shallow marshes in the northern San Joaquin Valley and in the wide irrigation ditches and rice fields of the Sacramento Valley. Native American peoples and early white settlers of the area referred to this reptile as a "water snake." It was shy, flighty, and always retreated to water, disappearing in and under the tules (water reeds). If grabbed, it had a reputation of biting viciously.

These snakes have a variable color pattern, with those in the north having a dark background color with a more prominent dorsal stripe. Those in the south generally lack the stripe but have a spotted (or checkered) background color ranging from brown through olive and a variable ventral surface (from cream to dark-colored). The narrow head of this species is very similar to that of the western aquatic garter snake (Sierra garter snake), *Thamnophis couchii*, the narrowhead garter, *T. rufipunctatus*, and members of the genus *Nerodia*, to which it is closely related. Remember, a narrow head is a common characteristic of predominantly fish-eating snakes.

Not a superspecialized feeder, the giant garter snake feeds on a wide variety of commonly accepted garter snake food items, particularly fishes of all kinds, frogs and other amphibians, and earthworms. Wright and Wright (1957) quote Fitch as saying that they will eat newts as well as frogs and fish. Brode (1988) and Hansen (pers. comm., 1992) list introduced fish including carp, *Cyprinis carpio*, the mosquito fish, *Gambusia affinis*, as well as larvae and young of the bullfrog, *Rana catesbeiana* (also introduced in California) which have replaced the native *Rana aurora*. In addition to their daytime activity, these snakes have been observed foraging at night by tactile means; once the snake's head comes in contact with a fish, it will be seized quickly (Hansen, pers. comm., 1992).

It is interesting to note that historical prey items such as Sacramento blackfish, thick-tailed chub, and red-legged frogs are now either extinct or very reduced in numbers (Hansen, pers. comm., 1992). This implies that introduced species may be critical to the continued survival of this threatened species in remaining suitable pockets of their range.

Virtually nothing has been reported about predators of this species, although the usual garter snake predators are suspects (e.g., raccoons, skunks, hawks, and other snakes).

Almost nothing was known about reproduction of these snakes until recently. Wright and Wright (1957) report finding a 19.1-cm (7.5-inch) specimen on 9 September and suspected it was a newborn. Since the same authors reported that these snakes are surface active from April through November, it is likely they breed in April or May, have a gestation period of 90–120 days as do other garter snakes and water snakes, and generally deliver their litters in late summer or early fall. This belief has been supported by recent observations. Between 10–46 young are born from mid-July to early September, with those from north of Sacramento bearing larger litters (14–46; average 26.3) and those from the San Joaquin Valley bearing smaller litters (10–26; average 17.4) (Hansen, pers. comm., 1992). Newborns range 20–30.6 cm (7.9–12 inches) in length (Hansen, pers. comm., 1992).

These small snakes grow rapidly. They range 58.4–66 cm (23–26 inches) in length by 20 months of age, and 76.2–94 cm (30–37 inches) in length by 32 months (Hansen, pers. comm., 1992). Since the smallest reproductively active female discovered was 92 cm (36.2 inches), these snakes may reach sexual maturity in 3 or more years, although this is unknown (Hansen, pers. comm., 1992).

The only note we have on the thermal ecology of this species is that both adults and juveniles may emerge from brumation and bask at temperatures above 21°C (70°F) (Hansen, pers. comm., 1992).

In captivity, they will do fairly well if treated much as other members of the genus, even though they require slightly more room. A 20–30-gallon long aquarium is a suitably sized enclosure for most. The basic cage setup using artificial carpet/turf as the substrate, a good hiding place, and a clean water bowl is satisfactory for this species, although other cage accessories may be added.

Temperatures suitable for other members of the genus are advisable, since there are no literature records for captive temperature ranges for this species. Hence, daily temperature fluctuations within the range of 17–35°C (63–95°F) are probably suitable for normal activity based on the work of Cunningham (1966), Fleharty (1967), and Hart (1979). A ventral heat source available on one side of the enclosure is advisable, as is a basking area with an incandescent bulb over it. Ultraviolet lights are probably not necessary for this species, as is the case with most other garter snakes.

Brumation is strongly advised at temperatures similar to those recommended in the general care section under brumation, since there are no specific data on this particular species available.

We also suspect that like their closest relatives, they will be very likely to consume scented rodents in captivity, especially because

---

SPECIES: *Thamnophis gigas*, Giant Garter Snake
MAINTENANCE DIFFICULTY INDEX: 3 (1 = easiest, 5 = most difficult)
AVERAGE SIZE: 120–152 cm (48–60 inches)
FOOD: Fish, tadpoles
CAGE SIZE: 20–30-gallon long aquarium
SUBSTRATE: Indoor-outdoor carpet or artificial turf
VENTRAL HEAT: Yes
UV LIGHT: No, but an incandescent bulb is useful
TEMPERATURE RANGE: 17–35°C (63–95°F)
SPECIAL CONSIDERATIONS: Protected species. Permit required for maintenance. Prefers fish but might take scented mice. Likely to be parasitized.

of the tactile feeding behavior described above. But this is unknown at the time of this writing. Hansen (pers. comm., 1992) reported that these snakes readily devoured both fish and tadpoles, especially bullfrog tadpoles, in captivity.

They are also very likely to be parasitized, and a fecal exam and the appropriate dewormings are advisable for intended long-term captives. Interestingly, Hansen (pers. comm., 1992) mentioned that numbers of these snakes had ulcers that he described as an "open area of swelling with a marble-sized cheesy exudate within." He thought this was possibly related to injuries from predation attempts. Based on our experience with other garter snakes, we believe further work may reveal abscesses secondary to subcutaneous tapeworms, as we have observed in two-striped garter snakes, *T. hammondii*. However, this is unknown at the present time.

Slavens and Slavens (1991) failed to list a single specimen of this snake in captivity, and no captive longevity was listed in either Slavens and Slavens (1991) or Snider and Bowler (1992).

We are especially indebted to Robert Hansen for taking the time to answer some of our questions on this species and allowing us to view the giant garter snake chapter in the manuscript of his soon-to-be-published book on the reptiles and amphibians of central California (Hansen and Tremper, in prep.).

Thamnophis hammondii
Two-striped Garter Snake

The two-striped garter snake ranges from Monterey Bay in southern California southward into Baja California, Mexico. Adults range 60–90 cm (24–36 inches) in length (Stebbins, 1985), although they may grow larger since one specimen with an incomplete tail was measured to

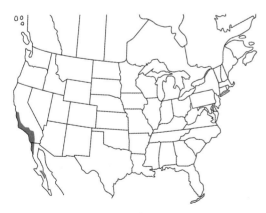

Thamnophis hammondii

have a SVL length of 84 cm (Rossman et al., 1996). They are easily recognizable and receive their name from the fact that they lack a central or vertebral stripe as seen in most other garter snakes. They do possess faint lateral (side) stripes (although some individuals can be melanistic), on a background color that varies from greenish to brownish. Many individuals have black spots dorsally and some at the northern end of the range may be nearly solid black.

The preferred habitat of this garter snake appears to be rocky streams, usually bordered by heavy vegetation (Wright and Wright, 1957; Stebbins, 1985; personal observations). Plant associations have been reported to include oak woodlands and mixed oak and chaparral, as well as sparse pines and cedars, scrub oak, and brush (Hansen and Tremper, in prep.). These snakes possess the characteristic long-jawed bug-eyed appearance that is common in very aquatic snakes.

Indeed, these snakes readily enter the water and consume a primarily aquatic fare that includes fish and their eggs, toads, frogs and their larvae (tadpoles), and earthworms (Wright and Wright, 1957; Stebbins, 1985; Rossman et al., 1996).

While there has been a great deal of discussion on general predation and defensive strategies of garter snakes (Sweeny, 1992; Rossman et al., 1996) there has been little specific data

Two-striped Garter Snake, *Thamnophis hammondii* (photo by Sean McKeown)

published on their predators. We could find no specific reference to the predators of this species.

Mating occurs in nature in April and May. We observed a pair copulating along a stream at Montana De Oro State Park in San Luis Obispo County, California, on 3 April 1992.

Birth of 3–36 young (average 15.6) has been recorded from late July through October (possibly through November) (Wright and Wright, 1957; Fitch, 1970; Stebbins, 1985; Hansen and Tremper, in prep.). The neonates from 7 litters measured 20.3–21.7 cm (8–8.5 inches).

Snakes demonstrate a huge variety of color patterns. There are probably many reasons why these patterns exist. This is a melanistic two-striped garter snake. Melanism may aid in thermoregulation or provide a different "search image" to some predators. The percentage of melanism in populations might therefore fluctuate. (photo by David G. Campbell)

SPECIES: *Thamnophis hammondii*, Two-striped Garter Snake
MAINTENANCE DIFFICULTY INDEX: 3 (1 = easiest, 5 = most difficult)
AVERAGE SIZE: 60–90 cm (24–36 inches)
FOOD: Fish, scented small mice
CAGE SIZE: 10–20-gallon aquarium
SUBSTRATE: Indoor-outdoor carpet or artificial turf
VENTRAL HEAT: Yes
UV LIGHT: No, but an incandescent bulb is useful
TEMPERATURE RANGE: 27–33°C (80–92°F)
SPECIAL CONSIDERATIONS: Will consume fish-scented mice. Likely to be heavily
  parasitized.

The temperatures at which individuals have been observed to be active and apparently their preferred temperature range has been reported as 19–32°C (66.2–89.6°F) (Cunningham, 1966).

In captivity, these snakes will do extremely well if cared for as other garter snakes. The basic cage design will suffice nicely for this species. Artificial carpet/turf is perhaps the best substrate for this species and probably most natricine snakes since it will not become a sloppy mess at feeding time. A stable hide box, clean water bowl, and well-ventilated top will complete the cage, although a few rocks and plastic plants would be nice additions. Ventral heat or heat from above in the form of an incandescent bulb is probably an excellent idea for long-term maintenance. Full-spectrum light is probably not necessary, but this is not known with certainty at this time. A 10-gallon aquarium is probably a suitably sized enclosure for most members of this species. House singly.

Air temperatures that allowed for growth and regular shedding for those specimens in our care fluctuated between 27 and 33°C (80 and 92°F) during the active part of the year. Nighttime lows during this time usually did not go below 23°C (74°F) during much of this active period. Brumation of these snakes was accomplished in the same cage. Temperatures at this time fluctuated between 3 and 18°C (38 and 65°F) and this lasted approximately 4 months.

As mentioned above, these snakes do prefer fish and amphibians and, in captivity, they will readily feed on these. Remember that they, like most garter snakes, are very scent-oriented and will usually take their food items frozen and thawed, which makes some parasite control possible. This also allows the keeper to try to train these snakes to consume fish-scented mice. Those in our care readily consumed fish-scented fuzzy mice regularly and would regularly consume unscented mice, thereby eliminating the need to feed any fish. Those in our care consumed about 50 fuzzies per year, although they generally stopped feeding in midsummer and from November until March. If you end up feeding nothing but frozen and thawed fish to these snakes, you will rapidly (within 4–6 months) note signs of a thiamin deficiency (usually neurological signs such as muscle tremors or seizures). The prevention and cure for this problem is discussed in the general care section.

One of the specimens examined by us from San Luis Obispo County, California, contained a number of subcutaneous tapeworms, some of which were found subepithelially in the mouth of this snake. Excision of as many worms as possible and the use of praziquantel (Droncit®) at a dose of 20 mg/kg IM twice at 2-week intervals appears to have resulted in elimination of these worms.

Captive breeding is rare, probably from a lack of effort. It can probably be accomplished as discussed in the general care section by placing the female in with the male right after brumation ends. Females gravid at the time of capture have delivered up to 36 young in the late summer and fall. These young may be raised similarly to other young garter snakes. See under the Santa Cruz garter snake.

One of these snakes was maintained for more than 7 years and 8 months in captivity (Slavens and Slavens, 1991; Snider and Bowler, 1993).

Overall, we have found these snakes to be relatively low-maintenance captives that eat regularly under the conditions described above and can probably be readily bred in captivity as well, although a special permit from the California Department of Fish and Game is needed to take them.

Thamnophis marcianus
Checkered Garter Snake

The checkered garter snake is a medium to large garter snake ranging 45–109.2 cm (18–43 inches) in length (Vial, 1957; Stebbins, 1985; Degenhardt et al., 1996). Some specimens are incredibly bulky and have been mistaken for bullsnakes from a distance.

These snakes have a variable background color, usually tan or olive, with a large number of squarish black blotches dorsally, hence the name. They possess a dorsal stripe that is usually cream to light yellow-colored, and lateral stripes (side stripes) almost entirely on scale row 3. Like the blackneck garter, they possess black blotches on the neck and crescent-shaped markings behind the angle of the mouth, but unlike that species they possess 21 scale rows (blacknecks have 19 and the lateral stripes are on scale rows 2 and 3).

They occupy a very extensive geographic area ranging from western Kansas southward through western Oklahoma, the majority of Texas, and westward through much of New Mexico and Arizona, with one population in extreme southeastern California. They also range well into Mexico, especially northeastern Mexico.

The preferred habitat of this species appears to be open grasslands and deserts in areas near permanent or semipermanent bodies of water (Wright and Wright, 1957; Fowlie, 1965; Webb, 1970; Tennant, 1984; Stebbins, 1985; Conant and Collins, 1991; Degenhardt et al., 1996). Tennant reports they also occur in the thorn brush thicket in the coastal area of Texas.

These snakes are not dietary specialists by any means. They are aggressive terrestrial snakes with a broad diet. Items listed in the literature have included invertebrates (slugs, earthworms, crayfish), fish, frogs (leopard frogs, *Rana* sp., spotted chorus frogs, *Pseudacris clarkii*), toads, (Couch's spadefoot, *Scaphiopus couchii*, and plains spadefoot, *S. bombifrons*, Woodhouse's toad, *Bufo woodhousii*, and green toad, *B. debilis*), tadpoles, salamanders (small-mouthed salamanders, *Ambystoma texanum*), lizards (speckled earless lizard, *Holbrookia maculata approximans*), snakes (Texas lined snake, *Tropidoclonion lineatum texanum*), and small mammals, as well as carrion (Wright and Wright, 1957; Fowlie, 1965; Webb, 1970; Tennant, 1984; Stebbins, 1985; Vermersch and Kuntz, 1986). We observed one instance of attempted cannibalism after food items were placed in with two of these snakes. In a feeding frenzy, the larger female seized the smaller male in the middle of his body. At that point we separated the two snakes. This species is believed to be largely a nighttime forager, as opposed to the blackneck garter snake which is diurnal (Wright and Wright, 1957; Tennant, 1984).

Collins (1993) listed large birds, mammals,

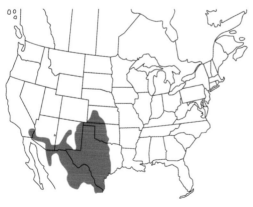

Thamnophis marcianus

Checkered Garter Snake, *Thamnophis marcianus* (photo by David G. Campbell)

and other snakes as predators of this species. Vermersch and Kuntz (1986) report numerous enemies including coyotes, armadillos, skunks, birds of prey, and ophiophagous snakes. Certainly many are killed by cars due to the snakes' nocturnal foraging tendencies.

Mating occurs in the spring, generally from March through May over most of the United States. However, Seigel et al. (1987) advised that southern populations may have a very long breeding season and actually breed more than once per year. Females from more northern latitudes mature later and produce larger clutches, however (Karges, 1982). Litters of 4–18 young (average 12.8) have been reported being born from late May through October over most of their range within the United States (Wright and Wright, 1957; Tennant, 1984; Stebbins, 1985; Mattison, 1988).

These young range 17.8–23.5 cm (7–9.25 inches) in length, and are colored similarly to the adults (Behler and King, 1979; Tennant, 1984). These young usually shed fairly soon after birth, sometimes within hours.

The checkered garter snake is perhaps one of the easiest of all the garter snakes (a group that

is already known for being relatively easy to care for) to keep in captivity. They are fantastically adaptable to a wide variety of housing arrangements but seem to do well in the basic (ideal) cage setup discussed in the general care section. Indeed, their adaptability to captivity seems to be a reflection of their adaptability in the wild. These snakes have been extending their range by using man-made environments (although recently there has been a decline of this species in certain western areas of the range) and so it seems only logical they would adapt well to the environments we create for them in captivity. At times, it seems they will thrive in captivity if they are just fed and kept clean.

Daytime air temperatures that have appeared acceptable to the checkered garter snakes in our care have fluctuated between 27 and 35°C (80 and 95°F). Nighttime temperatures during the active season ranged down to 23°C (74°F).

With regard to feeding, this species is definitely not finicky! They have a broad range of acceptable food items as listed above and the larger specimens seem especially fond of mice. Those feeding on mice may be fed weekly while those feeding on fish, amphibians, or worms will need to be fed at least twice weekly.

They sometimes seem insatiable. One specimen in our care swallowed a full-grown pig frog, *Rana gryllio*, one day and was actively patrolling her cage the following day, presumably looking for another meal. They will definitely fight other snakes for food or eat other snakes, including members of their own species, so they should be housed singly. In one instance following a routine feeding of two checkered garter snakes in our care, a large female attempted to swallow a smaller male that had been living in the cage for months.

In fact, the only food item refused by checkered garter snakes in our care were frozen and thawed crayfish.

Younger snakes may not be quite as likely to consume anything they can swallow, but will still eat the standard garter snake fare of worms, fish, and amphibians. Several have recorded chopped fish or lizards as consumed by juveniles. Indeed, fish- or lizard-scented pinkies may be consumed at a very young age. Eventually, they will consume mice readily.

As with other garter snakes, internal parasites are definitely something to be looked for and treated if found. Submit several fecal samples to your veterinarian initially and regularly thereafter. Remember that internal parasitism is the number one reason natricine snakes may fail to thrive and breed in captivity.

Usually a 10-gallon aquarium or similar size enclosure is a sufficiently large area in which to house all but the largest of these snakes.

As with many other snakes, they are quite prone to stop eating during the late fall and winter months. For this reason, and to improve breeding success, one should brumate these snakes. Brumation can be accomplished in the usual manner (see the section on brumation) in the regular cage. No modifications are necessary. Three to 4 months will usually be sufficient. Those in our care tolerated temperatures fluctuating from 3 to 18°C (38 to 65°F) for 4 months during the winter. However, others have determined that successful breeding may occur with only 7 weeks at 10°C (50°F) (Holtzman et al., 1989; Rossman et al., 1996). Furthermore, a temperature of 4°C (40°F) has been reported to "cause" some neurological signs (Rossman et al., 1996).

Captive breeding is rare or at least rarely reported. Tennant (1984) reported the successful captive breeding of this species by the late Eileen Morron for 3 successive years. Mating occurred consistently during the third week in May with birth consistently around 15 August, suggesting a gestation period around 90 days. Breeding should be attempted as described in the general care section. Keep in mind that with many of the natricine snakes, some have had more breeding success using a group of snakes rather than one pair. See the reproduction chart (Table 5) in the general care section.

Interestingly, some of these snakes may breed immediately after brumation ends, while others may breed 28 days after brumation ends. Ford and Cobb (1992) noted that those from Texas bred 28 days later, while those from southeastern Arizona bred the first day after brumation ended. Furthermore, it has been observed that females

---

SPECIES: *Thamnophis marcianus*, Checkered Garter Snake
MAINTENANCE DIFFICULTY INDEX: 2 (1 = easiest, 5 = most difficult)
AVERAGE SIZE: 45–105 cm (18–42 inches)
FOOD: Amphibians, mice
CAGE SIZE: 10–20-gallon long aquarium
SUBSTRATE: Indoor-outdoor carpet or artificial turf
VENTRAL HEAT: Yes
UV LIGHT: No, but an incandescent bulb is useful
TEMPERATURE RANGE: 27–35°C (80–95°F)
SPECIAL CONSIDERATIONS: Extremely aggressive feeders. Usually readily take small mice. Parasitism very likely. Very cannibalistic.

that are heavily fed prior to pregnancy will produce larger litters (Ford and Seigel, 1994).

The young, approximately 20.3 cm (8 inches) long at birth, present no special problems. Make sure to remove them from the mother right away, however, or she may eat them.

Overall, these snakes make interesting and attractive captives. They are not especially aggressive except when it comes to feeding, and this will eventually overcome the natural shy-ness that most snakes have at the time of capture. Long-term captives will come out of their hide boxes to greet you in anticipation of being fed and will readily take food from your hand. But be careful, large specimens may get excited and try to take your hand with it!

One of these snakes survived more than 7 years and 6 months in captivity (Snider and Bowler, 1992), but we suspect they can live much longer.

Thamnophis ordinoides
Northwestern Garter Snake

The northwestern garter snake is an extremely variably colored small garter snake, with adults ranging 32–96.5 cm (13–38 inches) in length. The background color may consist of bluish, grayish, greenish, brown, or black, with one, two, or three longitudinal stripes of red, orange, yellow, blue, brown, or black. In addition, the dorsal stripe may be well defined, faint, broken, or absent. Because of the incredible variety of color patterns in this species, the only way to really identify them is by doing a scale count (something that is really very easy, but which amateurs seem to hate doing and resist doing at almost any cost). The two meristic (scale counting) characteristics most reliable in distinguishing this species from the others are the number of dorsal scale rows (usually 17) and the number of upper labial (lip) scales (7). Other characteristics that may be helpful in identifying this snake are the relative size of the head and eyes. Generally, northwestern garter snakes have relatively small heads and small eyes compared with the other garter snakes with overlapping ranges.

This species ranges from southwestern British Columbia including Vancouver Island southward through western Washington and Oregon to northwestern California. Thus it has a fairly small range compared to most of the garter snakes. Only the shorthead, Mexican, and narrowhead garter snakes have smaller ranges within the United States and Canada.

The preferred habitat of this species has been described as meadows and open woodlands

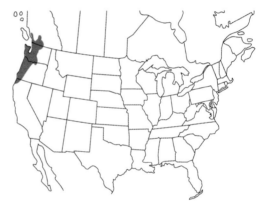

Thamnophis ordinoides

along the edges of humid forests, rarely far from some form of dense vegetation (Wright and Wright, 1957; Behler and King, 1979; Nussbaum et al., 1983; Rossman et al., 1996). Their habitat receives very heavy annual rainfall, often exceeding 100 inches of precipitation per year. This wet environment is ideal for moisture-loving animals, namely slugs, worms, frogs, and salamanders, and these are the items listed as the main foods for this species (Wright and Wright, 1957; Behler and King, 1979; Nussbaum et al., 1983; Stebbins, 1985). Slugs are apparently the preferred food item of both young and old northwestern garter snakes (Gregory, 1978; Nussbaum et al., 1983).

Natural predators of *T. ordinoides* include other snakes (*T. elegans*) (Rossman et al., 1996) and spotted owls (Nussbaum et al., 1983).

Northwestern Garter Snake, *Thamnophis ordinoides* (photo by David G. Campbell)

Mating occurs in the spring right after brumation (March to May) resulting in the birth of 3–20 (average 8–12) young from late July to mid-August (Nussbaum et al., 1983). Two other studies showed mean clutch sizes ranging 5.2–9.5 (Stewart, 1968; Brodie, 1989). These newborns generally measure 15–19 cm (6–7.5 inches) in length (Nussbaum et al., 1983). Mating has also been observed in late September and early October.

The temperature range at which these snakes are active is 17–34°C (62.6–93.2°F) with a preferred body temperature of 27°C (80°F) (Stewart, 1965). Basking behavior has been observed in wild snakes by a number of authors (Wright and Wright, 1957; Stebbins, 1985).

In captivity, the northwestern garter snake may represent a significant challenge for the snake keeper, at least initially. In fact, Mattison (1987) states that this snake is "notoriously difficult to keep." The reason for this difficulty is that their preferred diet is slugs.

However, after working with a number of these snakes, it is clear that many, if not all, can be trained to consume small prekilled mice that have been heavily scented with slugs; eventually they will consume unscented small mice.

Some individuals are quite stubborn, however, and may refuse the scented mice. For these individuals, we developed a technique we jokingly refer to as "slug hors d'oeuvres" in which a slug (live or frozen and thawed) was placed on the nose of a small fuzzy or pinky. For some reason, the slug itself was more than the stubborn snakes could resist. Perhaps they contained an ingredient or a texture that could not be transferred to the mouse by rubbing only. We also noted that some of these snakes would take live minnows initially, even though they might refuse dead ones. Some ate earthworms and others ignored them. In any case, some of the northwestern garter snakes we worked with would eventually consume unscented pinkies and fuzzies with the voracity of any rat snake (or the more widespread terrestrial garter snakes).

Housing for these snakes may be in exactly the same manner as the majority of terrestrial snakes; the basic setup will work well. Artificial carpet/turf is especially well suited for these snakes since it is unlikely to be accidentally ingested. A hide box is also essential for these snakes, which may be somewhat nervous though not especially so. A water bowl with clean water should be available at all times.

SPECIES: *Thamnophis ordinoides*, Northwestern Garter Snake
MAINTENANCE DIFFICULTY INDEX: 3 (1 = easiest, 5 = most difficult)
AVERAGE SIZE: 32–95 cm (13–38 inches)
FOOD: Slugs, mice
CAGE SIZE: 10–20-gallon aquarium
SUBSTRATE: Indoor-outdoor carpet or artificial turf
VENTRAL HEAT: Yes
UV LIGHT: No, but an incandescent bulb is strongly advisable
TEMPERATURE RANGE: 17–34°C (62–93°F)
SPECIAL CONSIDERATIONS: Often prefer slugs but eventually will take slug-scented mice,
   then unscented mice (pinkies or fuzzies).

A ventral heat source or a basking area created by an incandescent bulb is strongly advisable for these snakes. Those in our care seemed to thrive at temperatures fluctuating between 27 and 33°C (80 and 91.4°F) during the day with temperatures down to 23°C (73.4°F) at night during much of the active season. It is important to note, however, that we have not yet bred this snake in captivity and that it is quite possible these low nighttime temperatures may not be low enough. Time will tell.

Brumation temperatures fluctuated between 3 and 18°C (38 and 65°F) for 4 months. This was carried out in their regular cages. No modifications were necessary.

Interestingly, one small female we received demonstrated what appeared to be signs of metabolic bone disease. Her lower jaw was bowed and soft and she had what appeared to be several compression fractures of the spine. This snake was also small for her age. Upon questioning the donor, it was determined that this snake had been a captive for some time, and was offered earthworms only. Normally, earthworms represent a balanced diet for most snakes, but perhaps these worms were coming from an area with calcium-deficient soil (or soil too rich in something else that was competing with the absorption of calcium or binding the calcium, thereby preventing its absorption). This snake did improve once it was switched to pinky and fuzzy mice.

Overall, it has been our impression that these snakes are much more adaptable to captivity than most people think. Like some of the other garter snakes, they will often take food out of your hand and appear to feed readily once they become adjusted. We have not handled those in our care very much.

Our observations were supported by those at the Houston Zoo. According to Snider and Bowler (1992), one of these snakes, wild-caught as an adult, was maintained there for more than 15 years and 11 months. What was shocking to us was that this was the record longevity for all garter snakes. This northwestern garter snake had been maintained longer than any other species of garter snake in captivity, even the common garter snake.

Thamnophis proximus
Western Ribbon Snake

The western ribbon snake is a slimmer, more arboreal member of the garter snake group. They range 45–76 cm (18–30 inches) in length with a record of 123 cm (48.5 inches) (Stebbins, 1985; Conant and Collins, 1991).

Like the rest of the garter snake group, they have a preference for aquatic habitats but their slimmer proportions are thought to be an adaptation to life in the bushes and low trees. Hence, the habitats listed have included marshes,

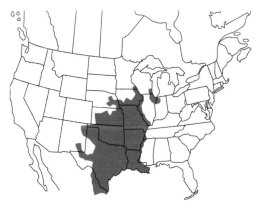

Thamnophis proximus

ponds, swamps, ditches, sloughs, creeks, brooks, rivers, wet prairies, and woodlands, where they are frequently found in low bushes, shrubs, or cattails along the edges (Wright and Wright, 1957; Webb, 1970; Behler and King, 1979; Tennant, 1984; Stebbins, 1985; Hudson, 1985; Ernst and Barbour, 1989; Dundee and Rossman, 1989; Christiansen and Bailey, 1990; Conant and Collins, 1991; Degenhardt et al., 1996; personal observations).

They are considered a very adaptable species as a whole, however, and six subspecies occupy a huge geographic area from southern Wisconsin to Costa Rica, entering many different habitat types. Only four of those subspecies are found in the United States. These include the arid land ribbon snake, *T. p. diabolicus*, the western ribbon snake, *T. p. proximus*, the Gulf Coast ribbon snake, *T. p. orarius*, and the redstripe ribbon snake, *T. p. rubrilineatus*. Most subspecies appear similar in their habitat and dietary preferences, although some variation is expected in a species occupying such a large area.

This species feeds largely on amphibians (frogs, *Hyla* sp., *Rana* sp., *Acris* sp. and their larvae, small toads, *Bufo* sp., salamanders and their larvae) and fish, but other food items such as lizards (*Scincella lateralis*, ground skinks), insects, smaller members of their own species, carrion, and small mice have been reported for wild snakes (Wright and Wright, 1957; Smith, 1961; Resetarits, 1983; Tennant, 1984; Ernst and Barbour, 1989; Dundee and Rossman, 1989).

These observations have extremely important implications for the captive maintenance of this species, which is discussed in detail below.

Interestingly, several authors have included earthworms in the diet of these snakes (Stebbins, 1985), while others state they will not consume earthworms (Dundee and Rossman, 1989; Tennant, 1985). Palmer and Fowler (1975) include earthworms in the wild diet of these snakes but reported they "will not eat them in captivity." Some have proposed that these snakes are avoiding competition in areas where they occur with garter snakes by eating primarily amphibians and not earthworms (Foquette, 1954) even though this varies from population to population. Those in our care showed no interest in earthworms.

Newly metamorphosed giant toads, *Bufo marinus*, may represent a suitable food for members of this species since they have been well accepted by eastern ribbon snakes in captivity (Rossi, 1981). We have also observed a Cuban tree frog, *Osteopilus septentrionalis*, being consumed by an eastern ribbon snake, so presumably this introduced species may represent a food source for wild or captive western ribbon snakes.

Predators of these snakes include large wading birds, hawks, raccoons, foxes, and ophiophagous snakes, such as kingsnakes and coral snakes.

Mating has been observed to occur in the springtime over much of their range within the United States and this results in the birth of 4–27 young sometime between July and October. Rossman et al. (1996) report a relatively low mean clutch size of 8.4–12.9. These young range 20–28 cm (8–11 inches) in length (Behler and King, 1979), and like most other members of the genus, they shed within several hours to days of their birth.

Very little is known about the thermal ecology of this species, but on the basis of the work of Jacobson and Whitford (1979), these snakes probably have an activity range of 20–30°C (68–86°F) with a critical thermal minimum of 4–8°C (39–46°F) and maximum of 39–42°C (102–107°F), depending on the temperature to which they were acclimated. One study found

Redstripe Ribbon Snake, *Thamnophis proximus rubrilineatus* (photo by David G. Campbell)

that they become active in midwinter only after several warm days (>15°C or 59°F) (Tinkel, 1957). These snakes are known to forage at night in warmer weather and during the day in cooler weather (Ernst and Barbour, 1989).

The western ribbon snake is not a difficult snake to maintain in captivity. They do have a nervous disposition even though in our experience they are not quite as high-strung as some of the eastern ribbon snakes we have worked with. With time, however, they will calm down nicely and make fascinating captives.

The basic (ideal) cage setup will work extremely well for this species. Artificial carpet/turf will definitely help them avoid getting blister disease. Other cage accessories should take into account their arboreal nature (although perhaps they are a little less so than their eastern relatives). These include a branch (or branches) and plastic plants. The branches and plants should be secure so they will not fall over, or the snakes may learn to avoid them. The branch should also be baked first at about 149°C (300°F) for 15 minutes in order to eliminate possible mites. A hide box is an absolute necessity for this alert and nervous snake. And, of course, a bowl of clean water should always be provided.

Remember that these snakes are likely to be parasitized at the time of capture and therefore should be checked for intestinal worms initially and regularly thereafter and dewormed as needed. One of these snakes we collected in Sanderson, Texas, had *Capillaria* (whipworm) eggs in its stool. See the general care section on dewormers.

Their preferred food appears to be amphibians but captive specimens will very rapidly switch to fish-scented, prekilled pinky mice (pinkies) and soon afterward, unscented pinkies. It is interesting to note that our captive breeding efforts were unsuccessful until we switched these snakes to the all-mouse diet. In addition, this made the stool firmer and less odoriferous, which made cleanup easier and more pleasant.

Of course, these snakes will also do well on a diet of bait shop minnows supplemented in some manner with thiamin (vitamin B_1). A diet of fish alone will predispose these snakes to a B_1 deficiency because the fish contain an enzyme called thiaminase, which if not neutralized will destroy most of the vitamin B_1. The fish may be treated by warming them to 80–90°C (176–194°F) for 5–10 minutes after thawing. However, we presently do not consider fish to be the diet of choice on the basis of the observations above.

In addition, feeding fresh fish to these snakes is not recommended because of the risk of parasitism. Freezing the fish for at least 3 days is a good way to eliminate many of these parasites. B_1 supplementation may either be in the form of a piece of brewer's yeast tablet placed in the mouth of the fish (Mehrtens, 1987) or by injection of liquid B_1 (we usually use an injectable B complex) into the fish or IM into the snake every 3–6 months.

If fish are fed, twice-weekly feedings are usually necessary, with the average-size adult consuming about six minnows twice weekly. Stay away from goldfish as they are considered by many to be too fatty. Pinky feeders may consume 3–4 pinkies and need to be fed only once weekly.

A UV light source is probably not necessary since we have successfully maintained and bred this snake without access to a UV light source.

Ventral heat does not appear necessary for this species but it certainly may have some benefit (see under temperature in the general care section). Alderton (1986) recommends maintaining the eastern ribbon snake at 22–26°C (72–79°F) during the active part of the year and this is probably suitable for this species as well. We have found they acclimate quite readily to higher temperatures and seem quite comfortable at temperatures that fluctuate between 26 and 35°C (79 and 95°F) on a daily basis.

Brumation of this species is strongly recommended and may be accomplished in the usual manner in their regular cage. Make sure to have a clean water source available as they will drink occasionally during this time. Those in our care were exposed to naturally fluctuating temperatures occurring in the Jacksonville, Florida, area such that they fluctuated from 3 to 18°C (38 to 65°F) for 4–5 months.

As in many other snakes, sexual maturity is usually reached in 2 or 3 years (probably the latter for most females of this species). Breeding can be accomplished in the usual manner as discussed in the general care section. A male and female housed together for nearly 2 years were brumated as mentioned above and produced 9 babies on 19 June 1992, and 10 babies on 24 September 1995. The babies in the first litter ranged 20–24.5 cm (7.9–9.6 inches) in length, and averaged 22.1 cm (8.5 inches) TL, while those in the second litter ranged 184.2–203.2 mm (7.25–8.0 inches) in length. The sex ratio of the babies in the second litter was 5:5. This is consistent with what is reported in literature (187–283 mm or 7.4–11.1 inches) (Bowers, 1967). The two shorter snakes in each litter appeared to have stubbed tails, however, and we suspect this may have been related to very high ambient temperatures during the mother's gestation period.

Double clutching has been reported a number of times in captive specimens, with the second clutch usually occurring in August (Neill in Fitch, 1970). It is interesting to note that the female mentioned above passed several slugs and a deformed embryo in mid-August following her June litter.

The young are hardy fish eaters, but are extremely prone to the thiamin deficiency discussed above and also to blister disease and septicemia if kept in cages that are too moist. Artificial carpet/turf works well as a substrate for them. Frequent feedings are also important with the young (2–3 times per week) if they are

---

SPECIES: *Thamnophis proximus*, Western Ribbon Snake
MAINTENANCE DIFFICULTY INDEX: 2 (1 = easiest, 5 = most difficult)
AVERAGE SIZE: 45–76 cm (18–30 inches)
FOOD: Fish, mice (pinkies)
CAGE SIZE: 10–20-gallon aquarium
SUBSTRATE: Indoor-outdoor carpet or artificial turf
VENTRAL HEAT: Not essential but helpful
UV LIGHT: No, but an incandescent bulb is useful
TEMPERATURE RANGE: 20–30°C (68–86°F)
SPECIAL CONSIDERATIONS: Can rapidly be switched to scented pinkies, then unscented.
    Arboreal (branches advisable).

to grow rapidly. Most will switch to fish-scented mouse tails within several months, and then eventually to prekilled pinkies.

These snakes are alert and inquisitive captives. They are generally a pleasure to watch if they are set up in an attractive terrarium as described above. They are excellent candidates for captive breeding, as they are being rapidly decimated by habitat destruction. The red- and orange-striped forms are particularly attractive,

and perhaps will become popular with herpeto-culturists in time.

Captive longevity has been reported at more than 3.5 years (Snider and Bowler, 1992), but they will probably survive much longer now that we have a better understanding of their dietary requirements and parasite problems. We have maintained a pair for 4 years and 1 month and they are still alive at the time of this writing.

Thamnophis radix
Plains Garter Snake

The plains garter snake is a very wide-ranging and adaptable member of the garter snake group. It is recognized fairly quickly over much of its range by a distinctive orange-yellow middorsal stripe, even though scale counts are necessary to be certain about the identification. This is presented in Stebbins (1985).

There are two subspecies. The eastern plains garter snake, *T. r. radix*, is found from western Indiana through northern Illinois and southern Wisconsin, westward through eastern Iowa and southeastern Minnesota. There is also an isolated population in central Ohio and another in southern Missouri and Illinois. The western plains garter snake, *T. r. haydenii*, spreads westward from there through southern Alberta and southward to northeastern New Mexico. They reach a fairly large size, with some individuals reaching more than 109 cm (43 inches) and becoming quite stout-bodied.

The preferred habitat of this species is basically grasslands (meadows, prairies, and farmlands) or other open areas near water, including vacant lots, ditches, and roadsides (Wright and Wright, 1957; Webb, 1970; Preston, 1982; Tennant, 1984; Hudson, 1985; Stebbins, 1985; Hammerson, 1986; Ernst and Barbour, 1989; Conant and Collins, 1991). Hence, it is well named.

In the wild, the plains garter snake appears to accept a wide variety of foods. These include insects (grasshoppers), earthworms, slugs,

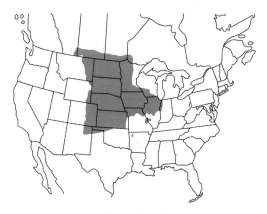

Thamnophis radix

leeches, snails, fish, and amphibians (wood frogs, *Rana sylvatica*, leopard frogs, *Rana* sp., bullfrogs, *Rana catesbeiana*, cricket frogs, *Acris* sp., chorus frogs, *Pseudacris* sp., gray tree frogs, *Hyla* sp., spadefoot toads, *Scaphiopus* sp., true toads, *Bufo* sp., and their tadpoles, and salamanders, *Ambystoma* sp.), as well as birds and mammals (Wright and Wright, 1957; Webb, 1970; Preston, 1982; Tennant, 1984; Stebbins, 1985; Hudson, 1985; Hammerson, 1986; Ernst and Barbour, 1989; Christiansen and Bailey, 1990; Degenhardt et al., 1996).

Predators of the plains garter snake include red-shouldered hawks, foxes, coyotes, skunks, minks, cats, and ophiophagous snakes (Ernst and Barbour, 1989).

Mating usually occurs in the spring (March

Plains Garter Snake, *Thamnophis radix* (photo by David G. Campbell)

to May), but may also occur in the fall (Wright and Wright, 1957; Tennant, 1984). This results in the birth of 2–60 young. Fitch (1970) listed 92 young for one clutch, apparently accepting the data given to Wright and Wright (1957). Tennant (1984) listed 95 young so perhaps larger litters occur, albeit rarely. Litters are apparently larger in northern and western populations (Fitch, 1985).

The young range 17.8–23.5 cm (7–9.25 inches) in length. The young grow rapidly (0.9–1.8 cm per week) for 2 years (Seibert and Hagen, 1947) and probably reach sexual maturity in 2 or 3 years.

This snake has been observed active on the surface most frequently at temperatures of 21–29°C (70–84.2°F) (Seibert and Hagen, 1947). Hart (1979) found that the snakes he studied were active at temperatures of 21–36°C (70–96.8°F) and had significantly higher body temperatures than common garter snakes.

The plains garter snake is not a difficult snake to maintain in captivity because of its broad diet and adaptable nature mentioned above. They do very well in the basic (ideal) cage arrangement if they are given a good dark hide box and a clean bowl of water. Ventral heat is recommended but may not be necessary if the snake is housed indoors and exposed to the usual fluctuations in room temperature. A heat lamp above may be very helpful, however, if one is not using ventral heat.

As stated above, their diet is very varied, but their favorite food appears to be earthworms. Adults will readily devour small mice and some amphibians if they are offered during the spring and summer, but commonly refuse anything but worms in the fall. A snake that refuses mice may be trained to accept them by feeding the snake a worm or two, then rubbing a worm over a pinky or fuzzy (prekilled) and offering it to them immediately afterward. Eventually, these snakes will take unflavored prekilled mice. Snakes that eat mice will need less frequent feedings, defecate less frequently, and are less likely to be parasitized, so getting the snake switched to mice is definitely a good objective for any serious snakekeeper.

Remember, these snakes are very likely to be parasitized, especially by *Strongyloides* worms, and therefore they should be checked for worms initially and regularly thereafter. If left

---

SPECIES: *Thamnophis radix*, Plains Garter Snake
MAINTENANCE DIFFICULTY INDEX: 2 (1 = easiest, 5 = most difficult)
AVERAGE SIZE: 51–71 cm (20–28 inches)
FOOD: Earthworms, mice
CAGE SIZE: 10–20-gallon aquarium
SUBSTRATE: Indoor-outdoor carpet or artificial turf
VENTRAL HEAT: Yes
UV LIGHT: No, but an incandescent bulb is useful
TEMPERATURE RANGE: 21–36°C (70–96°F)
SPECIAL CONSIDERATIONS: Adults usually take mice. May need to scent with
    earthworms initially.

---

untreated, they may fail to gain weight even though they may be eating. Also, untreated snakes are more prone to gastroenteritis (an infection of the gut that may eventually lead to an early death).

Brumation is strongly recommended for these snakes as they are very likely to stop eating in the winter regardless of the temperature at which they are kept, and this cooling off period will improve breeding success. Those in our care tolerated temperatures fluctuating between 2 and 38°C (36 and 65°F) for 4 months. Two of those months were usually at 2–7°C (36–45°F) since warmer temperatures often resulted in excessive wandering during the early part of the brumation period. These snakes were artificially brumated as described in the general care section.

Breeding may be accomplished in the usual manner following brumation. See the reproduction chart, Table 5.

As mentioned above, these snakes grow rapidly and will probably reach sexual maturity by their second year. The young are very prone to skin infections if kept too moist. They will readily consume earthworms until they are large enough to take pinkies, which usually occurs within 6 months.

Captive longevity for this species has been reported at only slightly more than 8 years and 5 months (Snider and Bowler, 1992) but they will probably survive much longer if dewormed and fed a good quality diet.

These snakes, with their distinctive orange stripes, are one of the more attractive garter snakes and they adapt well to captivity. Overall, we believe these snakes are one of the easiest of the garter snakes to maintain.

Thamnophis rufipunctatus
Narrowhead Garter Snake

The narrowhead garter snake is a small to medium-sized snake, with wild adults ranging 46–86 cm (18–34 inches) in length (Stebbins, 1985), however, one captive female in our care measured 94 cm (37 inches). They are brownish gray or olive-colored snakes with a variable number of reddish brown or blackish spots along the back that fade toward the tail. They have a distinctive head, with prominent or bulging eyes that face upward. This is thought to be an adaptation for a highly aquatic lifestyle (it probably reduces predation or aids the snake in ambushing amphibians by allowing the snake to keep less of its head above the water when it comes to the surface). The jaws are also longer and narrower than in more terrestrial garter snakes, a modification seen in other aquatic fish-eating species and thought to aid in the capture of that prey.

These highly aquatic snakes occupy permanent rocky streams in the upland forests of central and eastern Arizona and western New Mexico, with a disjunct population occupying a large area of Mexico's central highlands (Wright and Wright, 1957; Fowlie, 1965; Stebbins, 1985).

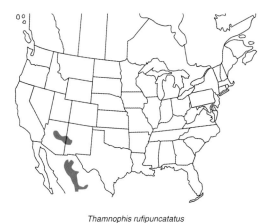

Thamnophis rufipuncatatus

As might be expected from such an aquatic form, the preferred foods of this snake are also aquatic and include fish and amphibians (frogs, toads, tadpoles, and salamanders) (Wright and Wright, 1957; Fowlie, 1965; Stebbins, 1985; Degenhardt et al., 1996).

In Arizona and New Mexico, 8–17 young, measuring approximately 15–20.5 cm (5.9–8 inches) SVL are born between mid-July and mid-August (Rosen and Schwalbe, 1988; Degenhardt et al., 1996). One long-term captive in our care gave birth to 2 young measuring 15.5 and 17.1 cm (6.1 and 6.7 inches) SVL. Our adults from Arizona mated repeatedly every March until April but very few young were produced. We suspect the pair was not cooled enough to produce normal litters.

The body temperatures of active individuals in the wild have been measured at 20–29°C (68–84°F) (Fleharty, 1967).

Suspected predators of this species include large fish, birds, raccoons, and other species of snakes.

Mating is believed to occur in early spring right after emergence from brumation. Fall breeding is certainly possible, however.

In captivity, the narrowhead garter snake may represent a real challenge. Although some who have worked with them have reported these snakes do poorly in captivity and may refuse to feed, we and others have found these snakes will thrive if set up properly. Remember, this snake is another long-jawed fish-eating snake, much like the western aquatic garter snake. Also remember that parasites are very likely to be a problem.

Indeed, about a half-dozen of these snakes have been maintained for more than 2 years at the Arizona-Sonora Desert Museum in Arizona. Reptile Curator Howard Lawler reported they were actually fairly easy to maintain, being similar in care to other garter snakes. They regularly consumed tiger salamander larvae, *Ambystoma tigrinum*, and fish. Our experience with this species is similar.

Interestingly, Curator Lawler pointed out that these snakes developed a heavy infestation of trematodes (flukes) in their oral cavities when they were fed the salamanders. Apparently these salamanders were intermediate hosts for the flukes. The problem was corrected by manually removing the flukes from the mouths on a regular basis and switching the snakes to a diet of fish only. It is important to note that attempted freezing of these amphibians had no major impact on the number of flukes. These cold-adapted parasites were controlled only by eliminating their source.

As stated above, this species prefers to eat fish. They will consume bait shop minnows and goldfish in captivity. They will also consume small prekilled scented mice as well, especially when offered with tongs in order to simulate a live prey item. Twice-weekly feedings will probably be necessary if fish are used, once per week is fine if mice are used.

With regard to housing, the basic cage design is strongly recommended for this species. A dark, stable hide box is very important. Artificial carpet/turf will work well as the substrate

Narrowhead Garter Snake, *Thamnophis rufipunctatus* (photo by David G. Campbell)

since fish will not stick to it and nothing can be ingested by accident. However, the Arizona-Sonora Desert Museum has used aspen shavings successfully for this species.

The use of ventral heat or an incandescent bulb to provide a hot spot is very strongly advised, even though cooler-than-usual room temperatures are well tolerated. Air temperatures at the upper end of those seen in wild specimens are recommended. Hence, air temperatures of 25–30°C (77–86°F) are advisable during the day, and a drop to 15–21°C (59–70°F) will probably be suitable at night (see below).

Of course, a stable nontippable water bowl with clean water should be provided at all times.

Brumation is strongly advised for these snakes as they are known to brumate in the wild. The average winter temperature (lowest and highest monthly average from October to April over several years) measured at 2700 m (7000 ft) in north central Arizona fluctuated between 10 and 17.6°C (14.4 and 62.3°F) according to the National Weather Service. It is

interesting to note that the monthly average low temperatures drop below 10°C (50°F) every month but July in this area. Similarly, May is the first month that nighttime temperatures average above freezing and July is the only month of the year with a daytime high above 27°C (80°F). These temperatures will give the snake keeper some idea of this snake's thermal environment. Indeed, these numbers should be checked for every species of snake with which one is unfamiliar and hopes to breed in captivity. In any case, brumation temperatures of 5–10°C (40–50°F) for 4 months or much lower will probably be suitable for this species.

We reported on a nearly successful captive breeding of this species (Rossi and Rossi, 1999a). These results are summarized here. One pair of narrow-headed garter snakes collected in Cottonwood, Arizona, was maintained in captivity for 8 years. These snakes were adults at the time of capture, making them at least 10 or 11 years old at the time of this mating. Repeated attempts at breeding following hibernation periods of 3 months at temperatures of 9.4–15°C (49–59°F) were met with repeated

---

SPECIES: *Thamnophis rufipunctatus*, Narowhead Garter Snake
MAINTENANCE DIFFICULTY INDEX: 3 (1 = easiest, 5 = most difficult)
AVERAGE SIZE: 46–86 cm (18–34 inches)
FOOD: Fish, amphibians, scented mice
CAGE SIZE: 10–20-gallon aquarium
SUBSTRATE: Indoor-outdoor carpet or artificial turf
VENTRAL HEAT: Yes
UV LIGHT: No, but an incandescent bulb is strongly advisable
TEMPERATURE RANGE: 25–30°C (77–86°F)
SPECIAL CONSIDERATIONS: Highly aquatic. Prefer fish but might take fish-scented
    pinkies. Cooler temperatures are well tolerated but cage should be dry.

---

failure, in spite of successful copulation each year. On two occasions the female gave birth to one male and several slugs. These were later believed to have been parthenogenic events.

During the winter of 1998–1999, the pair was brumated at 2.2–3.3°C (36–38°F) for 6 weeks, after a 4-week period at 15°C (59°F). Water was available at all times during hibernation. The snakes were removed from this low temperature and allowed to warm up to a temperature of 22.2°C (72°F) over 2 days. They were then separated and housed in aquariums for several days while they acclimated to the increasing temperatures and were offered food. They were placed together several times during this initial 2-week period, and no copulation was observed although the male made several breeding attempts. Two weeks later, on 17 April, the pair was placed together again, at which time copulation occurred. The pair was left together several more days and mating may have occurred repeatedly during this time.

The female ate voraciously for the next several months and began to demonstrate abdominal swelling. By July, her appetite had ceased but she continued to swell. By 4 July, several areas of epidermal separation were noted. These were believed to be areas of dysecdysis in the predelivery shed and a humidity box was placed in the aquarium. The female never left the heat source and maintained her body temperature at a constant 30°C (86°F). However, the areas of epidermal separation increased and she died on 7 July.

A necropsy was performed. The snake weighed 319 grams total, and her SVL was 73.7 cm (29 inches). Her TL was 94 cm (37 inches). Examination of internal organs revealed no abnormalities of the liver, kidneys, heart, or uterus. The lungs appeared hemorrhagic and somewhat edematous. The gut appeared thickened and with numerous nodules and fibrin tags. Histopathology revealed a large area of hemorrhage around the stomach and several sections of trematodes (flukes) in the blood vessels of the stomach.

The uterus contained 16 completely formed embryos, completely scaled and color patterned. There were no physical deformities. There were 8 males and 8 females, a sex ratio of 1:1. The babies, excluding membranes, weighed 34 grams, with an average weight of 2.1 grams. The SVL of the males was 15.08 cm (5.94 inches), and the TL was 19.05 cm (7.5 inches). The average SVL of the females was 15.44 cm (6.08 inches) and the average TL was 19.6 cm (7.72 inches).

Based upon the breeding date of April 17th, and an expected gestation period of 90 days, the neonates were approximately 10 days prepartum at the time of death. The size of these neonates, given 10 more growth days, would have correlated well with the size reported for neonates of this species collected in Arizona in late July and early August of 19.2–25.4 cm (7.6–10 inches) SVL (Rossman et al., 1996).

Even though successful breeding was not accomplished, these observations are significant. Firstly, the low temperatures required to produce a normal litter in this species appear to be lower than most species. This might be expected from their cold-water high altitude habitat. Temperatures normally used to induce normal gamete formation and maturation in other species of colubrids would represent those experienced by this species on an average summer night. Indeed, this pair failed to successfully reproduce for 8 successive years. Secondly, the cause of death appears to have been parasite-related: hemorrhagic septicemia secondary to trematode infestation of the stomach. Perhaps the circulatory compromise associated with late gestation contributed to bacterial overgrowth at the sites of tissue damage near parasites. Interestingly, a fecal exam had been performed on this animal in early gestation, and both tapeworms and amoeba were observed. This snake had been treated with 20 mg/kg of praziquantel (Droncit®) and 50 mg/kg of metronidazole (Flagenase®) orally on 5/21/99 and 6/7/99. Were either of these drugs responsible for the death of this snake nearly 1 month after the last dose? Had they been effective? Was the small size of the neonates and relatively low neonate weight compared to maternal body weight related to the parasites? This snake's maternal investment was 34–40 grams, which was less than 15% of her body weight. Many other colubrids produce litters that represent over twice that maternal investment, i.e., a snake this size might produce a litter weighing 60 or more grams. The observations presented here suggest that these parasites are not only capable of producing morbidity and mortality in their host, but also in their offspring. Even if the mother and neonates survived, the size and survivorship of the neonates might be affected. The provides further evidence for the importance of parasite control in captive animals.

Growth rate and age at sexual maturity are unknown but they will probably reach sexual maturity at 2–3 years in captivity.

No captive longevities have been reported for this species. The Arizona-Sonora Desert Museum has maintained some of these snakes for more than 2 years and we have maintained a male for 9 years and 2 months and he is still alive at the time of this writing. The snake was captured as an adult in the area of Cottonwood, Arizona.

Thamnophis sauritis
Eastern Ribbon Snake

The eastern ribbon snake is basically a thin arboreal member of the garter snake group. They are similarly colored, with dark brown or black forming the majority of the dorsal pattern and they possess three (sometimes four) variably colored longitudinal stripes. These stripes may be yellow, tan, light green, or blue. The belly is usually pale yellow to green; in many it is cream-colored. As mentioned above, they are fairly light-bodied, with the average ribbon snake usually not much thicker than a pencil. They usually range 45.7–66 cm (18–26 inches) in length with a record of 101.8 cm (40 inches) (Rossman et al., 1996).

There are four subspecies which range from southern Maine to Wisconsin, including southern Ontario, and southward to include every state east of the Mississippi River. There is also

Thamnophis sauritus

an isolated population in southern Nova Scotia. These four subspecies are the eastern ribbon snake, *T. s. sauritis*, the northern ribbon snake,

T. s. septentrionalis, the peninsula ribbon snake, *T. s. sackenii*, and the bluestripe ribbon snake, *T. s. nitae*. The vast majority of this range is occupied by the eastern ribbon snake, with the peninsula ribbon snake found only in peninsular Florida and southeastern Georgia, the bluestripe ribbon snake found only along the northern Gulf coast of Florida, and the northern ribbon snake found only in southern Wisconsin as well as northern Illinois.

The preferred habitat of the ribbon snake appears to be in areas of thick vegetation near water. Such habitats have been described as sloughs, ponds, swamps, bogs, meadows, marshes, brooks, streams, and rivers (Wright and Wright, 1957; Minton, 1972; Mount, 1975; Holman et al., 1990; Ernst and Barbour, 1989; Allen, 1992; Mitchell, 1994; Palmer and Braswell, 1995; Harding, 1997). We have also found them common in flooded prairies in northern Florida, as has Dalrymple (1988) in south Florida.

Body temperatures of active wild individuals have been measured between 12.6 and 34°C (54.7 and 93.2°F) (Carpenter, 1956), while bru-

mation temperatures have been measured at 5.4–5.8°C (41.7–42.5°F) (Carpenter, 1953).

The preferred food of the ribbon snake appears to be small amphibians, including tadpoles, as well as fish. Amphibians consumed have been reported to include 15 species of anurans (frogs and toads) and three species of salamanders (Rossman, 1963). The frogs and toads he reported included members of the genera *Bufo* (true toads), *Acris* (cricket frogs), *Pseudacris* (chorus frogs), *Hyla* (tree frogs), and *Rana* (true frogs), while the salamander genera included *Notophthalmus* (newts), *Ambystoma* (mole salamanders), and *Desmognathus* (dusky salamanders). Klemens (1993) reported that one of these snakes regurgitated a redback salamander, *Plethodon cinereus*, and these have been observed in specimens from Virginia (Mitchell, 1994). Much of the original research seemed to indicate a heavy preponderance of amphibians in the stomach contents of these snakes (Carpenter, 1952; Rossman, 1963; Mount, 1975; Brown, 1979; Dundee and Rossman, 1989), with other items such as leeches, insects, and spiders being reported

Eastern Ribbon Snake, *Thamnophis sauritus sauritus* (photo by Steve Barten)

only rarely. Earthworms are not thought to be taken by most populations of this snake.

Predators of these snakes include herons, hawks, minks, raccoons, otters, ophiophagous snakes, snapping turtles, bullfrogs, bass, and pickerel (Linzey and Clifford, 1981; Ernst and Barbour, 1989; Harding, 1997). Mitchell (1986) listed several incidents of cannibalism in captivity in which adult ribbon snakes consumed newborns or juveniles.

Interestingly, in an observation involving both habitat and food preference, we observed a large specimen in southern Florida approximately 1.2 m above the ground on a Brazilian pepper (*Schinus*) branch near a stream. The snake seized a medium-sized (approximately 2 cm [0.8 inch] SVL) Cuban treefrog, *Osteopilus septentrionalis*, and proceeded to swallow it, but rapidly released the frog and dropped off the branch when a large number of other Cuban treefrogs approached the calling amphibian.

Mating is thought to occur primarily in the spring, which may vary considerably in time of occurrence from north to south. The 3–26 young are usually born 3–4 months after mating and measure 16–24 cm (6.3–9.5 inches) in length (Fitch, 1970; Ernst and Barbour, 1989). Second litters have been reported in the same year for southern specimens (Neill, 1962), and the young of southern specimens are larger (Rossman, 1963).

The eastern ribbon snake is actually fairly easy to care for if you cater to its nervous disposition. The basic cage setup that works so well for the garter snakes also works well for this species. It is very arboreal, however, and therefore branches should be provided in its enclosure. Plastic plants are extremely beneficial in providing cover for the snake, thereby aiding in maintenance and breeding, as well as producing a beautiful terrarium. Unlike real plants, which can serve as a source of toxins or parasites, plastic plants can be thoroughly washed and disinfected. Both plastic plants and sticks should be mounted in such a way that they do not collapse, as accidents will contribute to the snake's nervousness, resulting in a loss of appetite or failure to bask. The branches you use should be baked at 300°F for about 15 minutes to kill parasites or other possible pathogens (harmful bacteria) before you place them in the cage. The cage size is not critical, but 10–20-gallon aquariums work very well. If the cage is too high or the plants are too dense, the snakes will have a difficult time seeing or capturing their prey. We have successfully used artificial carpet/turf for this species, but others have used newspaper or more natural substrates (e.g., cypress mulch) with success. Carpet/turf is extremely easy to clean and disinfect and doesn't get ingested by accident, so it is the substrate of choice for all ages of this species. Plastic hide boxes, which can be extremely small (the size of a box of playing cards) but don't have to be, are absolutely necessary for this species or you may get frequent vomiting.

SPECIES: *Thamnophis sauritus*, Eastern Ribbon Snake
MAINTENANCE DIFFICULTY INDEX: 3 (1 = easiest, 5 = most difficult)
AVERAGE SIZE: 46–66 cm (18–26 inches)
FOOD: Fish and small amphibians (treefrogs, cricket frogs, newly metamorphosed toads)
CAGE SIZE: 10–20-gallon long
SUBSTRATE: Artificial turf, indoor-outdoor carpet, or newspaper
VENTRAL HEAT: Yes
UV LIGHT: No
TEMPERATURE RANGE: 22–26°C (72–79°F)
SPECIAL CONSIDERATIONS: Arboreal (needs branches). Prone to parasitism and vitamin deficiency. Very nervous disposition.

Vitalites® or some other UV light source and ventral heat on one side of the cage are probably not necessary but may be helpful. Clean water, changed frequently, is necessary. A small to medium bowl will suffice.

They should be housed separately, except of course at the time of breeding. They reach sexual maturity at 2–3 years of age. Breeding occurs after brumation using the normal procedure described in the general care section. Brumation is a good idea, except for first year snakes, which may become dehydrated if you are not careful. If you are brumating babies, use a humidity box or place a small amount of mulch in one corner of the cage. Adults may be brumated in their regular cage, as with many other snakes. Just check the water frequently, and offer food if the air temperature rises for over a week.

Successfully feeding this species requires vitamin supplementation or (less preferably) a wide variety of food items. If these small snakes eat only fresh fish, they will develop a vitamin B deficiency fairly rapidly, leading to neurologic signs. (See the section on feeding.) The fish should be killed, frozen for several days, thawed, warmed up to at least 80°C (176°F) for 5 minutes, dipped in some sort of liquid reptile vitamin, and gently placed in the bottom of the cage in the late afternoon. Some of these snakes will approach and eat only moving objects, and for these specimens, a long pair of tongs can be used to dangle the fish in front of the snake.

If worse comes to worst, live fish and amphibians (*Hyla* sp., young *Bufo* sp., young *Rana* sp., and especially cricket frogs, *Acris gryllus*) can be utilized. Tadpoles can also be used. Don't be surprised if your snakes develop sparganosis (cutaneous or intramuscular lumps containing parasites) when you feed live amphibians and fish, however. Your veterinarian can treat this with Droncit® (praziquantel), but there may be other parasites introduced by feeding this way that are not so easy to treat. So do try to use frozen/heated or live fish if you can. If amphibians are used, they should be treated in the same manner. Please note that freezing/heating is not guaranteed to kill all pathogens, but performing this procedure will kill many and therefore reduce the likelihood for infection. Theoretically, parasites from more northern climates will not be so sensitive to freezing. Recently, some herpetologists have suggested microwaving food items which have had the abdomen sliced open to prevent gas-related abdominal ruptures. This may work, but no one knows the time or setting necessary to destroy any of these potential pathogens, or how much nutrient damage, if any, will occur when this is done. Perhaps freezing and microwaving could be combined in a standard procedure, and tested to determine if it results in a nutritionally complete and parasite-free food. At this time no one knows.

Young ribbon snakes are extremely sensitive to excess moisture in their cages. If the bottom of the cage is not kept dry, they can die within 3 days, presumably from a massive infection (septicemia) originating from cutaneous and respiratory sites (skin and lungs), since both blister disease and respiratory signs will be observed prior to death. This is the reason artificial carpet/turf with a nontippable or non-spillable water container is recommended. Use screen tops to help maintain good ventilation. Five- or 10-gallon aquariums work well for this species. Plastic shoe boxes do not. House the babies individually and feed them frequently, every 1 or 2 days. Pet store "feeder fish" can be purchased which are small enough for newborn babies. Most baby snakes will take dead fish (treated as mentioned above) and this is a good habit to maintain for reasons discussed above. Overall, this is a sensitive nervous snake but not that difficult to maintain or breed in captivity.

One of these snakes has been maintained for nearly 4 years at the Philadelphia Zoo (Snider and Bowler, 1992), but we imagine they may live much longer, now that we are aware of their parasite and vitamin problems.

We have housed this species and rough green snakes in the same tall terrarium for years. They seem to do quite well together as they don't compete for food. They are fascinating little snakes that bask frequently and hence are easy to observe among the branches during the day.

Thamnophis sirtalis
Common Garter Snake

The common garter snake is perhaps the most successful terrestrial snake in the world. It has one of the largest natural ranges known and certainly the largest range of any species within North America. There are 11 subspecies (at the time of this writing) that range from the Atlantic coast to the Pacific coast as far north as the northern borders of Alberta and Saskatchewan southward through southern California and Florida. The only areas not occupied by this species are some of the desert regions of the southwestern United States, and the only state without this species crossing its borders is Arizona.

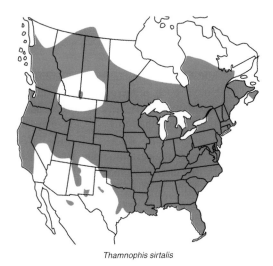

Thamnophis sirtalis

These 11 subspecies are as follows: The Texas garter snake, *T. s. annectans*, the red-spotted garter snake, *T. s. concinnus*, the New Mexico garter snake, *T. s. dorsalis*, the valley garter snake, *T. s. fitchi*, the California red-sided garter snake, *T. s. infernalis*, the maritime garter snake, *T. s. pallidulus*, the red-sided garter snake, *T. s. parietalis*, the Puget Sound garter snake, *T. s. pickeringii*, the Chicago garter snake, *T. s. semifasciatus*, the bluestripe garter snake, *T. s. similis*, and the eastern garter snake, *T. s. sir-*

talis. All of these snakes have large eyes, lateral stripes on rows 2 and 3, 19 scale rows at midbody, seven (sometimes eight) upper labials (lip scales), and big appetites. They are extremely variably colored, each with subspecies having some distinctive combination of pattern and scalation; a field guide should be consulted in order to identify the specimen in hand. Garter snake experts have recently made some major changes in the taxonomy of these animals (Rossman et al., 1996). The common garter snake subspecies have not been spared, and at the present time, the relationships and, hence, the biology of these are difficult to follow. We will do our best to summarize the natural history of this incredible species, although Rossman et al. (1996) say that attempts to do so may be "nearly impossible."

The common garter snake is a medium-sized snake, ranging 45.7–131.1 cm (18–51.6 inches) in length (Behler and King, 1979). As with most of the garter snakes, the females attain a larger size than the males (Fitch, 1981).

As one might expect from a snake with such a large distribution, the number of habitats occupied are numerous. Wright and Wright (1957) said 154 different habitat descriptions were collected in their research on this species. Some of the most common habitats listed include woodlands, lakes, meadows, swamps, rivers, creeks, sloughs, shrubby fields, quarries, trash dumps, vacant lots, and parks (Wright and Wright, 1957; Ernst and Barbour, 1989). Palmer and Braswell (1995) suggest that these snakes are most common in open grassy areas in North Carolina, and perhaps this is true for them throughout their range. Some subspecies appear to be more aquatic than others (Rossman et al., 1996).

The food items listed for this snake would fill several pages if listed down to species. It is an opportunistic generalist whose diet is summarized here. Items listed as food for this species

California Red-sided Garter Snake, *Thamnophis sirtalis infernalis* (photo by David G. Campbell)

have included earthworms, slugs, snails, insects, crayfish, fish, amphibians (true frogs, Rana sp., treefrogs, *Hyla* sp., spadefoots, *Scaphiopus* sp., narrow-mouthed frogs, *Gastrophryne* sp., woodland salamanders, *Plethodon* sp., brook salamanders, *Eurycea* sp., newts, *Notopthalmus* sp., waterdogs, *Necturus* sp.), other snakes (including members of their own species), nestling birds, mice, shrews, chipmunks, and more (Wright and Wright, 1957; Behler and King, 1979; Preston, 1982; Stebbins, 1985; Hammerson, 1986; Mitchell, 1986; Dundee and Rossman, 1989; Linder and Fichter, 1991; Conant and Collins, 1991).

Mating generally occurs in the spring right after emergence from brumation, which varies from March to July depending on latitude and altitude (Fitch, 1965, 1970; Ernst and Barbour, 1989), but may also occur in the fall over much of the western United States and Canada.

Spring mating generally results in the birth of 3–85 young (usually 11–26) 87–116 days later (Wright and Wright, 1957; Fitch, 1970, 1985; Ernst and Barbour, 1989). Litter sizes in the far west are fairly small, averaging 11–14 young, while those in the midwest and east are much larger, averaging 23–26 young (Fitch, 1985).

The young snakes are patterned similarly to the adults and range 13.5–23 cm (5.3–9.1 inches) in length (Ernst and Barbour, 1989; Conant and Collins, 1991).

There have been numerous studies on the thermal ecology of this species. From those studies it appears that this species may be active at temperatures of 9–35°C (48–95°F) but the preferred temperature range is 20–35°C (68–95°F) (Brattstrom, 1965; Kitchell, 1969). Brumation temperatures (cloacal temperatures of brumating snakes) were measured at 3.4–7°C (38–45°F) in Michigan (Carpenter, 1953). Another study of brumating garter snakes revealed body temperatures of 1.8–6.5°C (35.2–43.7°F) (MacCartney et al., 1989).

A wide variety of predators prey upon these snakes. Ernst and Barbour (1989) summarized the observations of many when compiling the following list. They reported the predators of garter snakes to include badgers, minks, weasels, raccoons, foxes, dogs, cats, chipmunks, shrews, hawks, owls, herons, bitterns, Virginia rails, goldeneye ducks, pheasants, chickens, turkeys, crows, robins, shrikes, other garter snakes, kingsnakes, racers, coral snakes, copperheads, milksnakes, box turtles, salamanders, bullfrogs, fish, large crayfish, and spiders.

Blue-striped Garter Snake, *Thamnophis sirtalis similis* (photo by David G. Campbell)

Garter snakes are relatively easy to maintain and breed in captivity and the common garter snake is probably the easiest member of the group. All subspecies appear to adapt readily to captivity as long as they are set up and fed properly. Unfortunately, most individuals try to set them up in moist environments with poor ventilation, and this often results in skin or respiratory infections.

The basic cage design using ventral heat, artificial carpet/turf, hide box, and a rock in an aquarium with a weighted screen top will work

Eastern Garter Snake, *Thamnophis sirtalis sirtalis* (photo by David G. Campbell)

Red-sided Garter Snake, *Thamnophis sirtalis parietalis* (photo by John Rossi)

well for this species. A 10-gallon aquarium is a suitable size for most. Much fancier cages have been used, as have a wide variety of substrates, but this adaptable species will usually thrive in the barest of basic cage designs. Nevertheless, some individuals are extremely nervous, and these animals will benefit tremendously by the presence of numerous hiding places in the cage. Plastic plants will also beautify the enclosure

and add a sense of security. A clean water bowl with fresh water should always be available.

After years of discussion and countless examples of long-term maintenance as well as several captive breedings, it now appears the common garter snake, like so many other North American snakes, does not require a UV light source. Indeed, some individual animals may show an increased appetite under these lights,

San Francisco Garter Snake, *Thamnophis sirtalis tetrataenia* (photo by John Rossi)

but this is now believed to be due to improved visualization of the prey items rather than any vitamin-producing ability. Even though UV light is not considered necessary, using an incandescent bulb to provide both light and heat (to form a hot spot) in the cage is an excellent idea for this species, as is a ventral heat source (see the upper end of the preferred temperature range above).

As alluded to earlier, their diet in nature consists largely of earthworms, amphibians, and fish, but most will also take mice. In fact, most of these snakes (of almost any age) may be easily trained to take mice, and a well-adjusted captive will do so with the voracity of a rat snake. They are easily tricked into swallowing things (which have included chopped beef, mice, small birds, etc.) by rubbing a fish or amphibian on the object intended for food; therefore, mice are the logical choice for this scent transfer. Diets of mice alone have proven safe for years for many of these snakes and it appears that the concerns about obesity and constipation were unwarranted.

Many neonates of this species will readily take foods which are usually not considered typical garter snake fare. We have seen neonates greedily consume unscented pinky parts, and rapidly move to ingesting whole pinkies. Many neonates will consume plain unscented pinkies or pinkie parts without any scenting, suggesting that this may be a natural prey item. This is particularly true of the western subspecies.

There are a number of excellent benefits derived from feeding mice. For the snake, it means a parasite-free nutritious meal that will need no vitamin supplementation, especially vitamin B_1 (thiamin). For the keeper, it means once-weekly feedings and cage cleanups more comparable to kingsnakes than water snakes. These snakes become bulkier, breed better, and seem calmer than those fed fish and amphibians. Lastly, the mice are easier to obtain than are amphibians and fish.

If small, scented, prekilled mice are refused, the more natural food items will be necessary for a short time until the snake can be trained to take the mice. Usually, frozen fish and frogs should be used both for the purpose of tricking the snakes and (after proper thawing and warming) as food itself. This will reduce but not eliminate the potential parasite problem inherent in feeding these items.

Earthworms are also an excellent captive food source, even though they may be a bit more tedious to administer and result in looser stools than are seen with mice. There is evidence now, however, suggesting earthworms do represent a balanced diet for small snakes, including garter snakes (Alpaugh, 1980; Rossi and Rossi, 1993c). Four or five worms every 10 days will support the average-sized garter snake (Alpaugh, 1980), and diets of worms alone have allowed reproduction in earth snakes (Rossi and Rossi, 1993c).

The combination of feeding mice to these snakes and a lack of exercise may lead to

---

SPECIES: *Thamnophis sirtalis*, Common Garter Snake
MAINTENANCE DIFFICULTY INDEX: 2 (1 = easiest, 5 = most difficult)
AVERAGE SIZE: 45–131 cm (18–51 inches)
FOOD: Fish, amphibians, mice
CAGE SIZE: 10–20-gallon aquarium
SUBSTRATE: Artificial turf or indoor-outdoor carpet
VENTRAL HEAT: Yes
UV LIGHT: No, but an incandescent bulb is useful
TEMPERATURE RANGE: 20–35°C (68–95°F)
SPECIAL CONSIDERATIONS: Readily consume small mice. Prone to blister disease if kept in moist cage. Likely to be parasitized.

problems in unbred, improperly brumated, female garter snakes, however. The production of "slugs" or infertile eggs on a regular basis appears to contribute to uterine or ovarian hyperplasia and possibly tumors, as we have seen several long-term captives with uterine/ovarian tumors that all had a history of heavy feeding and "slug" production.

Common garter snakes do best if housed singly, although they are not particularly aggressive to each other except during feeding. Sometimes, however, one snake will become dominant and take all the food—as has been observed previously in many other lizards and snakes—while another will waste away in the midst of plenty. In fact, it has been observed that submissive animals will not bask and may not thermoregulate. If they don't regulate their temperature, they will not have a normally functioning immune system or digestive system, so they get sick, refuse to eat, and ultimately die in the same cage with another garter snake that is doing well. Another simple reason is that these snakes are cannibalistic (Mitchell, 1986), and one may decide to eat a cagemate it has lived with for months.

Brumation and breeding should be accomplished as with other snakes. See the sections under general care. Canadian garter snakes (red-sided garter snakes) must be exposed to temperatures below 10°C (50°F) for at least 7 weeks if they are to show any interest in breeding (Crews and Garstka, 1982). Remember that the ambient temperature has also been shown to be a critical factor in inducing mating activity. This has been suspected in many reptiles but has been clearly demonstrated in this species. A temperature of 25°C (77°F) is necessary for many of these Canadian garter snakes to breed (Crews and Garstka, 1982).

Remember that garter snakes bear live young sometime in late summer or early fall. See the reproduction chart, Table 5.

Babies are voracious eaters, taking earthworms, amphibians, fish, or scented pinkies. All amphibians of appropriate size will be taken including several introduced species: young giant toads, *Bufo marinus*, greenhouse frogs, *Eleutherodactylus planirostris*, and Cuban treefrogs, *Osteopilus septentrionalis*.

House the babies in the same cage arrangement as mentioned for the adults. Just like ribbon snake young, garter snake babies are also very sensitive to cage moisture, so beware. Raise them separately.

One captive survived 14 years in captivity (Snider and Bowler, 1992).

These snakes are definitely not known for their handleability. However, a number of these snakes will be surprisingly calm after several years in captivity and do not seem to object to handling.

Trimorphodon biscutatus
Lyre Snake

The lyre snake is a tremendously interesting rear-fanged colubrid that does reasonably well in captivity. They are fairly attractive snakes but they have been largely ignored by herpetoculturists until recently.

The background color varies from gray to brown and they may have from 17–43 (depending on subspecies) hexagonal brown blotches along the back. They are relatively slender snakes with large spade-shaped heads and slender necks. The characteristic V marking on the top of the head is the source of the snake's common name but not all specimens have it. Perhaps the most attractive features are the disproportionately large yellow-brown eyes with elliptical pupils.

There are three subspecies in the United States. These include the California lyre snake, *T. b. vandenburghi*, the Sonoran lyre snake, *T. b. lambda*, and the Texas lyre snake, *T. b. vilkinsonii*. The former two are virtually indistinguishable by color pattern (although the California *may have* greater than 35 dorsal blotches while the Sonoran has fewer than 34) but may be identified by looking at the anal scale. In the California lyre snake, it is single, while in the Sonoran it is divided. The Texas lyre snake, which is protected in Texas, has the fewest number of blotches on a gray background and therefore looks much like an alterna morph gray-banded kingsnake.

Widespread across the southwest, but only common locally, the lyre snake ranges from southern California, southern Nevada and Utah, through much of Arizona, southern New Mexico, and western Texas. All three subspecies range down into northern Mexico, where other subspecies and species of lyre snake are found. They appear to be very shy, secretive, and nervous, but nonaggressive nocturnal snakes.

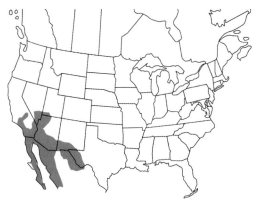

Trimorphodon biscutatus

The preferred habitat of the lyre snake is rocky areas, near the foothills of desert mountains, especially among large rocks with deep fissures that provide hiding places for these snakes (Wright and Wright, 1957; Fowlie, 1965; Shaw and Campbell, 1974; Tennant, 1984; Stebbins, 1985; Lowe et al., 1986). In a fascinating and detailed discussion of lyre snake behavior near Tuscon, Arizona, Repp (1998) pointed out that these snakes are "winter baskers." They select narrow, often vertical fissures that have deep retreats at the bases of their shelters. Their behavior throughout much of the winter, according to Repp, consists of moving forward, backward, up, or down in these crevices in order to thermoregulate. Up to three snakes have been seen in a single crevice. These observations may help to explain how these

snakes may breed in winter and thus improve our understanding of the species.

Vegetation varies from montane woodlands to desert grasslands and scrub (Degenhardt et al., 1996). They have also been found around human habitation and near bodies of water (Degenhardt et al., 1996; personal observations).

Food items reported for wild lyre snakes include lizards, (spiny lizards, *Sceloporus* sp., side-blotched lizards, *Uta stansburiana*, night lizards, *Xantusia* sp.), wild mice, bats, small birds, and small snakes (Wright and Wright, 1957; Fowlie, 1965; Tennant, 1984; Stebbins, 1985; Lowe et al., 1986). These snakes are known to forage at night for sleeping lizards (Tennant, 1984). This observation has been very useful in captive feeding efforts.

The natural predators of the lyre snake are unknown, but suspected predators include owls, coyotes, skunks, foxes, and other nocturnal carnivores including ophiophagous snakes.

Mating is believed to occur from early to midspring (March–May), but may occur in the fall or winter (Fitch, 1970). This results in the production of 7–20 eggs from March through September. These eggs generally hatch in 77–79 days into 20–23-cm (8–9-inch) young.

Little is known of the preferred temperature range in the wild; however, several specimens have been collected at night when the temperatures recorded were 17.7°C (64°F) and 18.8°C (66°F) (Wright and Wright, 1957). The senior author observed one crawling on the surface at 0200 hrs in the Gila Mountains of Arizona in late May. The temperature was approximately 18.3°C (65°F).

All but the largest of lyre snakes will do very well in a 10-gallon aquarium or an enclosure of similar size. The basic cage arrangement discussed in the general care section will work very well. Artificial carpet/turf is an excellent substrate as it allows these lithe snakes to obtain some traction when moving about the cage. Flat rocks, securely placed, and plastic plants will provide good hiding places and a small bowl of clean water will finish the cage. (It is critical that these rocks are secure. The snakes have been known to push rocks in such a way that they collapse and kill the snakes.)

Sonoran Lyre Snake, *Trimorphodon biscutatus lamda* (photo by David G. Campbell)

These snakes are very adaptable, however, and will readily use a plastic hide box if one is added. Ventral heat is a nice addition.

At this time it is unknown if these nocturnal snakes require any kind of special lighting, but it is unlikely. Weak fluorescent lighting or filtered natural light during the day will probably be sufficient for long-term maintenance. An incandescent bulb can be used to create a hot spot in the cage or ventral heat may be used to provide a thermal gradient. We believe ventral heat is more important for these nocturnal snakes since they rarely bask (and this should probably be available all year, even during brumation).

As mentioned above, the diet of lyre snakes in nature includes lizards, and unfortunately, they will often continue to include them in captivity. Small snakes have also been reported, although neither Degenhardt et al. (1996) nor we have found them to consume small snakes in captivity. Hatchling night snakes and ground snakes have been refused by those in our care. Serious herpetoculturists will usually be able to get a newly captured specimen switched to small mice without too much difficulty. Scent-transfer techniques (rubbing a lizard on a pinky) have worked well.

As with the night snake, we have found that the lyre snake is very fond of an introduced species, the Mediterranean gecko, *Hemidactylus turcicus*, which will be accepted dead or alive, making parasite control much easier. Degenhardt et al. (1996) reported that their captives consumed various iguanids, teids, skinks, and geckos as well as small rodents and bats including *Perognathus*, *Sigmodon*, *Mus*, and *Tadarida*. One Texas lyre snake in our care that had stubbornly refused domestic mice, rapidly struck, constricted, and consumed a much larger bat (species unidentified). Whatever food item is offered, remember this snake is nocturnal, and feeding success will probably be a little higher if it is offered at night. Certainly, well-adapted specimens may eat any time food is offered, just as the largely nocturnal kingsnakes and rat snakes do.

In our experience, the California lyre snakes are the most aggressive and adaptable of the three subspecies, often readily accepting small mice, while the Texas lyre snake is the least adaptable to captivity and will frequently refuse mice. "Supermeals" created by suturing a small prekilled mouse to a prekilled Mediterranean or banded gecko will allow these snakes to grow and do well until they begin taking plain (unscented) mice.

California Lyre Snake, *Trimorphodon biscutatus lyrophanes* (photo by David G. Campbell)

August "Gus" Rentfro of Brownsville, Texas, had success breeding the Texas lyre snake in captivity back in the 1970s. His observation that lyre snakes fed a diet of lizards only don't reproduce well is similar to our experience. We also both observed that Texas lyre snakes may be reluctant to feed on domestic mice. Gus solved this problem by offering them another introduced species, the house sparrow. Once he switched them over to nestling sparrows, his females gained weight rapidly and mated repeatedly in June. Seven eggs measuring approximately 3.0 cm (1.2 inches) in length were deposited in late July. These eggs hatched in 77 days when incubated at fluctuating temperatures. Gus noted that the young readily consumed young fence lizards, *Sceloporus* sp., and whiptail lizards, *Cnemidophorus* sp., after shedding, and soon after were consuming lizard-scented mice.

Brumation is strongly recommended for this species and is easily accomplished in the regular cage. Temperatures of 10–15°C (50–59°F) for 3–4 months are considered suitable. Those in our care have tolerated temperatures fluctuating from 3 to 18°C (38 to 65°F) for 4 months during the winter.

Captive breeding has occurred but only rarely at the time of this writing. The basic North American colubrid breeding scheme of placing the female in with the male after the first spring shedding may result in mating. Others have housed the pair together over the winter. The latter method may be safer since breeding may occur very early in the spring, or even in late winter according to some.

It is important to note that male lyre snakes may bite each other during the breeding season, much like male reticulated pythons. The "dominant" male in such a "dispute" mated with one of our females shortly thereafter. Thus, we advise housing these snakes singly, and never placing unsupervised males together during breeding season. These bites were not for show. They were deep and numerous. We removed the younger male from the older male's cage immediately.

A healthy inseminated female will then lay from 7–20 eggs in early summer which will hatch in about 2 months. The babies are approximately 20 cm (8 inches) long at birth and will readily consume small lizards as their first food, but can soon be switched to small mice. The babies are very thin and appear to have a high metabolic rate, as they require more frequent feedings (2–3 times per week) than might be expected for a kingsnake of a similar size. Doug Duerre of Las Cruces, New Mexico, has bred these snakes for several years and warns that the babies are the real challenge. He says the average person would have a difficult time raising large numbers of the babies since they will require 3–4 lizards per week for 4–5 months. Only then will they be large enough to consume pinky mice easily. In addition, they will usually not "fill out" until their second year (most grow lengthwise but stay fairly thin until about 2 years of age). In captivity, they will reach sexual maturity at this time also.

One pair of California lyre snakes in our care mated on 30 April, 1999. The female shed on 17 May and laid 10 eggs on 26 May. These eggs ranged 3.1–3.5 cm (1.2–1.4 inches) in length and 1.3–1.6 cm (0.5–0.6 inches) in width. These eggs were set up on vermiculite mixed with water at a 50:50 ratio by weight. At temperatures fluctuating from 22 to 33.3°C (72 to 92°F) 5 of them went full term but only 3 of them hatched on 28 August; the rest succumbed to a fungal infection. This suggests a short gestation period (26 days if the mating observed was the one that fertilized these eggs) and an incubation period of 93 days. Perhaps the average incubation temperature was too low or the medium was too moist to allow all of the eggs to develop. Perhaps this gave the fungus

an advantage over the embryos' immune systems. In any case, the surviving babies appeared normal. Interestingly one of these eggs contained twins. The 4 neonates measured 22.9 cm (9 inches), 20.32 cm (8 inches), 16.5 cm (6.5 inches) and 16.5 cm (6.5 inches) TL. They weighed 2 grams, 3 grams, 1 gram, and 1 gram respectively. The latter 2 were the twins. The color pattern of the twins was fascinating. One had darker markings on the left, the other had darker markings on the right. This color pattern difference may have been positional rather than genetic, but is was still very interesting. The neonates consumed anoles, *Anolis* sp., geckos, *Hemidactylus turcicus*, and gound skinks, *Scincella lateralis*, immediately after shedding.

One recently captured Sonoran lyre snake laid 6 eggs on 8 June that hatched on 24 August, an incubation period of 77 days. The neonates ranged 19–21.6 cm (7.5–8.5 inches) in TL. The SVLs of these lyre snakes ranged 16.5–19 cm (6.5–7.5 inches) with the two males (determined by the "popping" technique) having tail lengths of 3.2 and 3.8 cm (1.25 and 1.5 inches) and the four females having tail lengths of 2.5, 2.5, 2.7, and 2.7 cm (1.0, 1.0, 1.1, and 1.1 inches). The first shed occurred around 4 September, approximately 11 days later. Unlike hatchling night snakes, they do not appear to have sufficient energy reserves

Texas Lyre Snake, *Trimorphodon biscutatus vilkinsonii* (photo by David G. Campbell)

SPECIES: *Trimorphodon biscutatus*, Lyre Snake
MAINTENANCE DIFFICULTY INDEX: 3 (1 = easiest, 5 = most difficult)
AVERAGE SIZE: 46–76 cm (18–30 inches)
FOOD: Lizards, mice
CAGE SIZE: 10-gallon aquariums
SUBSTRATE: Indoor-outdoor carpet or artificial turf
VENTRAL HEAT: Yes
UV LIGHT: No, but an incandescent bulb is useful
TEMPERATURE RANGE: 20–35°C (68–95°F)
SPECIAL CONSIDERATIONS: Prefer lizards initially in most cases. Eventually takes mice.
   Nocturnal. Some are very aggressive mouse feeders.

to enter brumation immediately and not eat until the following spring. Hence, we advise feeding as soon as possible. Juvenile Mediterranean geckos and ground skinks were accepted as first food items, and feeding may begin right after shedding.

Parasites and diseases of the lyre snake are poorly known. Some blood parasites have been reported from some of these snakes in Mexico. We are presently attempting to determine what kinds of intestinal parasites are found in these snakes in the United States. One of the Sonoran lyre snakes in our care vomited a large hookworm, possibly *Kallicephalus* sp., shortly after capture. At the present time a standard deworming regimen (fenbendazole and metronidazole) is recommended for these snakes if they have been recently captured. Once dewormed, quality control of the diet and maintaining cage cleanliness will keep intestinal parasitism from being a serious problem in captive specimens. Fortunately, the lyre snake's broad diet and readiness to accept prekilled (frozen and thawed) food items make quality control of the diet much easier.

Remember that the lyre snake is a rear-fanged snake and possesses a mild venom that has been known to cause localized numbness, itching, and redness in people. Some states even apply their venomous snake restrictions on the sale and maintenance of this species. In our experience, however, the lyre snake is very unlikely to bite, and given the mild nature of the venom need not be treated any differently than a night snake. Of course, a bite may

become serious if one is allergic to the venom, so some caution is advisable. Check your state regulations on what is required in order to legally house this snake.

With regard to biting, the commonly available literature suggests these snakes are helpless during the day because they cannot strike accurately. Yet, we have discovered that these snakes strike extremely accurately during the day if they are striking at a lizard. In one daytime incident, a young California lyre snake struck 15 cm (approximately 6 inches) through a space 1.5 cm wide (approximately 0.5 inch wide) to grasp a prekilled Mediterranean gecko from Roxanne's hand. Hence, we now believe they can strike and hit exactly what they want to during the day, and their misses against people may be the equivalent of a hognose snake striking with its mouth closed (it is mostly a bluff). Most have refused to strike at us when handled, but even when bitten and even chewed upon, the senior author experienced no signs, so we do not feel they are particularly dangerous snakes.

Overall, the lyre snake makes a very interesting and attractive captive. In our opinion, however, they maintain their shy dispositions indefinitely and are not quite as curious as the night snakes appear to be. Still, a well-adapted specimen will take a favored food item right from your hand (tongs). Most lyre snakes will adapt very well to captivity and there are records of several surviving more than 10 years as captives. Snider and Bowler (1992) list a captive longevity record of 11 years and 10 months.

Tropidoclonion lineatum
Lined Snake

Outwardly similar to the garter snakes (because of the three longitudinal stripes from which they are named), but not closely related, the lined snake can be quickly identified by the double row of half-moons on the ventral surface. They occupy a huge range in the central part of the United States and appear to be primarily residents of open grassy areas where they can find cover and their favorite food— earthworms.

The lined snake is not a large snake. Most adults range 22–38 cm (8.75–15 inches) in length with a record of 54.4 cm (21.5 inches) (Conant and Collins, 1991). As mentioned above, they are found in the central United States, ranging from southern Illinois westward to eastern South Dakota and southward through much of eastern New Mexico and central Texas.

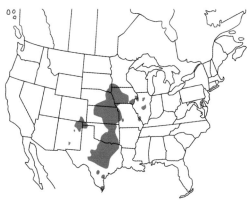

Tropidoclonion lineatum

Although this adaptable little snake was originally a prairie or grassland (as well as open woodlands) inhabitant, it can now be found in a number of disturbed habitats as well. These include city lots and suburbs where trash may provide the needed refuges (Stebbins, 1985; Ernst and Barbour, 1989; Conant and Collins, 1991). Degenhardt et al. (1996) point out that moisture is the limiting factor in western habi-

tats, with earthworms making the habitat adequate.

The preferred diet of these nocturnal snakes in the wild is earthworms, and little else aside from pillbugs or an occasional insect (Curtis, 1949; Wright and Wright, 1957; Tennant, 1984; Stebbins, 1985; Conant and Collins, 1991).

Although considered nocturnal, it appears the temperature preferences of the lined snake do not differ significantly from the large diurnal garter snakes. The temperature range of active individuals of this species has been measured at 19–33°C (66–91.4°F) with a preferred body temperature of 27°C (80°F) (Clark, 1968). They have been observed basking in the morning (Degenhardt et al., 1996).

Predators of the lined snake are known to include coral snakes, massasaugas, kingsnakes, birds, weasels, and skunks (Ernst and Barbour, 1989). Fitch (1999) found one in the stomach of a racer in eastern Kansas.

The lined snake is unusual among North American snakes in that spring mating is virtually unknown. Mating generally occurs in the fall soon after the birth of that year's litter. Sperm is stored over the winter and delayed fertilization occurs the following spring at the time of ovulation (Fox, 1956; Krohmer and Aldridge, 1985).

This results in the delivery of 2–13 young (frequently 7 or 8) babies ranging 7–13 cm (2.7–5.1 inches) in length the following August (Force, 1931; Funk and Tucker, 1978).

In captivity, they will do extremely well if given the same things wild snakes need: food and cover. There are, however, several peculiarities of behavior and reproduction in this species that are worth mentioning, and these are discussed below.

A 5–10-gallon aquarium is a suitable size enclosure for most members of this species. Cypress mulch appears to work well as a substrate, but a small area of rich soil on one side that is misted occasionally with water and into

Lined Snake, *Tropidoclonian lineatum* (photo by David G. Campbell)

which the worms can be placed is a good idea (see the photo of the wet/dry cage in the general care section). The soil may also be kept under a plastic cover or else in a plastic box in order to keep it from drying out too rapidly. These snakes are extremely susceptible to blister disease if kept in cages which are too moist, however, so be careful to avoid this by maintaining good cage ventilation. Do make sure to provide a bowl with clean water though.

No special lighting is required, but heat from above in the form of an incandescent bulb is strongly recommended. A 25-watt bulb is sufficient for a 10-gallon aquarium.

Daytime air temperatures of 27–33°C (80–93°F) during the active season have worked well for the lined snakes in our care, but spring and fall temperatures tolerated were lower. Nighttime temperatures tolerated by these snakes during their active season were 18–27°C (65–80°F).

As mentioned above, earthworms are the primary food item in the diet of the lined snake. Tennant mentioned they may also consume the toxic sowbug, but this is not thought to be a necessary inclusion in the diet of captive snakes. Mealworms and other soft-bodied insects have also been taken occasionally by captive specimens (Tennant, 1984). Also, unusual food items such as chopped meat have been reported being consumed when scented with earthworms (chopped meat is not recommended, however).

As with many other small worm-eating snakes in this size range, we have had great success offering two worms to each snake twice per week. These snakes are often shy eaters initially, so one should make every effort to avoid disturbing them while they eat. In captivity, they appear to be largely nocturnal, emerging onto the surface every evening and methodically searching through the soil for earthworms.

Brumation is strongly recommended for this species and may be accomplished in their regular cage (as described above). Brumation temperatures of 5–10°C (40–50°F) are suitable. Those in our care successfully brumated in their regular cages at air temperatures fluctuating from 3 to 18°C (38 to 65°F).

As mentioned above, these snakes have an unusual reproductive cycle compared to other

North American snakes. It appears they mate in August or September, right after the birth of the young. Hence, the keeper must be prepared to place a male in the cage immediately after the birth of the young (within 1–14 days of birth).

Some fascinating behaviors were noted when one female was observed giving birth. Babies were delivered every 5–11 minutes. As mentioned above the snake entered the soil side of the cage in order to have her babies. The following is a detailed description of a series of births by a captive female housed in a wet/dry cage with soil on one side and mulch on the other.

Prior to giving birth, the female became anorectic and spent more of her time in the soil end of the cage. One neonate was observed being born at 2:30 PM, another at 2:41. During the actual delivery, the mother had her tail in the soil and her head over the mulch. Babies were delivered by a slow and steady dorso-ventral compresison which pushed the babies toward the tail, and then a forceful lateral undulation to actually push the babies out. The mother left the soil for a short period, then reentered the soil at 3:01. Another baby was born at 3:07 and another at 3:12. The female then left the soil for several minutes but reentered it at 3:22 with an obvious cloacal bulge. By 3:27 she emergd from the soil without the cloacal bulge and did not reenter it. She submerged under the mulch and hid until observation was terminated. At 10:55 PM, this snake ate for the first time since 3 weeks prior to delivery.

One female in our care delivered young on 19 August and was observed mating on 22–25 August. Interestingly, she delivered her next litter on 10 July of the following year. This suggests that the warmer temperatures to which she was exposed (northern Florida is much warmer than central Texas) induced her to ovulate earlier than usual since this is the only record of which we are aware for lined snakes giving birth in July. All of the young were large healthy individuals showing no evidence of any defects.

The 4–5-inch long babies will consume small worms right away. These babies will shed almost immediately after birth. In fact, we noticed several newborns shedding within 5 minutes of birth. They may be set up exactly as the adults and should reach sexual maturity within 1 year in captivity.

Some of these snakes are fantastic feeders while others are quite fastidious, so make sure to house singly in order to avoid competition over food.

It is important to note that there is one instance of cannibalism reported for this species (Force, 1931). This involved a mother snake eating eight of her newborn babies within 8–24 hours after their birth. Hence, it is advisable to prepare for imminent delivery by providing plenty of hiding places for the babies, and once the babies are delivered, it is advisable to remove them from their mother's cage as soon as possible. A two-substrate cage (wet/dry cage with cypress mulch on one side and soil on the other) will assist in providing the

---

SPECIES: *Tropidoclonion lineatum*, Lined Snake
MAINTENANCE DIFFICULTY INDEX: 2 (1 = easiest, 5 = most difficult)
AVERAGE SIZE: 22–38 cm (8–15 inches)
FOOD: Earthworms
CAGE SIZE: 5–10-gallon aquarium
SUBSTRATE: Cypress mulch and soil
VENTRAL HEAT: No
UV LIGHT: No, but incandescent bulb is strongly advisable
TEMPERATURE RANGE: 27–33°C (80–93°F)
SPECIAL CONSIDERATIONS: Do well in captivity. Breed right after parturition, usually in
    August, resulting in birth 1 year later.

babies with hiding places and will also assist the mother with her delivery of those babies. Indeed, we have observed a female moving back and forth between the two substrates during the delivery process. Most of the young were delivered in the soil; a few were delivered in the mulch. One may predict delivery by observing the behavior of the female. Loss of appetite lasting from 3 weeks to 3 months may precede delivery. Females will generally hide under the substrate until several days before delivery, when they may move around more and be seen on the surface in unusual positions. Once the young are born, the females will usually feed heavily and may breed almost immediately after the litter is delivered.

In general, these small snakes have similar captive requirements to the earth snakes and brown snakes (and are about the same size), but are more frequently seen on the surface than the aforementioned species. Their disposition certainly appears calmer than many other small snakes, and they never bite. They are also considered more attractive by many and therefore may be one of the more desirable of the worm-eating snakes. Frequent handling must be avoided, however.

Interestingly, all of the specimens we have obtained thus far have been retrieved from "food snake" bins of a large reptile dealer. That appears to be all that these snakes are worth to herpetoculturists at the time of this writing. These snakes were suffering from bacterial dermatitis associated with high moisture and perhaps overcrowding in their cage. They were also suffering from intestinal amoebiasis, but this was successfully treated with metronidazole at the dose recommended in the general care section. Fenbendazole at a dose of 50 mg/kg was also used in these snakes and produced no apparent ill effects.

Captive longevity has not been reported for this species. We have maintained one female collected as an adult for 2 years and 2 months.

Virginia striatula
Rough Earth Snake

The rough earth snake is an inconspicuous snake. Its secretive nature, small size, and drab colors help it remain hidden among the leaf litter and surface debris. This strategy has been tremendously successful, however, as these snakes appear to be extremely common in some areas and have a very large geographic range extending from southeastern Virginia to northern Florida and westward to south central Missouri, eastern Oklahoma and eastern Texas, southward into Mexico (Conant and Collins, 1991). Solid brownish gray above, and pale white to tan below, these rough-scaled snakes have somewhat pointed snouts, and rarely exceed 25 cm (10 inches) in length, with the average individual ranging from 18 cm (7 inches) upward, and the record being 32.4 cm (12.75 inches) (Conant and Collins, 1991). They may be distinguished from most small snakes by the presence of keeled scales, not smooth scales, and from the other rough-scaled snakes

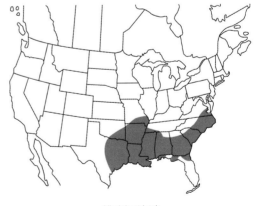

Virginia striatula

by scales of the head region. Brown snakes have seven upper labial (upper lip) scales and lack a loreal scale (see a field guide), while the rough earth snake has five upper labial scales and has a loreal scale. No subspecies are currently recognized.

Rough Earth Snake, *Virginia striatula* (photo by David G. Campbell)

The preferred habitat of these small snakes appears to be within either pine or hardwood woodlands and along their edges, wherever there is sufficient ground cover (Linzey and Clifford, 1981; Collins, 1993; Mitchell, 1994), but grasslands and vacant lots near cities have also been reported (Linzey and Clifford, 1981; Tennant, 1984; Mitchell, 1994; Palmer and Braswell, 1995). In fact, the greatest density of these snakes has been reported from very disturbed areas where there was a great deal of surface debris (Dundee and Rossman, 1989). We have found numerous young and adults under rocks along the edges of the Brazos River in central Texas. These areas had recently been flooded and earthworms were common in the rich soil there. They are believed to be primarily crepuscular or nocturnal, with most surface activity in the morning (Clark, 1964), but there are no recorded temperatures for active individuals in the wild. One torpid specimen was found 25 cm (10 inches) below the frozen surface, when the air temperature was 2.8°C (37°F) (Palmer and Braswell, 1995).

The preferred food of the rough earth snake is undoubtedly the earthworm throughout its range (Brown, 1979; Linzey and Clifford, 1981; Tennant, 1984; Vermersch and Kuntz, 1986; Dundee and Rossman, 1989; Mitchell, 1994), although other soil invertebrates such as snails, ant eggs, and soft-bodied insects have also been reported as have small vertebrates including small frogs and lizards (Mount, 1975; Ashton and Ashton, 1981; Linzey and Clifford, 1981; Collins, 1993).

Black racers, kingsnakes, and screech owls are known predators of rough earth snakes (Gehlbach and Baldridge, 1987; Palmer and Braswell, 1995). Suspected predators of this snake include raccoons and opossums and possibly many others.

Mating is known to occur primarily in the spring, but also in the fall, with most litters being born in mid- to late summer. The litters have ranged in size from 2 to 13 young with an average of 5 (Clark, 1964; Fitch, 1970; Behler and King, 1979; Linzey and Clifford, 1981). These dark-colored young range 7.6–12.1 cm (3–4.8 inches) in length (Behler and King, 1979; Conant and Collins, 1991; Palmer and Braswell, 1995).

The care of the rough earth snake is very similar to that of the brown snake and the smooth earth snake, but there are still many questions to be answered about all of these species, particularly the two earth snakes.

As mentioned above, the preferred food of this species is the earthworm; however, other soil invertebrates like insects, slugs, snails, and sowbugs have been found in the stomach contents of wild specimens. Ashton and Ashton (1981) reported that small frogs and ground skinks may also be taken by these snakes. In captivity, the only food which the snakes in our care would consume were earthworms. The worms should be offered twice per week. Generally, we will offer two worms per snake for each feeding. Feeding will rarely be observed, but the fact they are eating is evidenced by their growth and captive longevity. Just place the worms into the substrate, and the worms will be consumed as they are found. Based upon our work with the closely related smooth earth snakes, earthworms probably represent a balanced diet for this species as well (Rossi and Rossi, 1993c).

The substrate utilized successfully by some has been a combination of mulch and soil (50:50). This author has used cypress mulch only, or cypress mulch on one side and rich soil on the other. The worms can survive in this soil for some length of time and the snakes will enter it as needed to feed or for moisture. The latter arrangement is preferred for babies and smaller specimens, while the former is acceptable for adults. In either case, provide numerous hiding places; strips of bark work well for this. Plastic plants are also a nice addition. Make sure to provide clean water at all times.

Remember the warnings about the possibility of parasitism in worm-eating snakes, even though there is very little information available on the parasites of this species. A fecal exam performed on a specimen from northern Florida revealed rhabditiform larvae, an unidentified nematode, and an unidentified protozoan. The only other problem that has been noted with captive rough earth snakes is dysecdysis (difficult shedding), and this may be corrected by using the moist soil technique described above.

Blister disease has also been observed in this species when it is kept too moist.

Brumation and breeding may be attempted as described in the general care section. The snakes may be brumated in their regular cages since no changes are necessary. To our knowledge this species has not been bred in captivity, but females gravid when captured have given birth.

Two specimens in our care mated following brumation in early March, but the female died in early June. Inside her uterus were 3 70-mm long fully formed babies. Like the smooth earth snake, these snakes may have a great deal of difficulty near the end of gestation in captivity. Presently, the stress of captivity plus pregnancy are considered to have led to this snake's demise.

One of the fascinating and totally unexpected behaviors observed in this species is something we usually associated with "higher" animals. During the late gestation mentioned above, when the female was sitting on the surface for several days, the male remained close by. He was more well concealed than the female, but nevertheless, he kept his head and cranial part of his body above the surface near the female. When it became apparent to us that the female had died, he still remained near her body. When the senior author reached in to remove her, the male charged out of the mulch and appeared to be attacking his hand. For several days afterward he also "paced" around the cage perimeter, which was a highly unusual behavior for

---

SPECIES: *Virginia striatula*, Rough Earth Snake
MAINTENANCE DIFFICULTY INDEX: 3 (1 = easiest, 5 = most difficult)
AVERAGE SIZE: 18–25 cm (7–10 inches)
FOOD: Earthworms, occasional slugs, or other soft-bodied invertebrates
CAGE SIZE: 10-gallon aquarium
SUBSTRATE: Cypress mulch and topsoil mix (50:50) or straight cypress mulch. See text.
VENTRAL HEAT: Unknown but some heat from above may be helpful
UV LIGHT: Yes
TEMPERATURE RANGE: 23–25°C (73–77°F)
SPECIAL CONSIDERATIONS: Often refuse to eat for long periods, some never do. Prone to skin infections if kept too moist.

this secretive species and one which we had not observed before. We actually believed that he was looking for the female.

While highly unusual behavior, this is not the first time a snake has apparently defended its mate. We are struck by the story recounted in Ernst and Barbour (1989) of the three snakes that were found DOR back in 1925. A kingsnake was found with a glossy crayfish snake in its mouth. Attached to its neck, apparently biting the kingsnake on the side of the neck, was another glossy crayfish snake. All three snakes had been run over at the same time.

The young, about 7.7–10 cm (3–4 inches) at birth, will devour baby earthworms, offered twice per week. Place them into the soil side of the cage and the small snakes will find them. They grow rapidly and may reach sexual maturity (based upon their size) in 1 year. (Refer to Table 5, the reproduction chart.)

A 10-gallon aquarium is a suitably sized cage.

Refer to the section on smooth earth snakes for more information that may also be useful with this species.

In our opinion, these snakes are braver and more curious than the smooth earth snakes, and perhaps more stress-resistant. The authors have maintained one of these snakes in captivity for over 2 years this way.

One of these snakes survived 7 years and 3 months in captivity (Snider and Bowler, 1992).

Virginia valeriae
Smooth Earth Snake

Like the rough earth snake, the smooth earth snake is an inconspicuous resident of eastern woodlands. It is a small snake, ranging 18–25.4 cm (7–10 inches) in length with a record of 39.3 cm (15.4 inches) (Conant and Collins, 1991). They are generally reddish brown to tan-colored snakes above with longitudinal rows of small black dots, and an extremely inconspicuous pale stripe along the back in some specimens. The abdomen is usually cream-colored and the head is small and somewhat pointed. There are six upper labials (lip scales) and an elongated loreal scale, as opposed to five upper labials in the rough earth snake.

These snakes range from New Jersey southward to northern Florida and westward to southern Iowa, eastern Kansas, Oklahoma, and Texas. There is also an isolated population in south central Florida.

There are three subspecies, which are the eastern smooth earth snake, *V. v. valeriae*, the western smooth earth snake, *V. v. elegans*, and the mountain smooth earth snake, *V. v. pulchra*. The subspecies vary in the number of rows of scales and the amount of keel seen on the dorsal scales, with the eastern having the fewest scale rows (15), usually smooth, and the western

Virginia valeriae

having the greatest number of scale rows (17) usually keeled, and the mountain being intermediate in these characteristics. See Conant and Collins (1991) for more details.

The preferred habitat of the smooth earth snake appears to be woodlands, but they may be found in a wide variety of woodland situations, from deciduous to pine-dominated, wet to dry, and in those areas near woodlands, such as pastures, meadows, upland hammocks, and urban areas with litter (Wright and Wright, 1957; Linzey and Clifford, 1981; Tennant, 1984;

Smooth Earth Snake, *Virginia valeriae* (photo by David G. Campbell)

Ernst and Barbour, 1989; Allen, 1992; Collins, 1993). Both Minton (1972) and Collins (1993) mention the apparent preference for rocky slopes at the edge of such woodland situations. Fitch (1999) characterized the preferred habitat as moist woodland or woodland edge.

Body temperatures of two active individuals were measured at 23.5 and 31.0°C (74.3 and 87.8°F) (Fitch, 1956). Fitch also reported that these snakes were more cold-tolerant than ringneck snakes, although brumation temperatures have not been reported. These snakes are believed to be primarily nocturnal although some daytime activity has been reported (Minton, 1972).

Like the rough earth snake, the smooth earth snake seems to prey primarily upon earthworms, but other small invertebrates are occasionally taken. These have included insect larvae, small soft-bodied insects, snails, and slugs (Kelly et al., 1936; Cook, 1954; Wright and Wright, 1957; Ashton and Ashton, 1981; Linzey and Clifford, 1981). Many authors have found only remnants of earthworms, and no other prey in the snakes they examined (Brown, 1979; Blem and Blem, 1985; Collins, 1993), and earthworms have been shown to be a balanced diet for this species (Rossi and Rossi, 1993c).

Known predators of this species include other snakes (Hurst, 1963; Palmer and Bras-well, 1996). Predatory birds and mammals are suspected of preying upon these snakes.

Mating is known to occur in both the spring and fall (Collins, 1974; Vermersch and Kuntz, 1986; Collins, 1993). Birth of 2–14 young generally occurs 11–14 weeks later, usually sometime in August or September (Groves, 1961; Fitch, 1970, 1985; Morris and Walsh, 1991; Rossi and Rossi, 1992b). The darkly colored young range 7.6–11.4 cm (3–4.5 inches) in length at birth (Conant and Collins, 1991).

The smooth earth snake is best kept in straight cypress mulch or cypress mulch on one side and soil on the other, with plenty of refuges (bark or flat stones) on the surface.

It prefers earthworms but has been known to eat snails, slugs, and insects. It has similar problems in captivity to other small snakes, namely skin infections from being kept too moist and desiccation from being kept too dry, but these can be avoided by using the substrate described above (avoid artificial carpet/turf), and keeping away from high temperatures (29.4°C or 85°F plus) for long periods.

At this time, it is strongly suspected that a UV light source is not necessary, and the same can be said for ventral heat; however, a UV light will probably not hurt these snakes and may prove beneficial eventually, so we would recommend it. The authors have placed a "hot

SPECIES: *Virginia valeriae*, Smooth Earth Snake
MAINTENANCE DIFFICULTY INDEX: 3 (1 = easiest, 5 = most difficult)
AVERAGE SIZE: 18–25 cm (7–10 inches)
FOOD: Earthworms, occasional slugs, or other soft-bodied invertebrates
CAGE SIZE: 10-gallon aquarium
SUBSTRATE: Cypress mulch or mulch on one side and soil on the other
VENTRAL HEAT: Unknown but probably beneficial. See text.
UV LIGHT: Unknown but probably helpful
TEMPERATURE RANGE: 23–25°C (73–77°F)
SPECIAL CONSIDERATIONS: Like the rough earth snake, it may refuse to eat. Difficult to
  observe because of secretive nature. Prone to skin lesions if kept too moist. Very shy.

rock" on the surface of the mulch but never once observed young snakes under it or near it. It may still not be a bad idea for this or other small fossorial species, but it is too early to tell.

Like the rough earth snake, they can be offered about two earthworms twice a week. The young grow rapidly and three females born in captivity reached an average TL of 23.3 cm (9.2 inches) by 1 year of age (Rossi and Rossi, 1992b).

Some authors say that brumation is not necessary, but the same authors say that breeding has never been reported in captivity. We would recommend trying brumation as you would for other small snakes, in their regular mulch substrate cages at 10–15°C (50–60°F) with no additional light and no food. Just provide water.

Try breeding in the spring using the usual technique of placing the female in with the male right after brumation (after she sheds). Three brumated females in our care were placed in with a brumated male on 26 March. One female died in dystocia on 28 June. The other two had litters of 4 and 5 babies which were born on 1 and 2 July. This is slightly earlier than what is reported in the literature, and was probably related to slightly warmer than normal spring temperatures that year. In the wild, the young are usually born in August or September. (See Table 5, the reproduction chart.) Remember that the mother may stop eating during this time, as do many other female snakes during late gestation.

Delivery may be dependent upon substrate to push against and burrow through, as one female

kept on artificial carpet/turf died in dystocia, unable to deliver her babies. Compare this with smooth green snakes, known to die in a similar manner when they have no substrate in which to lay eggs. (See other warnings related to gravid smooth earth snakes below.)

Smooth earth snake babies may be raised in a cage with mulch on one side and moist soil on the other. The soil *should be misted every single day*, and the mulch can be left dry. A more practical option is to place a piece of plastic or rock over the moist soil to help retain the soil moisture. Live tubifex worms and tiny earthworms can be added to the soil twice weekly. Good ventilation is critical with this setup or the snakes may get blister disease from too much moisture. The young snakes will hide in the mulch, often under a piece of bark, the water dish, or a rock, and enter the soil to feed when they are hungry. Helping them along by throwing a worm directly in front of them once a week may help, but one must move extremely slowly and add the worm gently (or drop in gently) or the little snakes will flee. Gentle supplemental heat from above may be helpful, but do not overdo it. Three babies did excellently with no supplemental heat at all for over a year. As mentioned elsewhere, the size of the mulch chips may be a factor in success with this and other fossorial species. If the mulch pieces are cut too finely, they may be ingested with a meal and lead to intestinal impaction and death. Medium-sized cypress mulch chips (perhaps 1–3 cm long) are preferred by the authors. The young will rapidly approach the size of the mother by 1 year of age, and may breed at this time.

This is perhaps the most shy of all the snakes discussed in this book. These snakes are terrified by your movements, and even dropping in a large worm will send them scurrying. Be patient, move slowly, offer small worms, and eventually you will see them eat. In the meantime, just add worms to the substrate, and some will be captured by the snake.

This shy nature also takes its toll on the females when they are gravid. Handling them at this time or disturbing them has been known to cause spontaneous abortions. Since they will not eat anyway during this time (usually late July until early September), there is little reason to disturb them at this time. Just set them up in the correct environment as described above, with clean water and a few small worms initially, and never handle them unless absolutely necessary. After the babies are born, you may become slightly more aggressive in your attempts to watch this snake eat, etc., but they should never be handled very much.

Perhaps the smooth earth snake and the other fossorial secretive snakes in our backyard are not the most colorful or interesting of captives, but we owe it to these animals to learn how to take care of them. In addition, by learning how to best care for these species, which thankfully are not endangered at this time, we will learn how to better care for similar snakes on other continents, which may soon be endangered.

One of these snakes survived 6 years and 1 month in captivity (Snider and Bowler, 1992).

PART III

VENOMOUS SNAKES
NATURAL HISTORY AND CARE IN CAPTIVITY

Venomous Snakes: General Care and Safety

Keeping Venomous Reptiles

Keeping venomous snakes is not recommended for any amateur. It is very dangerous and it takes only one mistake to result in loss of limb or life. There are modifications in cage design and procedure, however, that can prevent excess contact with, and thus accidents with, venomous snakes. We cannot discriminate against keeping these animals just because they are venomous, since one of the chances of some for continued survival may be through captive maintenance and breeding.

Transportation

Transporting venomous snakes is similar to transporting nonvenomous snakes except that many states and provinces require the snake(s) to be placed inside of a locking box that is clearly marked VENOMOUS SNAKES and additionally labelled as to number and species. The snakes are best placed in a pillowcase first for double protection. Also, remember that many states and provinces require a special venomous snake permit in order to collect, transport, or keep venomous snakes. Other states and provinces do not allow the keeping of venomous snakes. Learn what the regulations are that affect you.

Maintaining Venomous Snakes: General Tips

The first thing to remember is that a person needs a separate room for venomous snakes that can be locked to prevent entry by unauthorized family members.

All of the vipers discussed in this book will do well with the basic cage setup discussed under the general care section. The modifications for venomous snakes should include:

1. A locking top.
2. A solid hide box with a bottom and locking door.
3. High sides.

These three modifications aid in preventing unauthorized departures of the snake or unauthorized entries into the cage by children, pets, etc. The hide box with a locking door and solid bottom facilitates cleaning because the snake can be locked inside the box while the cage is being cleaned. These modifications are not absolutely necessary for the safe maintenance of venomous snakes, but they are helpful.

A good snake hook is necessary for locking the box or closing the door (or any time the snake needs to be moved). One can purchase wonderfully light but solidly constructed manufactured snake hooks in all sizes now. You should own at least two snake hooks that will work for each snake.

Snake tongs can injure snakes easily, but if used properly, they are also an invaluable tool in moving these animals from one place to another, and they are absolutely necessary for some snakes that will not stay on the hooks.

Venomous snakes should be housed in either a separate building or in a separate room with a tight-fitting locked door (and window). This way, even if you forget to lock a cage lid, which you will (at least once), the snake will still be unable to escape.

Determine ahead of time the emergency procedure should someone be bitten. Locate the nearest hospital and find out if they have the appropriate antivenin.

Professional facilities keep the appropriate antivenins in stock and readily available in case someone is bitten. These operations also usually maintain a card or label their employees are instructed to grab and place in their pockets after they are bitten. This identifies the snake that was responsible and lists the proper antivenin to use. This saves time and perhaps a life if the person bitten loses consciousness and cannot identify the snake responsible. It also alerts the other keepers to check the cage of the snake involved to make sure the snake is still inside.

Strict protocols and routines for dealing with venomous snakes should be established and adhered to. One of the most important rules with our collection is that a venomous snake cage cannot be entered unless two people are present in the immediate vicinity. Certain times and days are best set aside for cleaning, feeding, watering, etc. These kinds of things should never be done on a rushed basis with these animals.

Basically, our routine involves unlocking one bank of cages, removing one snake at a time with snake tongs or hook and placing it in a secure garbage pail with a tight-fitting lid, and cleaning the cage thoroughly. The snake is then gently placed back in the cleaned cage with the tongs. In many cases, the entire hide box with the snake in it is removed with the tongs and placed in the pail.

Perhaps the most dangerous situation that may develop when dealing with venomous snakes is an escape. Although it has not happened to us at the time of this writing, it is a constant concern. If all of the guidelines above are followed, escapes are very unlikely. Re-

cently, we found that elastic cords may be easily slipped around cages and serve as an excellent back-up system should the lid come loose or the lock be forgotten.

Label all cages with bright-colored (red is good) warning signs: VENOMOUS.

DO NOT HANDLE WITHOUT THE PROPER EQUIPMENT FOR ANY REASON! EVEN FOR THE TREATMENT OF A MEDICAL PROBLEM, WHICH IS THE ONLY VALID REASON TO HANDLE, HANDLING SHOULD BE LIMITED TO MANEUVERING THE SNAKE INTO THE PROPER RESTRAINING DEVICE, LIKE A PLASTIC TUBE OR FOAM RUBBER AND PLEXIGLASS PLATE. See the section on handling in Part I.

See each species account for individual details on maintenance.

Agkistrodon contortrix
Copperhead

Nearly fluorescent pink to dull dark brown, the heavy-bodied copperhead is one of America's most recognizable snakes. It is named for its copper-toned unpatterned head, although there is a great deal of variation in the color and pattern within the species. The species has a huge geographic range, occupying some or all of 28 eastern and central states. It ranges from western Massachusetts southward to northern Florida and westward to southern Iowa, Nebraska, and much of Texas. Five subspecies are currently recognized. These are the northern copperhead, *A. c. mokasen*, the southern copperhead, *A. c. contortrix*, the Osage copperhead, *A. c. phaeogaster*, the broad-banded copperhead, *A. c. laticinctus*, and the Trans-Pecos copperhead, *A. c. pictigaster*.

The northern copperhead ranges from Massachusetts southward through the Appalachian Mountains as far south as northern Georgia and Alabama and then westward through southern Illinois. This dark-saddled snake definitely has the most distinctly "copper"-colored head of the group and was indeed the subspecies origi-

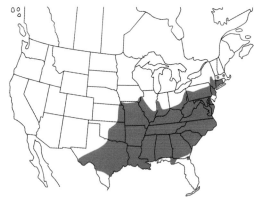

Agkistrodon contortrix

nally described by Linnaeus in 1766. The southern copperhead, which hybridizes with the northern copperhead over a wide area, is basically very similar, except that it is a much lighter color, usually pink, and rarely has a distinctly copper-colored head. It is also much more likely not to have complete bands across the back, and those bands that are complete are very narrow. This subspecies is found in lower

Southern Copperhead, *Agkistrodon contortrix contortrix* (photo by David G. Campbell)

coastal areas from Delaware and southern Maryland south to northern Florida and westward to Missouri, Arkansas, and eastern Texas. The Osage copperhead has a relatively small range, occupying most of Missouri, northern Arkansas, eastern Kansas, and Oklahoma. This subspecies may usually be distinguished by the white borders around the bands. From western Oklahoma through central Texas, the broad-banded copperhead is found. This subspecies is easily recognized by the fact that the bands are almost as wide on the back as they are on the sides. Lastly, the Trans-Pecos copperhead, which is found only in western Texas and adjacent Mexico, has a distinct pattern with light-colored areas in the center of each dorsal band that extend downward onto a very dark belly, producing a very strikingly colored belly, from which the subspecies name, *pictigaster*, was derived.

Among the five subspecies, there appears to be a trend toward smaller adults the farther south and west one travels. Adults of the northern copperhead range 61–90 cm (24–36 inches) in length with a record of 134.6 cm (53 inches), while adults of the Trans-Pecos copperhead range 51–76 cm (20–30 inches) in length with

a record of 83.5 cm (32.8 inches) (Conant and Collins, 1991).

With such a widely distributed species, a wide variety of habitats are utilized. Rocky hilly woodlands are the preferred habitat in the northeast, while low moist woodlands are areas where copperheads tend to be found in the greatest numbers in the southeast (Kelly et al., 1936; Wright and Wright, 1957; Mount, 1975; Linzey and Clifford, 1981; Jackson, 1983; Reinert, 1984; Petersen and Fritsch, 1986; Palmer, 1990; Allen, 1992; Klemens, 1993). In the western part of its range the copperhead tends to occur in open, dry, often rocky woodlands, but usually near water (Fitch, 1960; Minton, 1972; Tennant, 1984; Vermersch and Kuntz, 1986; Ernst, 1992; Collins, 1993).

The copperhead does not appear to be a specialized feeder. Food items included in wild specimens have included insects such as cicadas, beetles, grasshoppers, and caterpillars, as well as frogs and salamanders, lizards, snakes, turtles, birds, and mammals. A wide variety of each group has been reported, with at least 5 genera of frogs, 2 genera of salamanders, 6 genera of lizards, 7 genera of snakes, 7 genera of birds, and 18 genera of

Broad-banded Copperhead, *Agkistrodon contortrix laticinctus* (photo by David G. Campbell)

mammals (Ernst, 1992). Some of the more common and easily recognizable food items include leopard frogs, *Rana*, sp., small toads, *Bufo* sp., whiptails, *Cnemidophorus* sp., fence lizards, *Sceloporus* sp., skinks, *Eumeces* sp., glass lizards, *Ophisaurus* sp., worm snakes, *Carphophis* sp., garter snakes, *Thamnophis* sp., ringneck snakes, *Diadophis* sp., starlings, *Sturnus*, bats, shrews, mice, *Mus peromyscus*, *Microtus*, rats, chipmunks, squirrels, and small rabbits (Wright and Wright, 1957; Brown, 1979; Tennant, 1984; Ernst, 1992; Mitchell, 1994). Insects, amphibians, small snakes, and lizards are reportedly the preferred food of juveniles, while small mammals are preferred by adults (Fitch, 1960; Ernst, 1992).

Known predators of this species include amphibians such as bullfrogs, *Rana catesbeiana*, ophiophagous snakes such as racers, kingsnakes, milksnakes, and indigos, and birds such as broadwinged hawks, *Buteo platypterus*, and owls, *Bubo* sp., and predatory mammals such as moles, cats, coyotes, and opossums (Fitch, 1960; Ernst and Barbour, 1989; Ernst, 1992; Mitchell, 1994; Palmer and Braswell, 1995).

Fitch (1999) demonstrated that copperheads in Kansas were more abundant and had larger

adult body sizes in earlier successional stages (open areas with herbaceous vegetation) than they did in later stages, i.e., woods. This was believed to be due to increased numbers of rodents in the highly productive plants found in the earlier stages of succession. Many were found along the interface between field and forest. Regardless of habitat occupied, these snakes were observed to brumate in about the same place every year, usually a limestone outcrop with a southern exposure and deep fissures. In his Kansas study, Fitch found that there were no large denning aggregations and that many overwinter singly.

This species was also demonstrated to show a tremendous ontogenetic shift in food preference, with the first year young feeding largely on ectothermic prey, including ringneck snakes, western worm snakes, five-lined skinks, narrow-mouthed frogs, chorus frogs, and cicada nymphs. As they mature, Fitch found that the number of rodents taken increases, the type of rodent apparently depends upon the type of habitat occupied. Frog eating in these Kansas snakes was suspected to be the source of heavy parasitism; at least 35% of the copperheads in that study were found to contain lung flukes.

Northern Copperhead, *Agkistrodon contortrix mokasen* (photo by David G. Campbell)

In Kansas, copperheads mate in both fall and spring. The larger males engage in the well-described male combat, in which they try to push each other to the ground. The victor usually mates; however, females sometimes mate with more than one male. Females in Kansas generally gave birth for the first time as 4-year-olds, but some gave birth as early as 3 years of age. Birth in this population generally occurred from late August to early October. It is critical to note that those females that experienced prolonged confinement, without the opportunity to bask, often gave birth later than usual and possibly to stunted young. In some cases females produced litters consisting entirely of stunted or dead young (Fitch, 1999). Neonates in this study were generally observed to remain together for up to several weeks, suggesting sibling bonding. It is not uncommon in nature for toxic or venomous young to remain together. Predators attempting to prey on one may not attempt to prey upon others in the group. Interestingly, the estimated population density in one Kansas field varied from a high of 21.4 per hectare in 1977 to a low of 1.4 per hectare in 1988.

Mating may occur in either the spring or the fall, with 1–21 young (usually less than 10) being born sometime in the late summer or fall (Wright and Wright, 1957; Fitch, 1960; Ernst, 1992). Sperm storage has been shown in some cases (Schuett and Gillingham, 1986). The young range in size from 17 to 30 cm (6.7 to 11.8 inches) (Ernst, 1992), and have the characteristic yellow tail tip as seen in cottonmouths. This tail tip is believed to be used as a lure to draw amphibians into striking range. Females of the 3 western subspecies are known to produce smaller litters and have smaller young than the larger eastern subspecies (Fitch, 1985). These snakes may not give birth every year.

The copperhead can be somewhat more difficult to maintain in captivity than the other pit vipers. It usually eats well when placed in the same basic cage design as described in the general care section with venomous snake modification, but can undergo periods of inappetence for no apparent reason. John Breen (1974) proposed a possible explanation. He suggested that this snake has seasonal food preferences with birds being preferred in the spring, mice in the summer, and amphibians in the fall. This is probably a very widespread phenomenon in other snakes as well and cer-

SPECIES: *Agkistrodon contortrix*, Copperhead
MAINTENANCE DIFFICULTY INDEX: 3 (1 = easiest, 5 = most difficult)
AVERAGE SIZE: 61–91 cm (24–36 inches)
FOOD: Mice, chicks, amphibians. Babies have been reported to eat insects and pinkies.
CAGE SIZE: 20–30-gallon long
SUBSTRATE: Artificial turf, indoor-outdoor carpet, or newspaper
VENTRAL HEAT: Yes
UV LIGHT: Not essential but may be helpful
TEMPERATURE RANGE: 26–30°C (78.8–86°F)
SPECIAL CONSIDERATIONS: *VENOMOUS*. Usually good eater but can undergo periods of inappetence. Try changing food. Usually parasitized when captured. Permit required.

tainly something to be considered when any captive snake stops eating. If possible, however, one should attempt to feed only "clean" mice and chicks and avoid potentially parasitized amphibians. (See the section on food quality.) Copperheads will take dead food items, and many will eat well all year, so quality control of the food is possible.

Speaking of parasites, copperheads are very likely to be parasitized when first captured. Literature reports include tapeworms and roundworms.

Copperheads may breed either in the spring or fall. They reach sexual maturity at about 3 years of age, and females may breed only every other year. If breeding is successful, they will bear live young.

Brumation and breeding can be attempted as with other snakes. (See the section on winter cooldown [brumation and hibernation] and breeding under general care.)

Remember that Vitalites® or other UV light source and vipers go together. A UV light source really seems to stimulate and maintain the vipers' appetites, barring other problems; however, we have had many rattlesnakes and copperheads do well for many years. Ventral heat is a must as these snakes prefer to keep their temperature above 26.6°C (80°F).

Young copperheads should be offered pinkies after they shed, however, insects may be consumed. Cicadas and crickets should be tried on babies that refuse pinkies. Remember that insects are relatively calcium-deficient, and that they should be treated in the manner described in the general care feeding section. They are also more likely to be parasitized than captive-bred mice, rats, or chicks.

Remember to house separately and also have a fecal exam performed when the snake first arrives and regularly afterward. Mehrtens (1987) mentioned a specimen of this species that survived over 30 years in captivity!

Agkistrodon piscivorus
Cottonmouth

The cottonmouth may be considered the aquatic version of the copperhead, and the two species have many structural and genetic similarities. They are very heavy-bodied snakes with mottled markings, similar body scalation including the nine large scales on top of the head, similar numbers of teeth on the bones of the skull, and very similar chromosomes. The juveniles of the two species look very much alike, and even a trained herpetologist may need to take a second look to distinguish them from each other. Yet the cottonmouth, unlike any other member of this genus, has become an aquatic snake (Gloyd and Conant, 1990), and has become uniquely well adapted for that type of existence, even though they do not appear particularly well adapted for hunting in water (Savitzky, 1992).

The cottonmouth is widely distributed across the southern and central part of the United States. It ranges from southeastern Virginia southward through all of Florida and westward to southern Illinois, southern Indiana, Missouri,

Agkistrodon piscivorus

eastern Oklahoma, and much of eastern and central Texas. There are 3 subspecies, the eastern cottonmouth, *A. p. piscivorus*, the western cottonmouth, *A. p. leucostoma*, and the Florida cottonmouth, *A. p. conanti*. The eastern cottonmouth has the lightest color of the three subspecies, often retaining its banded pattern

Florida Cottonmouth, *Agkistrodon piscivorus conanti* (photo by David G. Campbell)

through adulthood. It ranges from southeastern Virginia to central Alabama. The western cottonmouth is dark-colored as an adult. It ranges from southern Alabama westward and northward to include the entire Mississippi Valley. It ranges from Indiana to Texas. The Florida cottonmouth is also darkly colored as an adult, but bears distinct vertical bars on the nose and chin areas which are absent in the other two subspecies. This subspecies ranges from southern Georgia to southern Alabama and southward through all of Florida. The authors have seen a large number of very light-colored cottonmouths in north central Florida however, with those in the area of the Osceola National Forest looking more like eastern cottonmouths.

Cottonmouths occur in an incredibly wide variety of habitats throughout their range. These have included bogs, swamps, sloughs, streams, rivers, lakes, ponds, and salt water marshes as well as offshore islands (Wright and Wright, 1957; Mount, 1975; Ashton and Ashton, 1981; Linzey and Clifford, 1981; Tennant, 1984; Dundee and Rossman, 1989; Palmer, 1990). Man-made habitats such as ditches, culverts, and retention ponds are heavily utilized in Florida (personal observation). They have

also been found far from water, over 1.6 km away from the nearest water (Gloyd and Conant, 1990).

Several studies on the thermal ecology of this species have been performed. Body temperatures of active wild individuals have ranged from 21.0 to 35.0°C (69.8 to 95.0°F) with an average of around 26–27°C (78.8–80.6°F) in two studies (Brattstrom, 1965; Bothner, 1973). Body temperatures of wild brumating cottonmouths in an underground den have been measured ranging from 4.2 to 16.5°C (39.6 to 61.7°F) (Wharton, 1969).

As might be expected for such a widely distributed habitat generalist, the cottonmouth also has an extremely broad diet. A list of prey items by species would run several pages. Basically, these snakes are known to consume insects, crayfish, snails, fish, amphibians, reptiles, birds, and mammals. Some of the more common and easily recognizable species include minnows, shiners, mosquito fish, mullets, eels, sunfish, catfish, mole salamanders, newts, sirens, amphiumas, true frogs, true toads, treefrogs, spadefoot toads, skinks, anoles, mud turtles, musk turtles, softshell turtles, snapping turtles, box turtles, hatchling gopher tortoises,

Florida Cottonmouth (juvenile), *Agkistrodon piscivorus conanti* (photo by David G. Campbell)

other cottonmouths, rattlesnakes, rat snakes, ringneck snakes, garter snakes, water snakes, brown snakes, baby alligators, nestling ibises and herons, ducks, a wide variety of passerine birds and their eggs, mice, rats, muskrats, shrews, moles, bats, squirrels, rabbits, and carrion (Clark, 1949; Wright and Wright, 1957; Bothner, 1973; Mount, 1975; Kofron, 1978; Brown, 1979; Ashton and Ashton, 1981; Tennant, 1984; Gloyd and Conant, 1990; Ernst,

Eastern Cottonmouth, *Agkistrodon piscivorus piscivorus* (photo by David G. Campbell)

1992; Butler, pers. comm., 1994; Mitchell, 1994; Palmer and Braswell, 1995). As in the copperhead, young cottonmouths are thought to engage in "caudal luring" behavior where the snake remains motionless and wiggles its bright yellow tail to attract amphibians to within striking distance.

Known predators include fish (gar, catfish, largemouth bass), snapping turtles, alligators, other snakes (kingsnakes, indigos, and larger cottonmouths), wading birds (egrets, herons, wood storks), predatory birds (hawks, owls, eagles), and mammals (raccoons, otters, cats, dogs, and humans) (Gloyd and Conant, 1990; Ernst, 1992).

The relationship between catfish and cottonmouths is interesting. Young snakes are prey to large catfish and vice versa. Sometimes, however, young snakes are killed when they attempt to prey upon catfish that are too large. We found one young specimen in Duval County, Florida, with a large catfish spine protruding through its side. It died 2 days later. It is possible that some snakes survive this, but it would certainly reduce their numbers.

Mating is known to occur at any time of the year (Wharton, 1966; Schuett, 1992), but is

Western Cottonmouth, *Agkistrodon piscivorus leucostoma*. The pattern of these snakes is generally very faded in the adults. (photo by Scott Cushnir)

most likely in the spring or fall in the northern part of the range, or presumably when cooler than normal winters occur in the southern part of the range (Linzey and Clifford, 1981; Vermersch and Kuntz, 1986; Dundee and Rossman, 1989; Collins, 1993). This usually results in the birth of 1–16 young (usually 6–8) measuring 20.3–35.0 cm (7.9–13.8 inches) in length, sometime in August through September (Gloyd and Conant, 1990; Conant and Collins, 1991). As in the copperhead, the larger eastern subspecies tend to have larger litters and larger young than the smaller western subspecies, and females may bear young only every other year, especially in the northern part of the range. As with most North American pit vipers, long-term sperm storage is possible (Schuett, 1992).

The cottonmouth is easy to care for at all stages of its life. Both young and old eat voraciously and have a broad diet. They will take food dead or alive, and hence it is easy to effect quality control of their diet. They require only the basic cage arrangement as described in the general care section plus venomous snake modifications. This includes artificial carpet/turf, ventral heat, hide box with lock, etc.

Since their diet is very broad, including fish, amphibians, other snakes, birds, and mammals, they are often parasitized when they first arrive in captivity. Some of the parasites found include hookworms, *Kalicephalus*, roundworms, tapeworms, *Ophiotaenia*, flukes, *Ochetostoma* and *Neorenifer*, and mites (Parker, 1941; Arny, 1949; Burkett, 1966; personal observations). A fecal exam should be performed as soon as possible and the snake should be treated if found to have worms or protozoan parasites. Your veterinarian can medicate a food item which you can then feed, thus avoiding the necessity of bringing the snake to a clinic. Even a hard-core herp vet like the senior author would appreciate this on most days! If it is necessary to bring the snake in, call ahead and make arrangements and follow transportation section procedures with venomous snake additions. As with other water snakes, a long quar-

---

SPECIES: *Agkistrodon piscivorus*, Cottonmouth
MAINTENANCE DIFFICULTY INDEX: 3 (1 = easiest, 5 = most difficult)
AVERAGE SIZE: 76–122 cm (30–48 inches)
FOOD: Mice, chicks, amphibians, fish and other snakes
CAGE SIZE: 40-gallon long aquarium
SUBSTRATE: Artificial turf, indoor-outdoor carpet, or newspaper
VENTRAL HEAT: Yes
UV LIGHT: Not essential but may be helpful
TEMPERATURE RANGE: 25–30°C (77–86°F)
SPECIAL CONSIDERATIONS: *VENOMOUS*. Good eaters at all ages. Likely to be
  parasitized when captured. Permit required.

---

antine (2 months) and good hygienic technique is critical to protect your other snakes and yourself.

In captivity, cottonmouths will rapidly devour mice, rats, and chicks, dead or alive. Babies will greedily devour pinkies and in fact will be able to swallow much larger mice than even an experienced herpetologist would expect, but we would not recommend very large meals at first. Avoid all ectothermic prey (fish, amphibians, and reptiles) because of the difficulty of controlling parasites.

Brumation and breeding may be accomplished as mentioned in the general care section. Cottonmouths usually reach sexual maturity by their third year and will probably bear young every year. (See Table 5, the reproduction chart.)

Housing the young is easily accomplished in a 10-gallon aquarium with appropriate locking top. The adults may require a display case or large homemade cage 1.8–2.4 m (6–8 feet)

long, at maturity. Ultraviolet light is probably not necessary but may be helpful.

These snakes are very unpredictable. A long-term captive specimen must not be "trusted" by its keeper. Always exercise extreme caution when working with these snakes and make sure to take all the precautions listed under keeping venomous reptiles. Even the beautifully marked young are dangerous and capable of delivering a nasty bite the minute they poke their heads through their birth sacs.

It is our impression that they are extremely hardy, adaptable snakes that are "hard to kill" with captive negligence. The only problem we have encountered is with recently captured young in the fall of the year. These juveniles may refuse feeding as they prepare for brumation. However, most will survive until spring if they are properly cooled down. Spring usually brings back a voracious appetite in these snakes.

One of these snakes survived 24 years and 4 months in captivity (Snider and Bowler, 1992).

Crotalus adamanteus
Eastern Diamondback Rattlesnake

Although the greatest diversity of rattlesnakes occurs in the western United States and Mexico, the most impressive member of this group is undoubtedly the eastern diamondback. Reaching up to 4 times the length and 10 times the weight of the smaller species of rattlesnakes, it

is truly a giant among North American snakes. Yet, its future is uncertain due to wholesale habitat destruction in the southeastern United States.

As mentioned above, the eastern diamondback (referred to as an "EDB" by local herpetologists), is the largest of the North American rattlesnakes, with an average adult ranging 84–183 cm (33–72 inches) in length with the record length being 244 cm (96.1 inches = 8 feet) (Conant and Collins, 1991; Ernst, 1992). Weights of up to 6.58 kg (14.5 pounds) have been reported (Palmer and Braswell, 1995). It ranges from southeastern North Carolina along the coastal plain southward to include all of Florida and westward to southern Mississippi and eastern Louisiana. Presently, no subspecies are recognized.

Crotalus adamanteus

These snakes are generally pale brown to greenish in background color with large light-bordered dark brown diamonds running down the length of the snake, but fading as they approach the tail. Near the tail, the diamonds again become darker, but narrow and encircle the tail forming brown rings, and ultimately a solid dark brown to black tail tip. There are generally some light-colored scales within the diamonds, which gives them a speckled appearance. The head has two prominent white stripes angling backward to the upper lip scales as seen in the western diamondback, and there are vertical stripes in the rostral area. As with all rattlesnakes, the pupils are elliptical and a large heat pit is present on each side of the face between the nostril and the eye.

The preferred habitat of the eastern diamondback appears to be dry, sandy-soiled, open woodlands, often dominated by pine or turkey oak, and especially those areas with thick palmetto growth, but also areas with wire grass or ferns as the predominant ground cover (Wright and Wright, 1957; Mount, 1975; Ashton and Ashton, 1981; Palmer, 1990; personal observation). Several authors have reported on the close association of these areas with water however (Ashton and Ashton, 1981; Dundee and Rossman, 1989; Palmer, 1990), and all of the specimens we can recall finding in the wild have been within several hundred meters of some water body. Many authors have reported on their ability to swim and their occupation of offshore islands (Wright and Wright, 1957; Ashton and Ashton, 1981). We have observed them on small islands of the St. Johns River. There is also a fairly common association of these snakes with gopher tortoise burrows, with numerous rattlesnakes being found in them and several reports of females giving birth in or near them (Cook, 1954; Wright and Wright, 1957; Ernst, 1992; Butler, pers. comm., 1994).

Food items taken by wild specimens have included mice, rats, cotton rats, squirrels, rabbits, and birds, including northern bobwhites and even a small wild turkey (Klauber, 1972; Jackson, 1983; Ernst, 1992)!

Known predators of the diamondback include large frogs (river frog), other snakes (kingsnakes, indigos, racers), predatory birds (hawks, owls, caracaras, and wood storks), and mammals (skunks, raccoons, bears, otters, cats, and dogs) (Ernst, 1992).

Mating is known to occur in the late winter or spring, but has also been observed in the fall (Kauffield, 1969; Meek, in Klauber, 1972). This results in the birth of 6–29 young snakes measuring 28–42.4 cm (11–16.6 inches) in length (Klauber, 1972; Jackson, 1983; Means, 1986; Dundee and Rossman, 1989; Conant and Collins, 1991; Palmer and Braswell, 1995) and weighing 35–48.5 grams (Murphy and Schadduck, 1978) sometime in midsummer to late fall (Klauber, 1972).

The eastern diamondback rattlesnake, the largest and most dangerous of all North American snakes, is also a dangerous and challenging captive. Only experienced herpetologists with adequate, safe, escape-proof facilities should attempt to maintain this snake.

If captured as an adult, this species has a reputation for staying nervous, eating poorly if

Eastern Diamondback Rattlesnake, *Crotalus admanteus* (photo by David G. Campbell)

at all, and wasting away in captivity. Newborns and juveniles, however, seem to thrive in captivity if they are treated correctly. The basic cage setup discussed under general care (plus the venomous snake modifications) works well for them.

Interestingly, the method of capture, and how stressful it is for these animals, seems to determine the rate of their adaptation to captivity (if they adapt at all). Particularly for this species, a smooth and gentle capture, accompanied by prompt transportation to the cage, will really help them adjust. (See the section under transportation and psychological factors.) Cover the front of the cage if necessary and make sure the hide box is dark-colored and acceptable to the captive. A UV light source is probably not necessary but may be helpful. Ventral heat is definitely a good idea.

Once adapted, these snakes will take their food (mice, rats, and rabbits) dead or alive, very readily. Therefore it is easy to keep parasites out of the food. (See the section on food quality.) Make sure to have a fecal exam performed on new captives, as wild prey consumed prior to capture may have infected them. In fact, these snakes are commonly infected

with untreatable (as yet) pentastomid worms. (See the section on cottonmouths for a possible treatment strategy.)

Brumation and breeding should be attempted in the usual manner, but can be very tricky. Breeding may not occur every year. In addition, breeding may occur in the fall or the spring. In captivity, sexual maturity may take only 2 years to reach (probably 3 for many), while wild specimens may take up to 5 years to reach sexual maturity. Breeding success may be enhanced by the "dirty spring cage approach" discussed in the breeding section under general care. Breeding this snake in captivity is apparently much more difficult than breeding the western diamondback.

In spite of the fact that this species may be difficult to breed in captivity, it can be done. Rob Crabtree of Jacksonville, Florida, has a special affinity for the diamondback and has been working on breeding them in captivity for several years. His first success is evident at the time of this writing, as he has just presented us with 7 neonates for measurements and sexing. This is how he did it.

A wild-caught gravid female captured near Callahan, Florida (Nassau County), gave birth on 7 September, 1997, to 4 males and 2 females. The same year, a female from Blount Island, Florida, gave birth to 5 neonates during the last week in August. One of these males reached 122 cm (4 feet) in length by 1.5 years of age, when it was placed in with the Callahan female. They lived with each other for nearly a year, housed in a wooden cage that was divided during feeding time. The cage measured 61 cm high × 61 cm deep × 122 cm long (2 feet high × 2 feet deep × 4 feet long). The substrate utilized was cypress mulch. The hide boxes were large plastic flowerpots, approximately 30 cm tall × 30 cm wide at the base (1 foot × 1 foot), turned upside down, with holes placed in one side at the substrate level. Crabtree stated that he kept the holes facing backward, away from the front of the cage, so the snakes wouldn't constantly see him.

They received no artificial heat or light, only naturally occurring temperatures and natural lighting that occurred in Jacksonville, Florida. In winter, the inside temperature was allowed to drop to about 10–15°F above the outside temperature. In early March 2000, the snakes were observed mating. Only one mating was observed, but Crabtree reported that copulation lasted for over 24 hours. He was unable to observe is the male withdrew and switched sides. He pointed out that this mating began within seconds of the female's first shed after brumation (hibernation). The male was actually following the female as she shed. The female stopped feeding by the first week in June, after becoming noticeably swollen in late May. Seven neonates were born to this female on 15 August. This would represent a gestation period of approximately 140 days, well within the range reported for large lowland rattlesnakes. The 7 babies ranged 35.6–38.1 cm (14–15 inches) in TL and 32.4–34.3 cm (12.75–13.5 inches) SVL. Their average TL was 36.8 cm (14.5 inches). Their weights ranged 40–48 grams with an average weight of 44.9 grams. There were four males and three females. The males had tail lengths of 3.8 cm (1.5 inches), while the females had full tail lengths of 2.5–3.2 cm (1.0–1.25 inches).

Note that the male in this successful captive breeding was born in captivity and had adjusted well to captivity. In fact, at the time of mating he was approximately 1.5 meters (5 feet) long. This snake was only a little over 2 years old at the time of mating. The female was also well adjusted to captivity. Many previous attempts at breeding this species in captivity have failed. Perhaps Rob Crabtree has discovered the necessary combination. When asked what he thought was the most important factor, he simply stated "give them a hide box and leave them alone." The authors would like to thank Rob Crabtree for sharing this information with us and allowing us to measure, weigh, and sex the neonates. It is this pioneering spirit—and the willingness to share information—that has resulted in the explosion of herpetocultural knowledge in the last 50 years.

SPECIES: *Crotalus adamanteus*, Eastern Diamondback Rattlesnake
MAINTENANCE DIFFICULTY INDEX: YOUNG: 2 ADULTS: 5 (1 = easiest, 5 = most difficult)
AVERAGE SIZE: 84–183 cm (33–72 inches)
FOOD: Mice, rats, and rabbits
CAGE SIZE: Display case 6–8′ long by 2–4′ wide
SUBSTRATE: Artificial turf, indoor-outdoor carpet, or newspaper
VENTRAL HEAT: Yes
UV LIGHT: Not essential but may be helpful
TEMPERATURE RANGE: 23–27°C (73.4–80.6°F)
SPECIAL CONSIDERATIONS: *VENOMOUS*. Adults adapt poorly. Young adapt readily. Very likely to be parasitized. Breeding in captivity and wild still poorly understood. Permit required.

A 10-gallon aquarium is sufficiently large for a newborn, but they will rapidly outgrow them, and adults will require a display case or large homemade cage 1.8–2.4 m (6–8 feet) in length in order to live comfortably. Some have done well in much smaller cages, however. Outdoor enclosures have also worked very well.

There is no question that these snakes have different personalities. Some of them seem calm right from the start and can be very adaptable, while others remain nervous in spite of your best efforts. Try to choose the calm ones for your breeding program.

Walt Timmerman has shown that these snakes have incredibly large home ranges (75 hectares for the males, 30 hectares for the females). Because of massive habitat destruction in the Southeast, this snake may become extinct throughout most of its range very rapidly. This places a greater emphasis on captive breeding as an important part of this snake's survival and implies that larger preserves are needed to protect these animals in the wild than was previously thought (Means, 1992). There is absolutely no justification for allowing the continuation of "rattlesnake roundups" anywhere within the snakes' range. Extinction may already be imminent. Why hasten it legally?

One of these snakes survived over 22 years in captivity (Snider and Bowler, 1992).

Crotalus atrox
Western Diamondback Rattlesnake

The western diamondback rattlesnake may best be described as being hardy and "hot." It is an extremely adaptable snake. We doubt that there will ever be a need for a captive breeding project to save it from extinction, but we discuss its care here for the sake of completeness and because we could be wrong. This species occupies a huge range from central Arkansas through most of Texas, New Mexico, and Arizona to southern California and southward through much of Mexico (Stebbins, 1985). They are habitat generalists and dietary generalists and do extremely well around human habitations, especially where other species of snakes have been eliminated (Wright and Wright, 1957; Fowlie, 1965; Webb, 1970; Behler and King, 1979; Tennant, 1984, 1985; Lowe et al., 1986; Stebbins, 1985; Ernst, 1992). Generally speaking however, desert, grassland, or open woodlands are preferred, wherever cover is found (Ernst, 1992).

This snake may be considered the corn snake of venomous snakes when it comes to adaptability in captivity. Like the corn snake, it will do very well in the basic cage setup with venomous snake modifications. Also, like the corn snake, adults will eat just about any endothermic prey and most will readily take other food items as well. Literature reports of prey items of wild snakes have included frogs, toads, lizards, other snakes (other diamondbacks and a blacktail rattlesnake have been reported), many species of birds and their eggs, mice, rats, rabbits, and squirrels (Wright and Wright, 1957; Fowlie, 1965; Klauber, 1972; Behler and King, 1979; Tennant, 1984; Stebbins, 1985; Lowe et al., 1986; Ernst, 1992). In captivity, they have even been known to consume raw beef and liver. The latter is not advisable for long-term maintenance, however, and the proper captive diet is discussed in more detail below.

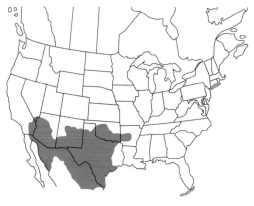

Crotalus atrox

Western Diamondback Rattlesnake, *Crotalus atrox* (photo by David G. Campbell)

Known predators of this snake include bull-frogs, other snakes such as whipsnakes, indigos, and larger rattlesnakes, as well as bobcats (Blair, 1954; Wilson, 1954; Shaw and Campbell, 1974; Clarkson and de Vos, 1986; Ernst, 1992). Suspected predators include kingsnakes, hawks, owls, roadrunners, wild pigs, skunks, and coyotes. The authors have observed coyotes feeding on a dead diamondback in Arizona, but this specimen was most likely a road kill.

In the wild, mating is known to peak in the spring with another smaller peak of activity in the fall (Wright and Wright, 1957; Lowe et al, 1986). This results in the birth of 2–25 young (usually around 10) from June to October (Tinkel, 1962; Armstrong and Murphy, 1979). These young range 21.5–33 cm (8.5–13 inches) in length. They grow rapidly and usually reach sexual maturity in 3 years.

The thermal preferences of this species have been well studied. Body temperatures of active individuals in the wild have been recorded at 18–34°C (65–93°F), and the preferred temperature range is thought to be 27–30°C (80–86°F) (Cowles and Bogert, 1944; Brattstrom, 1965). Like many other snakes, they seem to be diurnal in the spring and fall and nocturnal in the heat of summer. However, these snakes also appear to be active during much of the winter (Repp, 1998), and have been referred to as "winter baskers." These observations are critical in understanding the health and reproduction of this species. Accurate thermoregulation and early mating may be two of the major benefits they obtain.

In captivity, they rarely become ill, breed readily (almost any time of the year), and almost always seem to be preadapted for life in cages—much as the corn snake—but that is where the similarity ends.

The western diamondback is a deadly snake. This snake kills more people than any other snake in the area covered by this book (even more than the larger eastern diamondback). This is likely due to its more frequent occurrence around human habitations than many other species. It has a huge venom yield compared to many other rattlesnakes even though its venom is not especially toxic. Furthermore, most individuals have a very hot temperament when provoked and will readily bite. Extreme caution is advisable when dealing with this, or for that matter any, venomous species. See the beginning of the venomous snake section for safety precautions and methods of handling and restraint.

On the other hand, since this snake is so very adaptable, it eats well and is generally fairly easy to medicate by placing the medications in the food. This requires no handling at all, which is the best way to deal with a captive venomous snake. In addition, the fact that it is common takes the pressure off the keeper to engage in heroics to save an anorectic snake, which becomes very tempting with a less common snake. Thus, if one has decided to maintain a large rattlesnake, as for a small zoo, this snake may be an ideal candidate.

As mentioned above, the basic cage design with venomous snake modifications will work well for this species. Artificial carpet/turf, a locking hide box, and a water bowl are about all that are necessary to maintain these snakes. Ventral heat and UV light do not appear to be essential for long-term maintenance, but ventral heat is advisable. Plastic plants and rocks are nice additions. And of course, a locking cage is mandatory.

Remember that these are large snakes (up to 2.3 meters or 7 feet), the largest of western rattlesnakes, and adults will require fairly large sturdy cages. Still, they are relatively sedentary in captivity and seem to do well in cages that are not quite as large as one might expect for a snake of their size. Young ones may be successfully housed in a cage similar in size to a 10-gallon aquarium, while adults will do best in cages as large or larger than 30- or 40-gallon long aquariums. Be advised that very large tall cages are much safer when housing this very large and aggressive snake.

Feeding is rarely a problem. As discussed above, these snakes will readily consume a wide variety of food in captivity. But as with most other snakes, it is imperative to control the quality of the food. The only food items that should be offered to these snakes are captive-raised mice, rats, rabbits, and chicks. This will reduce the likelihood for parasitism and will usually result in healthy long-term captives. Also remember that these snakes will readily accept their prey prekilled, which is a safer and more manageable situation for both the snake and the keeper. There are many experienced herpetologists who have regretted placing a live rat into a venomous snake cage when the snake refused to eat. They ended up with an injured snake, a dead rat hidden somewhere in the cage, or a live angry rat in a poorly accessible cage in the presence of an angry rattlesnake. This last and most dangerous situation is best handled by locking up the snake first and then removing the rat and is best avoided by offering dead food. Furthermore, if the rat (or mouse) injures the snake, the snake may require treatment, which may require handling, leading to more risk. In summary, it makes very good sense to feed venomous snakes their food prekilled; in fact, many rattlesnakes we have worked with really seem to prefer it that way.

Those in our care and others have been the most consistent feeders of all the rattlesnakes, rarely turning down a meal except during the cooler months.

These snakes are commonly infested with

SPECIES: *Crotalus atrox*, Western Diamondback Rattlesnake
MAINTENANCE DIFFICULTY INDEX: 2 (1 = easiest, 5 = most difficult)
AVERAGE SIZE: 76–152 cm (30–60 inches)
FOOD: Mice, rats, rabbits
CAGE SIZE: 40-gallon long to display cases
SUBSTRATE: Indoor-outdoor carpet, artificial turf, or cypress mulch
VENTRAL HEAT: Yes
UV LIGHT: No, but an incandescent bulb is strongly advisable
TEMPERATURE RANGE: 27–30°C (80–86°F)
SPECIAL CONSIDERATIONS: *VENOMOUS*. Permit may be required. Aggressive
    disposition. Good eaters and breeders.

numerous parasites including roundworms, tapeworms, and pentastomids (Murphy and Armstrong, 1978). Tapeworm segments may be observed as tan- to white-colored spheres or strips in the stool, while pentastomid eggs and others may be detected on a fecal exam.

These snakes will breed readily in captivity following the standard techniques described in the general care section. Females may bear more than 20 young 3.5–5 months after mating. The young average around 30 cm (1 foot) long and will take small mice right away. The young have a bolder, more distinct pattern than the adults, but this soon fades in most snakes.

According to Snider and Bowler (1992), one of these snakes survived more than 25 years and 10 months in captivity. Ernst (1992) cites Lamar as having seen a 27-year captive.

Crotalus cerastes
Sidewinder

The sidewinder is our most desert-adapted viper, and as such it is widely distributed throughout much of the Mojave, Colorado, and Sonoran Deserts. Thus, they range from southeastern California through southern Nevada into extreme southwestern Utah and southward through much of southwestern Arizona into northwestern Mexico (Stebbins, 1985). There are three subspecies, the Mojave desert sidewinder, *C. c. cerastes*, the Sonoran sidewinder, *C. c. cercobombus*, and the Colorado desert sidewinder, *C. c. laterorepens*. The subspecies are somewhat difficult to tell apart at times (refer to Stebbins, 1985 and Ernst, 1992), but they are all easily recognized as sidewinders by their horn-like supraocular scales and, when they are out in open spaces, by their characteristic method of locomotion, sidewinding.

The sidewinder is not a large snake; in fact, individuals of 76 cm (30 inches) are considered huge for this species and the record is 82 cm (33 inches) (Stebbins, 1985). The majority of these snakes range 51–64 cm (20–25 inches) in length (Lowe et al., 1986).

The preferred habitat of the sidewinder appears to be loose, sandy lowlands, even though this desert dweller has occasionally been found in rocky areas (Wright and Wright, 1957; Lowe et al., 1986; Ernst, 1992). These snakes are known to migrate long distances and have large home ranges (Brown and Lillywhite, 1992; Secor, 1992).

Prey items reported taken by this species in the wild have included lizards, (side-blotched lizards, *Uta* sp., zebra-tailed lizards, *Callisaurus* sp., whiptails, *Cnemidophorus* sp., geckos, *Coleonyx* sp., desert iguanas, *Dipsosaurus* sp., leopard lizards, *Gambelia* sp., horned lizards, *Phrynosoma* sp., fringe-toed lizards, *Uma* sp., and tree or brush lizards, *Urosaurus* sp.), small snakes (glossy snake, *Arizona elegans*, shovel-nose snakes, *Chionactis* sp., other sidewinders, *Crotalus cerastes*, and ground snakes, *Sonora semiannulata*), mammals (pocket mice, house mice, harvest mice, white-footed mice, pocket gophers, shrews), and birds (sparrows and wrens) (Funk, 1965; Ernst, 1992). The juveniles are particularly fond of lizards (Ernst, 1992). Contrary to popular belief, it appears that many food items may be taken during the daytime (Brown and Lillywhite, 1992). The snakes appear to lie in surface pits, waiting in ambush for passing prey, although they may enter burrows and capture sleeping rodents.

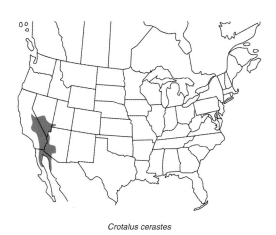

Crotalus cerastes

Mojave Desert Sidewinder, *Crotalus cerastes cerastes* (photo by David G. Campbell)

Potential predators of the sidewinder include the leopard lizard, other snakes including kingsnakes, longnose snakes, whipsnakes, and other sidewinders, many kinds of hawks, owls, eagles, roadrunners, and large passerine birds, and mammals including mice, skunks, coyotes, domestic dogs, foxes, bobcats, and domestic cats (Brown and Lillywhite, 1992). Known predators include coyotes, leopard lizards, snakes, and owls (Ernst, 1992). Many are killed by cars because of their habit of lying on roads, presumably to absorb retained heat from the asphalt. We found one specimen near Ajo, Arizona, lying motionless, stretched out as if it had fallen asleep on the road while it was crawling. It was 2330 hrs on 25 April. The air temperature was approximately 15°C (59°F). The snake appeared stiff and did not attempt to strike when picked up.

Mating generally occurs in the spring but some has been observed in the fall. This results in the birth of 4–18 young approximately 5 months after mating, which range 17–20 cm (6.5–8 inches) in length (Behler and King, 1979). The average litter size is around 9 (Klauber, 1956).

One female collected in southern California delivered 8 young on 11 September. These young ranged 18.5–20 cm (7.3–7.9 inches) in TL with an average TL of 19.25 cm (7.6 inches). The sex ratio was 1:1.

The preferred temperature range for members of this species appears to be 17.5–37°C (64–99°F) with a preferred temperature of 31.5°C (89°F) (Cowles and Bogert, 1944; Brattstrom, 1965). Brown and Lillywhite (1992) suggested that 31.5°C may be a summertime preference and it may vary seasonally. Winter temperatures in wild specimens have been measured down to 5°C (41°F).

The small size, unusual appearance, and attractive pastel patterns would seemingly make this a popular snake among herpetoculturists, but the sidewinder is perhaps one of the most difficult rattlesnakes to maintain in captivity. It's not that they are terribly difficult to house. They will do very well in the standard cage arrangement discussed in the general care section as long as they have a good heat source and good ventilation. They will also do well in a more natural enclosure using sand and rocks. The problem appears to be getting them to start feeding.

Indeed, numerous authorities, including the great rattlesnake expert Laurence Klauber, have listed the sidewinder as one of the most difficult rattlesnakes to maintain in captivity. Many of them are hard-core lizard eaters and may resist efforts to switch them to mice; some will readily take mice, however. These are indeed valuable snakes that are usually destined for a long healthy term in captivity. Once they start

Colorado Desert Sidewinder, *Crotalus cerastes laterorepens* (photo by David G. Campbell)

feeding on either mice or lizards, they generally do very well (although mice are easier to provide and they are better for the snakes).

Perhaps one of their favorite food items (in our experience) has been the western banded gecko, *Coleonyx variegatus*. These lizards will be taken prekilled, which permits some parasite control (via freezing), and will allow a keeper to train a sidewinder to take small prekilled mice. We usually use a part of a frozen and thawed gecko (leg, tail, piece of skin) in a fuzzy's mouth. Eventually, some specimens trained this way may take plain unflavored

mice. Unfortunately, the banded gecko is itself a beautiful and highly sought-after reptile by herpetoculturists, and this is reflected in their price when they become available in areas outside of their range.

Fortunately, the Mediterranean gecko, *Hemidactylus turcicus*, a widespread and common introduced species that is readily accepted by a number of other native snakes, is well liked by the sidewinder.

As a lizard eater, the recently captured sidewinder is very likely to be heavily parasitized. We have noted as many as five different species of parasites, including two species of coccidia in some specimens. Therefore, it is strongly recommended that these snakes be checked for parasites and dewormed immediately upon arrival. As with most rattlesnakes, broad-spectrum dewormers are best placed in the food items right away rather than waiting until the snake becomes anorectic, which will require handling in order to medicate.

Humidity has clearly been a critical factor in the maintenance of these snakes. Those housed in cages with poor ventilation and water bowls may become anorectic and develop skin lesions or respiratory infections. As yet, we don't know whether most cases of anorexia are directly related to the high humidity (is it an environmental cue that signals the snake to stop eating?) or indirectly related via resultant infections. In either case, loss of appetite has been observed

Sonoran Sidewinder, *Crotalus cerastes cercobombus* (photo by David G. Campbell)

SPECIES: *Crotalus cerastes*, Sidewinder
MAINTENANCE DIFFICULTY INDEX: 4 (1 = easiest, 5 = most difficult)
AVERAGE SIZE: 51–64 cm (20–25 inches)
FOOD: Lizards, mice
CAGE SIZE: 10-gallon aquarium
SUBSTRATE: Sand
VENTRAL HEAT: Yes
UV LIGHT: No, but an incandescent bulb is strongly advisable
TEMPERATURE RANGE: 17–37°C (64–99°F)
SPECIAL CONSIDERATIONS: *VENOMOUS*. Most wild-caught adults prefer lizards. Good
   ventilation essential. Some adapt readily. Others stubbornly refuse to feed.

---

when these snakes are maintained in cages with high humidity. This has led many to advise that water never be placed in with these snakes and this advice may indeed have a great deal of merit, since many of these snakes never drink anyway. Most keepers do offer water every week to several weeks, but only for a short time.

Brumation may be carried out for this species in their regular cage. Those in our care remained in a tight coil on the surface of the sand for 4–5 months while exposed to temperatures fluctuating from 3 to 18°C (38 to 65°F).

Captive reproduction of this species has, to date, been a rare occurrence. This is most likely due to the problems of maintenance mentioned above. Mating occurs both in the spring and fall (Lowe et al., 1986), with young being born in late summer. The young reportedly prefer lizards and invertebrates such as insects and scorpions, but can be trained to take pinky mice fairly soon. In one feeding trial we conducted with a litter of 8 young that were born in our care, 6 took live, unscented pinkies as their first

meal and never required scenting. Babies that are born in captivity and feed on pinkies immediately generally do extremely well in captivity and become excellent feeders and breeders.

As with other small venomous snakes, there is a tendency among keepers to treat these snakes with a little less respect than they might otherwise be treated because of their small size. Make no mistake, these snakes can produce a serious bite and they should be treated with due caution. In our experience these snakes have been very unpredictable and snappy, and their small size appears to be an advantage when it comes to speed and maneuverability.

All three subspecies have proven to be long-lived in captivity once they have adjusted. One Sonoran sidewinder has been maintained more than 10 years and 8 months in captivity, while a Mojave desert sidewinder has been maintained more than 11 years and 6 months and a Colorado desert sidewinder has been maintained more than 19 years and 8 months (Snider and Bowler, 1992).

Crotalus horridus
Timber Rattlesnake

The timber rattlesnake is the most widespread rattlesnake in eastern North America, but like the diamondback, it also appears to be suffering from habitat destruction. Hence, while looking at a range map may give the appearance of a very

common animal, they are actually only common in certain areas and rare or totally absent from many others. Either by design or accident, it appears that they have been largely exterminated from much of their historic range (Tyning, 1992).

Timber Rattlesnake, *Crotalus horridus* (photo by David G. Campbell)

The timber rattlesnake is another large rattlesnake, with adults ranging 90–152 cm (36–60 inches) in length and the record length being 189.2 cm (74.5 inches) (Conant and Collins, 1991). They are heavy-bodied pink, tan, yellow, or gray snakes with numerous black chevrons or blotches running down their entire length. Some specimens may be nearly solid black, thereby obscuring the crossbands. Light-colored specimens usually have an orange to rusty brown mid-dorsal stripe as well. The head is variably colored and may be yellow, olive, brown, gray, or black, and may or may not have a dark stripe behind the eye on each side.

The preferred habitat of those in the northern part of the range is rocky slopes at higher elevations or very hilly areas with ledges and bluffs, often near water, while the timber rattlesnakes in the southern part of the range seem to thrive in either open flat pine woods or dense hardwood forest near water such as swamps, floodplains, canebrakes, and bayheads (Mount, 1975; Linzey and Clifford, 1981; Allen, 1992; Martin, 1992a; Collins, 1993; Klemens, 1993). Petersen and Fritsch (1986) state that deciduous trees often dominate the area near timber rattle-

snake dens in Connecticut and indicated that their preferred habitat is often less densely forested than "copperhead country," while Martin (1992a) mentions that "closed-canopied" hardwoods were utilized in the southern part of the range. Hence, there is quite a bit of variation in the habitat type reportedly utilized by this species as well as the snakes that use them.

The body temperature of active timber rattlesnakes in the north has been found to range between 12.5 and 33.3°C (54.5 and 91.9°F), although the preferred temperature range is suspected of being 21.2–31.7°C (70.2–89.1°F) (Brattstrom, 1965; Brown, 1982; Reinert and Zappalorti, 1988; Oldfield and Keyler, 1989; Collins, 1993). Brumating timber rattlesnakes have been found at temperatures ranging from 4.3 to 15.7°C (39.7 to 60.3°F) with an average of 10.5°C (50.9°F) (Brown, 1982). Allen (1992) states that timber rattlesnakes in Pennsylvania will emerge from brumation when the ground temperature reaches 15.5–22.2°C (60–72°F).

Because of the variability of timber rattlesnakes across their range, and their spotty distribution, their taxonomic status is in dispute. For many years, two subspecies were considered to exist, the canebrake rattlesnake, *C. h. atricaudatus*, in the southern part of the range and the timber rattlesnake, *C. h. horridus*, in the northern part of the range. In 1973, Pisani et al. recommended against recognizing any subspecies. However, Martin (1992a) indicated that there were actually three readily distinguishable geographic groups, the eastern timber rattlesnake, the western timber rattlesnake, and the canebrake rattlesnake. The eastern group ranges from New England to northern Alabama and Georgia in mountainous regions, while the western group ranges from western Wisconsin southward along the Mississippi River through Iowa, Missouri, and Arkansas. The canebrake rattlesnake ranges from southeastern Virginia along the coastal plain all the way to eastern Texas, southern Arkansas, and southeastern Oklahoma. Only the northern part of peninsular Florida is occupied by the canebrake. Martin states that the western timber rattlesnake has "narrower and more angular bands or blotches than the eastern timber rattle-

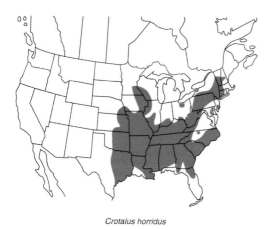

Crotalus horridus

snake and that the bands are usually outlined by a lighter color." Both the eastern and western timber rattlesnake have 23 rows of scales at midbody as opposed to the canebrake rattlesnake, which has 25 scale rows. Until more specimens are examined, the validity of these "groups" as subspecies will be questioned by many herpetologists. In the meantime, the timber rattlesnake may be considered an upland snake, while the canebrake is a lowland snake. See Mitchell (1994) and Palmer and Braswell (1995).

Food items taken by this species have included mice, rats, woodchucks, pocket gophers, chipmunks, squirrels, shrews, weasels, skunks, bats, rabbits, lizards, snakes, frogs, toads, and birds such as quail (Uhler et al., 1939; Clark, 1949; Cook, 1954; Myers, 1965; Wright and Wright, 1957; Klauber, 1972; Dundee and Rossman, 1989). These snakes appear to have a much stronger preference for endothermic prey than do copperheads (Petersen and Fritsch, 1986), although Collins (1993) reported that these snakes will often eat other smaller snakes, and Ernst (1992) lists numerous other ectothermic prey taken by wild specimens. Martin (1992a) presented an extremely detailed list of prey items which included many birds, and mammals including baby raccoons.

Predators of this species include predatory birds such as hawks, predatory mammals such as foxes, coyotes, dogs, bobcats, skunks, hogs, and snakes such as racers, cottonmouths, kingsnakes, indigos, and black rat snakes (Klauber, 1972; Ernst, 1992).

Mating may occur in spring or fall, but most mating is thought to occur during the late summer or fall (Brown, 1987, 1991; Martin, 1988). This results in the birth of 3–19 young (usually 6–10) sometime the following fall (sperm storage and delayed fertilization occurs) (Martof et al., 1980; Fitch, 1985; Martin, 1990). These young measure 19.7–41 cm (7.7–16 inches) in length (Conant and Collins, 1991). These young are born in a transparent membrane which the snakes usually rupture within several minutes. The young may remain with the mother up to 2 weeks (Martin, 1992a, b).

The timber rattlesnakes do well in captivity, given the same basic cage design as mentioned in the general care section with venomous snake modifications. They usually remain very nervous and aggressive but will eat readily if you cater to this nervous disposition by disturbing them as little as possible and providing a good, stable, dark hide box.

Their favorite food appears to be mammals (mice and rats), but they will take chicks (both of which they will take prekilled), although lizards, snakes, and amphibians may be taken by wild specimens. The young are also good eaters and may even take food before they shed

---

SPECIES: *Crotalus horridus*, Timber Rattlesnake
MAINTENANCE DIFFICULTY INDEX: 3 (1 = easiest, 5 = most difficult)
AVERAGE SIZE: 107–152 cm (42–60 inches)
FOOD: Mice and rats, chicks
CAGE SIZE: Display case 6–8′ long by 2–4′ wide
SUBSTRATE: Artificial turf, indoor-outdoor carpet, or newspaper
VENTRAL HEAT: Yes
UV LIGHT: Not essential but may be helpful
TEMPERATURE RANGE: 20–25°C (68–77°F)
SPECIAL CONSIDERATIONS: *VENOMOUS*. Prefer mammals. Good eaters. Likely to be
    parasitized. Nervous disposition. Permit required.

---

for the first time. Start with pinkies or fuzzies, and move rapidly to small mice.

Brumation and breeding may be accomplished as mentioned in the general care section. As with all of the vipers in this book, the females bear live young, usually in the late summer or early fall. Sexual maturity is usually reached at 3–4 years in captivity and females may only breed every other year. Interestingly, wild specimens are thought to take 8–10 years to reach sexual maturity.

As with the other vipers, a UV light source is an excellent idea, and may be helpful for long-term maintenance.

Remember that a fecal exam to check for parasites is necessary right after capture and should be done regularly thereafter.

A 10-gallon aquarium will suffice for new-borns, but adults will need at least a 40-gallon long aquarium and large specimens may need a display case or homemade cage 1.8–2.4 m (6–8 feet) long. Outdoor enclosures with hibernaculums built in may work well for this species, but this has been poorly studied.

Snider and Bowler (1992) mention a specimen that survived over 30 years in captivity, but Martin (1988) estimated that some wild snakes he studied might be as old as 50!

We would strongly advise individuals contemplating maintenance of these snakes to reconsider. They are considered endangered in many states, are protected in many, and are dangerous captives. Certainly, one of the smaller more common forms would be more appropriate for the serious herpetoculturist.

Crotalus lepidus
Rock Rattlesnake

The rock rattlesnake is perhaps one of the most popular and easily maintainable of all the North American rattlesnakes. Their small size, attractive coloration, and adaptability to captivity have endeared and will endear them to many herpetoculturists.

The rock rattlesnake is a small snake, rarely exceeding 61 cm (24 inches) TL, with a maximum recorded length of 83 cm (33 inches) (Ernst, 1992). They are generally bluish, greenish, or pinkish gray with dark contrasting cross-bands in the western subspecies (banded rock rattlesnake, *C. l. klauberi*) and lighter, sometimes barely visible crossbands in the eastern subspecies (mottled rock rattlesnake, *C. l. lepidus*). This snake ranges from western and central Texas westward through southern New Mexico and southeastern Arizona and southward through central Mexico, where two other subspecies are found. The eastern subspecies is thought to be a toxic model for the alterna morph gray-banded kingsnake, *L. alterna*,

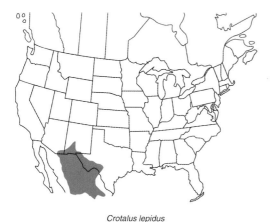

Crotalus lepidus

mimic, and indeed the two snakes' ranges overlap extensively. Also the habitats of the two species are similar in that they both prefer rocky areas (Wright and Wright, 1957; Fowlie, 1965; Klauber, 1972; Tennant, 1984, 1985; Lowe et al., 1986; Ernst, 1992), even though the mottled rock rattlesnake is occasionally found in hilly desert areas where cover is sufficient.

The preferred diet of this snake in the wild has been reported to include primarily lizards

(spiny lizards, *Sceloporus* sp., whiptails, *Cnemidophorus* sp., tree lizards, *Urosaurus* sp., horned lizards, *Phrynosoma* sp., earless lizards, *Holbrookia* sp.), but small snakes (hooknose snakes, *Gyalopion* sp., other rock rattlesnakes), frogs (cliff chirping frog, *Syrrhophus marnockii*), mice, and centipedes have been reported (Wright and Wright, 1957; Fowlie, 1965; Klauber, 1972; Lowe et al., 1986; Barker, pers. comm., 1992; Ernst, 1992).

Active wild individuals have been reported at air temperatures ranging from 24 to 35°C (75 to 95°F) (Klauber, 1972), but we have observed them basking at air temperatures of 22°C (72°F) in southeastern Arizona, and suspect they may be quite active at lower temperatures. The temperature of the rocks at that time was much higher than the air temperature and this is probably extremely important in determining the activity level.

There are few known predators of this species, but one specimen was consumed by a copperhead (Tennant, 1985). Other snakes, such as kingsnakes and whipsnakes, as well as predatory mammals and birds, are potential

Banded Rock Rattlesnake, *Crotalus lepidus klauberi* (photo by David G. Campbell)

Mottled Rock Rattlesnake, *Crotalus lepidus lepidus* (photo by Steve Barten)

predators. One juvenile rock rattlesnake was found wedged in the bark of a pine tree about 1.5 meters (5 feet) above the ground on a night when many coatimundis had been foraging in Carr Canyon of southeastern Arizona. Presumably the snake was trying to avoid being preyed upon (Rossi and Feldner, 1994).

Mating generally occurs in the fall, with 1–8 young being born late the following summer (July and August) (Armstrong and Murphy, 1979; Ernst, 1992). The young range 15.2–20.3 cm (6–8 inches) in length and weigh 6–8 grams (Tennant, 1984; Lowe et al., 1986; Ernst, 1992).

In captivity, the rock rattlesnake will thrive on a wide variety of substrates and in enclosures varying from the simplest and smallest aquariums with newspaper to complex zoo displays with ledges, flowing water, and live plants. They will do well in the basic cage design described in the general care section. Artificial carpet/turf is an excellent substrate but certainly not the only choice for this species, as a number of other substrates including newspaper, cypress mulch, aspen or pine shavings, clay beads, and others have worked well. Rocks and plastic plants are a nice addition regardless of the substrate chosen.

One of the more recent innovations in herpetoculture, namely the provision of a false floor with a number of small holes in it, has been used for this species and its mimic, the gray-banded kingsnake, with great success (Swinford, 1989). Apparently, this creates an artificial "subterranean" cavity in which the snakes feel more comfortable.

A heat source in the cage (ventral or overhead lamp) does not appear essential for the successful maintenance of this species, but is thought to be critical for captive reproduction, especially for gravid females over the winter and throughout gestation. Full-spectrum UV light sources do not appear essential for either maintenance or reproduction, nor does any artificial light. Natural light filtered through a window may suffice. Once again, however, one should be aware of the increased appetites of some vipers in captivity when full-spectrum lights are used.

Temperature ranges in which this snake has been maintained and bred successfully have included 10–19°C (50–67°F) in the winter and 20–35°C (68–95°F) in the summer (Swinford, 1989), but Tennant (1984) warns that larger healthier young will be produced if daytime air temperatures are maintained at 24.4–27°C (76–80°F) (*as long as ventral heat is provided*), with nighttime temperatures near or below 19°C (67°F) during their active season.

Brumation is also important for the long-term maintenance and reproduction of this species. Temperatures of 10–15°C (50–59°F) for at least 14 weeks are thought to be necessary.

Captive breeding has occurred numerous times in captivity, given several months at the lower temperatures described above. Captive breeding usually occurs in June, July, or August with 2–8 young being born the following

---

SPECIES: *Crotalus lepidus*, Rock Rattlesnake
MAINTENANCE DIFFICULTY INDEX: 2 (1 = easiest, 5 = most difficult)
AVERAGE SIZE: 38–83 cm (15–33 inches)
FOOD: Lizards, mice
CAGE SIZE: 10–20-gallon aquarium
SUBSTRATE: Indoor-outdoor carpet, artificial turf, or cypress mulch
VENTRAL HEAT: Yes
UV LIGHT: No, but an incandescent bulb is strongly advisable
TEMPERATURE RANGE: 20–35°C (68–95°F)
SPECIAL CONSIDERATIONS: Generally do well in captivity. False floor or numerous
   hiding places advisable. *VENOMOUS*.

---

summer. The gestation period ranges 10–12 months. Females should be placed in with the males following their first summer shed.

Most newborns will readily accept pinkies right from the start. If not, they will readily accept lizards and may be switched to pinkies by scent-transfer techniques described in the general care section. WARNING: There have been numerous incidents of cannibalism in captivity. Not only have adults, including the mother, been reported to eat babies, but the babies themselves have been reported to consume siblings (Mitchell, 1986). Large adults may also eat smaller adults. Thus, these snakes should be housed singly, and babies should be removed immediately from the parent's enclosure.

As seen above, these snakes are not picky eaters. A number of other food items have been reported for captives and are listed here in case a specimen refuses mice initially. These include tiger salamanders, *Ambystoma tigrinum*, skinks, *Eumeces* sp., and a rough earth snake, *Virginia striatula* (Ernst, 1992).

In our experience, these rattlesnakes settle down nicely and become calm good-eating captives that readily accept prekilled mice as food and rarely seem to have medical problems. Nevertheless, one must take all the precautions discussed in the general care section under venomous snakes, and their maintenance should be reserved for experienced herpetoculturists. The venom of the rock rattlesnake varies considerably in toxicity from one population to another, but those in the United States possess a very potent venom.

Captive longevity for the mottled rock rattlesnake has been reported at more than 17 years and 11 months, while captive longevity for the banded rock rattlesnake has been reported at more than 23 years and 3 months (Snider and Bowler, 1992). Tennant (1984) reported that William Woodin, former director of the Arizona-Sonora Desert Museum, had maintained one of these snakes for more than 30 years! This would make the banded rock rattlesnake the longest-lived captive among the western rattlesnakes. Only the timber rattlesnake has equaled this longevity among American rattlesnakes.

Crotalus mitchellii
Speckled Rattlesnake

The speckled rattlesnake is a variably patterned medium-sized rattlesnake of primarily rocky areas. It ranges over much of western Arizona, southern Nevada, and southern California down into Baja California and islands in the Gulf of California. The two subspecies in the United States are the southwestern speckled rattlesnake, *C. m. pyrrhus* and the panamint speckled rattlesnake, *C. m. stephensi*. The panamint is the more northern subspecies and may be rec-

Crotalus mitchellii

ognized by the creased or pitted supraocular scales and the absence of a row of small scales (an inverted U) between the prenasal scales and rostral scale, the latter being a characteristic of the southwestern speckled rattlesnake. Both subspecies are characterized by the speckling from which their name is derived, but the panamint generally has a lighter background color. Adults are generally 61–122 cm (24–48 inches) in length, with the maximum recorded length being 132 cm (52 inches). Although there are exceptions, they are generally considered one of the toughest rattlesnakes to get adjusted to captivity and to get to start feeding.

These snakes seem to prefer very hot, dry, upland rocky areas in the desert, such as canyons, mountain slopes, buttes, and erosion gullies, but may enter shrubby areas and open desert occasionally (Wright and Wright, 1957; Fowlie, 1965; Klauber, 1972; Armstrong and Murphy, 1979; Stebbins, 1985; Lowe et al., 1986; Ernst, 1992).

The preferred foods of this snake in the wild have been reported to include rodents (pocket mice, cactus mice, white-footed deer mice, kangaroo rats, wood rats, and ground squirrels), rabbits, birds, lizards (spiny, *Sceloporus* sp., side-blotched, *Uta* sp., skinks, *Eumeces* sp., whiptails, *Cnemidophorus* sp., zebra-tailed, *Callisaurus* sp., and chuckwalla, *Sauromalus* sp.), and other speckled rattlesnakes (Wright and Wright, 1957; Fowlie, 1965; Klauber, 1972; Lowe et al., 1986; Mitchell, 1986; Ernst, 1992). Moore (1978) thought these snakes ate primarily ground squirrels when they were active during the day and nocturnal rodents when they

were active at night, much like the timber rattlesnake is thought to eat chipmunks by day and other rodents by night.

Body temperatures of active wild individuals of this species have ranged from 18.8 to 39.3°C (66 to 103°F) (Moore, 1978) with an apparent preferred temperature of 31°C (88°F). This is quite a bit higher than the active temperature range reported by Brattstrom (1965). He found that free-ranging specimens had body temperatures ranging from 26.3 to 31.8°C (79 to 89°F) with an average temperature of 30.3°C (87°F). In any case, these snakes seem to like it fairly hot.

Known predators include foxes and bobcats (Ernst, 1992), but potential predators include a wide variety of birds and mammals, as well as ophiophagous snakes. Cannibalism has been reported in captive juveniles (Mitchell, 1986).

Mating generally occurs in the spring, usually April or May, but captive mating has been recorded in October, January, and March (Peterson, 1983), which results in the birth of 2–11 young 4–5 months later. The young range 20–30 cm (8–12 inches) long at birth (Lowe et al., 1986; Ernst, 1992).

The basic cage design with venomous snake modifications will work fairly well for this species. Artificial carpet/turf, wood chips, or newspaper will work well as the substrate, and a secure hide box is absolutely essential. Flat and stable rocks placed securely in the cage are a very nice addition and will often make the snake feel more secure and, in some cases, may stimulate the appetite of this frequently fastidious captive. Plastic plants are also a nice addition.

Water can be kept in the cage if the ventilation is good. Otherwise it should be placed in the cage only weekly or monthly for a short period of time in order for the snake to drink. If it is left in the cage permanently, it may lead to high humidity, which may lead to other problems. See the discussion on water in the section on the sidewinder.

Ventral heat is considered absolutely essential for this heat-loving reptile believed to have originated in Baja California. This will help to stimulate the appetite as well as help to prevent respiratory infections, a common malady of rattlesnakes in captivity.

Panamint Speckled Rattlesnake, *Crotalus mitchellii stephensii* (photo by David G. Campbell)

Heat from above in the form of an incandescent bulb is also advisable for this species, as is a UV light source, during the day. Making use of the temperature ranges reported for wild snakes (see above), one should provide ventral heat and a thermal gradient from one side of the cage to the other.

As mentioned above, this species ranks as one of the more difficult snakes to get to start

Southwestern Speckled Rattlesnake, *Crotalus mitchellii pyrrhus* (photo by Patrick Briggs)

feeding in captivity. The well-known rattlesnake expert Laurence Klauber commented on the difficulties of maintaining this species and the sidewinder (Klauber, 1972). Some individuals will start feeding on domestic mice or rats right away, but many refuse to eat and languish away in captivity. Sometimes the provision of natural prey items will induce an anorectic specimen to eat. If this fails, a number of tricks have been used to achieve the same end result. In either case, it makes sense to make use of the reptile disorientation syndrome discussed in the general care section. Feed heavily right after capture and make sure to routinely load the prekilled domestic rodents with broad-spectrum anthelminthics (such as fenbendazole or ivermectin) and antiprotozoal agents (such as metronidazole) at the doses recommended in the general care section. This may help avoid potential restraint, force-feeding, and medications later. These snakes are known to be hosts for roundworms such as *Thubunea cnemidophorus* (Babero and Emerson, 1974).

Prey items preferred by captives of this species have been listed by Lowe et al. (1986). See above for a summary. Domestic mice have been

Southwestern Speckled Rattlesnake (red phase), *Crotalus mitchellii pyrrhus* (photo by Patrick Briggs)

consumed by many captives, and if these are refused, they may be taken if scented with one of the prey items mentioned above.

Murphy and Armstrong (1978) also listed a number of tricks to induce captive rattlesnakes in general to feed and these may apply to this species as well. These include the following:

1. Offer a prekilled rodent with a long pair of forceps. The rodent should be positioned so the shoulder region is presented and to hopefully elicit a defensive strike, whereupon the rodent should be dropped and the snake left undisturbed.

2. Trim the whiskers and remove the skin from the nose of the rodent before offering it to the snake.

3. Leave prekilled prey in the cage overnight.

4. Use live prey, but remove within 30 minutes if uneaten.

5. Dip the live rodent in water first, whereupon the rodent will preen itself first and ignore the snake, and the snake will be stimulated to strike.

6. Place a flat rock in the cage that the snake may coil upon. The snake's elevated position may elicit a feeding response.

7. Mist the cage with water prior to feeding.

Mating usually occurs in the early spring following brumation, although Armstrong and Murphy (1979) reported a pair of a Mexican subspecies, *C. m. mitchellii*, mating in October. Two to 11 young measuring 20.3–27.9 cm (8–11 inches) are usually born in late July through September. The young are usually fond of lizards, but should be offered small mice initially or switched to them as soon as possible if they are refused initially. Most neonates will eat more readily in captivity than adults.

In summary, this is an aggressive nervous snake that has a fairly high venom yield with a medium to high toxicity (geographic variation occurs). It is definitely one of the more difficult rattlesnakes to maintain in captivity because it

SPECIES: *Crotalus mitchellii*, Speckled Rattlesnake
MAINTENANCE DIFFICULTY INDEX: 4 (1 = easiest, 5 = most difficult)
AVERAGE SIZE: 61–122 cm (24–48 inches)
FOOD: Mice, rats
CAGE SIZE: 10–20-gallon aquarium
SUBSTRATE: Indoor-outdoor carpet, artificial turf, or cypress mulch
VENTRAL HEAT: Yes
UV LIGHT: No, but an incandescent bulb is strongly advisable
TEMPERATURE RANGE: 18–39°C (66–103°F)
SPECIAL CONSIDERATIONS: *VENOMOUS*. Some specimens adapt readily to captivity
  while many fail to adapt at all. May well be the most difficult of rattlesnakes to maintain.

often refuses to eat. Since they are so nervous, they generally do not make good display animals in zoos (although there are exceptions), but private collectors with quiet and spacious facilities may often succeed with them. Avoid constant disturbances and vibrations with all rattlesnakes, but especially this one.

Inexperienced keepers of venomous reptiles are not advised to try to maintain this species. The cost or rarity of this species usually induces keepers to attempt force-feeding, which is a dangerous and sometimes futile effort if stress-related pathological changes have already begun. This is not to say that force-feeding is never justified or successful, but that it should be avoided by inexperienced keepers and attempted only after all other measures have been exhausted. Once an animal adapts

and begins feeding, it generally makes a good captive. Longevity for this species has been reported at more than 20 years and 3 months for a panamint rattlesnake and more than 22 years and 16 days for a southwestern speckled rattlesnake (Snider and Bowler, 1992).

It has been our experience and that of others that there is a difference in the personality and adaptability to captivity of the two subspecies within the United States. The southwestern speckled rattlesnake appears more aggressive (towards both people and feeding) than the panamint. The panamint rattlesnake may also be more sensitive to high humidity in its cage (Murphy and Armstrong, 1978). Hence, the southwestern speckled rattlesnake may be just a little easier to successfully maintain in captivity.

Crotalus molossus
Blacktail Rattlesnake

The blacktail rattlesnake is a fairly large snake reaching up to 126 cm (50 inches), but is usually 76–107 cm (30–42 inches) long (Stebbins, 1985; Conant and Collins, 1991). It is widely distributed from central Texas westward through central New Mexico and Arizona and southward through much of Mexico.

It receives its name and is easily recognizable by virtue of its black tail, although there is considerable variation in color pattern and the tail may be gray instead of black. The color

pattern may be very distinct, with regular blotches, bands, or diamonds, or completely absent as in the case of certain greenish or olive specimens. Others may be almost black. Some possess a black crown while others do not. Those with light yellow background color and charcoal black bands and crown are extremely attractive animals. These are most often found in southeastern Arizona.

Robust and highly adaptable snakes, they are found in a wide variety of habitats, but seem to

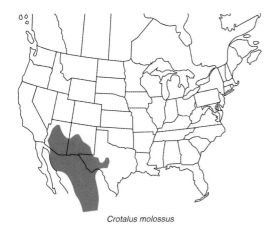

Crotalus molossus

prefer rocky areas in forests (Wright and Wright, 1957; Fowlie, 1965; Klauber, 1972; Lowe et al., 1986; Ernst, 1992; personal observations), especially south-facing slopes of mountains near streams. They may be active at any time of the day, but appear to be more nocturnal in the heat of summer.

Literature reports of food items taken by these snakes include a variety of mammals including pocket mice, white-footed mice, packrats, kangaroo rats, chipmunks, squirrels, rabbits, birds, lizards (including in one instance a Gila monster), and rarely other snakes and frogs (Wright and Wright, 1957; Funk, 1964; Klauber, 1972; Painter, 1985; Lowe et al., 1986; Ernst, 1992; Williamson et al., 1994).

While it is generally believed that most snakes can maintain themselves by eating 2–4 times their body weight per year, Beck (1995) showed that this species can survive by eating only 93% of its body weight in rodents per year.

The thermal ecology of this snake is perhaps the least studied of all rattlesnakes. The only references we could find to temperature for these snakes in the wild were as follows. Four specimens were collected on the surface at temperatures ranging from 21 to 32.2°C (70 to 90°F) (Klauber, 1972). They are apparently fairly cold-tolerant as one might expect from their mountain-dwelling habits. Tennant (1984) reported they might be active on nights when temperatures were 10–16°C (50–60°F), and Bogert (in Klauber, 1972) reported one specimen survived for 10 days at 4°C (39.2°F) with no ill effects. Indeed, Repp (1998) referred to this species as "winter active" and reported 14

of these snakes either basking or moving about during one winter, far removed from any obvious shelter. Beck (1995) reported that the average temperature when active individuals were observed was 29.5°C (85°F) during spring, summer, and fall observations.

We have found no records of natural predation; however, suspected predators include bobcats, coatimundis, coyotes, and birds of prey, as well as kingsnakes.

It is believed that mating in the wild occurs primarily in the late summer and fall, although spring or winter mating has been observed in Mexico (Wright and Wright, 1957; Armstrong and Murphy, 1979; Ernst, 1992; Degenhardt et al., 1996). Tennant (1984) believed this snake has a reproductive cycle similar to the other montane rattlesnakes—fall mating, followed by ovulation at that time or early the following spring, with birth of young in midsummer rather than late in the fall. The litter size ranges 3–16 but averages around 7 young (Klauber, 1972; Lowe et al., 1986).

The young range 21–31.4 cm (8–12.4 inches) in length and weigh 11–28 grams (Wright and Wright, 1957; Lowe et al., 1986; Ernst, 1992).

As one might expect from such a wide-ranging generalist, they will also adapt relatively quickly to captivity. The basic cage arrangement (with venomous snake modifications) including artificial carpet/turf or newspaper, hide box, and water bowl[1] will work well. Other substrates such as cypress mulch or washed soil will work as well but are more difficult to keep clean. Stable rocks are always a very welcome addition to the enclosure of a montane snake (by both the keeper and the

---

[1]The provision of water to a desert snake has been a subject of much discussion. Some have argued vehemently that one never needs to provide water to these snakes and that they obtain all the water they need from their food. And certainly, many desert snakes have survived years without any water in their cages. On the other hand, if offered water, many desert snakes, but by no means all, will drink. We prefer to offer water at all times in large cages that are well ventilated, but only offer water occasionally to desert snakes in small enclosures or where ventilation may not be adequate. Poor ventilation may predispose warm cages with water sources to develop high humidity resulting in skin or respiratory infections in these dry-adapted animals.

Blacktail Rattlesnake, *Crotalus molossus* (photo by David G. Campbell)

snake). They are very attractive and provide a more natural-appearing captive environment.

Ventral heat and a heat lamp under which these snakes can bask is considered very beneficial. A UV light source such as a Vitalite® may not be essential but has been known to stimulate appetite in some vipers.

Most healthy blacktails have a voracious appetite once they settle down and adjust to captivity. As mentioned above, captives will readily consume prekilled domestic mice and rats. An adult kept at 20–32°C (80–90°F) will be successfully maintained on two large mice per week. At room temperature, some individuals seem to thrive on only once-monthly feedings, but we would not advise this and suspect this kind of feeding schedule would not be sufficient for captive reproduction. Those individuals in our care did well at air temperatures fluctuating from 27 to 35°C (80 to 95°F) and nighttime temperatures dropping no lower than 23°C (73.5°F) during the active season. It is important to note, however, that captive breeding has not been attempted with these animals at the time of this writing, so a true evaluation of this temperature regime has not been performed.

These snakes may be heavily parasitized upon capture (Klauber, 1972; personal observations), and this may result in their demise in captivity if left untreated. In fact, we suspect that the commonly held belief among herpetologists that many of these snakes may be poor feeding, sensitive captives may actually be related to high parasite loads rather than an innate behavioral problem; thus, initial dewormings are strongly advised. Furthermore, it is much more advisable to use a broad-spectrum deworming agent such as fenbendazole in food items offered to newly captured specimens than to have to restrain and medicate long-term anorectic snakes later. This is easier on the snake and safer for the keeper. The most obvious worms are tapeworms, the segments of which may be visible in the stool. Interestingly, the segments may be spherical and not look wormlike at all, but microscopic examination of one of these crushed spheres (segments) reveals thousands of cestode eggs. Thus, the keeper is well advised to take note of little spheres in the stool of these snakes. Klauber (1956) noticed snake roundworms, probably *Ophidascaris* sp. See the general care section

---

SPECIES: *Crotalus molossus*, Blacktail Rattlesnake
MAINTENANCE DIFFICULTY INDEX: 3 (1 = easiest, 5 = most difficult)
AVERAGE SIZE: 76–107 cm (30–42 inches)
FOOD: Mice, rats
CAGE SIZE: 10–20-gallon long aquarium
SUBSTRATE: Indoor-outdoor carpet, artificial turf, or cypress mulch
VENTRAL HEAT: Yes
UV LIGHT: No, but an incandescent bulb is strongly advisable
TEMPERATURE RANGE: 20–32°C (80–90°F)
SPECIAL CONSIDERATIONS: *VENOMOUS*. Generally do well in captivity, but some are
    fastidious. Parasitism likely.

---

for drugs and doses that may be used against ophidian tapeworms and roundworms. Also remember to have fecal exams performed initially and regularly thereafter on wild-caught specimens, since these two worms are not the only threat and many of the other parasites are not visible with the naked eye.

Brumation is strongly advisable if breeding will be attempted and can be accomplished in their regular cage. Two to 4 months of temperatures in the 10–11°C (low 50s Fahrenheit) range will probably be sufficient for this species. Those in our care tolerated temperatures fluctuating from 3 to 18°C (38 to 65°F) for 4 months, but did have a ventral heat source available at all times.

The blacktail rattlesnake has been bred numerous times in captivity, but not many have been described. In fact, they breed so readily that in captivity they may mate with other species of rattlesnake, at times other than in spring. These kinds of breedings are interesting from a scientific standpoint, but are not very valuable from a conservation standpoint and we would advise against it. Ideally, the female should be placed in with the male following brumation, but also just before brumation. They also may be housed together.

Three to 16 young are usually born in summer or early fall. The newborns, often more distinctively colored than the adults, are usually just under 33 cm (12 inches) long. Most will consume small mice right away, although a difficult specimen may be induced to start feeding by offering lizards. Prior to offering lizards, however, we would advise offering rat pups, as some of the blacktails we have worked with seem to have a marked preference for rats.

In our experience, these snakes have been relatively easy to maintain. As noted by other authors, we have found these snakes to not be very aggressive, and as such might make good display animals for zoos and first-time venomous snake keepers. Remember, however, that this large snake possesses a very high venom yield and is therefore a very dangerous animal! The keeping of any venomous snake, including the blacktail, is not recommended for amateurs.

One of these snakes survived more than 20 years and 8 months in captivity (Snider and Bowler, 1992).

Crotalus pricei
Twin-spotted Rattlesnake

The twin-spotted rattlesnake is another small, beautiful, and, unfortunately, endangered rattlesnake in the United States. "Twin Spots" (as they are referred to by amateur herpers) are slender grayish snakes with two rows of dark (black or brown) spots running down the length of the back. Only about 61 cm (24 inches) as adults with a maximum of 66 cm (26 inches), they are one of the smallest of rattlesnakes. Lowe et al. (1986) reported that large adults usually weigh only 4–5 ounces. They are found only in four mountain ranges in southeastern Arizona and in other mountainous areas of northern Mexico. In the areas where they occur, they may be fairly abundant. But like so many other species of reptiles, they are particularly at risk because of the restricted habitat and range that they occupy and the relentless destruction of that habitat as the human population grows.

Crotalus pricei

As mentioned above, these are primarily mountain-dwelling rattlesnakes and they prefer rocky areas, particularly south-facing talus slopes at higher elevations, even though they have been found in grassy areas at higher elevations between the mountains (Wright and Wright, 1957; Fowlie, 1965; Klauber, 1972; Armstrong and Murphy, 1979; Lowe et al., 1986; personal observation).

As are most mountain-dwelling rattlesnakes, they are primarily diurnal and are very fond of eating other diurnally active reptiles, namely lizards, and particularly spiny lizards, *Sceloporus* sp. (Klauber, 1972; Armstrong and Murphy, 1979; Lowe et al., 1986; Ernst, 1992). Small rodents may also be consumed. Their preference for lizards is a very important factor to remember in their adjustment to captivity, as discussed below.

Another food item recently added to the list of prey taken by this species in the wild is nestling birds. Cumbert and Sullivan (1990)

reported that nestlings of the yellow-eyed junco, *Junco phaeonotus*, are commonly taken by these snakes in the Chiricahua Mountains.

As a high altitude mountain dweller, one would expect that these snakes are relatively cold-adapted. Indeed, body temperatures of active individuals of this species have ranged from 18 to 23.8°C (65 to 75°F) and they have been found on the surface when the air temperature was as low as 11°C (52°F) when there was still snow on the ground (Armstrong and Murphy, 1979; personal observation). It is important to note, however, that the surface temperatures available to these snakes often far exceed air temperatures. We have measured temperatures over 44°C (111°F) on the surface at the time of a capture of one of these snakes in the Chiricahuas, and the air temperature at that time was only 22.2°C (72°F).

Suspected predators of this species include skunks, coyotes, badgers, and birds of prey, as well as kingsnakes (Ernst, 1992).

Mating season is thought to occur in the late summer or fall, with young being born the following summer (July and August). The 3–9 young range from 12.7 to 20.3 cm (5 to 8 inches) in length (Lowe et al., 1986).

In captivity, the twin-spotted rattlesnake will do fairly well in the basic cage setup with venomous snake modifications. Artificial carpet/turf or newspaper will work well as the substrate, although more natural substrates such as washed soil or large smooth gravel has worked well for some. Regardless of substrate, large, flat, securely placed rocks are excellent and perhaps essential additions to the enclosure. They provide an unequaled sense of security for this small snake and may stimulate its appetite nicely. The same can be said for a dark-colored stable hide box; one of these should be used if the rocks do not form a dark secluded area. If the ventilation in the cage is good, a water bowl should be available at all times for this miniature rattlesnake. Ventral heat or heat from above in the form of an incandescent bulb is strongly advisable so that this snake may thermoregulate. Don't keep this montane rattlesnake in too high of a gradient. Brattstrom (1965) found that the body temperatures of wild *C. pricei* were 18–23.8°C (65–

Twin-spotted Rattlesnake, *Crotalus pricei* (photo by David G. Campbell)

74.8°F) with a mean of 21.1°C (69.9°F). A suitable cage size for most members of this species would be about the size of a 10–20-gallon aquarium. Remember the lock.

According to Arizona Game and Fish biologist Randy Babb, the twin-spotted rattlesnake can be one of the most difficult rattlesnakes to get feeding on rodents in captivity. As mentioned above, they prefer spiny lizards, and the Yarrow's spiny lizard, *Sceloporus jarrovii*, heads the list of food preferences in Arizona. Armstrong and Murphy (1979) reported that a crevice spiny lizard, *S. poinsettii*, was found in the stomach of one of these snakes from Mexico, and they have been reported to take *Sceloporus undulatus* (Kauffield, 1943). They also indicated that members of the following genera were suitable food items for this and other montane rattlesnakes: *Uta*, *Anolis*, and *Cnemidophorus* (Murphy and Armstrong, 1978). Fortunately, these lizards may be taken dead, so they can be frozen first, which allows for storage and some parasite control. Eventually, many twin-spots can be trained to accept small domestic mice in captivity using scent-transfer techniques, but some never will. Certainly, one may try several of the tricks discussed in the section on the speckled rattlesnake when trying to get these rattlesnakes to eat. Those we collected ate mice readily until early fall when they abruptly stopped eating as they prepared for brumation. They also seemed to prefer live fuzzies to prekilled fuzzies.

As tropical-dwelling lizard eaters, we would expect they are frequently parasitized. However, we have seen no mention of parasites in the literature regarding this species and have not communicated with anyone claiming to have identified parasites in this species. Repeated fecal exams on those in our care have not revealed parasite eggs to date.

This species has been bred in captivity, but only rarely because they are protected. Mating has been known to occur in the summer, with 3–9 young being born the following year, often in July or early August. The young are usually 12.8–20.5 cm (5–8 inches) long at birth, and may be the smallest rattlesnakes known (Lowe et al., 1986). As might be expected, these small young will often refuse pinkies, instead preferring small lizards. Eventually, however, they may be switched.

SPECIES: *Crotalus pricei*, Twin-spotted Rattlesnake
MAINTENANCE DIFFICULTY INDEX: 3 (1 = easiest, 5 = most difficult)
AVERAGE SIZE: 30–65 cm (12–26 inches)
FOOD: Lizards, mice
CAGE SIZE: 10-gallon aquarium
SUBSTRATE: Indoor-outdoor carpet, artificial turf, or cypress mulch
VENTRAL HEAT: Yes
UV LIGHT: No, but an incandescent bulb is strongly advisable
TEMPERATURE RANGE: 18–23°C (65–75°F)
SPECIAL CONSIDERATIONS: *VENOMOUS*. Nervous. Prefers lizards but many take mice
  as well. Protected species. Permit required.

Howard Lawler, curator of reptiles, amphibians, and invertebrates at the Arizona-Sonora Desert Museum, reported that one pair collected in northeastern Sonora, Mexico, mated on 10 July 1984, and that young were born on 19 July 1985. He believed that a warm spot in the cage during brumation was critical to successful overwintering and normal gestation.

One of these snakes survived more than 15 years and 8 months in captivity (Snider and Bowler, 1992). Like the other rattlesnakes, we suspect they may survive much longer in captivity. We still have a great deal to learn about maintaining and breeding this snake. Perhaps

an organized captive breeding program is in order for *C. pricei*.

Interestingly, there appears to be quite a bit of variation from one population to another of these snakes. This should not be surprising since Fowlie (1965) estimated that some of these populations may have been separated for as long as 100,000 years. Those twin-spots from the Pinalenos appear larger and darker-colored while those from the Chiricahuas seem smaller and lighter-colored. The snakes from the Pinalenos also are reportedly far more likely to consume mice readily than those snakes from the Chiricahuas.

Crotalus ruber (*exsul*)
Red Diamond Rattlesnake

The red diamond rattlesnake, a large and showy reddish rattlesnake of extreme southern California and Baja California, is another species whose taxonomy is in question. Some have proposed that the species name should be changed to *exsul* (Grismer et al., 1994). We will continue to use *ruber* until the matter is settled. Their range within the United States from San Bernardino County and Riverside County southward is being rapidly developed, leaving less and less suitable habitat for them. And like other venomous snakes, they are not well accepted in areas near human habitations where they might otherwise survive if left unmolested.

Fortunately, they will survive and breed very well in captivity.

The red diamond is definitely a lowland snake, primarily occupying hot valleys in southern California, but also along the coast and especially common in rocky areas with heavy brush and chaparral (Wright and Wright, 1957; Klauber, 1972; Armstrong and Murphy, 1979; Stebbins, 1985; Ernst, 1992).

They are fairly large snakes, ranging 75–162 cm (30–65 inches) in length. The northern red diamond rattlesnake, *C. r. ruber*, is the subspecies that occurs in the United States and is responsible for the common name. Indeed,

Crotalus ruber

these beautiful snakes do possess solid brick red to pinkish diamonds dorsally on a light pink to tan background color.

They are considered to be close relatives of the western diamondback rattlesnake, *C. atrox*, and like that species they are fond of rabbits, ground squirrels, other small rodents including mice (deer mice, voles, wild mice), kangaroo rats, and wood rats, as well as other mammals (in one case a spotted skunk was consumed). They have also been known to consume small birds and lizards (whiptails, *Cnemidophorus* sp.) (Wright and Wright, 1957; Klauber, 1972; Stebbins, 1985; Ernst, 1992). In one instance a

captive specimen ate a Southern Pacific rattlesnake, *C. v. helleri* (Klauber, 1972).

Suspected predators of this species include skunks, coyotes, and possibly domestic dogs, as well as birds of prey (Ernst, 1992).

These snakes usually mate from February to April, with a peak period in March. The 3–20 (average 8) grayish to brown-colored young are born about 5 months later (Klauber, 1972). These young range 30–35 cm (11.8–13.8 inches) in length (Ernst, 1992).

As with most other rattlesnakes and certainly many other snakes, they are diurnal during the cooler parts of the year and nocturnal during the hottest part of the summer. Air temperatures reported at the time active individuals have been observed have been 18–30°C (64–86°F) (Klauber in Wright and Wright, 1957). Brattstrom (1965) reported one specimen in the wild and in captivity had maintained its temperature at 24°C (75.2°F).

As mentioned above, these snakes will do extremely well in captivity. They can be housed in the basic cage arrangement discussed in the general care section, along with venomous snake modifications. Artificial carpet/turf or newspaper will work well as a substrate. Rocks and plastic plants are nice additions to the enclosure. Ventral heat or heat from above in

Red Diamond Rattlesnake, *Crotalus ruber* (*exsul*) (photo by David G. Campbell)

the form of an incandescent bulb is considered essential for long-term maintenance and captive reproduction of this species. A temperature range of 24–30°C (75–86°F) with a warmer spot somewhere in the cage would probably be suitable for these snakes. We have actually housed these snakes successfully at daytime air temperatures fluctuating from 27 to 35°C (80 to 95°F) during the active season, with nighttime temperatures no lower than 24°C (75°F).

A dark stable hiding place such as an inverted clay flowerpot (with drain hole widened) or one of the manufactured hide boxes now available commercially will provide these snakes with a sense of security and stimulate their appetite. Many have done very well in much simpler captive environments, however.

Feeding rarely presents a problem in captivity as these snakes will readily consume prekilled domestic mice and rats. In this respect, they are much like the western diamondbacks and perhaps many other lowland rattlesnakes.

Even though very few parasites have been described from this species, many of the same parasites affecting the closely related western diamondback and the other rattlesnakes are to be suspected. See the section on the western diamondback and the general care section for details on the types of parasites and treatment.

Brumation is advisable but apparently this species does not need a hard cold period in order to successfully breed. Two months at temperatures of 10–15°C (50–59°F) will work well. Ventral heat or an incandescent light creating a hot spot for basking purposes is a good idea, however. Using these supplemental heat sources, we have exposed these snakes to air temperatures fluctuating from 3 to 18°C (38 to 65°F) for 4 months with no ill effects.

This snake has been bred numerous times in captivity and breeding may be accomplished as discussed in the general care section. Just place the female in the male's cage soon after brumation ends. Feed the female heavily as she will often stop eating fairly soon into her gestation.

The young are generally born 141–190 days later. Most will readily accept small prekilled mice as their first meal, and if not, may be started on frozen and thawed lizards and switched to mice as soon as possible. However, 100% of the babies born in our care have consumed unscented prekilled fuzzies right after shedding their skins for the first time. They grow rapidly, reaching up to 70 cm (28 inches) near the end of their first summer and up to 94 cm (37 inches) by the third year. Sexual maturity may be reached in 3 years.

This snake's claim to fame among herpetologists is its good disposition (Klauber, 1972; Shaw and Campbell, 1974; Armstrong and Murphy, 1979; Stebbins, 1985). So tame may these snakes become that numerous herpetologists have become encouraged to handle them without the proper precautions. Remember, these snakes possess a large quantity of venom and fangs long enough to deliver it effectively. Therefore, under no circumstances should these snakes or any other venomous snakes be handled. As mentioned elsewhere in this book, the only valid reason for handling a venomous

---

SPECIES: *Crotalus ruber*, Red Diamond Rattlesnake
MAINTENANCE DIFFICULTY INDEX: 2 (1 = easiest, 5 = most difficult)
AVERAGE SIZE: 75–162 cm (30–65 inches)
FOOD: Mice, rats
CAGE SIZE: 20–30-gallon long aquarium
SUBSTRATE: Indoor-outdoor carpet, artificial turf, or cypress mulch
VENTRAL HEAT: Yes
UV LIGHT: No, but an incandescent bulb is strongly advisable
TEMPERATURE RANGE: 27–35°C (80–95°F)
SPECIAL CONSIDERATIONS: *VENOMOUS*. Good eaters. Generally nonaggressive. Breed readily.

snake is to provide medical treatment, and even this should be performed using the proper methods of restraint.

Regarding the personality of these snakes, there is presently a belief that only red diamonds from coastal areas have good dispositions. Those from inland desert areas are a bit more hot-tempered. This may have a basis in fact since these snakes may interbreed with western diamondbacks in some areas.

One of the first members of this species we had the opportunity to work with left large amounts of venom on the glass of its new cage as it struck at us with the aggressiveness of a western diamondback. Apparently, this *ruber* had not read the book.

As with most other rattlesnakes, it is advisable that they be administered the necessary routine deworming agents in their food when they first arrive in captivity and are still eating rather than wait until they become anorexic and require handling in order to medicate.

Overall, this snake is comparable to the western diamondback in terms of the ease with which they adjust to captivity. Combining that with their relatively mellow dispositions, they make ideal captives. Captive breeding is very strongly encouraged with this species because of the habitat destruction occurring in their range.

One pair in our care, housed together under naturally occurring conditions in northern Florida, was observed copulating on 24 February.

One of these snakes survived more than 19 years and 2 months in captivity (Snider and Bowler, 1992).

Crotalus scutulatus
Mojave Rattlesnake

The Mojave rattlesnake is perhaps the deadliest snake of North America. Although it does not rival the diamondbacks in terms of size, its venom is extremely potent, and in certain areas the neurotoxic component may approach cobra venom in its toxicity. Unlike the cobra, however, the Mojave possesses the long fangs and rapid delivery mechanism of a viper, which is what makes it even more dangerous. With these facts in mind, we would like to advise due caution to those maintaining or contemplating maintaining these snakes. Only experienced herpetologists with suitable escape-proof facilities and access to antivenin should maintain these snakes. This is not a snake for an inexperienced keeper of venomous snakes.

The Mojave rattlesnake is widely distributed throughout the southwest. They range from interior southern California, and parts of Nevada through much of Arizona southward through Mexico and the Big Bend region of Texas. These are medium to large snakes, reaching slightly over 129 cm (51 inches); however, most snakes range 61–91.4 cm (24–36 inches) in TL. The color and pattern of these

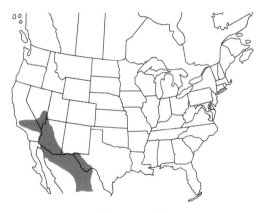

Crotalus scutulatus

snakes are very variable. The background color is usually greenish or greenish gray over most of their range in the United States. The dorsal pattern may consist of brown to gray diamonds, hexagons, or rounded blotches which usually contrast sharply with the greenish background. Perhaps the easiest way to recognize this snake is by the light-colored stripe behind the eye that curves backward and does not intersect the angle of the mouth (as it does in the western

Mojave Rattlesnake, *Crotalus scutulatus* (photo by David G. Campbell)

diamondback). Another easily recognizable feature is that the black rings on the tail are much narrower than the white rings (they are about the same size in the western diamondback).

The preferred habitat of the Mojave appears to be open desert dominated by creosote bush and mesquite. They are also found in open sandy areas but not as commonly as the sidewinder (Wright and Wright, 1957; Fowlie, 1965; Klauber, 1972; Armstrong and Murphy, 1979; Stebbins, 1985; Lowe et al., 1986; Ernst, 1992).

Their diets are fairly broad, with mammals, birds, amphibians, and reptiles being listed as part of their wild menu. Food items reported have included kangaroo rats, pocket mice, white-footed mice, packrats, wood rats, ground squirrels, rabbits, jackrabbits, birds and their eggs, whiptail lizards, *Cnemidophorus* sp., leaf-nose snakes, *Phyllorhynchus* sp., and an occasional spadefoot toad, *Scaphiopus* sp. (Wright and Wright, 1957; Fowlie, 1965; Klauber, 1972; Reynolds and Scott, 1982; Lowe et al., 1986; Ernst, 1992).

Body temperatures of active individuals in the wild ranged from 21.9 to 29.8°C (71.4 to 85.6°F) with an average of 26.5°C (79.7°F) (Pough, 1966). Other studies have recorded temperatures ranging from a low of 17°C (62.6°F) to a high temperature of 30°C (86°F). These snakes are considered to be largely nocturnal and therefore avoid extremely high temperatures in this manner.

Natural predators are unknown but suspected predators include hawks, owls, roadrunners, predatory mammals, kingsnakes.

Mating has been known to occur in both the spring and fall. Lowe et al (1986) indicated that breeding occurs primarily in the spring (late February through May). However, several observations have been made both in the wild and with captive specimens that suggest fall breeding may occur as well (Tennant, 1984; Jacobson, 1987). Spring mating will result in the birth of young approximately 5 months later (usually late July through September), while fall mating results in the birth of young approximately 9–11 months later. It is believed that the female stores the sperm but delays ovulation until the following spring. Hence, most young are born about the same time (late July until early September).

Litter size varies from 2 to 13 (average 8) and these young range 22–28.3 cm (8.6–11.1 inches) in length and average 25.6 cm (10 inches) (Klauber, 1972; Stebbins, 1985). These young generally weigh 7–9 grams (Lowe et al., 1986).

Mojave rattlesnakes will generally do extremely well in captivity if maintained in a basic cage setup (plus venomous snake modifications) with artificial carpet/turf or paper as the substrate, ventral heat, and a good stable place to hide. Water may be provided but remember that evaporation from a water bowl leading to high humidity within the cage may contribute to anorexia (a loss of appetite), a skin infection, or a respiratory infection. This is most likely to occur in a poorly ventilated enclosure (e.g., glass or wooden lids instead of screen or wire lids will restrict ventilation). Thus, good ventilation of the enclosure is a necessity for this desert-adapted animal. In fact, some keepers choose to provide water to these animals only once weekly for a short period of time regardless of the cage ventilation. See the discussion in the section on the sidewinder, *Crotalus cerastes*.

Air temperatures of 25–30°C (77–86°F) should be suitable for this snake's captive maintenance, although we have maintained them at daytime temperatures fluctuating from 27 to 35°C (80 to 95°F) and nighttime temperatures no lower than 24°C (75°F) during the active season.

As with most other lowland rattlesnakes, feeding in captivity is usually not a problem. Most of these snakes will readily consume prekilled domestic mice. Even most of the juveniles seem to show a preference for small rodents although some individuals may take lizards initially (but usually switch rapidly to rodents). Turner (in Tennant, 1984) observed one juvenile eating a Texas banded gecko, *Coleonyx brevis*, and believed they would also eat earless, *Cophosaurus* sp. or *Holbrookia* sp., canyon, and side-blotched, *Uta stansburiana*, lizards. Stubborn feeders may be enticed to feed by offering some of the natural food items mentioned above or by using some of the tricks discussed in the section on the twin-spotted rattlesnake, *Crotalus pricei*.

Very little is known about the parasites of this snake. The authors lost one of these snakes to amoebiasis (caused by *Entamoeba invadens*) following brumation one year. Apparently the snake was infected prior to brumation, harbored a heavy load throughout that period, and succumbed to the rapid growth of the organisms once warmed several months later. Certainly this kind of pattern has been noted when other sick snakes have been brumated and illustrates the importance of parasite control in these animals. In addition to amoeba, which is probably not normally found in the gut of free-ranging specimens, several metazoan parasites are likely in the Mojave rattlesnake. Babero and Emerson (1974) reported that the nematode *Thubunaea cnemidophorus* had been found in this snake. A large number of other worms including tapeworms (cestodes), hookworms (*Kalicephalus* sp. and *Oswaldocruzia* sp., stomach worms, *Physaloptera* sp., tongue-

---

SPECIES: *Crotalus scutulatus*, Mojave Rattlesnake
MAINTENANCE DIFFICULTY INDEX: 3 (1 = easiest, 5 = most difficult)
AVERAGE SIZE: 61–91 cm (24–36 inches)
FOOD: Mice, rats
CAGE SIZE: 10–20-gallon long aquarium
SUBSTRATE: Indoor-outdoor carpet, artificial turf, or cypress mulch
VENTRAL HEAT: Yes
UV LIGHT: No, but an incandescent bulb is strongly advisable
TEMPERATURE RANGE: 25–30°C (77–86°F)
SPECIAL CONSIDERATIONS: *VENOMOUS*. Some populations have extremely dangerous neurotoxin-containing venom. Nervous captives.

worms, Linguatulidae, and others may be found in these rattlesnakes since they have been found in others from the same area. As with most rattlesnakes, it is strongly advisable to administer anthelmintics in the food items when the snakes first arrive in captivity and are still eating rather than have to restrain an anorectic snake in order to medicate it later.

Captive breeding is a rarity with this species. As mentioned above, mating may occur in either the spring or the fall. One captive mating at the Fort Worth Zoo on 2 October resulted in the birth of young the following 23 July, 9.5 months later (Tennant, 1984). The young eat readily in captivity. If pinkies are refused, lizards may be necessary initially. See above.

Remember that brumation is advisable if breeding is to be attempted. Two to 4 months at temperatures between 10 and 15°C (50 and 59°F) will probably be satisfactory. Those in

our care have tolerated temperatures fluctuating from 3 to 18°C (38 to 65°F) for 4 months during the winter. No special requirements appear necessary as the snakes may be brumated in their regular cages. As alluded to above, snakes must be healthy in order to be brumated.

Overall, we have found the Mojave rattlesnake to be an unpredictable captive, seemingly mellow one day, irritable the next. Others have reported that these snakes are relatively unexcitable. Most do well in captivity.

One last word of caution is in order. Tennant (1984) reported that one of these snakes struck from a distance of more than 69.8 cm (27.5 inches) in order to deliver a bite, which proved fatal for Dr. Frederick Shannon. This is longer than the distance from top to bottom of most snake cages.

One of these snakes survived 14 years and 5 months in captivity (Snider and Bowler, 1992).

Crotalus tigris
Tiger Rattlesnake

The tiger rattlesnake is a relatively small, lowland, rock-dwelling resident of central and southern Arizona and Sonora, Mexico. Within their limited range they are fairly common.

These rattlesnakes are identified by their tiger stripes or bands that run transversely (crosswise) along their entire body. These bands may be dark brown to black against a variable background color. Perhaps the most distinguishing feature of this snake, however, is the very small head relative to the size of the body. In addition, the rattle is usually very large relative to the size of the body. Lowe et al. (1986) observed one of these snakes extract a dead cactus mouse from a narrow crevice and suspected the small head may be an adaptation for hunting in rocky areas. One can only guess why the rattle is so large. Perhaps the large rattle mimics the sound produced by a larger rattlesnake, thereby conferring some advantage to its owner. Indeed, the tiger is a relatively small snake. They are generally 45.7–77 cm (18–30 inches) in length with the record being

91 cm (36 inches) (Klauber, 1972; Stebbins, 1985).

As stated above, the preferred habitat of these snakes is rocky areas. These areas have been further characterized as rocky canyons, rocky foothills of mountains, rocky ravines, and essentially anywhere there is a rough, rugged, rocky terrain within the Arizona-

Crotalus tigris

Tiger Rattlesnake, *Crotalus tigris* (photo by David G. Campbell)

Sonoran Desert (Wright and Wright, 1957; Fowlie, 1965; Klauber, 1972; Armstrong and Murphy, 1979; Stebbins, 1985; Lowe et al., 1986; Ernst, 1992).

Their diet in the wild consists of a variety of rodents and lizards. These include pocket mice, deer mice, kangaroo rats, small woodrats, pocket gophers, whiptail lizards, *Cnemidophorus* sp., and spiny lizards, *Sceloporus* sp. (Ortenburger and Ortenburger, 1926; Fowlie, 1965; Klauber, 1972; Lowe et al., 1986; Ernst, 1992). Lowe et al. (1986) and Ernst (1992) suspected that lizards form a greater proportion of the diet of juvenile tiger rattlesnakes.

Virtually nothing is known of this snake's thermal ecology. They are rarely seen on the surface during much of the year and are generally considered crepuscular or nocturnal (Lowe et al., 1986; Armstrong and Murphy, 1979), although Repp (1998) reported seeing a total of four of these snakes basking during the winter. This has implications for captive snakes.

There are no reports of the natural predators of tiger rattlesnakes; however, suspected predators include hawks, owls, skunks, bobcats, coyotes, and ophiophagous snakes.

Mating is believed to occur primarily in the spring but may also occur in the fall. The 4–6 young are born from late June to September (Lowe et al., 1986). They range in size from 21 to 23.3 cm (8.3 to 9.2 inches) in length and weigh around 9 grams (Klauber, 1972; Lowe et al., 1986; Ernst, 1992).

In captivity, the tiger is very variable. Some appear to adapt extremely well, while others refuse to eat and traumatize their noses in attempts to escape. Many will do well in a wide variety of captive environments and cage sizes, but the basic cage setup discussed in the general care section will usually work very nicely. Artificial carpet/turf, paper, or wood chips (but not cedar) have proven satisfactory. Some have used large, smooth gravel. Ventral heat has been extremely beneficial, as has a good stable hide box. Flat stable rocks and plastic plants may be added to the enclosure to beautify it and increase the security of its occupant. A small water bowl may be provided if the ventilation is very good. Otherwise, water should be placed in the cage every several weeks to a month for a short period of time. Except for the largest of specimens, a cage the size of a 10-gallon aquarium will be suitable. Remember to include all of the venomous snake modifications.

House these snakes singly or they may be inhibited from feeding. In one instance in which a tiger had been housed with a speckled rattlesnake, the tiger stopped eating. Several weeks after the two snakes were separated, the tiger began feeding voraciously.

The preferred optimum temperature range of these snakes in the wild has not been determined, and therefore a daily temperature range for captive specimens is difficult to suggest. Other nocturnal snakes from the same habitat and other captive rattlesnakes (including members of this species) have done well in a temperature range of 25–30°C (77–86°F). One specimen in our care thrived at daytime air temperatures ranging from 27 to 35°C (80 to 95°F) with nighttime lows during this time of no lower than 23.8°C (75°F) during the summer. Yet this same snake maintained excellent body weight and fed regularly at air temperatures ranging down to 7.2°C (45°F) at night during the fall and early winter as long as it was provided with a constant source of ventral heat. Remember that wild tiger rattlesnakes have been observed basking in the winter (Repp, 1998).

The following year, this snake was not given a ventral heat source and it developed a respiratory infection. This cleared after ventral heat was provided and the snake then tolerated winter air temperatures down to 3°C (38°F) for short periods with no ill effects. Interestingly, this snake used the heat source on only rare occasions, but apparently this was enough. Winter temperatures ranged from 3 to 18°C (38 to 65°F) and lasted approximately 4 months.

As with other lowland rattlesnakes, these snakes seem to feed readily on domestic mice in captivity. They may refuse to take them prekilled, however; instead they are attracted by the natural motion of their prey, which appears to elicit a strike and a normal feeding response. Under these circumstances, it would behoove the keeper to offer smaller prey items to these snakes more frequently than larger items less frequently (there is a greater risk of injury to the snake from a larger mouse than a smaller one since live items are being offered). Contrary to popular belief, these snakes can easily consume a full-grown mouse. Regardless of the size offered, remember to remove the mouse fairly soon if the snake shows no interest in it. This is not to say that these snakes will not take prekilled mice. Indeed, most snakes will eventually take their food prekilled once they are well adapted, and a well-adapted tiger rattlesnake is no exception.

Virtually nothing is known about the parasites of these snakes. See the section on the Mojave rattlesnake, *Crotalus scutulatus*, for some information on the parasites of other rattlesnakes. Many of these parasites may be present in the tiger rattlesnake as well. An anorectic specimen in our care began feeding after ivermectin, metronidazole, and fenbendazole were administered at the doses mentioned in the general care section.

Brumation is advisable if breeding is to be attempted. It may be accomplished in the snake's regular cage as discussed above. No modifications of the cage are necessary at this time. As discussed above, ventral heat or a basking area is probably advisable during this period.

Very little is known about the reproduction of this snake either in the wild or captivity. Very few have bred these small rattlesnakes in captivity. As with many other rattlesnakes, it is believed they mate primarily in the spring, with

---

SPECIES: *Crotalus tigris*, Tiger Rattlesnake
MAINTENANCE DIFFICULTY INDEX: 2 (1 = easiest, 5 = most difficult)
AVERAGE SIZE: 45–77 cm (18–30 inches)
FOOD: Mice, rats
CAGE SIZE: 10–20-gallon long aquarium
SUBSTRATE: Indoor-outdoor carpet, artificial turf, or cypress mulch
VENTRAL HEAT: Yes
UV LIGHT: No, but an incandescent bulb is strongly advisable
TEMPERATURE RANGE: 27–35°C (80–95°F)
SPECIAL CONSIDERATIONS: *VENOMOUS*. Usually adapt to captivity and eat readily.
  Remain nervous and aggressive, however.

opportunistic mating at other times and a secondary peak of mating in the fall. Hence, the pair should be placed together in the spring soon after brumation ends and every so often afterward until the fall if no mating activity occurs earlier. The gestation period is probably around 5 months or 150 days, as it is for most other rattlesnakes (Klauber, 1972).

To date, there have been only two captive breedings of this species. The most recent occurred at the Knoxville Zoo. One pair copulated three times in late summer and the female delivered two young the following year on 11 July. The pair (one male and one female) measured 25.75 cm (10.1 inches) and weighed 2.4 grams. Tryon (1993) noted these animals were kept off display and disturbed minimally.

The female was also given a winter cooling period from November to February. The neonates shed at 7 and 9 days of age and consumed small furred mice at that time (Tryon, 1993).

In our experience and in the experience of others who have maintained this species, these snakes generally do very well in captivity. A few will refuse to eat, but most are hardy and consistent feeders and in time herpetoculturists should be able to successfully breed them in numbers. We can make no conclusions on their aggressiveness toward humans at this time. They appear to be fairly unpredictable from individual to individual and from day to day.

One of these snakes survived more than 15 years and 3 months in captivity (Snider and Bowler, 1992).

Crotalus viridis
Western Rattlesnake

The western rattlesnake is the most widely distributed venomous snake in North America. It is the only venomous snake that enters western Canada. Its huge range encompasses much of the territory between North Dakota southward through much of Texas and adjacent Mexico and westward from southwestern Canada to southern California and northern Baja California. At last count, there were eight subspecies in the United States and Canada, which vary considerably in coloration, size, toxicity, and behavior.

The eight subspecies are the prairie rattlesnake, *C. v. viridis*, Grand Canyon rattlesnake, *C. v. abyssus*, Arizona black rattlesnake, *C. v. cerberus*, midget faded rattlesnake, *C. v. concolor*, Southern Pacific rattlesnake, *C. v. helleri*, Great Basin rattlesnake, *C. v. lutosus*, Hopi rattlesnake, *C. v. nuntius*, and the Northern Pacific rattlesnake, *C. v. oreganus*. The largest subspecies, the Southern Pacific, can be easily more than 1.3 m (4 feet) long. The record for the species is 162 cm (65 inches) while the smallest, the Hopi rattlesnake, rarely reaches 61 cm (24 inches). The venom yield and its toxicity vary considerably also, with the midget

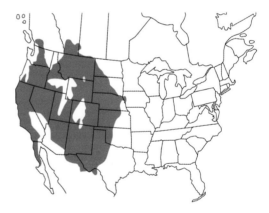

Crotalus viridis

faded rattlesnake having a toxicity up to 30 times that of the other subspecies (Lowe et al., 1986). Those who have kept many of the subspecies believe the Arizona black rattlesnake is the most docile subspecies, the prairie rattlesnake is the most aggressive, and the other subspecies are between these two extremes (Lowe et al., 1986). Perkins (in Klauber, 1972) believed the Great Basin was as mild tempered as a red diamond, and that many Southern Pacifics were very pugnacious.

Southern Pacific Rattlesnake, *Crotalus viridis helleri* (photo by David G. Campbell)

As might be expected from such a widely distributed snake, a variety of habitats are occupied. These have included brush-covered coastal dunes just past the tideline to coniferous forests at 3600 meters (11,000 feet), grasslands, woodlands, or wherever brumacula may be found, usually avoiding open deserts (except in the case of the Great Basin rattlesnake). Even the subspecies descriptions often indicate that this snake occupies numerous habitats within its range (Wright and Wright, 1957; Fowlie, 1965; Webb, 1970; Klauber, 1972; Basey, 1976; Lin-

Great Basin Rattlesnake, *Crotalus viridis lutosus* (photo by David G. Campbell)

Northern Pacific Rattlesnake, *Crotalus viridis oreganus* (photo by David G. Campbell)

der and Fichter, 1977; Armstrong and Murphy, 1979; Behler and King, 1979; Nussbaum et al., 1983; Tennant, 1984; Baxter and Stone, 1985; Stebbins, 1985; Hudson, 1985; Hammerson, 1986; Lowe et al., 1986; Conant and Collins, 1991; Ernst, 1992).

If identified down to species, the list of food items consumed by this species in the wild would form a small book. Hence, a summarized list is presented here. Mammals seem to be one of the preferred prey groups. They have included pocket mice, deer mice, voles, kangaroo rats, pocket gophers, chipmunks, wood rats, prairie dogs, ground squirrels, muskrats, marmots, rabbits, pikas, shrews, moles, and others.

Birds are also readily taken and these have included numerous sparrows, larks, doves, quail, numerous warblers, starlings, small pheasants, and even small owls. Lizards have included spiny, *Sceloporus* sp., skinks, *Eumeces* sp., collared, *Crotaphytus* sp., alligator lizard, *Gerrhonotus* sp., side-blotched, *Uta* sp., earless, *Holbrookia* sp., whiptails, *Cnemidophorus* sp., and horned lizards, *Phrynosoma* sp. Snakes have included other western rattlesnakes and kingsnakes, *Lampropeltis* sp., leopard frogs, *Rana* sp., and spadefoot toads, *Scaphiopus* sp. Fish and insects have also been reported as food items (Fowlie, 1965; Webb, 1970; Basey, 1976; Linder and Fichter, 1977; Nussbaum et al., 1983; Tennant, 1984; Gannon and Secoy, 1984; Hammerson, 1986; Lowe et al., 1986; Stebbins, 1985; Ernst, 1992).

The thermal ecology of this snake has been well studied. Basically, these snakes may be active on the surface at temperatures ranging from 20 to 35°C (68 to 95°F) and seem to have a preferred body temperature around 30°C (86°F); gravid females seek even higher temperatures and regulate their body temperatures more closely (Brattstrom, 1965; Klauber, 1972; Ernst, 1992).

Known predators of this widespread species include skunks, badgers, marmots, foxes, coyotes, domestic dogs, domestic cats, hawks, owls, eagles, roadrunners, and ophiophagous

Midget Faded Rattlesnake, *Crotalus viridis concolor* (photo by John Rossi)

Prairie Rattlesnake, *Crotalus viridis viridis* (photo by David G. Campbell)

snakes such as kingsnakes, racers, and whip-snakes (Ernst, 1992).

Mating in most populations of this species is believed to occur in the late summer or fall, but spring mating is also possible. Sperm are stored over the winter and ovulation and fertilization occur the following spring, with gestation from that point lasting approximately 4 months (Klauber, 1972; Diller and Wallace, 1984; Ernst, 1992). It is important to note that females may not eat much or at all during their pregnancy, instead relying upon fat reserves built up previously.

If all goes well, 1–25 young will be born in late summer or early fall (August through early October). The young range 17.8–30.5 cm (7–12 inches) in length at birth and grow rapidly to reach sexual maturity in 3–4 years. There is a tremendous variation in the size of the young from subspecies to subspecies and from north to south within a subspecies, just as there is with litter size. Furthermore, it appears that northern females may reproduce only every other year while those in the south may or may not reproduce annually depending upon their food intake that year. Litter size and size of young are listed in Table 12.

Table 12. Western Rattlesnake, *Crotalus viridis*, Litter Size and Size of Young

Subspecies	Litter Size	Average	Size of Young
Hopi	3–10	6.9	17.8 cm (7 in.)
Arizona Black	5–11	7.4	23–25 cm (9–10 in.)
Grand Canyon	5–13	8.0	23–25 cm (9–10 in.)
Great Basin	3–14	8.0	25–28 cm (10–11 in.)
Northern Pacific (N)	1–14	6.6	27–35 cm (11–12 in.)
(S)	2–14	8.3	
Southern Pacific	1–14	8.7	
Prairie	4–21	11.3	25–28 cm (10–11 in.)

Data from (Fitch, 1985; Lowe et al., 1986; Ernst, 1992).
N = northern California population; S = southern California population.

SPECIES: *Crotalus viridis*, Western Rattlesnake
MAINTENANCE DIFFICULTY INDEX: 2 (1 = easiest, 5 = most difficult)
AVERAGE SIZE: 37–162 cm (15–65 inches)
FOOD: Mice, rats
CAGE SIZE: 10–30-gallon long aquarium
SUBSTRATE: Indoor-outdoor carpet, artificial turf, or cypress mulch
VENTRAL HEAT: Yes
UV LIGHT: No, but an incandescent bulb is strongly advisable
TEMPERATURE RANGE: 20–35°C (68–95°F)
SPECIAL CONSIDERATIONS: *VENOMOUS*. Subspecies vary tremendously in size,
   disposition, and adaptability to captivity. Most do very well.

With this kind of variability in mind, one must be careful not to overgeneralize on the captive requirements and peculiarities of this species. Still, the basic rules of herpetoculture apply for every subspecies. These basics are discussed in detail in the general care section and include cleanliness, provision of a temperature gradient, proper substrate, parasite control, and proper diet. All subspecies of the western rattlesnake will do well in the basic cage design discussed in the general care section, with artificial carpet/turf or newspaper as the substrates of choice, a hide box, water bowl (see footnote 1 in the section on *Crotalus molossus* for a discussion on water), and ventral heat on one side. Special lighting does not appear necessary. Housing singly is strongly advisable to prevent competition for food, accidental ingestion of a cagemate that has grabbed the opposite end of the same food item, or blatant cannibalism (Mitchell, 1986). The latter is very rare. Most cases of cannibalism are of the former type. Klauber told of one prairie rattlesnake that ate another which had been a cagemate for years.

Cage size is not critical. A locked cage the size of a 10-gallon aquarium will work well for most members of this species; a 20–30 long will work for the giants.

In general, these snakes will eat readily in captivity. Although they have been reported to eat a wide variety of food in the wild, including amphibians, reptiles, birds, mammals, and even fish, in captivity these snakes will do very well on captive-bred domestic mice and small rats.

In fact, some snakes refusing mice initially may be induced to start feeding by using rat pups (fuzzies).

Others, including juveniles, may prefer lizards at first, but will eventually switch to mice. Also, one should expect those animals recently captured from more northern latitudes to become inappetent in the fall or even late summer, as do many other northern and montane snakes. Therefore, they should be fed heavily while they are feeding.

Brumation is very strongly advisable for most members of this species, especially if breeding is intended. Brumation has been accomplished in the usual manner, either using the same cage (seminatural method), or by placing the snake in a well-sealed but well-ventilated plastic box in a refrigerator (artificial method). Two to 4 months at 5–15°C (41–59°F) (5–10°C [41–50°F] for northern subspecies) should be sufficient. One Great Basin rattlesnake (from Nevada) in our care tolerated 2 months at 3–5°C (38–41°F). It was somewhat ataxic for several weeks after this, but it recovered fully.

Breeding has occurred numerous times in captivity, usually in the early spring but possibly in the fall, with up to 25 (usually 3–14) 18–30-cm (7–12-inch) young being born in late summer to midfall. As seen above, there is some variation in size, with the smaller subspecies tending to have smaller babies and smaller brood (litter) sizes.

The young often take pinkies, but may have to be started on lizards, as discussed above.

Table 13. Western Rattlesnake, *Crotalus viridis*, Longevities

Subspecies	Longevity
Hopi rattlesnake	12 years, 0 months, 24 days
Arizona black rattlesnake	12 years, 5 months, 4 days
Northern Pacific rattlesnake	14 years, 3 months, 10 days
Midget faded rattlesnake	14 years, 6 months, 28 day
Great Basin rattlesnake	19 years, 0 months, 20 days
Prairie rattlesnake	19 years, 3 months, 10 days
Southern Pacific rattlesnake	24 years, 1 month, 25 days

They will grow rapidly and will reach sexual maturity in 2–3 years (in captivity).

In our experience, these adaptable rattlesnakes make excellent captives that are usually good eaters and eventually calm down nicely (depending upon subspecies).

These snakes (like most rattlesnakes) may be quite long-lived in captivity. The record longevities for most subspecies are listed, in Table 13, according to Snider and Bowler (1992).

Ernst (1992) reported a prairie rattlesnake that had been maintained for 27 years and 9 months.

Crotalus willardi
Ridgenose Rattlesnake

The ridgenose rattlesnake is appropriately named. These small rattlesnakes are easily identified by the ridge on the nose, making them somewhat similar in appearance to the members of the genus *Agkistrodon* (cottonmouth and copperhead). The Arizona subspecies, *C. w. willardi*, also possesses distinctive solid white stripes on the face, lower jaw, and neck which contrast sharply with the chocolate brown color of those areas. The subspecies found in New Mexico, the New Mexico ridgenose rattlesnake, *C. w. obscurus*, is less boldly patterned and has numerous spots on the head. The body of both subspecies is generally rusty brown or rarely grayish with dorsal cream-colored crossbands, sometimes broken.

As mentioned above, these rattlesnakes are indeed small. They are generally 37–61 cm (15–24 inches) in length with the record being 64 cm (26 inches). They rarely weigh more than a quarter of a pound (0.1 kg). Thus, they are one of the smallest of the rattlesnakes, similar in size to the twin-spotted rattlesnake and slightly smaller than the rock rattlesnake and the sidewinder.

These snakes are one of the Mexican mountain rattlesnakes, found only in high mountain canyons in extreme southeastern Arizona and southwestern New Mexico and down into Mexico. Unlike the other montane rattlesnakes, however, they reportedly prefer cooler, more humid, pine/oak-dominated canyons to the drier slopes (Armstrong and Murphy, 1979). Armstrong and Murphy also reported they are generally active diurnally at temperatures rang-

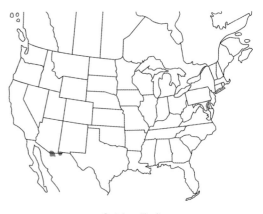

Crotalus willardi

Arizona Ridgenose Rattlesnake, *Crotalus willardi willardi* (photo by Steve Barten)

ing from 21 to 29°C (70 to 84°F), although they may be active at other times during the heat of summer (Lowe et al., 1986).

Like the other montane rattlesnakes, these snakes have a marked preference for lizards, particularly members of the genus *Sceloporus*, spiny lizards. The Yarrow's spiny lizard, *Sceloporus jarrovii*, is probably the main food item of these snakes in nature, although a variety of other food items have been reported. Klauber (1972) reported that a brush mouse, *Peromyscus boyli*, was found in one specimen, while Lowe et al. (1986) and Stebbins (1985) reported birds (rufous crowned sparrows), scorpions, and centipedes as well as mice. Lowe et al. mentioned one captive that ate a lyre snake, *Trimorphodon biscutatus*. Other food items reported have included a night snake, *Hypsiglena torquata*, and a tree lizard, *Urosaurus* sp. (Ernst, 1992).

Predators of this species are believed to include kingsnakes such as mountain kingsnakes, whipsnakes, hawks, and carnivorous mammals. One was found about 150 cm (60 inches) above the ground in a manzanita tree in the early morning after a large group of coatimundis had been observed there the night before (Rossi and Feldner, 1994).

Mating in the wild has been observed to occur in July (Lowe et al., 1986), but captives have also mated in April, June, August, September, and January (Martin, 1975, 1976; Tryon, 1978; Armstrong and Murphy, 1979). The young are born 13–16 months after mating, almost always from early August to early September. Litter size varies from 1 to 9 (Klauber, 1972; Martin, 1976; Quinn, 1977; Stebbins, 1985; Snead, pers. comm., 1991).

Newborn Arizona ridgenoses range 16.5–21.4 cm (6.5–8.5 inches) in size with an average size of 18.7 cm (7.4 inches). One litter of the New Mexico ridgenose ranged 20–21.2 cm (7.9–8.4 inches) in length with an average of 20.5 cm (8.1 inches) (Martin, 1976). The Arizona subspecies neonates weighed 5.4–7 grams (average 6.0), while the New Mexico subspecies neonates weighed 6.8–8.8 grams (average 7.4). It should be pointed out that we are probably comparing the young of one large female New Mexico ridgenose with a number of Arizona ridgenoses of varying sizes. Hence, there may be little difference in the size of neonates between the two U.S. subspecies. The young look similar, however. Those from the New Mexico subspecies usually have black

SPECIES: *Crotalus willardi*, Ridgenose Rattlesnake
MAINTENANCE DIFFICULTY INDEX: 2 (1 = easiest, 5 = most difficult)
AVERAGE SIZE: 37–61 cm (15–24 inches)
FOOD: Lizards, mice
CAGE SIZE: 10–20-gallon long aquarium
SUBSTRATE: Indoor-outdoor carpet, artificial turf, or cypress mulch
VENTRAL HEAT: Yes
UV LIGHT: No, but an incandescent bulb is strongly advisable
TEMPERATURE RANGE: 20–32°C (68–90°F)
SPECIAL CONSIDERATIONS: *VENOMOUS*. Protected species. Permit required.
  Semiarboreal. Provide sturdy branch.

tails, while those of the Arizona subspecies have yellowish tail tips.

These snakes will do extremely well in captivity in the basic cage arrangement discussed in the general care section with artificial carpet/turf, woodchip, or newspaper, a good hiding place, and a source of clean water. An enclosure the size of a 10-gallon aquarium will work well for most. Ventral heat and a heat lamp (incandescent bulb) above the enclosure is an excellent idea for long-term maintenance of these snakes. Stable rocks, especially a flat elevated rock on one side, will provide a sense of security and stimulate the appetite of these small shy snakes. Plastic hide boxes will also be well accepted. Water should be available regularly, as this species is known to drink frequently in captivity.

Air temperatures suitable for captive specimens have been reported by Tryon (1978) to range from 20 to 32°C (68 to 90°F) during the active season.

As mentioned above, mice are part of the regular diet of this rattlesnake, and they are usually not too terribly difficult to get to start feeding on these in captivity. If not, almost all captives will readily take spiny lizards (any species) initially and be switched to scented fuzzies in time. Murphy and Armstrong (1978) mentioned that newborn mice (pinkies) may not be consumed by some of the montane rattlesnakes although small furred mice (weight 7.5 grams) (fuzzies) were readily eaten. Native mice (*Peromyscus* sp.) may also be used for a specimen that refuses domestic mice. See the discussion under the speckled rattlesnake, *Crotalus mitchellii*, for tricks to use with an anorectic rattlesnake.

Remember, however, that gravid females may refuse to eat during the entire spring and summer prior to delivery of the young. Also be aware that recently captured adults may stop feeding in October or November in preparation for brumation. Hence, many cases of anorexia are not necessarily due to a lack of a suitable food source or a medical problem.

These snakes have been bred in captivity by Martin (1975) using techniques discussed in the general care section. As mentioned above, mating has occurred at different times, including June, July, August, September, and January. Tryon (1978) pointed out the importance of brumation for achieving successful captive breeding. He exposed the snakes in his care to temperatures fluctuating from 9 to 12°C (48 to 54°F) from December 1 until March or April, at which time the female was placed in the male's cage.

Mating does not usually occur, however, until after the female sheds for the first time after brumation (Martin, 1975; Tryon, 1978). Mating may occur several times, and if successful, the young will be born approximately 13 months later.

The young snakes are aggressive feeders, often taking pinky mice soon after birth and their first shed. Eating pinkies every 2–5 days, one newborn in our care grew from 21 to 24.5 cm (8.2 to 9.6 inches) in just over 1 month. This is an initial growth rate of approximately 1 mm per day.

Nine months later, this snake's TL was 43 cm

(17 inches), with an average growth rate over that time of about 0.7 mm per day. This female was observed mating in September at 13 months of age, and appeared to be gravid some 12 months later. However, she died in late gestation from what appeared to be a uterine infection. We have seen death in late gestation in a number of rattlesnakes including *C. durissus*.

In fact, the medical problems of this snake in captivity are numerous. Jarchow (1992b) attributed a number of problems to opportunistic pathogenic bacteria. The problems observed included stomatitis (mouth rot), infertility, osteomyelitis (bone infections), and others. Many reptile veterinarians believe captive stress results in immune suppression, which allows for the increase and spread of pathogenic bacteria such as *Salmonella*, *Arizona*, *Pseudomonas*, *Klebsiella*, and *Proteus*, with the resultant lesions mentioned above.

Overall, we have found these snakes to be good-eating adaptable captives. On the basis of the research reported above, it also appears these snakes can be bred fairly easily in captivity, although some have had considerable difficulty. This is only a statement of fact. We do not seek to encourage any illegal collecting activity of these endangered animals (see below).

The fate of these snakes in the wild is very much in question. Those who blame their demise in the wild primarily on illegal collection for the pet trade are not entirely correct, even though this is a very important factor (Baltosser and Hubbard, 1985). Mining and habitat destruction for development have also contributed greatly to their demise. Admittedly, overcollecting by a number of thoughtless selfish individuals hasn't helped and must be curtailed. However, federal and state officials must consider the benefits of a limited harvest for the purposes of captive breeding as recommended by Baltosser and Hubbard (1985).

On the other hand, private collectors must consider the necessity of working within the law. They must not act as individuals, capturing animals illegally at will, with the false belief that they alone will save a species by breeding one or two pairs. They cannot. However, professionals and amateurs can work together for the benefit of this and other species both in the wild and in captivity.

One Arizona ridgenose survived more than 21 years and 3 months in captivity, and a New Mexico ridgenose has been reported to have survived more than 8 years and 11 months in captivity (Snider and Bowler, 1992).

Micruroides euryxanthus
Western Coral Snake

The western coral snake is represented in the United States by its northernmost subspecies, the Arizona coral snake, *M. e. euryxanthus*. This beautiful little snake is found only in southern and central Arizona and extreme southwestern New Mexico and down into Mexico. The adults range in size from 33 to 38 cm (13 to 15 inches) usually, but specimens as large as 61.9 cm (24 inches) (Lowe et al., 1989) and 66 cm (26 inches) (Babb, pers. comm., 1991) have been reported. The 66-cm (26 inches) specimen died in June 2000, having been maintained in captivity for 17 years.

Like the eastern coral snake, they are very secretive, spending a great deal of time hidden

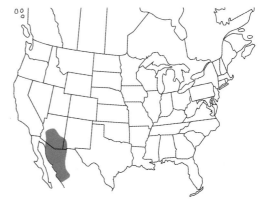

Micruroides euryxanthus

Arizona Coral Snake, *Micruroides euryxanthus euryxanthus* (photo by Jim Rorabaugh)

beneath the surface, emerging occasionally, day or night, for whatever reason. The preferred habitat of this species has been characterized as rocky and gravelly areas with many shrubs or clumps of grass (rocky upland deserts), especially near rivers or streams, but a wide variety of other habitats are occupied (Behler and King, 1979; Stebbins, 1985; Lowe et al., 1986; Ernst, 1992).

Also like its eastern relative and members of the family Elapidae (cobras, kraits, etc.) in general, they are very fond of eating snakes, but other reptiles (lizards) are relished in most cases. Food items reported for this species have included blind snakes, *Leptotyphlops* sp., blackhead snakes, *Tantilla* sp., ground snakes, *Sonora* sp., shovelnose snakes, *Chionactis* sp., leafnose snakes, *Phyllorhynchus* sp., night snakes, *Hypsiglena* sp., other coral snakes and hooknose snakes. Ernst (1992) stated *Ficimia* was also eaten but this was most likely the western hooknose, now *Gyalopion canum*. Finnegan (pers. comm., 1992) reported a roadkilled coral snake on Ruby Road in Santa Cruz County, Arizona, that contained a desert hooknose, *G. quadrangulare*. Those in captivity have also shown interest in the banded sand snake, *Chilomeniscus* sp., and the California

legless lizard, *Anniella* sp. (Wright and Wright, 1957; Fowlie, 1965; Vitt and Hulse, 1973; Behler and King, 1979; Stebbins, 1985; Lowe et al., 1986; Ernst, 1992; Babb, pers. comm., 1992). Fowlie (1965) reported that insect larvae may be also be eaten. Lizards reportedly consumed by wild specimens have included alligator lizards, *Gerrhonotus* sp., desert night lizards, *Xantusia* sp., young whiptails, *Cnemidophorus* sp., and skinks, *Eumeces* sp. (Lowe et al., 1986). Other items taken by captive specimens are listed below. Peccaries, coatis, and opossums are also likely predators of this species (Gehlbach, 1972).

Suspected predators include carnivorous mammals, birds including hawks, owls, and roadrunners, ophiophagous snakes, including kingsnakes and whipsnakes, and invertebrates such as tarantulas (Ernst, 1992).

Mating is believed to occur in the spring, but may also occur in the fall. This results in the deposition of 2–3 eggs sometime in July or August, which hatch in September. The young range 19–20.3 cm (7.5–8.0 inches) in length (Lowe et al., 1986).

Nothing is known on the thermal ecology of this snake, although at present it is believed they are primarily crepuscular or nocturnal during the summer, possibly more active in the morning at other times of the year (Ernst, 1992). Roze (1996) points out that most coral snakes surviving in hot dry areas with little vegetation are primarily nocturnal. Where trees provide more cover and at higher altitudes, these snakes tend to be more diurnal or crepuscular.

Maintaining the western coral snake in captivity is often difficult. They will do well in a desert terrarium with sand as the substrate. A 10-gallon aquarium with a secure tight-fitting lid is usually a suitable enclosure for this species. Heat from above in the form of an incandescent bulb is advisable. Water should be available on the side away from the heat source at all times, and the water may be allowed to overflow every once in a while. This will provide an area of moist sand much like what the coral snake seeks out in nature in order to find its favorite prey, the blind snakes, *Leptotyphlops humilis* and *L. dulcis*. It may also seek refuge in this area to avoid desiccation or overheating. Rocks and plastic cacti are nice additions to the enclosure and will beautify the terrarium.

Good ventilation of this cage arrangement is absolutely essential, or the humidity will rise to unhealthy levels very rapidly. Under no circumstances is the basic cage design considered suitable for this snake. They need the added security of a burrowing substrate or at least numerous deep crevices created by stable rocks. They generally will not accept standard hide boxes used so well by many other snakes.

Feeding the western coral snake does not generally present a problem as long as one can secure a sufficient number of snakes. As mentioned above, the all-time favorite food of this snake is blind snakes. In fact, Dr. Cecil Schwalbe, an Arizona herpetologist, referred to these as the "crème de la crème" on the western coral snake's captive menu. Those who maintain coral snakes are very protective of the location of their secret sources of blind snakes, he warned. Indeed, there are a number of indications that the coral snake is well adapted to prey exclusively upon these widespread little snakes. Their slender form is even suspected of being an adaptation so they may fit easily through the

burrows of their preferred prey (Lowe et al., 1986). So cued is the western coral snake on this particular snake that they will take just about anything else they can swallow that has been scented by them. According to Randy Babb, another herpetologist working for the Arizona Game and Fish Commission, they will usually readily consume small night snakes, *Hypsiglena torquata*, and small longnose snakes, *Rhinocheilus lecontei*, that have been treated in this manner. This is interesting because these two species were included among those items refused by other Arizona coral snakes in captivity, as reported by Vitt and Hulse (1973). Other food items that were refused by the snakes in their care included a glossy snake, garter snake, geckos, spiny lizards, side-blotched lizards, night lizards, and tree lizards. Again, Babb (pers. comm., 1992) noted that one specimen in his care would also consume geckos, side-blotched, tree lizards, night lizards, and earless lizards. Thus, even though this species may have a broad preference for snakes and lizards, there may be a great deal of individual variation.

Those in our care consumed ground snakes with great relish, but ignored hatchling night snakes. They also ignored five-lined skinks, *Eumeces fasciatus*, and ground skinks, *Scincella lateralis*. Others, including Howard Lawler, curator of the Arizona-Sonora Desert Museum, have had some success feeding ground skinks, even though some of these lizards had parasites that freezing did not eliminate and that may have been harmful to the snakes. In one of the first attempts to use a microwave oven to eliminate parasites, Lawler found that the lizards became unpalatable to the snakes, thereby negating any antiparasite value the technique may have held.

In any case, most of these snakes have a strong preference for blind snakes. They seem to prefer live prey but may take them dead, and this will allow long-term storage and some parasite control. It is not known how frequently or severely these snakes may be parasitized, however.

Like the eastern coral snake, the western coral snake may engage in feeding frenzy-type behavior. We have observed this with eastern

---

SPECIES: *Micruroides euryxanthus*, Western Coral Snake
MAINTENANCE DIFFICULTY INDEX: 5 (1 = easiest, 5 = most difficult)
AVERAGE SIZE: 33–38 cm (13–15 inches)
FOOD: Small snake (favorite food blind snake)
CAGE SIZE: 10-gallon aquarium
SUBSTRATE: Sand
VENTRAL HEAT: No
UV LIGHT: No, but an incandescent bulb is strongly advisable
TEMPERATURE RANGE: 20–30°C (77–86°F)
SPECIAL CONSIDERATIONS: *VENOMOUS*. Food (snakes and lizards) is often difficult to
   provide. Coral snakes are shy fossorial snakes that often refuse to eat.

---

coral snakes feeding on hatchling rat snakes, and Lowe et al. (1986) have observed this with the western species when offered a number of blind snakes. Basically, what happens is this: a coral snake that has not eaten for some time emerges from its hiding place and eats a number of snakes all at once, then goes back into hiding for another extended period of time even if other snakes are available in the cage. This feeding strategy may have developed to make use of short-lived abundance such as a nest of hatchlings or a breeding aggregation. In any case, the keeper is strongly advised to take advantage of this behavior by offering multiple meals when the snake is feeding.

Captive breeding of the western coral snake is a very rare occurrence. It is known that 2–3 eggs are laid from July to early August and that the eggs hatch sometime in September. Lowe et al. (1986) report that September newborns measured in the field are 19–20 cm (7.5–8 inches) long and weigh 1.5 grams (0.05 oz). The young presumably have the same taste preferences as adults and need to be fed smaller items more frequently, which makes feeding a juvenile coral snake even more of a challenge.

The following information is a summary of the only record of captive breeding of this species that we could locate. It is based on the notes of Larry Nienaber, related to us in 1997, nearly 20 years after the breeding occurred. All three coral snakes in this description were collected in Maricopa County, Arizona. The female, 48.25 cm (19 inches) TL, had been in captivity for 2 years. The first male (number 1),

35.6 cm (14 inches) TL, was captured on 9 September of the same year. Male number 1 was placed in the female's cage (5-gallon aquarium) on 11 August, and 30 minutes later copulation occurred and lasted 20 minutes. After mating, the female became aggressive toward the male and was removed. Male number 2 was placed in the female's cage on 11 September. Mating occurred immediately and lasted for 15 minutes. No aggressive behavior was observed and copulation was observed again on 16 September. The female continued to feed, eating four snakes in October and November. She was brumated from 2 December to 1 January, then the female was warmed and maintained at 25.5–26.6°C (78–80°F). At this temperature she fed on five more snakes from January through May. During May her abdomen began swelling and on 5 June 1 misshapen egg was laid followed by 3 normal eggs on 26 June. These eggs were incubated in moist vermiculite in a sealed plastic container at 29.4°C (85°F) and hatched on 27 August, an incubation period of 61 days. The 3 hatchlings had a combined weight of 5.08 grams, an average weight of 1.69 grams. Shortly before hatching, the eggs became transparent.

These observations suggest that mating may occur in the fall as well as the spring, and that delayed fertilization is possible.

As with the larger and more dangerous eastern coral snake, the keeper is advised to take all the precautions discussed in the general care section for venomous snakes. Admittedly, these snakes are not nearly as dangerous as any rattlesnake might be to a cautious adult. But once caged, it is the keeper's responsibility to prevent escape and avoid this snake's chance encounter with an unsuspecting child or adult.

The large specimen collected by Babb had been in captivity since 1983. Hence, the captive longevity of this specimen was 17 years, and it was collected as an adult, suggesting that it was at least 20 years old when it died.

Overall, this species is quite a challenge. The difficulty of procuring proper food needs to be taken into consideration. The fact that it is a venomous snake, albeit not a terribly dangerous one, needs to be considered. And last, one needs to remember that these are secretive snakes that appear quite sensitive to disturbance. Thus, only experienced keepers are advised to attempt to maintain this snake.

The authors would again like to thank Larry Nienaber, former supervisor of animal resources at Arizona State University, and James Badman, the current supervisor, for all of their help.

Micrurus fulvius
Eastern Coral Snake

Distinctively marked with red, yellow, and black, the eastern coral snake is one of the most attractive, albeit dangerous, North American snakes. The coral snake may be distinguished from its two mimics, the scarlet kingsnake, *Lampropeltis triangulum elapsoides*, and the scarlet snake, *Cemophora coccinea*, by the presence of a black snout as opposed to a red snout, and the presence of adjacent red and yellow bands along the rest of the body. Typically the mimics possess a red nose and have red bands (or saddles) separated from yellow bands by black bands. The eastern coral snake ranges from southeastern North Carolina southward through all of Florida and westward through southern Arkansas as well as eastern and southern Texas. It also ranges into adjacent Mexico. There are two subspecies within the United States. These include the eastern coral snake, *M. f. fulvius*, which is found east of the Mississippi River and possesses relatively little black pigmentation on the red bands, and the western coral snake, *M. f. tener*, which is found west of the Mississippi River and has more dark-colored pigment in each red band. However, there are a small number of other differences as well. Firstly, there is no overlap of the range of the two subspecies, and certainly no intergrades have been found. Secondly, the black nuchal (or neck) band of the eastern coral snake does not touch the back of the parietal scales, as it does in the western and all other members of this species. Thirdly, there is nearly twice as much protein in the venom of the eastern coral snake as there is in the wstern coral snake venom (Roze, 1996). Hence, there is some question as to whether these are really even the same species, much less subspecies!

These are medium-sized snakes, ranging from 51–76 cm (20–30 inches) in length, with a record length of 120.7 cm (47.5 inches) (Conant and Collins, 1991) for the eastern coral snake and 113.0 cm (44.5 inches) for the Texas coral snake (Roze, 1996).

Coral snakes are found in a wide variety of terrestrial habitats that have been categorized as dry or moist, open or densely vegetated, and dominated by broadleaf deciduous trees or pine trees (Mount, 1975; Jackson and Franz, 1981;

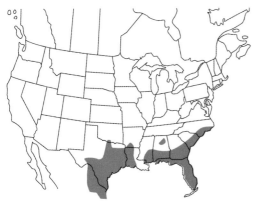

Micrurus fulvius

Eastern Coral Snake, *Micrurus fulvius* (photo by David G. Campbell)

Ashton and Ashton, 1981; Dundee and Rossman, 1989; Palmer, 1990; Roze, 1996). Mount (1975) stated that friable soil was a requirement for this species, and Tennant (1984) mentioned the importance of either rock crevice cover or thick terrestrial plant litter to provide hiding places for them and the snakes on which they prey. Indeed, with regard to habitat preference, this species would be considered a generalist, and it appears fairly adaptable to some of the changes made by humans. However, Roze (1996) strongly suspects that the dramatic environmental changes made by humans have ... had an influence on the activity patterns of both the eastern and Texas coral snakes. He suggests that this may be the reason these snakes are reported to be both diurnal and nocturnal in some areas.

The preferred food of the coral snake is definitely other snakes, with smooth-scaled snakes leading the list. These snakes do not appear to be specialized on one particular species, however, and over 30 species have been reported as food items for wild coral snakes (Wright and Wright, 1957; Jackson and Franz, 1981; Greene, 1984; Tennant, 1984; Vermersch and Kuntz, 1986; Dundee and Rossman, 1989; Ernst and Barbour, 1989; Palmer and Braswell, 1995). Legless lizards or those with reduced legs (e.g., glass lizards, *Ophisaurus*, racerunners, *Cnemidophorus*, skinks, *Eumeces*, sand skinks, *Neoseps*, ground skinks, *Scincella*, and fence lizards, *Sceloporus*) also seem to be taken readily by snakes from many areas, and

in some areas (northern Louisiana) appear to be preferable to other snakes (Clark, 1949). Frogs and small mice as well as centipedes have also been reported as food items for these snakes, although rarely. Another food item is the Florida worm lizard, *Rhineura floridana* (Jackson and Franz, 1981).

More specifically, the prey list for the eastern coral snake includes the following items: ringneck snake, *Diadophis punctatus*, black racer, *Coluber constrictor*, brown snake, *Storeria dekayi*, red-bellied snake, *Storeria occipitomaculata*, mud snake, *Farancia abacura*, crowned snakes, *Tantilla coronata*, *T. gracilis*, *T. relicta*, rough green snake, *Opheodrys aestivus*, smooth and rough earth snakes, *Virginia valeriae* and *V. striatula*, as well as young corn snakes, *Elaphe guttata*, young gray and yellow rat snakes, *Elaphe obsoleta*, young king snakes, *Lampropeltis getula*, and smaller coral snakes. Lizards consumed by the eastern coral snake include the five-lined skinks, *Eumeces fasciatus* and *E. inexpectatus*, the ground skink, *Scincella lateralis*, and the legless lizards, *Ophisaurus* sp. The prey list for the Texas coral snake based upon the research of numerous authors is as follows: rough earth snake, *Virginia striatula* (most common prey), smooth earth snake, *V. valeriae*, ground snake, *Sonora semiannulata*, Texas blind snake, *Leptotyphlops dulcis*, blackhead snakes, *Tantilla* sp., lined snake, *Tropidoclonion lineatum*, brown snake, *Storeria dekayi*, ringneck snake, *Diadophis punctatus*, rough green snake, *Opheodrys aestivus*, and young Texas rat snakes, *Elaphe obsoleta*, common king snakes, *Lampropeltis getula*, prairie kingsnakes, *Lampropeltis calligaster*, Texas patchnose snake, *Salvadora grahamiae*, coachwhip, *Masticophis flagellum*, racer, *Coluber constrictor*, diamondback water snake, *Nerodia rhombifer*, copperhead, *Agkistrodon contortrix*, and other coral snakes. Lizards reported to have been consumed by the Texas coral snake include the following: ground skink, *Scincella lateralis*, five-lined skink, *Eumeces fasciatus*, short-lined skink, *Eumeces tetragrammus*, fence lizards, *Sceloporus* sp., and whiptail lizards, *Cnemidophorus* sp.

The predatory behavior of coral snakes is fascinating. Many observers have described these snakes as alert observant predators that actually appear "intelligent." They may engage in either active foraging or a sit-and-wait mode. The actively foraging snake may rapidly move its head from side to side and probe into crevices as it travels. Neill (1957) reported that some specimens may even probe with their tails, and hypothesized that they were attempting to flush prey items out into their waiting jaws. Once prey is detected, a coral snake may act much like a cat stalking its prey. When the prey is stationary, they move very slowly, but when the prey attempts to flee, they rapidly follow it. Roze (1996) believes that prey is initially located by olfactory cues, especially pheromone trails. These "social hormones" are laid down by snakes, including other coral snakes, in order to communicate information to other snakes of the same species. Once prey is located, it is grasped in the coral snake's mouth and held firmly until it stops thrashing. With very small prey (snakes and lizards), the snake may rapidly walk its jaws toward the head of the prey without waiting for complete immobilization. Greene (1976) showed that coral snakes are able to distinguish the front end of a prey item by the direction of its overlapping scales. With larger prey items, the snake may actually bury its head under coils of its own body to protect itself from being struck by its struggling prey. For vigoriously struggling prey, the coral snake may actually use several loops of its body to hold it down. Struggles rarely last longer than 20 minutes. The bite of the coral snake is powerful and usually visibly compresses the prey animal. Swallowing is a rapid side-to-side motion which, as mentioned above, is almost always from the front of the prey item backward. Prey snakes are usually not released during the entire process, although this happens

Texas Coral Snake, *Micrurus fulvius tener* (photo by R. D. Bartlett)

occasionally. One of the interesting observations about coral snakes is that they appear to demonstrate a "feeding frenzy." Once they have fed, they appear to actively seek more, and may feed on a number of snakes at one time. Roze (1996) refers to this as a period of "feeding excitement," which is characterized by increased tongue flicking, head movement, and searching behavior. Then, after what appears to be a gluttonous meal, they stop as quickly as they started, seek shelter, and abstain from feeding for weeks. Greene (1984) reported that a coral snake may eat prey specimens weighing up to 130% of its body weight. One story about the closely related *M. corallinus* showed just how soon coral snakes become cannibalistic and how much they can eat. Eight hatchlings were placed in a cage overnight. The following morning only four snakes were found with the tails of their siblings protruding from their mouths. Soon afterward, even these four died, apparently from ingesting a meal too large!

As mentioned above, cannibalism is fairly common in both subspecies of *Micrurus fulvius*. Roze (1996) stated that 2% of the prey of *M. fulvius* was other *M. fulvius*, except in Florida where that number exceeds 4% of the prey taken.

Known predators include hawks, shrikes, other snakes including kingsnakes and other coral snakes, and fire ants (Jackson and Franz, 1981). One coral snake was eaten by a bullfrog (Minton, 1949).

The reproductive behavior of both subspecies of *Micrurus fulvius* has been fairly well studied. Mating usually occurs from fall through early spring and females may retain sperm and delay ovulation for several months (Quinn, 1979; Jackson and Franz, 1981). Male snakes may reach sexual maturity at 1 year of age (as early as 11 months for *M. f. fulvius* and 12 months for *M. f. tener*). Females may reach sexual maturity at 2 years, such that they can usually lay their first clutch of eggs during the summer of their third year, at a minimum size of 55 cm. The Texas coral snake may lay 2–12 eggs (usually 6–10), while the eastern coral snake may lay 2–13 eggs (usually 5–9) (Telford, 1955).

These eggs are usually deposited only once yearly, although oviposition may be delayed up to several weeks when appropriate conditions are not available or if the female is disturbed. Thus, a female coral snake may lay part of her clutch at one time, and several weeks later lay the rest. Therefore, the incubation period of coral snakes may vary tremendously depending on the time of fertilization and the time the fertilized eggs were retained in the oviduct, as well as the temperature and humidity the eggs are exposed to after they are deposited. Eggs of this species have hatched in 45–92 days depending primarily on the temperatures to which they were exposed during incubation. These eggs will nearly double in weight throughout their incubation. Rose (1996) warns that coral snake eggs laid in captivity frequently fail to hatch, presumably because of some disturbance of the mother or inadequate captive conditions.

Hatchlings of the eastern coral snake measure 18–23 cm (7–9 inches) TL while the hatchlings of the Texas coral snake measure 16.5–23.9 cm (6.5–9.4 inches) in TL (Campbell, 1973; Conant and Collins, 1991). Hatchlings may emerge within several hours or take over 24 hours to emerge from their eggs once they have "pipped." They usually shed within 2–20 days of age and often accept their first meal within 2 days of hatching (Rose, 1996). Neonates can be sexed by measuring tail lengths of each member of the clutch and dividing the hatchlings into two distinct size ranges. More specifically a tail length to total length ratio is very useful for determining the probable sex of the neonates. Counting subcaudal scales is another way to determine the sex of the individual in question. Males generally have 40–47 subcaudal scales while females generally have 30–37 subcaudal scales.

The eastern coral snake is the big challenge among our venomous snakes. It *cannot* be set up using the basic cage design or it will usually starve to death. It has been successfully maintained using cypress or pine mulch (not chips) with pieces of bark laid on top. (Mehrtens mentions that a glass or plastic plate may be used instead of bark to allow better visibility of the snake.) Pawley (1983) also mentions the successful use of a glass plate, but added that artificial plexiglass hollow logs were situated

---

SPECIES: *Micrurus fulvius*, Eastern Coral Snake
MAINTENANCE DIFFICULTY INDEX: 5 (1 = easiest, 5 = most difficult)
AVERAGE SIZE: 51–76 cm (20–30 inches)
FOOD: Crowned snakes, ringneck snakes, garter snakes, ground skinks, glass lizards,
    hatchling corn and rat snakes. Small frogs?
CAGE SIZE: 10–20-gallon long
SUBSTRATE: Cypress mulch or pine mulch
VENTRAL HEAT: Yes
UV LIGHT: Not essential but probably helpful
TEMPERATURE RANGE: 22–24°C (72–75°F)
SPECIAL CONSIDERATIONS: *VENOMOUS*. Can be very poor eater in captivity (some
    never will). Permit required.

---

over moist sphagnum moss topped with wood chips. This arrangement allowed the snakes to hide even though visible through the cage glass when the log was placed against it. It also allowed the snakes to hydroregulate. This is an important concept in herpetoculture which has only recently been addressed by snake keepers. In fact, Harvey Lillywhite, a well-known physiologist at the University of Florida, believes that many snakes succumb in captivity because of chronic dehydration due to the absence of suitable microhabitats. Indeed, Roze (1996) warns that captive coral snakes are very prone to dysecdysis (difficult shedding) if the case humidity is too low. In this captive environment, some will eat snakes of many different species, glass lizards, worm lizards, or small skinks (legless reptiles are apparently the preferred food), but others will flatly refuse to eat. "Okefenokee Joe" Flood said that one of his coral snakes would eat only tricolored snakes (scarlet kings, scarlets, and smaller coral snakes). This snake refused a black racer that had been painted to resemble a preferred species! In fact, when asked about techniques used to feed coral snakes in captivity, a well-respected herpetologically oriented head curator from a southeastern zoo said two words, "Force-feed!" As you might imagine, force-feeding is both a stressful and dangerous proposition with this snake and is not a viable alternative for a long-term breeding specimen.

Whether they are eating voluntarily or not, most of their preferred food items are not likely to be "clean" unless you are lucky enough to have one that eats pinkies, which you have rubbed with frozen reptiles. Therefore, it is recommended that the food items (probably mostly other snakes) be frozen and thawed as discussed in the general care section.

Specimens from northern Florida in our care ate hatchling rat snakes (yellow rat snakes, gray rat snakes, corn snakes) with great relish. They also consumed ribbon snakes, garter snakes, and striped whipsnake hatchlings. All of these were road kills that had been frozen and thawed, except for the whipsnakes. Those snakes that are eating voluntarily will often take dead food. You will improve the chances of a successful feeding by offering food in the morning or early evening since these snakes appear to be more active at these hours. Also remember that these snakes may refuse to eat for months, and patience as well as multiple food items will often result in a feeding snake.

A bowl of clean water should always be provided.

A UV light source is probably not necessary, but creating a horizontal temperature gradient with a heating pad and incandescent bulb may be of some value. A 10–20-gallon long aquarium is a good size for most of these snakes.

Brumation should be carried out as discussed in the general care section. Captive breedings are rare at this time, so attempt breeding as described in the general care section. (See Table 5, the reproduction chart.)

Also, because of the diet, this snake requires a fecal exam initially and regularly thereafter.

Tryon and McCrystal (1982) reported on one of the few successful captive breedings of the Texas coral snake. Mating was observed on 12 May and 8 eggs were deposited on 18 June, a gestation period of 37 days. All eggs hatched on 6 August at temperatures ranging from 25 to 32°C (77 to 90°F). The incubation period was 49 days. The 8 eggs weighted 28.3 grams, and the female after egg deposition weighed 32 grams. This represented a materal investment of 46.9%, which is similar to the maternal investment of many colubrid snakes.

Eggs should be removed and incubated in a plastic container with vermiculite. Roze (1996) recommends vermiculite moistened with an equal volume of water, which is a larger amount of water than we have used for most North American snakes. The eggs are generally very elongated, but the shape varies, as does the color. Some are yellowish, others are white, and some are nearly transparent.

Lastly, do not take shortcuts with cage security because of the small size and generally mellow disposition of this captive snake. It is a wonderful escape artist and it possesses a deadly neurotoxic venom which, if delivered, is more likely to kill you than any of our native eastern vipers' venoms. So use a locking top and all other venomous snake modifications and procedures. A permit is required to keep this snake in captivity in most states.

With regard to disposition, one word characterizes these snakes: nervous. Too much disturbance or an insufficient hiding area will result in an anorectic specimen. Cypress mulch of sufficient depth to allow burrowing and hiding areas as described will help tremendously. Handly only as necessary for medical treatment. Roze (1996) believes that the Texas coral snake is more nervous and aggressive than the eastern coral snake.

One individual was maintained for 10 years and 8 months at the Brookfield Zoo (Snider and Bowler, 1992). Ernst (1992) reported one that had been in captivity for 18 years at the Fort Worth Zoo.

Pelamis platurus
Yellowbelly Sea Snake

This is the most widespread snake in the world, ranging all the way from the western coast of southern Africa to northwestern South America, and northward to Japan and the southern coast of California (Heatwole, 1987). This range includes most of the coast of Southeast Asia and the northern and eastern coasts of Australia. They are often found far out at sea. In the United States, they have been found only as far north as San Clemente, California, in Orange County (Stebbins, 1985).

The preferred habitat of the yellowbelly sea snake appears to be shallow coastal waters, where the density of prey may be greater, and calmer warmer waters may be found (Ernst, 1992), particularly where there is surface debris such as seaweed and wood. The former also reported that they are usually found in waters ranging from 22 to 30°C (71.6 to 86°F).

These snakes are generally black or dark

Pelamis platurus

brown above and as the name indicates, yellow to pale yellow below. Occasionally, solid yellow specimens are observed (Tu, 1976). The tail is usually mottled or spotted with black, and is laterally compressed (oarlike). Adults range

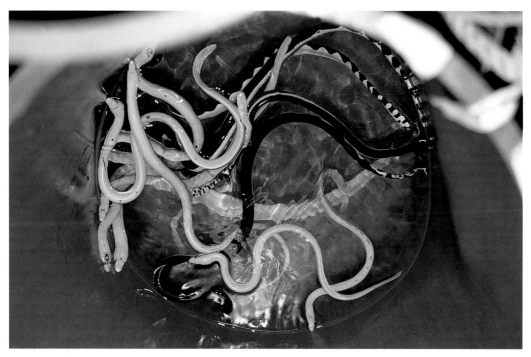

Yellow-bellied Sea Snake, *Pelamis platurus* (photo by Harold Voris)

50–113 cm (20–45 inches) in length (Stebbins, 1985).

The yellowbelly sea snake is a fascinating animal. Highly adapted for sea life, it possesses a tremendous number of morphological and physiological adaptations for survival. The morphological adaptations include dorsally placed nares (nostrils) with valves, smooth non-overlapping scales, and the broad flat tail mentioned above. Physiological adaptations include a high oxygen-carrying capacity of the blood, salt secretion via a sublingual salt gland, and skin impermeable to sodium (Pough and Lillywhite, 1984; Dunson and Dunson, 1975; Dunson and Robinson, 1976). *Pelamis* may be one of the few snakes that is both venomous and poisonous. Apparently, its meat is both distasteful and toxic to a number of predators, such that even when skinned and cut into pieces and colored differently, fish still refuse to eat it, or regurgitate it if they do (Heatwole, 1987). Hence, several authors have suggested that the bright yellow color is aposematic (warning) coloration. Known predators are rare, but include pufferfish and leopard seals (Heatwole,

1987). Other predators that have been observed to try eating these snakes in captivity usually regurgitate the snakes afterward or die, and hence they may not be true predators of this species in nature. Even the leopard seal mentioned above regurgitated the snake it had swallowed and appeared ill, according to Heatwole.

Parasites of the yellowbelly sea snake have been reported to include barnacles, but these are not true parasites since they do not derive any nourishment from the snakes. They may, however, interfere with vision or locomotion. Heatwole (1987) reported a turbellarian on one *Pelamis*. Other sea snakes have been found with intestinal nematodes, lungworms, ticks, and mites.

The preferred optimal temperature range for this snake appears to be 28–32°C (82.4–89.6°F) (Ernst, 1992), while the critical thermal minimum and maximum temperatures have been reported at 11.7°C and 36°C (53.1°F and 96.8°F) respectively (Graham et al., 1971).

The preferred diet of *Pelamis* is fish, almost any kind of fish and almost any size fish that it can swallow. Fish from nearly 20 families have been reported (Klawe, 1964; Kropach, 1975). They may also eat squid, cuttlefish, and crabs. Water currents and olfaction, but not vision, are believed to play a major role in food selection and capture (Heatwole, 1987).

Breeding is thought to occur most times of the year in tropical areas, and when the average monthly water temperature is above 20°C (68°F) in cooler areas (Dunson and Ehlert, 1971). Litter sizes range 1–8 and the neonates range 22–26 cm (8.6–10.2 inches) TL (Kropach, 1975). Kropach thought that the gestation period was at least 6 months, and possibly longer in many cases.

As might be expected, these snakes are rarely maintained in captivity, except in research laboratories or large public aquariums. However, this species can be maintained in captivity in a large aquarium with filtered seawater (real or synthetic) kept in the ranges discussed above. Mehrtens (1987) stated that a constant temperature of 29°C (85°F) was suitable, but we feel that some fluctuation would be well tolerated and possibly beneficial, especially on a seasonal basis.

Large aquariums with rounded corners are preferred because these snakes have a tendency to injure their noses in corners. In addition, floating real or plastic plants and floating driftwood or cork should be added to provide hiding or resting areas for these snakes. The bottom can be set up as any other salt water aquarium. These snakes probably should be housed individually if they are in a small aquarium, as they have been known to bite each other in a feeding frenzy.

In captivity, these snakes will readily feed on both live and dead fish. Dead fish are usually taken when shaken near the snake on a long pair of tongs. Interestingly, both salt- and freshwater fish will be consumed, even fish as common as goldfish.

Check your local regulations before attempting to acquire or maintain this snake. It is illegal to keep them in many states. They possess a potent venom and are highly dangerous.

Captive longevity has been reported at 3 years and 5 months and that specimen was still alive at the time of that report (Snider and Bowler, 1992). Several other members of this species have died at just over 2 years in captivity.

Sistrurus catenatus
Massasauga

The massasauga is a small to medium-sized rattlesnake, ranging 35.6–76.2 cm (14–30 inches) in length, with a record of 100.3 cm (39.5 inches). They may be quickly distinguished from all other rattlesnakes except the pygmy by the nine large plates on top of the head (which is the reason they have been placed in the genus *Sistrurus* with the pygmy rattlesnake rather than the genus *Crotalus* with all of the other rattlesnakes) and the two elongated spots that extend from the head onto the neck. Otherwise, they are similar in overall appearance to many other rattlesnakes in that they have a series of large brown or black saddles or blotches along the back and smaller spots along the sides. In some cases however, they may be solid black.

There are three subspecies that vary considerably in size and coloration. The three subspecies are: the eastern massasauga, *S. c. catenatus*, the western massasauga, *S. c. tergeminus*, and the desert massasauga, *S. c. edwardsii*. Basically, the eastern subspecies is the largest and darkest colored of the three, with the ventral color usually being black or gray. The western subspecies is smaller and lighter colored, usually having a light-colored ventral surface with dark spots along the edges. The desert subspecies is the smallest of the three (a dwarf subspecies) and has a plain light-colored ventral surface with few or no black spots. The eastern massasauga is found from central New York and southern Ontario southward and westward into eastern Iowa and Missouri. The western massasauga ranges from western Iowa and Missouri southward through central Texas where it inter-

Sistrurus catenatus

grades with the desert massasauga. The desert massasauga is found in southern and western Texas and westward through southeastern Arizona and southeastern Colorado (where it intergrades with the western massasauga).

The habitat varies somewhat from subspecies to subspecies, but basically this appears to be a snake of open wet areas such as swamps in the east, wet prairies centrally, and grasslands in the west (Wright and Wright, 1957; Fowlie, 1965; Webb, 1970; Klauber, 1972; Behler and King, 1979; Tennant, 1984; Hudson, 1985; Stebbins, 1985; Hammerson, 1986; Lowe et al., 1986; Holman et al., 1990; Christiansen and Bailey, 1990; Conant and Collins, 1991; Ernst, 1992; Degenhardt et al., 1996).

The massasauga has taken a plethora of food items in the wild. These have included fish, amphibians (treefrogs, *Hyla* sp., true frogs, *Rana* sp., toads, *Bufo* sp.), reptiles (whiptail lizards, *Cnemidophorus* sp., earless lizards, *Holbrookia* sp., leopard lizards, *Gambelia* sp., Texas spiny lizard, *Sceloporus olivaceus*, garter snakes, *Thamnophis* sp., ground snakes, *Sonora semiannulata*, lined snake, *Tropidoclonion lineatum*, brown or redbelly snakes, *Storeria* sp., hognose snakes, *Heterodon* sp.), birds (field sparrows, lark sparrows and their eggs, redwinged blackbird), mammals (pocket mice, voles, deer mice, shrews), insects, centipedes, and crayfish (Wright and Wright, 1957; Fowlie, 1965; Klauber, 1972; Keenlyne and Beer, 1973; Lardie, 1976; Best, 1978; Tennant, 1984; Stebbins, 1985; Brush and Ferguson, 1986; Lowe et al., 1986; Seigel, 1986; Conant and Collins,

1991; Ernst, 1992). One long-term captive also ate a young rabbit, chicks, a bat, a mole, two racerunners, a collared lizard, and pieces of meat of various kinds (Loewen in Klauber, 1972). There appears to be a considerable amount of variation in the diet of these snakes, with those from drier areas consuming more reptilian prey and those from moister areas consuming more amphibian prey, with all groups studied to date being rodent eaters and some almost exclusively rodent eaters.

Predators are known to include loggerhead shrikes (Chapman and Casto, 1972), blue racers (Minton, 1972), and domestic hogs (Harding, 1997). Suspected predators include herons, egrets, hawks, raccoons, skunks, foxes, cats, bobcats, and badgers (Ernst, 1992). This species is considered threatened in most states due primarily to habitat destruction.

Mating in the wild has been recorded only in the late summer and fall, although captive breedings have occurred in the spring and numerous authors have reported that spring breeding may occur in the wild also (Fitch, 1970; Chiszar et al., 1976; Lowe et al., 1986; Hammerson, 1986; Ernst, 1992). Litters of 2–19 (8–10 usually) are born in mid- to late summer after a gestation period of around 4 months (delayed fertilization and ovulation occur if mating occurs in the fall).

Eastern Massasauga, *Sistrurus catenatus catenatus* (photo by Steve Barten)

Western Massasauga, *Sistrurus catentus tergeminus* (photo by David G. Campbell)

The young snakes range 14–25 cm (5.5–10 inches) in length. The smallest subspecies, the desert massasauga, has the smallest young, but not much smaller than the large eastern massasauga. Lowe et al. (1986) reported that the juveniles of this subspecies were relatively large, less than an inch shorter than the smallest newborn of the larger races.

Very little is recorded in the literature on the thermal ecology of these snakes. It is known that they experience seasonal activity shifts from diurnal to nocturnal during the warm season (Seigel, 1986), as appears common with many other snakes.

The massasauga is not at all a difficult snake to maintain. It is similar to the pygmy rattlesnake in its adaptability to captivity, except that the young massasaugas are easier to care for. Clarence Wright, former reptile curator at the Lincoln Park Zoo in Chicago, stated that the babies did so well in captivity that they had to find places to "get rid of some." The massasauga requires the same basic cage arrangement as discussed in the general care section, with

the venomous snake additions. As with the other vipers, a UV light source seems really helpful as does ventral heat.

Air temperatures suitable for the maintenance of these snakes probably safely ranges from 24 to 33°C (75 to 91°F) during the day and down to 18–20°C (64–68°F) at night. One desert massasauga in our care thrived at daytime air temperatures ranging from 20 to 35°C (80 to 95°F) and 24–27°C (75–80°F) at night. Interestingly, when this snake first arrived, it experienced an unexpected drop to 10°C (50°F) for 2 nights. The absence of a ventral heat source and perhaps the stress of the recent environmental change resulted in a severe respiratory infection. Fortunately, the snake responded nicely to supplemental heat and a course of amikacin at the usual dose. After the addition of the ventral heat source, this snake recovered completely and ate regularly thereafter. This is not meant to imply that these snakes cannot tolerate lower temperatures than this, only that a ventral heat source may be a valuable cage addition for these animals. In

---

SPECIES: *Sistrurus catenatus*, Massasauga
MAINTENANCE DIFFICULTY INDEX: 2 (1 = easiest, 5 = most difficult)
AVERAGE SIZE: 35–76 cm (14–30 inches)
FOOD: Mice
CAGE SIZE: 10–20-gallon aquarium
SUBSTRATE: Indoor-outdoor carpet, artificial turf, or cypress mulch
VENTRAL HEAT: Yes
UV LIGHT: Yes
TEMPERATURE RANGE: 24–33°C (75–91°F)
SPECIAL CONSIDERATIONS: *VENOMOUS*. Nervous initially but generally adapts nicely to
    captivity. Good eaters. Protected species in some states. Permit needed.

---

deed, this snake and others will normally undergo temperatures much lower than this during brumation.

Even though in the wild they will take amphibians, fish, other snakes, small bird eggs, crayfish, and insects, their preferred food (in captivity) appears to be mice, and small mice seem to be favored. In addition, most will readily take their food dead, which facilitates quality control of the diet.

Clarence Wright also warns that massasaugas are commonly parasitized, with both external (mites) and internal parasites. Thus, a fecal exam should be performed initially and regularly thereafter. The mites can be treated with an ivermectin-loaded mouse as discussed in the section on speckled rattlesnakes and others (this will work for many of the internal parasites as well). Placing the snake in 5% Sevin dust for 3–8 hours has also been useful in helping to eliminate mites.

Females will usually reach sexual maturity in their third year. Please note that this species may breed only every other year. Breeding has occurred numerous times in captivity and can be accomplished as described in the general care section, right after brumation. Brumation can be carried out in the regular cage in the usual manner discussed in the general care section. Like the other pit vipers, massasaugas bear live young, which are ready to eat almost immediately. The preferred food of the babies is pinkies.

Unlike some other rattlesnakes, adult massasaugas adjust rapidly to captivity. However, many will stop eating if they do not have a hide box, Wright warns. It has been our experience that these snakes are inquisitive voracious feeders in spite of their high-strung personality. Perhaps their most characteristic behavior is a sudden change in the position of their head when they see something of interest. This cocking of the head occurs so rapidly and smartly that one often wonders if it really happened or if it was imagined. Yet it has been observed by us with both the eastern and desert subspecies.

Another common behavior when food is added to the cage is the mouth gaping and shaking that has been observed in other rattlesnakes. The purpose of this gape and shake has been suggested to aid the snake in picking up airborne particles by increasing the amount of air exposed to the vomeronasal organ. First-time keepers will often falsely diagnose a massasauga as having a respiratory infection because of this sneezinglike activity.

Bites from this species are generally not fatal but can be painful. The junior author received a bite on the thumb from a western massasauga. Pain, swelling, and numbness were mild and of short duration, but it is possible that this was primarily a dry bite. Other bites have caused severe pain, nausea, cold sweats, and death (Ernst, 1992).

These snakes may be quite long-lived in captivity. One eastern massasauga survived more than 11 years and 8 months, while a desert massasauga survived more than 12 years and 3 months and a western massasauga survived 20 years and 0 months (Snider and Bowler, 1992).

Sistrurus miliarius
Pygmy Rattlesnake

The pygmy rattlesnake is so named because it is the smallest of the eastern rattlesnakes. Individuals of this species rarely exceed 61 cm (24 inches) with most ranging from 38–53 cm (15–22 inches) and the record length being 80.3 cm (31.5 inches) (Conant and Collins, 1991). These snakes are usually tan to gray in background color, but may be reddish in some areas, with a series of dark brown to black rounded blotches running the length of the back. They also usually have a series of smaller dark blotches running lengthwise along each side. The head is marked with two diagonal dark stripes angling backward from the eye in most specimens, and they usually have two dark stripes on top of the head which extend onto the neck, as seen in their closest relative, the massasauga, *S. catenatus*. Like that species, they have nine large scales on the top of the head rather than many small ones as seen in most of the other rattlesnakes (*Crotalus* sp.).

The species ranges widely in the southeastern part of the United States from northern North Carolina southward to include all of Florida and westward through extreme southern Tennessee, western Kentucky, Missouri, Oklahoma, and eastern Texas. There are three

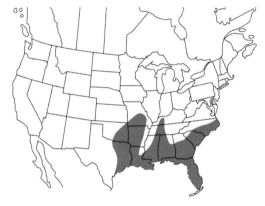

Sistrurus miliarius

Dusky Pygmy Rattlesnake, *Sistrurus miliarius barbouri* (photo by David G. Campbell)

Carolina Pygmy Rattlesnake (red phase),
Sistrurus miliarius miliarius (photo by R. D.
Bartlett)

subspecies, the Carolina pygmy rattlesnake, *S. m. miliarius*, the dusky pygmy rattlesnake, *S. m. barbouri*, and the western pygmy rattlesnake, *S. m. streckeri*. The Carolina pygmy ranges from the Carolinas westward through northern Alabama and may be recognized by its relatively clean pattern with only one or two rows of lateral blotches. It and the dusky pygmy have 25 scale rows toward the middle to front half of the body and 23 scale rows toward the back half. The dusky pygmy ranges from extreme southeastern South Carolina southward throughout Florida and westward to southern Alabama. This subspecies is recognized by its mottled or dusty appearance due to the presence of two or three rows of indistinct lateral blotches and dark stippling over much of the body. The western pygmy rattlesnake ranges westward from western Alabama to occupy Mississippi, western Tennessee, and Kentucky and all areas to the west in which this species occurs. It may be recognized by its light ground color, clean pattern, and usually transverse bars instead of blotches along the back, as well as a slightly lower scale row count (23 toward the front, 21 toward the back).

The preferred habitat of the pygmy rattlesnake appears to be any area near water and has included a wide variety of vegetational types. These have included pine flatwoods, mixed pine and hardwood forest, scrub pinewoods, wiregrass flatwoods, palmetto flatwoods, and cutover pine woods (Wright and Wright, 1957; Mount, 1975; Ashton and Ashton, 1981; Palmer, 1990). Mount (1975) states that the habitats for all three subspecies in Alabama appear to be similar. However, it follows riparian corridors and other moist woodland areas (Tennant,

Western Pygmy Rattlesnake, *Sistrurus miliarius streckeri* (photo by R. D. Bartlett)

SPECIES: *Sistrurus miliarius*, Pygmy Rattlesnake
MAINTENANCE DIFFICULTY INDEX: 2 (1 = easiest, 5 = most difficult)
AVERAGE SIZE: 38–56 cm (15–22 inches)
FOOD: Mice, frogs, lizards
CAGE SIZE: 10–20-gallon long
SUBSTRATE: Artificial turf, indoor-outdoor carpet, or newspaper
VENTRAL HEAT: Yes
UV LIGHT: Not essential but may be helpful
TEMPERATURE RANGE: 20–25°C (68–77°F)
SPECIAL CONSIDERATIONS: *VENOMOUS*. May refuse pinkies when very young, but
   great eaters as they mature. Easiest venomous snake to keep. Permit required.

1984), until in the extreme western part of its range, the pygmy rattlesnake is apparently restricted to moist grasslands (Ernst, 1992). It may also be found in rocky areas (Dundee and Rossman, 1989). Surface cover, including logs, rocks, or thick vegetation, is considered critical for the survival of these snakes in some areas, and they are commonly found under both natural and man-made objects during the day. The senior author once found a pair of pygmy rattlesnakes under a large concrete slab in the Tampa, Florida, area. They also reportedly climb into trees occasionally (Klauber, 1972). We observed a juvenile specimen basking on top of a palmetto leaf at a height of approximately 1 meter near a small clearing just north of Gainesville, Florida. Other small species of rattlesnakes have been observed to climb in an apparent effort to escape predation (Rossi and Feldner, 1994), and perhaps these snakes do so as well.

The food of this small rattlesnake has been reported to include frogs, lizards, small snakes, mice, small birds, insects, centipedes, and spiders (Clark, 1949; Wright and Wright, 1957; Tennant, 1984). In fact, young captives readily consume crickets and lizards (Verkerk, 1987; personal observation). More specifically, anoles, *Anolis* sp., and skinks, *Scincella* and *Eumeces*, have been consumed, as have ringneck snakes, *Diadophis* sp., water snakes, *Nerodia* sp., ribbon snakes, *Thamnophis* sp., as well as other pygmy rattlesnakes.

Known predators of this species include other snakes such as kingsnakes and indigo snakes, predatory mammals, such as skunks, opossums, cats, dogs, and predatory birds (Ernst, 1992).

Mating is known to occur in both the spring and the fall, with 3–10 young being born in the fall following mating (Anderson, 1965; Mount, 1975; Fitch, 1985). The young range 10–22 cm (4.0–7.5 inches) in length at birth (Behler and King, 1979; Conant and Collins, 1991).

The pygmy rattlesnake is not a difficult snake to maintain in captivity. It will do well with the basic cage setup as described under general care, with venomous snake modifications. Mehrtens states that some individuals prefer a pile of leaves or pine needles rather than a hide box, but the individuals we worked with did fine with small dark hideboxes. They will eat live or dead captive-raised mice, and so it is easy to effect quality control of their food.

They can be brumated and bred relatively easily using the techniques described in the general care section, but they seem to do well even if not brumated. A UV light source is recommended but probably not essential for this species. The females bear live young in the late summer.

The big problem with the pygmy rattlesnakes is getting the babies to start eating, according to Fred Antonio, experienced reptile curator, and we must agree. "If they won't eat pinkies, they may consume frogs or lizards, but many won't switch over," says Fred. "But once they get started they are hard to kill," he added. Wild specimens have been known to eat a wide variety of food items including insects, spiders, centipedes, snakes and birds, in addition to mice, according to Ernst and Barbour (1989).

In our experience, babies will readily accept skinks and anoles (except Cuban anoles, *Anolis sagrei*) but refuse pinkies until after their first brumation period.

It has been our experience that these snakes are very hardy consistently feeding and shedding captives that would make perfect pets if they weren't venomous! Because of their small size, they will do very well in a 10–20-gallon aquarium with a weighted and locking screen top. House them singly.

A fecal exam should be performed on recent captives in order to head off potential parasite problems. Also don't forget to follow the general rules for venomous snakes. Do not allow yourself to become careless because of the snake's small size! *IT IS VENOMOUS AND CAN INFLICT A SERIOUS BITE!!*

Mattison states that an occasional misting may be of some value.

One of these specimens has survived over 16 years in captivity (Snider and Bowler, 1992).

REFERENCES

Acha, P. N., and B. Szyfres. 1980. Zoonoses and Communicable Diseases Common to Man and Animals. Pan American Health Organization WHO, Washington, DC.

Adler, K. K., and S. G. Tilley. 1960. A fish and a snail in the diet of *Natrix septemvittata* (Say). J. Ohio Herpetol. Soc. 2:28–29.

Alderton, D. 1986. A Petkeepers Guide to Reptiles and Amphibians. Salamander Books Limited, New York, 117 pp.

Aldridge, R. D. 1992. Oviductal anatomy and seasonal sperm storage in the southeastern crowned snakes. (*Tantilla coronata*). Copeia 1992:1103–1106.

Allen, M. E. 1989. Dietary induction and prevention of osteodystrophy in an insectivorous reptile *Eublepharis macularius*: Characterization by radiography and histopathology, pp. 83–84. Third International Colloquium on the Pathology of Reptile and Amphibians Abstracts.

Allen, W. B., Jr. 1992. The Snakes of Pennsylvania. Reptile and Amphibian Magazine, Pottsville, PA.

Alpaugh, W. C. 1980. Earthworm (*Lumbricus terrestris*) consumption in captive garter snakes, *Thamnophis sirtalis*. Herp. Review 11:93.

Anderson, C. 1992. Care and Captive Breeding of the Desert Glossy Snake, *Arizona elegans eburnata*. New England Herpetol. Soc. Newsletter 14(1):1–3.

Anderson, P. K. 1965. The Reptiles of Missouri. University of Missouri Press, Columbia, MO, 330 pp.

Annandale, N. 1907. Notes on the fauna of a desert tract in southern India. Part I. Batrachians and reptiles of the desert region of the Northwest frontier. Mem. Asiatic Soc. Bengal 1:183–202.

Applegate, R. 1987. Captive breeding of the Durango Mountain Kingsnake, *Lampropeltis mexicana greeri*, and the Arizona Mountain Kingsnake, *L. pyromelana*. In R. O. Gowan (Ed.), Proceedings of the Third Northern California Herpetological Society's Conference on the Captive Propagation of Reptiles and Amphibians, pp. 87–95.

——. 1989. Methodology for obtaining multiple clutches of eggs in one season from Colubrid snakes. In Northern California Herpetol. Soc. Sp. Publ. No. 5, Captive Propagation of Reptiles and Amphibians.

——. 1992. The General Care and Maintenance of Milk Snakes. Advanced Vivarium Systems, Lakeside, CA, 71 pp.

Armstrong, B. L., and J. B. Murphy. 1979. The natural history of Mexican rattlesnakes. Univ. Kansas Publ. Mus. Nat. Hist. Special Publ. No. 5, pp. 1–88.

Arnold, S. J. 1977. Polymorphism and geographic variation in the feeding behavior of the garter snake, *Thamnophis elegans*. Science 197:676–678.

——. 1980. The microevolution of feeding behavior. In A. Kamil and T. Sargent (Eds.), Foraging Ecology: Ecological, Ethological, and Psychological Approaches. Garland Press, New York, pp. 409–455.

Arny, S. A. 1949. A survey of the reptiles and amphibians of the Delta National Wildlife Refuge. Unpublished Master's Thesis, 1948, Tulane Univ. Abstracts of Theses: 97–98.

Ashton R. E., and P. S. Ashton. 1981. Handbook of Reptiles and Amphibians of Florida. Part One, The Snakes. Windward Publishing, Miami, FL.

Asplund, K. K. 1963. Ecological factors in

the distribution of *Thamnophis brachystoma* (Cope). Herpetologica 19:128–132.

Assetto, R., Jr. 1978. Reproduction of the gray-banded kingsnake, *Lampropeltis mexicana alterna.* Herp. Review 9:56–57.

Babero, B. B., and F. H. Emerson. 1974. *Thubunaea cnemidopborus* in Nevada rattlesnakes. J. Parasitol. 60:595.

Backner, B. 1990. The effect of calcium/ phosphate and vitamin D3 supplementation on growth rates of hatching rat snakes. In Alan W. Zulich (Ed.), Proceedings of the 14th International Herpetological Symposium, Dallas-Fort Worth.

Ball, R. L. 1990. Captive propagation of the Kansas glossy snake, *Arizona e. elegans.* In Alan W. Zulich (Ed.), Proceedings of the 14th International Herpetological Symposium, Dallas-Fort Worth.

Baltosser, W. H., and J. P. Hubbard. 1985. New Mexico Ridgenose Rattlesnake Recovery Program. U.S. Fish and Wildlife Service, Albuquerque, NM.

Barnard, S. M. 1985. Reptile care: relating to the inquiring novice. Parts 1–14. Animal Keepers Forum. American Association of Zoo Keepers, Topeka, KS.

Barten, S. L. 1980. The consumption of turtle eggs by a western hognose snake, *Heterodon nasicus*: A field observation. Bull. Chicago Herp. Soc. 15:97–98.

——. 1981. Reproduction of *Lampropeltis triangulum elapsoides* from Onslow County, North Carolina. Herp. Review 12:62.

Bartlett, R. 1998. Herping in Texas, the sequel: Bartlett returns. Reptiles 6(10): 32–38.

Basey, H. E. 1976. Discovering Sierra reptiles and amphibians. Yosemite Association and the U.S. Department of Interior, pp. 1–50.

Baxter, G. T., and M. D. Stone. 1985. Amphibians and Reptiles of Wyoming. Wyoming Game and Fish Commission, pp. 1–137.

Bechtel, B., and E. Bechtel. 1978. Heredity of pattern mutation in the corn snake,

Elaphe guttata, demonstrated in captive breedings. Copeia 1978(3):719–721.

Beck, D. D. 1995. Ecology and energetics of three sympatric rattlesnake species in the Sonoran Desert. J. Herpetol. 29(2):211–223.

Behler, J. L., and F. W. King. 1979. The Audubon Society Field Guide to North American Reptiles and Amphibians. Alfred E. Knopf, New York, 719 pp.

Bels, V. L. 1989. Health problems of captive reptiles. Proceedings of the Third International Colloquium on the Pathology of Reptiles and Amphibians, pp. 13–15.

Bennion, R. S., and W. S. Parker. 1976. Field observations on courtship and aggressive behavior in desert striped whipsnakes, *Masticophis t. taeniatus.* Herpetologica 32:30–35.

Best, I. B. 1978. Field sparrow reproductive success and nesting ecology. Auk 95: 9–22.

Black, J. H. 1983. Red-tailed hawks captures prairie kingsnake. Bull. Oklahoma Herpetol. Soc. 8:63–65.

Blair, C. L., and F. Schitoskey, Jr. 1982. Breeding biology and diet of the ferruginus hawk in South Dakota. Wilson Bull. 94:46–54.

Blair, W. 1954. Mammals of the mesquite plains biotic district in Texas and Oklahoma, and speciation in the central grasslands. Texas J. Sci. 6:235–264.

Blanchard, F. N. 1933. Eggs and young of the smooth green snake, *Liopeltis vernalis* (Harlan). Pap. Michigan Acad. Sci. Arts Lett. 17:493–508.

——. 1937. Data on the natural history of the red-bellied snake, *Storeria occipitomaculata*, in northern Michigan. Copeia 1937:151–162.

Blem, C. R. and L. B. Blem. 1985. Notes on *Virginia* (Reptilia, Colubridae) in Virginia. Brimleyanna (11):87–95.

—— and L. B. Blem. 1990. Lipid reserves of the brown water snake, *Nerodia taxispilota.* Comp. Biochem. Physiol. 97A:367–372.

Bogert, C. M., and R. B. Cowles. 1947. Results of the Archbold expeditions, No.

58. Moisture loss in relation to habitat selection in some Floridian reptiles. Bull. Am. Mus. Novit. (1358):1–34.

Bothner, R. C. 1963. A hibernaculum of the short-headed garter snake, *Thamnophis brachystoma* (Cope). Copeia 1963:572–573.

———. 1973. Temperatures of *Agkistrodon p. piscivorus* and *Lampropeltis g. getulus* in Georgia. Hiss News-J. 1:24–25.

Boundy, J. 1990. Biogeography and Variation in Southern Populations of the Garter Snake, *Thamnophis atratus*, with a synopsis of the *T. couchii* complex. Master's thesis, San Jose State University, San Jose, CA.

———. 2000. In: Crother et al. (eds.), Scientific and Standard English Names of Amphibians and Reptiles of North America North of Mexico, with Comments Regarding Confidence in Our Understanding. *Thamnophis atratus zaxanthus* Boundy, 1999. SSAR Herpetological Circular No. 29, p. 72.

Bowers, J. H. 1967. A record litter of *Thamnophis sirtalis proximus*. Southwestern Nat. 12(2):200.

Bowler, J. K. 1977. Longevity of reptiles and amphibians in North American collections. Soc. Stud. Amph. Rept. Misc. Publ. Herpetol. Circ. (6):1–32.

Bragg, A. 1960. Is *Heterodon* venomous? Herpetologica 16:121–123.

Branson, B. A., and E. C. Baker. 1974. An ecological study of the queen snake, *Regina septemvittata* (Say) in Kentucky, Tulane Stud. Zool. Bat. 18:153–171.

Brattstrom, B. H. 1965. Body temperatures of reptiles. Am. Midland Nat. 73:376–422.

——— and R. Swenkmeyer. 1965. Notes of the natural history of the worm snake, *Leptotyphlops humilis*. Herpetologica 7:193–196.

Brecke, B. J., J. B. Murphy, and W. Seifert. 1976. An Inventory of reproduction and social behavior in captive Baird's ratsnakes, *Elaphe obsoleta bairdi*. Herpetologica 32:389–395.

Breen, J. F. 1974. Encyclopedia of Reptiles and Amphibians. T. F. H. Publications, Neptune City, NJ, 576 pp.

Brode, J. M. 1988. Natural history of the giant garter snake, *Thamnophis couchii gigas*. Proceedings of the Conference on California Herpetology. Spec. Publ. No. 4, Southwestern Herpetol. Soc., pp. 25–28.

Brode, W. E., and P. Allison. 1958. Burrowing snakes of the panhandle counties of Mississippi. Herpetologica 14:37–40.

Brodie, E. D., III. 1989. Behavioral modification as a means of reducing the cost of reproduction. Am. Natur. 134:225–238.

Brown, B. C. 1937. Notes on *Coniophanes imperialis*. Copeia 1937:234.

———. 1939. The effect of *Coniophanes* poisoning in man. Copeia 1939(2):109.

Brown, E. E. 1978. A note on food and young in *Natrix rigida*. Bull. Maryland Herp. Soc. 14:91–92.

———. 1979. Some snake food records from the Carolinas. Brimleyanna (1):113–124.

———. 1992. Notes on amphibians and reptiles of the western piedmont of North Carolina. J. Elisha Mitchell Scientific Soc. 109(1):38–54.

Brown, P. 1997. A Field Guide to the Snakes of California. Gulf Publishing Co., Houston. 215 pp.

Brown, T. W., and H. B. Lillywhite. 1992. Autecology of the Mojave Desert sidewinder, *Crotalus cerastes cerastes*, at Kelso Dunes, Mojave Desert, California, USA. In Campbell and Brodie (Eds.), Biology of the Pitvipers. Selva, Tyler, TX, pp. 279–308.

Brown, W. S. 1982. Overwintering body temperatures of timber rattlesnakes, *Crotalus horridus*, in northeastern New York. J. Herpetol. 16:145–150.

———. 1987. Hidden life of the timber rattler. National Geographic 172:128–138.

———. 1991. Female reproductive ecology in a northern population of the timber rattlesnakes *Crotalus horridus*. Herpetologica 47:101–115.

———. 1992. Biology and conservation of the timber rattlesnake. In T. F. Tyning (Ed.),

Conservation of the Timber Rattlesnake in the Northeast. Massachusetts Audubon Society, Lincoln, MA.

—— and W. S. Parker. 1976. Movement ecology of *Coluber constrictor* near communal hibernacula. Copeia 1976 (2):225–242.

—— and W. S. Parker. 1982. Niche dimensions and resource partitioning in a Great Basin desert snake community. In N. J. Scott, Jr. (Ed.), Herpetological Communities. U.S. Fish and Wildlife Service. Wildlife Research Report. 13:59–81.

Brush, S. W., and G. W. Ferguson. 1986. Predation of lark sparrow eggs by a massasauga rattlesnake. Southwestern Nat. 31:260–261.

Bruyndonckx, H. 1984. Refrigerator hibernation. Litteratura Sepentium 4:146–148.

Burchfield, P. 1993. An unusual dietary inclusion for the cat-eyed snake, *Leptodeira septentrionalis septentrionalis*. Bull. Chicago Herp. Soc. 28(12):266–267.

Burger, J., R. T. Zappalorti, J. Dowdell, T. Georgiadis, J. Hill, and M. Gochfeld. 1992. Subterranean predation on pine snakes, *Pituophis melanoleucus*. J. Herpetol. 26:259–263.

Burkett, R. D. 1966. Natural history of the cottonmouth moccasin, *Agkistrodon piscivorus* (Reptilia). Univ. Kansas Publ. Mus. Nat. Hist. 17:435–491.

Burt, C. E., and W. L. Hoyle. 1935. Additional records of reptiles of the central prairie region of the United States. Trans. Kansas Acad. Sci. 37:193–212.

Butler, R. 1985. The captive care and breeding of *Thamnophis elegans terrestris*. Herptile 10:34–38.

Cagle, F. 1946. *Typhlops braminus* in the Marianas islands. Copeia 1946:101.

Campbell, J. A. 1972. Reproduction in captive Trans-Pecos ratsnakes, *Elaphe subocularis*. Herp. Review 4:129–130.

——. 1973. A captive hatchling of *Micrurus fulvius tenere* (Serpentes: Elapidae). J. Herpetol. 7:312–315.

Carl, G. 1981. Reproduction in the captive Brazos water snake, *Nerodia harteri*. Texas J. Sci. 33:77–78.

Carpenter, C. C. 1952. Comparative ecology of the common garter snake, *Thamnophis s. sirtalis*, the ribbon snake, *Thamnophis s. sauritus*, and Butler's garter snake, *Thamnophis butleri*, in mixed populations. Ecol. Monogr. 23:235–258.

——. 1953. A study of hibernacula and hibernating associations of snakes and amphibians in Michigan. Ecology 43: 74–80.

——. 1956. Body temperatures of three species of *Thamnophis*. Ecology 37:732–735.

——. 1985. *Lampropeltis calligaster calligaster* (prairie kingsnake). reproduction. Herp. Review 16:81.

Carson, H. L. 1945. Delayed fertilization in a captive indigo snake with notes on feeding and shedding. Copeia 1945:222–225.

Catling, P. M., and B. Freedman. 1980. Variation in distribution and abundance of four sympatric species of snake at Amherstburg, Ontario. Can. Field-Natur. 94:19–27.

Chapman, B. R., and S. D. Casto. 1972. Additional vertebrate prey of the loggerhead shrike. Wilson Bull. 84(4): 496–497.

Chiszar, D., K. Scudder, H. M. Smith, and C. W. Radcliffe. 1976. Observations of courtship behavior in the western Massasauga, *Sistrurus catenatus tergeminus*. Herpetologica 32:337–338.

Christiansen, J. L., and R. M. Bailey. 1990. The Snakes of Iowa. Iowa Department of Natural Resources, Des Moines, IA.

Clark, D., and C. Lieb. 1973. Notes on reproduction in the night snake (*Hypsiglena torquata*). Southwest Nat. 18(2):248–252.

Clark, D. R., Jr. 1964. Reproduction and sexual dimorphism in a population of the rough earth snake *Virginia striatula* (Linnaeus). Texas J. Sci. 16:265–295.

——. 1967. Experiments into selection of soil type, soil moisture level and temperature by five species of small snake. Trans. Kansas Acad. Sci. 70:490–496.

——. 1968. A proposal of specific status for the western worm snake, *Carphophis amoenus vermis* (Kennicott). Herpetologica 24:104–112.

——. 1970. Ecological study of the worm snake, *Carphophis vermis* (Kennicott). Univ. Kansas Publ. Mus. Nat. Hist. 19(2):85–194.

Clark, H. 1953. Eggs, egg laying and incubation of the snake *Elaphe emoryi* (Baird and Girard). Copeia 1953(2):90–92.

Clark, R. E. 1949. Snakes of the hill parishes of Louisiana. J. Tennessee Acad. Sci. 24:244–261.

Clarkson, R., and J. de Vos. 1986. The bullfrog, *Rana catesbeiana* (Shaw), in the lower Colorado River, Arizona-California. J. Herpetol. 20:42–49.

Clausen, H. J. 1936. Observations on the brown snake, *Storeria dekayi* (Holbrook), with especial reference to the habits and birth of the young. Copeia 1936:98–102.

Cochran, P. A. 1994. A longevity record for the eastern hognose snake, *Heterodon platirhinos*. Bull. Chicago Herp. Soc. 29(6):117–118.

Collins, J. T. 1974. Amphibians and reptiles in Kansas. Univ. Kansas Publ. Mus. Nat. Hist. Publ. Ed. Ser. (1):1–283.

——. 1990. Standard Common and Current Scientific Names for North American Amphibians and Reptiles. Third edition. SSAR Circ. No. 19.

——. 1993. Amphibians and Reptiles in Kansas. Univ. Kansas Mus. Nat. Hist., Lawrence, KS, 397 pp.

——. 1997. Standard Common and Current Scientific Names for North American Amphibians and Reptiles. Fourth edition. SSAR Circ. No. 25.

Conant, R. 1943. Studies on North American water snakes. I: *Natrix kirtlandii* (Kennicott). Am. Midland Nat. 29:313–341.

——. 1965. Notes on reproduction in two natricine snakes from Mexico. Herpetologica 21:140–144.

—— and J. T. Collins. 1991. A Field Guide to the Reptiles and Amphibians of Eastern and Central North America. Houghton Mifflin, Boston, MA, 450 pp.

—— and A. Downs, Jr. 1940. Miscellaneous notes on the eggs and young of reptiles. Zoologica. 25:33–48.

—— and J. D. Lazell, Jr. 1973. The Carolina salt marsh snake: A distinct form of *Natrix sipedon*. Breviora (400):1–13.

Cook, F. A. 1954. Snakes of Mississippi. Mississippi Game and Fish Commission, Jackson, MS, 40 pp.

Coote, J. 1984. Second generation captive breeding of the California mountain kingsnake, *Lampropeltis zonata multicincta*. In Proceedings of the International Herpetological Symposium, pp. 2–6.

Cowan, D. F. 1980. Adaptation, Maladaptation and Disease. In J. B. Murphy and J. T. Collins (Eds.), Reproductive Biology and Diseases of Captive Reptiles. SSAR.

Cowles, R. B., and C. M. Bogert. 1944. A preliminary study of the thermal requirements of desert reptiles. Bull. Am. Mus. Nat. Hist. 83(5):261–296.

Cranston, T. 1985. Notes on the natural history and husbandry of the gray-banded kingsnake. Northern California Herp. Soc. Newsletter 4(1):4.

——. 1989a. Natural history and captive husbandry of the western green rat snake, *Senticolis triaspis*. Vivarium 2(1):8–11.

——. 1989b. Captive propagation and husbandry of the western green rat snake, *Senticolis triaspis intermedia*: The untold story. In R. L. Gowan (Ed.), Captive Propagation and Husbandry of Reptile and Amphibians. Northern California Herp. Soc. Special Publ. No. 5.

——. 1991. Notes on the natural history, husbandry, and breeding of the gray-banded king snake. Vivarium 3(2):7–10.

——. 1993. The natural history and captive husbandry of the Trans-Pecos rat snake, *Bogertophis subocularis*. Vivarium 4(5):18–21.

Crews, D. and W. R. Garstka. 1982. The ecological physiology of a garter snake. Sci. American 247(5):159–168.

Criddle, S. 1937. Snakes from an anthill. Copeia 1937(2):142.

Crimmins, M. L. 1937. A case of *Oxybelis* poisoning in man. Copeia 1937(4):233.

Crother, B. I., J. Boundy, J. A. Campbell, K. de Queiroz, D. R. Frost, R. Highton, J. B. Iverson, P. A. Meylan, T. W. Reeder, M. E. Seidel, J. W. Sites, Jr., T. W. Taggart, S. G. Tilley, and D. B. Wake. 2000. Scientific and Standard English Names of Amphibians and Reptiles of North America North of Mexico, with Comments Regarding Confidence in Our Understanding. SSAR Herpetological Circular No. 29. SSAR, iv + 82 pp.

Cumbert, T. C., and K. A. Sullivan. 1990. Predation on yellow-eyed junco nestings by twin-spotted rattlesnake. Southwestern Nat. 35:367–368.

Cunningham, J. D. 1966. Additional observations on the body temperatures of reptiles. Herpetologica 2:184–489.

Curtis, L. 1949. The snakes of Dallas County, Texas. Field and Lad. 17:1–13.

Dalrymple, G. H. 1988. The herpetofauna of Long Pine Key, Everglades National Park, in relation to vegetation and hydrology. In R. C. Szaro, K. E. Severson, and D. R. Patton (Eds.), Management of Amphibians, Reptiles, and Small Mammals in North America, pp. 72–86. USDA Forest Service General Tech. Rep. RM-166.

Daniel, J. 1983. The Book of Indian reptiles. Bombay Nat. Hist. Soc., 141 pp.

Deckert, R. F. 1918. A list of reptiles from Jacksonville, Florida. Copeia (54):30–33.

Degenhardt, W. G., and P. B. Degenhardt. 1965. The host-parasite relationship between *Elaphe subocularis* (Reptilia: Colubridae) and *Aponomma elaphensis* (Acarina: Ixodidae). Southwestern Nat. 10(3):167–178.

——, C. W. Painter, and A. H. Price. 1996. Amphibians & Reptiles of New Mexico. University of New Mexico Press, Albuquerque, NM, 431 pp.

de Vosjoli, P. 1995. Basic Care of Rough Green Snakes Including Notes on the Care of Brown Snakes and Ringneck Snakes. Advanced Vivarium Systems, Santee, CA, 16 pp.

Diller, L., and R. Wallace. 1984. Reproductive biology of the northern Pacific rattlesnake, *Crotalus viridis oreganus*, in northern Idaho. Herpetologica 40:182–193.

Ditmars, R. L. 1931. Snakes of the World. Macmillan, New York.

——. 1936. The Reptiles of North America. Doubleday, Doran, Garden City, NY.

——. 1939. A Field Book of North American Snakes. Doubleday, Doran, New York.

Dixon, J. R., B. D. Greene, and M. J. Whiting. 1991. Annual report: Concho water snake natural history study. Colorado River Municipal Water District, Big Spring, TX.

Dowling, H. G. 1950. Studies of the black swamp snake, *Seminatrix pygaea* (Cope), with descriptions of two new subspecies. Misc. Publ. Mus. Zool., Univ. Michigan (76):1–38.

Duellman, W. E. 1958. A monographic study of the colubrid snake genus *Leptodeira*. Bull Am. Mus. Nat. Hist. 114(1):1–152.

—— and A. Schwartz. 1958. Amphibians and reptiles of southern Florida. Bull. St. Mus. Biol. Sci. 3:181–324.

Dundee, H. A., and D. A. Rossman. 1989. The amphibians and reptiles of Louisiana. Louisiana State University Press, Baton Rouge, LA.

Dunson, M., and W. Dunson. 1975. The relation between plasma Na+/K+ ATPase content in the diamondback terrapin and the yellowbelly sea snake. J. Comp. Physiol. 101:89–97.

—— and G. Ehlert. 1971. Effects of temperature, salinity and surface water flow on distribution of the sea snake *Pelamis*. Limnol. Oceanogr. 16:845–853.

—— and G. Robinson. 1976. Sea snake skin: Permeable to water but not to sodium. J. Comp. Physiol. 108:303–311.

Edgren, R. A. 1955. The natural history of the hognosed snakes, genus *Heterodon*: A review. Herpetologica 11:105–117.

Ernst, C. H. 1992. Venomous Reptiles of North America. Smithsonian Institution Press, Washington, DC, 236 pp.

—— and R. W. Barbour. 1989. Snakes of Eastern North America. George Mason University Press, Fairfax, VA.

——, S. W. Gotte, and J. E. Lovich. 1985. Reproduction in the mole kingsnake, *Lampropeltis calligaster rhombomaculata*. Bull. Maryland Herpetol. Soc. 21:16–22.

Evans, H., and R. Roecker. 1951. Notes on the herpetology of Ontario, Canada. Herpetologica 7:69–71.

Fantham, H. B., and A. Porter. 1952. The endoparasites of some North American snakes and their effects on the ophidia. Proc. Zool. Soc. Lond. 123:867–899.

Finnegan, D. 1984. Hibernation and hibernaculum construction. Northern California Herp. Soc. Newsletter 3(9):4.

Finneran, L. C. 1949. A sexual aggregation of the garter snake *Thamnophis butleri* (Cope). Copeia 1949:141–144.

Fitch, H. S. 1940. A biogeographical study of the ordinoides artenkreis of garter snakes (genus *Thamnophis*). Univ. California Publ. Zool. 44:1–150.

——. 1949. Study of snake populations in central California. Am. Midland Nat. 41(3):513–579.

——. 1956. Temperature responses in free-living amphibians and reptiles in northeastern Kansas. Univ. Kansas. Publ. Mus. Nat. Hist. 8:417–476.

——. 1960. Autecology of the copperhead. Univ. Kansas Publ. Mus. Nat. Hist. 13:85–288.

——. 1963. Natural history of the racer, *Coluber constrictor*. Univ. Kansas Publ. Mus. Nat. Hist. 15:351–468.

——. 1965. An ecological study of the garter snake *Thamnophis sirtalis*. Univ. Kansas Publ. Mus. Nat. Hist. 15(10):493–564.

——. 1970. Reproductive cycles in lizards and snakes. Univ. Kansas Publ. Mus. Nat. Hist. 52:1–247.

——. 1975. A demographic study of the ringneck snake, *Diadophis punctatus*, in Kansas. Univ. Kansas Publ. Mus. Nat. Hist. 62:1–53.

——. 1978. A field study of the prairie kingsnake, *Lampropeltis calligaster*. Trans. Kansas Acad. Sci. 81:354–362.

——. 1981. Sexual size differences in reptiles. Univ. Kansas Publ. Mus. Nat. Hist. 70:1–72.

——. 1985. Variation in clutch and litter size in new world reptiles. Univ. Kansas Publ. Mus. Nat. Hist. 76:1–76.

——. 1999. A Kansas Snake Community: Composition and Changes over 50 Years. Krieger, Malabar, FL, 165 pp.

——, and R. R. Fleet. 1970. Natural history of the milk snake *Lampropeltis triangulum* in northeastern Kansas. Herpetologica 26:387–396.

Flanigan, A. B. 1971. Predation on snakes by eastern bluebird and brown thrasher. Wilson Bull. 83:441.

Fleharty, E. D. 1967. Comparative ecology of *Thamnophis elegans*, *T. cyrtopsis*, and *T. rufipunctatus* in New Mexico. Southwestern. Nat. 12:207–230.

Fogel, D. 1997. Captive Husbandry and Propagation of the Boa Constrictors and Related Boas. Krieger, Malabar, FL, 98 pp.

Foquette, M. J., Jr. 1954. Food competition among four sympatric species of garter snakes, genus *Thamnophis*. Texas J. Sci. 6:172–188.

Force, E. R. 1931. Habits and birth of young of the lined snake, *Tropidoclonion lineatum*. Copeia 1931(2):51–53.

——. 1935. A local study of the opisthoglyph snake, *Tantilla gracilis* (Baird and Girard). Pap. Michigan Acad. Sci. Arts. Lett. 21:613–617.

Ford, N. B. 1982. Species specificity of sex pheromone trails of sympatric and allopatric garter snakes, *Thamnophis*. Copeia 1982:10–13.

——, and V. A. Cobb. 1992. Timing of courtship in two Colubrid snakes of the southern United States. Copeia 1992:573–577.

——, and R. A. Seigel. 1994. Phenotypic plasticity: Implications for captive-breeding and conservation programs. In J. B. Murphy, J. T. Collins and K. Adler (Eds.), Captive Management and Conservation of Amphibians and Reptiles. SSAR Publ., pp. 175–182.

Fowlie, J. 1965. The Snakes of Arizona. McGraw-Hill, New York, 164 pp.

Fox, W. 1956. Seminal receptacles of snakes. Anat. Rec. 124:519–540.

Frank, W. 1979. Boas and Other Non-Venomous Snakes. T. F. H. Publications, Neptune City, NJ, 91 pp.

Franz, R. 1977. Observations on the food, feeding behavior, and parasites of the striped swamp snake, *Regina alleni*. Herpetologica 33:91–94.

Freedman, W., and P. Catling. 1978. Population size and structure of four sympatric species of snakes at Amherstburg, Ontario. Can. Field Natur. 92:167–173.

Frye, F. L. 1979. Reptile Medicine and Husbandry. In Veterinary Clinics of North America: Small Animal Practice. 9(3):415–428. W. B. Saunders, Philadelphia, PA.

———. 1981. Biomedical and Surgical Aspects of Captive Reptile Husbandry. Veterinary Medicine Pub., Edwardsville, KS, 456 pp.

———. 1991. Biomedicine and Surgical Aspects of Captive Reptile Husbandry. Vol. I and II. Krieger, Malabar, FL, 637 pp.

Funk, R. 1964. On the food of *Crotalus m. molossus*. Herpetologica 20:134.

———. 1965. Food of *Crotalus cerastes laterorepens* in Yuma County, Arizona. Herpetologica 21:15–17.

———. 1967. A new colubrid snake of the genus *Chionactis* from Arizona. Southwestern Nat. 12(2):180–188.

——— and J. K. Tucker. 1978. Variation in a large brood of lined snakes, *Tropidoclonion lineatum* (Reptilia, Serpentes, Colubridae). J. Herpetol. 12:115–117.

Gannon, V. P. J., and D. M. Secoy. 1984. Growth and reproductive rate of a northern population of the prairie rattlesnake *Crotalus v. viridis*. J. Herpetol. 18:13–19.

Gehlbach, F. R. 1972. Coral snake mimicry reconsidered: The strategy of self-mimicry. Forma et Functio 5:311–320.

———. 1974. Evolutionary relations of southwestern ringneck snakes, *Diadophis punctatus*. Herpetologica 3:140–148.

——— 1981. Mountain Islands and Desert Seas: A Natural History of the U.S.-Mexican Borderland. Texas A&M University Press, College Station, TX.

———, and R. S. Baldridge. 1987. Live blind snakes, *Leptotyphlops dulcis*, in eastern screech owls, *Otus asio*, nests: A novel commensalism. Oecologia 71:560–563.

Gibbon, J. W., J. W. Coker, and T. M. Murphy, Jr. 1977. Selected aspects of the life history of the rainbow snake, *Farancia erytrogramma*. Herpetologica 33:276–281.

Gillingham, J. C. 1974. Reproductive behavior of the western fox snake, *Elaphe vulpina* (Baird and Girard). Herpetologica 30:309–313.

———. 1976. Early egg deposition by southern black racer, *Coluber constrictor priapus*. Herp. Review 7:115.

———. 1979. Reproductive behavior of rat snakes in eastern North America, genus *Elaphe*. Copeia 1979(2):319–331.

———. 1987. Social behavior. In R. A. Siegel, J. T. Collins, and S. S. Novak (Eds.), Snakes: Ecology and Evolutionary Biology. McGraw-Hill, New York, pp. 184–209.

Gloyd, H. K., and R. Conant. 1990. Snakes of the *Agkistrodon* complex. A monographic review. SSAR Contrib. Herp. G: Vit., 614 pp.

Godley, J. S. 1980. Foraging ecology of the striped swamp snake, *Regina alleni*, in southern Florida. Ecol. Monogr. 50:411–436.

———. 1982. Predation and defensive behavior of the striped swamp snake, *Regina alleni*. Florida Field Natur. 10:31–36.

Goin, C. J. 1947. A note on the food of *Heterodon simus*. Copeia 1947:275.

Goldberg, S. R. 1995. Reproduction in the western patchnose snake, *Salvadora hexalepis*, and the mountain patchnose, *S. grahamiae* (Colubridae), from Arizona. Southwestern Nat. 40(1):119–120.

Graham, J., I. Rubinoff, and M. Hecht. 1971. Temperature physiology of the sea snake *Pelamis platurus*: An index of its colonization potential in the Atlantic Ocean. Proc. Nat. Acad. Sci. 68:1360–1363.

Greene, H. W. 1976. Scale overlap, a directional sign stimulus for prey ingestion by ophiphagous snakes. Z. Tierpsychol. 41:113–120.

———. 1984. Feeding behavior and diet of the eastern coral snake, *Micrurus fulvius*. Univ. Kansas Mus. Nat. Hist. Spl. Publ. (10):147–162.

——— and G. M. Burghardt. 1978. Behavior and phylogeny: Constriction in ancient and modern snakes. Science 200:74–77.

——— and G. V. Oliver, Jr. 1965. Notes on the natural history of the western massasauga. Herpetologica 21:225–228.

Gregory, P. T. 1977. Life history observations of three species of snakes in Manitoba. Can. Field Natur. 91:19–27.

———. 1978. Feeding habits and diet overlap of three species of garter snakes (*Thamnophis*) on Vancouver Island. Can. J. Zool. 56:1967–1974.

———. 1983. Identification of sex of small snakes in the field. Herp. Review 14:42–43.

Grismer, L., J. McGuire, and B. Hollingsworth. 1994. A report on the herpetofauna of the Vizcaino Peninsula, Baja California, Mexico, with a discussion of its biogeographic and taxonomic implications. Bull. Southern California Acad. Sci. 93:45–80.

Gritis, P. 1993. The rough green snake: Aspects of its natural history and life in captivity. Reptile and Amphibian Magazine March/April:54–57.

Groves, F. 1961. Notes in two large broods of *Haldea v. valeriae*. (Baird and Girard). Herpetologica 17:71.

Groves, J. D., and P. S. Sachs. 1973. Eggs and young of the scarlet kingsnake, *Lampropeltis triangulum elapsoides*. J. Herpetol. 7:389–390.

Guidry, E. V. 1953. Herpetological notes from southeastern Texas. Herpetologica 9:49–56.

Guthrie, J. E. 1932. Snakes versus birds: birds versus snakes. Wilson Bull. 44:88–101.

Hall, R. J. 1969. Ecological observations on Graham's watersnake, *Regina grahamii*. Am. Midland Nat. 81:156–163.

Hamilton, W. J. Jr., and J. A. Pollack. 1956. The food of some crotalid snakes from Fort Benning, Georgia. Ecology 37:519–526.

Hammack, S. H. 1991. New concepts in colubrid egg incubation—a preliminary report. In M. J. Uricheck (Ed.), 15th International Herpetological Symposium on Captive Propagation and Husbandry, Seattle, WA, pp. 103–108.

Hammerson, G. A. 1977. Head-body temperature differences monitored by telemetry and the snake, *Masticophis flagellum piceus*. Comp. Biochem. Physiol. 57:399–402.

———. 1978. Observations on the reproduction, courtship, and aggressive behavior of the striped racer, *Masticophis lateralis euryxanthus* (Reptilia, Serpentes, Colubridae). J. Herpetol. 12:253–255.

———. 1986. Amphibians and Reptiles in Colorado. Colorado Division of Wildlife Pub. No. DOW-M-I-3-86.

Hansen, R. W., and R. L. Tremper. In Prep. Amphibians and Reptiles of Central California. University of California Press, Berkeley, CA.

Harding, J. H. 1997. Amphibians and Reptiles of the Great Lakes Region. University of Michigan Press, Ann Arbor, MI, 378 pp.

Hardy, D. L., Sr. (Ed.). 1992. Collected Papers of the Tucson Herpetological Society 1988–1991. Tucson Herpetol. Soc., Tucson, AZ.

Hart, D. R. 1979. Niche relationships of *Thamnophis radix* and *Thamnophis sirtalis parietalis* in the Interlake District of Manitoba. Tulane Stud. Zool. Bot. 21:125–140.

Heatwole, H. 1987. Sea Snakes. New South Wales University Press, Kensington, Australia, 85 pp.

Henderson, R. W. 1970. Feeding behavior, digestion, and water requirements of

Diadophis punctatus arnyi Kennicott. Herpetologica 26:520–525.

——. 1974. Aspects of the ecology of the netropical vine snake, *Oxybelis aeneus*. Herpetologica 30:19–24.

——, M. H. Binder, R. A. Sajdak, and J. A. Buday. 1980. Aggregating behavior and exploitation of subterranean habitat by gravid eastern milksnakes (*Lampropeltis t. triangulum*). Milwaukee Publ. Mus. Contrib. Biol. Geol. (32):1–9.

Hensley, M. 1962. Another snake recorded in the diet of the bull frog. Herpetologica 18:141.

Hibbard, C. W. 1964. A brooding colony of the blind snake, *Leptotyphlops dulcis dissecta*. Copeia 1964(1):222.

Hirth, H. F., and A. C. King. 1969. Body temperatures of snakes in different seasons. J. Herpetol. 3:101–102.

Holman, J. A. 2000. Fossil Snakes of North America. Indiana University Press, Bloomington, IN, 357 pp.

——, J. H. Harding, M. M. Hensley, and G. R. Dudderar. 1990. Michigan Snakes. Michigan State University Cooperative Extension Service, East Lansing, MI, 72 pp.

Holtzman, D. A., G. R. Ten Eyck, and D. Begon. 1989. Artificial hibernation of garter, *Thamnophis* sp., and corn, *Elaphe guttata guttata*, snakes. Herp. Review 20:67–69.

Honegger, R. 1992. Undesirable trends in captive management and conservation in reptiles. Bull. Chicago Herp. Soc. 27(10):207–210.

Hoyer, R. F., and R. M. Storm. 1991. Reproductive biology of the rubber boa, *Charina bottae*. In M. J. Uricheck (Ed.), Proceedings of the 15th International Herpetological Symposium on Captive Propagation and Husbandry, Seattle, WA, pp. 109–118.

Hudson, G. E. 1985. The Amphibians and Reptiles of Nebraska. University of Nebraska, Lincoln, NE, 146 pp.

Huheey, J. E. 1959. Distribution and variation in the glossy water snake, *Natrix rigida* (Say). Copeia 1959:303–311.

Hunter, M. L., Jr., J. Albright, and J. Arbuckle. 1992. The Amphibians and Reptiles of Maine. University of Maine, Orono, ME.

Hurst, G. A. 1963. A phenological study of the herpetofauna of William B. Umstead and Reedy Creek State Parks, Wake County, North Carolina. M.S. thesis, North Carolina State University, Raleigh, NC.

Ippoliti, S. 1980. Cannibalism in a corn snake hatchling, *Elaphe guttata*. Bull. Philadelphia Herpetol. Soc. 28:14.

Iverson, J. B. 1975. Notes on Nebraska reptiles. Trans. Kansas Acad. Sci. 78:51–62.

——. 1990. Nesting and parental care in the mud turtle, *Kinosternon flavescens*. Can. J. Zool. 68:230–233.

Jackson, D. L., and R. Franz. 1981. Ecology of the eastern coral snake, *Micrurus fulvius*, in northern peninsular Florida. Herpetologica 37:213–288.

——. 1971. Intraspecific predation in *Coluber constrictor*. J. Herpetol. 5:196.

Jackson, J. J. 1983. Snakes of the southeastern United States. University of Georgia College of Agriculture, Athens, GA, 111 pp.

Jacobson, E. R. 1987. Reptiles. In Veterinary Clinics of North America. Small Animal Practice. Vol. 17, No. 5, September 1987. W. B. Saunders, Philadelphia, PA.

——, and W. G. Whitford, 1970. The effect of acclimation on physiological responses to temperature in snakes. *Thamnophis proximus* and *Natrix rhombifera*. Comp. Biochem. Physiol. 35:439–449.

——, and W. G. Whitford, 1971. Physiological responses to temperature in the patch-nosed snake, *Salvadora hexalepis*. Herpetologica 27:289–295.

Jarchow, J. L. 1988. Hospital Care of the Reptile Patient. In E. R. Jacobson and A. Kollias (Eds.), Exotic Animals. Churchill Livingstone, New York.

Jarchow, J. 1992a. Herp health. In D. L. Hardy, Sr. (Ed.), Collected Papers of the Tucson Herpetological Society 1988–1991. Tucson Herpetol. Soc., Tucson, AZ. pp. 113–119.

——. 1992b. Causes of disease in captive reptiles and how they relate to wild populations. In D. L. Hardy, Sr. (Ed.), Collected Papers of the Tucson Herpetological Society 1988–1991. Tucson Herpetol. Soc., Tucson, AZ. pp. 65–70.

——, H. McCrystal, and D. F. Retes. 1992. Reptiles in captivity: a roundtable discussion. In D. L. Hardy, Sr. (Ed.), Collected Papers of the Tucson Herpetological Society 1988–1991. Tucson Herpetol. Soc., Tucson, AZ. pp. 239–245.

Jensen, J. 2000. In Stepzinski, T., Snake species slither into Georgia. The Times Union. October 30, 2000. Jacksonville, FL. p. B-3.

Johnson, T. 1980. The Snakes of Missouri. Missouri Department of Conservation. Jefferson City, Missouri, (pamphlet) 12 pp.

Jones, K. B. 1990. Habitat use and predatory behavior of Thamnophis cyrtopsis (Serpentes: Colubridae) in a seasonally variable aquatic environment. Southwestern Nat. 35:115–122.

Jones, L. 1976. Field data on Heterodon p. platirhinos in Prince George's County, Maryland. Bull. Maryland Herp. Soc. 12:29–32.

Karges, J. P. 1982. Geographic variation in reproductive cycles and strategies of Thamnophis marcianus. In Abstracts of SSAR 1982 Meeting, Raleigh, NC.

Kassing, E. F. 1961. A life history study of the Great Plains ground snake, Sonora episcopa episcopa (Kennicott). Texas J. Sci. 13:185–203.

Kauffield C. 1943. Grown and feeding of newborn Price's and green rock rattlesnakes. Am. Midland Nat. 29:607–614.

Kauffield C. 1948. Notes on a hooknose snake from Texas. Copeia 1984(4):301.

——. 1969. Snakes, the Keeper and the Kept. Doubleday, New York, 248 pp. (Reprinted, 1995. Krieger, Malabar, FL.)

Keenlyne, K. D., and J. R. Beer. 1973. Food habits of Sistrurus catenatus catenatus. J. Herpetol. 7:382–384.

Kelly, H. A., A. W. Davis, and H. C. Robertson. 1936. Snakes of Maryland. Nat. Hist. Soc. of Maryland

Kennedy, J. P. 1964. Natural history notes on some snakes of eastern Texas. Texas J. Sci. 16:210–215.

Keogh, J. S. 1992. The fox snake, Elaphe vulpina: The "other" rat snake. Vivarium 4(2):23–24.

Kitchell, J. F. 1969. Thermophilic and thermophobic response of snakes in a thermal gradient. Copeia 1969:189–191.

Klauber, L. M. 1940. The snakes of the genus Leptotyphlops in the United States and northern Mexico. Trans. San Diego Soc. Nat. Hist. 9:87–162.

——. 1941. The longnose snakes of the genus Rhinocheilus. Trans. San Diego Soc. Nat. Hist. 9:289–332.

——. 1956 (1972). Rattlesnakes: Their Habits, Life Histories, and Influence on Mankind. 2nd. edition. University of California Press, Berkeley, CA, 1533 pp.

Klawe, W. 1964. Food of the black and yellow sea snake, Pelamis platurus, from Ecuadorian coastal waters. Copeia 1964: 712–713.

Klemens, M. W. 1993. Amphibians and reptiles of Connecticut and adjacent regions. State Geological and Natural History Survey of Connecticut.

Klimstra, W. D. 1959. Food habits of the yellow-bellied water snake in southern Illinois. Herpetologica 15:1–5.

Klingenberg, R. J. 1991. Egg binding in colubrid snakes. Vivarium 3(2):32–35.

——. 1993. Understanding Reptile Parasites. Advanced Vivarium Systems, Lakeside, CA. 81 pp.

Knable, A. E. 1970. Food habits of red fox (Vulpes fulva) in Union County, Illinois. Trans. Illinois St. Acad. Sci. 63:359–365.

Kochman, H. I. 1992. Atlantic salt marsh snake, Nerodia clarkii taeniata (Cope). In P. E. Moler (Ed.), R. E. Ashton, Jr. (Series Ed.), Rare and Endangered Biota of Florida. Vol. III Amphibians and Reptiles. University Press of Florida, Gainesville, FL.

Kofron, C. P. 1978. Foods and habitats of aquatic snakes (Reptilia, Serpentes) in a

Louisiana swamp. J. Herpetol. 12:543–554.

——. 1979. Reproduction of aquatic snakes in south-central Louisiana. Herpetologica 35:44–50.

—— and J. R. Dixon. 1980. Observations on aquatic colubrid snakes in Texas. Southwestern Nat. 25:107–109.

Krohmer, R., and R. Aldridge. 1985. Female reproduction cycle of the lined snake *Tropidoclonion lineatum*. Herpetologica 41(1):39–44.

Kronen, D. 1980. Notes on the eggs and hatchlings of the longnose snake, *Rhinocheilus lecontei*, including the occurrence of a semi-striped pattern. Bull. Chicago Herp. Soc. 15:54–56.

Kropach, C. 1975. The yellow-bellied sea snake, *Pelamis*, in the eastern Pacific. In W. Dunson (Ed.), The Biology of Sea Snakes. University Park Press, Baltimore, MD.

Lang, J. 1969. Hibernation and movements of *Storeria occipitomaculata* in northern Minnesota. J. Herpetol. 3:196–197.

Lardie, R. L. 1965. Eggs and young of *Rhinocheilus lecontei tessellatus*. Copeia 1965(3):366.

——. 1976. Large centipede eaten by a western massasauga. Bull. Oklahoma Herpetol. Soc. 1:40.

Laslow, J. 1979. Notes on reproductive patterns of reptiles in relation to captive breeding. In P. J. S. Olney (Ed.), International Zoo Yearbook 19:22–27. The Zoological Society of London, London.

——. 1983. Further notes on reproductive patterns of amphibians and reptiles in relation to captive breeding. In P. J. S. Olney (Ed.), International Zoo Yearbook 23:166–174. The Zoological Society of London, London.

Laszlo, J. 1977. Probing as a practical method of sex recognition of reptiles, primarily snakes. Proc. 2nd Ann. Symp. on Captive Propagation and Husbandry, pp. 20–25.

Lawler, H. 1992. Riparian Herpetofauna in the Sonoran Desert. In D. L. Hardy, Sr. (Ed.), Collected Papers of the Tucson Herpeptological Society, 1988–1991.

Tucson Herpetol. Soc., Tuscon, AZ, pp. 43–45.

Levell, J. P. 1992. Eradicating snake mites: A brief history with the report of another method. Bull. Chicago Herp. Soc. 27(10):205–206.

Lillywhite, H. B., and R. W. Henderson. 1993. Behavioral and functional ecology of arboreal snakes. In R. A. Seigel and J. T. Collins (Eds.), Snakes Ecology and Behavior. McGraw-Hill, New York.

Linder, A., and E. Fichter. 1977. The Amphibians and Reptiles of Idaho. Idaho State University Press, Pocatello, ID, 78 pp.

Linder, A. D., and E. Fichter. 1991. The Amphibians and Reptiles of Idaho. Idaho State University Press, Pocatello, ID, pp. 1–78.

Liner, E. 1954. The herpetofauna of LaFayette, Terrebonne, and Vermillion Parishes, Louisiana. Proc. Louisiana Acad. Sci. 17:65–85.

Linzey, D. W., and M. J. Clifford. 1981. Snakes of Virginia. The University Press of Virginia.

Logier, E. B. S. 1958. The snakes of Ontario. University of Toronto Press, Toronto, 99 pp.

Low, J. 1993. Colubrids: successful snakes. Reptile and Amphibian Magazine Jan.–Feb., 1993:30–41.

Lowe, C. H., C. R. Schwalbe, and T. B. Johnson. 1986. The Venomous Reptiles of Arizona. Arizona Game and Fish Commission, Phoenix, AZ, 155 pp.

MacCartney, J. M., K. W., Larsen, and P. T. Gregory, 1989. Body temperatures and movements of hibernating snakes (*Crotalus* and *Thamnophis*) and thermal gradients of natural hibernacula. Can. J. Zool. 67:108–114.

Mara, W. P. 1994a. First captive breeding of the scarlet snake with notes on care. Captive Breeding 3(1):8–11.

——. 1994b. The scarlet snake. Reptile and Amphibian Magazine Mar.–Apr. 1994: 17–20.

Markel, R. G. 1990. Kingsnakes and Milk Snakes. T. F. H. Publishers, Neptune City, NJ.

Markezich, A. 1962. Ophiophagy in western fox snakes, *Elaphe v. vulpina.* Bull. Philadelphia Herpetol. Soc. 10(4):5.

Martin, B. E. 1975. An occurrence of the Arizona ridge-nosed rattlesnake, *Crotalus willardi willardi* observed feeding in nature. Bull. Maryland Herp. Soc. 11:187–189.

———. 1976. A reproductive record for the New Mexican ridgenosed rattlesnake (*Crotalus willardi obscurus*). Bull. Maryland Herpetol. Soc. 12(4):126–128.

Martin, W. H. 1988. Life history of the timber rattlesnake. Catesbeiana 8(1):9–12.

———. 1990. The timber rattlesnake, *Crotalus horridus*, in the Appalachian Mountains of eastern North America. Catesbeiana 10:49.

———. 1992a. The timber rattlesnake: Its distribution and natural history. In T. F. Tyning (Ed.), Conservation of the timber rattlesnakes in the northeast. Massachusetts Audubon Society, Lincoln, MA.

———. 1992b. Phenology of the timber rattlesnake, *Crotalus horridus*, in an unglaciated section of the Appalachian Mountains. In Campbell and Brodie (Eds.), Biology of the Pitvipers. Selva, Tyler, TX, pp. 259–278.

Martof, B. S., W. M. Palmer, J. R. Bailey, J. R. Harrison, II, and J. Dermid. 1980. Amphibians and Reptiles of the Carolinas and Virginia. University of North Carolina Press, Chapel Hill, NC.

Mattison, C. 1986. Snakes of the world. Facts on File, New York, 190 pp.

———. 1987. The Care of Reptiles and Amphibians in Captivity. Sterling Publishing Co., New York, 317 pp.

———. 1988. Keeping and Breeding Snakes. Blandford Press, London, 184 pp.

———. 1990. A to Z of Snake Keeping. Sterling, New York, 143 pp.

———. 1991. A–Z of Snake Keeping. Sterling Publishing Co., New York, 143 pp.

McCoy, C. J., Jr. 1975. Cave-associated snakes, *Elaphe guttata*. Oklahoma Bull. Natl. Speleol. Soc. 37(2):41.

McCoy, C., and F. Gehlbach. 1967. Cloacal hemorrhage and the defense display of the colubrid snake *Rhinochielus lecontei.* Texas J. Sci. 19(4)349–352.

McDiarmid, R. W. 1968. Variation, distribution, and systematic status of the blackheaded snake, *Tantilla yaquia*. Smith. Bull. Southern California Acad. Sci. 67(3):159–177.

McEachern, M. J. 1991. A Color Guide to the Corn Snakes Captive Bred in the United States. Advanced Vivarium Systems, Lakeside, CA, 49 pp.

McGurty, B. M. 1982. Hatching snake eggs: Substrate considerations. San Diego Herp. Soc. Newsletter 4:4–5.

———. 1988. Natural history of the California mountain kingsnake, *Lampropeltis zonata*. Proceedings of the Conference on California Herpetology. Spec. Publ. No. 4: 73–88.

McIntyre, D. C. 1977. Reproductive habits of captive Trans-Pecos rat snakes, *Elaphe subocularis*. J. Northern Ohio Assoc. Herp. 3:20–22.

Meade, G. P. 1934. Some Observations on Captive Snakes. Copeia 1934:4–5.

Means, D. B. 1986, Eastern diamondback rattlesnake, *Crotatus adamanteus* Beauvois. In R. H. Mount (Ed.), Vertebrate Animals of Alabama in Need of Special Attention. Alabama Agricultural Experiment Station, Auburn University, AL, pp. 48–49.

Means, D. B. 1992. Mole snake *Lampropeltis calligaster rhombomaculata* (Holbrook). In P. E. Moler (Ed.), R. E. Ashton, Jr. (Series Ed.), Rare and Endangered Biota of Florida. Volume III. Amphibians and Reptiles. University Press of Florida, Gainesville, FL.

Mehrtens, J. M. 1987. Living Snakes of the World. Sterling, New York, 480 pp.

Miller, D. 1979. A life history study of the gray-banded kingsnake, *Lampropeltis mexicana alterna*, in Texas. Chihuahuan Desert Res. Inst. Cont. No. 87. Alpine, TX, 48 pp.

Miller, L. 1987. An investigation of four rare snakes in south central Kansas. Report Kansas Wildlife and Parks Commission, 24 pp.

Mills, T. 1989. To scent or not to scent. Vivarium (2):8–20.

Millstead, W. W. 1953. Geographic variation in the garter snake *Thamnophis cyrtopsis*. Texas J. Sci. 5:348–379.

Minton, J. E. 1949. Coral snake preyed upon by a bullfrog. Copeia 1949:288.

Minton, S. A., Jr. 1959. Observations on amphibians and reptiles of the Big Bend region of Texas. Southwestern Nat. 3:28–54.

——. 1972. Amphibians and Reptiles of Indiana. Indiana Acad. Sci. Monogr. (3):1–346.

Mitchell, J. C. 1986. Cannibalism in reptiles: A worldwide review. SSAR.

——. 1994. The Reptiles of Virginia. Smithsonian Institution Press, Washington, DC, 352 pp.

Moore, R. G. 1978. Seasonal and daily activity patterns and thermoregulation in the southwestern speckled rattlesnake, *Crotalus mitchellii pyrrhus* and the Colorado Desert sidewinder, *Crotalus cerastes laterorepens*. Copeia 1978(3):439–442.

Morris, M. A. 1974. Observations on a large litter of the snake *Storeria dekayi*. Trans. Illinois St. Acad. Sci. 67:359–360.

—— and K. Vail. 1991. Courtship and mating of captive rough green snakes, *Opheodrys aestivus*, from Illinois. Bull. Chicago Herp. Soc. 26(2):34.

—— and S. J. Walsh. 1991. Reproduction in a western smooth earth snake, *Virginia valeriae elegans*, from western Kentucky. Bull. Chicago Herp. Soc. 26(6):133.

Moulis, R. 1976. Autecology of the eastern indigo snake, *Drymarchon corais couperi*. Herp. Bull. New York Herp. Soc. 12(3–4):14–23.

Mount, R. H. 1975. The Reptiles and Amphibians of Alabama. Auburn University Agricultural Experiment Station, Auburn University, AL.

Moyle, M. 1989. Vitamin D and UV radiation: Guidelines for the herpeticulturist. In M. J. Uricheck (Ed.), Thirteenth International Herpetological Symposium on Captive Propagation and Husbandry, Phoenix, AZ, pp. 61–70.

Murphy, J. B., and B. L. Armstrong. 1978. Maintenance of rattlesnakes in captivity. Special Publ. Univ. Kansas Mus. Nat. His. 3:1–40.

—— and J. A. Schadduck. 1978. Reproduction in the eastern diamondback rattlesnake, *Crotalus adamanteus*, in captivity, with comments regarding taratoid birth anomaly. British J. Herpetol. 5:727–733.

Mushinsky, H. R. 1984. Observations of the feeding habits of the short-tailed snake, *Stilosoma extenuatum*, in captivity. Herp. Review 15:67–68.

—— and J. J. Hebrard. 1977. Food partitioning by five species of water snake in Louisiana. Herpetologica 33:162–166.

——, J. J. Hebrard, and D. S. Vodopich. 1982. Ontogeny of water snake foraging ecology. Ecology 63:1424–1629.

——, J. J. Hebrard, and M. S. Walley. 1980. The role of temperature on the behavioral and ecological associations of sympatric water snakes. Copeia 1980:744–754.

—— and K. H. Lotz. 1980. Chemoreceptive responses of two sympatric water snakes to extracts of commonly ingested prey species. Ontogenetic and Ecological Considerations. J. Chem. Ecol. 6:523–535.

Myers, C. W. 1965. Biology of the ringneck snake, *Diadophis punctatus*, in Florida. Bull. Florida St. Mus. Biol. Soc. 10:43–90.

——. 1967. The pine woods snake, *Rhadinaea flavilata* (Cope). Bull. Florida St. Mus. Biol. Sci. 11:47–97.

Neill, W. T. 1948. Hibernation of amphibians and reptiles in Richmond County, Georgia. Herpetologica 4:107–114.

——. 1951. Notes on the natural history of certain North American snakes. Publ. Res. Div. Ross Allen's Rept. Inst. 1:47–60.

——. 1954. Evidence of venom in snakes of the genera *Alsophis* and *Rhadinaea*. Copeia 1954:59–60.

——. 1957. Some misconceptions regarding the eastern coral snake, *Micrurus fulvius*. Herpetologica 13:111–118.

——. 1962. The reproductive cycle of snakes in a tropical region, British

Honduras. Quart. J. Florida Acad. Sci. 25(3):234–253.

——. 1963. Polychromatism in snakes. Quart. J. Florida Acad. Sci. 26:194–216.

——. 1964. Taxonomy, natural history, and zoogeography of the rainbow snake *Farancia erytrogramma* (Palisot de Beauvois). Am. Midland Nat. 71:257–295.

——. 1965. Notes of aquatic snakes, *Natrix* and *Tretanorhinus*, in Cuba. Herpetologica 21:62–67.

Nelson, D. H., and J. W. Gibbons. 1972. Ecology, abundance, and seasonal activity of the scarlet snake, *Cemophora coccinea*. Copeia 1972:582–584.

Nussbaum, R. A., E. D. Brodie, and R. M. Storm. 1983. Amphibians and Reptiles of the Pacific Northwest. University Press of Idaho, Moscow, ID, 332 pp.

Obst, F. J., K. Richter, and U. Jacob. 1988. The Completely Illustrated Atlas of Reptiles and Amphibians for the Terrarium. T. F. H. Publications, Neptune City, NJ, 831 pp.

O'Connor, P. F. 1991. Captive propagation and post-copulatory plugs of the eastern indigo snake, *Drymarchon corais couperi*. Vivarium 3(3):32–35.

Oldfield, B. L., and D. E. Keyler. 1989. Survey of timber rattlesnake, *Crotalus horridus*, distribution along the Mississippi River in western Wisconsin. Trans. Wisconsin Acad. Sci. Arts. Lett. 77:27–34.

—— and J. J. Moriarty 1994. Amphibians & Reptiles Native to Minnesota. University of Minnesota Press, Minneapolis, MN, 237 pp.

Ortenburger, A., and R. Ortenburger. 1926. Field observations on some amphibians and reptiles of Pima County, Arizona. Proc. Oklahoma Acad. Sci. 6:101–121.

Osgood, D. W. 1970. Thermoregulation in water snake studied by telemetry. Copeia 1970:568–571.

Owens, V. 1949. An overwintering colony of *Coluber c. constrictor* (Say) and *Elaphe o. obsoleta* (Say). Herpetologica 5:90.

Painter, C. W. 1985. Herpetology of the Gila and San Francisco river drainages of southwestern New Mexico. Unpubl. Rept. New Mexico Dept. Game and Fish, Santa Fe, NM, 333 pp.

Palmer, L. E., and H. S. Fowler. 1975. Fieldbook of Natural History. McGraw-Hill, New York, 779 pp.

Palmer, W. M. 1990. Poisonous Snakes of North Carolina. State Mus. of Natur. Sci. N.C. Dept. of Agriculture, 22 pp.

—— and A. L. Braswell. 1995. Reptiles of North Carolina. University of North Carolina Press, Chapel Hill, NC, 412 pp.

—— and A. L. Braswell. 1996. Reptiles of North Carolina. The University of North Carolina Press, 412 pp.

—— and G. Tregembo. 1970. Notes on the natural history of the scarlet snake, *Cemophora coccinea copei* Jan. in North Carolina. Herpetologica 26:300–302.

—— and G. M. Williamson. 1971. Observations on the natural history of the Carolina pigmy rattlesnake, *Sistrurus miliarius miliarius* Linnaeus. J. Elisha Mitchell Sci. Soc. 87(1):20–25.

Parker, M. V. 1941. The trematode parasites from a collection of amphibians and reptiles. J. Tennessee Acad. Sci. 16:27–45.

Pawley, R. 1983. Husbandry of the eastern coral snake (*Micrurus fulvius*) at Brookfield Zoo. Proc. 6th Reptile Symp., on Captive Propagation and Husbandry. Washington, DC.

Pendlebury, G. B. 1976. The Western hognose snake, *Heterodon nasicus nasicus*, in Alberta. Can. Field Nat. 90:416–422.

Peterson, C. R. 1987. Daily body temperature variation in free ranging garter snakes, *Thamnophis elegans vagrans*. Ecology 68(1):160–169.

Peterson, H. W. 1956. A record of viviparity in a normally oviparous snake. Herpetologica 12:52.

Peterson, K. H. 1983. Reproduction of *Crotalus mitchellii mitchellii* and *Crotalus durissus* at the Houston Zoological Gardens. Proc. Rept. Symp. Capt. Prop. Husb. 6:323–327.

Peterson, R. C., and R. W. Fritsch. 1986. Connecticut's venomous snakes! The timber rattlesnake and northern copperhead. Bull. State Geol. Nat. Hist. Surv. Connecticut 111:1–48.

Pisani, G. R. 1967. Notes on the courtship and mating behavior of *Thamnophis brachystoma* (Cope). Herpetologica 23:112–115.

—— and R. C. Bothner. 1970. The annual reproductive cycle of *Thamnophis brachystoma*. Sci. Stud. St. Bonaventure Univ. 26:15–34.

—— J. T. Collins, and S. R. Edwards. 1973. A re-evaluation of the subspecies of *Crotatus horridus*. Trans. Kansas Acad. Sci. 75:255–263.

Platt, D. R. 1969. Natural history of the hognose snakes *Heterodon platirhinos* and *Heterodon nasicus*. Univ. Kansas Publ. Mus. Nat. Hist. 18:253–420.

Plummer, M. V. 1981. Habitat utilization, diet and movements of a temperate arboreal snake, *Opheodrys aestivus*. J. Herpetol. 15:425–432.

——. 1983. Annual variation in stored lipids and reproduction in green snakes, *Opheodrys aestivus*. Copeia 1983:741–745.

——. 1984. Female reproduction in an Arkansas population of rough green snakes, *Opheodrys aestivus*. Herpetologica 41:373–381.

——. 1991. Rough green snake diet, metabolism and feces. J. Herpetol. 25(2):222–226.

——. 1993. Thermal ecology of arboreal green snakes, *Opheodiys aestivus*. J. Herpetol. 27(3):254–260.

Porter, K. R. 1972. Herpetology. W. B. Saunders, Philadelphia, PA, 524 pp.

Pough, F. H. 1966. Ecological relationships in southeastern Arizona with notes on other species. Copeia 1966(4):676–683.

—— and H. Lillywhite. 1984. Blood volume and blood oxygen capacity of sea snakes. Physiol. Zool. 57:32–39.

Preston, W. B. 1982. The Amphibians and Reptiles of Manitoba. Manitoba Museum of Science and History, pp. 1–128.

Price, W. H., and L. C. Carr. 1943. Eggs of *Heterodon simus*. Copeia 1943:193.

Punzo, E. 1974. Comparative analysis of the feeding habits of two species of Arizona blind snakes, *Leptotyphlops h. humilis* and *L. d. dulcis*. J. Herpetol. 8:153–156.

Quinn, H. R. 1977. Further notes on the reproduction in *Crotalus willardi* (Reptilia, Serpentes, Crotalidae). Bull. Maryland Herp. Soc. 13:111.

——. 1979. Reproduction and growth of the Texas coral snake, *Micrurus fulvius tener*. Copeia 1979:453–463.

Radcliffe, C. W., and D. Chiszar. 1983. Clear plastic hiding boxes as a husbandry device for nervous snakes. Herp. Review 14(1):18.

Recchio, I. 1998. Incubation of western blind snake eggs. Vivarium 9(1):26.

Reinert, H. K. 1984. Habitat separation between sympatric snake populations. Ecology 65:478–486.

——, and R. T. Zappalorti. 1988. Timber rattlesnakes, *Crotalus horridus*, of the Pine Barrens: Their movement patterns and habitat preference. Copeia 1988:964–978.

Repp, R. 1998. Winter time observations on five species of reptiles in the Tucson area: Sheltersite selections/fidelity to sheltersites, notes on behavior. Bull. Chicago Herp. Soc. 33(3):49–56.

Resetarits, W. J., Jr. 1983. *Thamnophis proximus proximus* (western ribbon snake) food. Herp. Review 14:75.

Retes, F. 1989. A non-scientific (behavioral) approach to reptile reproduction. In D. L. Hardy, Sr. (Ed.), Collected Papers of the Tucson Herpetological Society 1988–1991. Tucson Herpetol. Soc., Tucson, AZ, pp. 61–64.

Reynolds, R. P., and N. J. Scott, Jr. 1982. Use of a mammalian resource by a Chihuahuan snake community. In N. J. Scott, Jr. (Ed.), Herpetological Communities. U.S. Dept. Interior, Fish and Wildl. Serv., Wildl. Res. Rep. 13:99–118. 239 pp.

Richmond, N. D. 1945. The habits of the rainbow snake in Virginia. Copeia 1945:28–30.

——. 1956. Autumn mating of the rough green snake. Herpetologica 12:325.

Rojas, N. N., and J. S. Godley. 1979. Tooth morphology in crayfish-eating snakes, genus *Regina*. In Abstracts, Joint Annual Meeting, Herpetologists League, Society for the Study of Amphibians and Reptiles, University of Tennessee (Knoxville), p. 52.

Rosen, P. C. 1991. Comparative field study of thermal referenda in garter snakes, *Thamnophis*. J. Herpetol. 25(3):301–312.

——, and C. R. Schwalbe. 1988. Status of the Mexican and narrowheaded garter snakes, *Thamnophis eques megalops* and *Thamnophis rufipuntatus*, in Arizona. Unpubl. Report U.S. Fish & Wildlife Service.

Ross, R. A., and G. Marzec. 1990. The Reproductive Husbandry of Pythons and Boas. Institute for Herpetological Research, Stanford, CA, 270 pp.

Rossi J. V. 1981. *Bufo marinus* in Florida. Some natural history and its impact on native vertebrates. Master's thesis, University of South Florida, Tampa, FL, 75 pp.

——. 1992. Snakes of the United States and Canada: Keeping Them Healthy in Captivity. Vol. I Eastern Area. Krieger. Malabar, FL, 209 pp.

—— and F. Feldner. 1994. *Crotalus willardi* and *Crotalus lepidus klauberi*, arboreal behavior. Herp. Review 24(1):35.

—— and R. Lewis. 1994. *Drymarchon corais couperi* (eastern indigo snake). Unusual dietary inclusion. Herp. Review 25(3):123–124.

—— and R. Rossi. 1991. Notes on the captive reproduction of the southern hognose snake, *Heterodon simus*. Bull. Chicago Herp. Soc. 26(12):265–266.

—— and R. Rossi. 1992a. Notes on the natural history, husbandry, and breeding of the southern hognose snake, *Heterodon simus*. Vivarium 3(6):16–27.

—— and R. Rossi. 1992b. Notes on the captive reproduction of the smooth earth snake, *Virginia valeriae*. Bull. Chicago Herp. Soc. 27(1):7–8.

—— and R. Rossi. 1992c. The incredible edible gecko, *Hemidactylus turcicus*: A new food source for snakes. Vivarium 4(3):12–13.

—— and R. Rossi. 1993a. Notes on the natural history and husbandry of the short-tailed snake, *Stilosoma extenuatum*: Primitive mini-kingsnake of the Florida sand hills. League of Florida Herpetological Societies. September 1993.

—— and R. Rossi. 1993b. Notes on the captive maintenance and feeding behavior of a juvenile short-tailed snake, *Stilosoma extenuatum*. Herp. Review 24(3):100–103.

—— and R. Rossi. 1993c. Earthworms: A balanced diet for small snakes? Herp. Review 24(2):56.

—— and R. Rossi. 1995a. Notes on the mangrove salt marsh snake, *Nerodia clarkii compressicauda*. Reptiles 2(3): 16–23.

—— and R. Rossi. 1995b. Snakes of the United States and Canada: Keeping Them Healthy in Captivity. Vol. II Western Area. Krieger Publishing, 325 pp.

—— and R. Rossi. 1996. What's Wrong With My Snake? Advanced Vivarium Systems, Santee, CA, 150 pp.

—— and R. Rossi. 1999a. Notes on a nearly successful captive breeding and the parasite-related death of a narrow-headed garter snake, *Thamnophis rufipunctatus*. Bull. Chicago Herp. Soc. 34(9):210.

—— and R. Rossi. 1999b. Notes on the reproduction of the black-striped snake, *Coniophanes imperialis*, from Texas. Bull. Chicago Herp. Soc. 34(10):227.

—— and R. Rossi. 1999c. A population survey of the Brazos water snake, *Nerodia harteri harteri*, and other water snakes on the Brazos River, Texas, with notes on a captive breeding and release program. Bull. Chicago Herp. Soc. 34(11):251–253.

—— and R. Rossi. 2000a. Fall Survey of the Brazos water snake, *Nerodia harteri harteri*, and other snakes on the Brazos River, Palo Pinto County, Texas, with notes on the survival of a captive-born neonates. Bull. Chicago Herp. Soc. 35(1):1–2.

—— and R. Rossi. 2000b. Comparison of

growth, behavior, parasites and oral bacteria of related neonate water snakes, *Nerodia harteri harteri*, raised in an outdoor enclosure with those raised indoors. Bul. Chicago Herp. Soc. 35(10):221–228.

—— and R. Rossi. 2000c. Preliminary report on the survival, growth and problems of captive born Brazos water snakes, *Nerodia harteri harteri*, released into the wild, with implications for head starting and species survival. Proceedings of the Annual Meeting of the Assoc. of Reptilian and Amphibian Veterinarians. October 14–18, Reno, Nevada.

Rossman, D. A. 1963. The colubrid snake genus *Thamnophis*. A revision of the *sauritus* group. Bull. Fl. St. Mus. Biol. Sci. 7:99–178.

—— and P. A. Myer. 1990. Behavioral and morphological adaptations for snail extraction in the North American brown snakes, genus *Storeria*. J. Herpetol. 24(4):434–438.

—— and G. R. Stewart. 1987. Taxonomic reevaluation of *Thamnophis couchii* (Serpentes, Colubridae). Occ. Papers Mus. Zool. Louisiana State Univ. (63):1–25.

——, N. B. Ford, and R. A. Seigel. 1996. The Garter Snakes: Evolution and Ecology. University of Oklahoma Press, Norman, OK, 332 pp.

Rothman, N. 1961. Mud, rainbow, and black swamp snakes in captivity. Bull. Philadelphia Herpetol. Soc. 9(3):17–20.

Roze, J. A. 1996. Coral Snakes of the Americas: Biology, Identification, and Venoms. Krieger, Malabar, FL, 328 pp.

Ruben, J. A. 1976. Aerobic and anaerobic metabolism during activity in snakes. J. Comp. Physiol. 109:147–157.

Rubio, M. 1998. Rattlesnake, Portrait of a Predator. Smithsonian Institution Press, Washington, DC, 240 pp.

Sabath, M., and R. Worthington. 1959. Eggs and young of certain Texas reptiles. Herpetologica 15:31–32.

Savitzky B. A. C. 1992. Laboratory studies on piscivory in an opportunistic pitviper, the cottonmouth, *Agkistrodon piscivorus*.

In J. A. Campbell and E. D. Brodie, Jr. (Eds.), Biology of the Pitvipers. Selva, Tyler, TX, pp. 347–368.

Schroder, R. C. 1950. Hibernation of blue racers and bull snakes in western Illinois. Natur. Hist. Misc. (75):1–2.

Schuett, G. W. 1992. Is long-term sperm storage an important component of the reproductive biology of temperate pitvipers? In J. A. Campbell and E. D. Brodie, Jr. (Eds.), Biology of the Pitvipers. Selva, Tyler, TX, pp. 169–184.

—— and J. C. Gillingham. 1986. Sperm storage and multiple paternity in the copperhead, *Agkistrodon contortrix*. Copeia 1986:807–811.

Scott, J. R. 1978. Thermal biology of the wandering garter snake. Ph.D. dissertation, Colorado State University, Fort Collins, CO.

——, C. R. Tracy, and D. Pettus. 1982. A biophysical analysis of daily and seasonal utilization of climate space by a montane snake. Ecology 63:482–493.

Scott, N. J., B. D. Greene, T. C. Maxwell, A. H. Price, and O. Thornton. 1993. Concho water snake recovery plan. U.S. Fish and Wildlife Service. Albuquerque, NM, 65 pp.

——, T. C. Maxwell, O. Thornton, L. A. Fitzgerald, and J. W. Flury. 1989. Distribution, habitat and future of Harter's water snake, *Nerodia harteri*, in Texas. J. Herpetol. 23(4):373–389.

Secor, S. M. 1992. A preliminary analysis of the movement and home range size of the sidewinder, *Crotalus cerastes*. In J. A. Campbell and E. D. Brodie, Jr. (Eds.), Biology of the Pitvipers. Selva, Tyler, TX, pp. 389–394.

Seib, R. L. 1984. Prey use in three syntopic neotropical racers. J. Herpetol. 18:412–420.

Seibert, H., and C. Hagan. 1947. Studies on a population of snakes in Illinois. Copeia 1947:6–22.

Seigel, R. 1986. Ecology and conservation of the endangered rattlesnake *Sistrurus catenatus* in Missouri, U.S.A. Biol. Conserv. 35:333–346.

Seigel, R. A., J. T. Collins, and S. Novak.

(Eds.). 1987. Snakes, Ecology and Evolutionary Biology. McGraw-Hill, New York, 529 pp.

Semlitsch, R. D., and G. B. Moran. 1984. Ecology of the redbelly snake, *Storeria occipitomaculata*, using mesic habitats in South Carolina. Am. Midland Nat. 111: 33–40.

———, H. K. Pechman, and J. W. Gibbons. 1988. Annual emergence of juvenile mud snakes, *Faranacia abacura*, in aquatic habitats. Copeia 1988(1):243–245.

Shaw, C. E., and S. Campbell. 1974. Snakes of the American West. Alfred E. Knopf, New York. 332 pp.

Skehan, P., Jr. 1960. Feeding notes on captive reptiles. Herpetologica 16:32.

Slavens, F. L., and K. Slavens. 1990. Reptiles and Amphibians in Captivity. Breeding Longevity. Slaveware, Seattle, WA, 516 pp.

———, and K. Slavens. 1991. Reptiles and Amphibians in Captivity. Breeding Longevity. Slaveware, Seattle, WA, 505 pp.

Slevin, J. R. 1951. A high birth rate for *Natrix sipedon sipedon* (Linne). Herpetologica 7:132.

Smith, H. M., D. Chiszar, J. R. Staley, II, and K. Tepedelen. 1994. Populational relationships in the corn snake, *Elaphe guttata* (Reptilia, Serpentes). Texas J. Sci. 46(3):259–292.

Smith, P. W. 1961. The amphibians and reptiles of Illinois. Illinois Nat. Hist. Survey Bull. 28:1–298.

Snider, A. T., and J. K. Bowler. 1992. Longevity of Reptiles and Amphibians in North American Collections. SSAR Herpetological Circular No. 21.

Spiess, P. 1997. Popular Arizona natives in herpetoculture, Part 1: Rosy boas. Vivarium. 8(5):54–55, 69.

Spitieri, D. E. 1991. The subspecies of *Lichanura trivirgata*: Why the confusion? Bull. Chicago Herp. Soc. 26(7):153–156.

———. 1992. The questionable status of *Lichanura trivirgata bostici*, the Cedros Island Boa. Bull. Chicago Herp. Soc. 27(9):181.

———. 1998. The geographic variability of the species *Lichanura trivirgata* and a description of a new subspecies. In Proceedings of the Conference on California Herpetology. Special Publ. No. 4, pp. 113–130.

Staedeli, J. H. 1964. Eggs and young of the vermillion-lined ground snake, *Sonora semiannulata linearis*. Copeia 1964(3):581–582.

Staszko, R., and J. Walls. 1994. Rat Snakes: A Hobbyist's Guide to *Elaphe* and Kin. T. F. H. Publishers, Neptune City, NJ, 208 pp.

Stebbins, R. C. 1954. Amphibians and Reptiles of Western North America. McGraw-Hill, New York, 536 pp.

———. 1972. California Amphibians and Reptiles. University of California Press, Berkeley, CA, 152 pp.

———. 1985. A Field Guide to Western Reptiles and Amphibians. Houghton Mifflin, Boston, MA, 336 pp.

Stengel, R. 1998. The beautiful scarlet snake. Reptiles Magazine April 1998:100.

Stevenson, R. D., C. R. Peterson, and J. S. Tsuji. 1985. The thermal dependence of locomotion, tongue flicking, digestion and oxygen consumption in the wandering garter snake. Physiol. Zool. 58:46–57.

Stewart, G. R. 1965. Thermal ecology of the garter snakes, *Thamnophis sirtalis concinnus* and *T. ordinoides*. Herpetologica 21:81–102.

———. 1968. Some observations on the natural history of two Oregon garter snakes, genus *Thamnophis*. J. Herpetol. 2: 71–86.

———. 1988. The rubber boa, *Charina bottae*, in California, with particular reference to the southern subspecies, *C. b. umbratica*. In Proceedings of the Conference on California Herpetology. Spec. Publ. No. 4. Southwestern Herpetol. Soc., pp. 131–138.

Stewart, J. 1989. Techniques for sex identification in reptiles. In Captive Propagation and Husbandry of Amphibians and Reptiles. Northern California Herp. Soc. Spec. Publ. No. 5: 99–104.

Stoskopf, M. K., and R. Hudson. 1982. Commercial feed frogs as a source of trematode infection in reptile collections. Herp. Review 13:125.

Strecker, J. K. 1926. On the habits of southern snakes. Contrib. Baylor Univ. Mus. 4:1–11.

——. 1927. Observations on the food habits of Texas amphibians and reptiles. Copeia 1927(2):6–7.

Swanson, P. L. 1948. *Natrix sipedon compressicauda* at Key West, Florida. Herpetologica 4:105–106.

——. 1952. The reptiles of Venango County, Pennsylvania. Am. Midland Natur. 47:161–182.

Sweeny, R. 1992. Garter Snakes: Their Natural History and Care in Captivity. Blandford Press, London, 128 pp.

Swinford, G. W. 1989. Captive reproduction of the banded rock rattlesnake, *Crotalus lepidus klauberi*. In M. J. Uricheck (Ed.), Proceedings of the 13th International Herpetological Symposium on Captive Propagation and Husbandry, pp. 99–110.

Switak, K. H. 1984. The Life of Desert Reptiles and Amphibians. Karl Switak, San Francisco, 31 pp.

Telford, S. R. 1955. A description of the eggs of the coral snake, *Micrurus f. fulvius*. Copeia 1955(3):258.

Tennant, A. 1984. The Snakes of Texas. Texas Monthly Press, Austin, TX, 561 pp.

——. 1985. A Field Guide to Texas Snakes. Texas Monthly Press, Austin, TX, 260 pp.

——. 1997. A Field Guide to the Snakes of Florida. Gulf Publishing Co., Houston. 257 pp.

Tinkel, D. W. 1957. Ecology, maturation and reproduction of *Thamnophis sauritus proximus*. Ecology 38:69–77.

——. 1962. Reproductive potential and cycles in female *Crotalus atrox* from northwestern Texas. Copeia 1962(2):306–313.

Tomkins, J. R. 1965. Swallow-tailed kite and snake: An unusual encounter. Wilson Bull. 77:294.

Trapido, H. 1940. Mating time and sperm viability in *Storeria*. Copeia 1940:107–109.

Tresott, E., Jr. 1998. The short-tailed snake, *Stilosoma extenuatum*. Reptiles 6(3):32–37.

Trutnau L. 1981. Nonvenomous Snakes. Barrons, Woodbury, NJ, 191 pp.

Tryon, B. W. 1976. Second generation reproduction and courtship behavior in Trans-pecos ratsnakes, *Elaphe subocularis*. Herp. Review 7:156–157.

——. 1978. Reproduction in a pair of captive Arizona ridge-nosed rattlesnakes, *.Crotalus willardi willardi* (Reptilia, Serpentes, Crotalidae). Bull. Maryland Herp. Soc. 14:83–88.

——. 1993. Tiger rattlesnakes bred at Knoxville Zoo. The Desert Monitor 23(3):7.

—— and G. Carl. 1980. Reproduction in the mole kingsnakes, *Lampropeltis calligaster rhombomaculata* (Serpentes, Colubridae). Trans. Kansas Acad. Sci. 83:66–73.

—— and H. K. McCrystal. 1982. *Micrurus fulvius tenere* (Texas coral snake) reproduction. Herp. Review 13(2):47–48.

—— and J. B. Murphy. 1982. Miscellaneous notes on the reproductive biology of reptiles. Thirteen varieties of the genus *Lampropeltis*, species *mexicana*, *triangulum*, and *zonata*. Trans. Kansas Acad. Sci. 85:96–119.

Tu, A. 1976. Investigation of the sea snake, *Pelamis platurus* (Reptilia, Serpentes, Hydrophiidae), on the Pacific coast of Costa Rica, Central America. J. Herpetol. 10:13–18.

Tucker, J. K. 1977. Notes on the food habits of Kirtland's water snake, *Clonophis kirtlandii*. Bull. Maryland Herpetol. Soc. 13:193–195.

—— 1994. *Clonophis kirtlandii* (Kirtland's snake). Subterranean prey capture. Herp. Review 25(3):122–123.

Tyning, T. F. (Ed.) 1992. Conservation of the timber rattlesnake in the northeast. Massachusetts Audubon Society, Lincoln, MA.

Uhler, F. M., C. Cottan, and T. E. Clarke. 1939. Food of snakes of the George Washington National Forest, Virginia.

Trans. 4th North American Wildl. Conf.:605–622.

Vaeth, R. H. 1980. Observation of ophinophagy in the western hooknose snake, *Gyalopion canum*. Bull. Maryland Herpetol Soc. 16(3):94–96.

Van Denburgh J. 1922. The reptiles of western North America. Vol. II: Snakes and turtles. California Acad. Sci. (10):617–1028.

Van Devender, T. R., and G. L. Bradley. 1994. Late quaternary amphibians and reptiles from Maravillas Canyon Cave, Texas, with discussion of the biogeography and evolution of the Chihuahuan Desert herpetofauna, pp. 23–53. In P. R. Brown and J. W. Wright (Eds.), Herpetology of the North American deserts: Proceedings of a symposium. Spec. Publ. 5, Southwest Herpetol. Soc., Van Nuys, CA, iv + 311 pp.

Van Duyn, G. 1937. Snakes that "play possum". Nature 29:215–217.

Van Hyning, O. C. 1931. Reproduction of some Florida snakes. Copeia 1931:59–60.

———. 1932. Food of some Florida snakes. Copeia 1932:37.

Vaughan, R., J. Dixon, and R. Thomas. 1996. A reevaluation of the corn snake *Elaphe guttata* in Texas. Texas J. Sci. 48(3):175–190.

Verkerk, J. W. 1987. Enkele aanvullende opmerkingen over het gedrag van de dwergertelslang, *Sistrurus miliarus barbouri*. Lacerta 45:142–143.

Vermersch, T. G., and R. E. Kuntz. 1986. Snakes of South-Central Texas. Eakin Press, 137 pp.

Vest, D. K. 1981. Envenomation following the bite of a wandering garter snake, *Thamnophis elegans vagrans*. Clinical Toxicology 18:573.

Vial, J. L. 1957. A new size record for *Thamnophis marcainus* Baird and Girard. Copeia 1957b(2):143.

Viosca, P., Jr. 1926. A snake tragedy. Copeia 151:109.

Vitt, L. J. 1974. Body temperatures of high latitude reptiles. Copeia 1974:225–256.

———, and A. C. Hulse. 1973. Observations on feeding habits and tail display of the Sonoran coral snake, *Micruroides euryxanthus*. Herpetologica 29:302–304.

Vogt, R. C. 1981. Natural History of Amphibians and Reptiles of Wisconsin. Milwaukee Public Museum, Milwaukee, WI, 205 pp.

Webb, R. G. 1970. The Reptiles of Oklahoma. University of Oklahoma Press, Norman, OK, 370 pp.

Werler, J., and J. Dixon. 2000. Texas Snakes: Identification, Distribution, and Natural History. University of Texas Press, Austin, TX, 437 pp.

Wharton, C. H. 1966. Reproduction and growth in the cottonmouth, *Agkistrodon piscivorus* Lacepede, of Cedar Keys, Florida. Copeia 1966:149–161.

——— 1969. The cottonmouth moccasin on Sea Horse Key, Florida. Bull. Florida St. Mus. Biol. Sci. 14:272–277.

Wheeler, W. 1984. Duck egg predation by fox snakes in Wisconsin. Wildlife Soc. Bull. 12:77–78.

Willard, D. E. 1977. Constricting methods of snakes. Copeia 1977:379–382.

Williams, K. L. 1988. Systematics and Natural History of the American Milk Snakes, *Lampropeltis triangulum*. Milwaukee Public Museum, Milwaukee, WI, 176 pp.

Williamson, M. A., P. W. Hyder, and J. S. Applegarth. 1994. Snakes, Lizards, Turtles, Frogs, Toads & Salamanders of New Mexico: A Field Guide. Sunstone Press, Santa Fe, NM, 176 pp.

Wilson, S. 1954. Snake fight. Texas Game & Fish 12(5):16–17.

Witwer , M. 1996. Rosy boas. Reptile and Amphibian Magazine. Nov–Dec:58–69.

Wood, H. W. 1994. Captive care of the rough-scaled green snake. Newsletter Arizona Herp. Assoc. 25(3).

Wood, J. T. 1949. Observations on *Natrix sepemvittata* (Say) in southwestern Ohio. Am. Midland Natur. 42:744–750.

Wozniak, E. M., and R. C. Bothner. 1966. Some ecological comparisons between *Thamnophis brachystoma* and *Thamnophis sirtalis sirtalis* on the Allegheny High Plateau. J. Ohio Herp. Soc. 5:164–165.

Wright, A. H., and A. A. Wright. 1957. Handbook of Snakes of the United States and Canada. Vol. I and II. Comstock, Ithaca, NY, 1105 pp.

Zappalorti, R. T., E. W. Johnson, and Z. Leszcynski. 1983. The ecology of the northern pine snake, *Pituophis melanoleucus melanoleucus* (Davdin) (Reptilia, Serpentes, Colubridae) in southern New Jersey, with special notes on habitat and nesting behavior. Bull. Chicago Herp. Soc. 18:57–72.

Zehr, D. 1969. Mating, ejaculate, egg laying, and hatching of the fox snake, *Elaphe vulpina vulpina*. J. Herpetol. 3:180–181.

Zimmerman, E. 1986. Breeding Terrarium Animals. T. F. H. Publications, Neptune City, NJ, 384 pp.

Zug, G. R., S. B. Hedges, and S. Sunkel. 1979. Variation in reproductive parameters of three neotropical snakes, *Coniophanes fissidens*, *Dipsas catesbyi*, and *Imantodes cenchoa*. Smithsonian Contrib. Zool. 300: 1–20.

Zwart, P., B. Langerwerf, H. Claessen, J. Leunisse, J. Mennes, C. Van Riel, L. Lambrechts, and M. Kik. 1989. Health aspects in breeding and rearing insectivorous lizards from moderate climate zones. Third International Colloquium on the Pathology of Reptiles and Amphibians, Orlando, FL, p. 82.

Zweifel, R. G. 1980. Aspects of the biology of a laboratory population of kingsnakes. In Reproductive Biology and Diseases of Captive Reptiles. SSAR Contrib. Herpetol. 1:141–152.

APPENDIX OF COMMON TO SCIENTIFIC NAMES
AT THE SPECIES LEVEL

Arizona mountain kingsnake	*Lampropeltis pryomelana*
Baird's rat snake	*Elaphe bairdi*
Baja California rat snake	*Bogertrophis rosaliae*
Banded sand snake	*Chilomeniscus cinctus*
Big Bend patchnose snake	*Salvadora deserticola*
Blackhead snakes	*Tantilla* sp.
Blackneck garter snake	*Thamnophis cyrtopsis*
Blacktail rattlesnake	*Crotalus molossus*
Black-striped snake	*Coniophanes imperialis*
Black swamp snake	*Seminatrix pygaea*
Blind snake, Brahminy	*Rhamphotyphlops braminus*
Blind snake, Texas	*Leptotyphlops dulcis*
Blind snake, western	*Leptotyphlops humilis*
Blotched water snake	*Nerodia erythrogaster*
Brazos water snake	*Nerodia harteri*
Brown snake	*Storeria dekayi*
Brown water snake	*Nerodia taxispilota*
Bull snake	*Pituophis catenifer*
Butler's garter snake	*Thamnophis butleri*
California mountain kingsnake	*Lampropeltis zonata*
Checkered garter snake	*Thamnophis marcianus*
Coachwhip	*Masticophis flagellum*
Common garter snake	*Thamnophis sirtalis*
Common kingsnake	*Lampropeltis getula*
Common rat snake	*Elaphe obsoleta*
Copperhead	*Agkistrodon contortrix*
Concho water snake	*Nerodia paucimaculata*
Corn snake	*Elaphe guttata*
Cottonmouth	*Agkistrodon piscivorus*
Crowned snakes	*Tantilla* sp.
Desert hooknose snake	*Gyalopion quadrangulare*
Diamondback water snake	*Nerodia rhombifer*
Eastern coral snake	*Micrurus fulvius*
Eastern diamondback rattlesnake	*Crotalus admanteus*
Eastern fox snake	*Elaphe gloydi*
Eastern hognose snake	*Heterodon platirhinos*
Eastern indigo snake	*Drymarchon couperi*
Eastern ribbon snake	*Thamnophis sauritis*
Eastern worm snake	*Carphophis amoenus*
Flathead snake	*Tantilla gracilis*
Florida green water snake	*Nerodia floridana*
Giant garter snake	*Thamnophis gigas*

509

Glossy crayfish snake	*Regina rigida*
Glossy snake	*Arizona elegans*
Gopher snake	*Pituophis catenifer*
Graham's crayfish snake	*Regina grahamii*
Gray-banded kingsnake	*Lampropeltis alterna*
Green rat snake	*Senticolis triaspis*
Ground snake	*Sonora semiannulata*
Kirtland's snake	*Clonophis kirtlandi*
Longnose snake	*Rhinocheilus lecontei*
Lined snake	*Tropidoclonion lineatum*
Lyre snake	*Trimorphodon biscutatus*
Massasauga	*Sistrurus catenatus*
Mexican garter snake	*Thamnophis eques*
Mexican hooknose snake	*Ficimia streckeri*
Mexican vine snake	*Oxybelis aenus*
Mississippi green water snake	*Nerodia cyclopion*
Milk snake	*Lampropeltis triangulum*
Mole kingsnake	*Lampropeltis calligaster*
Mountain patchnose snake	*Salvadora grahamiae*
Mountain shovelnose snake	*Chionactis saxatilis*
Mud snake	*Farancia abacura*
Narrowhead garter snake	*Thamnophis rufipunctatus*
Night snake	*Hypsiglena torquata*
Northern cat-eyed snake	*Leptodeira septentrionalis*
Northern water snake	*Nerodia sipedon*
Northwestern garter snake	*Thamnophis ordinoides*
Pacific coast aquatic garter snake	*Thamnophis atratus*
Plainbelly water snake	*Nerodia erythrogaster*
Plains garter snake	*Thamnophis radix*
Prairie kingsnake	*Lampropeltis calligaster*
Pine snake	*Pituophis melanoleucus*
Pine woods snake	*Rhadinea flavilata*
Pygmy rattlesnake	*Sistrurus miliarius*
Queen snake	*Regina septemvittata*
Racer	*Coluber constrictor*
Rainbow snake	*Farancia erytrogramma*
Red diamond rattlesnake	*Crotalus ruber (exsul)*
Redbelly snake	*Storeria occipitomaculata*
Ridgenose rattlesnake	*Crotalus willardi*
Ringneck snake	*Diadophis punctatus*
Rock rattlesnake	*Crotalus lepidus*
Rosy boa	*Lichanura trivirgata*
Rough earth snake	*Virginia striatula*
Rough green snake	*Opheodrys aestivus*
Rubber boa	*Charina (Lichanura) bottae*
Saddled leafnose snake	*Phyllorhynchus browni*
Salt marsh snake	*Nerodia clarkii*
Scarlet snake	*Cemophora coccinea*
Sharptail snake	*Contia tenuis*
Shorthead garter snake	*Thamnophis brachystoma*

Short-tailed snake	*Stilosoma extenuatum*
Sidewinder	*Crotalus cerastes*
Smooth earth snake	*Virginia valeriae*
Smooth green snake	*Opheodrys (Liochlorophis) vernalis*
Sonoran shovelnose snake	*Chionactis palarostris*
Sonoran whipsnake	*Masticiphis bilineatus*
Southern hognose snake	*Heterodon simus*
Southern water snake	*Nerodia fasciata*
Speckled racer	*Drymobius margaritiferus*
Speckled rattlesnake	*Crotalus mitchelii*
Spotted leafnose snake	*Phyllorhynchus decurtatus*
Striped crayfish snake	*Regina alleni*
Striped racer	*Masticophus lateralis*
Striped whipsnake	*Masticophus taeniatus*
Texas blind snake	*Leptotyphlops dulcis*
Texas indigo snake	*Drymarchon corais erebennus*
Texas patchnose snake	*Salvadora grahamiae*
Tiger rattlesnake	*Crotalus tigris*
Timber rattlesnake	*Crotalus horridus*
Trans-Pecos rat snake	*Bogertrophis subocularis*
Twin-spotted rattlesnake	*Crotalus pricei*
Two-striped garter snake	*Thamnophis hammondii*
Western aquatic garter snake	*Thamnophis couchii*
Western blind snake	*Leptotyphlops humilis*
Western coral snake	*Micruoides euryxanthus*
Western diamondback rattlesnake	*Crotalus atrox*
Western hognose snake	*Heterodon nasicus*
Western indigo snake	*Drymarchon erebennus*
Western patchnose snake	*Salvadora hexalepis*
Western hooknose snake	*Gyalopion canum*
Western ribbon snake	*Thamnophis proximus*
Western shovelnose snake	*Chionactis occipitalis*
Western terrestrial garter snake	*Thamnophis elegans*
Western worm snake	*Carphophis vermis*
Yellowbelly sea snake	*Pelamis platurus*

SUBJECT INDEX

Note: Page numbers followed by t refer to tables.